# Real Estate Law Fundamentals

# Real Estate Law Fundamentals

**Alice Hart Hughes**
Attorney at Law

**Thomas F. Goldman**
Attorney at Law
Professor Emeritus
Bucks County Community College

**Charles P. Nemeth**
J.D., Ph.D, LL.M.

**PEARSON**

Boston   Columbus   Indianapolis   New York   San Francisco   Upper Saddle River
Amsterdam   Cape Town   Dubai   London   Madrid   Milan   Munich   Paris   Montréal   Toronto
Delhi   Mexico City   São Paulo   Sydney   Hong Kong   Seoul   Singapore   Taipei   Tokyo

**Editorial Director:** Vernon Anthony
**Acquisitions Editor:** Gary Bauer
**Editorial Assistant:** Tanika Henderson
**Director of Marketing:** David Gesell
**Senior Marketing Manager:** Stacey Martinez
**Senior Marketing Coordinator:** Alicia Wozniak
**Senior Marketing Assistant:** Les Roberts
**Senior Managing Editor:** JoEllen Gohr
**Project Manager:** Jessica H. Sykes
**Senior Operations Supervisor:** Pat Tonneman
**Senior Art Director:** Jayne Conte

**Cover Designer:** Suzanne Duda
**Cover Art:** David Graham
**Chapter Opener Photographs:** David Graham
**Lead Media Project Manager:** Karen Bretz
**Full-Service Project Management:**
    Christina Taylor/Integra Software Services
**Composition:** Integra Software Services
**Printer/Binder:** Edwards Brothers Malloy
**Cover Printer:** Lehigh-Phoenix Color
**Text Font:** 11/13, Goudy

Microsoft® and Windows® are registered trademarks of the Microsoft Corporation in the U.S.A. and other countries. Screen shots and icons reprinted with permission from the Microsoft Corporation. This book is not sponsored or endorsed by or affiliated with the Microsoft Corporation.

Many of the designations by manufacturers and sellers to distinguish their products are claimed as trademarks. Where those designations appear in this book, and the publisher was aware of a trademark claim, the designations have been printed in initial caps or all caps.

**Library of Congress Cataloging-in-Publication Data is available from the Publisher upon request.**

10 9 8 7 6 5 4 3 2 1

ISBN 10:    0-13-336236-1
ISBN 13: 978-0-13-336236-7

To my mentors who, through their teaching, encouragement and expectation of the best, made this book possible: in real estate, the Pasquarellas, Val, Jr., Joe, Art, Val, Sr., and Uncle Art; in law, Wayne N. Cordes and Martin J. King, and; in education and publishing, Thomas F. Goldman.

—AHH

For Henry Joseph, may you bring your father joy he has brought me.

—CT

# BRIEF CONTENTS

# CONTENTS

### CHAPTER 11

## Closing    243

# UNIT IV
# SPECIAL REAL ESTATE   274

### CHAPTER 12

## Landlord-Tenant Law   277

### CHAPTER 13

## Common Interest Communities   299

### CHAPTER 14

## Real Estate Development and Investment   315

# ABOUT THE AUTHORS

**THOMAS F. GOLDMAN, JD,** is an experienced trial attorney who has represented nationally known insurance companies and corporations. At Thomas Edison State College, he developed the Advanced Litigation Support and Technology Certificate Program, and was a member of the Paralegal Studies Program Advisory Board and a mentor. He is Professor Emeritus of Bucks County Community College, where he was a professor of Law and Management, former Director of the Center for Legal Studies, and former Director of the ABA approved Paralegal Studies Program.

Dr. Goldman is an author of textbooks in paralegal studies and technology, including *The Paralegal Professional*, in its fourth edition; *Civil Litigation: Process and Procedure*, in its second edition *Litigation Concepts*; *Accounting and Taxation for Paralegals*; and *Technology in the Law Office*, in its third edition; *AbacusLaw Tutorial and Guide; and SmartDraw Tutorial and Guide*; and the executive producer of the Paralegal Professional video series as well as the creator and executive producer of the Virtual Law Office Experience.

An accounting and economics graduate of Boston University and of Temple University School of Law, Professor Goldman has an active international law, technology law, and litigation practice. He has worked extensively with paralegals and received the award of the Legal Support Staff Guild. He was elected the Legal Secretaries Association Boss of the Year for his contribution to cooperative education by encouraging the use of paralegals and legal assistants in law offices. He also received the Bucks County Community College Alumni Association Professional Achievement Award. He has been an educational consultant on technology to educational institutions and major corporations and a frequent speaker and lecturer on educational, legal, and technology issues. He was appointed to the American Association for Paralegal Education Board of Directors in October 2005, and served as the founding chair of the Technology Task Force, where he initiated the Train the Trainer program.

**ALICE HART HUGHES, JD,** is a practicing attorney and experienced litigator. She is a former Adjunct Professor of Paralegal Studies at Bucks County Community College where she taught Civil Litigation, Legal Research and Writing, Accounting for Paralegals, Introduction to Paralegal Studies, Negligence, and Family Law.

After receiving a Bachelors of Business Administration in finance and real estate from Temple University, Dr. Hughes began her career in the real estate industry conducting market analysis for residential and commercial real estate appraisals. She received both a real estate salesperson's and title insurance agent's license and began marketing and managing residential real estate and managing a title insurance agency. During these early years of her professional career she taught Real Estate Fundamentals and Real Estate Practices at the Montgomery County Community College and at local realty boards. Her career in real estate was a natural lead-in to pursue a law degree, also from Temple University.

She has practiced real estate law and civil litigation extensively, working in mid-sized, multi-office law firms. She is currently a sole practitioner with her practice being limited to estate planning, administration and litigation. She is the co-author of *Civil Litigation: Process and Procedures*, in its second edition, and has been extensively involved in the script writing and production of the Paralegal Video Law Office Experience. Most recently, she was appointed to the Pennsylvania Board of Dentistry and lectures frequently on estate planning and ethical issues.

# PREFACE

## ■ FROM THE AUTHOR

*Real Estate Fundamentals* has been designed to provide a real-world hands-on approach to the typical real estate transaction. Few students taking a real estate law class have ever had any actual contact with the purchase and sale of real estate. In the real world the process can be slow, highly detailed and a bit of a mystery because of the number of professionals involved from beginning to end. We have in the text and in the supplements opened the doors to the process and the procedures of the real world of the real estate transaction.

We have attempted to open the doors and reveal the mysteries of real estate with the extensive use of a video scenario. This video follows the steps in a traditional real estate transaction, from the signing of the listing contract and agreement of sale, through the mortgage application, home inspection and settlement process. These scenarios form the basis for discussion and appreciation of the interconnection of ethics of the profession with actual practice and procedures.

Sample forms are provided for each stage of the real estate transaction. Within the text the forms are completed to coincide with the video scenario. These completed forms can be used as a guideline to complete the blank forms, available in the text and on-line, for one of the additional real estate transactions described in the appendix.

This text is more than a how-to guide. Although a how-to guide is what allows one to hit the ground running upon entering the work force, knowledge of essential real estate concepts is also important. We have provided a solid foundation of real estate law concepts that paralegals and others working in the real estate profession must be familiar with in order to function effectively. For each concept we have tried to include practical examples that will make the concept more easily grasped for the student.

Each chapter also includes an ethical consideration frequently encountered in the practice of real estate law.

Our goal is to offer a well rounded approach, legal concepts, ethics and practical applications that will stimulate both student and teacher in the learning environment. It has been written as a teaching text and as a practice reference manual.

A common set of facts is used throughout the text as a learning aid, in understanding traditional real estate concepts and in preparing the documents related to the real estate transaction. This fact pattern is based on a real case that is similar to the real estate transactions fact patterns described in the appendix providing for additional practice. The examples are designed to assist the reader in moving through the case study assignments that are spread throughout the chapters. They are intended to offer a real-life work environment—a mini-internship—with print-outs that can be used as a portfolio to demonstrate knowledge of the entire real estate transaction and as a reference set for future on-the-job references.

Alice Hart Hughes, JD
Thomas F. Goldman, JD

# KEY THEMES EXPLORED THROUGHOUT THIS TEXT

## ■ UNDERSTANDING THE INTERCONNECTEDNESS OF LEGAL AND REAL ESTATE PROFESSIONS

The real estate industry has evolved such that legal professionals frequently work with real estate professionals. For many years a friendly competition existed between these two professions. As the complexity of real estate transaction has grown these former competitors have seen the need to work together. To successfully work together, it is important for each to understand the nature and extent of the skills and services the other provides.

## ■ UNDERSTANDING REAL ESTATE LAW CONCEPTS

Real estate law derives from centuries of common law. We seek to clarify the most important real estate concepts in terms that are easily understandable for the student. A thorough understanding of the concepts allows the student to identify the rights and obligations of owners, buyers and sellers of real estate. This knowledge lays the foundation for the practical skills that are required in any real estate transaction.

## ■ DEVELOPING PRACTICAL REAL ESTATE LAW PRACTICAL SKILLS THROUGH HANDS-ON PRACTICE

Preparation of and understanding all the forms associated with a real estate transaction is a key component of learning. Sample forms are completed for the transaction and the significance of those forms is explained in easy to understand terms.

## ■ DEVELOPING CRITICAL THINKING AND PROCEDURAL SKILLS

End-of-chapter material focuses on developing critical-thinking and hands-on skills and includes exercises and assignments broken down into two sections:

> Concept Review and Reinforcement
> Key Terms
> Chapter Summary
> Review Questions and Exercises
> Video Case Study
> Internet and Technology Exercises
> Real Estate Portfolio Exercises Virtual Law Office Experience
> Assignments

## ■ DEVELOPING PRACTICAL LAW OFFICE SKILLS THROUGH HANDS-ON PRACTICE

End-of-chapter practice materials, continuing case studies, and a comprehensive case study reflect the actual activities of paralegals working in the real estate law office. Samples are placed throughout the chapters for reference and guidance in preparing the assignments.

## ■ UNDERSTANDING HOW TO HANDLE ETHICAL SITUATIONS IN REAL ESTATE LAW PRACTICE

The text and package are designed to build a strong foundational understanding of the ethical principles that apply to the members of the legal team in actual practice. Resources include references to national and individual states' codes of legal ethics and professional responsibility, ethical perspectives boxes integrated throughout the textbook.

# ORGANIZATION OF THE BOOK

The book is divided into four units:

- Essentials of Real Estate Practice Overview
- Real Estate Transfer
- Real Estate Closing
- Special Real Estate Interests

**UNIT ONE—ESSENTIALS OF REAL ESTATE PRACTICE OVERVIEW** provides a description of the real estate industry including the wide array of employment opportunities within the industry. The section defines and describes real estate law concepts, such as concurrent ownership, the rights and obligations of owners of real estate, and restrictions on real property use. These elements make up the foundation of real estate law and despite their ancient origin, each concept is explained in clear terms and supported with real world examples for better understanding.

**UNIT TWO—REAL ESTATE TRANSFER** is designed to explain the ways in which real estate is transferred. The unit begins with a chapter describing the voluntary and involuntary ways in which real estate is transferred. Then three chapters focus on the process followed for the primary method of real estate transfer, sale with the assistance of a real estate professional. The first explains the process of listing and marketing residential real estate and entering an agreement of sale. The next chapter describes the title searching process and why public records and the recording of documents affecting legal title are key to the valid transfer of real estate. The final chapter considers the role of mortgage lending to the real estate transfer process and includes information on the pre-approval, loan application, qualification and approval processes. For most, the purchase of real estate would be impossible without mortgage lending. For the paralegal an understanding of the lending process and requirements will assist in understanding how realtors assist buyers in locating the real estate ultimately purchased.

**UNIT THREE—REAL ESTATE CLOSING** is written with the goal of equipping each student with the ability to describe and complete the documents associated with the typical residential real estate transaction. Chapter 10 familiarizes students with the components of deeds, promissory notes and mortgages, giving them the ability to explain and prepare the documents essential to the sale and transfer of real estate. In Chapter 11 students will encounter the process for clearing title in accordance with the terms of an agreement of sale and as may be required by a lender. Calculations of closing costs and preparation of the real estate settlement sheet are covered in depth so students can develop an understanding and ability to complete these tasks.

**UNIT FOUR—SPECIAL REAL ESTATE INTERESTS** seeks to describe three areas of real estate law that are most frequently encountered, other than real estate sales. Chapter 12 explains the area of Landlord-Tenant law defining the rights, duties and remedies of the landlord and the tenant. This chapter includes a discussion of the use of leases for purchase of real estate from both the seller's and the buyer's perspectives. The next chapter covers common interest communities, condominiums, co-operatives, including an examination of hybrid ownership interests, such as time shares and retirement communities. With a growing older population these non-traditional forms of ownership are becoming more commonplace and the chapter is designed to provide the student with sufficient knowledge to understand and explain these ownership forms. The final chapter is devoted to explaining the real estate development process, from planning and land acquisition to approvals, construction and ultimate sale of the property, students will acquire an appreciation for the numerous components and professionals that participate in the land development process.

# CHAPTER PEDAGOGY AND FEATURES

Real Estate Fundamental follows the same design used in the authors' Civil Litigation Process and Procedures, Litigation Concepts and Technology in Practice text to provide a consistent look and feel for those using this family of texts. Chapter features include:

## ■ COMMON LAW TERMS

A feature that explains the signifcance of the common law terms is utilized to acknowledge the source of our real estate law but prevent getting bogged down in archaic terms that have fallen out of use in many jurisdictions.

## ■ ETHICAL CONSIDERATIONS BOXES

These features raise students' awareness of ethical issues encountered by the legal team and direct the students to resources to resolve those issues

## ■ WORDS OF THE COURT

Students are provided with case decisions to read which are relevant to a particular real estate law principle.

## ■ PRACTICAL TIPS

The goal of this feature is to provide practical tips for the real estate legal team based on experience. Typical advice can incorporate the simple (*always check the local rules*), the practical (*call the courthouse to determine the date electronic filing for deeds began*), and the obtuse (*contact the mortgage lender to determine the form of payment required when paying off a mortgage*).

## ■ SKILL BUILDING EXERCISES USING CASE RESOURCE MATERIALS

End-of-chapter practice materials and a comprehensive case study reflect the actual activities of professional working in the real estate law office. Samples are placed throughout the chapters for reference and guidance in preparing the assignments.

## ■ VIDEO CASE STUDIES

*Real Estate Fundamentals* is supported by scenario-based video segments dealing with sale, purchase, practice, procedures, and ethical issues in real estate practice that allow you to bring the world of the practicing paralegal into the classroom. The video series tracks a single real estate transaction from beginning to end.

## ■ BUILDING YOUR PROFESSIONAL PORTFOLIO

One of the key outcomes of this course is the building of a professional portfolio of documents that can be shown to prospective employers and functions as a reference on the job.

# STUDENT RESOURCES ONLINE

Case Study Videos supported by case material and forms are available for student access at www.pearsonhighered.com/careers.

## ■ REAL ESTATE CASE STUDY VIDEOS

Students watch realistic video scenarios, work with case files and documents to do the work a paralegal will be asked to do in practice. Throughout the course students build a portfolio of work that demonstrates that they have the training and experience employers are looking for.

## ■ FORMS AND CASE MATERIALS

Examples of forms and documents needed to complete assignments are available online for student download.

 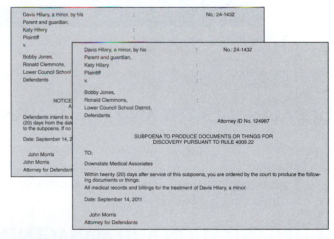

ACCIDENT SCENE

# LEGAL SOFTWARE RESOURCES

Students can download the latest (time-limited) versions of the most popular legal software from the Technology Resources Website at www.pearsonhighered.com/Goldman. There you will find links to software tutorials, video overviews, teaching notes, and a variety of other useful resources, including forms for requesting lab copies of software from venders.

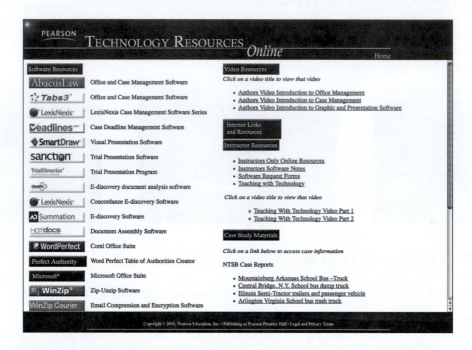

http://media.pearsoncmg.com/ph/chet/chet_goldman_techresources_2/pages/index.html

## ■ OFFICE MANAGEMENT AND ACCOUNTING SOFTWARE

Office management and accounting software is used extensively in most law firms, from the sole practitioner to large, multi-office practices. It is used to keep accurate calendars of appointments, schedules, and deadlines; to track time and billing information, client funds, and costs; and prepare accurate billing records. One of the most popular and best supported is **AbacusLaw.**

## ■ CASE ORGANIZATION AND MANAGEMENT SOFTWARE

Case management software can be used to organize the cast of characters in a case, the documents, the relevant timetables, issues, legal authority, and other desired information. Top programs included here are **LexisNexis CaseMap** and **LexisNexis TimeMap.**

## ■ EXTENDED USAGE SOFTWARE PACKAGES:

AbacusLaw Tutorial and Guide with 3 year Access Code ISBN: 0-13-249071-4
     Check with you local Pearson representative to find out about other new tutorial guides with extended software.

## ■ INSTRUCTOR'S MANUAL

The *Instructor's Manual*, written by Alice Hart Hughes, contains sample syllabi, chapter outline and summary, answers to questions and exercises, and teaching notes.

## ■ MY TEST

The My Test allows you to generate quizzes and tests composed of questions from the Test Item File, modify them, and add your own.

## ■ POWERPOINT LECTURE PRESENTATION

The PowerPoint Lecture Presentation includes key concept screens and exhibits from the textbook.

The Instructor's Manual, Test Generator, and PPT package can be downloaded from our Instructor's Resource Center. To access supplementary materials online, instructors need to request an instructor access code. Go to **www.pearsonhighered.com/irc**, where you can register for an instructor access code. Within 48 hours of registering you will receive a confirming e-mail including an instructor access code. Once you have received your code, locate your text in the online catalog and click on the Instructor Resources button on the left side of the catalog product page. Select a supplement and a log-in page will appear. Once you have logged in, you can access instructor material for all Pearson textbooks.

# ACKNOWLEDGMENTS

This text incorporates material from *Reality of Real Estate*, 3rd Edition, written by Charles Nemeth. We would like to thank Charles for his contribution to this project.

Our appreciation goes out to all the students over the years who have taught us the lessons on presenting the material covered in this text. The tips and practice pointers are gleaned from many years of handling real estate settlements, the simple, the difficult and the ones that fall through, for those, we thank realtors, opposing counsel everywhere and the judges before whom we have practiced.

To Charlie and Harry Hughes, Alice's son and husband, for yet another summer when a manuscript had to come before fun.

To William Mulkeen, Esquire, Community College of Philadelphia, Paralegal Studies Program, for his thoughtful comments and suggestions, which he will recognize incorporated in these pages.

Alice Hart Hughes,
Thomas F. Goldman,
Charles P. Nemeth

# UNIT I   Essentials of Real Estate Practice: Overview

## OVERVIEW OF THE RESIDENTIAL REAL ESTATE TRANSACTION

The typical real estate sale and purchase involves a number of people; the seller and the buyer of the real estate are the principals who may use the services of agents such as lawyers, real estate brokers, appraisers, inspectors, mortgage brokers, or other professionals.

In the United States, the real estate industry has evolved such that legal professionals frequently work with real estate professionals. In some jurisdictions, depending on applicable law and custom, real estate professionals may perform real estate functions without any input or review by a legal professional. Where the two professions work together, it is important for each to understand the nature and extent of the skills and services the other provides. For the professional working in the real estate field, it is essential to have a firm foundation in the fundamentals of real estate law, procedure, and local practice customs. This includes an appreciation of the different types of property, personal and real; the way in which property is transferred; and the attendant rights and obligations of each form of ownership.

The typical real estate transaction starts with a seller listing a property for sale with a real estate broker. In some cases, the seller may also retain the services of a lawyer. The real estate broker has a duty as the agent of the seller to sell the property for the best possible price to a qualified buyer. In contemporary practice, this is usually done by listing the property with a real estate listing service that makes available information on properties that are for sale in the local area; these services may be called a multiple listing bureau or multiple listing service, or known by their initials MLB or MLS. Frequently, the listing service will show the property information on an Internet website as part of the service to market the property, either directly or indirectly using the listing broker's website. Buyers usually retain the services of a real estate broker as their agent, to locate and show them properties within their price range with the features and location they desire. The buyer's real estate broker will usually try to qualify the buyers' financial ability and coordinate that ability to obtain a mortgage with the type of property, location, or special needs of the buyer. In this Internet age, buyers sometimes use the Internet first and, when they find something they think they like, contact the listing agent or another real estate professional to arrange to see the property. Buyers may retain the services of a lawyer before a property is located, but more frequently a lawyer is consulted after the agreement of sale is signed by the seller and the buyer.

In some jurisdictions, the law provides a period of time for lawyers for the buyer and seller to review the sales agreement before it becomes binding. In other states, there is no review period, and the parties are bound to the agreement of sale as soon as they sign it.

Depending on local custom or procedure, a title or closing company, lawyer, or escrow agent will be hired to check on the title, or ownership, of the property and any claims that may impact the buyer obtaining good or full title.

In addition to real estate purchased for personal or business use, it is also a popular investment for individuals and businesses. Renting and managing residential, commercial, and industrial property is an area within the industry in which many legal and real estate professionals specialize. Professionals in this area of practice have ongoing relationships tied to the length of the leases or rental agreements. This may include finding tenants, drafting leases, collecting rents, arranging repairs and maintenance, and sometimes instituting litigation to collect rents or evict tenants.

Real estate development is also an area of specialization for the real estate and legal professional. It may involve the location of appropriate raw land or suitable structures for development or conversion. Working in this area of specialty may include acting as a straw party for the developer during the assembly of a number of tracts of land or negotiating a better price if the developer is a well-known and successful business from whom sellers would demand a higher price. Typically, legal professionals for developers spend time in public meetings before local governmental agencies and follow up where necessary with the litigation for appeals.

## LEARNING OBJECTIVES

*Upon completion of this chapter, you should be able to*

1. Describe the employment opportunities in the real estate industry.

2. Explain the difference between real and personal property.

3. Explain the difference between fixtures and real property.

4. List and describe the rights included in real property.

# Overview of Real Estate | CHAPTER 1

## ■ INTRODUCTION

The term *real estate* has multiple meanings. It is used to describe real property or land, and it is used to describe the real estate industry, including residential, commercial, and industrial real estate. Many employment opportunities exist in the real estate industry for individuals with a firm foundation in the fundamentals, an understanding of the substantive areas of real estate law, and training in the procedural side of real estate law practice. Understanding this area of law begins with learning to differentiate and define items of real property, personal property, and fixtures, as well as understanding the unique rights and duties of ownership associated with the different types of property ownership and possession.

## ■ THE REAL ESTATE INDUSTRY

The term **real estate** has multiple meanings. It is used to describe real property that someone owns, such as his or her home. It is also used to describe the real estate industry, which includes the residential market for housing, the commercial market for office and retail space, and the industrial market for warehouse and manufacturing space. To work successfully in the real estate industry requires, at the very least, education and specialized training. In some states, to work in real estate sales, inspection, title examination, or financing, an individual must

**LEARNING OBJECTIVE 1**
Describe the employment opportunities in the real estate industry.

## DIGITAL RESOURCES

Introduction to Timekeeping with Abacus.

Author Introduction to Real Estate.

Law Librarian Advice on Using Forms.

Overview of the Residential Real Estate Transaction.

Welcome to the Law Firm.

**real estate**
real property that someone owns

be licensed. Obtaining a license may require certain formal education and passing a statewide examination that tests knowledge and understanding of related real estate fundamentals and procedure.

In the United States, the real estate industry has evolved such that legal professionals frequently work with real estate professionals. In some jurisdictions, depending on applicable law and local practice and custom, real estate professionals may perform real estate functions without any input or review by the legal community. Where the two professions work together, it is important for each to understand the nature and extent of the skills and services the other provides.

## Legal Professionals

Real estate law is a dynamic industry and area of practice. Virtually every general practice law firm will have some portion of its practice devoted to real estate matters. It is an area of practice that affords opportunities limited only by an individual's skills and willingness to take on additional responsibility.

In many law firms, real estate law is secondary to the primary area of practice. For example, in firms that handle decedents' estates and family law, the firm will handle the traditional purchase and sale of a residence because most decedents' estates and divorce cases have a home that must be sold or transferred. In firms that serve business clients, the matters handled may include the acquisition and sale of commercial real estate and assistance in arranging financing.

**transactional real estate law**
negotiating and drafting documents, but not litigation that may arise from the transactions

Some law firms limit their practice to **transactional real estate law**; that is, the clients they represent are involved in the purchase, sale, or development of real estate. These law firms work on all aspects of the transaction, such as negotiating and drafting documents, but do not handle any litigation that may arise from the transactions.

Other law firms handle real estate development, from the acquisition of raw, undeveloped land through the planning, zoning approval, development, and ultimate sale process. This practice is geared more toward transactions, but with some elements of litigation involved. For example, when a request for zoning approval is presented to a local zoning hearing board and the request is opposed by members of the community, the legal team will need to prepare for a zoning hearing conducted before the local zoning board or local government board. Zoning and land use disputes not resolved at the local level may be litigated before the state trial and appellate courts.

Finally, there are firms that handle the litigation aspects of real estate law. These firms might represent property owners in zoning challenges and in disputes about the rights and duties of owners of real estate, including boundary lines, usage and maintenance of easements, and contribution to the repairs of jointly owned real estate.

Paralegals employed in real estate law practices may perform the tasks listed below:

- Drafting documents, such as agreements of sale, installment sale contracts, loan commitment documents, deeds, leases, and correspondence
- Reviewing title searches and reports
- Reviewing and preparing a summaries of the important terms in contracts such as agreements of sale and leases
- Assuming closing, settlement, and post-closing responsibilities
- Recording mortgage, deed, assignment, release, and other documents

- Preparing tax filings
- Securing zoning permits and applications
- Preparing legal descriptions
- Arranging for payoff of notes and release of mortgages
- Notarizing documents at closing, if qualified
- Arranging for liability and hazard insurance
- Ordering and conducting lien searches
- Assessing and analyzing ownership, whether sole or joint
- Assessing and analyzing types of realty
- Assuring compliance with governmental requirements
- Communicating with clients and other professionals involved in the real estate transaction

## Real Estate Professionals

In many states, properly licensed **real estate professionals** are authorized by state statute to perform many of the tasks that the legal team performs, such as drafting documents and performing title searches. State statutes and regulations set a standard for the minimum required training, education, testing, and other licensing requirements to offer real estate brokerage, sales, inspection, and title services to the public. In many cases, real estate professionals provide their services without use of or consultation with members of the legal profession. However, with more complex real estate transactions, legal and real estate professionals find themselves working together more often.

**Real estate brokerage** and **real estate sales** involve the marketing and sale of real estate. Real estate brokers and salespersons or sales agents are licensed under state law and regulated by a state real estate commission or licensing board. Typically, there are separate requirements, education, and testing for licensed real estate brokers and licensed real estate salespersons. Real estate brokers have the same authority as salespersons, with the added responsibility of managing a real estate brokerage, including supervision of real estate salespersons. Salespersons are employed by real estate brokers, subject to the brokers' supervision, and generally do anything related to the listing and sale of real estate. Like members of other professions, real estate professionals have a national association that requires adherence to a code of ethics. The National Association of Realtors requires its members to abide by a code of conduct or ethics and provides its members marketing tools and forms for real estate transactions.

Exhibit 1.1 is the Preamble to the National Association of Realtors Code of Ethics.

**Real estate rental management** involves the marketing of rental property, including obtaining and qualifying tenants; collecting rents; supervising work, maintenance, and repairs; and resolving tenant complaints. In many jurisdictions, real estate management is a function that may only be performed by licensed real estate salespersons and brokers. The Institute of Real Estate Management is an affiliate of the National Association of Realtors, which offers education and certification for those working in real estate management.

**Real Estate Finance** involves reviewing applications for the financing of the purchase, development, and construction of real property. Real estate financing is conducted by financial institutions such as banks and credit unions. Real estate finance is heavily regulated by federal and state statutes. Financial institutions are licensed under federal and state law.

**real estate professionals**
those authorized by state statute to perform many of the real estate tasks that lawyers perform, such as drafting documents and performing title searches

**real estate sales**
the marketing and sale of real estate

 **WEB EXPLORATION**
Check the National Association of Realtors website for the services provided: http://www.realtor.org/

**real estate rental management**
the marketing of rental property, including obtaining and qualifying tenants; collecting rents; supervising work, maintenance, and repairs; and resolving tenant complaints

 **WEB EXPLORATION**
Check the Institute of Real Estate Management website for the certification requirements and benefits: http://www.irem.org/

**Real Estate Finance**
reviewing applications for the financing of the purchase, development, and construction of real property

**Exhibit 1.1** National Association of Realtors Preamble to the Code of Ethics

While the Code of Ethics establishes obligations that may be higher than those mandated by law, in any instance where the Code of Ethics and the law conflict, the obligations of the law must take precedence.

**Preamble**

Under all is the land. Upon its wise utilization and widely allocated ownership depend the survival and growth of free institutions and of our civilization. REALTORS® should recognize that the interests of the nation and its citizens require the highest and best use of the land and the widest distribution of land ownership. They require the creation of adequate housing, the building of functioning cities, the development of productive industries and farms, and the preservation of a healthful environment.

Such interests impose obligations beyond those of ordinary commerce. They impose grave social responsibility and a patriotic duty to which REALTORS® should dedicate themselves, and for which they should be diligent in preparing themselves. REALTORS®, therefore, are zealous to maintain and improve the standards of their calling and share with their fellow REALTORS® a common responsibility for its integrity and honor.

In recognition and appreciation of their obligations to clients, customers, the public, and each other, REALTORS® continuously strive to become and remain informed on issues affecting real estate and, as knowledgeable professionals, they willingly share the fruit of their experience and study with others. They identify and take steps, through enforcement of this Code of Ethics and by assisting appropriate regulatory bodies, to eliminate practices which may damage the public or which might discredit or bring dishonor to the real estate profession. REALTORS® having direct personal knowledge of conduct that may violate the Code of Ethics involving misappropriation of client or customer funds or property, willful discrimination, or fraud resulting in substantial economic harm, bring such matters to the attention of the appropriate Board or Association of REALTORS®. *(Amended 1/00)*

Realizing that cooperation with other real estate professionals promotes the best interests of those who utilize their services, REALTORS® urge exclusive representation of clients; do not attempt to gain any unfair advantage over their competitors; and they refrain from making unsolicited comments about other practitioners. In instances where their opinion is sought, or where REALTORS® believe that comment is necessary, their opinion is offered in an objective, professional manner, uninfluenced by any personal motivation or potential advantage or gain.

The term REALTOR® has come to connote competency, fairness, and high integrity resulting from adherence to a lofty ideal of moral conduct in business relations. No inducement of profit and no instruction from clients ever can justify departure from this ideal.

In the interpretation of this obligation, REALTORS® can take no safer guide than that which has been handed down through the centuries, embodied in the Golden Rule, "Whatsoever ye would that others should do to you, do ye even so to them."

**mortgage broker**
individual licensed by the state or states who assists buyers in obtaining financing from financial institutions

**Mortgage brokers** are generally individuals licensed by the state or states who assist buyers in obtaining financing from financial institutions. States vary widely in their requirements and regulation of mortgage brokers. Licensing typically requires some education and a test to establish minimum knowledge and skills, as stated by the *Mortgage News Daily*:

> The uniqueness of the mortgage licensing laws of each state is expressed in the diversity of the laws, rules, regulations that each state adopts. The states differ on whether a Mortgage Broker even needs a mortgage license, whether the Mortgage Broker can loan on both 1st and 2nd mortgages, or whether a physical office in the state is required. As business over the internet increases, the mortgage licensing laws are becoming more lenient on this physical office requirement. States also differ on how much continuing education they require of the Mortgage Brokers. The various mortgage licensing laws also pertain to the employees of the Mortgage Brokers, and whether they, too, need a mortgage license.

**WEB EXPLORATION**
Check the website below for the mortgage broker requirements in your state
http://www.mortgagenewsdaily.com/Mortgage_License/

*Source:* http://www.mortgagenewsdaily.com/Mortgage_License/

**Exhibit 1.2** Appraisal Institute Preamble to the Code of Professional Ethics and Standards of Professional Appraisal Practice

> Real estate is one of the basic sources of wealth in the global economy. Therefore, homeowners, business entities, governments, individuals, and others who own, manage, sell, purchase, invest in, or lend money on the security of real estate must have ready access to the services of Appraisal Institute Members who provide unbiased opinions of value, as well as sound information, analyses, and advice on a wide range of real estate-related issues. Members of the Appraisal Institute also are increasingly called upon to use their expertise to value other property types such as personal property, machinery and equipment, and businesses. Therefore, the services of Appraisal Institute Members are vital to the well being of our society and the global economy, and foster economic growth, stability, and public confidence.
>
> *Source:* http://www.appraisalinstitute.org/membership/downloads/cpe/CPE.pdf

**Real estate development** involves acquiring structures for conversion or rehabilitation; acquiring raw, undeveloped land; developing a plan to improve the land for residential, commercial, or industrial use; and implementing that plan through the development and construction process and, ultimately, by selling the individual units. There is generally no specific requirement for real estate developers to be licensed or have specialized knowledge or training. Certainly knowledge of real estate law, finance, construction, and business principles will assist one who is engaged in the development process.

**Real estate appraisal** involves determining the value of real property, independent of any existing agreement of sale or loan application related to it. Appraisers generally are licensed under state law by the state real estate board and have professional organizations, most notably the Appraisal Institute, which grants designations or certifications for the appraisal of certain types of real estate—residential, commercial, or industrial. This professional organization also has a code of conduct or ethics that governs those who are members of the profession. Exhibit 1.2 is the preamble to the Appraisal Institute's Code of Professional Ethics.

**Real estate inspection** involves inspection services to determine whether any deficiencies or defects exist with the structural and mechanical components of real estate. In many states, there are licensing requirements. To receive a designation from professional associations such as the American Society of Home Inspectors or the National Association of Home Inspectors, inspectors go through significant training and education. The Code of Ethics of the American Society of Home Inspectors appears in Exhibit 1.3.

**Title insurance** agents' services involve determining ownership of real estate by conducting title searches and examinations, issuing title reports and title insurance, and conducting insured real estate closings. Title insurance agents, like all insurance agents, are regulated by the state, usually through the state insurance commissions. Education and testing are required to obtain a license. Title insurance rates are controlled by the state regulatory commission. In addition, membership in a professional association such as the American Land Title

**Real estate development**
acquiring structures for conversion or rehabilitation; acquiring raw, undeveloped land; developing a plan to improve the land for residential, commercial, or industrial use; and implementing that plan through the development and construction process and, ultimately, by selling the individual units

 **WEB EXPLORATION**
The Urban Land Institute is an educational and research group that studies the development of land in urban areas.

See the Urban Land Institute website for information on green planning: http://www.uli.org/

**real estate appraisal**
determining the value of real property, independent of any existing agreement of sale or loan application related to it

 **WEB EXPLORATION**
Review the requirements for the SRA designation from the Appraisal Institute: http://www.appraisalinstitute.org/

**real estate inspection**
services to determine whether any deficiencies or defects exist with the structural and mechanical components of real estate

 **WEB EXPLORATION**
Review the training and education requirements for home inspectors at the following websites: http://www.nahi.org/public/department13 and http://www.ashi.org/6.cfm

**title insurance**
insurance insuring the quality of the ownership after title searches and examinations have been conducted

## Exhibit 1.3 American Society of Home Inspectors, Code of Ethics

American Society of Home Inspectors
Code of Ethics
Effective on June 13, 2004

The ASHI Code of Ethics details the core guidelines of home inspection professionalism and home inspection ethics. Covering crucial issues such as conflicts of interest, good faith and public perception, these home inspection ethics are central pillars of home inspection professionalism for the entire industry.

Integrity, honesty, and objectivity are fundamental principles embodied by this Code, which sets forth obligations of ethical conduct for the home inspection profession. The Membership of ASHI has adopted this Code to provide high ethical standards to safeguard the public and the profession.

Inspectors shall comply with this Code, shall avoid association with any enterprise whose practices violate this Code, and shall strive to uphold, maintain, and improve the integrity, reputation, and practice of the home inspection profession.

All inspector members of ASHI have agreed to abide by this Code of Ethics:

1. Inspectors shall avoid conflicts of interest or activities that compromise, or appear to compromise, professional independence, objectivity, or inspection integrity.
   A. Inspectors shall not inspect properties for compensation in which they have, or expect to have, a financial interest.
   B. Inspectors shall not inspect properties under contingent arrangements whereby any compensation or future referrals are dependent on reported findings or on the sale of a property.
   C. Inspectors shall not directly or indirectly compensate realty agents, or other parties having a financial interest in closing or settlement of real estate transactions, for the referral of inspections or for inclusion on a list of recommended inspectors, preferred providers, or similar arrangements.
   D. Inspectors shall not receive compensation for an inspection from more than one party unless agreed to by the client(s).
   E. Inspectors shall not accept compensation, directly or indirectly, for recommending contractors, services, or products to inspection clients or other parties having an interest in inspected properties.
   F. Inspectors shall not repair, replace, or upgrade, for compensation, systems or components covered by ASHI Standards of Practice, for one year after the inspection.

2. Inspectors shall act in good faith toward each client and other interested parties.
   A. Inspectors shall perform services and express opinions based on genuine conviction and only within their areas of education, training, or experience.
   B. Inspectors shall be objective in their reporting and not knowingly understate or overstate the significance of reported conditions.
   C. Inspectors shall not disclose inspection results or client information without client approval. Inspectors, at their discretion, may disclose observed immediate safety hazards to occupants exposed to such hazards, when feasible.

3. Inspectors shall avoid activities that may harm the public, discredit themselves, or reduce public confidence in the profession.
   A. Advertising, marketing, and promotion of inspectors' services or qualifications shall not be fraudulent, false, deceptive, or misleading.
   B. Inspectors shall report substantive and willful violations of this Code to the Society.

American Society of Home Inspectors, Inc.® Effective on June 13, 2004
©2004 American Society of Home Inspectors, Inc.® All Rights Reserved.

*Source:* http://www.homeinspector.org/codeofethics/default.aspx

Association has served to standardize the industry nationwide with uniform forms, as set forth below:

> The American Land Title Association first created its policy forms eight decades ago in order to standardize title insurance coverage across the country. These uniform policy forms have become the gold standard of the industry and have allowed universal acceptance of title insurance written on ALTA policy forms. ALTA continues to improve and adapt the forms to address current marketplace needs.

Source: http://www.alta.org/membership/Intro.cfm

**WEB EXPLORATION**
View the requirements for and benefits of membership in the American Land Title Association: http://www.alta .org/membership/Intro.cfm

## ◼ ISSUES IN REAL ESTATE PRACTICE

The real estate industry is highly localized. It is important to understand the state law and industry practice, customs, and procedures in each state and in each locality where a particular piece of real property is located. Within the same state, different practice customs and procedures may be followed by those in different parts of the state, such as north and south New Jersey. Some state statutes require lawyers to handle certain aspects of a real estate transaction. In other states, real estate professionals may perform those same functions without the involvement of lawyers. A primary area of concern for those involved is the unauthorized practice of law, or UPL. Unless authorized by statute to do so, an individual who completes for others the standardized preprinted forms used in real estate transactions may commit the unauthorized practice of law. While they may appear to be simple fill-in-the-blank forms, each entry has the potential to impact the rights of others, a factor that is usually included in the definition of the practice of law for UPL purposes. Knowledge and observance of ethical codes are equally important to legal and real estate professionals engaged in real estate, because the failure to observe them may lead to a loss of license to practice.

### Unauthorized Practice of Law

The **unauthorized practice of law (UPL)** is a crime in most states—usually a misdemeanor, punishable by a jail term of less than one year and/or a fine. Applicable statutes were designed with consumer protection in mind, to protect the public from having their legal rights impacted by those who are not licensed attorneys. Anyone not otherwise authorized who gives legal advice that affects the legal rights of another can be charged with the unauthorized practice of law. Even filling in the blanks to complete a preprinted Agreement to Purchase and Sell Real Estate form can constitute the unauthorized practice of law, because the information included or excluded can affect the legal rights of the parties. Under their licensing statutes, real estate professionals may perform certain activities without committing the unauthorized practice of law. For example, licensed real estate sales agents and brokers complete listing and sales contracts for the benefit of the seller or buyer for whom they are working. The Virginia State Bar issued a detailed statement, which appears below, of what services a Settlement Agent may provide without risk of committing the unauthorized practice of law. In Virginia, Settlement Agents include licensed real estate brokers, title insurance agents, financial institutions, and licensed attorneys.

**unauthorized practice of law (UPL)**
the offering of legal advice that affects the legal rights of another without the proper authorization

In connection with a real estate closing, the Virginia State Bar in its rules prohibiting the unauthorized practice of law, has stated that the following tasks, among others, may be performed by a non-lawyer Settlement Agent and do not involve the practice of law:

> ordering a survey, termite or other inspection(s), casualty insurance or certificates of insurance, lien payoff figures, loan checks or title insurance;
>
> creating or preparing a title abstract;
>
> determining the status of utility services and assisting in their transfer;
>
> making mathematical calculations involving the proration of taxes, insurance, rent, interest and the like in accordance with the contract or local custom;
>
> completing form documents selected by and in accordance with the instructions of the parties to the transaction, but not drafting or selecting such documents;
>
> obtaining lien waivers from mechanics or material men in a form acceptable to the parties in interest, but not drafting such waivers or giving advice as to the legal sufficiency thereof;
>
> preparing settlement statements, such as the HUD-1;
>
> receiving and disbursing settlement funds;
>
> drafting receipts and certificates of satisfaction, but not deeds, deeds of trust, deed of trust notes, or deeds of release;
>
> completing other forms such as the Owner's/Seller's Affidavit, Notice of Availability, and tax reporting forms.

*Source:* http://www.vsb.org/site/regulation/
upl-guidelines-for-real-estate-settlement-agents/

While statutes provide exemption for some real estate professionals and others may be exempt under licensing statutes, there is generally no exemption for the paralegal.

Paralegals must be vigilant and take affirmative action to avoid even the appearance that they are practicing law. Five golden rules are as follows:

1. Always identify yourself as a paralegal and not a lawyer.
2. Never give advice or your opinion about what to do.
3. Never issue draft documents that the supervising attorney has not reviewed.
4. Never issue forms you have completed that the supervising attorney has not reviewed.
5. When in doubt, always refer the client to the attorney or indicate that the attorney will get back to the client.

Like the paralegal, the real estate professional should make sure to indicate that he or she is not a lawyer and that perhaps a lawyer should be consulted. A few states recognize the quandary and provide a statutory attorney review period after any contract is signed before it becomes binding. This requirement encourages parties to consult with lawyers early in the process and protects the real estate professional from being placed in a position that might be UPL.

## ■ REAL PROPERTY

**LEARNING OBJECTIVE 2**
Explain the difference between real and personal property.

**Personal property** may be tangible or intangible and generally is movable. A car is personal property and so are jewelry, bank accounts, and a professional practice such as a dental or law office. **Tangible personal property** is property you can touch—for instance, a car and jewelry—and is movable. **Intangible personal property** is property that you cannot touch—such as a bank account or a professional practice—but that also is movable. Keep in mind that a medical or legal practice is not the office in which it operates, but rather the unique knowledge, training, and skills the professional possesses. These are movable, as they go with the professionals wherever they are.

**Real property** is anything that is not personal property. Simply, real property is land, which is not movable in the way personal property is. Land does not wear out or fall out of vogue, and there isn't any more being made. But real property is more than just land. Real property includes whatever is permanently attached to the land and certain rights that are associated with the land. A building is attached to the land in such a way as to become permanent and, thus, part of the real property. Generally, landscaping elements such as ornamental trees and shrubs are considered part of the real property. Different rules apply to a farmer's growing crops, which under local state law may be considered personal property, the theory being that crops are planted with the intent of being harvested and may be used by the farmer as collateral for a loan.

**personal property**
property that is tangible or intangible and that generally is movable

**tangible personal property**
property you can touch

**intangible personal property**
property you cannot touch

**real property**
anything that is not personal property

## Fixtures

**Fixtures** are items of personal property that, once attached to the real property, become part of the real property because the removal of a fixture might cause substantial harm or damage. There is a wide spectrum of items that are fixtures; some clearly become part of the real property, but for others it may not be so clear. Think of a central heating and air conditioning unit. The furnace, blower, ducts, compressor, and condenser are each an individual tangible item of personal property. Once installed in a home, they become an integral part of the real property; removal would be impractical and certainly cause substantial harm. At the opposite end of the spectrum are curtain rods. Although attached to the wall of the home, curtain rods are easily removable without causing substantial harm. The curtain rods are personal property. What about a swimming pool? The answer depends on whether the swimming pool is in ground or above ground. The factors to consider in determining whether something, such as the swimming pool, is a fixture that becomes part of the real property are summarized below:

**LEARNING OBJECTIVE 3**
Explain the difference between fixtures and real property.

**fixtures**
items of personal property that, once attached to the real property, become part of the real property

1. The means and method of attachment (e.g., in-ground swimming pool dug into earth)
2. The adaptation of the object outside the real property (e.g., an in-ground pool cannot be moved or relocated, while one that is above ground can)
3. The intent of the party who originally attached the object (e.g., an in-ground pool is not a temporary addition)
4. The relationship of the parties involved (e.g., owners of real property)
5. The existence of an agreement that defines whether the object is part of the real property or not (e.g., agreement of sale, which may or may not include the pool)

In the swimming pool example, the in-ground pool is a fixture, while the above-ground pool, because it is removable, is personal property, not a fixture.

## Bundle of Rights

Real property includes the land itself, anything affixed to the land, and the rights that accompany ownership of the land. **Rights appurtenant** to the land are the rights that accompany the ownership or possession of land, such as air rights,

**rights appurtenant**
rights that accompany ownership of land

**LEARNING OBJECTIVE 4**
List and describe the rights included in real property.

### Exhibit 1.4 Interests in land

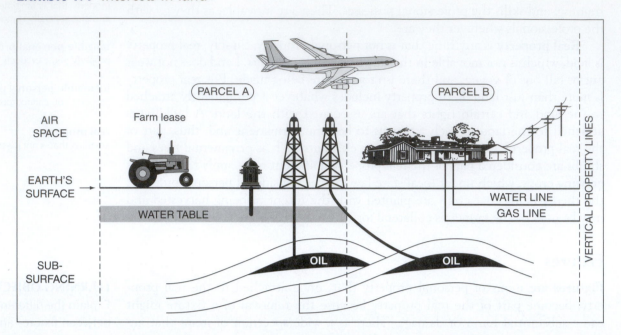

**bundle of rights**
the rights that accompany the ownership or possession of land, such as air rights, mineral rights, and riparian (river or stream) rights

mineral rights, or riparian (river or stream) rights. These rights are often referred to as a **bundle of rights**. The individual rights are like a handful of pick-up sticks. When held together, they represent the entire bundle, but each is separate and distinct from the others. Ownership of real property includes all the rights. The party having the bundle of rights is sometimes said to have **title**. The entire bundle of rights can be sold or transferred, or an individual right can be separated and sold or transferred to another. Exhibit 1.4 depicts the various rights related to the land itself.

**title**
term used interchangeably with ownership of real property

**Surface rights** include the right to possess or occupy a parcel of real estate. The individual right may be transferred to another through a lease or rental agreement. Surface rights include the right to build on the land and to farm or cultivate the land. In fact, many farmers do not own but rather rent the land they farm.

**surface rights**
right to possess or occupy a parcel of real estate

**air rights**
the rights in the air above the land

**Air rights** are the rights in the air above the land. This includes the right to erect a structure to a particular height. One might be inclined to think, "If I own the real property and it includes the airspace, don't I own the air rights above my property to the ends of the universe?" However, airspace does have its limits. Such limits are determined by technological advancement: how high a structure can be built and remain safe, airways needing to be clear for airplanes, etc.

**mineral rights**
subsurface rights, including the right to use or take any of the minerals found in the earth's crust

**Mineral rights** or subsurface rights include the right to use or take any of the minerals found in the earth's crust. Mineral rights include the rights to drill for water, oil, natural gas, stone, rock, and precious metals such as gold, silver, and copper. The rights to remove each of these individual minerals can be leased, transferred, or sold to another.

## Riparian rights

**riparian rights**
the rights associated with the access to and usage and control of water that flows over land

Water is found on land in the form of lakes, rivers, streams, and oceans. Riparian rights are the rights associated with the access to and usage and control of water

## Exhibit 1.5 Riparian rights

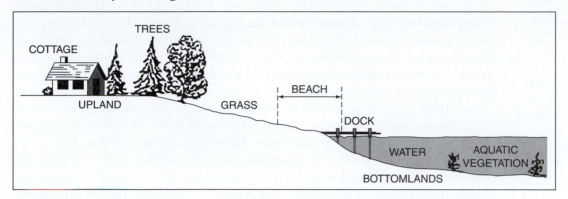

that flows over land. With riparian rights, there are competing rights: the rights of the individual landowners over whose land the water flows and the rights of the adjoining landowners and the public at large who are also granted the rights to use and enjoy the water.

Exhibit 1.5 depicts a typical setting with riparian rights.

Riparian rights are multidimensional and include the following:

- The right of access to the water. Access is the "first and most basic right of the riparian owner," under which all other riparian rights are created and protected. The right of access (1) ensures the riparian owner's "right to be and remain a riparian proprietor," (2) protects the riparian owner's ability to reach the navigable portions of adjacent waters without unreasonable impediment, (3) supports the riparian owner's right to wharf out onto the waterway, (4) includes the right to erect structures in aid of navigation, and (5) underlies the riparian owner's right to take title to lands that accrete beyond the mean high-water mark.
- The right to erect a dock or wharf to gain access to the water
- The right to acquire accretions left behind by the water
- The right to fill
- The right to the continued flow of water
- The right to preservation of the view of the water

Of all these rights, questions involving the appropriation of water are some of the most common. Appropriation determines who has the lawful right to access the water supply, what standards dictate ownership of the water, and what standards permit individual or larger usage by a community. For the most part, statewide agencies and legislatures lay out rules and regulations regarding these rights.

## The Statute of Frauds

The **Statute of Frauds** was originally created under the common law of England as a method of preventing individuals from committing fraud on the courts. Individuals would present a dispute to the court without any documentation and lie to the court, claiming rights in real estate. Generally, these were claims by the aristocracy, who often relied upon their elevated status to give them greater

**Statute of Frauds**
the requirement that certain contracts be in writing to be enforceable in a court of law

credibility than the word of a mere commoner. To prevent the court from being turned into a war of words won by social status, the Statute of Frauds was enacted. Every state has enacted some form of the Statute of Frauds. The underlying theory of current statutes of fraud laws is that certain transactions are so significant that they must be written—to provide a reliable record of the transaction and, of course, to prevent fraud. If a transaction involves any interest in real property, an activity that cannot be completed within one year, or property of a certain value, there must be a written document signed by the person against whom enforcement might be sought. The purchase of a home or rental of an apartment involves an interest in real estate. These transactions are of such a serious consequence that they should be written, as memories fade and what someone may have said and how they said it should not impact the terms of an agreement. These are not interests where a dispute, if it arises, should be decided on one person's word versus that of another.

For the real estate team, whether legal or real estate professionals, the terms of agreements should be in writing. There are many reasons for this requirement. Depending on the jurisdiction, the Statute of Frauds may require that certain types of contracts be in writing to prevent disputes over the terms of the agreement, such as the rights and duties of the parties. Employment contracts are another example that may need to be in writing to prevent misunderstanding, involving obligations and rates of compensation.

California requires employment agreements for sale or leasing of real estate to be in writing.

> The following contracts are invalid, unless they, or some note or memorandum thereof, are in writing and subscribed by the party to be charged or by the party's agent:
>
> (4) An agreement authorizing or employing an agent, broker, or any other person to purchase or sell real estate, or to lease real estate for a longer period than one year, or to procure, introduce, or find a purchaser or seller of real estate or a lessee or lessor of real estate where the lease is for a longer period than one year, for compensation or a commission.
>
> Cal. Civ. Code 1624(a)(4)

# ETHICAL Considerations

**WEB EXPLORATION**

Ethical Note:
The rules of professional conduct for the legal professions require the supervision of all members of the legal team by a supervising attorney and by the managing partners. Check the link to your state's ethics code from the American Bar Association listings at http://www.americanbar.org/groups/professional_responsibility/resources/links_of_interest.html

## SUPERVISION

Non-lawyer employees include paralegals, legal assistants, secretarial staff, bookkeepers, file clerks, and information technologists. Non-lawyer personnel are required to abide by the same rules of professional conduct as lawyers. There is an affirmative duty on the attorney overseeing the work of the non-lawyer to make sure that those rules are adhered to. In those jurisdictions where there is a UPL statute, the supervising attorney must be certain the work produced by the non-lawyer is reviewed before it is issued. This simple yet time-consuming review process protects the non-lawyer from committing UPL and the attorney from violating the ethical duty to supervise non-lawyer work product.

The non-lawyer employee should be assertive in seeking review and approval from the supervising attorney of work produced that will impact the rights or legal interests of the client.

## KEY TERMS

## CHAPTER SUMMARY

| | |
|---|---|
| Introduction | *Real estate* has multiple meanings. It is used to describe real property or land, and it is used to describe the real estate industry—residential, commercial, and industrial. |
| The Real Estate Industry | The real estate industry includes the residential market for housing, the commercial market for office and retail space, and the industrial market for warehouse and manufacturing space. In some states, to work in real estate sales, inspection, title examination, or financing, an individual must be licensed. |
| Legal Professionals | Virtually every general practice law firm will have some portion of its practice devoted to real estate matters. Some law firms limit their practice to transactional real estate law, while other firms handle the litigation aspects of real estate law. |
| Real Estate Professionals | In many states, properly licensed real estate professionals are authorized by state statute to perform many of the tasks that the legal team performs, such as drafting documents and performing title searches. |
| Real Estate Brokerage and Sales | Involves the marketing and sale of real estate. |
| Ethical Concerns for the Real Estate Team | Like members of other professions, real estate professionals have a national association that requires adherence to a code of ethics for its members. |
| Real Estate Rental Management | Involves the marketing of rental property, including obtaining and qualifying tenants; collecting rents; supervising work, maintenance, and repairs; and resolving tenant complaints. |
| Real Estate Finance | Involves reviewing applications and approving financing for the purchase, development, and construction of real property. |
| Real Estate Development | Involves acquiring raw, undeveloped land; developing a plan to improve the land for residential, commercial or industrial use; and implementing that plan through the development and construction process and, ultimately, by selling the individual units. |

| Real Estate Appraisal | Involves determining the value of real property, independent of any existing agreement of sale or loan application related to it. |
|---|---|
| Real Estate Inspection | Involves inspection services to determine whether any deficiencies or defects exist with the structural and mechanical components of real estate. In many states, there are licensing requirements. |
| Title Insurance | Involves determining ownership of real estate by conducting title searches and examinations, issuing title reports and title insurance, and conducting insured real estate closings. |
| Real Estate Custom and Procedure | The real estate industry is highly localized. It is important to understand the state law and industry custom and procedure in each state and in each locality where the real estate is located. |
| Unauthorized Practice of Law | These statutes were designed with consumer protection in mind, to protect the public from having their legal rights impacted by those who are not licensed attorneys. Under their licensing statutes, real estate professionals may perform certain activities without committing the unauthorized practice of law. |
| Real Property | Real property is anything that is not personal property. Simply, real property is land, which is not movable in the way personal property is. |
| Fixtures | Fixtures are items of personal property that, once attached to the real property, become part of the real property. |
| Bundle of Rights | Real property includes the land itself, anything affixed to the land, and the rights that accompany ownership of the land. |
| Surface Rights | Include the right to possess or occupy the parcel of real estate. |
| Air Rights | The rights in the air above the land. |
| Mineral Rights | Subsurface rights include the right to use or take any of the minerals found in the earth's crust. |
| Riparian Rights | The rights associated with the access to and usage and control of water that flows over land. |
| The Statute of Frauds | The underlying theory of current statutes of fraud laws is that certain transactions are so significant that they must be written to provide a reliable record of the transaction and, of course, to prevent fraud. |

## REVIEW QUESTIONS AND EXERCISES

1. Define the term *real estate*.
2. What functions does the real estate industry perform?
3. What are the types of real estate practice in which a law firm may be engaged?
4. What types of activities and tasks might a paralegal perform in a real estate law practice?
5. What is the purpose of Unauthorized Practice of Law statutes?
6. Define, describe, and provide an example of the different forms of personal property.
7. Define real property.
8. What is a fixture? Give examples of items that are fixtures and those that may or may not be fixtures, and explain why.
9. What characteristics make a fixture part of real property rather than personal property?
10. To what does the term *bundle of rights* refer?
11. What are surface rights? Air rights? Mineral rights? Riparian rights?

## VIDEO CASE STUDY

Go to www.pearsonhighered.com/careers to view the following videos.

### Welcome to the Law Firm

The intern is welcomed to the firm by the supervising attorney to whom they will be reporting in the virtual law office.

### Author Introduction to Real Estate

Author video introduction to chapter coverage.

### Overview of the Residential Real Estate Transaction

Overview of the Residential Real Estate Transaction, including all the parties involved and the process from the signing of the listing contract to attending the real estate closing.

### Law Librarian Advice on Using Forms

The law librarian offers advice and warnings on the use of sample forms, templates.

## INTERNET AND TECHNOLOGY EXERCISES

1. Obtain contact information, including the URL, for your local realty board, and determine what forms, if any, are available.
2. Determine what state government agency regulates real estate sales and brokerage, and obtain the requirements that must be met to be licensed in your state.
3. Obtain your state's statute for Unauthorized Practice of Law. Is UPL a crime in your state? If so, what is the punishment?

## REAL ESTATE PORTFOLIO EXERCISES

**Overview of Real Estate**

**To:** Paralegal Intern
**From:** Human Resources Director
**Re:** Personal Calendar and Timekeeping

**Welcome to the firm**

As a member of the firm you are expected to keep accurate time records for all time spent working on any activity related to your internship. Please download and install AbacusLaw on your computer and set yourself up as a timekeeper.

You should set up a separate client record in Abacus as new assignments are given to you, identifying the client by name and the type of case or matter.

Also set up your instructor as a client and "course activity" as the matter. Any time spent in the course not on a specific client file can be entered into this general category so you can track all time spent in all activity related to the course.

**Calendars**

We also need to know your schedule for the semester. We all use the calendaring option in the time keeping program to indicate our appointments and other time commitments.

In the AbacusLaw calendar feature please enter your important personal dates for the next four months, including test dates, vacation days, and other important dates and deadlines.

You will be required to submit a printout of your calendar and time records summaries during the internship and at the end.

Portfolio item produced:
Calendar for the next four months

Go to www.pearsonhighered.com/careers to download instructions.

## LEARNING OBJECTIVES

*Upon completion of this chapter, you should be able to*

1. Describe the types of freehold estates.

2. Describe the types of non-freehold estates.

## CHAPTER 2

# Estates in Land

## ■ INTRODUCTION TO ESTATES IN LAND

In real estate law, the word **estate** means the bundle of individual rights of ownership in real estate, such as the right to own, occupy, use, sell, and transfer real estate.

Estates can be classified as either **freehold estates** or **non-freehold estates.** Freehold estates are those that include possession and ownership for an indefinite period of time. The freehold estate with the greatest number of rights is the fee simple estate. Fee simple ownership is the most common way that real estate is owned. However, fee simple ownership and the rights included with that form of ownership are not absolute; those rights can be limited by the federal, state, and local governments.

Non-freehold estates are leasehold estates that include possession for a definite period of time but not ownership. For example, the rights that an apartment renter has: The renter has possession of the real property for a period of time but does not own the property. The duration of the leasehold estate is for a fixed period of time.

Real Estate Law has its deepest roots in the feudal system found in Europe and particularly England. The feudal system was designed to allow the aristocracy—the wealthy and titled—to acquire, control, and keep land. The terminology and many of the concepts used in feudal times to describe interests in land have survived as part of the English common law adopted in the United States, such as the terms *freehold* and *non-freehold* estates. Other terms have fallen out of use: **seizen,** the feudal term for one who has possession of and title to real estate has been replaced with the modern term *title and possession*; **fee tail**, a form of ownership of

**estate**
the bundle of individual rights of ownership in real estate, such as the right to own, occupy, use, sell, and transfer real estate

**freehold estates**
forms of ownership that include present possession and ownership for an indefinite or unknown period of time

**COMMON LAW TERMS**

**seizen**
the feudal term for one who has possession of and title to real estate; has been replaced with the modern term *title and possession*

**fee tail**
a form of ownership of real estate where title is passed only on the death of the owner and only to legitimate heirs to assure continued ownership of the land within a particular bloodline

## DIGITAL RESOURCES

Author Introduction to Estates in Land.

Seller's First Meeting with Attorney.

Sample forms and templates.

real estate where title passed only on the death of the owner and only to legitimate heirs to assure continued ownership of the land within a particular bloodline has also fallen out of use.

## ◼ FREEHOLD ESTATES

**LEARNING OBJECTIVE 1**
Describe the types of free-hold estates.

**Freehold estates** are those forms of ownership that include present possession and ownership for an indefinite or unknown period of time. The duration of owner-ship is generally the lifetime of the owner, a time period that is never certain and therefore is said to be indefinite. There are four types of freehold estates:

1. fee simple absolute
2. fee simple determinable
3. fee simple conditional
4. life estate

As described below, each of the freehold estates lasts for an indefinite period of time and may have other conditions or limitations on the use or possession of the real property.

## Fee Simple Absolute

**fee simple absolute estate**
a freehold estate without limitation or restriction of any kind for an indefinite period of time, the life of the owner

**inherit**
the right to receive the property of another upon that person's death

**title**
often used interchangeably with the term *estate* to describe the entire bundle of rights that the owner of a fee simple absolute estate has

**deed**
the written document that is usually used to transfer an estate or title to real property

**grantor**
the person transferring the title

**grantee**
the person to whom the title is transferred

A **fee simple absolute estate** is a freehold estate without limitation or restriction of any kind for an indefinite period of time, the life of the owner. The owner has the present right to exclusively possess and enjoy the property. The owner of a fee simple absolute estate has the right to determine who will **inherit** or receive the property at his or her death.

The owner of the fee simple absolute estate is sometimes said to have title to the property. **Title** is often used interchangeably with the term *estate* to describe the entire bundle of rights that the owner of a fee simple absolute estate has. The bundle of rights may be transferred, in whole or in part, during the lifetime of the owner by a deed or upon death by a testamentary writing or will.

A **deed** is the written document that is usually used to transfer an estate or title to real property. Exhibit 2.1 is a deed showing the transfer of a fee simple absolute estate. The parties in a deed are the **grantor,** the person transferring the title, and the **grantee,** the person to whom the the title is transferred. The deed also includes the type of estate being transferred, such as fee simple absolute, as shown in Exhibit 2.1.

In Exhibit 2.1, Molly Taylor is the grantor and Daniel Schan is the grantee. The grantor is transferring a fee simple absolute ownership (title). The fee simple absolute title comes with the unlimited use of the real property and the power to transfer grantee's title during his life or upon his death.

A fee simple absolute estate has the greatest number of rights and is often said to represent the full bundle of rights of real estate ownership. The fee simple absolute owner may do whatever he wishes with his property; subject to local, state, and federal government control, the land can be farmed or left untouched, improved with the construction of buildings, excavated to uncover and remove minerals and gases that lie beneath the surface, or sold, leased, or gifted. Thus, the fee simple absolute estate is said to be complete, unrestricted ownership.

There are limits to ownership rights. The Common Law recognizes that the owner of a fee simple absolute estate has the right to peaceful and quiet

## Exhibit 2.1  Fee simple absolute deed

**THIS INDENTURE,** MADE this day of 201 ,

BETWEEN                                    **MOLLY TAYLOR**
                                           (hereinafter called the Grantor),

                                           **AND**

                                           **DANIEL SCHAN**
                                           (hereinafter called the Grantee),

**WITNESSETH** That the said Grantor for and in consideration of the sum of Three Hundred and EIGHT Thousand ($308,000.00) Dollars lawful money of the United States of America, unto her well and truly paid by the Grantee, at or before the sealing and delivery hereof, the receipt whereof is hereby acknowledged, hath granted, bargained and sold, released and confirmed, and by these presents doth grant, bargain and sell, release and confirm unto the said Grantee, his heirs and assigns, in fee.

ALL THAT PARCEL OF LAND IN THE TOWNSHIP OF NEWTOWNE, AS MORE FULLY DESCRIBED IN DEED BOOK 1673, PAGE 21, ID# 55-24-157, BEING KNOWN AND DESIGNATED AS:

BEGINNING AT A POINT ON THE NORTHWESTERLY SIDE OF JEFFERSON STREET(50 FEET WIDE), A CORNER OF LOT #166 ON AFOREMENTIONED PLAN, SAID POINT BEING MEASURED THE FOUR FOLLOWING COURSES AND DISTANCES FROM A POINT OF CURVE ON THE NORTHEASTERLY SIDE OF LIBERTY STREET (60 FEET WIDE), (1) LEAVING SAID SIDE OF LIBERTY STREET ON THE ARC OF A CIRCLE CURVING TO THE LEFT, NORTHEASTWARDLY, HAVING A RADIUS OF 20.00 FEET THE ARC DISTANCE OF 31.42 FEET TO A POINT OF TANGENT ON AFORESAID SIDE OF JEFFERSON STREET, (2) ALONG SAID SIDE OF JEFFERSON STREET NORTH 19 DEGREES 40 MINUTES 45 SECONDS EAST 61.90 FEET TO A POINT OF CURVE, (3) ON THE ARC OF A CIRCLE CURVING TO THE RIGHT, NORTHEASTWARDLY, HAVING A RADIUS OF 175.00 FEET THE ARC DISTANCE OF 176.77 FEET TO A POINT OF TANGENT AND (4) NORTH 77 DEGREES 33 MINUTES 15 SECONDS EAST 284.34 FEET TO POINT OF BEGINNING. BEING LOT #489.

BEING THE SAME PREMISES WHICH FELIX J. KNOWLES AND ANNA F. KNOWLES BY DEED DATED SEPTEMBER 11. 1968, AND RECORDED AT DEED BOOK 1673 PAGE 21 CONVEYED UNTO ROBERT J. TAYLOR AND MOLLY TAYLOR, IN FEE.

AND THE SAID ROBERT J. TAYLOR DEPARTED THIS LIFE ON _____

**TOGETHER** with all land singular the buildings, improvements, ways, streets, alleys, driveways, passages, water, water-courses, rights, liberties, privileges, hereditaments and appurtenances, whatsoever unto the hereby granted premises belonging or in any wise appertaining, and the reversions and remainders, rents, issues, and profits thereof; and all the estate, right, title, interest, property, claim and demand whatsoever of the said Grantor, as well at law as in equity, of, in and to the same.

**TO HAVE AND TO HOLD** the said lot or piece of ground above described with the buildings and improvements thereon erected, hereditaments and premises hereby granted, or mentioned and intended so to be, with the appurtenances, unto the said Grantee, his heirs and assigns, to and for the only proper use and behoof of the said Grantee, his heirs and assigns forever.

AND the said Grantor, for herself, her heirs and assigns do, by these presents, covenant, grant and agree to and with the said Grantee, his heirs and assigns, that she the said Grantor, her heirs and assigns all and singular the hereditaments and premises herein above described and granted or mentioned and intended so to be with the appurtenances, unto the said Grantee, his heirs and assigns against her, the said Grantor, her heirs and assigns and against all and every person or persons whomsoever lawfully claiming the same or any part thereof, by, from or under him, her, them, or any of them shall and will by these presents WARRANT and forever DEFEND.

*(continued)*

## Exhibit 2.1 Continued

**IN WITNESS WHEREOF,** The said Grantor has caused these presents to be duly executed the day and year first herein above written.

SEALED AND DELIVERED
IN THE PRESENCE OF US:

_____                          _____ (SEAL)
                                                                     MOLLY TAYLOR


COUNTY OF

      On this, the day of 201 , before me, the undersigned officer, personally appeared MOLLY TAYLOR, known to me (or satisfactorily proven) to be the person whose name is subscribed to the within instrument, and acknowledged that he executed the same for the purposes therein contained.

      IN WITNESS WHEREOF, I hereunto set my hand and official seal.

_____
          NOTARY PUBLIC


The address of the above-named Grantee is:
469 Jefferson Street
Newtowne, YS


_____

On behalf of the Grantee

---

enjoyment of the property, as long as that peaceful and quiet enjoyment does not interfere with the rights of the adjoining real estate owners. For example, the right to farm is subject to the adjoining property owners' right to be free from excess water runoff or risks inherent from hazardous activities from a neighbor's use of their property, such as blasting.

    In addition, federal, state, and local governments have the power to control and regulate the development and use of land. Federal statutes may limit use or require cleanup of land that has been contaminated with hazardous materials, such as cancer-causing chemicals. State statutes limit or even prohibit development of forested land and wetlands. Local governments control the development of their municipalities with building codes that require construction conform to minimum construction standards with approved materials, and with zoning codes that limit the land use in certain areas to specific uses. These uses include residential, commercial, and industrial; and limitations include the size of building lots; the height of buildings; and a minimum number of parking spaces.

### Defeasible Fee Simple Estates

A **defeasible fee simple estate** is a freehold estate in land that ends upon the occurrence of a future event that was specified by the grantor when the title to

**defeasible fee simple estate**
a freehold estate in land that ends upon the occurrence of a future event that was specified by the grantor when the title to the land was transferred

## Exhibit 2.2  Fee simple determinable deed

**THIS INDENTURE**, MADE this 12th day of 2013,

BETWEEN                         AMY BALWIN
                                (HEREINAFTER CALLED THE GRANTOR),

                                AND

                                NEW TOWNE ELEMENTARY SCHOOL COMMITTEE
                                (HEREINAFTER CALLED THE GRANTEE),

WITNESSETH That the said Grantor for and in consideration of the sum of Three Hundred Thousand ($300,000.00) Dollars lawful money of the United States of America, unto her well and truly paid by the Grantee, at or before the sealing and delivery hereof, the receipt whereof is hereby acknowledged, hath granted, bargained and sold, released and confirmed, and by these presents doth grant, bargain and sell, release and confirm unto the said Grantee, their successors and assigns, is fee, so long as the property is used as and for a school.

the land was transferred. There are two defeasible fee simple estates: the **fee simple determinable** and the fee simple conditional. A defeasible fee simple estate is a freehold estate that terminates if an event specified by the grantor occurs or a specific use specified by the grantor ends.

**fee simple determinable**
a freehold estate that terminates if an event specified by the grantor occurs, or a specific use specified by the grantor ends

The language used to created the fee simple determinable ownership is shown in Exhibit 2.2.

In this example, New Towne Elementary School Committee and its successors have been transferred title to a fee simple defeasible estate. They will continue as the owners until the property is no longer used as a school. The interest is for an indefinite or undetermined period of time, and the rights are limited to a specific use.

The New Towne Elementary School Committee, as the grantee, may build on the land, sell it, or otherwise transfer the property. However, when the property is no longer used as a school, the ownership right will terminate. The ownership of the property will automatically go back to the grantor if still alive or the grantor's heirs or assigns. The possibility of the property coming back in the future to the grantor, or the heirs or assigns, is called the **possibility of reverter or reversion.** The property remains in the possession of the grantee Committee as long as it is used for the specific purpose, as a school. The use of the property is restricted. This means that the Committee, its successors, and anyone to whom it may transfer the property is subject to the same limitation—that the property can only be used as a school. The limitation on the use for the specified purpose is said to "run with the land." Once the property is no longer used as a school, the possibility arises of reverter or reversion to the grantor and her heirs. Words that may indicate that a fee simple determinable is intended include "so long as," "during," "while," and "until."

**possibility of reverter or reversion**
the ownership of the property will automatically go back to the grantor if still alive or to the grantor's heirs or assigns

Because of the potential unfair outcome of an automatic termination, many states have abolished the fee simple determinable and replaced it with the fee simple conditional, described below. In the case of *Willhite v. Masters*, 965 S.W.2d 406 (MO Ct App 1998), the event that would result in reversion was the failure of the grantee to supply electricity to the grantor's flour mill. The flour mill was destroyed by fire and not rebuilt, and therefore the grantee could not supply electricity. The court held that it was not fair for the property to revert to the original grantor, not because the grantee failed to provide the required electric, but because the grantee had been prevented from doing so by the grantor, who did not rebuild after the fire, and the grantor therefore should not benefit from its own actions. The case appears below.

# IN THE WORDS OF THE COURT

## *Willhite v. Masters,* 965 S.W.2d 406 (MO Ct App 1998)

"The trial court in a quiet title action must 'ascertain and determine the rights of the parties under the pleadings and the evidence, grant such relief as may be proper and determine the 'better' title, as between the parties to the proceeding, though a title superior to the rights of either party may be held by a stranger.'" Manard, 952 S.W.2d at 389-90. "[T]he trial court is compelled to 'adjudicate the respective interests of the parties regardless of which party is entitled to it.'" Id. at 390...

In 1925, Mr. W.A. Whinrey executed a warranty deed, as party of the first part, conveying to Ozark Utilities Company, party of the second part, the disputed property in question. The warranty deed contained certain conditions, in pertinent part as follows:

It is a condition and part of the consideration hereof that the second party will furnish to the first party or his assigns energy to a maximum of forty (40) horse power for the operation of a flour mill at Caplinger Mills where the present flour mill is now located for the purpose of grinding and milling flour meal and feed only said power to be furnished by electricity or by direct connection to water wheel. The power right and privilege herein reserved by first parties (sic) is a right and privilege belonging to and to be used exclusively in the operation of a flouring mill and first party shall have the right and privilege to sell assign or transfer said power right with and only with said flouring mill. If operation of the flouring mill is at any time suspended for a period of two (2) years the power right herein reserved by first party shall cease and be thereafter non-effective; if second party or its assigns fail or refuse to furnish said forty (40) horse power to said first party as herein provided then this deed to be null and void and property above conveyed shall revert back to said first party or his assigns.

...the trial court received exhibits supporting the respective parties' chronological chains of title and stipulations were entered into by the parties. In one stipulation the parties agreed that Empire District Electric Company, successor in title to Ozark Utilities Company, provided electricity pursuant to the terms of the 1925 deed until 1953.

In the second stipulation, the parties agreed that the Whinrey Flouring Mill burned in 1947, was rebuilt and then burned for the second time on June 3, 1953, and was not rebuilt. Thereafter, there was no provision made for electricity to the mill site.

These stipulations are generally considered as "controlling and conclusive, and courts are bound to enforce them." *City of Jennings v. Division of Emp. Sec.,* 943 S.W.2d 330, 335–36 (Mo.App.1997). "Stipulations designed to simplify or shorten the litigation and reduce expenses to the parties are to be encouraged by courts, and enforced unless good cause is shown to the contrary." Id.

Donehue instructs that a determinable fee simple estate is one that automatically terminates upon the occurrence of a specified event or the cessation of use for a specified purpose and will revert to the grantor without any entry or other act. Id. 266 S.W.2d at 554–55; see also *City of Carthage v. United Missouri Bank*, 873 S.W.2d 610, 613 (Mo.App.1994).

Upon the creation of a determinable fee simple estate the grantor retains an interest known as a "possibility of reverter" which is both alienable and devisable. Id. at 613. This future interest should be contrasted, however, with a defeasible fee simple estate, which gives rise to a right of entry for a condition broken, id. at 614, i.e., "the right of entry for condition broken retained by the grantor of a fee upon condition subsequent." Id. at 614. "[T]he fee conveyed does not automatically terminate upon condition broken." Id. (citing *Chouteau v. City of St. Louis*, 331 Mo. 781, 55 S.W.2d 299, 301 (1932)). It necessarily requires an affirmative act of forfeiture because such a "condition operates upon an estate already created and vested, and renders it liable to be defeated." *Polette v. Williams*, 456 S.W.2d 328, 331 (Mo.1970) (emphasis added). At common law it is neither assignable, devisable or alienable, although it is descendible to the heirs of the grantor. Id.

Although the distinction between the two types of estates would otherwise be pertinent to the resolution of the instant matter (the first type of estate is alienable/assignable while the latter is not), we need not reach the question as to the correctness of Appellant's argument that the 1925 deed created a determinable fee simple estate. This is because, as discussed below, the triggering mechanism that would either automatically terminate the estate created by the 1925 deed, or subject it to forfeiture, has been nullified.

"The intention of the parties must be determined from the language used in the deed where the intention is clearly expressed." *St. Joseph Lead Co. v. Fuhrmeister*, 353 Mo. 232, 182 S.W.2d 273, 278 (1944). "It is the totality of the language in the instrument which determines the interest conveyed." *Fischer v. Trentmann*, 672 S.W.2d 139, 141 (Mo.App.1984). "The agreements or conditions of a deed bind a person who accepts the deed, the grantor, a purchaser from the grantor with notice. and any assignee or grantee of the grantee in whom the estate on condition is vested." 26 C.J.S. Deeds § 149 (1956).

As a general rule "[f]orfeitures are not favored, and all conditions or provisions in contracts providing for them must be strictly construed." *Robinson v. Cannon*, 346 Mo. 1126, 145 S.W.2d 146, 149 (1940). "[C]onditions subsequent are not favored in law, and are construed strictly, because they tend to destroy estates." *University City v. Chicago, R.I. & P. Ry. Co.*, 347 Mo. 814, 149 S.W.2d 321, 324 (1941). "When relied on to work a forfeiture, they must be created in express terms or by clear implication." Id.; *Miller v. Atchison, Topeka and Santa Fe Railway Co.*, 325 F.Supp. 604, 606 (E.D.Mo.1971) ("conditions subsequent and reverters are not favorites of the law").

The clear language of the 1925 deed, emphasized, supra, provides in part, that if the "operation of the flouring mill is at any time suspended for a period of two (2) years the power right [the right to receive electrical power] herein reserved by first party shall cease and be thereafter non-effective." By the clear terms of the deed, then, the non-operation of the flouring mill for a period of two years nullified the requirement that the utility furnish electric power to the flouring mill site.

…"A condition in a deed is not binding if its performance has been rendered impossible by act of the grantor or the party to be benefited thereby, by act of God, or by prohibition or operation of law." 26 C.J.S. Deeds § 156 (1956); see also *Turner v. Turner*, 186 Ga. 223, 197 S.E. 771, 772 (1938)("[c]onditions subsequent in deeds, although not favored, will be given effect, when they are clearly created, are not inconsistent with the other terms of the conveyance, and are not rendered impossible of performance by the act of God or by the subsequent conduct of the grantor").

## Exhibit 2.3 Fee simple conditional deed

THIS INDENTURE, MADE this 12th day of 2013,

BETWEEN           AMY BALWIN
                  (HEREINAFTER CALLED THE GRANTOR),

                  AND

                  ANDREW SPENCER
                  (HEREINAFTER CALLED THE GRANTEE),

WITNESSETH That the said Grantor for and in consideration of the sum of Two Hundred Thousand ($200,000.00) Dollars lawful money of the United States of America, unto her well and truly paid by the Grantee, at or before the sealing and delivery hereof, the receipt whereof is hereby acknowledged, hath granted, bargained and sold, released and confirmed, and by these presents doth grant, bargain and sell, release and confirm unto the said Grantee, his heirs and assigns, is fee, so long as no alcoholic beverages are brewed, distilled or served on the property.

**fee simple conditional**
freehold estate that continues uninterrupted until the occurrence of an event in the future

**condition subsequent**
future event

**right of reentry**
grantor's future interest that requires an affirmative action by the grantor, her heirs, or her assigns to reassert the ownership based on the violation of the specific terms of the original grant limiting the use of the property

**Fee simple conditional** or fee simple subject to a **condition subsequent** is a freehold estate that continues uninterrupted until the occurrence of an event in the future. Unlike the fee simple defeasible, there is no automatic reversion of the property to the grantor. Once the event occurs, the grantor, her heirs, or her assigns, has the potential right of entry, exercisable by filing a lawsuit to evict the grantee of the property for failure to follow the terms of the original transfer. The language used to create the fee simple determinable ownership might read as shown in the deed in Exhibit 2.3.

In the fee simple conditional deed in Exhibit 2.3, the grantee, Andrew, continues as the owner until the property is used for brewing, distilling, or serving of alcoholic beverages. The future event, or **condition subsequent**, that may impact the ownership is the brewing, distilling, or serving of alcohol. The grantee, his heirs, and his assigns have a present possessory interest for an indefinite or undetermined period of time and the right of use unlimited except for use as related to brewing, distilling, or serving alcoholic beverages, which may end the grantee's ownership. The grantor's future interest is called the **right of reentry,** which requires an affirmative action by the grantor, her heirs, or her assigns to reassert the ownership based on the violation of the specific terms of the original grant limiting the use of the property. The property remains in the possession of the grantee unless and until the grantor files suit to reenter and repossess the land. As with the fee simple determinable, many years may pass before the right to reentry may arise. Andrew and Amy may both be long dead. The condition is said to "run with the land." This means that Andrew, his heirs, and beneficiaries and anyone he may transfer the property to are subject to the same condition: No alcohol may be brewed, distilled, or served on the property. Once that occurs, Amy's right to reentry extends to her, her estate, and heirs.

To distinguish, the fee simple determinable tends to limit the use of the property to a particular purpose, such as a school. The fee simple conditional tends to permit all uses except the one described, such as brewing, distilling, and serving alcohol. The fee simple determinable ends automatically with the land reverting to the original owner or her heirs or estate. By contrast, the fee simple conditional does not automatically terminate unless and until the original owner or her heirs or estate take some legal action to reenter and repossess the property.

## Life Estate

A **life estate** is a freehold estate limited in duration to the life of a designated individual. The designated individual whose lifetime will determine the length of the life estate is called the **measuring life.** The person who receives a life estate is called the **life tenant.** The measuring life can be that of the grantor, the grantee (life tenant), or another individual. Because the length of a life is not certain, the duration of the life estate is for an indefinite time. A life estate is used as a method of planning and control over the distribution of real estate—for example, to provide use of a home to a child and then ownership of the home to grandchildren.

There are a number of ways in which a life estate may be created. The language that creates the life estate will determine the types of interests of the parties. Exhibit 2.4 is a deed granting a life estate.

In Exhibit 2.4, Amy is the grantor, and Andrew is the grantee. Andrew is the life tenant. Andrew's life is also the measuring life; upon Andrew's death, the life estate will end. On the death of the measuring life, the property will revert automatically to the grantor. Amy's future interest is a **reversionary interest,** and it belongs to her, her heirs, and her assigns. By giving a life estate to Andrew, Amy can ensure that Andrew has someplace to live during his lifetime. The purpose may be to protect him. He might be disabled in a way that prevents him from working and being able to provide suitable housing for himself. He might be irresponsible with his finances, and, by giving him a life estate, his home during his lifetime cannot be attacked by creditors. Amy provides a home for Andrew, and upon his death, the property goes to her heirs.

**life estate**
a freehold estate limited in duration to the life of a designated individual

**measuring life**
the designated individual whose lifetime will determine the duration of the life estate

**life tenant**
person who receives a life estate

**reversionary interest**
on the death of the measuring life, the property will revert automatically to the grantor

## Exhibit 2.4  Deed creating a life estate

**THIS INDENTURE**, MADE this 15th day of June, 2013,

BETWEEN                    AMY BALWIN
                          (HEREINAFTER CALLED THE GRANTOR),

                          AND

                          ANDREW SPENCER, for life
                          (HEREINAFTER CALLED THE GRANTEE),

WITNESSETH That the said Grantor for and in consideration of the sum of One (1.00) Dollar lawful money of the United States of America, unto her well and truly paid by the Grantee, at or before the sealing and delivery hereof, the receipt whereof is hereby acknowledged, hath granted, bargained and sold, released and confirmed, and by these presents doth grant, bargain and sell, release and confirm unto the said Grantee, his assigns, in fee, for life.

### Remainder Interest

**remainder interest**
a future interest following the end of a limited possessory estate

A **remainder interest** is a future interest following the end of a limited possessory estate, as shown in Exhibit 2.5.

In Exhibit 2.5, Amy is the grantor, and Andrew is the grantee who receives a life estate. Andrew is the life tenant and the measuring life. Upon Andrew's death, the property will pass to Eric. Eric has a future interest known as the remainder interest, and he is called a **remainderman.** The remainder interest belongs to Eric, his heirs, and his estate. Upon Andrew's death, Amy and her heirs have no rights or interest. In this case, Amy's goal for Andrew remains the same: to provide suitable housing for him during his lifetime. Upon Andrew's death, Amy's goal is to benefit Eric with the fee simple absolute ownership interest.

**remainderman**
the person to whom the remainder interest will pass

**Life estate *pur autre vie*** is a special form of life estate that literally translates "for another's life."

**life estate *pur autre vie***
a special form of life estate that literally translates "for another's life"

Exhibit 2.6 is a special form of life estate called a life estate *pur autre vie*, which literally translates "for another's life." As with the preceding examples, Amy is the grantor, Andrew is the grantee who receives a life estate, and he is the life tenant. The measuring life is Wayne's, and upon Wayne's death, the property reverts to Amy.

In Exhibit 2.7, a life estate *pur autre vie* deed with remainderman, Amy is the grantor, and Andrew is the grantee who receives a life estate and is the life tenant. Eric is the remainderman, and Wayne is the measuring life.

In each example, the life estate lasts only as long as the measuring life. It is a freehold estate, in which the life tenant is the freehold owner, owning the property freely and unreservedly for that time.

### Present v. Future Interest

With every life estate, there are two concurrent interests in the real estate: the present interest and the future interest.

**present interest**
the right to currently own, possess, use, and enjoy the property

The **present interest** is the right to currently own, possess, use, and enjoy the property. This right of present possession belongs to the life tenant, Andrew, in Exhibits 2.4, 2.5, 2.6, and 2.7.

## Exhibit 2.5  Deed with remainder interest

THIS INDENTURE, MADE this 15th day of June, 2013,

BETWEEN          AMY BALWIN
                 (HEREINAFTER CALLED THE GRANTOR),

                 AND

                 ANDREW SPENCER, for life

                 AND

                 ERIC HILLS,
                 As Remainderman
                 (HEREINAFTER CALLED THE GRANTEES),

WITNESSETH That the said Grantor for and in consideration of the sum of One (1.00) Dollar lawful money of the United States of America, unto her well and truly paid by the Grantees, at or before the sealing and delivery hereof, the receipt whereof is hereby acknowledged, hath granted, bargained and sold, released and confirmed, and by these presents doth grant, bargain and sell, release and confirm unto the said Grantee, Andrew Spencer, his assigns, in fee, for life and then to Eric Hills, his heirs and assigns, in fee.

## Exhibit 2.6 Life estate *pur autre vie* deed

THIS INDENTURE, MADE this 15th day of June, 2013,

BETWEEN        AMY BALWIN
(HEREINAFTER CALLED THE GRANTOR),

AND

ANDREW SPENCER, for the life of Wayne Spencer
(HEREINAFTER CALLED THE GRANTEES),

WITNESSETH That the said Grantor for and in consideration of the sum of One (1.00) Dollar lawful money of the United States of America, unto her well and truly paid by the Grantee, at or before the sealing and delivery hereof, the receipt whereof is hereby acknowledged, hath granted, bargained and sold, released and confirmed, and by these presents doth grant, bargain and sell, release and confirm unto the said Grantee, his assigns, in fee, for the life of Wayne Spencer.

The **future interest** is the right to own the property at some unknown time in the future. Possession, use, and enjoyment are deferred until the future, specifically at the end of the measuring life. The future interest can be a reversion to the original grantor and his heirs, Amy in Exhibit 2.4, or a remainder to a third party—Eric in Exhibits 2.5 and 2.7.

**future interest**
the right to own the property at some unknown time in the future

### Rights and Duties of Life Tenant

The life tenant is treated as the owner during the measuring life. The life tenant has the right to possess, use, occupy, and enjoy the property. This includes the right to improve it, use it as collateral for loans, or sell the life interest. While difficult to calculate, a life estate has a monetary value. Consider what you would pay for the right to be a life tenant at an oceanfront or mountain lake vacation home. The value lies somewhere between the cost to purchase comparable property and the cost to rent the same property. Let's assume the cost to purchase is $1,000,000 and the rent is $24,000 per year. The value of

## Exhibit 2.7 Life estate *pur autre vie* deed with remainderman

THIS INDENTURE, MADE this 15th day of June, 2013,

BETWEEN        AMY BALWIN
(HEREINAFTER CALLED THE GRANTOR),

AND

ANDREW SPENCER, for the life of Wayne Spencer
and ERIC HILLS, as Remainderman
(HEREINAFTER CALLED THE GRANTEES),

WITNESSETH That the said Grantor for and in consideration of the sum of One (1.00) Dollar lawful money of the United States of America, unto her well and truly paid by the Grantee, at or before the sealing and delivery hereof, the receipt whereof is hereby acknowledged, hath granted, bargained and sold, released and confirmed, and by these presents doth grant, bargain and sell, release and confirm unto the said Grantee, Andrew Spencer, his assigns, in fee, for the life of Wayne Spencer and then to Eric Hills, his heirs and assigns, in fee.

the life estate would be less than the full purchase price, because you are not receiving an interest for an unlimited time, as you would if it were a fee simple absolute freehold estate. The value of the life estate would be more than one year's rent, because the possibility exists that the measuring life is greater than one year. The spread between these two extremes, $24,000 and $1,000,000, can be further narrowed in determining value of the life estate. The value may be the estimated **life expectancy** of the measuring life times the annual rental value. Life expectancy tables, like the Social Security table in Exhibit 2.8, can be used to estimate the remaining years of life of the average person based on his or her current age.

The longer the life expectancy of the measuring life, the longer the life estate will potentially last and thus the greater the value of the life estate. If the individual with the measuring life has a life expectancy of 10 years, the potential value is 10 times the $24,000 annual rental, or $240,000. But if the life expectancy is 30 years, the value is $720,000.

The life tenant has certain duties, including paying all expenses, utilities, maintenance, repairs, and real estate taxes. The life tenant must refrain from damaging the property or generating waste. **Waste** is anything the life tenant does that would interfere with, detract from, or negatively impact upon the value of the remainder interest. Waste can occur from inaction, such as failing to make repairs to a leaking roof that causes water damage to the inside of the house. Waste can occur from action, such as demolishing a structure like a garage whose removal negatively impacts the value of the property.

### Rights and Duties of Remainder/Reversion Interest

The person with the remainder or reversion interest has the right to receive the property in fee simple absolute from the life tenant at the end of the measuring life. Like the life estate, the remainder interest can be sold. The owner of the remainder interest has the right to expect the property to be in the same condition, subject to normal wear and tear. The remainder interest has the right to enforce the duties that are imposed upon the life tenant, such as making repairs. Where the taxes and expenses go unpaid, the remaindermen may file an action to force the life tenant to pay those items. Where the life tenant creates waste, whether through action or inaction, the remaindermen may file suit to prevent or stop that waste, seeking monetary damages and an order to force the life tenant to repair and correct any waste that has occurred. The remainder/reversion interest may not otherwise interfere with the rights of the life tenant.

### Dower and Curtesy

*Dower* and *curtesy* are two old English common law traditions used to protect a spouse upon the death of the other spouse. **Dower** was the life estate right a wife had in her husband's estate upon his death. The right arose out of a desire to protect women from being homeless and destitute. Dower ensured that a widowed woman had a roof over her head for the rest of her life. **Curtesy** was the husband's right to a life estate in his wife's individually owned real property upon her death.

Both these common law concepts have been replaced in most states with statutory provisions to protect the interest of the surviving spouse. **Intestate Statutes** set up a statutory scheme of inheritance used when one fails to write a

---

**life expectancy**
estimate of the remaining years of life of the average person based on his or her current age

**waste**
the action or inaction of the life tenant, which causes the value of the remainder interest to decrease

**COMMON LAW TERMS**

**dower**
the life estate right a wife had in her husband's estate upon his death

**curtesy**
the husband's right to a life estate in his wife's individually owned real property upon her death

**Intestate Statutes**
statutory scheme of inheritance used when one fails to write a will

## Exhibit 2.8 Social Security Actuarial Life Table 2007

**Actuarial Life Table**

A period life table is based on the mortality experience of a population during a relatively short period of time. Here we present the 2007 period life table for the Social Security area population. For this table, the period life expectancy at a given age represents the average number of years of life remaining if a group of persons at that age were to experience the mortality rates for 2007 over the course of their remaining life.

| | Period Life Table, 2007 | | | | | |
|---|---|---|---|---|---|---|
| | Male | | | Female | | |
| Exact age | Death probability[a] | Number of lives [b] | Life expectancy | Death probability[a] | Number of lives[b] | Life expectancy |
| 0 | 0.007379 | 100,000 | 75.38 | 0.006096 | 100,000 | 80.43 |
| 1 | 0.000494 | 99,262 | 74.94 | 0.000434 | 99,390 | 79.92 |
| 2 | 0.000317 | 99,213 | 73.98 | 0.000256 | 99,347 | 78.95 |
| 3 | 0.000241 | 99,182 | 73.00 | 0.000192 | 99,322 | 77.97 |
| 4 | 0.000200 | 99,158 | 72.02 | 0.000148 | 99,303 | 76.99 |
| 5 | 0.000179 | 99,138 | 71.03 | 0.000136 | 99,288 | 76.00 |
| 6 | 0.000166 | 99,120 | 70.04 | 0.000128 | 99,275 | 75.01 |
| 7 | 0.000152 | 99,104 | 69.05 | 0.000122 | 99,262 | 74.02 |
| 8 | 0.000133 | 99,089 | 68.06 | 0.000115 | 99,250 | 73.03 |
| 9 | 0.000108 | 99,075 | 67.07 | 0.000106 | 99,238 | 72.04 |
| 10 | 0.000089 | 99,065 | 66.08 | 0.000100 | 99,228 | 71.04 |
| 11 | 0.000094 | 99,056 | 65.09 | 0.000102 | 99,218 | 70.05 |
| 12 | 0.000145 | 99,047 | 64.09 | 0.000120 | 99,208 | 69.06 |
| 13 | 0.000252 | 99,032 | 63.10 | 0.000157 | 99,196 | 68.07 |
| 14 | 0.000401 | 99,007 | 62.12 | 0.000209 | 99,180 | 67.08 |
| 15 | 0.000563 | 98,968 | 61.14 | 0.000267 | 99,160 | 66.09 |
| 16 | 0.000719 | 98,912 | 60.18 | 0.000323 | 99,133 | 65.11 |
| 17 | 0.000873 | 98,841 | 59.22 | 0.000369 | 99,101 | 64.13 |
| 18 | 0.001017 | 98,754 | 58.27 | 0.000401 | 99,064 | 63.15 |
| 19 | 0.001148 | 98,654 | 57.33 | 0.000422 | 99,025 | 62.18 |
| 20 | 0.001285 | 98,541 | 56.40 | 0.000441 | 98,983 | 61.20 |
| 21 | 0.001412 | 98,414 | 55.47 | 0.000463 | 98,939 | 60.23 |
| 22 | 0.001493 | 98,275 | 54.54 | 0.000483 | 98,894 | 59.26 |
| 23 | 0.001513 | 98,128 | 53.63 | 0.000499 | 98,846 | 58.29 |
| 24 | 0.001487 | 97,980 | 52.71 | 0.000513 | 98,796 | 57.32 |
| 25 | 0.001446 | 97,834 | 51.78 | 0.000528 | 98,746 | 56.35 |
| 26 | 0.001412 | 97,693 | 50.86 | 0.000544 | 98,694 | 55.38 |

*(continued)*

## Exhibit 2.8 Continued

| | Period Life Table, 2007 | | | | | |
|---|---|---|---|---|---|---|
| | Male | | | Female | | |
| Exact age | Death probability[a] | Number of lives [b] | Life expectancy | Death probability[a] | Number of lives[b] | Life expectancy |
| 27 | 0.001389 | 97,555 | 49.93 | 0.000563 | 98,640 | 54.40 |
| 28 | 0.001388 | 97,419 | 49.00 | 0.000585 | 98,584 | 53.44 |
| 29 | 0.001405 | 97,284 | 48.07 | 0.000612 | 98,527 | 52.47 |
| 30 | 0.001428 | 97,147 | 47.13 | 0.000642 | 98,466 | 51.50 |
| 31 | 0.001453 | 97,009 | 46.20 | 0.000678 | 98,403 | 50.53 |
| 32 | 0.001487 | 96,868 | 45.27 | 0.000721 | 98,336 | 49.56 |
| 33 | 0.001529 | 96,724 | 44.33 | 0.000771 | 98,266 | 48.60 |
| 34 | 0.001584 | 96,576 | 43.40 | 0.000830 | 98,190 | 47.64 |
| 35 | 0.001651 | 96,423 | 42.47 | 0.000896 | 98,108 | 46.68 |
| 36 | 0.001737 | 96,264 | 41.54 | 0.000971 | 98,020 | 45.72 |
| 37 | 0.001845 | 96,096 | 40.61 | 0.001056 | 97,925 | 44.76 |
| 38 | 0.001979 | 95,919 | 39.68 | 0.001153 | 97,822 | 43.81 |
| 39 | 0.002140 | 95,729 | 38.76 | 0.001260 | 97,709 | 42.86 |
| 40 | 0.002323 | 95,525 | 37.84 | 0.001377 | 97,586 | 41.91 |
| 41 | 0.002526 | 95,303 | 36.93 | 0.001506 | 97,452 | 40.97 |
| 42 | 0.002750 | 95,062 | 36.02 | 0.001650 | 97,305 | 40.03 |
| 43 | 0.002993 | 94,800 | 35.12 | 0.001810 | 97,144 | 39.10 |
| 44 | 0.003257 | 94,517 | 34.22 | 0.001985 | 96,968 | 38.17 |
| 45 | 0.003543 | 94,209 | 33.33 | 0.002174 | 96,776 | 37.24 |
| 46 | 0.003856 | 93,875 | 32.45 | 0.002375 | 96,566 | 36.32 |
| 47 | 0.004208 | 93,513 | 31.57 | 0.002582 | 96,336 | 35.41 |
| 48 | 0.004603 | 93,120 | 30.71 | 0.002794 | 96,087 | 34.50 |
| 49 | 0.005037 | 92,691 | 29.84 | 0.003012 | 95,819 | 33.59 |
| 50 | 0.005512 | 92,224 | 28.99 | 0.003255 | 95,530 | 32.69 |
| 51 | 0.006008 | 91,716 | 28.15 | 0.003517 | 95,219 | 31.80 |
| 52 | 0.006500 | 91,165 | 27.32 | 0.003782 | 94,885 | 30.91 |
| 53 | 0.006977 | 90,572 | 26.49 | 0.004045 | 94,526 | 30.02 |
| 54 | 0.007456 | 89,940 | 25.68 | 0.004318 | 94,143 | 29.14 |
| 55 | 0.007975 | 89,270 | 24.87 | 0.004619 | 93,737 | 28.27 |
| 56 | 0.008551 | 88,558 | 24.06 | 0.004965 | 93,304 | 27.40 |
| 57 | 0.009174 | 87,800 | 23.26 | 0.005366 | 92,841 | 26.53 |
| 58 | 0.009848 | 86,995 | 22.48 | 0.005830 | 92,342 | 25.67 |

*Source*: http://www.ssa.gov/oact/STATS/table4c6.html

will. They may also be used when there is no provision made in a will for a surviving spouse. The Intestate Statutes generally leave the entire or a significant portion of the estate to the surviving spouse.

## ■ NON-FREEHOLD ESTATES

A **non-freehold estate** is an estate in real property that has a definite time period and is limited to present possessory rights. The owner of the freehold estate, known as the **lessor or landlord,** transfers the right of possession, usually by way of a written lease agreement, to the owner of the non-freehold estate. The owner of the non-freehold estate is the **lessee or tenant.** The non-freehold estate is also referred to as the **leasehold estate.** Renters of apartments and office space are examples of owners of non-freehold estates. There are other uses of this special type of tenancy, such as **ground leases.** A religious, environmental, or nonprofit group that owns a large tract of land may issue a long-term ground lease to permit certain types of use, such as farm preservation, low-income housing, or recreation. Through the issuance of leases, the organization can control who joins the community and the types of uses that will be permitted on its land.

### Tenancy for Years

A **tenancy for years** is any leasehold interest of a specific duration, no matter how long or short. The leasehold terminates automatically upon expiration of the time stated in the lease. It is called a tenancy for years even though the duration is less than one (1) year, because it is a term certain.

### Periodic Tenancy

A **periodic tenancy** is an agreement with no stated duration of lease period, but rental payments are due at particular intervals. A periodic tenancy terminates upon notice at the end of a payment interval.

John's tenancy for years has become a periodic tenancy. So long as the tenant pays the rent, there is a month-to-month lease. Either John or the landlord could give notice to terminate the tenancy at the end of the next periodic payment period.

### Tenancy at Will

A **tenancy at will,** also called an **estate at will,** is an informal lease arrangement where the landlord allows a tenant to stay on a month-to-month basis and which may be terminated at any time by the landlord or the tenant.

### Tenancy at Sufferance

A **tenancy at sufferance** is a tenancy created when a tenant retains possession after expiration of a valid tenancy. The lessee is also called a **holdover tenant.** Tenants who stay beyond either the month-to-month period or an exact term of years are deemed in an **estate at sufferance.** Often considered the lowest form of estate, a tenant at sufferance has no title to and has wrongly retained possession of the real property. A tenant at sufferance is distinguished from a trespasser or squatter by the permission he had at the commencement of his tenancy. Sufferance commences only when the tenant had an original right to possess, the right to possess has ended, and the tenant, thereafter, remains in possession. The lessee remains responsible for rent payment. The landlord will likely need to pursue legal action to evict the lessee and regain possession of the property.

## Rights and Duties of Landlords and Tenants

**habitable condition**
property is free from defects that would
render it uninhabitable

The rights and duties of a landlord and tenant will depend in great part on the terms of the written lease agreement. Generally, the landlord agrees to provide the space, and in case of a residential property, guarantees that the premises will be in a **habitable condition.** *Habitable condition* means the property is free from defects that would render it uninhabitable, such as rodent infestation, plumbing defects, or lack of heat. The tenant has the right to occupy the property and use it in any way that is permissible under the terms of the lease agreement so long as the use is not illegal and does not interfere with the rights of adjoining owners and occupiers. The tenant must return the property at the end of the lease term in the same condition, with only normal wear and tear. In exchange for the right of occupancy, the tenant is obligated to pay the stated rental payment. Lease agreements may also have provisions that indicate who is responsible for maintenance and repair of common areas such as parking lots, sidewalks, and hallways.

# ETHICAL Considerations

### RULES OF PROFESSIONAL CONDUCT

For legal professionals, the requirement of a written fee agreement with the client will depend on the rules of professional conduct adopted in the state in which they practice. The American Bar Association has set forth a model code of professional conduct that the individual states have adopted in whole or in part and in many instances have modified. American Bar Association Rule 1.5(b) states:

> The scope of the representation and the basis or rate of the fee and expenses for which the client will be responsible shall be communicated to the client, *preferably in writing,* before or within a reasonable time after commencing the representation, except when the lawyer will charge a regularly represented client on the same basis or rate. Any changes in the basis or rate of the fee or expenses shall also be communicated to the client. [ABA Model Rule 1.5(b); emphasis added]

By contrast, the rule for lawyers in Pennsylvania requires that all fee agreements be written:

> When the lawyer has not regularly represented the client, the basis or rate of the fee *shall be communicated to the client, in writing,* before or within a reasonable time after commencing the representation. [Pa. R. Prof. C. 1.5(b); emphasis added]

For lawyers hired to represent parties in a real estate transaction, the fee agreement will generally be based on an hourly rate. Exhibit 2.9 is a sample lawyer's hourly fee agreement for real estate purchase.

Similarly, real estate professionals, sales agents, and brokers have a code of professional conduct that requires all agreements for employment, whether they are serving as the representatives for the seller, buyer, landlord, or tenant.

> …for the protection of all parties, shall assure whenever possible that *all agreements* related to real estate transactions including, but not limited to, listing and representation agreements, purchase contracts, and leases *are in writing* in clear and understandable language expressing the specific terms, conditions, obligations and commitments of the parties. A copy of each agreement shall be furnished to each party to such agreements upon their signing or initialing. (Amended 1/04) (Code of Ethics and Standards of Practice National Association of Realtors, Article 9; emphasis added).

See the other forms on the website of the Texas Association of Realtors at http://www.sahomelocator.com/files/BuyerRep.pdf

Exhibit 2.10 is a real estate agent's written agreement to represent a buyer in a real estate purchase.

**Exhibit 2.9** Lawyer's hourly fee agreement for real estate purchase

April 15, 2013

Mr. & Mrs. Daniel Schan
12 Centre Street
New Towne, Your State 99999

Re:    Real Estate Purchase
       4890 Jefferson Street

Dear Mr. & Mrs. Schan:

Pursuant to our initial client conference of April 12, 2013, I have agreed to represent you in connection with your real estate purchase of 4890 Jefferson Street, New Towne.

I want to thank you for placing your trust in me and selecting my law firm to represent you in this matter.

I also wish to set forth our agreement as to payment of legal fees and costs. My fees for legal services are $200.00 per hour. In addition, you will be responsible for any costs or expenses that may be incurred, such as filing fees, copying costs, postage, and related expenses. You will be billed on a monthly basis, depending upon the amount of work that was done on your file during that period of time. At this point in the case, it is difficult to estimate the amount of time and expense that will be necessary to adequately represent you in this case.

This agreement is limited to matters related to the purchase of real estate. It is not intended to cover representation in the event of litigation. Should a dispute arise and the parties proceed to litigation, arbitration, mediation, or other means of dispute resolution, a new fee agreement must be prepared.

I have agreed to waive the customary requirement of a retainer.

I will send you pleadings, documents, correspondence, and other information throughout your representation to keep you advised of the progress in your purchase of the property. These copies will be your file copies. Please retain them. I will also keep the information in a file in my office, which will be my file. Please bring your copy of the file to all of our meetings so that we both have all the necessary information in front of us. When I have completed all the legal work necessary for your case, I will close my file and return original documents to you. I will then store the file for approximately two years. I will destroy the file after that period of time unless you instruct me in writing now to keep your file longer.

A copy of this letter is enclosed for your review, signature, and return to me in the postage-paid envelope. If any of the information in this letter is not consistent with your understanding of our agreement, please contact me before signing the letter. Otherwise, please sign the enclosed copy of this letter and return it to me.

If you have any questions, please contact me at your convenience.

Very truly yours,


I have read this letter and agree to the terms set forth herein.


_____               _____
Daniel Schan                                   Date


_____               _____
Sara Schan                                     Date

**Exhibit 2.10** Real estate agents' fee agreement for representing a buyer

STATE OF MARYLAND
REAL ESTATE COMMISSION
## Understanding Whom Real Estate Agents Represent
**At the Time of the First Scheduled Face to Face Contact with You, the Real Estate Licensee Who is Assisting You is Required by Law to Provide this Notice to You. This Notice is Not a Contract or Agreement and Creates No Obligation on Your Part.**

**Before you decide to sell or buy or rent a home you need to consider the following information**

*In this form "seller" includes "landlord"; "buyer" includes "tenant"; and "purchase" or "sale" includes "lease"*

**Agents Who Represent the Seller**

**Seller's Agent:** A seller's agent works for the real estate company that lists and markets the property for the sellers and exclusively represents the sellers. That means that the Seller's agent may assist the buyer in purchasing the property, but his or her duty of loyalty is only to the sellers.

**Cooperating Agent:** A cooperating agent works for a real estate company different from the company for which the seller's agent works. The cooperating agent can assist a buyer in purchasing a property, but his or her duty of loyalty is only to the sellers.

<u>**If you are viewing a property listed by the company with whom the agent accompanying you is affiliated, and you have not signed a "Consent for Dual Agency" form, that agent is representing the seller**</u>

**Agents Who Represent the Buyer**

**Presumed Buyer's Agent (no written agreement):** When a person goes to a real estate agent for assistance in finding a home to purchase, the agent is presumed to be representing the buyer and can show the buyer properties that are *NOT* listed by the agent's real estate company. A presumed buyer's agent may *not* make or prepare an offer or negotiate a sale for the buyer. The buyer does *not* have an obligation to pay anything to the presumed agent.

If for any reason the buyer does not want the agent to represent him or her as a presumed agent, either *initially* or *at any time,* the buyer can decline or terminate a presumed agency relationship simply by saying so.

**Buyer's Agent (by written agreement):** A buyer may enter into a written contract with a real estate agent which provides that the agent will represent the buyer in locating a property to buy. The agent is then known as the buyer's agent. That agent assists the buyer in evaluating properties and preparing offers, and negotiates in the best interests of the buyer. The agent's fee is paid according to the written agreement between the agent and the buyer. If you as a buyer wish to have an agent represent you, you must enter into a written buyer agency agreement before a contract offer can be prepared.

**Dual Agents**

The possibility of **dual agency** arises when the buyer's agent and the seller's agent both work for the same real estate company, and the buyer is interested in property listed by that company. The real estate broker or the broker's designee, is called the "dual agent." Dual agents do not act exclusively in the interests of either the seller or buyer, and therefore cannot give undivided loyalty to either party. There may be a conflict of interest because the interests of the seller and buyer may be different or adverse.

**If both seller and buyer agree to dual agency** by signing a Consent For Dual Agency form, then the "dual agent" (the broker or the broker's designee) will assign one agent to represent the seller (the seller's "intra-company agent") and another agent to represent the buyer (the buyer's "intra-company agent"). Intra-company agents may provide the same services to their clients as exclusive seller's or buyer's agents, including advising their clients as to price and negotiation strategy, provided the clients have both consented to be represented by dual agency.

## Exhibit 2.10  Continued

**If either party does not agree to dual agency**, the real estate company must withdraw the agency agreement for that particular property with either the buyer or seller, or both. If the seller's agreement is terminated, the seller must then either represent him or herself or arrange to be represented by an agent from another real estate company. If the buyer's agreement is terminated, the buyer may choose to enter into a written buyer agency agreement with an agent from a different company. Alternatively, the buyer may choose not to be represented by an agent of his or her own but simply to receive assistance from the seller's agent, from another agent in that company, or from a cooperating agent from another company.

No matter what type of agent you choose to work with, you have the following rights and responsibilities in selling or buying property:

>Real estate agents are obligated by law to treat all parties to a real estate transaction honestly and fairly. They must exercise reasonable care and diligence and maintain the confidentiality of clients. They must not discriminate in the offering of properties; they must promptly present each written offer or counteroffer to   the other party; and they must answer questions truthfully.

>Real estate agents must disclose all material facts that they know or should know relating to a property.   An agent's duty to maintain confidentiality does not apply to the disclosure of material facts about a property.

>All agreements with real estate brokers and agents should be in writing and should explain the duties and obligations of both the broker and the agent. The agreement should explain how the broker and agent will be paid and any fee-sharing agreements with other brokers and agents.

>You have the responsibility to protect your own interests. You should carefully read all agreements to make sure they accurately reflect your understanding. A real estate agent is qualified to advise you on real estate matters only. If you need legal or tax advice, it is your responsibility to consult a licensed attorney or accountant.

Any complaints about a real estate agent may be filed with the Real Estate Commission at 500 North Calvert Street, Baltimore, MD 21202. (410) 230-6206.

We, the  □ Sellers/Landlord   □ Buyers/Tenants acknowledge receipt of a copy of this disclosure and

that _____(firm name)

and _____(salesperson) are working as:

**(You may check more than one box but not more than two)**

□ seller/landlord's agent
□ co-operating agent  (representing seller/landlord)
□ buyer's /tenant's agent
□ intra-company agent/dual agent  ( **CHECK BOX ONLY IF CONSENT FOR DUAL AGENCY FORM HAS BEEN SIGNED** )

_____          _____
Signature                          (Date)          Signature                          (Date)

\* \* \* \* \* \* \* \* \* \* \* \* \* \* \* \* \* \* \* \* \* \* \* \* \* \* \* \* \* \*

I certify that on this date I made the required agency disclosure to the individuals identified below and they were **unable or unwilling** to acknowledge receipt of a copy of this disclosure statement

_____          _____
Name of Individual to whom disclosure made          Name of Individual to whom disclosure made

_____          _____
Agent's Signature                                    (Date)

## KEY TERMS

## CHAPTER SUMMARY

| | |
|---|---|
| Introduction | Estates can be classified as either freehold estates or non-freeehold estates. |
| Freehold Estates | Freehold estates are those forms of ownership that include present possession for an indefinite or unknown period of time. Freehold estates include fee simple absolute, fee simple determinable, fee simple conditional, and life estate. |
| Fee Simple Absolute | A freehold estate without limitation or restriction of any kind on ownership, which lasts for an indefinite period of time. The owner may freely transfer his interest. Limitations may be imposed by federal, state, and local governments and the rights of adjoining property owners. |
| Defeasible Fee Simple Estates | The fee simple determinable limits the use of a property to a particular purpose and is usually accompanied by the possibility of reverter. The fee simple conditional permits all uses except the one described and is accompanied by the right of reentry. |
| Life Estate | A freehold estate that is limited in time to the life of a designated individual. |
| Present v. Future Interest | The present interest is the right to currently own, possess, use, and enjoy the property. This right of present possession belongs to the life tenant. The future interest is the right to own the property at some unknown time in the future. Possession, use, and enjoyment are deferred until the future, specifically at the end of the measuring life; this is the remainder interest. |
| Rights and Duties of Life Tenant | The life tenant has the right to possess, use, occupy, and enjoy the property. This includes the right to improve it, use it as collateral for loans, or sell the life interest. The life tenant has certain duties, including paying all expenses, utilities, maintenance, repairs, and real estate taxes. The life tenant must refrain from damaging the property or generating waste. |

| | |
|---|---|
| Rights and Duties of Remainder/Reversion Interest | The person with the remainder or reversion interest has the right to receive the property in fee simple absolute from the life tenant at the end of the measuring life. Like the life estate, the remainder interest can be sold. The owner of the remainder interest has the right to expect the property to be in the same condition, with only normal wear and tear. |
| Dower and Curtesy | Dower and curtesy are two old English common law traditions used to protect a spouse upon the death of the other spouse. Dower was the life estate right a wife had in her husband's estate upon his death. Curtesy was the husband's right to a life estate in his wife's individually owned real property upon her death. |
| Non-freehold Estates | A non-freehold estate is an estate in real property that has a definite time period and is limited to present possessory rights. |
| Tenancy for Years | A tenancy for years is any leasehold interest of a specific duration, no matter how long or short. |
| Periodic Tenancy | A periodic tenancy is an agreement with no stated duration of lease period, but rental payments are due at particular intervals. |
| Tenancy at Will | A tenancy at will, also called an estate at will, is an informal lease arrangement where the landlord allows a tenant to stay on a month-to-month basis and which may be terminated at any time by the landlord or the tenant. |
| Tenancy at Sufferance | A tenancy at sufferance is a tenancy created when a tenant retains possession after expiration of a valid tenancy. |
| Rights and Duties of Landlords and Tenants | Generally, the landlord agrees to provide the space, and in case of a residential property, guarantees that the premises will be in a habitable condition. The tenant has the right to occupy the property and use it in any way that is permissible under the terms of the lease agreement so long as the use is not illegal and does not interfere with the rights of adjoining owners and occupiers. The tenant must return the property at the end of the lease term in the same condition, with only normal wear and tear. |
| Ethics | The terms of the agreements should be in writing. There are many reasons for this requirement. Depending on the jurisdiction, the Statute of Frauds may require that certain types of contracts be in writing to prevent disputes over the terms of the agreements. |

## REVIEW QUESTIONS AND EXERCISES

1. Explain the differences between a freehold and non-freehold estate.
2. List and describe the freehold estates.
3. Distinguish between a fee simple determinable and a fee simple conditional.
4. Why have some states abolished the fee simple determinable?
5. What is a life estate?
6. Is the life tenant always the measuring life? Why or why not?
7. Describe and contrast the present and future interests in a life estate.
8. What is waste?
9. Define and distinguish between dower and curtesy.
10. List and describe the non-freehold estates.
11. What are the rights and duties of the landlord?
12. What are the rights and duties of the tenant?

## VIDEO CASE STUDY

Go to www.pearsonhighered.com/careers to view the following videos.

### Author Introduction to Estates in Land

Author video introduction to chapter coverage.

### Seller's First Meeting with Attorney

A seller meets with her attorney to discuss a listing agreement for the sale of her home.

## INTERNET AND TECHNOLOGY EXERCISES

1. Check your state's requirement for written fee agreements for lawyers and for real estate agents. Is the provision statutory, a rule of professional conduct, or both?

2. Determine whether your state recognizes the following interests in real estate:
   a. fee simple determinable
   b. dower
   c. curtesy

## REAL ESTATE PORTFOLIO EXERCISES

**Estates in Land**

| | |
|---|---|
| **To:** | Paralegal Intern: |
| **From:** | Charles Hart, Esq. |
| **Case Name:** | Mrs. Taylor |
| **Re:** | Home Sale |

**Thank you for sitting on the interview with Mrs. Taylor. Please:**

1. Set her up in the time and billing program
2. Prepare a fee agreement. We will charge ½% of the sales price
3. Notify brokers and buyers attorney of our representation
4. Request information from Title Company on requirements for settlement.

Portfolio items produced:

1. Letter of representation and fee agreement.
2. Letter notifying others involved in the transaction of the representation.
3. Letter requesting information.

Go to www.pearsonhighered.com/careers to download instructions.

## LEARNING OBJECTIVES

*Upon completion of this chapter, you should be able to*

1. List and explain the differences between types of real estate owners.

2. List and explain the differences between the forms of concurrent ownership.

# Concurrent Ownership | CHAPTER 3

---

## ■ INTRODUCTION TO CONCURRENT OWNERSHIP

**Concurrent ownership** is when two or more legal entities have an ownership interest in the same property *at the same time*. Legal entities that can own real estate include individuals, partnerships, corporations, and other types of business organizations. Each legal entity may own property in its own name or jointly with one or more other types of owners. The rights and obligations of each joint owner are determined by the form of ownership of the property. The three major types of concurrent ownership are: tenants in common, joint tenants with right of survivorship, and tenants by the entirety.

**concurrent ownership**
when two or more **legal entities** have an ownership interest in the same property *at the same time*

## ■ WHO CAN OWN REAL ESTATE?

### Individuals

Under current law in most states, any person over the age of majority—generally 18 years of age—and under no disability that would bar them from entering into a valid contract, may own real estate. This has not always been the case in the United States. The rights of women, African Americans, and other minorities were limited in many ways through the 1960s, with rights of ownership controlled by the individual states, territories, and in some instances, by private

**LEARNING OBJECTIVE 1**
List and explain the differences between types of real estate owners.

---

## DIGITAL RESOURCES

Author Introduction to Concurrent Ownership.

agreements. In many communities, it was common to place restrictions by private agreement in deeds, forbidding the sale of the real estate to certain groups, based on race, religion, or national origin. Federal civil rights legislation and decisions of the United States Supreme Court in the 1960s and 1970s eliminated these types of limitations.

For most individuals, the primary reason to acquire real estate is for the purpose of home ownership. Real estate is also acquired by some individuals as an investment for the potential appreciation in value and generation of income. Income may be generated from the rents and fees received for the use of an investment property, which could include an apartment or office rental, or the extraction of minerals and other materials.

## Partnerships

There are two types of partnerships: general and limited.

**partnership or general partnership**
the voluntary association of two or more individuals or legal entities for carrying on a business as co-owners

A **partnership or general partnership** is the voluntary association of two or more individuals or legal entities for carrying on a business as co-owners. General partners are personally liable for the debts and obligations of the partnership. The agreement to form a partnership may be oral, written, or implied from the conduct of the partners. A written partnership agreement is called a partnership agreement or articles of partnership. Partners can agree to almost any lawful terms, and those terms may be concise and brief or complex and lengthy. If no agreement exists or an agreement fails to cover an essential term, the Uniform Partnership Act, as adopted by the state, will control the operation of the partnership. General business partnerships frequently buy real estate for the operation of their business, such as doctors buying a property from which to operate their practice. Real estate partnerships may be formed for the business purpose of owning real estate.

In general partnerships, the partners share operating profits and losses and management responsibilities as determined in their agreement. Each partner has unlimited liability for partnership debts and obligations. For tax purposes, general partnerships are treated as "pass through" organizations. That is, the partnership reports income and losses but pays no taxes as a partnership. Instead, those profits and losses are passed through to each partner, who then reports income or claims deductions on his or her individual tax return, based on the respective portion of profit and loss. General partners share control and participate equally in management of the partnership.

**limited partnerships**
a special form of partnership, created by statute. Unlike general partnerships, they are considered legal entities distinct from their individual partners.

**Limited partnerships** are a special form of partnership, created by statute. Unlike general partnerships, they are considered legal entities distinct from their individual partners. A limited partnership must have one or more general partners who, like general partners in a general partnership, have unlimited liability. A limited partnership must also have one or more limited partners. Limited partners may invest cash, property, or services in exchange for a limited ownership interest in the partnership. The limited partner's liability is limited to the amount of his or her respective investment. Limited partners do not participate in the management of the business.

Limited partnerships are used for investment, especially in the area of real estate development.

Limited partnerships include the following characteristics:

■ A limited partnership is an entity distinct from its partners.
■ It must contain both general partners and limited partners.

- A person can serve as a general and limited partner.
- A partnership agreement governs relations among the partners and between the partners and the partnership.
- It achieves both limited liability and partnership principles.
- A limited partnership has the power to sue, be sued, and defend in its own name and to maintain an action against a partner for harm caused to the limited partnership by a breach of the partnership agreement or violation of a duty to the partnership.

## Corporations

A **corporation** is a legal entity, sometimes referred to as an *artificial person*, created by statute. The corporation is a legal entity separate and distinct from it owners, called stockholders or shareholders. Corporations can sue or be sued, enter into and enforce contracts, hold title to and transfer property, and be found civilly and criminally liable for violation of law. Management of the corporation is by a board of directors elected by the shareholders. Day-to-day activities are managed by officers of the corporation selected by the board of directors. The advantages of the corporation include:

1. Perpetual existence: the death of a shareholder, director, or officer will not affect the existence of the corporation
2. Limited liability: shareholders are not liable for the debts and obligations of the corporation
3. Ownership interest: shares are transferable

**corporation**
a legal entity, sometimes referred to as an artificial person, created by statute

## Joint Ventures

A **joint venture** is an unincorporated association created by the co-owners of a business venture, usually to carry out a particular venture. It is also known as a joint adventure, co-adventure, business consortium, syndicate, group, pool, joint enterprise, joint undertaking, or joint speculation. Joint ventures are frequently used for real estate investment that involves some inherent risk—for example, exploration for oil and gas reserves. In some states, the joint venture is called a joint stock association. It may operate like a corporation, issuing shares and carrying out the business of the association with annual meetings and typical protocols, but it remains unincorporated and generally is taxed like a partnership.

**joint venture**
an unincorporated association created by the co-owners of a business venture, usually to carry out a particular venture

## Real Estate Investment Trusts

A **Real Estate Investment Trust (REIT)** is a company that buys, develops, manages, and sells real estate assets. The REIT issues fractional, divisible investment shares based on the amount of each owner's investment. REITs invest in blocks of real estate and issue shares proportionate to the investment. It is a sort of mutual fund for real estate investors. REITs may be public or private in design, and some REITs are actually traded on the various stock exchanges. REITs allow individuals and business entities to invest in a portfolio of real estate properties. REITs usually qualify as pass-through entities, companies who are able to distribute the majority of income cash flows to

**Real Estate Investment Trust (REIT)**
a company that buys, develops, manages, and sells real estate assets

investors without traditional taxation at the personal level. There are three basic forms of REITs generally seen in the marketplace.

- **Equity REITs:** Equity REITs invest in and own properties and derive income principally from their properties' rents.
- **Mortgage REITs:** Mortgage REITs deal in investment and ownership of property mortgages. This type of REIT loans money for mortgages. Revenue is generated from the interest paid on the mortgages.
- **Hybrid REITs:** Hybrid REITs dabble in both the equity and mortgage sides of the business.

## ■ CONCURRENT OWNERSHIP

**LEARNING OBJECTIVE 2**
List and explain the differences between the forms of concurrent ownership.

**cotenant**
two or more parties that have an ownership interest in the same property at the same time

**Unity of Time**
the ownership or title interests are received at the same time, upon the creation of the ownership freehold

**Unity of Title**
each of the cotenants or owners acquired title from the same source

**Unity of Interest**
each cotenant has the same or equal ownership interest; for example, each is an owner in fee as opposed to one having ownership in fee and the other being a tenant of a leasehold interest

**Unity of Possession**
an equal right to possess the whole property for possessory purposes only

**Unity of Person**
concurrent ownership by husband and wife

**tenants in common**
a form of concurrent ownership that may, but is not required to, have all five unities

**Concurrent ownership** is the simultaneous ownership of the same property by more than one individual or legal entity, each of which is called a **cotenant.**

Concurrent ownership is characterized by one or more of the following:

1. **Unity of Time**
2. **Unity of Title**
3. **Unity of Interest**
4. **Unity of Possession**
5. **Unity of Person**

Unity of Time means that the ownership or title interests are received at the same time, upon the creation of the ownership freehold.

Unity of Title means that each of the cotenants or owners acquired title from the same source.

Unity of Interest means that each cotenant has the same or equal ownership interest; for example, each is an owner in fee as opposed to one who owns in fee and the other being a tenant of a leasehold interest.

Unity of Possession means an equal right to possess the whole property for possessory purposes only.

Unity of Person applies to concurrent ownership by husband and wife.

The combination of the different characteristics of these unities will determine the form of the concurrent ownership.

### Tenants in Common

**Tenants in common** is a form of concurrent ownership that may, but is not required to, have all five unities. Tenants in common do not have to be spouses, take title at the same time, receive title from the same source, or have equal interests. The one unity tenants in common do share is the equal right to possess and occupy the property. Each cotenant has the right to individually, without the agreement of the other tenant in common, transfer his or her interest, whether by sale, by gift, or at the time of death though a provision in a will.

For example, in Exhibit 3.1, Alice and Ed are brother and sister and own a parcel of real estate; each owns one-half as tenants in common. Alice decides to make a gift of her interest to her two children, Jesse and Thomas, who now own one-fourth each as tenants in common and together are tenants in common with Ed, who still owns his one-half interest. Ed then dies and leaves his interest to his three children, James, Maureen, and Robert, who now each own one-sixth as tenants in common and collectively are tenants in common with Jesse and Thomas. The one unity they share is the equal right to possess

## Exhibit 3.1

> **THIS INDENTURE,** MADE this 15th day of June, 2013,
>
> BETWEEN                    AMY BALWIN
>                            (HEREINAFTER CALLED THE GRANTOR),
>
>                            AND
>
>                            ALICE DONNELLY and EDWARD O'HARA
>                            (HEREINAFTER CALLED THE GRANTEES),
>
> WITNESSETH That the said Grantor for and in consideration of the sum of ONE HUNDRED FIFTY THOUSAND ($150,000.00) Dollars lawful money of the United States of America, unto her well and truly paid by the Grantee, at or before the sealing and delivery hereof, the receipt whereof is hereby acknowledged, hath granted, bargained and sold, released and confirmed, and by these presents doth grant, bargain and sell, release and confirm unto the said Grantees, their heirs and assigns, in fee, as tenants in common.

and occupy the property, because they took title at different times, derived it from different sources, have unequal interests, and are none of them are married to one another.

The tenancy in common, even though a concurrent, joint ownership form, does not include an automatic right of survivorship. Each tenant in common owns and possesses an undivided interest in the whole property, which passes to their respective statutory heirs in the event of intestacy. Each tenant in common may transfer, encumber, or devise his or her interest by provision in a will.

In addition to the equal right to possess the property, tenants in common must contribute to the upkeep, maintenance, repair, and taxes in accordance with their respective ownership interests. In the example above, Jesse and Thomas will be required to contribute one-fourth each to the expenses, and James, Maureen, and Robert will contribute one-sixth each. Failure to pay one's fair share grants the other cotenants the right to sue the noncontributing cotenant for **contribution,** the legal right of cotenants to enforce the obligation of each of the other cotenants to pay his or her fair share of the expenses.

**contribution**
the legal right of cotenants to enforce the obligation of each of the other cotenants to pay his or her fair share of the expenses

Tenancy in common in real estate ownership is like a partnership, where the tenants in common together must define a method and manner for use of the property. In the example of an investment property such as an apartment house that would be rented, rents are collected, expenses deducted from the rents, and net income distributed among the cotenants in accordance with their ownership interest. With a non-investment vacation home, it can be difficult to decide who and when someone can use the property when there are multiple owners—such as Jesse, Thomas, James, Maureen, and Robert in the above example. Often, the parties will reach a mutually acceptable use schedule. If they are unable to, they may seek court intervention in an action called **partition.** In a partition action, the court is asked to resolve the disputes concerning ownership, use, and possessory interests that the cotenants are unable to resolve. The court can order the sale of the real estate and that the proceeds of the sale be distributed in accordance with the ownership interest. Each cotenant has the right to purchase the property through the partition sale, but in reality the cotenant may not have the financial ability to do so.

**partition**
a cause of action to resolve the disputes concerning ownership, use, and possessory interests that the cotenants are unable to resolve

## Joint Tenants with Rights of Survivorship

**joint tenants with the rights of survivorship**
concurrent ownership in which surviving cotenants automatically succeed to the ownership interest of a deceased cotenant

**Joint tenants with the rights of survivorship** is a form of concurrent ownership in which surviving cotenants automatically succeed to the ownership interest of a deceased cotenant. This form of cotenancy requires four of the five unities but does not require the cotenants to be spouses. The joint tenants must take title at the same time, from the same source, and with equal interests. Joint tenants have an equal right to possess and occupy the property. When all these unities are present and the language of the conveyance is clear, indicating that the parties take title as "joint tenants with right of survivorship," then the joint tenancy is created. Joint tenants have the right to freely transfer their respective interests; but when they do, there is no longer a joint tenancy, because the unities of time and same source disappear. The concurrent ownership will become a tenancy in common.

Let's use the example above and add some different facts. Alice and Ed are brother and sister. They own a parcel of real estate that they purchased together as joint tenants with the rights of survivorship. Exhibit 3.2 is the relevant portion of the deed for that purchase. Each owns an undivided one-half interest. They have taken title at the same time from the same source and with equal interests. When Ed dies, Alice, by right of survivorship, becomes the sole owner. In this manner, Ed's children, James, Maureen and Robert, are disinherited. And this automatic transfer to someone other than the natural benefactors of one's wealth, effectively disinheriting one's children, is why joint tenancy is disfavored, never assumed, and must always be specifically stated in the deed.

Should Alice make her gift to her children, Jesse and Thomas, before Ed dies, the joint tenancy ends. Jesse and Thomas now own one-fourth each as tenants in common, and together they are tenants in common with Ed, who still owns his one-half interest.

Like tenants in common, joint tenants must contribute to the upkeep, maintenance, repair, and taxes in accordance with their respective ownership interests. Failure to do so gives the other joint tenants the right to sue the noncontributing joint tenant for contribution. Like tenants in common, joint tenants must define a method and manner for use of the property, which can be difficult with multiple owners. In contentious circumstances, the cotenants or joint tenants may turn

## Exhibit 3.2

THIS INDENTURE, MADE this 15th day of June, 2013,

BETWEEN            AMY BALWIN
                          (HEREINAFTER CALLED THE GRANTOR),

                          AND

                          ALICE DONNELLY and EDWARD O'HARA
                          (HEREINAFTER CALLED THE GRANTEES),

WITNESSETH That the said Grantor for and in consideration of the sum of ONE HUNDRED FIFTY THOUSAND ($150,000.00) Dollars lawful money of the United States of America, unto her well and truly paid by the Grantee, at or before the sealing and delivery hereof, the receipt whereof is hereby acknowledged, hath granted, bargained and sold, released and confirmed, and by these presents doth grant, bargain and sell, release and confirm unto the said Grantees, their heirs and assigns, in fee, as joint tenants with the rights of survivorship and not as tenants in common.

## Exhibit 3.3

THIS INDENTURE, MADE this 15th day of June, 2013,

BETWEEN                MOLLY TAYLOR
                       (HEREINAFTER CALLED THE GRANTOR),

                       AND

                       DANIEL SCHAN and SARA SCHAN, husband and wife
                       (HEREINAFTER CALLED THE GRANTEES),

WITNESSETH That the said Grantor for and in consideration of the sum of THREE HUNDRED AND EIGHT THOUSAND ($308,000.00) Dollars lawful money of the United States of America, unto her well and truly paid by the Grantees, at or before the sealing and delivery hereof, the receipt whereof is hereby acknowledged, hath granted, bargained and sold, released and confirmed, and by these presents doth grant, bargain and sell, release and confirm unto the said Grantees, their heirs and assigns, in fee as tenants by the entireties.

to the courts for resolution of disagreements. In situations where division of the property is an issue, an action for partition may be instituted. In partition, the court will determine how to divide the interests. Because it is difficult to physically divide a house, in many instances the court may order the property sold and the proceeds of sale divided in accordance with the ownership interests. The owners have the right to purchase the property just as anyone else would.

## Tenants by the Entireties

**Tenants by the entireties** is a form of concurrent ownership, like joint tenancy with a right of survivorship, but limited to married individuals. This form of concurrent ownership is the only form that shares all five of the unities. As shown in Exhibit 3.3, the parties must take title at the same time, from the same source, and with equal interests, as well as have an equal right to possess and occupy the property, and they must be married to one another at the time they take title. Under common law and subsequently codified by statute, there is a presumption of tenancy by the entireties when a married couple takes title together; the idea is that the individual spouses, once married, become a single marital unit.

**tenants by the entireties**
a form of concurrent ownership, like joint tenancy with a right of survivorship, but limited to married individuals

The most important feature of tenancy by the entireties is the absolute, unequivocal right of survivorship the remaining spouse has in the event of the other's death. When one dies, the other living spouse retains all, not some divisible portion. During their lifetime, neither spouse may individually sell, transfer, or give the property to another without the consent and participation of both spouses.

## ■ SPECIAL TYPES OF CONCURRENT OWNERSHIP

## Community Property

**Community property** is a statutory provision that defines assets that are the property of a marital unit. Community property laws replace the common law presumptions of tenants by the entireties. Just nine states—Arizona, California, Idaho, Louisiana, Nevada, New Mexico, Texas, Washington, and

**community property**
a statutory provision that defines assets that are the property of a marital unit

Wisconsin—have community property statutes. Community property generally includes all property acquired by either spouse during the time of the marriage. In this sense, real property is community property if acquired during a period of marriage and not the result of gift, inheritance, or other devise. As a rule, all property owned or acquired prior to marriage, in whatever form, remains the separate and individual property of the spouse and is not community property.

Much like tenancy by the entireties, upon the death of one spouse, his one-half of the community property inures to the benefit of the surviving spouse. In certain jurisdictions, all community property remains with the surviving spouse. Community property practice and procedure is highly localized, and reference to the particular statute is required.

For example, in California, Texas, Washington, and Louisiana, surviving spouses may not take a full and unbridled interest in the real property upon the death of the spouse.

## Condominium

**condominium**
a creation of statute that allows legal entities to own individual units in a building, with common elements in fee simple and a percentage of the common elements as tenants in common with other unit owners

**Condominium** ownership is a creation of statute that allows legal entities to own individual units in a building with common elements in fee simple and a percentage of the common elements (hallways and recreation areas) as tenants in common with other unit owners. Thus, each owner of a unit in a condominium is a concurrent owner with other owners in the project. Owners pay monthly fees for maintenance and repair of common areas.

The burdens of repair, maintenance of common areas, and other drudgeries of home ownership are replaced by or delegated to an association—a collective of owners—who wish to avoid these recurring responsibilities.

# ETHICAL Considerations

 **WEB EXPLORATION**
Review Model Rules of Professional Conduct at:
www.abanet.org/cpr

For the legal professional, it is important to know and understand the concepts related to real estate ownership. This is the duty of competence, providing competent representation to clients, set forth in the American Bar Association (ABA) Model Rules of Professional Conduct, Rule 1.1.

Competent representation considers the legal knowledge and skill that may be required for thorough representation of the client. It is not necessary that one be an expert in a particular area of law, but that one possess the skills to research, learn, and understand that area before undertaking the representation. Competence also requires effectively communicating with the client and non-legal members of the legal team. Suppose an attorney whose practice focuses on estate planning, administration, and litigation is handling an estate with a parcel of real estate that the Environmental Protection Agency (EPA) claims was contaminated by a predecessor in title to the deceased person. Should the estate's practitioner handle the EPA claim? Probably not. This goes to the ethical obligation to use competence, reasonable skill, and diligence in the representation of the client's best interests. The client would be better served if an attorney knowledgeable in dealing with the EPA handled this aspect of the estate.

## KEY TERMS

## CHAPTER SUMMARY

| | |
|---|---|
| **Introduction to Concurrent Ownership** | Concurrent ownership is when two or more legal entities have an ownership interest in the same property *at the same time*. Legal entities that can own real estate include individuals, partnerships, corporations, and other types of business organizations. |
| Who Can Own Real Estate<br><br>Individuals | Under current law in most states, any person over the age of majority—generally 18 years of age—and under no disability that would bar them from entering into a valid contract, may own real estate. |
| Partnerships | There are two types of partnerships: general and limited.<br>A partnership or general partnership is the voluntary association of two or more individuals or legal entities for carrying on a business as co-owners. General partners are personally liable for the debts and obligations of the partnership.<br>Limited partnerships are a special form of partnership, created by statute. Unlike general partnerships, they are considered legal entities distinct from their individual partners. A limited partnership must have one or more general partners who, like general partners in a general partnership, have unlimited liability. |
| Corporations | A corporation is a legal entity, sometimes referred to as an artificial person, created by statute. The corporation is a legal entity separate and distinct from it owners, called stockholders or shareholders. |
| Joint Ventures | A joint venture is an unincorporated association created by the co-owners of a business venture, usually to carry out a particular venture. It is also known as a joint adventure, co-adventure, business consortium, syndicate, group, pool, joint enterprise, joint undertaking, or joint speculation. |

| | |
|---|---|
| REIT | A Real Estate Investment Trust (REIT) is a company that buys, develops, manages, and sells real estate assets. The REIT issues fractional, divisible investment shares based on the amount of each owner's investment. REITs invest in blocks of real estate and issue shares proportionate to the investment. It is a sort of mutual fund for real estate investors. |
| Concurrent Ownership | Concurrent ownership is the simultaneous ownership of the same property by more than one individual or legal entity, each of which is called a cotenant.<br><br>Concurrent ownership is characterized by<br>1. Unity of Time<br>2. Unity of Title<br>3. Unity of Interest<br>4. Unity of Possession<br>5. Unity of Person |
| Tenants in Common | Tenants in common is a form of concurrent ownership that may, but is not required to, have all five unities. Tenants in common do not have to be spouses, take title at the same time, get title from the same source, or have equal interests. The one unity tenants in common do share is the equal right to possess and occupy the property. |
| Joint Tenants with Rights of Survivorship | Joint tenants with the rights of survivorship is a form of concurrent ownership in which surviving cotenants automatically succeed to the ownership interest of a deceased cotenant. This form of cotenancy requires four of the five unities but does not require the cotenants to be spouses. |
| Tenants by the Entireties | Tenants by the entireties is a form of concurrent ownership, like joint tenancy with a right of survivorship, but limited to married individuals. This form of concurrent ownership is the only form that shares all five of the unities. |
| Community Property | Community property is a statutory provision that defines assets that are the property of a marital unit. Community property laws replace the common law presumptions of tenants by the entireties. Just nine states—Arizona, California, Idaho, Louisiana, Nevada, New Mexico, Texas, Washington, and Wisconsin—have community property statutes. |
| Condominium | Condominium ownership is a creation of statute that allows legal entities to own individual units in a building, with common elements in fee simple and a percentage of the common elements (hallways and recreation areas) as tenants in common with other unit owners. |

## REVIEW QUESTIONS AND EXERCISES

1. For what reasons would an individual own real estate?
2. What is a general partnership?
3. What is a limited partnership? How is it similar to a general partnership? How is it different?
4. What are the benefits of being a corporation rather than a partnership?
5. What is a joint venture? What form of business entity is it most similar to?
6. What is an REIT? How does an REIT own real estate interests?
7. What is concurrent ownership?
8. What are the five unities?
9. Describe the characteristics of tenants in common ownership.
10. Describe the characteristics of joint tenants with the rights of survivorship ownership.
11. Describe the characteristics of tenants by the entireties ownership.
12. Describe the characteristics of community property ownership.
13. Describe the characteristics of condominium ownership.
14. What is contribution?
15. What is partition?

## VIDEO CASE STUDY

Go to www.pearsonhighered.com/careers to view the following videos.

### Author Introduction to Concurrent Ownership
Author video introduction to chapter coverage.

## INTERNET AND TECHNOLOGY EXERCISES

1. Using the Internet, find your state's requirements for creating a limited partnership.
2. Using the Internet, find your state's requirements for creating a corporation.

## REAL ESTATE PORTFOLIO EXERCISES

Concurrent Ownership

| | |
|---|---|
| **To:** | Paralegal Intern |
| **From:** | Charles Hart, Esq. |
| **Case Name:** | Christine Magee and Rochelle Church |
| **Re:** | Ownership by non-married parties |

I have a request from my partner, Mr. Chancellor, who is doing estate planning for a same-sex couple residing in a state that does not recognize same sex marriage.

They are planning on buying a house together. I need to prepare a memorandum of law for him on the different forms of ownership and recommendations on the best method of ownership for this couple. It must provide for the property interest of one to go to the other on the death of the first.

Please research and prepare a memorandum showing the forms of possible ownership and their differences.

Portfolio item produced:
Memorandum of law on the different forms of real estate property ownership and those that a same sex couple might use to get the same result as ownership by a married couple.

Go to www.pearsonhighered.com/careers to download instructions.

## LEARNING OBJECTIVES

*Upon completion of this chapter, you should be able to*

1. Describe the rights inherent in fee simple real estate ownership and the way in which those rights may be severed from the fee simple ownership.

2. Describe the obligations that flow from the rights inherent in fee simple ownership of real estate.

3. Identify the violations of the rights of real property owners.

4. Understand the remedies available to real property owners whose rights have been violated.

# Rights and Obligations of Real Property Owners

## CHAPTER 4

## ■ INTRODUCTION TO RIGHTS AND OBLIGATIONS OF REAL PROPERTY OWNERS

Fee simple real estate ownership comes with an owner's "bundle of rights," including the right to occupy, use, improve, mortgage, lease, donate, or sell the property. Together, these individual rights represent the entire bundle, or fee simple. Each of these individual rights has its own value and can be transferred to another from the fee simple ownership.

Property is not owned in isolation; with rights come obligations and duties. Each landowner has an obligation to refrain from interfering with the adjoining or neighboring property owners' rights. This obligation is reciprocal: rights held by one owner give rise to duties from neighboring landowners. An example is the right to improve one's property by installing a paved driveway that may hinder water absorption, causing flooding on the neighboring property. With that right to improve one's property comes the duty to control excess rainwater runoff onto a neighboring property so that it does not cause flooding of the neighboring property.

## ■ RIGHTS OF REAL PROPERTY OWNERS

### Use, Possess, and Occupy

The terms *use*, *possess*, and *occupy* are often used synonymously. However, each has a separate meaning with regard to the ownership of real property. Each represents an identifiable right associated with fee simple absolute ownership—a

**LEARNING OBJECTIVE 1**
Describe the rights inherent in fee simple real estate ownership and the way in which those rights may be severed from the fee simple ownership.

## DIGITAL RESOURCES

Author Introduction to Rights and Obligations of Real Property Owners.

**COMMON LAW TERMS**

Under the common law, one who holds title and possession is said to *be seized of the real estate* or to *enjoy the right of seizen.*

**sever**
to separate and transfer one of the rights associated with ownership of real property, such as when the right to occupy is severed by a lease

**possess**
exercising control over the property

**use**
the right to profit from the land

**COMMON LAW TERMS**

Under the common law, the right to take from or use the land of another for the purpose of profit is called profit *a prendre.*

**license**
an agreement that grants another the right to engage in a specific profit-generating activity on the land

**occupy**
the right one has to live or reside on the land in whatever manner one wishes

**quiet enjoyment**
the right to be free from interference from others—to peacefully use, possess, and occupy the real estate

**alienate**
the right of the fee simple owner to freely transfer his or her interest to another

right that can be held by the fee simple owner or **severed,** that is, transferred to another. Upon severance of any individual right, the fee simple absolute estate ceases and a lesser estate comes into existence.

To **possess** the property, one controls its use and occupancy. Possession is demonstrated by exercising control over the property, such as erecting a fence along the boundary lines of the property, tilling the soil, or constructing a home. Possession can be severed from the fee simple ownership with the creation of a life estate. In a life estate, the life tenant has the right to control the use and occupancy of the property for the duration of the measuring life so long as the life tenant does nothing to negatively impact the value of the remainder interest. Upon the severance of possession, there is no longer a fee simple estate. In the example of a life estate, the fee simple estate is converted to a life estate with a remainder.

To **use** the property, one has the right to profit from the land. One profits from the land by constructing and selling a home; cutting and selling the timber located on the land; planting, raising, harvesting, and selling crops; and extracting, refining, and selling minerals, oil, and gas. The requirement is that the activity be undertaken for earning money. The fee simple owner has the right to do or not do any of these things. This right to use the property for profit making can be severed from the fee simple estate by use of a **license.** A license is an agreement that grants to another the right to engage in a specific profit-generating activity on the land, such as a license to drill for natural gas. The licensee pays a royalty fee to the landowner. The fee simple estate is converted to a fee simple subject to a license.

To **occupy** the property is the right one has to live or reside on the land in whatever manner one wishes. Constructing a home and pitching a tent are equally methods of occupying a property. The right of occupancy is severed from the fee simple estate through the use of a residential lease. The fee simple estate is then converted to a leasehold estate.

## Quiet Enjoyment

**Quiet enjoyment** is the right to be free from interference from others—to peacefully use, possess, and occupy the real estate. With regard to fee simple ownership, it also means there are no adverse or hostile claims to the ownership of the property; there are no others who have an interest of any kind in the real estate. In essence, the fee simple owner has not severed and transferred any of the individual rights. Each property owner is said to enjoy the right to peaceful use, possession, and occupancy of his or her real estate. From this concept arises the reciprocal right of quiet enjoyment between adjoining property owners. You may have heard the adage that your right to punch the air with your fist ends at the tip of my nose. All of the rights of our individual freedoms must coexist and take into account the same equal rights of other citizens. The same is true of real estate and the adjoining and neighboring property owners' right of quiet enjoyment.

## Alienate and Encumber

The right to **alienate** is the right of the fee simple owner to freely transfer his interest to another. This right includes the right to transfer any of the individual rights, such as occupancy and use, through a lease. This right also includes the right to transfer the property in its entirety by sale, by gift, by inheritance, or through the terms contained in a will provision. Generally, there are no limitations on the rights of the fee simple owner to transfer an interest in whole or in part. The limitations that do impact the right of alienation are directly related to other rights that may have been severed from the estate. For example, the owner of the fee simple estate who has severed the right to occupy the property through a lease can transfer only that which the owner continues to own. That is, the fee simple is subject to the leasehold interest of the tenant.

The right to **encumber** is the right of the fee simple owner to burden the property with a restriction of some kind, called an **encumbrance.** The encumbrance limits the unrestricted use of the property in some way. A typical encumbrance is a **lien,** or debt, against the property. A mortgage, where the property has been used as collateral to secure repayment of money borrowed, is an encumbrance. The right of alienation will be subject to the existence of the mortgage, and in most instances, the mortgage must be paid in full before the property can be transferred free of encumbrances. An encumbrance can also be an agreement, such as a covenant that forbids the land to be used as a slaughterhouse, or an easement that allows another the right to cross over the property. In each case, the covenant or easement impacts use of the land.

## Riparian Rights

**Riparian rights** are the rights of landowners related to water that flows on, over, adjacent to, or as a boundary line of their land. Water is a finite resource necessary to sustain life. The issues of what land and water may be used and how are part of riparian rights.

Riparian rights are rooted in both statutory and common law principles. In the most generic sense, riparian rights deal with both individual and collective rights to water in rivers, groundwater, and beachfronts. Riparian rights are multidimensional and include:

- Access to the water
- The right to erect a dock or wharf for water access
- The right to acquire land deposits that result from flowing water
- The right to fill
- The right to continued water flow
- The right to preservation of the view of the water

The right of access to the water is the "first and most basic right of the riparian owner," under which all other riparian rights are created and protected. The right of access (1) ensures the riparian owner's "right to be and remain a riparian proprietor," (2) protects the riparian owner's ability to reach the navigable portions of adjacent waters without unreasonable impediment, (3) supports the riparian owner's right to wharf out, (4) includes the right to erect structures in aid of navigation, and (5) underlies the riparian owner's right to take title to lands that accrete beyond the mean high-water mark.

Of all these rights, questions involving the appropriation of water are very common. Appropriation determines who has the lawful right to access the water supply, what standards dictate ownership of the water, and what standards permit individual or larger usage by a community. For the most part, statewide agencies and legislatures lay out rules and regulations regarding these rights.

Riparian rights are especially sensitive to the coequal rights of other property owners. What happens on a stream or river can significantly impact the riparian rights of those who are upstream or downstream from the event. Building a dam has two results: (1) for landowners whose lands are upstream from the dam, their lands may be flooded; and (2) for landowners whose lands are downstream, they may be deprived of water. Using pesticides that run off into the stream can result

**COMMON LAW TERMS**

Under the common law, the transfer of title and possession was referred to as *livery of seizen.*

**encumber**
the right of the fee simple owner to burden the property with a restriction of some kind

**encumbrance**
restriction of some kind

**lien**
an encumbrance that is usually financial in nature, such as a mortgage

**riparian rights**
rights of landowners related to water that flows on, over, adjacent to, or as a boundary line of their land

in contaminated water downstream. Both of these actions, erection of a dam and the use of pesticides, would be controlled or perhaps prohibited by the federal, state, or local government to protect the coequal rights of those downstream.

## Air Rights

**air rights**
the rights in the air above the land

**Air rights** are the rights in the air above the land. They represent the right to erect a structure to a particular height, such as three, four, or five stories. One might be inclined to think, "If I own the real property and it includes the airspace, don't I own the air rights above my property to the ends of the universe?" However, airspace does have its limits. Such limits are determined by technological advancement. How high can a structure be built and remain safe? Also, airways must be clear for airplanes. Airspace rights can be severed from the fee simple estate by granting a license for use such as to a company erecting cell phone towers.

## Mineral Rights

**mineral or subsurface rights**
rights to use or take any of the minerals found in the earth's crust

**Mineral or subsurface rights** are the rights to use or take any of the minerals found in the earth's crust. Mineral rights include the right to drill for water, oil, natural gas, stone, rock, and precious metals such as gold, silver, and copper. The rights for each of these individual minerals can be leased, transferred, or sold to another.

## ■ OBLIGATIONS OF REAL PROPERTY OWNERS

**LEARNING OBJECTIVE 2**
Describe the obligations that flow from the rights inherent in fee simple ownership of real estate.

Fee simple absolute ownership rights do not exist in a vacuum. Although the word "absolute" is included in the term, fee simple ownership is not absolute. If one's home is one's castle, one certainly does not rule with the authority of a king or queen. Government controls, presumably for the good of the public, impact the rights of the property owner.

Ownership is subject to the statutes, regulations, and obligations imposed by federal, state, and local governments. Each in its own way limits the rights of the owner. Study of federal and state statutes, federal and state administrative regulations, and local ordinances defining the obligations of landowners could encompass an entire semester of study. For the landowner, it is possible for ownership rights to be subject to regulation and control from all three—federal, state, and local government. For the real estate team, an understanding of the general nature and purpose of these limitations is helpful.

Federal enactments, from both the Congress and administrative agencies, have impacted the rights of property owners particularly in the past 50 years, most significantly in the areas of racial discrimination and environmental protection.

By declaring unenforceable deed covenants or restrictions prohibiting sale or lease of property based on race or national origin, the Fair Housing Act of 1968 outlawed discrimination in the sale or leasing of residential real estate. Rather than race, the financial ability of the individual to purchase or lease the property was to be considered. Even with the provisions of the Fair Housing Act, however, discrimination remained in lending. Impoverished communities, usually populated by a single ethnic group unable to qualify for financing to purchase a home, became blighted. If you looked at a map of where banks were making loans and where they weren't, it was as if a red line had been drawn around the impoverished inner-city communities—a red line to indicate "we don't lend there." The Community Reinvestment Act of 1977 was intended to stimulate financial institutions to meet the needs of all borrowers, even those in low- and moderate-income communities, and to stimulate the cherished goal of home ownership.

Equally important are the Clean Air Act of 1970 and Clean Water Act of 1972. These statutes were designed to control the discharge of pollutants into our air and water supply, set standards for the cleanup of any contaminated site, and establish a system of fines and penalties for polluters. The Environmental Protection Agency (EPA) is the administrative agency that oversees and regulates this area, with enactment and enforcement of regulations.

It is easy to see now, some 40 years later, the good that has resulted from these federal restrictions on the rights of property owners. But at the time, owners and operators of industrial and manufacturing businesses fought their imposition, as the requirements interfered with their use of the land and significantly impacted their cost of doing business.

Similar to federal enactments, state legislatures have enacted antidiscrimination laws and environmental protection laws. In many instances, the states laws were "on the books" or enacted before any federal government action was taken. Pennsylvania first enacted its Human Relations Act prohibiting discrimination in the sale or lease of real estate based on race, color, religious creed, ancestry, or national origin in 1955 and its Clean Water Act of 1971. States also enact legislation that delegates to local municipalities the rights to control land development and use.

Local governments seek to control the development and use of land within their jurisdictions through zoning codes. These highly localized enactments define districts within the municipality for specific uses: residential single family, residential multifamily/apartment, and office space; shops, restaurants, and bars; hospitals and schools; and manufacturing and warehouses. The goal is to keep similar uses together and protect residential owners from having uses that are offensive close to their homes. You wouldn't want your home next to a trucking company where the noise of the diesel engines idling begins at 5:00 a.m. and the fumes from the diesel fuel are unpleasant. Zoning ordinances may also define the minimum lot sizes within the particular districts, the maximum building heights, and the positioning of the building on an individual lot by limiting the setback from the street, front, side, and rear boundary lines of the property. All of these rules limit the free use of the real property, particularly with regard to how the property can be used and what can be erected.

Some communities may further control construction by having a building code in place. The goal in adopting a building code is to have buildings erected with certain safety concerns addressed. This can include requirements for fire-resistant siding as well as for the electric service to be of a particular amperage, wiring, and number of circuit breakers, including special provisions for any electric outlet that is near water in the bathroom or kitchen.

## Adjoining and Neighboring Property Owners

In addition to fulfilling the obligations owed to the federal, state, and local government, property owners have obligations to adjoining and neighboring property owners. An old adage states that "my rights end where your rights begin." The same is true when the rights of real property owners are compared. The right of one owner is limited by the same, coequal rights of an adjoining property owner. One owner cannot do something that will interfere with those rights. "Do unto others as you would have them do unto you" might be the motto to live by to establish good relations with your neighbors.

You, as a property owner, have the right to have large, beautiful shade trees on your property, but those trees cannot interfere with the rights of an adjoining property owner. With large tree there are many concerns. The limbs and branches may overhang the boundary line and create some risk of damage. A limb could be blown off in high winds and land on the car parked in the neighbor's driveway. Maybe it is a fruit-bearing tree, and when the fruit on the branches hanging over the boundary line ripens, it drops on the neighbor's property, rots, and attracts rodents and bees, both unpleasant for the neighbor. Or even more insidious is the deep, thick root system of the beautiful shade tree that seeks water underground and has found your neighbor's sewage lines. Every year the same thing happens: The tree roots block the line and sewage cannot flow out of the house. Instead, the sewage backs up the drains into the neighbor's basement.

In circumstances such as these, one would hope the adjoining property owners would find a mutually agreeable solution, but if not, they will resort to legal action.

## ■ VIOLATIONS OF RIGHTS OF REAL PROPERTY OWNERS

### Nuisance

**LEARNING OBJECTIVE 3**
Identify the violations of the rights of real property owners

**nuisance**
unreasonable interference with another property owner's right to peaceful and quiet enjoyment of his or her property

**private nuisance**
nuisance that occurs between adjacent landowners but does not include physical trespass or entrance onto the land of another

**public nuisance**
nuisance that harms the public safety and welfare generally

**trespass to land**
direct and intentional interference with the rights of the real property owner

**Nuisance** is the unreasonable interference with another property owner's right to peaceful and quiet enjoyment of his or her property. Nuisance has both a private and a public form.

A **private nuisance** is one that occurs between adjacent landowners but does not include physical trespass or entrance onto the land of another. For a nuisance to be actionable—that is, for the court to intervene and order the nuisance to be stopped—the harm caused must be more than a mere inconvenience or annoyance. The newborn infant with colic who cries endlessly every night might be an annoyance but is not a nuisance. An example of a private nuisance might be the dust and fumes related to stripping, sanding, and refinishing furniture.

A **public nuisance** is one that harms the public safety and welfare generally. In many jurisdictions, there are statutes that define public nuisance. Exhibit 4.1 is the public nuisance statute from California, which is written in broad general terms. Exhibit 4.2 is the definition of just one of 15 public nuisance definitions found in New York statute.

### Trespass

**Trespass to land** is the direct and intentional interference with the rights of the real property owner. Generally, the property owner has granted permission to another for

### Exhibit 4.1 California Public Nuisance Statute

> Anything which is injurious to health, including, but not limited to, the illegal sale of controlled substances, or is indecent or offensive to the senses, or an obstruction to the free use of property, so as to interfere with the comfortable enjoyment of life or property, or unlawfully obstructs the free passage or use, in the customary manner, of any navigable lake, or river, bay, stream, canal, or basin, or any public park, square, street, or highway, is a nuisance. (Cal. Civ. Code §3479)

**Exhibit 4.2** New York Public Nuisance Statute

The following are declared to be public nuisances:

(a) Any building, erection or place, including one- or two-family dwellings, used for the purpose of prostitution as defined in section 230.00 of the penal law. Two or more criminal convictions of persons for acts of prostitution in the building, erection or place, including one- or two-family dwellings, within the one-year period preceding the commencement of an action under this chapter, shall be presumptive evidence that the building, erection or place, including one- or two-family dwellings, is a public nuisance. In any action under this subdivision, evidence of the common fame and general reputation of the building, erection or place, including one- or two-family dwellings, of the inmates or occupants thereof, or of those resorting thereto, shall be competent evidence to prove the existence of the public nuisance. If evidence of the general reputation of the building, erection or place, including one- or two-family dwellings, or of the inmates or occupants thereof, is sufficient to establish the existence of the public nuisance, it shall be prima facie evidence of knowledge thereof and acquiescence and participation therein and responsibility for the nuisance, on the part of the owners, lessors, lessees and all those in possession of or having charge of, as agent or otherwise, or having any interest in any form in the property, real or personal, used in conducting or maintaining the public nuisance; [N.Y. ADC. Law §7-703(a)]

a specific purpose. When that purpose ends or the person does something beyond the specific purpose for which permission has been granted, trespass occurs.

Think of a landowner who leases the land to a farmer for purposes of raising corn each year. Harvest season coincides with hunting season. The farmer will commit trespass should the farmer hunt and kill deer when he or she should be tending to the crops. The farmer has then gone beyond the authorized use of the land.

## Encroachment

**Encroachment** occurs when a property owner builds or erects something on the land of an adjoining property owner. Encroachments are often referred to as boundary line disputes. The item may be placed intentionally or inadvertently. Examples include overhanging tree limbs, fences and shrubs installed for the purposes of demarking the boundary line but that have gone beyond it, or the installation of a structure such as a shed or doghouse that is over the property line.

**encroachment**
when a property owner builds or erects something on the land of an adjoining property owner

## ■ REMEDIES

## Self-Help

In limited circumstances, the law recognizes **self-help,** the right of property owners to correct, on their own and at their own expense, violations of their property rights. The idea is to permit the correction of the violation without resort to court intervention. Where shrubbery and tree limbs encroach, or hang over, the boundary line, the adjoining property owner has the right to cut and trim, at his own expense, those shrubs and tree limbs to the boundary line. Self-help is permissible, but in performing the action, one may not damage the other person's property or the item being trimmed. Trimming can be to the boundary line only.

**LEARNING OBJECTIVE 4**
Understand the remedies available to real property owners whose rights have been violated.

**self-help**
right of property owners to correct, on their own and at their own expense, violations of their property rights

In the interest of maintaining good relations, the better practice is to contact the neighbor with the offending trees or shrubs to arrange a solution that can be worked on together and involves sharing the expense.

## Monetary Damages

**monetary damages**
monetary awards as a result of a lawsuit, to compensate someone financially for a loss or harm sustained

**Monetary damages** are monetary awards as a result of a lawsuit to compensate someone financially for a loss or harm sustained. There must be an actual compensable harm that is capable of calculation. If the neighbor's overhanging tree limb falls off and comes through your roof, the cost to repair the damage to your roof is something that can easily be calculated.

## Specific Performance

**specific performance**
order to do something (remove an encroachment) or stop doing something (nuisance), when monetary award is not sufficient remedy

Because each parcel of real estate is unique, there may be no way to financially compensate for wrongs done. In those cases, a lawsuit will seek specific performance as a remedy for the violation. **Specific performance** asks the court to order someone to do something (remove an encroachment) or stop doing something (nuisance).

Suppose your neighbor recently erected a fence on the boundary line of your properties. The neighbor did so without obtaining a survey to accurately determine the location of the boundary line. The result, you later discover, is that the fence is on your property, about five feet beyond the property line. In essence, your lot has lost five feet on that side, and the neighbor has gained five feet. If the neighbor is unwilling to move the fence, there is no adequate financial compensation for the reduction in the size of your property. You would seek an order from the court for specific performance, directing the neighbor to remove and relocate the fence at his own expense.

Now assume instead that the neighbor has recently installed a sump pump that pumps storm water out of his basement when heavy rain falls. The discharge pipe for the pump goes into you backyard. Unfortunately, the water discharged is an odd color and smells. The area of the lawn where the water is discharged has begun to die off. If the neighbor is unwilling to change the location of the discharge pipe, there is no adequate financial compensation for the pollutants being placed on your land. You would seek an order from the court for specific performance, ordering the neighbor to stop the discharge of water onto your land.

# ETHICAL Consideration

### DILIGENCE

Often, violations of the rights of property owners go on for long periods of time before they are suspected, investigated, and confirmed. This delay can be the result of the property owner's reliance on visual cues to establish boundary lines for erecting fences and installing shrubs rather than referring back to the legal description, which defines with particularity the boundary lines. For the legal profession, time and its passage can bring an end to the right to seek recovery. You may be familiar with the statute of limitations that defines the time within which a lawsuit may be brought to seek recovery for a personal injury or a breach of contract. With real estate, the time to seek recovery may not necessarily have a fixed limitation, such as two years. Rather, a common law principal will be applied to determine whether the delay in discovery of the violation and the institution of the lawsuit is reasonable under the circumstances.

Rule 1.3 of the American Bar Association Model Rules of Professional Conduct requires the lawyer to act with "diligence and promptness." This rule seeks to avoid procrastination and delay in investigating the client's claim and, where necessary, filing a lawsuit on behalf of the client. While the client's delay in uncovering an encroachment on his or her property line may be reasonable under the circumstances, once the client has engaged legal counsel, the lawyer must see to it that there are no further delays in seeking to correct that wrong.

## KEY TERMS

License   58
Sever   58
Use   58
Possess   58
Occupy   58
Quiet enjoyment   58
Alienate   58
Encumber   59

Encumbrance   59
Riparian rights   59
Lien   59
Air rights   60
Mineral or subsurface
  rights   60
Nuisance   62

Private nuisance   62
Public nuisance   62
Trespass to land   62
Encroachment   63
Self-help   63
Monetary damages   64
Specific performance   64

## CHAPTER SUMMARY

| | |
|---|---|
| Introduction to Rights and Obligations of Real Property Owners | Fee simple real estate ownership comes with a "bundle of rights" that the owner has, including the right to occupy, use, improve, mortgage, lease, donate, or sell the property. Property is not owned in isolation; with rights come obligations and duties. Each landowner has an obligation to refrain from interfering with the adjoining or neighboring property owners' rights. |
| RIGHTS OF PROPERTY OWNERS<br>Use, Possess, and Occupy | The terms *use*, *possess*, and *occupy* are often used synonymously.<br>To possess the property, one controls its use and occupancy.<br>To use the property, one has the right to profit from the land.<br>To occupy the property is the right one has to live or reside on the land in whatever manner one wishes. |
| Quiet Enjoyment | Quiet enjoyment is the right to be free from interference from others and to peacefully use, possess, and occupy the real estate. |
| Alienate and Encumber | The right to alienate is the right of the fee simple owner to freely transfer his or her interest to another. The right to encumber is the right of the fee simple owner to burden the property with a restriction of some kind, called an encumbrance. |
| Riparian Rights | Riparian rights are the rights of landowners related to water that flows on, over, adjacent to, or as a boundary line of their land. |
| Airspace Rights | Airspace rights are the rights in the air above the land. |
| Mineral Rights | Mineral or subsurface rights are the rights to use or take any of the minerals found in the earth's crust. Mineral rights include the right to drill for water, oil, natural gas, stone, rock, and precious metals such as gold, silver, and copper. |

| Obligations of Property Owners | Ownership is subject to the statutes, regulations, and obligations imposed by federal, state, and local governments. |
|---|---|
| Adjoining and Neighboring Property Owners | Property owners have obligations to adjoining and neighboring property owners. |
| VIOLATIONS OF RIGHTS OF REAL PROPERTY OWNERS | |
| Nuisance | Nuisance is the unreasonable interference with another property owner's right to peaceful and quiet enjoyment of his or her property. Nuisance has both a private and a public form. A private nuisance is one that occurs between adjacent landowners but does not include physical trespass or entrance onto the land of another. A public nuisance is one that harms the public safety and welfare generally. |
| Trespass | Trespass to land is the direct and intentional interference with the rights of the real property owner. |
| Encroachment | Encroachment occurs when a property owner builds or erects something on the land of an adjoining property owner. |
| REMEDIES | |
| Self-Help | Self-help is the right of property owners to correct, on their own and at their own expense, violations of their property rights. |
| Monetary Damages | Monetary damages are awarded as a result of a lawsuit, and they seek to compensate someone for a loss or harm sustained. |
| Specific Performance | Specific performance asks the court to order someone to do something (remove an encroachment) or stop doing something (nuisance). |

## REVIEW QUESTIONS AND EXERCISES

1. What are the individual rights included in the bundle of rights held by a fee simple owner of real estate?
2. How are these individual rights severed from the fee simple estate? What impact does severing the rights have on the fee simple estate?
3. How are the terms *use, possess,* and *occupy* different with regard to rights of fee simple ownership?
4. What does quiet enjoyment mean?
5. How does one alienate an interest in real estate?
6. How does one encumber an interest in real estate?
7. What are riparian rights?
8. Distinguish between airspace and mineral rights. How are they severed from the fee simple ownership?
9. Describe federal government obligations that all landowners must abide by and how they impact the rights of ownership.
10. Describe the local government obligations that landowners must adhere to and how they impact the rights of ownership.
11. What obligations does a landowner have to the adjoining and neighboring property owners?
12. What is a nuisance?
13. What is trespass?
14. What is an encroachment?
15. Describe the circumstances under which self-help would be an appropriate remedy for violation of one's property rights.
16. Why are monetary damages inadequate to compensate the property owner in most real estate disputes?
17. Describe the types of specific performance.

## INTERNET AND TECHNOLOGY EXERCISES

1. Check online for the availability of your municipality's zoning code. If not available online, how can a copy be obtained? What is the cost?
2. Check online for the availability of your municipality's building code. If not available online, how can a copy be obtained? What is the cost?

3. Using the Internet, locate your state's statute that defines public nuisance. Is the statute specific or general in its definition?

## VIDEO CASE STUDY

Go to www.pearsonhighered.com/careers to view the following videos.

### Author Introduction to Rights and Obligations of Real Property Owners
Author video introduction to chapter coverage.

## REAL ESTATE PORTFOLIO EXERCISES

**Rights and Obligations of Real Property Owners**

**To:** Paralegal Intern
**From:** Supervising Attorney
**Re:** Water runoff

Our client's neighbor has expanded his driveway and the area around his garage by paving it with asphalt. The local building codes limit this impervious cover to 10% of the total property area.

From our calculations, this is now over 40%. The neighbor uses his property to work on cars that he races every weekend. The asphalt-covered area is on higher ground than our client's property. Before the additional asphalt was put down, the rain runoff was absorbed by the bare ground, now it is now running off onto our client's property, flooding his basement every time there is a heavy rain. Worse yet, the chemicals and petroleum products used on the cars are running into his lawn and the area in which his young children play.

He wants to know what his rights are to stop this excess runoff of water and chemicals.

Portfolio item produced:
1. Memorandum of law on right to stop excess water runoff
2. Opinion letter to client

**To:** Paralegal Intern
**From:** Supervising Attorney
**Re:** Tree overhang

Our client's neighbor has a very large tree along the property line. During the last storm, a few lower-level branches broke off the tree and fell on our client's property, causing minor damage that the neighbor paid for. He has asked the neighbor to allow him to cut down the very large branches that still hang over onto his side of the property. They are over the bedroom of his house and over the garage and he is afraid if they break off it will cause substantial damage, and someone might get hurt.

Can he cut the branches off that are on his side of the property line, or can he make the neighbor cut down the tree or the branches on his side of the property line?

Portfolio item produced:
1. Memorandum of law on remedies available for overhanging branches
2. Opinion letter to client

Go to www.pearsonhighered.com/careers to download instructions.

## LEARNING OBJECTIVES

*Upon completion of this chapter, you should be able to*

1. Explain how restrictions on land use are created by private agreement.

2. Explain how government action can restrict land use.

# Restrictions on Real Property Use

## CHAPTER 5

## ■ INTRODUCTION TO RESTRICTIONS ON REAL PROPERTY USE

The ownership of real property does not include the absolute right to use it without restriction. Generally, limits are created through an agreement of parties, defining the private restrictions on use. Voluntary agreements between real property owners and government action may impose restrictions on the use of the land, such as conservation restrictions.

Agreements of parties that create private restrictions on use are generally referred to as *servitudes*. The three major servitudes are easements, covenants, and licenses.

Police power is the right of state governments to define and control activities to promote the health, safety, and general welfare of its citizens. Governmental restrictions limit the use of property through zoning regulations, building codes, and environmental protection regulations implemented to control the use and development of real property.

## ■ SERVITUDES

A **servitude** is anything that burdens the use of real property. Generally, servitudes are created through an agreement of parties defining the private restrictions on use. The three major servitudes are as follows:

- Easements
- Covenants
- License

**LEARNING OBJECTIVE 1**
Explain how restrictions on land use are created by private agreement.

**servitude**
anything that burdens the use of real property

## DIGITAL RESOURCES

Author Introduction to Restrictions on Use of Real Property.

Sample forms and templates.

**COMMON LAW TERMS**

Under the English common law, the term for license was *profit a prendre*.

All three share three characteristics. They

- run with the land.
- create a dominant estate and a servient estate.
- allow nonowners a limited right of use of land.

Servitudes are created for a number of reasons: for utility companies to provide service, such as underground electric service; for the mutual benefit of adjoining property owners, such as sharing a driveway; for providing a convenient access to a property; for the preservation of open space for recreation; or for preservation of the historic character of a neighborhood.

Servitudes are sometime referred to as encumbrances. An encumbrance affects the quality of the title to the real estate; it can be an easement, covenant or license, as each does affect the owner's title. More accurately, an encumbrance has a financial impact; that is, it must be paid or satisfied by the owner of the real property before the property can be transferred.

## Easements

**easements**
a limited right to enter real property owned by another, which allows one party to use some portion of the real property of another but comes with no right of ownership

**Easements** provide a limited right to enter real property owned by another, which allows one party to use some portion of the real property of another but comes with no right of ownership. Utility easements provide the right to enter the land of another to install and service electric, gas, cable, telephone, water and sewer, and other utilities. Land developers frequently grant utility easements so the raw land being developed is served by the needed utilities. Homeowners may also grant an easement to a utility to obtain or upgrade utility service, such as having an in-ground natural gas line installed for heating.

### Dominant Estate and Servient Estate

**dominant estate**
the party with the right to use the property of another

**servient estate**
the property that the party with the dominant estate may use

Every easement grants a right and imposes a burden. The party with the right to use the property of another possesses the **dominant estate.** The property that the party with the dominant estate may use is the **servient estate.** The dominant estate has the right to use the easement in such a way as to not interfere with the servient estate's ownership interest. For example, the holder of the dominant estate, granted an easement to use a driveway, does not have the right to block the driveway and is obligated to maintain the easement in a reasonable manner.

Easements fall into two categories.

**easements in gross**
also called commercial easements; characterized by the existence of one parcel of real estate that is the servient estate, but there is no specified parcel of real estate receiving a benefit from the easement

**Easements in gross,** also called commercial easements, are characterized by the existence of one parcel of real estate that is the servient estate, but there is no specified parcel of real estate receiving a benefit from the easement. Rather, an entity such as the telephone company possesses the dominant estate, owning the right to use the property for the purpose granted in the easement, such as installing telephone poles and running lines.

Easements in gross are generally granted where the access is needed for a permanent installation, such as an electric power transmission line or pipeline and where access is needed to service and repair the installed equipment. Easements in gross may be sold or transferred.

**appurtenant easements**
characterized by two parcels of land, usually adjoining, with each parcel having a different owner

**Appurtenant easements** are characterized by two parcels of land, usually adjoining, with each parcel having a different owner. The easement benefits one parcel, the dominant estate, and runs with the land, benefiting all future owners. Likewise, the property over which the easement runs is the servient estate, and that burden runs with the land to all successor owners. The most common example is a driveway. Another example is the land on either side of a state-owned roadway, which may have an easement permitting maintenance and widening of the road.

### Easement Creation

Easements may be created in three ways: by agreement, by necessity, and by prescription. An **easement by agreement** is one negotiated by the parties. It defines the specific land over which the easement will be granted. It may also define in very limited terms the types of access permitted and what rights, if any, the servient estate has in the event of damage to the land. The easement agreement is generally recorded in the land records or recorder of deeds office for the county or parish in which the property is located. Utility and shared driveway easements are typical easements by agreement. Exhibit 5.1 is a Utility Easement Agreement.

**easement by agreement**
an easement negotiated by the parties

An **easement by necessity** is created where one parcel of land is **landlocked,** or has no access to a public roadway. The underlying concept is that every owner of real property must be able to enter and leave their property and gain access to public roadways.

**easement by necessity**
created where one parcel of land has no access to a public roadway

In Exhibit 5.2, a landowner has divided his land into four lots for development purposes from what was originally one lot. In doing so, lots 18-A and 18-B have no access from the lot to the public roadway. An easement would have to be created so those lots have access.

**landlocked**
where one parcel of land has no access to a public roadway

## Exhibit 5.1  Utility Easement Agreement

**THIS INDENTURE,** made this 16th day of January 1996, between **DELUCA ENTERPRISES, INC.,** a Pennsylvania Corporation, (hereinafter Grantor) and **PECO ENERGY COMPANY**, a Pennsylvania Corporation (hereinafter Company),

**WHEREAS**, the Grantor is the owner of premises situated on the southwesterly side of Street Road, in the Township of Buckingham, County of Bucks, Commonwealth of Pennsylvania, as more particularly described in Deed dated September 15, 1995 and recorded in the Office of the Recorder of Deeds, in the aforesaid County, in Deed Book 1121, page 717 & c.,

**NOW, THEREFORE, THIS INDENTURE WITNESSETH:**

That the said Grantor for and in consideration of the sum of ONE ($1.00) DOLLAR, the receipt whereof is hereby acknowledged, does hereby grant to the Company, the full, free, and uninterrupted right, liberty, privilege and authority to locate, relocate, construct, erect, install, renew, replace, add to, operate and maintain on, over, under, along, across and within said premises such electric, gas and communication transmission and distribution facilities (hereinafter Facilities) as from time to time the Company shall determine are necessary or proper to supply said premises and those adjacent thereto with electricity, gas and communication services, together with the right of ingress and egress across the premises and the right to trim and keep trimmed, cut down and remove, in a workmanlike manner, all trees, roots and branches of trees to the extent determined necessary by said Company, to provide sufficient clearance for the protection of the Facilities; together with the right to attach said Facilities to the buildings erected or to be erected on the said premises.

**Exhibit 5.2** Land subdivision

| STATE GAME LANDS | | | State Game Land Service Yard and Garage Lot 19-32 1,200 Acres |
|---|---|---|---|
| Goodland Dairy Farm Lot 17 150 Acres | Lot 18-A 10.5 Acres | Lot 18-B 10.5 Acres | |
| | Lot 18-C 10.1 Acres | Lot 18-D 10.1 Acres | |
| County | | | |
| Road 232 | | | |

Exhibit 5.3 shows one way in which such an easement by necessity would be created. In that exhibit, Lots 18-C and 18-D are servient estates, while lots 18-A ansd 18-B are dominant estates.

Where the original common landowner does not create an easement by a written agreement, the law imposes an unwritten easement, creating a dominant and servient estate. The original landowner had an obligation to create access to a public roadway for each lot—thus the necessity for the easement. In the event that a road is later built that grants road access to lots 18-A and/or 18-B, the easement over the servient estates will be **extinguished,** or ended.

An **easement by prescription** is an easement created by common law and/or statute when a person without right or authorization uses or occupies the real estate of another for the statutorily prescribed time, usually 21 years. The wrongful or unauthorized use must be open, visible, and notorious—sufficient to put the owner on notice of the unauthorized use. The wrongful or unauthorized use must be actual and exclusive, continuous, and peaceful during the prescribed time period, without the express or implied permission of the rightful owner. The resulting easement by prescription results in the right to use that portion of the land only. An example

**extinguished**
ended

**easement by prescription**
an easement created by common law and/or statute when a person without right or authorization uses or occupies the real estate of another for the statutorily prescribed time

**Exhibit 5.3** Plan for easement by necessity

| STATE GAME LANDS | | | | | State Game Land Service Yard and Garage Lot 19-32 1,200 Acres |
|---|---|---|---|---|---|
| Goodland Dairy Farm Lot 17 150 Acres | Lot 18-A 10.5 Acres | | Lot 18-B 10.5 Acres | | |
| | Lot 18-C 10.1 Acres | EASEMENT | EASEMENT | Lot 18-D 10.1 Acres | |
| County | | | | | |
| Road 232 | | | | | |

might be a shortcut used by one neighbor over another neighbor's farm to get to town. Over the statutory period of years, a pathway is worn, from repeated use, over the other neighbor's land. This could result in an easement by prescription.

A lawsuit will be required to confirm the existence of the easement by prescription after the statutory time period has passed. *Putts & Divots, L.P., et al. v. McGonigal* is an interesting case involving a golf course developed with homes surrounding it. The tee for hole 5 was located on the land of one of the private homes, but there was never an easement created for access to the tee. After years of golf carts tearing up the backyard, golf balls breaking windows, and irritation with golfers in her backyard, the landowner erected a fence on her property lines, which blocked the tee. The owner of the golf course successfully argued that the fence should be removed so that it could use the tee, by reason that it possessed an easement by prescription.

# IN THE WORDS OF THE COURT

## *Putts & Divots, L.P., et al. v. McGonigal,* 85 Bucks Co. L. Rep. 485 (CCP 2012).

Plaintiff Putts & Divots is a Pennsylvania Limited Partnership and owns the Fairways Golf Course. McGonigal resides in a single-family residential dwelling referred to as "Parcel D," upon which a golf cart pathway and the men's and ladies' tees for the 5th hole of the Fairways Golf Course are located.

Putts & Divots initiated the instant action alleging that although they had "prescriptive easement rights over and on the rear portion of Parcel D," McGonigal had "erected a temporary fence in the rear of Parcel D so as to totally prevent the use of the Men's tee box and Ladies' tee box, as well as to prevent the use of the golf cart pathway as access thereto." Putts & Divots therefore requested relief in the form of a declaration of their permanent easement rights over Parcel D, as well as an entry of Preliminary and Mandatory Injunctions directing McGonigal to remove the temporary fence and "enjoining her from maintaining any fence or other structure, and/or the installation or construction of any other structure and/or engaging in any other conduct" which would interfere with access to the Men's and Ladies' tee boxes and the utilization of the golf cart pathway.

Under Pennsylvania Law,

> An easement by prescription arises by adverse, open, continuous, notorious and uninterrupted use of the land for a period of twenty-one years. *Bodman v. Bodman*, 456 Pa. 421,414, 321 A.2d 910 (1974); *Waltimyer v. Smith,* 383 Pa. Super. 291, 294, 556 A.2d 912, 913 (1989); *Burkett v. Smyder*, 369 Pa. Super. 519, 522, 535 A.2d 671, 673 (1988); *Wally v. Iraca*, 360 Pa. Super. 436, 441, 520 A.2d 886, 889 (1987). Necessity is not a requirement to the establishment of a prescriptive easement. *Boyd v. Teeple*, 460 Pa. 91, 94, 331 A.2d 433, 434 (1975). A landowner may "tack" the period of use by his predecessor in title onto his own period in order to establish continuous possession for the required twenty-one years. *Lednak v. Swatsworth*, 33 D.&C.3d 535, 537-538 (1984). "Tacking" is only permissible, however, where privity exists between the adverse possessors by the sale of the property by each owner to his successor. *Id.* Finally, in order to establish continuous possession, the adverse possessor need not illustrate constant use, and instead, may establish continuity by a settled course of conduct which shows an attitude of mind on the part of the user or users that the use is the exercise of a property right. *Burkett v. Smyder, supra*, 369 Pa. Super. at 522, 535 A.2d at 673.

*McCormick v. Camp Pocono Ridge, Inc. II*, 781 F. Supp. 328, 322 (M. D. Pa., 1991).

*(continued)*

The evidence presented at the hearing revealed that the easement over McGonigal's property used to access the tee areas for the 5th fairway had been in constant use since the inception of the golf course in 1966. More importantly, the course of conduct in accessing those tees continued unabated after Parcel D was subdivided from the original golf course property in 1985 and continued up until 2010 when McGonigal erected the privacy fence and prevented access to those tees. McGonigal's purchase of her residence from Keith Sink established the required privity, and by "tacking" the period of use of that easement during the Sinks' ownership of Parcel D, beginning in 1985, to that which occurred during McGonigal's ownership up to 2010, it is clear that the period of use necessary for the establishment of a prescriptive easement exceeded the required 21 years.

McGonigal did not present evidence in an attempt to convince this Court that the use of the easement has been interrupted due to the alleged closing or nonuse of the 5th fairway tees. We are aware, however, that the Superior Court of Pennsylvania has observed that:

> [a]nother factor for establishing a prescriptive easement that is somewhat less stringent than that required for adverse possession is the "continuous use" of the property. In establishing a prescriptive easement, constant use need not be demonstrated in order to establish the continuity of the use. Rather, "continuity is established if the evidence shows a settled course of conduct indicating an attitude of mind on the part of the user or users that the use is the exercise of a property right." *Minteer v. Wolfe,* 300 Pa. Super. 234, 240, 446 A.2d 316, 319 (1982), quoting *Keefer v. Jones,* 467 Pa. 544, 584, 359 A.2d 735, 737 (1976).

> *Newell Rod and Gun Club, Inc. v. Bauer,* 597 A.2d 667, 670 (Pa. Super., 1991).

This Court did not find the testimony of McGonigal or Keith Sink regarding either their alleged permission to use the tee boxes or the alleged closing of the tee box area for "at least one season" in "the early-mid 90's" to be credible, especially when contrasted to that of Jeffry Castle, Joseph Donnelly, Joseph Lightkep and Ronald Gorniak. We concluded that a "settled course of conduct" in accessing the 5th fairway tees over an easement on McGonigal's property has been established over a period of time well exceeding the requisite 21 years, and that the evidence demonstrated that that course of conduct, which involved numerous golfers, a well-recognized golf course and residential dwellings in close proximity to that golf course, had been clearly adverse, open and notorious.

McGonigal also alleges that this Court "abused its discretion in determining that McGonigal moved to the nuisance" because this factor was "entirely irrelevant to whether Plaintiff's motion for preliminary injunction should be granted."

McGonigal apparently implies that it is impermissible for this Court to equitably consider evidence that she was well aware of the activities of which she complains prior to the purchase of her residence, and that these lawful activities had been established well before she purchased her property. We disagree.

Our sister jurisdiction, the Court of Common Pleas of Washington County, encountered a similar situation in *Weishner v. Washington County Golf and Country Club,* 11 Pa. D.&C.3d 458 (Pa. Com. Pl., 1979), in which plaintiff homeowners attempted to enjoin defendant golf club from operating "the number one tee on its golf course." In denying plaintiffs the requested injunctive relief, the Court observed in relevant part:

> Finally, we consider the fact that plaintiffs by the purchase of their plot of ground in its present location have "come to the nuisance" which they now seek to enjoin. Obviously when plaintiffs purchased their land in 1977, they

were aware of the existence and location of the golf course. As reasonable people they realized, or should have realized, the potential hazard of locating a house in such close proximity to a golf course. During excavation they found evidence that would warn them of what they might expect with reference to golf balls landing on their property. The fact that defendant is making reasonable and normal use of its premises and that plaintiffs voluntarily chose to purchase adjoining property without making responsible inquiry as to probable or potential hazard must work against plaintiffs. Also, we must consider the fact that no other homeowners in the vicinity have complained of the activities of the defendant's members, nor have they testified on plaintiff's behalf.

*Id.* At 461.

There is clearly no legal basis, as McGonigal suggests, to prohibit this Court from equitably considering the fact that she was well aware of the well-established golf course activities surrounding and encroaching on Parcel D, and yet still chose to purchase the property, and then over five years later, attempted to enjoin those very activities while transferring her problematic situation onto her neighbors.

For the foregoing reasons we granted the preliminary injunction requested by the Plaintiffs.

### Conservation Easements

**Conservation easements** are restrictions created for the specific purpose of land preservation programs. By offering favorable tax treatment—or in some instances, exemption from real estate taxes—state and local governments encourage property owners to place their properties into land preservation programs. In both historic districts and open land settings, owners of these parcels may agree to restrict the use of the property or convey buildings or lands to designated governmental authorities. Thus, if an owner of five acres of forestland wishes to preserve it and the surrounding community wishes to foster pristine open space, the conservation easement is the mechanism to formalize these mutual desires. As in other transactions, the grantor of the easement would note its conservation purpose directly in the deed. Exhibit 5.4 is a sample conservation easement.

> **conservation easements**
> restrictions created for the specific purpose of land preservation

## Covenants

**Restrictive covenants or covenants** are agreements between the sellers and buyers of land usually related to the use of the land. Covenants represent the earliest form of controlling land use. For example, before the existence of municipal planning or zoning, use of property within a particular neighborhood or community was controlled by restrictive covenants placed in deeds. Below is a sample of a restrictive covenant taken from a deed for a property located in Ocean City, New Jersey:

> **restrictive covenants or covenants**
> agreements between the sellers and buyers of land, usually related to the use of the land

> And also under and subject to the express conditions and restrictions that no building of any description whatever shall be erected within ten feet of the front line of said avenue, nor within four feet of sidelines of said lot…, and also that no building, or any part thereof, erected upon the said lot or lots, shall be used or occupied as a livery or sales stable, dye-house, bone-boiling or skin dressing establishment, soap, candle, glue, starch, lamp-jack, poudrette or fish-guano manufactory, slaughter-house, piggery, or tannery. Nor shall any building be used or occupied as a drug store, without the written consent of the said party of the first part hereto.
> *Barton v. Slifer,* 72 N.J. Eq. 812, 66 A. 899 (1907).

Covenants and restrictive covenants are considered a contract between the parties to the agreement and enforceable unless they violate public policy or law.

## Exhibit 5.4 Deed of Conservation Easement

**DEED OF CONSERVATION EASEMENT**

**THIS DEED OF CONSERVATION EASEMENT** ("Conservation Easement") made this _____ day of _____, 200_, by and between _____, ("Grantor(s)"), and The State of Maryland to the use of the Department of Natural Resources ("Grantee"),

**WITNESSETH**

**WHEREAS**, by Contract of Sale approved by the Board of Public Works on February 9, 2000, the Pennsylvania Electric Company agreed to sell and the State of Maryland agreed to buy the bed of Deep Creek Lake and certain surrounding parcels of property, known collectively as Parcel 2, subject to the imposition of a conservation easement upon the State's resale of certain portions of the property;

**WHEREAS**, of the property purchased from Pennsylvania Electric Company, the State has determined to retain a portion of Parcel 2 contiguous to Deep Creek Lake to be reserved for public use and additional land as necessary to protect the Lake's natural, recreational, scenic, and aesthetic resources, and to delineate boundary lines, or to provide for public access to the Lake;

**WHEREAS**, of the remaining portions of Parcel 2, the State has determined to resell to contiguous property owners, certain parcels, subject to this Conservation Easement;

**WHEREAS**, Grantors herein own in fee simple real property situate, lying and being in Garrett County, Maryland, contiguous to Deep Creek Lake, thereby making them eligible to purchase a portion of Parcel 2 subject to this Conservation Easement; and

**WHEREAS**, the within Grantors have availed themselves of the opportunity to purchase property ("Property") and are willing to grant this Conservation Easement on the Property, thereby restricting and limiting the use of the Property as hereinafter provided in this Conservation Easement for the purposes set forth below.

**WHEREAS**, the purpose of the Conservation Easement is to prevent development and maintain the beauty and recreational purpose and to conserve the natural and scenic qualities of the environment of Deep Creek Lake and the surrounding area;

**NOW, THEREFORE**, in consideration of the facts stated in the above paragraphs and the covenants, terms, conditions and restrictions (the "Terms") hereinafter set forth, the receipt and sufficiency of which are hereby acknowledged by the parties, the Grantors unconditionally and irrevocably hereby grant and convey unto the Grantee, its successors and assigns, forever and in perpetuity a Conservation Easement of the nature and character and to the extent hereinafter set forth, with respect to the Property:

**ARTICLE I. DURATION OF EASEMENT**

This Conservation Easement shall be perpetual. It is an easement in gross and runs with the land as an incorporeal interest in the Property, enforceable with respect to the Property by the Grantee against the Grantors and their personal representatives, heirs, successors and assigns.

**ARTICLE II. PROHIBITED AND RESTRICTED ACTIVITIES**

**A. *Industrial or Commercial Activities on the Property***

Industrial or commercial activities are prohibited on the Property, except, with the approval of the Grantee, for activities necessary to support and gain access to lake-related, commercial and recreational uses permitted by the State of Maryland on immediately contiguous State land or on Deep Creek Lake, at the time of the proposed activity.

**B. *Construction and Improvements***

No building, facility, means of access, fence or other structure shall be permitted on the Property, except: (1) pedestrian pathways or stairways constructed with wood, stone or permeable surfaces of natural materials to provide access to the lake or improvements on the Property from the contiguous property; (2) with the approval of the Grantee, utilities to serve commercial or recreational facilities on the contiguous State land; (3) structures identified on a plat of Parcel 2 as recorded among the Land Records of Garrett County, Maryland in Plat Drawer P, File 134 or in the records of the Department of Natural Resources and those structures identified on the individual plats prepared by the surveyor and recorded with each conveyance, provided that such structures were permitted by the Department or its predecessor in title prior to the Grantor's ownership of the Property; and (4) as subject to the approval of the Grantee, temporary structures with a footprint no greater than 120 square feet.

**C. *Transferable, Cluster and Other Development Rights***

The Grantors hereby grant to the Grantee all transferable, cluster or other development rights under any present or future law that are now or hereafter allocated to, implied, reserved or inherent in the Property, and the parties agree that such rights are terminated and extinguished, and may not be used or transferred to any portion of the Property, or to any other property, nor used for the purpose of calculating permissible size or lot yield of the Property or any other property.

**D. *Trees***

There shall be no burning, cutting, removal or destruction of trees, shrubs and other woody vegetation (collectively "Vegetation"), except: subject to the approval of the Grantee (1) Vegetation that is dead, infested or diseased; (2) Vegetation necessary to control erosion; (3) Vegetation necessary to provide reasonable access to Deep Creek Lake; and (4) Vegetation cut, maintained, or removed pursuant to a forest management plan that has been approved by the Grantee and prepared by a professional forester registered in Maryland. Trimming and maintenance of Vegetation that has been planted by the Grantor or a predecessor in title to the Grantor on the Property is permitted; provided, that the Grantor or the Grantor's predecessor provides written documentation to the Grantee of the type and location of the Vegetation prior to maintenance or trimming.

**E. *Dumping, Placement or Storage of Materials***

No materials may be dumped or stored on the Property, including, but not limited to, ashes, trash, garbage, rubbish, abandoned vehicles, abandoned vessels, abandoned appliances, and abandoned machinery.

**F. *Excavation of Materials***

Excavation or mining of the Property is prohibited, including, but not limited to, removal of soil or sand, except, with the approval of the Grantee, for temporary excavation: (1) to maintain access to Deep Creek Lake; or (2) to repair and extend a septic system or well that has failed on a contiguous property, so long as the failure is not due to increased use, occupancy, or size of the contiguous dwelling that the septic system or well serves, in violation of any health laws, ordinances, regulations or permits.

**G. *Wetlands***

No diking, draining, filling, dredging or removal of any wetland or wetlands is permitted. "Wetland" or "wetlands" means portions of the Property defined by any State or federal laws as a wetland or wetlands at the time of the proposed activity.

*(continued)*

# Exhibit 5.4  Continued

**H.** *Signs and Billboards*

No signs, billboards, or outdoor advertising displays may be erected, displayed, placed or maintained on the Property except temporary signs not exceeding six square feet to advertise the property's sale or rental.

**I.** *Public Access*

This Conservation Easement does not grant the public any right to access or any right of use of the Property.

**J.** *Reserved Rights*

Except to the extent that prior written approval of the Grantee is required by any paragraph of this Article, all rights not prohibited by this Conservation Easement are considered to be consistent with the Terms of this Conservation Easement and require no prior notification or approval. If the Grantors have any doubt with respect to whether or not any particular use of the Property is prohibited by the Terms of this Conservation Easement, the Grantors may submit a written request to the Grantee for consideration and approval of such use.

## ARTICLE III. ENFORCEMENT AND REMEDIES

**A.** *Remedies*

Upon any breach of the Terms of this Conservation Easement by the Grantors, the Grantee may exercise any or all of the following remedies:

1. institute suits to enjoin any breach or enforce any covenant by temporary and/or permanent injunction either prohibitive or mandatory; and

2. require that the Property be restored promptly to the condition required by this Conservation Easement.

The Grantee's remedies shall be cumulative and shall be in addition to any other rights and remedies available to the Grantee at law or equity. If the Grantors are found to have breached any of the Terms under this Conservation Easement, the Grantors shall reimburse the Grantee for any costs or expenses incurred by the Grantee, including court costs and reasonable attorney's fees.

**B.** *Effect of Failure to Enforce*

No failure on the part of the Grantee to enforce any Term hereof shall discharge or invalidate such Term or any other Term hereof or affect the right of the Grantee to enforce the same in the event of a subsequent breach or default.

**C.** *Right of Inspection*

The State of Maryland, acting by and through the Department of Natural Resources, the Grantee, their respective employees and agents, have the right, with reasonable notice to the Grantors, to enter the Property at reasonable times for the purpose of inspecting the Property to determine whether the Grantors are complying with the Terms of this Conservation Easement.

## ARTICLE IV. MISCELLANEOUS

**A.** *Future Transfers*

By executing this Conservation Easement, the Grantors acknowledge that this Conservation Easement is permanent and is binding on their heirs, personal representatives, successors or assigns.

**B.** *Effect of Laws Imposing Affirmative Obligations on the Grantors*

In the event that any applicable State or federal law imposes affirmative obligations on owners of land which if complied with by the Grantors would be a violation of a Term of this Conservation Easement, the Grantors shall: (i) if said law requires a specific act without any discretion on the part of the Grantors, comply with said law and give the Grantee written notice of the Grantors' compliance as soon as reasonably possible, but in no event more than thirty (30) days from the time the Grantors begin to comply; or (ii) if said law leaves to the Grantors discretion over how to comply with said law, use the method most protective of the purpose of this Conservation Easement set forth in the recitals herein.

**C.** *Notices to the Grantee*

Any notices by the Grantors to the Grantee pursuant to any Term hereof shall be sent by registered or certified mail, return receipt requested, addressed to the current address of the Secretary, Department of Natural Resources, with a copy to Manager, Deep Creek Lake Natural Resources Management Area.

**D.** *Approval of the Grantee*

In any case where the terms of this Conservation Easement require the approval of the Grantee, such approval shall be requested by written notice to the Grantee. After consultation with the Deep Creek Lake Policy Review Board, approval or disapproval shall be given promptly and in writing; in the event the request is disapproved, a statement of the reasons for the disapproval shall be given.

**E.** *Condemnation*

Whenever all or part of the Property is taken in the exercise of eminent domain, so as to abrogate, in whole or in part, the restrictions imposed by this Conservation Easement, or this Conservation Easement is extinguished, in whole or in part, by other judicial proceeding, the Grantors and the Grantee shall be entitled to proceeds payable in connection with the condemnation or other judicial proceedings in any amount equal to the current fair market value of their relative real estate interests. Any costs of a judicial proceeding allocated by a court to the Grantors and the Grantee shall be allocated in the same manner as the proceeds are allocated.

**F.** *Construction*

This Conservation Easement shall be construed pursuant to the purpose of this Conservation Easement and the purposes of Section 2-118 of the Real Property Article of the Annotated Code of Maryland, and to the laws of the State of Maryland generally.

**G.** *Effect of Laws and Other Restrictions on the Property*

The Terms of this Conservation Easement shall be in addition to any local, State or federal laws imposing restrictions on the Property and any real estate interests imposing restrictions on the Property.

**H.** *Entire Agreement and Severability of the Terms*

This instrument sets forth the entire agreement of the parties with respect to the Conservation Easement and supersedes all prior discussions, negotiations, understanding or agreements relating to the Conservation Easement. If any Term is found to be invalid, the remainder of the Terms of this Conservation Easement, and the application of such Term to persons or circumstances other than those as to which it is found to be invalid, shall not be affected thereby.

**I.** *Successors*

The terms "Grantors" and "Grantee" wherever used herein, and any pronouns used in place thereof, shall include, respectively,

*(continued)*

## Exhibit 5.4 Continued

the above-named Grantors and their personal representatives, heirs, successors, and assigns and the above-named Grantee and their successors and assigns.

**J. *Real Property Taxes***
Except to the extent provided for by State or local law, nothing herein contained shall relieve the Grantors of the obligation to pay taxes in connection with the ownership of the Property.

**K. *Captions***
The captions in this Conservation Easement have been inserted solely for convenience of reference and are not a part of this instrument. Accordingly, the captions shall have no effect upon the construction or interpretation of the Terms of this Conservation Easement.

**IN WITNESS THEREOF**, the Grantors have hereunto set their hands and seals in the day and year above written.

WITNESS/ATTEST:                                    GRANTORS:

_____                    _____(SEAL)
_____                    _____(SEAL)


**STATE OF MARYLAND,**
_____ of _____ TO WIT:
**I HEREBY CERTIFY**, that on this _____ day of _____, 200__, before me the subscriber, a Notary Public of the State aforesaid, personally appeared _____, known to me (or satisfactorily proven) to be a Grantor of the foregoing Deed of Conservation Easement and acknowledged that he/she executed the same for the purposes therein contained and in my presence signed and sealed the same.
WITNESS my hand and Notarial Seal.
Notary Public
My Commission Expires: _____
(Use a separate notary for each Grantor's signature and modify the above certificate if any entity, such as a corporation, is a Grantor.)
I hereby certify that this Deed of Conservation Easement was prepared and reviewed for legal form and sufficiency by _____, an attorney admitted to practice before the Court of Appeals of Maryland.

_____
ASSISTANT ATTORNEY GENERAL

---

This contract concept of covenants was used for segregation purposes to prohibit the sale of land to minorities in the United States.

> No person or persons of Asiatic, African or Negro blood, lineage, or extraction shall be permitted to occupy a portion of said property.

In 1948, the United States Supreme Court ruled that these provisions were invalid. However, racial discrimination in housing continued until the Congress passed the Housing Act of 1968.

The most frequent use of restrictive covenants today is in land development. Large tracts of land are developed, with hundreds of houses. To control building lot size, exercise the right to further divide the land, and build only single-family residential units, the land developer will include these items as restrictive covenants in the deeds of purchasers. These restrictive covenants are particularly important where there is an absence of zoning limitations or where there is a zoning code, but the developer wants to be more restrictive about the land use and development. Frequently during the development process, an additional covenant will restrict the resale of the land, requiring that any sale within a certain time period be a sale back to the developer only.

Covenants are said to **run with the land.** Regardless of who owns the land or how many times ownership is transferred over time, the covenant continues to exist, or "run with the land." The covenant is a restriction on the land and its future use, regardless of who owns the land.

## License

A **license** is the common law right to remove natural resources, such as minerals and timber, from the property of another. Profit in the common law was limited

**WEB EXPLORATION**
For a review of the use of covenants to discriminate against minorities see: http://depts.washington.edu/civilr/covenants.htm

---

**COMMON LAW TERMS**

*Profit* or *profit a prendre* is the common law term for what is called a license in contemporary law.

---

**run with the land**
a restriction on the land and its future use, regardless of who owns the land

**license**
the right to profit from the land belonging to another, typically through the removal of natural resources, such as minerals and timber

to items taken from the soil. The term has been replaced by the broader term license. A license is the privilege to use land for a specific, profit-making purpose not limited to taking from the soil. Examples include removal of oil and gas, construction, and similar activity. Mineral rights are a common subject matter for the license. A mineral right is a right to extract a mineral from the earth and make a payment, in the form of royalty, for the extraction. *Mineral* may have different meanings, depending on the context. Although there is no universal definition, the term generally includes the following:

- Fossil fuels—oil, natural gas, and coal
- Metals and metal-bearing ores such as gold, copper, and iron
- Nonmetallic minerals and mineable rock products such as limestone, gypsum, building stones, and salt
- Sand and gravel, peat, marl, and so on

A license allows a licensee to do something on land that except for the license would be considered trespass. Licenses are generally granted for an extremely limited purpose, such as mining coal, cutting trees, or growing a crop. A license is personal, temporary, and limited to the licensed activity. Subsequent buyers of the license have no assurance that the owner of the property will continue the license. The consent of the landowner is required for the effective transfer of the license. The owner of the real estate continues to maintain exclusive control of the real estate during the life of the license. Compared to an easement, the license is **incidental** to the land, meaning that it does not run with the land.

**incidental**
a right to use the land of another is incidental when it does not run with the land but requires the approval of the owner for future or continued use

## Judgment Liens

A **judgment** is a final decision from a court, which assesses liability against a party to a lawsuit. Many judgments are for monetary damages, to compensate one of the parties to the lawsuit. The person being compensated is the judgment creditor. The person who owes the money as a result of the lawsuit is the judgment debtor. The judgment is filed in the office for recording property liens for the court in which the property is located and, when properly filed, represents a lien against all the real property owned by the judgment debtor. A **judgment lien** is an encumbrance which creates a limitation on the ability of the owner of the property to sell it or borrow money using the property as collateral until the judgment lien is paid in full and satisfied of record in the courthouse records. Unpaid income and real estate taxes and municipal charges for water and sewer can become judgment liens. Judgment liens are involuntarily created.

**judgment**
final decision from a court, which assesses liability against a party to a lawsuit

**judgment lien**
limitation on the ability of the owner of a property to sell it or to borrow money using the property as collateral until the judgment lien is paid in full and satisfied of record in the courthouse records

An encumbrance or lien may be voluntarily created by the owner of real property. A **mortgage** is a lien voluntarily created by the owner using the real property as collateral for the promise to repay the mortgage debt.

**mortgage**
lien voluntarily created by the owner using the real property as collateral for the promise to repay a debt

## ■ POLICE POWER AND GOVERNMENT RESTRICTIONS

**Police power** is the right of state governments to define and control activities to promote the health, safety, and general welfare of their citizens. Anything that is not within the exclusive jurisdiction of the federal government is subject to the police power of the state. This power includes the right to establish a police department and promote the general welfare. Through the implementation of laws and regulations, the state defines acceptable and unacceptable behavior. This includes imposing restrictions on the use of private property through building and zoning codes. Each state also has the authority to delegate certain powers to local communities.

**LEARNING OBJECTIVE 2**
Explain how government action can restrict land use.

**police power**
right of state governments to define and control activities to promote the health, safety, and general welfare of their citizens

## Zoning and Building Codes

**zoning codes**
laws enacted by municipalities to control the use and development of the land in the community

 **WEB EXPLORATION**

For more information on the municipalities in Pennsylvania, see http://www.pamunicipalitiesinfo.com/

**enabling acts**
state statutes authorizing a municipality to adopt laws and regulations

**Zoning codes** are enacted by municipalities to control the use and development of the land in the community. These are highly localized in nature. For example, Pennsylvania is divided into 67 counties that are further divided into 2,563 local municipalities such as cities, townships, boroughs, and villages with potentially 2,563 different zoning codes.

Under state statutes called **enabling acts,** each municipality is authorized to adopt a zoning code to control the use and development of land within its borders. Some municipalities elect not to enact zoning codes; this could be because the amount of land or number of residents is so small that there is no concern about land development. In some instances, a group of municipalities located in close proximity to each other will form a joint zoning plan to coordinate growth and development across a larger area. This type of long-range planning is found frequently in areas adjacent to cities and large metropolitan areas where suburban communities seek to control urban sprawl. Most municipalities do enact a zoning code that will determine the following items:

1. The definition of residential, commercial, institutional, and industrial uses permitted within the borders of the municipality
2. The definitions of permitted uses, such as apartment house, manufacturing, convenience store, or beer distributor
3. Where the permitted uses may be located—for example, a commercial shopping district, a commercial office district, a light industrial district
4. The minimum lot size for a single-family dwelling, setback lines from the street and other property lines, the maximum height of any dwelling, and the percentage of a lot that can be paved
5. For commercial, industrial, and institutional uses, the lot size, building height, and required parking that must be provided based on the square footage of the building or structure erected

The list above is just a sampling of the restrictions placed on real estate through zoning. A review of the zoning requirements in the community in which the real property is located will determine what, if anything, can be done to develop raw land or improve an existing building.

### Zoning Litigation

The area of zoning is a highly litigated matter. Most zoning codes have provisions to allow for making exceptions to the rules contained in the code. There is a very specific procedure that must be followed to request an exception or be granted a variance from the zoning provisions. The application for the exception or variance is made to the governing body, usually the zoning hearing board. Notice must be given to all interested parties, usually the owners of adjoining and nearby properties, who are given the right to attend the zoning hearing board meeting when the application is reviewed. Generally, the applicant will establish that there is no substantial harm caused by granting the exception and that to refuse the request would represent a hardship.

A good example is the request to waive a side yard requirement of 20 feet to permit an addition to a house. The proposed addition will reduce the side yard from 20 to 15 feet. This is not a significant violation of the requirement and will not result in great harm to the neighboring property owner. But if the neighbor objects, the request may not be so easily granted.

**Building code** restrictions and specifications to be used for construction and repairs of structures are enacted by local municipalities to ensure safety in the construction of buildings and improvements attached to land. The International Code Council has developed a nationwide model building code that is based on model building codes enacted by three regional groups—the Building Officials Code Administrators (North and Midwest), Southern Building Code Congress International (South), and the International Conference of Building Officials (West). It is these model codes that have been enacted by local municipalities. The goal is the construction of buildings and improvements that withstand certain known stresses such as hurricane-force winds, wildfires, and earthquakes. Windows must be shatter resistant. Siding must be fire resistant. Roofs must withstand the weight of a heavy snowfall. Obviously, the geographic location of the property will determine which risks are most important to protect against. One that all communities agree on is the erection of a fence around a pool to prevent small children from drowning. The building code will set standards for quality of materials used as well as the standard measurements for support beams and the interval at which they can be set. The building code will also control features on the interior of the building. For example, homes that exceed a particular height will be required to include a fire suppression system.

**Building codes**
laws enacted by local municipalities to ensure safety in the construction of buildings and improvements attached to land

## Taxation

In our society, the government provides services—police and fire protection, pools and recreation centers, trash and garbage removal, public school systems—that are paid for through taxation. For many municipalities, tax revenues have been based on real estate taxes. Each parcel of real estate is appraised and an **assessed value** assigned based on the market value of the property. School districts and county and local governments determine a tax rate, which is then applied to the assessed value to determine the real estate taxes due.

**assessed value**
a value assigned to a property by the municipality, based on market value

$$\text{Assessed Value} \times \text{Tax Rate} = \text{Real Estate Taxes}$$
$$\$77,000.00 \times 3.47\% = \$2,671.90$$

For the government, there are two ways to increase tax revenues. One way is to raise tax rates.

$$\text{Assessed Value} \times \text{Tax Rate} = \text{New Real Estate Tax}$$
$$\$77,000.00 \times 3.78\% = \$2,910.60$$

Another way to increase tax revenues is to **reassess**, or change the value of the properties. Assessed values are determined by reviewing recent sales within a particular neighborhood to set a new assessed value for all the properties in that neighborhood. This process can result in unfair treatment, as there is no accounting for the condition of any particular property. Another method is to conduct a countywide reassessment where every property is inspected and an estimate of value prepared. Some properties will go up in value and others will go down. Where values go up, imposition of the existing tax rate can be burdensome on the property owner.

**reassess**
to change the value of properties

$$\text{Assessed Value} \times \text{Tax Rate} = \text{New Real Estate Tax}$$
$$\$110,000.00 \times 3.47\% = \$3,817.00$$

But not every property will have the same large increase in value. For that reason, there is usually a modest reduction of the tax rate in conjunction with any reassessment. In this example, the tax rate might be reduced to 3.11% and the taxes still increase to $3,421.00—a significant increase for the property owner.

For those on a fixed income, real estate taxes can become a financial burden. Income taxes seem fairer, as they are based on the amount of income received. With a fixed income, such as a pension or Social Security, people do not control the amount of income received through their labor. As real estate taxes increase, they become a greater share of that fixed income, leaving less funds available for food, clothing, utilities, and home repairs. For this reason, high taxes can result in quality schools and services making a community a desirable place to live. But those same high taxes can also make a community unaffordable, and less desirable.

## Environmental

Federal and state governments control and restrict the right to use property by the imposition of environmental regulations. There are standards related to the release of pollutants into the air, water, and ground. The goal, of course, is to protect the general welfare and safety of our citizens from materials that are harmful to our health. For manufacturers, there may be limitations related to emissions from smokestacks to protect and preserve clean air. For farmers, there are limitations on the use of chemical pesticides that are helpful in preventing crop destruction but run off the land and into the water supply when it rains. In both cases, known pollutants are rigorously controlled by state and federal environmental agencies. Both the farmer and the manufacturer know of these costs of doing business.

For individual home ownership, it is hard to imagine that federal and state environmental controls could affect the rights of ownership. However, there are things once thought safe but which are now declared unsafe conditions or contaminants that must be removed. For years, home heating units were oil fired in the eastern United States. Unsightly oil storage tanks were buried underground, with a pumping mechanism forcing oil into the heating unit as needed. Over many years, it was discovered that seals on the seams of those storage tanks were failing and that oil was leaching into the soil surrounding the buried storage tanks. For homeowners with oil-fired heating systems, the ability to sell their homes was suddenly dependent on removal of the buried tank, relocation of the tank, soil tests to determine the presence of contaminated soil, and cleanup of that contamination. Depending on the levels of soil contamination, there might also be the requirement to test the groundwater supply to determine whether that had been contaminated. This process can be a huge expense and time consuming. It can also render a property unmarketable, because many buyers would be fearful of the safety of a previously contaminated property.

# ETHICAL Consideration

### HAZARDOUS MATERIAL

Consider the dilemma of a lawyer whose client has, in confidence, revealed the existence of hazardous material on the property currently being sold. Does the attorney–client privilege and the duty of confidentiality bar the lawyer from revealing the potential hazard to the buyer and the buyer's lawyer or representative?

Does the Model Code of Professional Responsibility allow the disclosure because of the potential for harm to another?

What if the information does not involve a hazard to life, but only to the economic value of the property, such as the fact that the water well has dried up and the buyer has not checked or inspected that feature?

## KEY TERMS

## CHAPTER SUMMARY

| | |
|---|---|
| Introduction to Restrictions on Real Property Use | The ownership of real property does not include the absolute right to use it without restriction. Voluntary agreements between real property owners and government action may impose restrictions on the use of the land. |
| Servitudes | A servitude is anything that burdens the use of real property. Generally servitudes are created through an agreement of parties defining the private restrictions on use. The three major servitudes are easements, covenants, and profits. |
| Easements | Easements provide a limited right to enter real property owned by another, which allows one party to use some portion of the real property of another but comes with no right of ownership. Every easement grants a right and imposes a burden. The party with the right to use the property of another possesses the dominant estate. The property that the party with the dominant estate may use has the servient estate. Easements fall into two categories. Easements in gross, also called commercial easements, are characterized by the existence of one parcel of real estate that is the servient estate, but there is no specified parcel of real estate receiving a benefit from the easement. Appurtenant easements are characterized by two parcels of land, usually adjoining, with each parcel having a different owner. The easement benefits one parcel, the dominant estate, and runs with the land. |
| Easement Creation | Easements may be created in three ways: by agreement, by necessity, and by prescription. An easement by necessity is created where one parcel of land is landlocked, or has no access to a public roadway. An easement by prescription is an easement created by common law and/or statute when a person without right or authorization uses or occupies the real estate of another for the statutorily prescribed time, usually 21 years. |

| | |
|---|---|
| Conservation Easements | Conservation easements are created for the specific purpose of land preservation programs. |
| Covenants | Covenants are agreements between the sellers and buyers of land, usually related to the use of the land. Covenants represent the earliest form of controlling land use. For example, before the existence of municipal planning or zoning, use of property within a particular neighborhood or community was controlled by restrictive covenants placed in deeds. |
| Profits and Licenses | A *profit* or *profit a prendre* is the common law right to remove natural resources, such as minerals and timber, from the property of another. A license is the privilege to use land for a specific profit-making purpose not limited to taking from the soil. |
| Judgment Liens | Judgment liens, whether created as a result of a court proceeding or voluntarily, are encumbrances which can impact thte ability to transfer real estate. |
| Police Power and Government Restrictions | Police power is the right of state governments to define and control activities to promote the health, safety, and general welfare of their citizens. Anything that is not within the exclusive jurisdiction of the federal government is subject to the police power of the state. |
| Zoning and Building Codes | Zoning codes are enacted by municipalities to control the use and development of the land in the community. These are highly localized in nature. Building codes are enacted by local municipalities to ensure safety in the construction of buildings and improvements attached to land. The International Code Council has developed a nationwide model building code that is based on model building codes enacted by three regional groups—the Building Officials Code Administrators (North and Midwest), Southern Building Code Congress International (South), and the International Conference of Building Officials (West). It is these model codes that have been enacted by local municipalities. |
| Taxation | For many municipalities, tax revenues have been based on real estate taxes. Each parcel of real estate is assessed a value, and the county and local governments determine a tax rate. The rate is then applied to the assessed value to determine the real estate taxes due.<br>Assessed Value $\times$ Tax Rate = Real Estate Taxes |
| Environmental | Federal and state governments control and restrict the right to use property by the imposition of environmental regulations. There are standards related to the release of pollutants into the air, water, and ground. The goal, of course, is to protect the general welfare and safety of our citizens from materials that are harmful to our health. |

## REVIEW QUESTIONS AND EXERCISES

1. What is a servitude?
2. Define the three main types of servitudes.
3. What is the difference between the dominant and servient estates?
4. What does it mean for a servitude to "run with the land"?
5. How are an easement in gross and an appurtenant easement similar? How are they different?
6. Describe the three ways an easement may be created.
7. What is a conservation easement?
8. What is a covenant, and how are covenants most frequently used? How does a covenant differ from an easement?
9. What is a profit or license? How does a profit or license differ from a covenant? From an easement?
10. How is a judgment lien created? How does a judgment lien restrict real property ownership?
11. What is police power?
12. Describe how zoning codes restrict the use of real property.
13. Describe how building codes restrict the use of real property.
14. How can taxation based on real estate values impact real property rights?
15. How do environmental regulations restrict real property ownership rights?

## VIDEO CASE STUDY

Go to www.pearsonhighered.com/careers to view the following videos.

**Author Introduction to Restrictions on Use of Real Property.**
Author video introduction to chapter coverage.

## INTERNET AND TECHNOLOGY EXERCISES

1. Using the Internet, determine the number of local municipalities in your state. How many of those do not have a zoning ordinance?
2. Using the Internet, locate a service provider for testing and removal of oil storage tanks and soil remediation for homeowners.
3. Using the Internet, find the website for your local electric utility provider. Determine whether there is an easement that allows the company to trim and/or remove trees within a certain distance of transmission lines.

## REAL ESTATE PORTFOLIO EXERCISES

**Restrictions on Use of Real Property**

**To:**        Paralegal Intern:
**From:**      Supervising Attorney
**Case Name:** Sheldon Todd
**Re:**        Driveway Easement

Our client has a shared driveway easement with the next door property owner. The neighbor has blocked a portion of the driveway, preventing our client from driving down the driveway. Attached are the original easement that was recorded, and a surveyor drawing.
   Can our client force the neighbor to allow him to use the driveway to drive his large pickup truck down the drive way?
   Research the right of adjoining landowners with a recorded easement to block the easement.
   Prepare an opinion letter to the client for my review explaining his rights.

Portfolio items produced
1. Memorandum of law on right to use driveway under terms of easement
2. Opinion letter to client

Go to www.pearsonhighered.com/careers to download instructions.

# UNIT II   Real Estate Transfer

# OVERVIEW OF THE RESIDENTIAL REAL ESTATE TRANSFER PROCESS

The typical real estate transaction starts with a seller listing a property for sale with a real estate broker. In some cases, the seller may also retain the services of a lawyer. The real estate broker has a duty as the agent of the seller to sell the property for the best possible price to a qualified buyer. In contemporary practice, this is usually done by listing the property with a real estate listing service that makes available information on properties that are for sale in the local area; these services may be called a multiple listing bureau or multiple listing service, or known by their initials MLB or MLS. Frequently, the listing service will show the property information on an Internet website as part of the service to market the property, either directly or indirectly using the listing broker's website. Buyers usually retain the services of a real estate broker as their agent, to locate and show them properties within their price range with the features and location they desire. The buyer's real estate broker will usually try to qualify the buyers' financial ability and coordinate that ability to obtain a mortgage with the type of property, location, or special needs of the buyer. In this Internet age, buyers sometimes use the Internet first and, when they find something they think they like, contact the listing agent or another real estate professional to arrange to see the property. Buyers may retain the services of a lawyer before a property is located, but more frequently, a lawyer is consulted after the agreement of sale is signed by the seller and the buyer.

In some jurisdictions, the law provides a period of time for lawyers for the buyer and seller to review the sales agreement before it becomes binding. In other states, there is no review period, and the parties are bound to the agreement of sale as soon as they sign it.

Unless it is a cash purchase, the buyers will usually meet with a mortgage solicitor or representative of a mortgage company or bank to secure financing. In some cases, buyers may be preapproved for a mortgage before they start looking at properties. Once an agreement of sale is signed, the buyer must complete the loan application process to financially qualify for the loan to purchase the property.

## LEARNING OBJECTIVES

*Upon completion of this chapter, you should be able to*

1. Explain the importance of an accurate legal description for real estate.

2. Explain how real estate is transferred voluntarily.

3. Describe how real estate is transferred involuntarily.

# Transferring Real Property | CHAPTER 6

## ■ INTRODUCTION TO TRANSFERRING REAL PROPERTY

Transferring real property requires that the land be described with accuracy. The methods of describing and identifying parcels of land have changed as methods of measurement have become more accurate and systematized by government regulations.

In some areas of the country, generally east of the Mississippi, traditional methods and terminology have persisted, while western states have embraced the federal government system utilized during the westward expansion surveys.

Real property can be transferred either voluntarily or involuntarily.

The most common type of voluntary transfer of real property is the voluntary sale by the owner. Other methods of voluntary transfer include lifetime gifts and leaving the property to someone at the time of death, usually through a provision contained in the owner's will.

An involuntary transfer occurs when a property owner is either forced to convey the property to another person or entity or the property is taken by a government action. An owner who fails to make mortgage payments will be forced to transfer the property to the mortgage lender through mortgage foreclosure proceedings. Property may be taken from the owner by some entity—such as the government or a utility company—through eminent domain and condemnation proceedings.

## DIGITAL RESOURCES

Author Introduction to Transferring Real Property.

Buyers' First Meeting with Attorney.

Author Explains Conflict of Interest.

Sample forms and templates.

# ■ LAND DESCRIPTION

**LEARNING OBJECTIVE 1**
Explain the importance of an accurate legal description for real estate.

**legal description**
describes the property based on its boundary lines and distances

Description of a parcel of real estate is called a **legal description.** The legal description describes the property based on its boundary lines and distances or, in common law terms, its metes and bounds. Traditionally, legal descriptions were prepared by land surveyors and engineers. A legal description includes the length of each boundary (side) of the property and the direction traveled along that boundary, using compass headings starting from and returning to a known point, usually a physical monument or an artificial marker.

Early surveys were created using metal chains with links, cloth and metal tape measures, and handheld compasses. The land survey profession has seen a major transition from the use of traditional tools to modern technology using computers and global positioning satellite (GPS) equipment to measure and describe properties with great accuracy.

The accuracy of the legal description is critical. Only the land described is transferred. If the description is not accurate and part of the parcel is omitted, the portion omitted is not transferred and remains in the ownership of the grantor. Consider the sale of a 10-acre parcel of land sold for development of a shopping center. Suppose a mistake is made in describing the property conveyed; a strip of land is omitted and not conveyed to the developer. That strip of land supplies needed access from the property to the highway. But because of an error in the description, that portion of the property may remain in the hands of the grantor or his heirs. The new owners would not have access to the property from the highway, which is essential for customer access to the shopping center. Without the land, the customers are required to use a more obscure route, which they may not be willing to take. This would deny the developers the economic benefit of customers having easy access. So the careful preparation and review of the legal description for accuracy is important. In the case of a metes and bounds description where the boundary lines do not return to the same starting point, a question remains as to the accuracy of the description and what was intended to be conveyed.

## LINEAR MEASUREMENT

1 chain = 100 links or 66 feet
1 mile = 80 chains or 5,280 feet
1 mile = 1.61 kilometers

## AREA MEASUREMENT

1 acre = 10 sq. chains or 43,560 sq. feet
1 square mile = 640 acres
2.47 acres = 1 hectar

For the members of the real estate team to be able to create new descriptions using modern measurements and determine what was conveyed in older conveyances where the older terms of measurement were used, familiarity with the terminology used in traditional and modern surveying is important (such as *chains* for a term of measurement).

**chain of title**
refers to a list of deeds transferring ownership of a parcel of land from one person to the next over a period of time

**Chain of title** refers to a list of deeds transferring ownership of a parcel of land from one owner to the next over a period of time. Research on a parcel of land includes review of all the prior deeds for the same parcel. Each of the prior deeds is checked to confirm the identity of the prior grantors and grantees, the legal description of the property conveyed, and any restrictive covenants or easements.

## Monuments

**monument**
a natural or artificial object permanently affixed to the land, used as a marker along the boundaries of a property

A **monument** is a natural or artificial object permanently affixed to the land, used as a marker along the boundaries of a property. The earliest method of land description was to walk the boundaries of the land and mark certain points along the way: natural objects, such as streams; large, naturally occurring items in the land, such as trees or boulders; or objects permanently affixed to the land, such as roads and bridges. Modern survey practice is to avoid the use of natural monuments in favor of concrete or metal markers. The use of natural objects can be seen in Exhibit 6.1.

## Exhibit 6.1 Sketch depicting legal description by monuments

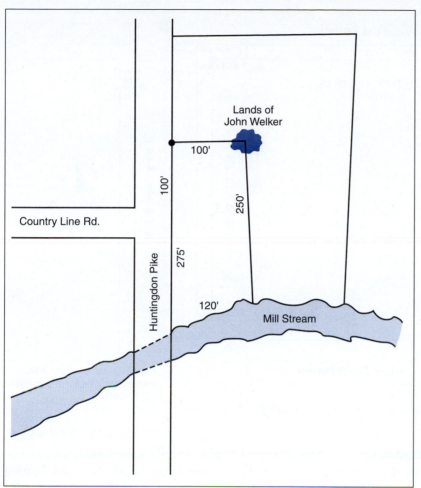

Below is the legal description for the parcel of land depicted in Exhibit 6.1:

BEGINNING at the intersection of the Huntingdon Pike with Country Line Road and heading northerly 100 feet to the point and place of beginning; thence extending easterly parallel to lands of John Welker, 150 paces, approximately 100 feet to *sycamore tree*, thence extending southerly 300 paces, approximately 250 feet to a *stream*, thence along the *bed of the stream* westerly 175 paces, approximately 120 feet to the Huntingdon Pike thence along the Huntingdon Pike 275 paces to the point and place of beginning.

## Metes and Bounds

**Metes and bounds** are the distances and boundary lines of the property, starting from a designated marker or monument. In many communities across the United States, surveys have been conducted of all the land within the county or township. Monuments have been replaced by in-ground concrete markers or iron pins. These markers or pins may be placed on the boundary line between lands of different owners or at the location of a natural monument. The markers or pins become a permanent reference point for all future surveyors. This is a common form of land description in the eastern portion of the United States. As seen in Exhibit 6.2, each marker or reference point is shown with the corresponding direction and distance.

**metes and bounds**
the distances and boundary lines of the property, starting from a designated marker or monument

### Exhibit 6.2 Metes and bounds drawing

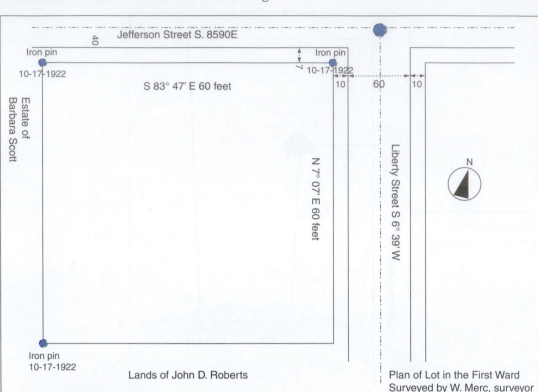

Jefferson Street S. 8590E
40
Iron pin
10-17-1922
Iron pin
10-17-1922
10
60
10
S 83° 47' E 60 feet
Estate of Barbara Scott
N 7° 07' E 60 feet
Liberty Street S 6° 39' W
N
Iron pin
10-17-1922
Lands of John D. Roberts
Plan of Lot in the First Ward
Surveyed by W. Merc, surveyor
10-17-1992

Each legal description uses a starting point—usually a monument or marker. The compass direction to the next marker or monument is called a **point bearing** and is set using traditional compass direction in degrees, minutes, and seconds (30° 45' 30") as well as a distance measurement usually in feet and inches. Additional bearing points and distances are used until the boundary description returns to the beginning point. Descriptions by bearing points and distance may be combined with other descriptions, such as "adjacent to the lands of John Smith," or monuments, such as the intersection of streets or the existence of a waterway. Property that has curved boundaries, as in the case of homes located on a circular street, may include descriptions based on geometry measurements such as arc, curve, and radius.

Below is a metes and bounds legal description for the piece of land depicted in Exhibit 6.2.

BEGINNING at a point on the northwesterly side of Jefferson Street (50 feet wide), a corner of lot #166 on aforementioned plan, said point being measured the four following courses and distances from a point of curve on the northeasterly side of Liberty Street (60 feet wide), (1) leaving said side of Liberty Street on the arc of a circle curving to the left, northeastwardly, having a radius of 20.00 feet the arc distance of 31.42 feet to a point of tangent on aforesaid side of Jefferson Street, (2) along said side of Jefferson Street north 19 degrees 40 minutes 45 seconds east 61.90 feet to a point of curve, (3) on the arc of a circle curving to the right, northeastwardly, having a radius of 175.00 feet the arc distance of 176.77 feet to a point of tangent and (4) north 77 degrees 33 minutes 15 seconds east 284.34 feet to point of BEGINNING.

THENCE the four following courses and distances (1) along the said side of Jefferson Street South 83° 47' East 60 feet to a corner, marked by an iron pin; (2) from said pin along the lands now or late of Barbara Scott South 7° 7' South

60 feet to a corner, marked by an iron pin; (3) from said pin along the lands now or late of John D. Roberts North 83° 47' West 60 feet to a corner, and: (4) along the said side of Liberty Street North 7° 7'North 60 feet to the first mentioned point and place of BEGINNING.

## Plat Maps

A **plat map** is a map of a subdivision or municipality that includes a metes and bounds description for every piece of real estate, usually including a lot and block number or tax parcel number. The plat may be created by a developer when a large tract of land is subdivided for a housing development. The plat is prepared based on a land survey, following metes and bounds descriptions to identify the individual lots. The map is divided into sections called blocks, and each lot is assigned a number. The plat map is recorded in the recorder of deeds, land registry, or tax assessor's office. Any lot located within the subdivision can be identified by reference to the recorded plat map, the page of the map if there are multiple pages, and the block and lot number of the individual parcel of land.

Similar to plat maps are tax maps. Many municipalities have prepared tax maps that identify every parcel of land within their borders. The maps are similar to plat maps. Each parcel is assigned a tax parcel number that identifies where on the tax maps the parcel is located. For example, the tax parcel number may be 09-28-004-27-6. Each number in the sequence helps to locate the property: 09 is the county identifier, 28 is the township identifier, 004 is the page number from the maps for the township, 27 is the block, and 6 is the particular lot. For purposes of transferring property, all that is required is reference to the lot and block numbers. Exhibit 6.3 is a plat map.

## Government Rectangular Survey

**Government Rectangular Survey** is a system of describing real property used primarily in areas of the United States west of the Mississippi River. As part of the westward expansion of the United States, the government surveyed the land and from that survey identified individual parcels that were granted to settlers.

The system is based on basic geographic concepts of longitude and latitude. Lines of **longitude** are imaginary parallel lines running from the North Pole to the South Pole. Lines of **latitude** run perpendicular to lines of longitude, circling the globe from east to west as shown in Exhibit 6.4.

The Government Rectangular Survey divides the lands west of the Mississippi River using meridians and base lines. **Meridians** run north and south like longitude, and **base lines** run east and west, parallel to latitude lines. These lines create a grid system.

The basic unit of division is called a **range** and represents 24 square miles defined by a principal meridian and base line. This 24-square-mile unit is then divided into four 6-square-mile units called **townships.** Each 6-square-mile township is then divided into 36 lots that are 1 square mile each, called **sections.** Each section is then divided into quarters and can be divided again and again until the desired individual lot size for a home or business is achieved.

Lots are identified based on a system of numbering that is standardized for all lots in the Government Survey. There is an identifying number for the range that indicates distance from a starting point. Exhibit 6.5 shows the rectangular survey system depicting a range, township and section, and Exhibit 6.6 depicts a plan for numbering a section.

**plat map**
map of a subdivision or municipality that includes a metes and bounds description for every piece of real estate

**Government Rectangular Survey**
system of describing real property used primarily in areas of the United States west of the Mississippi River

**longitude**
imaginary parallel lines running from the North Pole to the South Pole

**latitude**
imaginary lines perpendicular to lines of longitude, circling the globe from east to west

**meridians**
run north and south like longitude

**base lines**
run east and west, parallel to latitude lines

**range**
basic unit of division, which represents 24 square miles defined by a principal meridian and base line

**townships**
the result of dividing a range into four 6-square-mile units

**sections**
6-square-mile township divided into 36 lots that are 1 square mile each

## Exhibit 6.3 Plat map

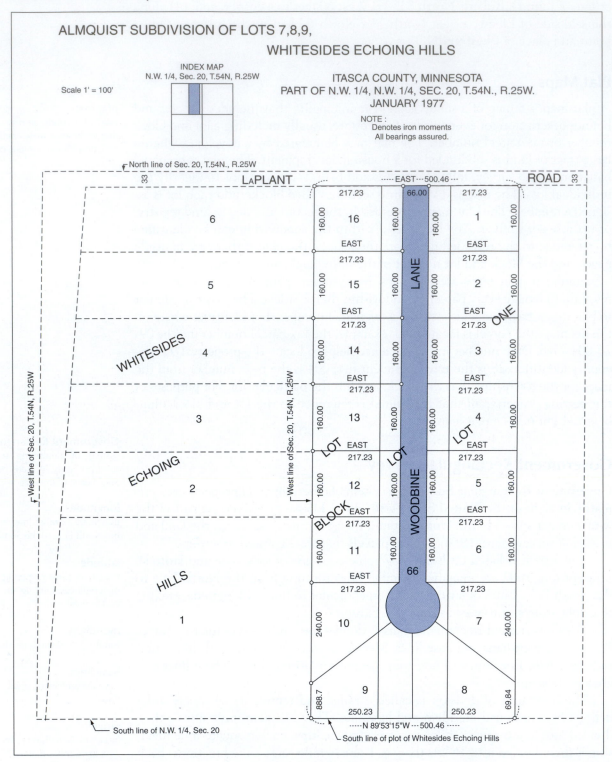

**Exhibit 6.4**  Map depicting the United States and showing lines of latitude and longitude

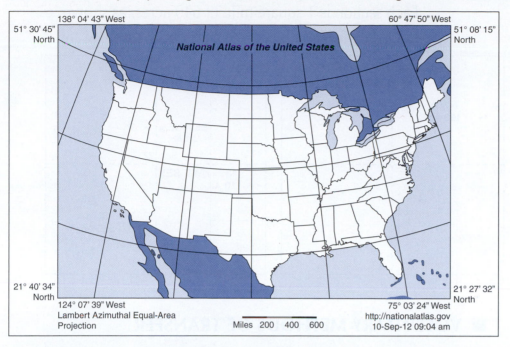

**Exhibit 6.5**  Depiction of the Government Rectangular Survey System

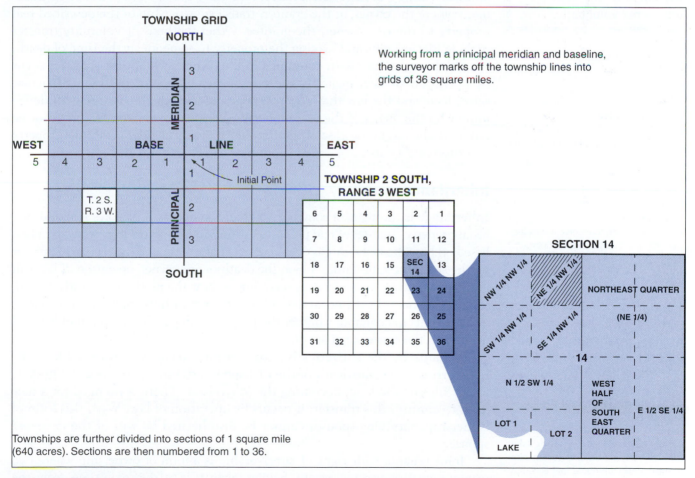

*Source:* www.blm.gov
For additional information, see the Bureau of Land Management at www.blm.gov or LandPrints at www.landprints.com

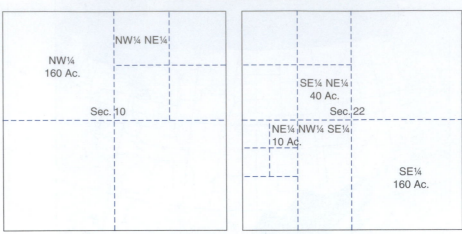

**Exhibit 6.6** Plan of numbering sections
Each section is 1 square mile of 640 acres, as shown
in the plat map for sections 10 and 23.

## ■ VOLUNTARY METHODS OF TRANSFER

**LEARNING OBJECTIVE 2**
Explain how real estate is transferred voluntarily.

The most common method of voluntary transfer of real property is the sale by an owner using a **deed of conveyance.** A deed of conveyance is a written document where the owner, as the grantor, transfers ownership of the described real property to the new owner, the grantee. Other methods of voluntary transfer include lifetime gifts and leaving the property to someone at the time of death, usually through a provision contained in the owner's will. Some transfers occur by **operation of law,** meaning the new owner is determined by a particular set of facts and the law that governs; applying the law to the facts will determine who the owner of the real property is. A deed of conveyance may not be required, such as in the case of the transfer of tenants by the entireties property to a surviving spouse.

**deed of conveyance**
method of voluntary transfer of real property

**operation of law**
transfer of ownership determined by a particular set of facts and the law that governs

### Inheritance

**inheritance**
right of someone to receive a deceased person's real and personal property

**Inheritance** is the right of someone to receive a deceased person's real and personal property. Transfer of real property by inheritance occurs by operation of law, based on how the real estate is owned or titled at the time of the owner's death, or on the state intestate statute. Upon the death of one owner, operation of law will determine who the new owner is according to how the property is jointly owned, such as in tenants by the entireties or joint tenants with the right of survivorship. With tenants in common, whether the property will pass by operation of law will depend on the existence of a will.

**tenants by the entireties**
form of joint ownership reserved for married parties

**Tenants by the entireties** is a form of joint ownership reserved for married parties. Upon the death of the first spouse, the surviving spouse automatically inherits the land, becoming the sole owner. There is no need for a new deed to confirm this transfer; it occurs by operation of law. With this form of ownership, surviving spouses cannot be disinherited by will of the deceased spouse.

**joint tenants with right of survivorship**
form of ownership where two or more entities own real estate, having taken title at the same time, from the same grantor, and with equal interests, having specifically stated their intention to take title with the right of survivorship

**Joint tenants with right of survivorship** is a form of ownership where two or more entities own real estate, having taken title at the same time, from the same grantor, and with equal interests, having specifically stated their intention to take title with the right of survivorship. With real property owned as joint tenants with right of survivorship, the surviving joint tenants become the new owners, and their proportional interests change accordingly. For example Kathy, Doug, and Wayne are joint tenants with the right of survivorship, each owning a one-third interest in the real estate. When Wayne dies, Kathy and Doug are the surviving owners, each now owning a one-half interest. Again, there is no requirement that a new deed be prepared to confirm the transfer; it occurs by operation of law. And there is nothing Wayne could have included in his will that would have overridden the survivorship attribute of joint tenancy with the right of survivorship.

**Tenants in common** is form of ownership where two or more parties own the real estate without any right of survivorship. Each tenant in common has a share of ownership that can be transferred or sold, independent of the other owners. With real property owned as tenants in common, the heirs of the deceased owner will stand in his or her shoes. Unless the deceased co-owner had a will, the transfer of the real estate will be governed by the state **intestacy law.** Every state has an intestacy law, a statutory scheme that determines who will inherit someone's property if there is no will. The intestacy law prefers close family relations, starting with the surviving spouse of the deceased; and if there is none, then the property goes to the children of the deceased; if no children, then to parents; if no parents, then to the brothers and sisters of the deceased. In the tenants in common situation or for real property owned individually by the deceased, the property will be inherited based on the intestate statute in effect in the state where the real estate is located. For this transfer, a deed must be prepared, signed by the administrator of the estate of the deceased owner, and recorded in the land registry or recorder of deeds office to confirm the new ownership of the real estate.

## Gift

A **gift** is the voluntary transfer of property by the **donor** (owner) to the **donee** (the recipient of the gift). A gift is characterized by a lack of consideration; nothing is given in exchange for the item received. Gifts can be made during someone's lifetime or at the time of death.

A **lifetime gift** is one that is given while someone is alive. An outright gift would be a present transfer of the property to another without any limitations. A gift of real estate is made by a deed to convey whatever interest the grantor-donor owns in the real estate to the recipient grantee-donee, usually a fee simple estate.

The donor may choose to place restrictions on the gift or limit what is given. Property can be transferred and a right or interest retained, such as giving the property to a child but retaining a life estate—the right to continue to live in the property until death. In Exhibit 6.7, the donee has received a gift of the remainder interest, while the donor has retained the right to live in or use the property during her lifetime.

Another way of limiting the gift would be to place it in trust. A trust agreement would be prepared to limit how the property can be used and by whom, under what circumstances the trust terminates, and what happens to the property at termination of the trust. When real estate is placed in trust, it may be because the recipient of the benefits of ownership is financially irresponsible. The real estate is placed in trust, and the donee is the beneficiary of the trust who has the right to receive the income generated by the property or perhaps reside in the property.

---

**PRACTICE TIP**
While a deed is not required, it is good practice to prepare and record one in the land registry or recorder of deeds office.

**tenants in common**
form of ownership where two or more parties own the real estate without any right of survivorship

**intestacy law**
statutory scheme that determines who will inherit someone's property if there is no will

**gift**
voluntary transfer of property without consideration

**donor**
the owner and giver of a gift

**donee**
the recipient of a gift

**lifetime gift**
gift that is given while someone is alive

### Exhibit 6.7  Deed gift of the remainder interest

**THIS INDENTURE**, MADE this 15th day of June, 2013,

BETWEEN                    AMY BALWIN
                           (HEREINAFTER CALLED THE GRANTOR),

                           AND

                           AMY BALWIN, for life and
                           ANDREW SPENCER, as Remainderman
                           (HEREINAFTER CALLED THE GRANTEES),

WITNESSETH That the said Grantor for and in consideration of the sum of One (1.00) Dollar lawful money of the United States of America, unto her well and truly paid by the Grantees, at or before the sealing and delivery hereof, the receipt whereof is hereby acknowledged, hath granted, bargained and sold, released and confirmed, and by these presents doth grant, bargain and sell, release and confirm unto the said Grantee, Amy Spencer, her assigns, in fee, for life and then unto the said Grantee Andrew Spencer, his heirs and assigns, in fee.

**will**
a written document that disposes of all property, real and personal, owned by someone at the time of death

Gifts made at the time of death are governed by the provisions contained in the will of the deceased. A **will** is a written document that disposes of all property, real and personal, owned by someone at the time of death. With a will, an individual may leave property to whomever he or she wishes—family, friends, charities, etc. There is no requirement that one's belongings be left to family members, although that is what we presume. Exhibit 6.8 is a portion of a will containing provisions giving real estate to the named beneficiaries at the owner's death.

In some instances, the deceased person may want to exercise some control over the use of the real property after his or her death. Real estate and other assets are sometimes placed in a trust under the terms of the will. The reasons for doing this may be related to tax benefits, but there may also be concern about family members and their financial responsibility. It is not unheard of that a spouse can spend money faster than it can be made. The deceased spouse may have such a situation in mind when placing assets in trust, out of the reach of the spendthrift spouse and insuring that the next generation receives the benefit of his or her wealth.

## Sale

**sale**
the transfer for good and valuable consideration, usually the sale price

Sale of real estate is the most common form of voluntary transfer of real estate. A **sale** is the transfer of real estate for good and valuable consideration, usually the sale price. Sales can occur privately between a seller and a purchaser. More likely, however, a sale occurs with the assistance of real estate professionals such as real estate sales agents and brokers. Real estate agents and brokers will assist the seller in determining the asking price for the property, market the property, show it to potential purchasers, assist in preparing a written contract for the sale of the real estate, and assist the seller through the closing process, where title to the property is transferred with a deed to the purchaser.

## Exhibit 6.8 Will

# LAST WILL AND TESTAMENT

I, **AMY BALDWIN**, a resident of Bucks County in the Commonwealth of Virginia, being of sound and disposing mind, memory and understanding, do hereby make, publish and declare this to be my Last Will and Testament. I revoke any and all wills and codicils that I have previously made.

**ARTICLE ONE:** I direct the expenses of my last illness and funeral, the expense of the administration of my estate, and all estate, inheritance and similar taxes payable with respect to the property included in my estate, whether or not passing under this will, and any interest or penalties thereon, shall be paid out of the residue of my estate, without apportionment and with no rights of reimbursement from any recipient of any such property (including reimbursement under Section 2207B of the Internal Revenue Code).

**ARTICLE TWO:** I give all my articles of personal and household use, including automobiles, and all insurance on that property, to my Executor, to be retained or distributed by him in accordance with my wishes which I have made known to him during my lifetime.

**ARTICLE THREE:** I give, devise and bequeath my real estate known as 17 Ocean Avenue, Virginia Beach, Virginia to my children, Joseph Gaitner and Rebecca Gaitner, as joint tenants with the rights of survivorship and not as tenants in common.

**ARTICLE FOUR:** I give, devise and bequeath my real estate known as 3224 University Avenue, State College, Virginia to the University of Virginia.

**ARTICLE FIVE:** All the rest of the real estate that I may own at the time of my death I give to my Executor and direct that each parcel be sold and the proceeds distributed in accordance with Article Six of this my last will and testament.

**ARTICLE SIX:** All the rest, residue and remainder of my estate, real and personal and wheresoever situated I give, devise and bequeath in equal shares to my beloved granddaughter, SUZANNE SHIELDS and my beloved grandson, DAVID BINGHAM, or to the survivor of them.

**ARTICLE SEVEN:** The interests of the beneficiaries hereunder shall not be subject to anticipation or to voluntary or involuntary alienation until distribution is actually made.

**ARTICLE EIGHT:** In addition to the powers granted by law, my fiduciaries, executors, administrator and trustees appointed herein shall have the following powers, exercisable at their discretion from time to time without court approval, with respect to both principal and accumulated income, and such powers shall continue until distribution is actually made:

A. To sell at public or private sale, exchange or lease for any period of time any real or personal property and to give options for sales or leases.
B. To compromise claims, and to disclaim any interest which I may have in an estate or trust.
C. To accept in kind, retain and invest in any form of property without regard to any principal of diversification as to any property owned by me at my death.
D. To make distributions in kind or in cash.
E. If any interest created hereunder vests in a minor or incompetent, my fiduciaries, without court authorization, may distribute the interest in whole or in part to the guardian of the said minor or incompetent.
F. To exercise any options available in determining and paying death taxes in my estate as my executor deems appropriate without requiring adjustments between income and principal.
G. The determination of my fiduciaries as to the amount or advisability of any discretionary payment shall be final and conclusive on all persons, whether or not then in being, having or claiming any interest.

*(continued)*

## Exhibit 6.8 Continued

**ARTICLE NINE:** I appoint my grandson DAVID BINGHAM, Executor of this my last will and testament. In the event my grandson DAVID BINGHAM shall predecease me, or should fail or be unable to qualify or having qualified should resign or die, then I appoint my granddaughter SUZANNE SHIELDS, alternate Executrix in his place and stead with all of the rights and powers as though originally appointed.
No Executor appointed hereunder shall be required to furnish bond.

**IN WITNESS WHEREOF,** I have hereunto written my name in the margin of the foregoing two pages of this my last will and testament and set my hand and seal at the end hereof this _____ day of _____, 2013.

_____
AMY BALDWIN

**SIGNED, SEALED, PUBLISHED and DECLARED** by the above named Testatrix, AMY BALDWIN, as and for her last will and testament, in the presence of us, who in her presence and in the presence of each other, all being present at the same time and at her request, have subscribed our names as witnesses hereto.

_____          _____
Sign above and print name                Sign above and print name
And address below:                       And address below:
_____          _____
_____          _____
_____          _____


COMMONWEALTH OF VIRGINIA          )
                                  ) ss:
COUNTY OF                         )

I, AMY BALDWIN, Testatrix, whose name is signed to the attached or foregoing instrument, having been duly qualified according to law, do hereby acknowledge that I have signed and executed the instrument as my last will; that I signed it willingly; and that I signed it as my free and voluntary act for the purposes therein expressed.

_____
AMY BALDWIN

SWORN TO AND SUBSCRIBED:
Before me this _____ day of
_____, 2013:

_____
NOTARY PUBLIC


COMMONWEALTH OF VIRGINIA          )
                                  ) ss:
COUNTY OF                         )

We, _____ and _____, the witnesses whose names are signed to the attached or foregoing instrument, being duly qualified according to law, do depose and say that we were present and saw the Testatrix sign and execute the instrument as her last will; that the said Testatrix, AMY BALDWIN, signed willingly and that the Testatrix executed it as her sole and voluntary act for the purposes therein expressed; that each of us in the hearing and sight of the Testatrix signed the Will as witnesses; and that to the best of our knowledge the Testatrix was at the time eighteen or more years of age, of sound mind and under no constraint or undue influence.

_____
_____

SWORN TO AND SUBSCRIBED:
Before me this _____ day of
_____, 2013:

_____
NOTARY PUBLIC

# ■ INVOLUNTARY METHODS OF TRANSFER

## Eminent Domain

**Eminent domain** is the right of the government to take private property for uses that will benefit the general public. The right belongs to the federal, state, and local governments and can be granted by the government to certain businesses and agencies that provide public services, such as utility companies.

The Fifth Amendment to the U.S. Constitution prohibits the federal government from depriving a person of "life, liberty or property, without due process of law; nor shall private property be taken for public use, without just compensation."

The Fourteenth Amendment makes the Fifth Amendment equally applicable to actions of the individual states. Combined, these provisions have been interpreted to require the government to conduct a legal proceeding before taking property by eminent domain, and if the property is taken, the property owner is entitled to compensation for the property. The legal proceeding necessary for the government to take privately owned property by eminent domain is called a **condemnation proceeding.**

The process begins with the government making a determination that a location or parcel of land would be a suitable location for a use that will benefit the health, safety, or general welfare of the citizenry. Examples of such beneficial uses could be a new highway, a rapid transit railway, an expanded roadway, a new sports stadium, a school, a hospital, or a public park system. After defining the intended purpose and location, the government will attempt to privately purchase the affected lands from the individual owners. This portion of the process would include communication and negotiation of a price for the government to acquire the land. Successful negotiation would result in deeds being prepared for transfer of the real estate to the government body and payment of the fair market value of the land to its owner.

Where the private landowner and the government are unable to reach an agreement, the government must begin an eminent domain or condemnation proceeding. A hearing will be conducted to establish that the government body has contacted the landowner and attempted to reach a negotiated agreement but been unsuccessful, and provide evidence that the acquisition of the land will serve a beneficial purpose for the general public. The landowner has the right to challenge the positions the government puts forward. Frequent challenges allege that there is another, more appropriate or less offensive placement of the suggested use, or that the intended use will benefit a limited segment of the community rather than the general population.

If the government is successful, a hearing is then conducted to determine the **fair value** or **just compensation** to which the landowner is entitled. While these terms can be used interchangeably, they are to be distinguished from **fair market value.** Fair market value represents what a willing buyer will pay a willing seller in an arms-length transaction to purchase the real estate. Fair value or just compensation will include fair market value, plus it will compensate for additional losses related to being forced to relocate. For a homeowner, there may be a delay in finding another suitable home, and the cost of short-term alternate housing may be significantly more than the fair market value of the home. Those components would be included in determining just compensation. For a business owner, lost business as the result of forced relocation may be part of the calculation of just compensation.

**eminent domain**
right of the government to take private property for uses that will benefit the general public

**condemnation proceeding**
eminent domain legal proceeding which determines whether a location or parcel of land would be a suitable location for a use that will benefit the health, safety, or general welfare of the citizenry

**fair value or just compensation**
the compensation assigned to a parcel of land acquired through condemnation proceedings, it can include fair market value plus compensate for additional losses related to being forced to relocate

**fair market value**
represents what a willing buyer will pay a willing seller in an arms-length transaction to purchase the real estate

# IN THE WORDS OF THE COURT

## *Kelo v. City of New London, Connecticut, 545 U.S. 469 (2005)*

### JUSTICE STEVENS delivered the opinion of the Court.

In 2000, the city of New London approved a development plan that, in the words of the Supreme Court of Connecticut, was "projected to create in excess of 1,000 jobs, to increase tax and other revenues, and to revitalize an economically distressed city, including its downtown and waterfront areas." 268 Conn. 1, 5, 843 A. 2d 500, 507 (2004). In assembling the land needed for this project, the city's development agent has purchased property from willing sellers and proposes to use the power of eminent domain to acquire the remainder of the property from unwilling owners in exchange for just compensation. The question presented is whether the city's proposed disposition of this property qualifies as a "public use" within the meaning of the Takings Clause of the Fifth Amendment to the Constitution.

Two polar propositions are perfectly clear. On the one hand, it has long been accepted that the sovereign may not take the property of *A* for the sole purpose of transferring it to another private party *B*, even though *A* is paid just compensation. On the other hand, it is equally clear that a State may transfer property from one private party to another if future "use by the public" is the purpose of the taking; the condemnation of land for a railroad with common-carrier duties is a familiar example. Neither of these propositions, however, determines the disposition of this case.

As for the first proposition, the City would no doubt be forbidden from taking petitioners' land for the purpose of conferring a private benefit on a particular private party. See *Midkiff,* 467 U. S., at 245 ("A purely private taking could not withstand the scrutiny of the public use requirement; it would serve no legitimate purpose of government and would thus be void"); *Missouri Pacific R. Co. v. Nebraska,* 164 U. S. 403 (1896). Nor would the City be allowed to take property under the mere pretext of a public purpose, when its actual purpose was to bestow a private benefit. The takings before us, however, would be executed pursuant to a "carefully considered" development plan. 268 Conn., at 54, 843 A. 2d, at 536. The trial judge and all the members of the Supreme Court of Connecticut agreed that there was no evidence of an illegitimate purpose in this case. Therefore, as was true of the statute challenged in *Midkiff,* 467 U. S., at 245, the City's development plan was not adopted "to benefit a particular class of identifiable individuals."

On the other hand, this is not a case in which the City is planning to open the condemned land - at least not in its entirety - to use by the general public. Nor will the private lessees of the land in any sense be required to operate like common carriers, making their services available to all comers. But although such a projected use would be sufficient to satisfy the public use requirement, this "Court long ago rejected any literal requirement that condemned property be put into use for the general public." *Id.,* at 244. Indeed, while many state courts in the mid-19th century endorsed "use by the public" as the proper definition of public use, that narrow view steadily eroded over time. Not only was the "use by the public" test difficult to administer (*e.g.,* what proportion of the public need have access to the property? at what price?), but it proved to be impractical given the diverse and always evolving needs of society. Accordingly, when this Court began applying the Fifth Amendment to the States at the close of the 19th century, it embraced the broader and more natural interpretation of public use as "public purpose." See, *e.g., Fallbrook Irrigation Dist. v. Bradley,* 164 U. S. 112, 158.164 (1896). Thus, in a case upholding a mining company's use of an aerial bucket line to transport ore over property it did not own, Justice Holmes' opinion for the Court stressed "the inadequacy of use by the general public as a universal test." *Strickley v. Highland Boy Gold Mining Co.,* 200 U. S. 527, 531 (1906). We have repeatedly and consistently rejected that narrow test ever since.

The disposition of this case therefore turns on the question whether the City's development plan serves a "public purpose." Without exception, our cases have defined that concept broadly, reflecting our longstanding policy of deference to legislative judgments in this field.

In *Berman v. Parker,* 348 U. S. 26 (1954), this Court upheld a redevelopment plan targeting a blighted area of Washington, D. C., in which most of the housing for the area's 5,000 inhabitants was beyond repair. Under the plan, the area would be condemned and part of it utilized for the construction of streets, schools, and other public facilities. The remainder of the land would be leased or sold to private parties for the purpose of redevelopment, including the construction of low-cost housing.

The owner of a department store located in the area challenged the condemnation, pointing out that his store was not itself blighted and arguing that the creation of a "better balanced, more attractive community" was not a valid public use. *Id.,* at 31. Writing for a unanimous Court, Justice Douglas refused to evaluate this claim in isolation, deferring instead to the legislative and agency judgment that the area "must be planned as a whole" for the plan to be successful. *Id.,* at 34. The Court explained that "community redevelopment programs need not, by force of the Constitution, be on a piecemeal basis - lot by lot, building by building." *Id.,* at 35. The public use underlying the taking was unequivocally affirmed:

> We do not sit to determine whether a particular housing project is or is not desirable. The concept of the public welfare is broad and inclusive.... The values it represents are spiritual as well as physical, aesthetic as well as monetary. It is within the power of the legislature to determine that the community should be beautiful as well as healthy, spacious as well as clean, well-balanced as well as carefully patrolled. In the present case, the Congress and its authorized agencies have made determinations that take into account a wide variety of values. It is not for us to reappraise them. If those who govern the District of Columbia decide that the Nation's Capital should be beautiful as well as sanitary, there is nothing in the Fifth Amendment that stands in the way. *Id.,* at 33.

Viewed as a whole, our jurisprudence has recognized that the needs of society have varied between different parts of the Nation, just as they have evolved over time in response to changed circumstances. Our earliest cases in particular embodied a strong theme of federalism, emphasizing the "great respect" that we owe to state legislatures and state courts in discerning local public needs. See *Hairston v. Danville & Western R. Co.,* 208 U. S. 598, 606. 607 (1908) (noting that these needs were likely to vary depending on a State's "resources, the capacity of the soil, the relative importance of industries to the general public welfare, and the long-established methods and habits of the people"). For more than a century, our public use jurisprudence has wisely eschewed rigid formulas and intrusive scrutiny in favor of affording legislatures broad latitude in determining what public needs justify the use of the takings power.

Those who govern the City were not confronted with the need to remove blight in the Fort Trumbull area, but their determination that the area was sufficiently distressed to justify a program of economic rejuvenation is entitled to our deference. The City has carefully formulated an economic development plan that it believes will provide appreciable benefits to the community, including - but by no means limited to - new jobs and increased tax revenue. As with other exercises in urban planning and development, the City is endeavoring to coordinate a variety of commercial, residential, and recreational uses of land, with the hope that they will form a whole greater than the sum of its parts. To effectuate this plan,

*(continued)*

the City has invoked a state statute that specifically authorizes the use of eminent domain to promote economic development. Given the comprehensive character of the plan, the thorough deliberation that preceded its adoption, and the limited scope of our review, it is appropriate for us, as it was in *Berman*, to resolve the challenges of the individual owners, not on a piecemeal basis, but rather in light of the entire plan. Because that plan unquestionably serves a public purpose, the takings challenged here satisfy the public use requirement of the Fifth Amendment.

The judgment of the Supreme Court of Connecticut is affirmed.

Not every eminent domain proceeding results in condemnation of the entire property. When the entire property is included, it is termed a **full or complete taking.** When a portion of a property is sought, it is called a **partial taking.** Partial taking occurs most frequently with road-widening programs that require the government to take a portion of the front or rear of the landowner's property. The same process is followed, but the compensation will be limited to the fair value of the strip of land. In some instances, the government may pay the fair value and, at its own expense, erect sound and safety barriers to protect the homeowner from the harms associated with heavily traveled roadways.

Either the landowner or the government has the right to appeal the decisions rendered in court as they relate to the condemnation and determination of the fair value. As demonstrated in *Kelo v. City of New London*, 545 U.S. 469 (2005), recent litigation has focused on whether government appropriation of entire communities considered abandoned and blighted for purposes of urban redevelopment by private, rather than government, entities is eminent domain.

## Adverse Possession

**Adverse possession** is an involuntary taking of ownership of another's land, without a deed. Adverse possession is granted following a court proceeding that confirms the transfer based on use by another party that is adverse to the interests of the landowner. Adverse possession may be determined by common law or local statutory provisions. At common law, all of the following elements of adverse possession must be established.

- Wrongful possession is for the prescribed time, usually 21 years.
- Wrongful possession must be open, visible, and notorious, giving the landowner, or anyone for that matter, notice of the wrongful possession.
- Wrongful possession must be actual, using the property in the way the landowner reasonably would, and exclusive, excluding the landowner from physical possession of the land.
- Wrongful possession must be continuous and peaceful for the statutory period.
- Wrongful possession must be hostile and adverse, without the express or implied permission of the rightful owner.

The resulting ownership is limited to that portion of the land adversely used and possessed—for example, a driveway over a 40-acre property.

## Foreclosure

**Foreclosure** is the process by which a **mortgagee** (lender) terminates the interest of the **mortgagor** (borrower) in real property. The mortgagee's right to do so arises when the mortgagor **defaults**—that is, fails to meet any of the obligations

**full or complete taking**
condemnation of an entire property

**partial taking**
condemnation of a portion of a property

**adverse possession**
an involuntary taking of ownership of another's land, without a deed

**foreclosure**
the process by which a mortgagee (lender) terminates the interest of the mortgagor (borrower) in real property

**defaults**
fails to meet any of the obligations under the terms of the mortgage loan agreement

under the terms of the mortgage loan agreement. A mortgagor might default under the terms of the mortgage document by failing to pay property taxes, by failing to maintain property insurance, or by damaging the property (sometimes called "committing waste"). The most common cause of default is the mortgagor's failure to make regular payments on the debt that the mortgage secures.

The fact that a mortgagor is in default does not, however, always mean that the mortgage will be foreclosed. The foreclosure process begins solely at the mortgagee's option. A mortgagee might, for example, wait to begin foreclosure proceedings in hopes that the mortgagee will resume making payments. When the mortgagee intends to begin foreclosure proceedings (or wants to spur payment from the borrower), the lender will issue a notice of default to the mortgagor. The notice will include a statement that the borrower is in default, say what steps can be taken to cure the default, provide information on credit counseling services in the community, provide information on the existence of special programs available from the lender or the government to assist distressed borrowers, and describe the lender's right to take the property to satisfy the default. Exhibit 6.9 is a sample notice of a default letter.

## Exhibit 6.9 Notice of Default

**Notice of Default Required by Massachusetts, 209 CMR 56.03, the (150 / 90 Day)"Right to Cure Your Mortgage Default"**

❖ **This is an important notice concerning your right to live in your home. Have it translated at once.**
❖ **Esta carta explica sus derechos legales para permanezer en su propiedad de vivienda. Por favor traduzca esta notificacion imediatamente.**
❖ **Este é um aviso importante em relação ao seu dereito de morar na sua residência. Por favor, tem tradizido imediatamente.**
❖ **C'est une notification importante concernant votre droit de vivre chez vous. Faites-la traduire immédiatement.**
❖ **这是一则关於您居住权的重要通知, 请儘快安排翻译。**

January 1, 2013

VIA: FIRST CLASS MAIL and
        CERTIFIED MAIL RETURN RECEIPT REQUESTED

Katherine Thomas
767 Cobalt Drive
Oldetown, AnyState

RE: 767 Cobalt Drive
        Loan Account No. 42599 with National Bank & Trust

To Katherine Thomas:

We are contacting you because you did not make your monthly loan payment[s] due on October 1, November 1, and December 1, 2012 to National Bank & Trust. Your last payment received was on September 1, 2012. You must pay the past due amount of $9,728.25 on or before May 31, 2013, which is 150 days from the date of this notice. The past due amount on the date of this notice is specified below:

☐ UNPAID MORTGAGE PAYMENTS AND DELINQUENCY DATES

| | | |
|---|---|---|
| October 1, 2012 | $2,287.00 delinquent on October 15, 2012 | |
| November 1, 2012 | $2,287.00 delinquent on November 15, 2012 | |
| December 1, 2012 | $2,287.00 delinquent on December 15, 2012 | |

*(continued)*

**Exhibit 6.9** Continued

☐ INTEREST ACCRUED/PER DIEM INTEREST
$1,285.20 calculated based on $9.52 per day per missed payment

☐ APPLICABLE UNPAID ESCROW CONTRIBUTIONS
$1,239.00 calculated at $413.00 per missed payment

☐ OTHER LATE CHARGES OR FEES
$343.05 calculated at 5% late fee for each missed payment

If you pay the past due amount, and any additional monthly payments, late charges, or fees that may become due between the date of this notice and the date when you make your payment, your account will be considered up-to-date and you can continue to make your regular monthly payments.

Make your payment directly to:
Jane Greer
Loan Default Specialist
National Bank & Trust
123 Avenue of the Arts
Center City, Any State

Please consider the following:

☐ You should contact the Homeownership Preservation Foundation (888-995-HOPE) to speak with counselors who can provide assistance and may be able to help you work with your lender to avoid foreclosure. There may be other homeownership assistance available through your lender or servicer;

☐ You may also contact the Division of Banks (617-956-1500) or visit www.mass.gov/foreclosures to find a foreclosure prevention program near you;

☐ After May 1, 2013, you can still avoid foreclosure by paying the total past due amount before a foreclosure sale takes place. Depending on the terms of the loan, there may also be other ways to avoid foreclosure, such as selling your property, refinancing your loan, or voluntarily transferring ownership of the property to National Bank & Trust.

**If you do not pay the total past due amount of $9,728.25 and any additional payments that may become due by May 31, 2013, you may be evicted from your home after a foreclosure sale. If National Bank & Trust forecloses on this property, it means the mortgagee or a new buyer will take over the ownership of your home.**

If you have questions, or disagree with the calculation of your past due balance, please contact National Bank & Trust at 555-555-5555 TOLL FREE, or at the address listed above.

Sincerely,

**acceleration clause**
gives the mortgagee the right to declare the entire loan amount due immediately because the mortgagor is in default on the loan

An **acceleration clause** gives the mortgagee the right to declare the entire loan amount due immediately because the mortgagor is in default on the loan. Most mortgages have this type of clause, which is permitted in all states. Most jurisdictions require the mortgagee to send a notice to the mortgagor of the intent to accelerate; this can be included in the default notice, or a separate notice may be required in some jurisdictions. Because the result of acceleration is so harsh, many jurisdictions permit the borrower to cure the default and stop the acceleration by paying the amount in default at any time prior to a foreclosure sale.

**judicial foreclosure**
the process by which mortgaged property is sold under the supervision of a court

**Judicial foreclosure** is the process by which mortgaged property is sold under the supervision of a court. This type of foreclosure is available in all states, and it is the dominant method of foreclosure in almost half of the states.

Judicial foreclosure begins with a title search to determine who must be given notice of the foreclosure action. This may include other parties with a claim against the property. The result of the action is that a judgment is entered and the mortgagee is granted the right to execute on the judgment. To execute on the judgment, the lender will follow the local procedure for having the property listed for judicial or sheriff's sale. The purchaser of the property at a judicial sale receives the property title as it existed at the time the mortgagor executed the mortgage. The mortgagor's interest in the property and those of others—**junior lienholders,** parties who have a claim, such as a second mortgage, and who were notified of and included in the foreclosure action—are extinguished. If the proceeds from the sale are not enough to cover the outstanding debt, the lender may have the right to a **deficiency judgment,** a claim against the mortgagor for the balance of the mortgage debt that was not recovered by the lender through the foreclosure sale.

**junior lienholders**
parties who have a claim, such as a second mortgage, and who are notified of and included in the foreclosure action, whose interest may be extinguished

**deficiency judgment**
a claim against the mortgagor for the balance of the mortgage debt that was not recovered by the lender through the foreclosure sale

The mortgagee has the right to attend the sheriff's sale and purchase the property. Lenders will purchase the property when the bids at the sale are too low to pay the amount of the debt. The mortgagor also has the right to attend the sale and purchase the property, but this is unlikely.

Proceeds from the sale are disbursed in the following order:

1. Expenses of the foreclosure
2. Payment of the mortgage debt
3. Satisfaction of other judgments or liens in order of their priority

Any sums left after payment of these expenses belong to the mortgagor.

If the sale proceeds are not enough to pay the mortgage debt, the mortgagee may bring an action for a deficiency judgment against the mortgagor. Generally, this judgment can be obtained during (or shortly after) a judicial foreclosure action. The sale price usually determines how much is applied to reduce the debt and how much remains unpaid for which a deficiency judgment can be sought.

Because a deficiency judgment can be enforced against other property of the mortgagor, as in the case of any other judgment, there are a number of procedural requirements that the mortgagee must surmount before receiving the judgment. Many states have rigorous notice requirements and strictly limit the time within which the mortgagee must bring suit to obtain a deficiency judgment. In fact, under a principle known as the **one-action rule**, some states *require* the mortgagee to bring an action for a deficiency judgment at the same time as the foreclosure action, on pain of being forever barred from pursuing this type of judgment.

**one-action rule**
a rule that requires a deficiency action be brought at the same time as the mortgage foreclosure action

**Redemption** or the **equity right of redemption** is the right of the mortgagor to recover the property after default by paying the outstanding debt. This equitable right to redeem property before foreclosure exists in all states. But, unlike statutory redemption, equitable redemption terminates at the foreclosure sale.

**redemption or the equity right of redemption**
right of the mortgagor to recover the property after default by paying the outstanding debt

More than half the states allow the mortgagor a window of time (generally 6 to 12 months) to buy back the foreclosed property, usually by paying the sale price. This is known as **statutory redemption** because it is a legislative creation. This legislation has been criticized on the grounds that it removes an incentive for timely mortgage payments since the mortgagor knows that the property can be recovered after foreclosure. On the other hand, statutory redemption gives the mortgagor needed breathing space to arrange new financing to recover the property. It also encourages potential purchasers to make fair bids for the property; if they bid too low, they may lose the property.

**statutory redemption**
state's law allowing the mortgagor a window of time to buy back the foreclosed property, usually by paying the sale price

# ETHICAL Considerations

### CONFLICT OF INTEREST: SELF-DEALING

An attorney represents a homeowner who is involved in a mortgage foreclosure proceeding. The attorney has worked diligently to protect the rights of his client homeowner. In the event of a foreclosure sale, the attorney has successfully negotiated with the lender, and the lender has agreed to waive any claim for a deficiency judgment against the homeowner—a good result.

Driving back and forth to the courthouse, the attorney has long admired his client's historic home. With knowledge of the amount owed on the mortgage, he has decided that he can purchase the home for much less than its market value by attending the mortgage foreclosure sale. Is there any reason why he shouldn't take advantage of the bargain?

Rule 1.7 of the ABA Model Rules of Professional Conduct controls. Rule 1.7 discusses the conflict of interest and the duty of loyalty the attorney owes to the client. When the lawyer's own interests conflict with those of the client, the lawyer is barred from representing the client. But from the facts, it appears that the representation is concluded, with a successful result achieved. However, it is not the success of the result that matters, and the representation is not complete until the sale is concluded. Clearly there is a conflict between the interests of the client and the lawyer's self-interest. The lawyer has some options: (1) do not attend the foreclosure sale to purchase the home; (2) advise the client of his interests and how his personal interest interferes with his ability to represent the client, giving the client the ability to seek alternate representation; and (3) prepare a written waiver of conflict of interest for the client to sign if the client still wants the lawyer to represent him after being advised of the conflict.

If a paralegal in the office learns of the sale, can the paralegal use the information to make the purchase?

## KEY TERMS

## CHAPTER SUMMARY

| | |
|---|---|
| Introduction to Transferring Real Property | Transferring real property requires that the land be described with accuracy. Real property can be transferred either voluntarily or involuntarily. |
| Land Description | The legal description describes the property based on its boundary lines and distances or, in common law terms, its metes and bounds. The accuracy of the legal description is critical. Only the actual land parcel described is transferred. If the description is not accurate and part of the original parcel not included, the portion omitted is not transferred and remains in the ownership of the grantor. |
| Chain of Title | Chain of title refers to a list of deeds transferring ownership of a parcel of land from one person to the next. |
| Monuments | A monument is a natural or artificial object permanently affixed to the land, used as a marker along the boundaries of a property. |
| Metes and Bounds | Metes and bounds are the distances and boundary lines of the property, starting from a designated marker or monument. |
| Plat Map | A plat map is a map of a subdivision or municipality that includes a metes and bounds description for every piece of real estate, usually including a lot and block number or tax parcel number. |
| Government Rectangular Survey | Government Rectangular Survey is a system of describing real property used primarily in areas of the United States west of the Mississippi River. |
| Voluntary Methods of Transfer | The most common method of voluntary transfer of real property is the sale by an owner using a deed of conveyance. |
| Inheritance | Inheritance is the right of someone to receive a deceased person's real and personal property. |
| Gift | A gift is the voluntary transfer of property by the donor (owner) to the donee (the recipient of the gift). A gift is characterized by a lack of consideration; nothing is given in exchange for the item received. Gifts can be made during someone's lifetime or at the time of death. |
| Sale | Sale of real estate is the most common form of voluntary transfer of real estate. A sale is the transfer of real estate for good and valuable consideration, usually the sale price. |
| Involuntary Methods of Transfer | The most common methods of involuntary transfer of real property are eminent domain, adverse possession, and foreclosure. |

| Eminent Domain | Eminent domain is the right of the government to take private property for uses that will benefit the general public. The right belongs to the federal, state, and local governments and can be granted by the government to certain businesses and agencies that provide public services, such as utility companies. |
| --- | --- |
| Adverse Possession | Adverse possession is an involuntary taking of ownership of another's land, without a deed. Adverse possession is granted following a court proceeding that confirms the transfer based on use by another party that is adverse to the interests of the landowner. |
| Foreclosure | Foreclosure is the process by which a mortgagee (lender) terminates interest of the the mortgagor (borrower) in real property. The mortgagee's right to do so arises when the mortgagor defaults—that is, fails to meet any of the obligations under the terms of the mortgage loan agreement. |

## REVIEW QUESTIONS AND EXERCISES

1. What is the purpose of land description?
2. Why is an accurate description essential?
3. What are monuments? What role do they play in land description?
4. What are metes and bounds? What role do they play in land description? Does use of metes and bounds descriptions eliminate the reference to monuments?
5. What is a plat map? How is it similar to a tax map? How are they different?
6. What is the Government Rectangular Survey Method? Where is it most used?
7. What is the difference between voluntary and involuntary transfer of real property?
8. How does one inherit real property?
9. Is inheriting property the same as receiving it from a provision contained in a will? Why or why not?
10. Who are the parties in a gift transaction? What distinguishes a gift from an inheritance?
11. What distinguishes a sale of real estate from a gift?
12. What is eminent domain? Who has the power to exercise eminent domain and under what circumstances?
13. What is a condemnation proceeding? When is a condemnation proceeding necessary?
14. What is fair compensation? How does it differ from fair market value?
15. What is the difference between a full taking and a partial taking?
16. What is adverse possession?
17. On what grounds might a mortgagee bring a mortgage foreclosure action?
18. Why is an acceleration clause considered a harsh provision in a mortgage?
19. What is the difference between the right to cure default, the equitable right of redemption, and the statutory right of redemption?
20. What is a deficiency judgment?

## VIDEO CASE STUDY

Go to www.pearsonhighered.com/careers to view the following videos.

### Author Introduction to Transferring Real Property
Author video introduction to chapter coverage

### Author Explains Conflict Of Interest
Because this video series offers the opportunity to view the real estate transaction from both the sellers' and the buyers' perspective an explanation of the conflict of interest potential is explained.

### Buyers First Meeting With Attorney
Buyers meet with attorney to discuss agreement of sale and inspection contingencies.

## INTERNET AND TECHNOLOGY EXERCISES

1. Using the Internet, determine whether your state requires one action for a deficiency judgment.
2. Using the Internet, determine whether your municipality uses monuments, metes and bounds, the plat map, the lot and block method of land description, the Government Rectangular Survey Method, or some combination of these.

## REAL ESTATE PORTFOLIO EXERCISES

**Transferring Real Estate**

To:        Paralegal Intern
From:      Paul Saunders
Case Name: Mr. & Mrs. Schan
Re:        Home Purchase

1. Set up client in the time and billing program (AbacusLaw).
2. Prepare a fee agreement.
3. Prepare a cover letter to client for the fee agreement Letters to brokers and Title Company.

Portfolio items produced:
1. Fee Agreement
2. Letters to other parties advising of representation.

Go to www.pearsonhighered.com/careers to download instructions.

## LEARNING OBJECTIVES

*Upon completion of this chapter, you should be able to*

1. Describe the requirements for a valid contract.

2. Explain the rights and duties of agents and principals to each other.

3. Describe the purpose and components of the listing contract between the seller and real estate broker.

4. Describe the purpose and components of the sales agreement between the seller and purchaser of real estate.

# Real Estate Sales

## ■ INTRODUCTION TO REAL ESTATE SALES

Contracts play a major role in real estate transactions. In the typical real estate transaction, there are two significant contracts: (1) the listing agreement between a seller and a realtor and (2) the agreement of sale between the seller and the purchaser setting out the purchase price and any terms and conditions of their agreement.

Most sales of residential real estate are completed with the assistance of a real estate broker acting as an agent of the seller in marketing the property. Buyers also usually work with a legal or real estate professional who acts as their agent in negotiating the terms and conditions of the sales contract. Occasionally, the same agent represents both buyer and seller.

The initial agreement with the seller is the listing agreement setting out the rights and obligations of the seller and the real estate broker, typically giving the broker an exclusive right to market and sell the property in exchange for a sales commission.

## ■ CONTRACT LAW

The Statute of Frauds requires contracts involving real estate to be in writing, and some states require that the agreement of representation between sellers or buyers and their legal or real estate professional also be in writing. The basic concepts of contract law apply to these real estate contracts.

**LEARNING OBJECTIVE 1**
Describe the requirements for a valid contract.

## DIGITAL RESOURCES

Author Introduction to Real Estate Sales.

Seller's Second Meeting with Attorney.

Sample forms and templates.

**contract**
sometimes called a valid contract; an enforceable agreement between competent parties, supported by consideration for a lawful purpose

A **contract** (sometimes called a valid contract) is an enforceable agreement between competent parties, supported by consideration for a lawful purpose. The elements of the valid contract are discussed below.

## Agreement

**agreement**
an offer and an acceptance

Every contract starts with an **agreement**, an offer and an acceptance of that specific offer. If the agreement meets the other requirements for a contract—competent parties, consideration, and lawful purpose—it is a contract. The difference between an agreement and a contract is that every contract is enforceable in a court of law, but an agreement, because it lacks one of the necessary elements, is not enforceable in court; an example would be an agreement to commit an unlawful act such as selling alcohol to a minor.

**offer**
a communication by the offeror containing the terms and conditions under which he or she is willing to enter into a contract

An **offer** is a communication by the offeror containing the terms and conditions under which he or she is willing to enter into a contract. The offer must be communicated in such a way that the other person (the offeree) understands that an offer is being made that the offeree is invited to accept or reject. The terms contained in the offer must be definite or reasonably certain. Once made, the offer may be accepted or rejected by the offeree. The offer may be revoked by the offeror anytime before it is accepted by the offeree, or, depending on the circumstances, it will expire as an outstanding offer by a passage of time. For example, the time to accept an offer for sale of a perishable product such as fresh tomatoes will be shorter than one for the sale of a staple such as a keg of nails.

**revoke**
the offeror's withdrawal of an offer

The offeror may **revoke** the offer at any time before the offeree accepts the offer, by communicating the revocation to the offeree. However, once the offeree properly and timely accepts the offer, the offer cannot be revoked.

**reject**
the offeree's decision not to accept or counter the offer

The offeree may **reject** the offer by communicating the rejection to the offeror. The offeree may make a counteroffer. A counteroffer is anything that changes any of the terms or conditions of the original offer. For example, I accept your offer but will only pay half the price asked. A counteroffer acts as a rejection of the offer. The counteroffer and its terms then become the offer that the other side may accept or reject. Changing even one term of the offer is a counteroffer. The original offeror is now the offeree and may reject, accept, or create another counteroffer. The process continues until there is an acceptance of the last offer or counteroffer.

**acceptance**
agreement by the offeree to accept the specific terms of the offer

**Acceptance** is the agreement by the offeree to accept the specific terms of the offer. The acceptance must be **communicated** by the offeree as specified in the offer as the required method of acceptance—for example, by certified mail or overnight courier service. If no method of communication is specified, the acceptance may be communicated by any reasonable method, such as mail or e-mail. The acceptance must be of all of the terms of the offer; otherwise, it is not an acceptance, but rather a rejection and counteroffer.

**communicate**
the required manner in which the offer must be accepted

## Consideration

**consideration**
in contract law, anything of value given in exchange for a promise

Every contract must be accompanied by consideration. **Consideration** in contract law is anything of value given in exchange for a promise. It can be monetary, such as the sale price given by the buyer to the seller in exchange for the seller transferring the real estate to the buyer. It can also be nonmonetary, such as the performance of an act or the promise not to perform an act.

## Capacity

A contract requires competent parties or ones who have legal capacity. Contracts in which either or both of the parties lacks capacity are called **voidable contracts**, because the party claiming a lack of capacity may be able to avoid the contract being enforced against them. **Capacity** is the legal ability to enter into a contract, including these characteristics: being of legal age, called the **age of majority**, typically 18 today; possessing mental capacity sufficient at the time of contracting to understand the consequences of one's actions; and not being under any other legal disability, such as having been declared incompetent by a court.

Those under the age of majority—under the age of 18—are considered minors and have limited capacity to enter contracts. Most contracts entered into by a minor are voidable contracts and may be disaffirmed by the minor during their minority or for a reasonable period after reaching the age of majority. To disaffirm a contract, the other party must be notified and the subject matter of the contract returned. The exception is contracts for necessaries, such as food, clothing, and shelter, and in some states, education suitable to the minor's economic station in life—where the minor may be held to the contract but may only be required to pay a fair price and not the contract price. Those who enter contracts with minors run the risk that the contract will be disaffirmed by the minor.

In some cases, a person who lacks mental capacity will enter into a contract and later seek to disaffirm the contract as voidable. Intoxication may represent a sufficient disability that will permit the disaffirmance of an otherwise valid contract. The person who claims to lack capacity to enter a contract, such as due to intoxication, has the burden of proof that they were intoxicated to the extent that it prevented them from understanding the nature of the contract. Contracts entered by those with a mental deficiency may also be disaffirmed. Those with mental incapacity arising from mental illness, brain damage, mental retardation, senility, and similar conditions may not understand the consequences of their actions in entering into a contract and may claim that the contract is void. However, the contract may be valid if the person entered into the contract during a lucid interval and understood the nature of the contract at that time or received a benefit from the contract. The burden of proof of the mental disability at the time of contracting is on the person claiming the disability. Persons declared mentally incompetent by a court have no contractual capacity, and any purported contract with them is void.

## Legality of Purpose

A contract requires that the object or purpose of the contract be legal. For example, two students enter an agreement: Sam agrees to sell alcohol to Pat, who is under the drinking age; Pat agrees to pay Sam $25. They are both over the age of 18 and not under any disability. Sam delivers the alcohol, but Pat refuses to pay. Sam may not sue Pat for the $25 because the subject matter—selling alcohol to a person under the required age, normally 21—is illegal, and a court will not enforce the contract. A contract to perform any activity that is illegal or against public policy will not be enforceable.

**voidable contracts**
contracts in which either or both of the parties lack contractual capacity

**capacity**
the legal ability to enter into a contract, including being of legal age, called the age of majority

**age of majority**
the legal age for entering into a contract

**COMMON LAW TERMS**

Under the common law, the age of majority was 21, but this has been reduced to 18 by the states. In some states, pressure is being exerted to further reduce the age or allow greater contractual ability at younger ages.

# ■ THE RELATIONSHIP BETWEEN THE SELLER AND BROKER

**LEARNING OBJECTIVE 2**
Explain the rights and duties of agents and principals to each other.

A seller typically uses a real estate professional to help market and sell the property and will sign a listing agreement or listing contract. A **listing agreement** or **listing contract** is a contract that describes the rights and obligations of the seller and the real estate broker, typically giving the broker an exclusive right to market and sell the property in exchange for a sales commission. The listing contract is an agency relationship contract between the seller (the principal) and the broker (the agent). The agency relationship imposes rights and duties on both the agent and the principal.

**listing agreement or listing contract**
contract that describes the rights and obligations of the seller and the real estate broker

## Creation of the Agency Relationship

A listing contract creates an agency relationship between the seller and the real estate broker. An agency relationship is formed by mutual agreement where one party, the principal, agrees that another, the agent, shall act on his or her behalf, at the principal's direction, and under the principal's control. In the listing contract, the seller is the principal and the real estate broker or sales person is the agent. Often, the term *real estate agent* will be used to identify the broker or salesperson. The most common form of agency relationship between the seller and the broker is the **exclusive agency**, in which the seller gives the broker the exclusive right to market the property and receive a commission upon the sale of the property.

**exclusive agency**
the seller gives the broker the exclusive right to market the property and receive a commission upon the sale of the property

The agency relationship imposes certain duties upon the agent in all the agent's actions and undertakings on behalf of the principal. These are the duties of loyalty, obedience, disclosure, confidentiality, reasonable care and diligence, and accounting.

**loyalty**
agent's duty to act solely in the best interests of the principal

**Loyalty** requires the real estate agent to act solely in the best interests of the seller, excluding all other interests, including the interests of the broker.

**obedience**
agent's duty follow the lawful requests and instructions of the principal

**Obedience** requires the real estate agent to follow the lawful requests and instructions of the seller.

**disclosure**
agent's duty to communicate all information that affects the principal

**Disclosure** requires that the real estate agent communicate to the seller in a prompt manner all information that affects the value of the property and all offers to purchase the property.

**confidentiality**
agent's duty to keep information about the principal from others

**Confidentiality** requires the real estate agent to respect a seller's privacy and overall position. An agent should never divulge what he or she thinks the seller will do, nor reveal conversations the agent has had with the seller. Real estate agents are required to use their best efforts, based upon their training and experience in the industry, reasonable care, and diligence in carrying out the wishes of the seller.

**commingle**
combining the client's funds with those of the agent

Finally, the agent may not **commingle** the client's funds with the agent's own. By law in most states, client funds must be kept in a separate account. The agent must provide an **accounting** of those funds when requested or at the time those funds are distributed, such as at the time of final settlement or closing.

**accounting**
a report of the funds of the principal

In a listing contract, the real estate agent's primary obligation is to the seller. However, in the real estate industry it is not uncommon to find an agent representing both the seller and the buyer. This is a special agency relationship called **dual agency**, where one person may act as the agent for two parties with potentially conflicting interests, provided each is aware of the dual agency and agrees.

**dual agency**
when an agent represents both parties in a transaction

*Dual agency*

Dual agency occurs when a broker/agent represents both the buyer and seller in a real estate transaction. Intuitively, it seems impossible that a broker could properly honor his or her obligations of loyalty to the seller and buyer at the same time. The interests of the buyer and seller are inherently opposite to one another: The seller wants to sell a home for the highest possible price, while the buyer wants to purchase the home for the lowest price possible. Exhibit 7.1 summarizes the conflicting interests a broker/agent may face when representing both parties to a sales transaction.

However, it is the nature of the real estate industry that brokers/agents will be in the position to represent both buyers and sellers. "For sale" signs posted on a property and advertisements in the media identify the name and phone number for the listing agent. Interested buyers naturally begin the process by contacting that agent. In most states, this representation of both the seller and the buyer is permissible where there is disclosure of the potential for and the existence of the dual representation. Both the buyer and seller are placed on notice that this type of representation can arise, that they understand it means the broker's duties may be in conflict, and that they agree to go forward with the assistance of that broker. Exhibit 7.2 is a dual agency agreement from the State of Ohio.

## Exhibit 7.1 Summary comparison of agent's duties to seller and buyer

| Seller's Agent | Buyer's Agent |
|---|---|
| Must do everything possible to gain an advantage for the seller. | Must do everything possible to gain an advantage for the buyer. |
| Must obey all lawful instructions of the seller; is not obligated to obey instructions from the buyer. | Must obey all lawful instructions of the buyer; is not obligated to obey instructions from the seller. |
| Must reveal any known material defects in the property. | Must tell buyer everything agent can find out about the seller, including the motivation for selling and any reasons the seller may have for wanting a quick sale. |
| Must NOT reveal information about traffic problems, poor school system, declining property values, etc., since these items might make the property less desirable to buyers. | Must tell buyer everything agent can find out about the property, including traffic problems, poor school system, high crime rates, etc. |
| Must tell the seller everything they can find out about the buyer, including all financial details they can obtain, divorce, etc. | Must keep all information about the buyer confidential, including the buyer's ability or willingness to pay more for the property than they are offering as well as the buyer's motivation for buying. |
| Must be prepared through education and study to competently represent the seller in all matters. | Must be prepared through education and study to competently represent the buyer in all matters. |
| Must account to seller for any money or documents entrusted to him or her. | Must account to buyer for any money or documents entrusted to him or her. |

**Exhibit 7.2** Dual agency agreement

# AGENCY DISCLOSURE STATEMENT

EQUAL HOUSING
OPPORTUNITY

**The real estate agent who is providing you with this form is required to do so by Ohio law. You will not be bound to pay the agent or the agent's brokerage by merely signing this form.** Instead, the purpose of this form is to confirm that you have been advised of the role of the agent(s) in the transaction proposed below. (For purposes of this form, the term "seller" includes a landlord and the term "buyer" includes a tenant.)

Property Address: _____

Buyer(s): _____

Seller(s): _____

## I. TRANSACTION INVOLVING TWO AGENTS IN TWO DIFFERENT BROKERAGES

The buyer will be represented by _____, and _____.
<br>                                        AGENT(S)                                        BROKERAGE

The seller will be represented by _____, and _____.
<br>                                        AGENT(S)                                        BROKERAGE

## II. TRANSACTION INVOLVING TWO AGENTS IN THE SAME BROKERAGE

If two agents in the real estate brokerage _____
represent both the buyer and the seller, check the following relationship that will apply:

☐   Agent(s)_____ work(s) for the buyer and
Agent(s)_____ work(s) for the seller. Unless personally
involved in the transaction, the broker and managers will be "dual agents", which is further explained on the back of this form.
As dual agents they will maintain a neutral position in the transaction and they will protect all parties' confidential information.

☐   Every agent in the brokerage represents every "client" of the brokerage. Therefore, agents _____
and _____ will be working for both the buyer and seller as "dual agents". Dual agency is explained
on the back of this form. As dual agents they will maintain a neutral position in the transaction and they will protect all parties'
confidential information. Unless indicated below, neither the agent(s) nor the brokerage acting as a dual agent in this transaction
has a personal, family or business relationship with either the buyer or seller. *If such a relationship does exist, explain:*
_____.

## III. TRANSACTION INVOLVING ONLY ONE REAL ESTATE AGENT

Agent(s) _____ and real estate brokerage _____ will

☐   be "dual agents" representing both parties in this transaction in a neutral capacity. Dual agency is further explained on the back of
this form. As dual agents they will maintain a neutral position in the transaction and they will protect all parties' confidential
information. Unless indicated below, neither the agent(s) nor the brokerage acting as a dual agent in this transaction has a
personal, family or business relationship with either the buyer or seller. *If such a relationship does exist, explain:* _____
_____.

☐   represent only the (*check one*) ☐ **seller** or ☐ **buyer** in this transaction as a client. The other party is not represented and agrees to
represent his/her own best interest. Any information provided the agent may be disclosed to the agent's client.

## CONSENT

I (we) consent to the above relationships as we enter into this real estate transaction. If there is a dual agency in this transaction, I
(we) acknowledge reading the information regarding dual agency explained on the back of this form.

_____   _____   _____   _____
BUYER/TENANT                          DATE           SELLER/LANDLORD                     DATE

_____   _____   _____   _____
BUYER/TENANT                          DATE           SELLER/LANDLORD                     DATE

Effective 01/01/05

**Exhibit 7.2** Continued

# DUAL AGENCY

Ohio law permits a real estate agent and brokerage to represent both the seller and buyer in a real estate transaction as long as this is disclosed to both parties and they both agree. This is known as dual agency. As a dual agent, a real estate agent and brokerage represent two clients whose interests are, or at times could be, different or adverse. For this reason, the dual agent(s) may not be able to advocate on behalf of the client to the same extent the agent may have if the agent represented only one client.

**As a dual agent, the agent(s) and brokerage shall:**
- Treat both clients honestly;
- Disclose latent (not readily observable) material defects to the purchaser, if known by the agent(s) or brokerage;
- Provide information regarding lenders, inspectors and other professionals, if requested;
- Provide market information available from a property listing service or public records, if requested;
- Prepare and present all offers and counteroffers at the direction of the parties;
- Assist both parties in completing the steps necessary to fulfill the terms of any contract, if requested.

**As a dual agent, the agent(s) and brokerage shall not:**
- Disclose information that is confidential, or that would have an adverse effect on one party's position in the transaction, unless such disclosure is authorized by the client or required by law;
- Advocate or negotiate on behalf of either the buyer or seller;
- Suggest or recommend specific terms, including price, or disclose the terms or price a buyer is willing to offer or that a seller is willing to accept;
- Engage in conduct that is contrary to the instructions of either party and may not act in a biased manner on behalf of one party.

**Compensation:** Unless agreed otherwise, the brokerage will be compensated per the agency agreement.

**Management Level Licensees:** Generally the broker and managers in a brokerage also represent the interests of any buyer or seller represented by an agent affiliated with that brokerage. Therefore, if both buyer and seller are represented by agents in the same brokerage, the broker and manager are dual agents. There are two exceptions to this. The first is where the broker or manager is personally representing one of the parties. The second is where the broker or manager is selling or buying his own real estate. These exceptions only apply if there is another broker or manager to supervise the other agent involved in the transaction.

**Responsibilities of the Parties:** The duties of the agent and brokerage in a real estate transaction do not relieve the buyer and seller from the responsibility to protect their own interests. The buyer and seller are advised to carefully read all agreements to assure that they adequately express their understanding of the transaction. The agent and brokerage are qualified to advise on real estate matters. IF LEGAL OR TAX ADVICE IS DESIRED, YOU SHOULD CONSULT THE APPROPRIATE PROFESSIONAL.

**Consent:** By signing on the reverse side, you acknowledge that you have read and understand this form and are giving your voluntary, informed consent to the agency relationship disclosed. If you do not agree to the agent(s) and/or brokerage acting as a dual agent, you are not required to consent to this agreement and you may either request a separate agent in the brokerage to be appointed to represent your interests or you may terminate your agency relationship and obtain representation from another brokerage.

Any questions regarding the role or responsibilities of the brokerage or its agents should be directed to an attorney or to:
Ohio Department of Commerce
Division of Real Estate & Professional Licensing
77 S. High Street, 20th Floor
Columbus, OH 43215-6133
(614) 466-4100

EQUAL HOUSING OPPORTUNITY

Effective 01/01/05

## The Listing Contract

**LEARNING OBJECTIVE 3**
Describe the purpose and
components of the listing
contract between the seller
and real estate broker.

The listing contract gives the broker/agent the right, under agreed terms and conditions, to sell a property in exchange for payment in the form of a sales commission. The types of listing agreements are related to the way in which the compensation is calculated, who may receive a commission, or both.

### Open Listing

**open listing**
the seller grants the right to market
and sell the property to a number of
brokers at the same time

In an **open listing**, the seller grants the right to market and sell the property to a number of brokers at the same time. The seller also reserves the right to sell the property on his or her own, and if the seller does, he or she has no obligation to pay a commission. Understandably, brokers do not favor this arrangement; the seller or another agent may collect the full commission despite the broker's efforts.

### Flat Fee Listing

**flat fee listing**
the seller and broker/agent agree to a
set compensation amount unrelated to
the sale price

In a **flat fee listing**, the seller and broker/agent agree to a set compensation amount unrelated to the sale price. Generally where compensation is set as a percentage of the sale price, the broker is encouraged to obtain the highest price for the seller, as a higher price will yield higher compensation. With a flat fee, there is no incentive to obtain a higher price. In fact, a flat fee may result in the broker limiting the services he or she provides. The property may be included in the multiple listing service or bureau, but advertising in newspapers may be eliminated, as it can be very costly. Sometimes, the seller will be required to take on the responsibilities of the sale, such as showing the property to potential purchasers.

### Net Listing

**net listing**
the broker/agent earns a commission
only on the part of the sales price that
exceeds a stated price

In a **net listing**, the broker/agent earns a commission only on the part of the sales price that exceeds a stated price. Here, the broker/agent is rewarded for an aggressive sales price.

### Exclusive Agency

**exclusive agency agreement**
the broker is the sole, exclusive agent

In an **exclusive agency agreement**, the broker is the sole, exclusive agent, with the exclusive right to sell the property. This type of agreement gives the broker the exclusive right to market the property. Generally, compensation is set as a percentage of the sale price of the property. This method encourages brokers to obtain the highest price for the seller, as a higher price will yield higher compensation. These agreements also secure the broker's compensation no matter who obtains a buyer. Whether there is another broker/agent involved or the seller obtains a buyer, the listing broker in the exclusive agency will receive his or her compensation. Thus, exclusive agency is the preferred listing arrangement of real estate professionals. Exhibit 7.3 represents the usual exclusive listing agreement.

Let's review of some of the important provisions in the agreement:

Paragraph 3.6 defines the length of time for which the listing agreement will be in effect.

Paragraph 5, "Brokerage Duties," defines the duty of the broker to market the property, to present offers and all communication relevant to the property to the seller in a timely manner, and to keep confidential the willingness of the seller to accept a price less than the listing price and the seller's motivation for sale. These duties track the duties of loyalty an agent owes his or her principal.

## Exhibit 7.3 Colorado Exclusive Right-to-Sell Contract

<table>
<tr><td>1<br>2<br>3</td><td>The printed portions of this form, except differentiated additions, have been approved by the Colorado Real Estate Commission. (LC50-8-10) (Mandatory 1-11)</td></tr>
</table>

4 **THIS IS A BINDING CONTRACT. THIS FORM HAS IMPORTANT LEGAL CONSEQUENCES AND THE PARTIES SHOULD**
5 **CONSULT LEGAL AND TAX OR OTHER COUNSEL BEFORE SIGNING.**

6 **Compensation charged by brokerage firms is not set by law. Such charges are established by each real estate**
7 **brokerage firm.**

8 **DIFFERENT BROKERAGE RELATIONSHIPS ARE AVAILABLE WHICH INCLUDE BUYER AGENCY, SELLER AGENCY, OR**
9 **TRANSACTION-BROKERAGE.**
10

11 # EXCLUSIVE RIGHT-TO-SELL LISTING CONTRACT

12 ☐ **SELLER AGENCY** ☐ **TRANSACTION-BROKERAGE**
13

14 Date: _____

15 **1. AGREEMENT.** Seller and Brokerage Firm enter into this exclusive, irrevocable contract (Seller Listing Contract) as of the
16 date set forth above.

17 **2. BROKER AND BROKERAGE FIRM.**
18 ☐ **2.1. Multiple-Person Firm.** If this box is checked, the individual designated by Brokerage Firm to serve as the broker of
19 Seller and to perform the services for Seller required by this Seller Listing Contract is called Broker. If more than one individual is
20 so designated, then references in this Seller Listing Contract to Broker shall include all persons so designated, including substitute
21 or additional brokers. The brokerage relationship exists only with Broker and does not extend to the employing broker, Brokerage
22 Firm or to any other brokers employed or engaged by Brokerage Firm who are not so designated.
23 ☐ **2.2. One-Person Firm.** If this box is checked, Broker is a real estate brokerage firm with only one licensed natural person.
24 References in this Seller Listing Contract to Broker or Brokerage Firm mean both the licensed natural person and brokerage firm
25 who shall serve as the broker of Seller and perform the services for Seller required by this Seller Listing Contract.

26 **3. DEFINED TERMS.**
27 **3.1. Seller:** _____

28 **3.2. Brokerage Firm:** _____

29 **3.3. Broker:** _____

30 **3.4. Property.** The Property is the following legally described real estate in the County of _____, Colorado:
31
32
33
34 known as No. _____,
35           Street Address           City           State           Zip

36 together with the interests, easements, rights, benefits, improvements and attached fixtures appurtenant thereto, and all interest of
37 Seller in vacated streets and alleys adjacent thereto, except as herein excluded.
38 **3.5. Sale.**
39 **3.5.1.** A Sale is the voluntary transfer or exchange of any interest in the Property or the voluntary creation of the
40 obligation to convey any interest in the Property, including a contract or lease. It also includes an agreement to transfer any
41 ownership interest in an entity which owns the Property.
42 ☐ **3.5.2.** If this box is checked, Seller authorizes Broker to negotiate leasing the Property. Lease of the Property or
43 Lease means any lease of an interest in the Property.
44 **3.6. Listing Period.** The Listing Period of this Seller Listing Contract shall begin on _____, and
45 shall continue through the earlier of (1) completion of the Sale of the Property or (2) _____.
46 Broker shall continue to assist in the completion of any sale or lease for which compensation is payable to Brokerage Firm under
47 § 7 of this Seller Listing Contract.
48 **3.7. Applicability of Terms.** A check or similar mark in a box means that such provision is applicable. The abbreviation
49 "N/A" or the word "Deleted" means not applicable. The abbreviation "MEC" (mutual execution of this contract) means the date upon
50 which both parties have signed this Seller Listing Contract.

*(continued)*

## Exhibit 7.3 Continued

51     **3.8.**   **Day; Computation of Period of Days, Deadline.**
52         **3.8.1.**   **Day.** As used in this Seller Listing Contract, the term "day" shall mean the entire day ending at 11:59 p.m.,
53 United States Mountain Time (Standard or Daylight Savings as applicable).
54         **3.8.2.**   **Computation of Period of Days, Deadline.** In computing a period of days, when the ending date is not
55 specified, the first day is excluded and the last day is included, e.g., three days after MEC. If any deadline falls on a Saturday,
56 Sunday or federal or Colorado state holiday (Holiday), such deadline ☐ **Shall** ☐ **Shall Not** be extended to the next day that is
57 not a Saturday, Sunday or Holiday. Should neither box be checked, the deadline shall not be extended.

58 **4.**   **BROKERAGE RELATIONSHIP.**
59     **4.1.**   If the Seller Agency box at the top of page 1 is checked, Broker shall represent Seller as a Seller's limited agent
60 (Seller's Agent). If the Transaction-Brokerage box at the top of page 1 is checked, Broker shall act as a Transaction-Broker.
61     **4.2.**   **In-Company Transaction – Different Brokers.** When Seller and buyer in a transaction are working with different
62 brokers, those brokers continue to conduct themselves consistent with the brokerage relationships they have established. Seller
63 acknowledges that Brokerage Firm is allowed to offer and pay compensation to brokers within Brokerage Firm working with a
64 buyer.
65     **4.3.**   **In-Company Transaction – One Broker.** If Seller and buyer are both working with the same broker, Broker shall
66 function as:
67         **4.3.1.**   **Seller's Agent.** If the Seller Agency box at the top of page 1 is checked, the parties agree the following applies:
68             **4.3.1.1.**   **Seller Agency Only.** Unless the box in § 4.3.1.2 (**Seller Agency Unless Brokerage Relationship**
69 **with Both**) is checked, Broker shall represent Seller as Seller's Agent and shall treat the buyer as a customer. A customer is a
70 party to a transaction with whom Broker has no brokerage relationship. Broker shall disclose to such customer Broker's
71 relationship with Seller.
72         ☐   **4.3.1.2.**   **Seller Agency Unless Brokerage Relationship with Both.** If this box is checked, Broker shall
73 represent Seller as Seller's Agent and shall treat the buyer as a customer, unless Broker currently has or enters into an agency or
74 Transaction-Brokerage relationship with the buyer, in which case Broker shall act as a Transaction-Broker.
75         **4.3.2.**   **Transaction-Broker.** If the Transaction-Brokerage box at the top of page 1 is checked, or in the event neither
76 box is checked, Broker shall work with Seller as a Transaction-Broker. A Transaction-Broker shall perform the duties described in
77 § 5 and facilitate sales transactions without being an advocate or agent for either party. If Seller and buyer are working with the
78 same broker, Broker shall continue to function as a Transaction-Broker.

79 **5.**   **BROKERAGE DUTIES.** Brokerage Firm, acting through Broker, as either a Transaction-Broker or a Seller's Agent, shall
80 perform the following **Uniform Duties** when working with Seller:
81     **5.1.**   Broker shall exercise reasonable skill and care for Seller, including, but not limited to the following:
82         **5.1.1.**   Performing the terms of any written or oral agreement with Seller;
83         **5.1.2.**   Presenting all offers to and from Seller in a timely manner regardless of whether the Property is subject to a
84 contract for Sale;
85         **5.1.3.**   Disclosing to Seller adverse material facts actually known by Broker;
86         **5.1.4.**   Advising Seller regarding the transaction and advising Seller to obtain expert advice as to material matters
87 about which Broker knows but the specifics of which are beyond the expertise of Broker;
88         **5.1.5.**   Accounting in a timely manner for all money and property received; and
89         **5.1.6.**   Keeping Seller fully informed regarding the transaction.
90     **5.2.**   Broker shall not disclose the following information without the informed consent of Seller:
91         **5.2.1.**   That Seller is willing to accept less than the asking price for the Property;
92         **5.2.2.**   What the motivating factors are for Seller to sell the Property;
93         **5.2.3.**   That Seller will agree to financing terms other than those offered;
94         **5.2.4.**   Any material information about Seller unless disclosure is required by law or failure to disclose such
95 information would constitute fraud or dishonest dealing; or
96         **5.2.5.**   Any facts or suspicions regarding circumstances that could psychologically impact or stigmatize the Property.
97     **5.3.**   Seller consents to Broker's disclosure of Seller's confidential information to the supervising broker or designee for the
98 purpose of proper supervision, provided such supervising broker or designee shall not further disclose such information without
99 consent of Seller, or use such information to the detriment of Seller.
100     **5.4.**   Brokerage Firm may have agreements with other sellers to market and sell their property. Broker may show alternative
101 properties not owned by Seller to other prospective buyers and list competing properties for sale.
102     **5.5.**   Broker shall not be obligated to seek additional offers to purchase the Property while the Property is subject to a
103 contract for Sale.
104     **5.6.**   Broker has no duty to conduct an independent inspection of the Property for the benefit of a buyer and has no duty to
105 independently verify the accuracy or completeness of statements made by Seller or independent inspectors. Broker has no duty to
106 conduct an independent investigation of a buyer's financial condition or to verify the accuracy or completeness of any statement
107 made by a buyer.

# Exhibit 7.3 Continued

| | |
|---|---|
| 108 | **5.7.** Seller understands that Seller shall not be liable for Broker's acts or omissions that have not been approved, directed, or |
| 109 | ratified by Seller. |
| 110 | **5.8.** When asked, Broker ☐ **Shall** ☐ **Shall Not** disclose to prospective buyers and cooperating brokers the existence of |
| 111 | offers on the Property and whether the offers were obtained by Broker, a broker within Brokerage Firm or by another broker. |

| | |
|---|---|
| 112 | **6. ADDITIONAL DUTIES OF SELLER'S AGENT.** If the Seller Agency box at the top of page 1 is checked, Broker is |
| 113 | Seller's Agent, with the following additional duties: |
| 114 | **6.1.** Promoting the interests of Seller with the utmost good faith, loyalty and fidelity; |
| 115 | **6.2.** Seeking a price and terms that are set forth in this Seller Listing Contract; and |
| 116 | **6.3.** Counseling Seller as to any material benefits or risks of a transaction that are actually known by Broker. |

| | |
|---|---|
| 117 | **7. COMPENSATION TO BROKERAGE FIRM; COMPENSATION TO COOPERATIVE BROKER.** Seller agrees that |
| 118 | any Brokerage Firm compensation that is conditioned upon the Sale of the Property shall be earned by Brokerage Firm as set forth |
| 119 | herein without any discount or allowance for any efforts made by Seller or by any other person in connection with the Sale of the |
| 120 | Property. |
| 121 | **7.1. Amount.** In consideration of the services to be performed by Broker, Seller agrees to pay Brokerage Firm as follows: |
| 122 | **7.1.1. Sale Commission.** (1) _____% of the gross purchase price or (2) _____, |
| 123 | in U.S. dollars. |
| 124 | **7.1.2. Lease Commission.** If the box in § 3.5.2 is checked, Brokerage Firm shall be paid a fee equal to (1) _____% |
| 125 | of the gross rent under the lease, or (2) _____, in U.S. dollars, payable |
| 126 | as follows: _____. |
| 127 | **7.2. When Earned.** Such commission shall be earned upon the occurrence of any of the following: |
| 128 | **7.2.1.** Any Sale of the Property within the Listing Period by Seller, by Broker or by any other person; |
| 129 | **7.2.2.** Broker finding a buyer who is ready, willing and able to complete the sale or lease as specified in this Seller |
| 130 | Listing Contract; or |
| 131 | **7.2.3.** Any Sale (or Lease if § 3.5.2 is checked) of the Property within _____ calendar days subsequent to the |
| 132 | expiration of the Listing Period (Holdover Period) (1) to anyone with whom Broker negotiated and (2) whose name was submitted, |
| 133 | in writing, to Seller by Broker during the Listing Period, including any extensions thereof, (Submitted Prospect). Provided, |
| 134 | however, Seller ☐ **Shall** ☐ **Shall Not** owe the commission to Brokerage Firm under this § 7.2.3 if a commission is earned by |
| 135 | another licensed real estate brokerage firm acting pursuant to an exclusive agreement entered into during the Holdover Period and |
| 136 | a Sale or Lease to a Submitted Prospect is consummated. If no box is checked above in this § 7.2.3, then Seller shall not owe the |
| 137 | commission to Brokerage Firm. |
| 138 | **7.3. When Applicable and Payable.** The commission obligation shall apply to a Sale made during the Listing Period or |
| 139 | any extension of such original or extended term. The commission described in § 7.1.1 shall be payable at the time of the closing of |
| 140 | the Sale, or, if there is no closing (due to the refusal or neglect of Seller) then on the contracted date of closing, as contemplated by |
| 141 | § 7.2.1 or § 7.2.3, or upon fulfillment of § 7.2.2 where the offer made by such buyer is not accepted by Seller. |
| 142 | **7.4. Other Compensation.** _____ |
| 143 | **7.5. Cooperative Broker Compensation.** Broker shall seek assistance from, and Brokerage Firm offers compensation to, |
| 144 | outside brokerage firms, whose brokers are acting as: |
| 145 | ☐ **Buyer Agents:** _____% of the gross sales price or _____, in U.S. dollars. |
| 146 | ☐ **Transaction-Brokers:** _____% of the gross sales price or _____, in U.S. dollars. |

| | |
|---|---|
| 147 | **8. LIMITATION ON THIRD-PARTY COMPENSATION.** Neither Broker nor the Brokerage Firm, except as set forth in |
| 148 | § 7, shall accept compensation from any other person or entity in connection with the Property without the written consent of |
| 149 | Seller. Additionally, neither Broker nor Brokerage Firm shall assess or receive mark-ups or other compensation for services |
| 150 | performed by any third party or affiliated business entity unless Seller signs a separate written consent. |

| | |
|---|---|
| 151 | **9. OTHER BROKERS' ASSISTANCE, MULTIPLE LISTING SERVICES AND MARKETING.** Seller has been advised |
| 152 | by Broker of the advantages and disadvantages of various marketing methods, including advertising and the use of multiple listing |
| 153 | services (MLS) and various methods of making the Property accessible by other brokerage firms (e.g., using lock boxes, by- |
| 154 | appointment-only showings, etc.), and whether some methods may limit the ability of another broker to show the Property. After |
| 155 | having been so advised, Seller has chosen the following (check all that apply): |
| 156 | **9.1. MLS/Information Exchange.** |
| 157 | **9.1.1.** The Property ☐ **Shall** ☐ **Shall Not** be submitted to one or more MLS and ☐ **Shall** ☐ **Shall Not** be |
| 158 | submitted to one or more property information exchanges. If submitted, Seller authorizes Broker to provide timely notice of any |
| 159 | status change to such MLS and information exchanges. Upon transfer of deed from Seller to buyer, Seller authorizes Broker to |
| 160 | provide sales information to such MLS and information exchanges. |
| 161 | **9.1.2.** Seller authorizes the use of electronic and all other marketing methods except: _____. |
| 162 | **9.1.3.** Seller further authorizes use of the data by MLS and property information exchanges, if any. |

LC50-8-10. **EXCLUSIVE RIGHT-TO-SELL LISTING CONTRACT** Page 3 of 7

*(continued)*

**Exhibit 7.3** Continued

| | | |
|---|---|---|
| 163 | **9.1.4.** | The Property Address ☐ **Shall** ☐ **Shall Not** be displayed on the Internet. |
| 164 | **9.1.5.** | The Property Listing ☐ **Shall** ☐ **Shall Not** be displayed on the Internet. |

165 **9.2. Property Access.** Access to the Property may be by:
166 ☐ Lock Box
167 ☐ _____
168 Other instructions: _____
169 **9.3. Broker Marketing.** The following specific marketing tasks shall be performed by Broker:
170
171
172 **9.4. Brokerage Services.** The Broker shall provide brokerage services to Seller.

173 **10. SELLER'S OBLIGATIONS TO BROKER; DISCLOSURES AND CONSENT.**
174 **10.1. Negotiations and Communication.** Seller agrees to conduct all negotiations for the Sale of the Property only through
175 Broker, and to refer to Broker all communications received in any form from real estate brokers, prospective buyers, tenants or any
176 other source during the Listing Period of this Seller Listing Contract.
177 **10.2. Advertising.** Seller agrees that any advertising of the Property by Seller (e.g., Internet, print and signage) shall first be
178 approved by Broker.
179 **10.3. No Existing Listing Agreement.** Seller represents that Seller ☐ **Is** ☐ **Is Not** currently a party to any listing
180 agreement with any other broker to sell the Property.
181 **10.4. Ownership of Materials and Consent.** Seller represents that all materials (including all photographs, renderings,
182 images or other creative items) supplied to Broker by or on behalf of Seller are owned by Seller, except as Seller has disclosed in
183 writing to Broker. Seller is authorized to and grants to Broker, Brokerage Firm and any MLS (that Broker submits the Property to)
184 a nonexclusive irrevocable, royalty-free license to use such material for marketing of the Property, reporting as required and the
185 publishing, display and reproduction of such material, compilation and data. This license shall survive the termination of this
186 Seller Listing Contract.
187 **10.5. Colorado Foreclosure Protection Act.** The Colorado Foreclosure Protection Act (Act) generally applies if (1) the
188 Property is residential (2) Seller resides in the Property as Seller's principal residence (3) Buyer's purpose in purchase of the
189 Property is not to use the Property as Buyer's personal residence and (4) the Property is in foreclosure or Buyer has notice that any
190 loan secured by the Property is at least thirty days delinquent or in default. If all requirements 1, 2, 3 and 4 are met and the Act
191 otherwise applies, then a contract, between Buyer and Seller for the sale of the Property, that complies with the provisions of the
192 Act is required. If the transaction is a Short Sale transaction and a Short Sale Addendum is part of the Contract between Seller and
193 Buyer, the Act does not apply. It is recommended that Seller consult with an attorney.

194 **11. PRICE AND TERMS.** The following Price and Terms are acceptable to Seller:
195 **11.1. Price.** U.S. $_____
196 **11.2. Terms.** ☐ **Cash** ☐ **Conventional** ☐ **FHA** ☐ **VA** ☐ **Other:** _____
197 **11.3. Loan Discount Points.** _____
198 **11.4. Buyer's Closing Costs (FHA/VA).** Seller shall pay closing costs and fees, not to exceed $_____, that Buyer
199 is not allowed by law to pay, for tax service and _____.
200 **11.5. Earnest Money.** Minimum amount of earnest money deposit U.S. $_____ in the form of _____
201 **11.6. Seller Proceeds.** Seller will receive net proceeds of closing as indicated: ☐ **Cashier's Check** at Seller's expense;
202 ☐ **Funds Electronically Transferred (Wire Transfer)** to an account specified by Seller, at Seller's expense; or ☐ **Closing**
203 **Company's Trust Account Check.**
204 **11.7. Advisory: Tax Withholding.** The Internal Revenue Service and the Colorado Department of Revenue may require
205 closing company to withhold a substantial portion of the proceeds of this Sale when Seller either (1) is a foreign person or (2) will
206 not be a Colorado resident after closing. Seller should inquire of Seller's tax advisor to determine if withholding applies or if an
207 exemption exists.

208 **12. DEPOSITS.** Brokerage Firm is authorized to accept earnest money deposits received by Broker pursuant to a proposed Sale
209 contract. Brokerage Firm is authorized to deliver the earnest money deposit to the closing agent, if any, at or before the closing of
210 the Sale contract.

211 **13. INCLUSIONS AND EXCLUSIONS.**
212 **13.1. Inclusions.** The Purchase Price includes the following items (Inclusions):
213 **13.1.1. Fixtures.** If attached to the Property on the date of this Seller Listing Contract, lighting, heating, plumbing,
214 ventilating, and air conditioning fixtures, TV antennas, inside telephone, network and coaxial (cable) wiring and connecting
215 blocks/jacks, plants, mirrors, floor coverings, intercom systems, built-in kitchen appliances, sprinkler systems and controls, built-in
216 vacuum systems (including accessories), garage door openers including _____ remote controls; and
217

## Exhibit 7.3 Continued

218       **13.1.2. Personal Property.** If on the Property whether attached or not on the date of this Seller Listing Contract:
219 storm windows, storm doors, window and porch shades, awnings, blinds, screens, window coverings, curtain rods, drapery rods,
220 fireplace inserts, fireplace screens, fireplace grates, heating stoves, storage sheds, and all keys. If checked, the following are
221 included: ☐ **Water Softeners** ☐ **Smoke/Fire Detectors** ☐ **Security Systems** ☐ **Satellite Systems** (including satellite
222 dishes); and

223
224

225     The Personal Property to be conveyed at closing shall be conveyed by Seller free and clear of all taxes (except personal
226 property taxes for the year of closing), liens and encumbrances, except _____.
227 Conveyance shall be by bill of sale or other applicable legal instrument.
228       **13.1.3. Trade Fixtures.** The following trade fixtures: _____
229     The Trade Fixtures to be conveyed at closing shall be conveyed by Seller, free and clear of all taxes (except personal property
230 taxes for the year of closing), liens and encumbrances, except _____.
231 Conveyance shall be by bill of sale or other applicable legal instrument.
232       **13.1.4. Parking and Storage Facilities.** ☐ **Use Only** ☐ **Ownership** of the following parking facilities: _____
233 _____; and ☐ **Use Only** ☐ **Ownership** of the following storage facilities: _____.
234       **13.1.5. Water Rights.** The following legally described water rights:

235
236

237     Any water rights shall be conveyed by _____ deed or other applicable legal instrument. The Well
238 Permit # is _____.
239       **13.1.6. Growing Crops.** The following growing crops:

240
241

242     **13.2. Exclusions.** The following are excluded (Exclusions): _____

243     **14. TITLE AND ENCUMBRANCES.** Seller represents to Broker that title to the Property is solely in Seller's name. Seller shall
244 deliver to Broker true copies of all relevant title materials, leases, improvement location certificates and surveys in Seller's
245 possession and shall disclose to Broker all easements, liens and other encumbrances, if any, on the Property, of which Seller has
246 knowledge. Seller authorizes the holder of any obligation secured by an encumbrance on the Property to disclose to Broker the
247 amount owing on said encumbrance and the terms thereof. In case of Sale, Seller agrees to convey, by a _____
248 deed, only that title Seller has in the Property. Property shall be conveyed free and clear of all taxes, except the general taxes for
249 the year of closing.
250     All monetary encumbrances (such as mortgages, deeds of trust, liens, financing statements) shall be paid by Seller and released
251 except as Seller and buyer may otherwise agree. Existing monetary encumbrances are as follows: _____.
252     The Property is subject to the following leases and tenancies: _____.
253     If the Property has been or will be subject to any governmental liens for special improvements installed at the time of signing
254 a Sale contract, Seller shall be responsible for payment of same, unless otherwise agreed. Brokerage Firm may terminate this Seller
255 Listing Contract upon written notice to Seller that title is not satisfactory to Brokerage Firm.

256     **15. EVIDENCE OF TITLE.** Seller agrees to furnish buyer, at Seller's expense, a current commitment and an owner's title
257 insurance policy in an amount equal to the Purchase Price in the form specified in the Sale contract, or if this box is checked,
258 ☐ **An Abstract of Title** certified to a current date.

259     **16. ASSOCIATION ASSESSMENTS.** Seller represents that the amount of the regular owners' association assessment is
260 currently payable at $_____ per _____ and that there are no unpaid regular or special assessments against
261 the Property except the current regular assessments and except _____. Seller agrees to promptly
262 request the owners' association to deliver to buyer before date of closing a current statement of assessments against the Property.

263     **17. POSSESSION.** Possession of the Property shall be delivered to buyer as follows: _____,
264 subject to leases and tenancies as described in § 14.

265     **18. MATERIAL DEFECTS, DISCLOSURES AND INSPECTION.**
266     **18.1. Broker's Obligations.** Colorado law requires a broker to disclose to any prospective buyer all adverse material facts
267 actually known by such broker including but not limited to adverse material facts pertaining to the title to the Property and the
268 physical condition of the Property, any material defects in the Property, and any environmental hazards affecting the Property which
269 are required by law to be disclosed. These types of disclosures may include such matters as structural defects, soil conditions,
270 violations of health, zoning or building laws, and nonconforming uses and zoning variances. Seller agrees that any buyer may have
271 the Property and Inclusions inspected and authorizes Broker to disclose any facts actually known by Broker about the Property.

---

LC50-8-10. **EXCLUSIVE RIGHT-TO-SELL LISTING CONTRACT**                             **Page 5 of 7**

*(continued)*

## Exhibit 7.3 Continued

272     **18.2. Seller's Obligations.**
273         **18.2.1. Seller's Property Disclosure Form.** A seller is not required by law to provide a written disclosure of adverse
274 matters regarding the Property. However, disclosure of known material latent (not obvious) defects is required by law. Seller
275 ☐ **Agrees** ☐ **Does Not Agree** to provide a Seller's Property Disclosure form completed to Seller's current, actual knowledge.
276         **18.2.2. Lead-Based Paint.** Unless exempt, if the improvements on the Property include one or more residential
277 dwellings for which a building permit was issued prior to January 1, 1978, a completed Lead-Based Paint Disclosure (Sales) form
278 must be signed by Seller and the real estate licensees, and given to any potential buyer in a timely manner.
279         **18.2.3. Carbon Monoxide Alarms.** Note: If the improvements on the Property have a fuel-fired heater or appliance, a
280 fireplace, or an attached garage and one or more rooms lawfully used for sleeping purposes (Bedroom), Seller understands that
281 Colorado law requires that Seller assure the Property has an operational carbon monoxide alarm installed within fifteen feet of the
282 entrance to each Bedroom or in a location as required by the applicable building code, prior to offering the Property for sale or lease.
283     **18.3. Right of Broker to Terminate.** Although Broker has no obligation to investigate or inspect the Property, and no duty
284 to verify statements made, Broker shall have the right to terminate this Seller Listing Contract if the physical condition of the
285 Property, Inclusions, any proposed or existing transportation project, road, street or highway, or any other activity, odor or noise
286 (whether on or off the Property) and its effect or expected effect on the Property or its occupants, or if any facts or suspicions
287 regarding circumstances that could psychologically impact or stigmatize the Property are unsatisfactory to Broker.

288 **19. FORFEITURE OF PAYMENTS.** In the event of a forfeiture of payments made by a buyer, the sums received shall be
289 divided between Brokerage Firm and Seller, one-half thereof to Brokerage Firm but not to exceed the Brokerage Firm
290 compensation agreed upon herein, and the balance to Seller. Any forfeiture of payment under this section shall not reduce any
291 Brokerage Firm compensation owed, earned and payable under § 7.

292 **20. COST OF SERVICES AND REIMBURSEMENT.** Unless otherwise agreed upon in writing, Brokerage Firm shall bear all
293 expenses incurred by Brokerage Firm, if any, to market the Property and to compensate cooperating brokerage firms, if any.
294 Neither Broker nor Brokerage Firm shall obtain or order any other products or services unless Seller agrees in writing to pay for
295 them promptly when due (examples: surveys, radon tests, soil tests, title reports, engineering studies). Unless otherwise agreed,
296 neither Broker nor Brokerage Firm shall be obligated to advance funds for the benefit of Seller in order to complete a closing.
297 Seller shall reimburse Brokerage Firm for payments made by Brokerage Firm for such products or services authorized by Seller.

298 **21. DISCLOSURE OF SETTLEMENT COSTS.** Seller acknowledges that costs, quality, and extent of service vary between
299 different settlement service providers (e.g., attorneys, lenders, inspectors and title companies).

300 **22. MAINTENANCE OF THE PROPERTY.** Neither Broker nor Brokerage Firm shall be responsible for maintenance of the
301 Property nor shall they be liable for damage of any kind occurring to the Property, unless such damage shall be caused by their
302 negligence or intentional misconduct.

303 **23. NONDISCRIMINATION.** The parties agree not to discriminate unlawfully against any prospective buyer because of the
304 race, creed, color, sex, sexual orientation, marital status, familial status, physical or mental disability, handicap, religion, national
305 origin or ancestry of such person.

306 **24. RECOMMENDATION OF LEGAL AND TAX COUNSEL.** By signing this document, Seller acknowledges that Broker
307 has advised that this document has important legal consequences and has recommended consultation with legal and tax or other
308 counsel before signing this Seller Listing Contract.

309 **25. MEDIATION.** If a dispute arises relating to this Seller Listing Contract, prior to or after closing, and is not resolved, the
310 parties shall first proceed in good faith to submit the matter to mediation. Mediation is a process in which the parties meet with an
311 impartial person who helps to resolve the dispute informally and confidentially. Mediators cannot impose binding decisions. The
312 parties to the dispute must agree, in writing, before any settlement is binding. The parties will jointly appoint an acceptable
313 mediator and will share equally in the cost of such mediation. The mediation, unless otherwise agreed, shall terminate in the event
314 the entire dispute is not resolved within 30 calendar days of the date written notice requesting mediation is delivered by one party
315 to the other at the party's last known address.

316 **26. ATTORNEY FEES.** In the event of any arbitration or litigation relating to this Seller Listing Contract, the arbitrator or court
317 shall award to the prevailing party all reasonable costs and expenses, including attorney and legal fees.

318 **27. ADDITIONAL PROVISIONS.** (The following additional provisions have not been approved by the Colorado Real Estate Commission.)
319
320
321

# Exhibit 7.3 Continued

322 **28. ATTACHMENTS.** The following are a part of this Seller Listing Contract:
323
324

325 **29. NO OTHER PARTY OR INTENDED BENEFICIARIES.** Nothing in this Seller Listing Contract shall be deemed to inure
326 to the benefit of any person other than Seller, Broker and Brokerage Firm.

327 **30. NOTICE, DELIVERY AND CHOICE OF LAW.**
328    **30.1. Physical Delivery.** All notices must be in writing, except as provided in § 30.2. Any document, including a signed
329 document or notice, delivered to the other party to this Seller Listing Contract, is effective upon physical receipt. Delivery to Seller
330 shall be effective when physically received by Seller, any signator on behalf of Seller, any named individual of Seller or
331 representative of Seller.
332    **30.2. Electronic Delivery.** As an alternative to physical delivery, any document, including any signed document or written
333 notice may be delivered in electronic form only by the following indicated methods: ☐ **Facsimile** ☐ **Email** ☐ **Internet** ☐ **No**
334 **Electronic Delivery.** Documents with original signatures shall be provided upon request of any party.
335    **30.3. Choice of Law.** This Seller Listing Contract and all disputes arising hereunder shall be governed by and construed in
336 accordance with the laws of the State of Colorado that would be applicable to Colorado residents who sign a contract in this state
337 for property located in Colorado.

338 **31. MODIFICATION OF THIS SELLER LISTING CONTRACT.** No subsequent modification of any of the terms of this
339 Seller Listing Contract shall be valid, binding upon the parties, or enforceable unless made in writing and signed by the parties.

340 **32. COUNTERPARTS.** If more than one person is named as a Seller herein, this Seller Listing Contract may be executed by
341 each Seller, separately, and when so executed, such copies taken together with one executed by Broker on behalf of Brokerage
342 Firm shall be deemed to be a full and complete contract between the parties.

343 **33. ENTIRE AGREEMENT.** This agreement constitutes the entire contract between the parties, and any prior agreements,
344 whether oral or written, have been merged and integrated into this Seller Listing Contract.

345 **34. COPY OF CONTRACT.** Seller acknowledges receipt of a copy of this Seller Listing Contract signed by Broker, including
346 all attachments.

347 Brokerage Firm authorizes Broker to execute this Seller Listing Contract on behalf of Brokerage Firm.

Seller's Name: _____    Broker's Name: _____

Seller's Signature _____ Date _____    Broker's Signature _____ Date _____

Address: _____    Address: _____

Phone No.: _____    Phone No.: _____
Fax No: _____    Fax No: _____
Electronic Address: _____    Electronic Address: _____

Brokerage
Firm's Name: _____
Address: _____

Phone No.: _____
Fax No.: _____
Electronic Address: _____

348

Paragraph 7, "Compensation," describes how the sales commission will be calculated and when it is payable. It also addresses how the commission will be split if another broker/agent procures the buyer.

Paragraph 9, "Other Brokers' Assistance, Multiple Listing Services and Marketing," describes the advantages and disadvantages of marketing methods. Marketing of real estate is conducted in a variety of ways, some traditional and others taking advantage of technology. Traditional marketing is conducted through advertisements in newspapers and local publications. Advertisements usually refer to the location of the property, may include a photograph and description of the property, and give contact information for the broker/agent. Sunday afternoon open house events are also a traditional means of marketing. The agent or broker will ask the seller to clean up and leave the house for the day. Advertisements and signs will be posted to attract potential buyers who then can leisurely browse through the home. The desired outcome is that one of those potential buyers will be serious enough to purchase the home.

The multiple listing service (MLS or MLB) represents a traditional form of marketing that has certainly changed with the times. These services used to publish booklets of available real estate, by community in which the properties were located, and within that community from lowest to highest prices. Because of the time to print and distribute the printed booklet, there was a delay from the time of reporting the available property to the time it would be included in the publication. With the Internet, all this information is online for members to access. Properties placed on websites can be viewed by members the same day. Brokers themselves have become Internet savvy, too. Many brokers maintain a website that lists all the properties that are under listing contract with one of the agents or brokers in their office. Each property will have a description, photographs, and a "virtual tour" of the property. Potential home buyers can have a look at the homes available from a particular real estate broker's office without ever leaving their living rooms.

The seller may place some limits on the marketing efforts the agent can utilize. Some sellers do not want to have people wandering through their home when they are not there, and for them the open house is out of the question. Some sellers may, for privacy reasons, limit what information can be placed on the Internet.

Paragraph 11, "Price and Terms," sets the listing price for the real estate and other terms that will be acceptable to the seller, such as the type of financing and whether the seller has a willingness to assist the purchaser by paying all or a portion of the purchaser's closing or loan costs. The determination of the listing price for the property is a purely subjective one. For the seller, who loves the home he or she has lived and raised a family in, the property and the memories found there may be priceless. In many instances, there may be a bottom line price the seller needs to receive on the sale of the home. The seller's bottom line can be related to his or her ability to purchase another home, or it could represent an entrance fee into a senior life care community. The broker/agent will work with the seller to determine the suggested listing price and likely selling price, with the goal of achieving the seller's bottom line.

The broker/agent will consult public records, as well as records from the MLS, to find properties with similar characteristics that have recently sold or are currently on the market. The most important factor to consider is the specific location, community, or development. The list of recent sales or current listings in the same community will then be narrowed down to those that have a similar style of house, bedroom and bath count, lot size, features such as garage and swimming pool, etc. The more similar the properties, the more accurately they reflect the value of the seller's home. In most areas, the MLS will track listing prices, reduction to those prices over the course of the listing contract, and the final sales price. These factors will also bear on the broker's recommended listing price. Typically, the listing price will be higher than the sales price, to allow room for negotiation with potential buyers. The broker will prepare and present a report with the sales and current listing information, which will assist the seller in understanding why the broker recommends a particular price point.

Paragraph 13, "Inclusions and Exclusions," is an important clause to prevent confusion at a later point in the marketing and sales process. It lists what items are included or excluded from the sale, such as appliances, draperies, etc.

Paragraph 23, "Nondiscrimination," prohibits the seller and the broker from discriminating against potential purchasers. This requirement has its roots in federal, state, and local laws. Under the Fair Housing Act, the real estate agent or broker may not refuse to show properties to an individual based on race, sex, religion, or national origin. Brokers and agents are also prohibited from directing buyers only to communities that are occupied by people of the same race, sex, religion, or national origin—a practice called steering. Furthermore, should a seller indicate that he or she will not sell to someone based on that person's race, sex, religion, or national origin, the broker/agent has an obligation to refuse that request.

Paragraph 25, "Mediation," describes the process for resolution of any dispute that arises out of the listing contract and requires the parties to first submit any dispute to **mediation.** Mediation is an alternative dispute resolution method where the parties present their dispute to an independent third party, who assists them in coming to a mutually agreeable resolution of their dispute. Use of mediation is informal and nonbinding. The parties may agree to accept the result of mediation, in which case the dispute is quickly resolved rather than the parties suffering the delays associated with filing a lawsuit.

**mediation**
an alternative dispute resolution method where the parties present their dispute to an independent third party who assists them in achieving a mutually agreed resolution

## Seller's Disclosure

In conjunction with the listing contract, many states also require a Seller's Disclosure Statement. This is a detailed statement prepared by the seller concerning the property and its condition. This type of disclosure form has become common in most states. The purchase of a home represents the largest purchase most people will make. An educated purchaser will be less likely to find fault at some point in the future should a problem arise after the home is purchased. The goal is for buyers to make an educated decision about the real estate. The person with the greatest knowledge about the property and its condition is the seller. Thus, it has becomes the duty of the seller to disclose the condition of the property. Exhibit 7.4 is a Seller's Property Disclosure for the State of Colorado.

The form represents a checklist and covers everything from the construction of the house to the water service to any environmental contamination that may exist. The questions ask about present and past conditions. The seller affirms the condition of the property and discloses known defects honestly and in good faith. Agents and brokers bear a similar duty and cannot hide behind a claim of ignorance about the condition of the property.

# Exhibit 7.4 Seller's Property Disclosure statement

The printed portions of this form, except differentiated additions, have been approved by the Colorado Real Estate Commission. (SPD29-8-10) (Mandatory 1-11)

**THIS FORM HAS IMPORTANT LEGAL CONSEQUENCES AND THE PARTIES SHOULD CONSULT LEGAL AND TAX OR OTHER COUNSEL BEFORE SIGNING.**

## SELLER'S PROPERTY DISCLOSURE
## (RESIDENTIAL)

### THIS DISCLOSURE SHOULD BE COMPLETED BY SELLER, NOT BY BROKER.

Seller states that the information contained in this Disclosure is correct to Seller's CURRENT ACTUAL KNOWLEDGE as of this Date. **Any changes will be disclosed by Seller to Buyer promptly after discovery.** Seller hereby receipts for a copy of this Disclosure. **If the Property is part of a Common Interest Community, this Disclosure is limited to the Property or Unit itself, except as stated in Section L.** Broker may deliver a copy of this Disclosure to prospective buyers.

Note: If an item is not present at the Property or if an item is not to be included in the sale, mark the "N/A" column. The Contract to Buy and Sell Real Estate, not this Disclosure form, determines whether an item is included or excluded; if there is an inconsistency between this form and the Contract, the Contract controls.

Date: _____

Property Address: _____

Seller: _____

| | I. IMPROVEMENTS | | | | | |
|---|---|---|---|---|---|---|

| **A.** | **STRUCTURAL CONDITIONS** Do any of the following conditions **now exist or have they ever existed:** | **Yes** | **No** | **Do Not Know** | **N/A** | **Comments** |
|---|---|---|---|---|---|---|
| 1 | Structural problems | | | | | |
| 2 | Moisture and/or water problems | | | | | |
| 3 | Damage due to termites, other insects, birds, animals or rodents | | | | | |
| 4 | Damage due to hail, wind, fire or flood | | | | | |
| 5 | Cracks, heaving or settling problems | | | | | |
| 6 | Exterior wall or window problems | | | | | |
| 7 | Exterior Artificial Stucco (EIFS) | | | | | |
| 8 | Any additions or alterations made | | | | | |
| 9 | Building code, city or county violations | | | | | |

| **B.** | **ROOF** Do any of the following conditions **now exist:** | **Yes** | **No** | **Do Not Know** | **N/A** | **Comments** |
|---|---|---|---|---|---|---|
| 1 | Roof problems | | | | | |
| 2 | Roof material: _____ Age _____ <br> Roof material: _____ Age _____ | | | | | |
| 3 | Roof leak:  Past | | | | | |
| 4 | Roof leak:  Present | | | | | |
| 5 | Damage to roof:  Past | | | | | |
| 6 | Damage to roof:  Present | | | | | |
| 7 | Roof under warranty until _____. <br> Transferable _____ | | | | | |
| 8 | Roof work done while under current roof warranty | | | | | |
| 9 | Skylight problems | | | | | |
| 10 | Gutter or downspout problems | | | | | |

## Exhibit 7.4 Continued

| C. | APPLIANCES<br>Are the following **now** in working condition: | IN WORKING CONDITION | | | Age If Known | N/A | Comments |
|---|---|---|---|---|---|---|---|
| | | Yes | No | Do Not Know | | | |
| 1 | Built-in vacuum system & accessories | | | | | | |
| 2 | Clothes dryer | | | | | | |
| 3 | Clothes washer | | | | | | |
| 4 | Dishwasher | | | | | | |
| 5 | Disposal | | | | | | |
| 6 | Freezer | | | | | | |
| 7 | Gas grill | | | | | | |
| 8 | Hood | | | | | | |
| 9 | Microwave oven | | | | | | |
| 10 | Oven | | | | | | |
| 11 | Range | | | | | | |
| 12 | Refrigerator | | | | | | |
| 13 | T.V. antenna: ☐ Owned ☐ Leased | | | | | | |
| 14 | Satellite system or DSS dish: ☐ Owned<br>☐ Leased | | | | | | |
| 15 | Trash compactor | | | | | | |

| D. | ELECTRICAL & TELECOMMUNICATIONS<br>Are the following **now** in working condition: | IN WORKING CONDITION | | | Age If Known | N/A | Comments |
|---|---|---|---|---|---|---|---|
| | | Yes | No | Do Not Know | | | |
| 1 | Security system: ☐ Owned ☐ Leased | | | | | | |
| 2 | Smoke/fire detectors: ☐ Battery ☐ Hardwire | | | | | | |
| 3 | Carbon Monoxide Alarm: ☐ Battery ☐ Hardwire | | | | | | |
| 4 | Light fixtures | | | | | | |
| 5 | Switches & outlets | | | | | | |
| 6 | Aluminum wiring (110) | | | | | | |
| 7 | Electrical: _____ Amps _____ | | | | | | |
| 8 | Telecommunications (T1, fiber, cable, satellite) | | | | | | |
| 9 | Inside telephone wiring & blocks/jacks | | | | | | |
| 10 | Ceiling fans | | | | | | |
| 11 | Garage door opener | | | | | | |
| 12 | Garage door control(s) #_____ | | | | | | |
| 13 | Intercom/doorbell | | | | | | |
| 14 | In-wall speakers | | | | | | |
| 15 | 220 volt service | | | | | | |
| 16 | Landscape lighting | | | | | | |

| E. | MECHANICAL<br>Are the following **now** in working condition: | IN WORKING CONDITION | | | Age If Known | N/A | Comments |
|---|---|---|---|---|---|---|---|
| | | Yes | No | Do Not Know | | | |
| 1 | Air conditioning: | | | | | | |
| | Evaporative cooler | | | | | | |
| | Window units | | | | | | |
| | Central | | | | | | |
| 2 | Attic/whole house fan | | | | | | |
| 3 | Vent fans | | | | | | |
| 4 | Humidifier | | | | | | |

*(continued)*

# Exhibit 7.4 Continued

| | | | | | | | |
|---|---|---|---|---|---|---|---|
| 5 | Air purifier | | | | | | |
| 6 | Sauna | | | | | | |
| 7 | Hot tub or spa | | | | | | |
| 8 | Steam room/shower | | | | | | |
| 9 | Pool | | | | | | |
| 10 | Heating system: Type _____<br>Fuel _____<br>Type _____<br>Fuel _____ | | | | | | |
| 11 | Water heater: Number of _____<br>Fuel type _____ Capacity _____ | | | | | | |
| 12 | Fireplace: Type _____<br>Fuel _____ | | | | | | |
| 13 | Fireplace insert | | | | | | |
| 14 | Stove: Type _____<br>Fuel _____ | | | | | | |
| 15 | When was fireplace/wood stove, chimney/flue last cleaned:  Date: _____ ☐ Do not know | | | | | | |
| 16 | Fuel tanks: ☐ Owned ☐ Leased | | | | | | |
| 17 | Radiant heating system: ☐ Interior ☐ Exterior<br>Hose Type _____ | | | | | | |
| 18 | Overhead door | | | | | | |
| 19 | Entry gate system | | | | | | |
| 20 | Elevator | | | | | | |

| | | IN WORKING CONDITION | | | | | |
|---|---|---|---|---|---|---|---|
| **F.** | **WATER, SEWER & OTHER UTILITIES**<br>Are the following **now** in working condition: | **Yes** | **No** | **Do Not Know** | **Age If Known** | **N/A** | **Comments** |
| 1 | Water filter system: ☐ Owned ☐ Leased | | | | | | |
| 2 | Water softener: ☐ Owned ☐ Leased | | | | | | |
| 3 | Sewage problems: ☐ Yes ☐ No ☐ Do not know | | | | | | |
| 4 | Lift station (sewage ejector pump) | | | | | | |
| 5 | Drainage, storm sewers, retention ponds | | | | | | |
| 6 | Grey water storage/use | | | | | | |
| 7 | Plumbing problems: ☐ Yes ☐ No ☐ Do not know | | | | | | |
| 8 | Sump pump | | | | | | |
| 9 | Underground sprinkler system | | | | | | |
| 10 | Fire sprinkler system | | | | | | |
| 11 | Polybutylene pipe: ☐ Yes ☐ No ☐ Do not know | | | | | | |
| 12 | Galvanized pipe: ☐ Yes ☐ No ☐ Do not know | | | | | | |
| 13 | Backflow prevention device: ☐ Domestic<br>☐ Irrigation ☐ Fire ☐ Sewage | | | | | | |
| 14 | Irrigation pump | | | | | | |
| 15 | Well pump | | | | | | |

| | | IN WORKING CONDITION | | | | | |
|---|---|---|---|---|---|---|---|
| **G.** | **OTHER DISCLOSURES – IMPROVEMENTS** | **Yes** | **No** | **Do Not Know** | **Age If Known** | **N/A** | **Comments** |
| 1 | Included fixtures and equipment **now** in working condition | | | | | | |
| | | | | | | | |

# Exhibit 7.4 Continued

| | | | | | | |
|---|---|---|---|---|---|---|
| | | | | | | |
| | | | | | | |

| II. GENERAL | | | | | | |
|---|---|---|---|---|---|---|
| **H.** | **USE, ZONING & LEGAL ISSUES**<br>Do any of the following conditions **now exist**: | **Yes** | **No** | **Do Not Know** | **N/A** | **Comments** |
| 1 | Zoning violation, variance, conditional use, violation of an enforceable PUD or non-conforming use | | | | | |
| 2 | Notice or threat of condemnation proceedings | | | | | |
| 3 | Notice of any adverse conditions from any governmental or quasi-governmental agency that have not been resolved | | | | | |
| 4 | Violation of restrictive covenants or owners' association rules or regulations | | | | | |
| 5 | Any building or improvements constructed within the past one year from this Date without approval by the Association or the designated approving body | | | | | |
| 6 | Notice of zoning action related to the Property | | | | | |
| 7 | Other legal action | | | | | |

| **I.** | **ACCESS, PARKING, DRAINAGE & SIGNAGE**<br>Do any of the following conditions **now exist**: | **Yes** | **No** | **Do Not Know** | **N/A** | **Comments** |
|---|---|---|---|---|---|---|
| 1 | Any access problems | | | | | |
| 2 | Roads, driveways, trails or paths through the Property used by others | | | | | |
| 3 | Public highway or county road bordering the Property | | | | | |
| 4 | Any proposed or existing transportation project that affects or is expected to affect the Property | | | | | |
| 5 | Encroachments, boundary disputes or unrecorded easements | | | | | |
| 6 | Shared or common areas with adjoining properties | | | | | |
| 7 | Requirements for curb, gravel/paving, landscaping | | | | | |
| 8 | Flooding or drainage problems: Past | | | | | |
| 9 | Flooding or drainage problems: Present | | | | | |

| **J.** | **WATER & SEWER SUPPLY**<br>Do any of the following conditions **now exist**: | **Yes** | **No** | **Do Not Know** | **N/A** | **Comments** |
|---|---|---|---|---|---|---|
| 1 | Water Rights: Type _____ | | | | | |
| 2 | Water tap fees paid in full | | | | | |
| 3 | Sewer tap fees paid in full | | | | | |
| 4 | Subject to augmentation plan | | | ▓▓▓ | | |
| 5 | Well required to be metered | | | ▓▓▓ | | |

6 | Type of water supply: ☐ Public ☐ Community ☐ Well ☐ Shared Well ☐ Cistern ☐ None
If the Property is served by a Well, a copy of the Well Permit ☐ **Is** ☐ **Is Not attached**. Well Permit #: _____
☐ Drilling Records ☐ Are ☐ Are not attached. Shared Well Agreement ☐ **Yes** ☐ **No**.
The **Water Provider** for the Property can be contacted at:
Name: _____ Address: _____
Web Site: _____ Phone No.: _____
☐ There is neither a Well nor a Water Provider for the Property. The source of potable water for the Property is [describe source]:

**SOME WATER PROVIDERS RELY, TO VARYING DEGREES, ON NONRENEWABLE GROUND WATER. YOU MAY WISH TO CONTACT YOUR PROVIDER (OR INVESTIGATE THE DESCRIBED SOURCE) TO DETERMINE THE LONG-TERM SUFFICIENCY OF THE PROVIDER'S WATER SUPPLIES.**

7 | Type of sanitary sewer service: ☐ Public ☐ Community ☐ Septic System ☐ None ☐ Other _____
If the Property is served by an on-site septic system, supply to buyer a copy of the permit.
Type of septic system: ☐ Tank ☐ Leach ☐ Lagoon

*(continued)*

## Exhibit 7.4 Continued

| K. | ENVIRONMENTAL CONDITIONS Do any of the following conditions **now exist or have they ever existed**: | Yes | No | Do Not Know | N/A | Comments |
|---|---|---|---|---|---|---|
| 1 | Hazardous materials on the Property, such as radioactive, toxic, or biohazardous materials, asbestos, pesticides, herbicides, wastewater sludge, radon, methane, mill tailings, solvents or petroleum products | | | | | |
| 2 | Underground storage tanks | | | | | |
| 3 | Aboveground storage tanks | | | | | |
| 4 | Underground transmission lines | | | | | |
| 5 | Pets kept on the Property | | | | | |
| 6 | Property used as, situated on, or adjoining a dump, land fill or municipal solid waste land fill | | | | | |
| 7 | Monitoring wells or test equipment | | | | | |
| 8 | Sliding, settling, upheaval, movement or instability of earth or expansive soils on the Property | | | | | |
| 9 | Mine shafts, tunnels or abandoned wells on the Property | | | | | |
| 10 | Within governmentally designated geological hazard or sensitive area | | | | | |
| 11 | Within governmentally designated flood plain or wetland area | | | | | |
| 12 | Dead, diseased or infested trees or shrubs | | | | | |
| 13 | Environmental assessments, studies or reports done involving the physical condition of the Property | | | | | |
| 14 | Property used for any mining, graveling, or other natural resource extraction operations such as oil and gas wells | | | | | |
| 15 | Interior of improvements of Property tobacco smoke-free | | | | | |
| 16 | Other environmental problems | | | | | |

| L. | COMMON INTEREST COMMUNITY – ASSOCIATION PROPERTY Do any of the following conditions **now exist**: | Yes | No | Do Not Know | N/A | Comments |
|---|---|---|---|---|---|---|
| 1 | Property is part of an owners' association | | | | | |
| 2 | Special assessments or increases in regular assessments approved by owners' association but not yet implemented | | | | | |
| 3 | Has the Association made demand or commenced a lawsuit against a builder or contractor alleging defective construction of improvements of the Association Property (common area or property owned or controlled by the Association but outside the Seller's Property or Unit). | | | | | |

| M. | OTHER DISCLOSURES – GENERAL Do any of the following conditions **now exist**: | Yes | No | Do Not Know | N/A | Comments |
|---|---|---|---|---|---|---|
| 1 | Any part of the Property leased to others (written or oral) | | | | | |
| 2 | Written reports of any building, site, roofing, soils or engineering investigations or studies of the Property | | | | | |
| 3 | Any property insurance claim submitted (whether paid or not) | | | | | |
| 4 | Structural, architectural and engineering plans and/or specifications for any existing improvements | | | | | |
| 5 | Property was previously used as a methamphetamine laboratory and not remediated to state standards | | | | | |
| 6 | Government special improvements approved, but not yet installed, that may become a lien against the Property | | | | | |
| | | | | | | |
| | | | | | | |

# Exhibit 7.4 Continued

Seller and Buyer understand that the real estate brokers do not warrant or guarantee the above information on the Property. Property inspection services may be purchased and are advisable. This form is **not** intended as a substitute for an inspection of the Property.

**ADVISORY TO SELLER:**

**Failure to disclose a known material defect may result in legal liability.**

The information contained in this Disclosure has been furnished by Seller, who certifies to the truth thereof based on Seller's CURRENT ACTUAL KNOWLEDGE.

_____     _____
Seller                    Date          Seller                    Date

**ADVISORY TO BUYER:**

1.      Even though Seller has answered the above questions to Seller's current actual knowledge, Buyer should thoroughly inspect the Property and obtain expert assistance to accurately and fully evaluate the Property to confirm the status of the following matters:
   a.   the physical condition of the Property;
   b.   the presence of mold or other biological hazards;
   c.   the presence of rodents, insects and vermin including termites;
   d.   the legal use of the Property and legal access to the Property;
   e.   the availability and source of water, sewer, and utilities;
   f.   the environmental and geological condition of the Property;
   g.   the presence of noxious weeds; and
   h.   any other matters that may affect Buyer's use and ownership of the Property that are important to Buyer as Buyer decides whether to purchase the Property.

2.      Seller states that the information is correct to "Seller's current actual knowledge" as of the date of this form. The term "current actual knowledge" is intended to limit Seller's disclosure only to facts actually known by the Seller and does not include "constructive knowledge" or "common knowledge" or what Seller "should have known" about the Property. The Seller has no duty to inspect the Property when this Disclosure is filled in and signed.

3.      Valuable information may be obtained from various local/state/federal agencies, and other experts may assist Buyer by performing more specific evaluations and inspections of the Property.

4.      Boundaries, location and ownership of fences, driveways, hedges, and similar features of the Property may become the subjects of a dispute between a property owner and a neighbor. A survey may be used to determine the likelihood of such problems.

5.      Whether any item is included or excluded is determined by the contract between Buyer and Seller and not this Seller's Property Disclosure.

6.      Buyer acknowledges that Seller does not warrant that the Property is fit for Buyer's intended purposes or use of the Property. Buyer acknowledges that Seller's indication that an item is "working" is not to be construed as a warranty of its continued operability or as a representation or warranty that such item is fit for Buyer's intended purposes.

7.      Buyer hereby receipts for a copy of this Disclosure.

_____     _____
Buyer                    Date          Buyer                    Date

## ■ SALES AGREEMENT

**LEARNING OBJECTIVE 4**
Describe the purpose and components of the sales agreement between the seller and purchaser of real estate.

**Sales Agreement or Agreement of Sale**
written contract between the seller and the buyer that sets the terms for the purchase and sale of real property

**PRACTICE TIP**

When using forms, caution should be exercised and the form reviewed to be certain it meets the needs of the buyer and seller and, where necessary, clauses are deleted, modified, or added.

**offer to purchase**
the Agreement of Sale, which is prepared by the buyer's agent and presented to the seller

**attorney review period**
a statutory time period during which the buyer and seller may retain the services of an attorney to review the Agreement of Sale

The **Sales Agreement** or **Agreement of Sale** is the written contract between the seller and the buyer that sets the terms for the purchase and sale of real property. As the agreement affects an interest in land, it must be in writing as required by the Statute of Frauds.

All states, through their Board of Realtors, have adopted an Agreement of Sale form to be used when an agent or broker represents either the seller or buyer. The state forms are frequently updated and revised to meet the needs of an ever-changing real estate market. The forms seek to cover every potential issue that can arise from the time the agreement is signed until the property is transferred to the buyer. And because of this thorough coverage, the forms have become so commonplace that they are frequently used in private transactions where no broker or agent is involved. Exhibit 7.5 is a standard Agreement of Sale form for the State of Colorado.

### Offer to Purchase

The drafting of an Agreement of Sale is generally handled by the agent for the buyer. When completed, it is referred to as an **offer to purchase** the real estate, which is presented to the seller.

The agreement is drafted, setting forth the identification of the parties, seller and buyer, the identification of the real estate to be purchased, the purchase price and how it will be paid (including a deposit at the time the agreement is signed by the buyer and an additional deposit due within a certain number of days following the seller accepting the offer to purchase by signing the contract). The terms of financing and the list of inspections the buyer may desire are also included.

This draft of the Agreement of Sale represents the buyer's offer to purchase the property. The buyer's agent or broker will present the offer to the seller's agent or broker. The seller's agent is then obligated to present the offer to the seller.

Rarely does an offer come in with the seller's full list price, and sometimes the conditions and inspections may not be acceptable to the seller. The seller can accept the offer by signing it, and a binding contract for the sale of the real estate is entered. The seller can reject the offer, and the property then stays on the market. More likely, the seller will respond with a counteroffer, changing one or more of the terms the buyer has proposed. Thus begins the negotiations for the purchase of real estate.

In most cases, there will be several counteroffers before the agreement is signed and becomes a binding contract. Each change of terms, no matter how small or insignificant, represents a counteroffer. In addition to the sale price, items that are frequently changed are the settlement date and the seller's obligation, if any, to make corrections or repairs. Once the terms have been settled with the back and forth of offer, counteroffer of seller, and counteroffer of buyer, the agreement will be signed and becomes a binding contract.

Some jurisdictions have an **attorney review period,** which means that both the buyer and the seller have the right to have the agreement reviewed by an attorney within a certain number of days. During that time, the attorney can review and make recommendations to change the terms of the agreement. Those changes must be approved by the other party, just like any other counteroffer.

# Exhibit 7.5 Standard Agreement of Sale form

| | |
|---|---|
| 1 | The printed portions of this form, except differentiated additions, have been approved by the Colorado Real Estate Commission. |
| 2 | (CBS1-10-11) (Mandatory 1-12) |

3

4 **THIS FORM HAS IMPORTANT LEGAL CONSEQUENCES AND THE PARTIES SHOULD CONSULT LEGAL AND TAX OR**
5 **OTHER COUNSEL BEFORE SIGNING.**

6

7 ## CONTRACT TO BUY AND SELL REAL ESTATE
8 ## (RESIDENTIAL)

9

10 Date: _____

11 | **AGREEMENT** |

12 **1.    AGREEMENT.** Buyer, identified in § 2.1, agrees to buy, and Seller, identified in § 2.3, agrees to sell, the Property
13 described below on the terms and conditions set forth in this contract (Contract).

14 **2.    PARTIES AND PROPERTY.**
15     **2.1.    Buyer.** Buyer, _____, will take title to the Property
16 described below as ☐ **Joint Tenants** ☐ **Tenants In Common** ☐ **Other** _____.
17     **2.2.    Assignability and Inurement.** This Contract ☐ **Shall** ☐ **Shall Not** be assignable by Buyer without Seller's prior
18 written consent. Except as so restricted, this Contract shall inure to the benefit of and be binding upon the heirs, personal
19 representatives, successors and assigns of the parties.
20     **2.3.    Seller.** Seller, _____, is the current owner of the
21 Property described below.
22     **2.4.    Property.** The Property is the following legally described real estate in the County of _____, Colorado:
23
24
25
26
27 known as No. _____,
28           Street Address          City          State          Zip

29 together with the interests, easements, rights, benefits, improvements and attached fixtures appurtenant thereto, and all interest of
30 Seller in vacated streets and alleys adjacent thereto, except as herein excluded (Property).
31     **2.5.    Inclusions.** The Purchase Price includes the following items (Inclusions):
32         **2.5.1.    Fixtures.** If attached to the Property on the date of this Contract: lighting, heating, plumbing, ventilating
33 and air conditioning fixtures, TV antennas, inside telephone, network and coaxial (cable) wiring and connecting blocks/jacks,
34 plants, mirrors, floor coverings, intercom systems, built-in kitchen appliances, sprinkler systems and controls, built-in vacuum
35 systems (including accessories), garage door openers including _____ remote controls.
36 **Other Fixtures:**
37
38
39 If any fixtures are attached to the Property after the date of this Contract, such additional fixtures are also included in the Purchase
40 Price.
41         **2.5.2.    Personal Property.** If on the Property whether attached or not on the date of this Contract: storm windows,
42 storm doors, window and porch shades, awnings, blinds, screens, window coverings, curtain rods, drapery rods, fireplace inserts,
43 fireplace screens, fireplace grates, heating stoves, storage sheds, and all keys. If checked, the following are included: ☐ **Water**
44 **Softeners** ☐ **Smoke/Fire Detectors** ☐ **Security Systems** ☐ **Satellite Systems** (including satellite dishes).
45 **Other Personal Property:**
46
47
48         The Personal Property to be conveyed at Closing shall be conveyed by Seller free and clear of all taxes (except
49 personal property taxes for the year of Closing), liens and encumbrances, except _____.
50 Conveyance shall be by bill of sale or other applicable legal instrument.
51         **2.5.3.    Parking and Storage Facilities.** ☐ **Use Only** ☐ **Ownership** of the following parking facilities:
52 _____; and ☐ **Use Only** ☐ **Ownership** of the following storage facilities: _____.

CBS1-10-11.  **CONTRACT TO BUY AND SELL REAL ESTATE (RESIDENTIAL)**                    Page 1 of 15

*(continued)*

# Exhibit 7.5 Continued

53       2.5.4. **Water Rights, Water and Sewer Taps.**
54           2.5.4.1. **Deeded Water Rights.** The following legally described water rights:
55
56
57       Any water rights shall be conveyed by ☐ _____ **Deed** ☐ **Other** applicable legal instrument.
58 ☐       **2.5.4.2. Well Rights.** If any water well is to be transferred to Buyer, Seller agrees to supply required
59 information about such well to Buyer. Buyer understands that if the well to be transferred is a Small Capacity Well or a Domestic
60 Exempt Water Well used for ordinary household purposes, Buyer shall, prior to or at Closing, complete a Change in Ownership
61 form for the well. If an existing well has not been registered with the Colorado Division of Water Resources in the Department of
62 Natural Resources (Division), Buyer shall complete a registration of existing well form for the well and pay the cost of
63 registration. If no person will be providing a closing service in connection with the transaction, Buyer shall file the form with the
64 Division within sixty days after Closing. The Well Permit # is _____.
65       **2.5.4.3.** ☐ **Water Stock Certificates:**
66
67
68       **2.5.4.4.** ☐ **Water Tap**     ☐ **Sewer Tap**
69 **Note: Buyer is advised to obtain, from the provider, written confirmation of the amount remaining to be paid, if any, time**
70 **and other restrictions for transfer and use of the tap.**
71       **2.5.4.5. Other Rights:**
72
73
74     **2.6.**    **Exclusions.** The following items are excluded (Exclusions):
75
76

77 **3. DATES AND DEADLINES.**

| Item No. | Reference | Event | Date or Deadline |
|---|---|---|---|
| 1 | § 4.2 | Alternative Earnest Money Deadline | |
| | | **Title and Association** | |
| 2 | § 7.1 | Record Title Deadline | |
| 3 | § 7.2 | Exceptions Request Deadline | |
| 4 | § 8.1 | Record Title Objection Deadline | |
| 5 | § 8.2 | Off-Record Title Deadline | |
| 6 | § 8.2 | Off-Record Title Objection Deadline | |
| 7 | § 8.3 | Title Resolution Deadline | |
| 8 | § 7.3 | Association Documents Deadline | |
| 9 | § 7.3 | Association Documents Objection Deadline | |
| 10 | § 8.5 | Right of First Refusal Deadline | |
| | | **Seller's Property Disclosure** | |
| 11 | § 10.1 | Seller's Property Disclosure Deadline | |
| | | **Loan and Credit** | |
| 12 | § 5.1 | Loan Application Deadline | |
| 13 | § 5.2 | Loan Conditions Deadline | |
| 14 | § 5.3 | Buyer's Credit Information Deadline | |
| 15 | § 5.3 | Disapproval of Buyer's Credit Information Deadline | |
| 16 | § 5.4 | Existing Loan Documents Deadline | |
| 17 | § 5.4 | Existing Loan Documents Objection Deadline | |
| 18 | § 5.4 | Loan Transfer Approval Deadline | |
| | | **Appraisal** | |
| 19 | § 6.2 | Appraisal Deadline | |
| 20 | § 6.2 | Appraisal Objection Deadline | |
| | | **Survey** | |
| 21 | § 9.1 | Current Survey Deadline | |
| 22 | § 9.2 | Current Survey Objection Deadline | |
| | | **Inspection and Due Diligence** | |
| 23 | § 10.2 | Inspection Objection Deadline | |
| 24 | § 10.3 | Inspection Resolution Deadline | |

# Exhibit 7.5  Continued

| | | | |
|---|---|---|---|
| 25 | § 10.5 | Property Insurance Objection Deadline | |
| 26 | § 10.6 | Due Diligence Documents Delivery Deadline | |
| 27 | § 10.7 | Due Diligence Documents Objection Deadline | |
| | | **Closing and Possession** | |
| 28 | § 12.3 | **Closing Date** | |
| 29 | § 17 | Possession Date | |
| 30 | § 17 | Possession Time | |
| 31 | § 28 | **Acceptance Deadline Date** | |
| 32 | § 28 | **Acceptance Deadline Time** | |
| | | | |
| | | | |

78  **Note: Applicability of Terms.**
79  Any box, blank or line in this Contract left blank or completed with the abbreviation "N/A", or the word "Deleted" means such
80  provision in **Dates and Deadlines** (§ 3), including any deadline, is not applicable and the corresponding provision of this Contract
81  to which reference is made is deleted.

82  The abbreviation "MEC" (mutual execution of this Contract) means the date upon which both parties have signed this Contract.

83  **Note:** If **FHA** or **VA** loan boxes are checked in § 4.5.3 (Loan Limitations), the **Appraisal Deadline** (§ 3) does **Not** apply to **FHA**
84  insured or **VA** guaranteed loans.

85  **4.    PURCHASE PRICE AND TERMS.**
86      **4.1.    Price and Terms.** The Purchase Price set forth below shall be payable in U.S. Dollars by Buyer as follows:

| Item No. | Reference | Item | Amount | Amount |
|---|---|---|---|---|
| 1 | § 4.1 | Purchase Price | $ | |
| 2 | § 4.2 | Earnest Money | | $ |
| 3 | § 4.5 | New Loan | | |
| 4 | § 4.6 | Assumption Balance | | |
| 5 | § 4.7 | Seller or Private Financing | | |
| 6 | | | | |
| 7 | | | | |
| 8 | § 4.3 | Cash at Closing | | |
| 9 | | **TOTAL** | $ | $ |

87      **4.2.    Earnest Money.** The Earnest Money set forth in this section, in the form of _____, shall be
88  payable to and held by _____ (Earnest Money Holder), in its trust account, on behalf of
89  both Seller and Buyer. The Earnest Money deposit shall be tendered with this Contract unless the parties mutually agree to an
90  **Alternative Earnest Money Deadline** (§ 3) for its payment. If Earnest Money Holder is other than the Brokerage Firm identified
91  in § 33 or § 34, Closing Instructions signed by Buyer, Seller and Earnest Money Holder must be obtained on or before delivery of
92  Earnest Money to Earnest Money Holder. The parties authorize delivery of the Earnest Money deposit to the company conducting
93  the Closing (Closing Company), if any, at or before Closing. In the event Earnest Money Holder has agreed to have interest on
94  Earnest Money deposits transferred to a fund established for the purpose of providing affordable housing to Colorado residents,
95  Seller and Buyer acknowledge and agree that any interest accruing on the Earnest Money deposited with the Earnest Money
96  Holder in this transaction shall be transferred to such fund.
97      **4.2.1.    Alternative Earnest Money Deadline.** The deadline for delivering the Earnest Money, if other than at the
98  time of tender of this Contract is as set forth as the **Alternative Earnest Money Deadline** (§ 3).
99      **4.2.2.    Return of Earnest Money.** If Buyer has a Right to Terminate and timely terminates, Buyer shall be
100  entitled to the return of Earnest Money as provided in this Contract. If this Contract is terminated as set forth in § 25 and, except as
101  provided in § 24, if the Earnest Money has not already been returned following receipt of a Notice to Terminate, Seller agrees to
102  execute and return to Buyer or Broker working with Buyer, written mutual instructions, i.e., Earnest Money Release form, within
103  three days of Seller's receipt of such form.
104      **4.3.    Form of Funds; Time of Payment; Funds Available.**
105      **4.3.1.    Good Funds.** All amounts payable by the parties at Closing, including any loan proceeds, Cash at Closing
106  and closing costs, shall be in funds that comply with all applicable Colorado laws, including electronic transfer funds, certified
107  check, savings and loan teller's check and cashier's check (Good Funds).
108      **4.3.2.    Available Funds.** All funds required to be paid at Closing or as otherwise agreed in writing between the
109  parties shall be timely paid to allow disbursement by Closing Company at Closing **OR SUCH PARTY SHALL BE IN DEFAULT**.

*(continued)*

## Exhibit 7.5 Continued

110  Buyer represents that Buyer, as of the date of this Contract, ☐ **Does** ☐ **Does Not** have funds that are immediately verifiable and
111  available in an amount not less than the amount stated as Cash at Closing in § 4.1.
112    **4.4.    Seller Concession.** Seller, at Closing, shall credit, as directed by Buyer, an amount of $_____ to assist
113  with Buyer's closing costs, loan discount points, loan origination fees, prepaid items (including any amounts that Seller agrees to
114  pay because Buyer is not allowed to pay due to FHA, CHFA, VA, etc.), and any other fee, cost, charge, expense or expenditure
115  related to Buyer's New Loan or other allowable Seller concession (collectively, Seller Concession). Seller Concession is in
116  addition to any sum Seller has agreed to pay or credit Buyer elsewhere in this Contract. Seller Concession shall be reduced to the
117  extent it exceeds the amount allowed by Buyer's lender as set forth in the Closing Statement or HUD-1, at Closing.
118    **4.5.    New Loan.**
119        **4.5.1.    Buyer to Pay Loan Costs.** Buyer, except as provided in § 4.4, if applicable, shall timely pay Buyer's loan
120  costs, loan discount points, prepaid items and loan origination fees, as required by lender.
121        **4.5.2.    Buyer May Select Financing.** Buyer may pay in cash or select financing appropriate and acceptable to
122  Buyer, including a different loan than initially sought, except as restricted in § 4.5.3 or § 30 (Additional Provisions).
123        **4.5.3.    Loan Limitations.** Buyer may purchase the Property using any of the following types of loan:
124  ☐ **Conventional** ☐ **FHA** ☐ **VA** ☐ **Bond** ☐ **Other** _____.
125        **4.5.4.    Good Faith Estimate – Monthly Payment and Loan Costs.** Buyer is advised to review the terms, conditions
126  and costs of Buyer's New Loan carefully. If Buyer is applying for a residential loan, the lender generally must provide Buyer with
127  a good faith estimate of Buyer's closing costs within three days after Buyer completes a loan application. Buyer should also obtain
128  an estimate of the amount of Buyer's monthly mortgage payment. If the New Loan is unsatisfactory to Buyer, Buyer shall have the
129  Right to Terminate under § 25.1, on or before **Loan Conditions Deadline** (§ 3).
130    **4.6.    Assumption.** Buyer agrees to assume and pay an existing loan in the approximate amount of the Assumption
131  Balance set forth in § 4.1, presently payable at $_____ per _____ including principal and interest
132  presently at the rate of _____% per annum, and also including escrow for the following as indicated: ☐ **Real Estate Taxes**
133  ☐ **Property Insurance Premium** ☐ **Mortgage Insurance Premium** and ☐ _____.
134    Buyer agrees to pay a loan transfer fee not to exceed $_____. At the time of assumption, the new interest rate shall
135  not exceed _____% per annum and the new payment shall not exceed $_____ per _____ principal and
136  interest, plus escrow, if any. If the actual principal balance of the existing loan at Closing is less than the Assumption Balance,
137  which causes the amount of cash required from Buyer at Closing to be increased by more than $_____, then Buyer shall
138  have the Right to Terminate under § 25.1, on or before **Closing Date** (§ 3), based on the reduced amount of the actual principal
139  balance.
140    Seller ☐ **Shall** ☐ **Shall Not** be released from liability on said loan. If applicable, compliance with the requirements for
141  release from liability shall be evidenced by delivery ☐ **on or before Loan Transfer Approval Deadline** (§ 3) ☐ **at Closing** of
142  an appropriate letter of commitment from lender. Any cost payable for release of liability shall be paid by _____
143  in an amount not to exceed $_____.
144    **4.7.    Seller or Private Financing.** Buyer agrees to execute a promissory note payable to _____,
145  as ☐ **Joint Tenants** ☐ **Tenants In Common** ☐ **Other** _____, on the note form as indicated:
146  ☐ **(Default Rate)** NTD81-10-06 ☐ **Other** _____ secured by a _____
147  (1st, 2nd, etc.) deed of trust encumbering the Property, using the form as indicated:
148  ☐ **Due on Transfer – Strict** (TD72-8-10) ☐ **Due on Transfer – Creditworthy** (TD73-8-10) ☐ **Assumable – Not Due on**
149  **Transfer** (TD74-8-10) ☐ **Other** _____.
150    The promissory note shall be amortized on the basis of _____ ☐ **Years** ☐ **Months**, payable at $_____
151  per _____ including principal and interest at the rate of _____% per annum. Payments shall commence
152  _____ and shall be due on the _____ day of each succeeding _____. If not sooner
153  paid, the balance of principal and accrued interest shall be due and payable _____ after Closing.
154  Payments ☐ **Shall** ☐ **Shall Not** be increased by _____ of estimated annual real estate taxes, and ☐ **Shall** ☐ **Shall**
155  **Not** be increased by _____ of estimated annual property insurance premium. The loan shall also contain the following
156  terms: (1) if any payment is not received within _____ days after its due date, a late charge of _____% of such payment
157  shall be due; (2) interest on lender disbursements under the deed of trust shall be _____% per annum; (3) default interest rate
158  shall be _____% per annum; (4) Buyer may prepay without a penalty except _____;
159  and (5) Buyer ☐ **Shall** ☐ **Shall Not** execute and deliver, at Closing, a Security Agreement and UCC-1 Financing Statement
160  granting the holder of the promissory note a _____ (1st, 2nd, etc.) lien on the personal property included in this sale.
161    Buyer ☐ **Shall** ☐ **Shall Not** provide a mortgagee's title insurance policy, at Buyer's expense.

# Exhibit 7.5 Continued

<table>
<tr><td>162</td><td colspan="2" align="center">**TRANSACTION PROVISIONS**</td></tr>
</table>

163 **5.    FINANCING CONDITIONS AND OBLIGATIONS.**

164    **5.1.    Loan Application.** If Buyer is to pay all or part of the Purchase Price by obtaining one or more new loans (New
165 Loan), or if an existing loan is not to be released at Closing, Buyer, if required by such lender, shall make an application verifiable
166 by such lender, on or before **Loan Application Deadline** (§ 3) and exercise reasonable efforts to obtain such loan or approval.

167    **5.2.    Loan Conditions.** If Buyer is to pay all or part of the Purchase Price with a New Loan, this Contract is conditional
168 upon Buyer determining, in Buyer's sole subjective discretion, whether the New Loan is satisfactory to Buyer, including its
169 availability, payments, interest rate, terms, conditions, and cost of such New Loan. This condition is for the benefit of Buyer.
170 Buyer shall have the Right to Terminate under § 25.1, on or before **Loan Conditions Deadline** (§ 3), if the New Loan is not
171 satisfactory to Buyer, in Buyer's sole subjective discretion. **IF SELLER DOES NOT TIMELY RECEIVE WRITTEN NOTICE**
172 **TO TERMINATE, BUYER'S EARNEST MONEY SHALL BE NONREFUNDABLE,** except as otherwise provided in this
173 Contract (e.g., Appraisal, Title, Survey).

174    **5.3.    Credit Information and Buyer's New Senior Loan.** If Buyer is to pay all or part of the Purchase Price by
175 executing a promissory note in favor of Seller, or if an existing loan is not to be released at Closing, this Contract is conditional
176 (for the benefit of Seller) upon Seller's approval of Buyer's financial ability and creditworthiness, which approval shall be at
177 Seller's sole subjective discretion. In such case: (1) Buyer shall supply to Seller by **Buyer's Credit Information Deadline** (§ 3),
178 at Buyer's expense, information and documents (including a current credit report) concerning Buyer's financial, employment and
179 credit condition and Buyer's New Senior Loan, defined below, if any; (2) Buyer consents that Seller may verify Buyer's financial
180 ability and creditworthiness; (3) any such information and documents received by Seller shall be held by Seller in confidence, and
181 not released to others except to protect Seller's interest in this transaction; and (4) in the event Buyer is to execute a promissory
182 note secured by a deed of trust in favor of Seller, this Contract is conditional (for the benefit of Seller) upon Seller's approval of
183 the terms and conditions of any New Loan to be obtained by Buyer if the deed of trust to Seller is to be subordinate to Buyer's
184 New Loan (Buyer's New Senior Loan). If the Cash at Closing is less than as set forth in § 4.1 of this Contract or Buyer's New
185 Senior Loan changes from that approved by Seller, Seller shall have the Right to Terminate under § 25.1, at or before Closing. If
186 Seller disapproves of Buyer's financial ability, creditworthiness or Buyer's New Senior Loan, in Seller's sole subjective discretion,
187 Seller shall have the Right to Terminate under § 25.1, on or before **Disapproval of Buyer's Credit Information Deadline** (§ 3).

188    **5.4.    Existing Loan Review.** If an existing loan is not to be released at Closing, Seller shall deliver copies of the loan
189 documents (including note, deed of trust, and any modifications) to Buyer by **Existing Loan Documents Deadline** (§ 3). For the
190 benefit of Buyer, this Contract is conditional upon Buyer's review and approval of the provisions of such loan documents. Buyer
191 shall have the Right to Terminate under § 25.1, on or before **Existing Loan Documents Objection Deadline** (§ 3), based on any
192 unsatisfactory provision of such loan documents, in Buyer's sole subjective discretion. If the lender's approval of a transfer of the
193 Property is required, this Contract is conditional upon Buyer's obtaining such approval without change in the terms of such loan,
194 except as set forth in § 4.6. If lender's approval is not obtained by **Loan Transfer Approval Deadline** (§ 3), this Contract shall
195 terminate on such deadline. Seller shall have the Right to Terminate under § 25.1, on or before Closing, in Seller's sole subjective
196 discretion, if Seller is to be released from liability under such existing loan and Buyer does not obtain such compliance as set forth
197 in § 4.6.

198 **6.    APPRAISAL PROVISIONS.**

199    **6.1.    Lender Property Requirements.** If the lender imposes any requirements or repairs (Requirements) to be made to
200 the Property (e.g., roof repair, repainting), beyond those matters already agreed to by Seller in this Contract, Seller shall have the
201 Right to Terminate under § 25.1, (notwithstanding § 10 of this Contract), on or before three days following Seller's receipt of the
202 Requirements, based on any unsatisfactory Requirements, in Seller's sole subjective discretion. Seller's Right to Terminate in this
203 § 6.1 shall not apply if, on or before any termination by Seller pursuant to this § 6.1: (1) the parties enter into a written agreement
204 regarding the Requirements; or (2) the Requirements have been completed; or (3) the satisfaction of the Requirements is waived in
205 writing by Buyer.

206    **6.2.    Appraisal Condition.** The applicable Appraisal provision set forth below shall apply to the respective loan type set
207 forth in § 4.5.3, or if a cash transaction, i.e. no financing, § 6.2.1 shall apply.

208        **6.2.1.    Conventional/Other.** Buyer shall have the sole option and election to terminate this Contract if the
209 Property's valuation is less than the Purchase Price determined by an appraiser engaged on behalf of _____
210 The appraisal shall be received by Buyer or Buyer's lender on or before **Appraisal Deadline** (§ 3). Buyer shall have the Right to
211 Terminate under § 25.1, on or before **Appraisal Objection Deadline** (§ 3), if the Property's valuation is less than the Purchase
212 Price and Seller's receipt of either a copy of such appraisal or written notice from lender that confirms the Property's valuation is
213 less than the Purchase Price.

214        **6.2.2.    FHA.** It is expressly agreed that, notwithstanding any other provisions of this Contract, the Purchaser
215 (Buyer) shall not be obligated to complete the purchase of the Property described herein or to incur any penalty by forfeiture of
216 Earnest Money deposits or otherwise unless the Purchaser (Buyer) has been given in accordance with HUD/FHA or VA
217 requirements a written statement issued by the Federal Housing Commissioner, Department of Veterans Affairs, or a Direct

---

CBS1-10-11.  **CONTRACT TO BUY AND SELL REAL ESTATE (RESIDENTIAL)**                                Page 5 of 15

*(continued)*

# Exhibit 7.5 Continued

218 Endorsement lender, setting forth the appraised value of the Property of not less than $_____. The Purchaser (Buyer)
219 shall have the privilege and option of proceeding with the consummation of this Contract without regard to the amount of the
220 appraised valuation. The appraised valuation is arrived at to determine the maximum mortgage the Department of Housing and
221 Urban Development will insure. HUD does not warrant the value nor the condition of the Property. The Purchaser (Buyer) should
222 satisfy himself/herself that the price and condition of the Property are acceptable.
223       **6.2.3.**    **VA.** It is expressly agreed that, notwithstanding any other provisions of this Contract, the purchaser (Buyer)
224 shall not incur any penalty by forfeiture of Earnest Money or otherwise or be obligated to complete the purchase of the Property
225 described herein, if the Contract Purchase Price or cost exceeds the reasonable value of the Property established by the Department
226 of Veterans Affairs. The purchaser (Buyer) shall, however, have the privilege and option of proceeding with the consummation of
227 this Contract without regard to the amount of the reasonable value established by the Department of Veterans Affairs.
228       **6.3.**    **Cost of Appraisal.** Cost of any appraisal to be obtained after the date of this Contract shall be timely paid by
229 ☐ **Buyer** ☐ **Seller**.

230 **7.**    **EVIDENCE OF TITLE AND ASSOCIATION DOCUMENTS.**
231       **7.1.**    **Evidence of Title.** On or before **Record Title Deadline** (§ 3), Seller shall cause to be furnished to Buyer, at Seller's
232 expense, a current commitment for owner's title insurance policy (Title Commitment) in an amount equal to the Purchase Price, or
233 if this box is checked, ☐ **An Abstract** of title certified to a current date. If title insurance is furnished, Seller shall also deliver to
234 Buyer copies of any abstracts of title covering all or any portion of the Property (Abstract) in Seller's possession. At Seller's
235 expense, Seller shall cause the title insurance policy to be issued and delivered to Buyer as soon as practicable at or after Closing.
236 The title insurance commitment ☐ **Shall** ☐ **Shall Not** commit to delete or insure over the standard exceptions which relate to:
237 (1) parties in possession, (2) unrecorded easements, (3) survey matters, (4) unrecorded mechanics' liens, (5) gap period (effective
238 date of commitment to date deed is recorded), and (6) unpaid taxes, assessments and unredeemed tax sales prior to the year of
239 Closing. Any additional premium expense to obtain this additional coverage shall be paid by ☐ **Buyer** ☐ **Seller**.
240 **Note:** The title insurance company may not agree to delete or insure over any or all of the standard exceptions. Buyer shall have
241 the right to review the Title Commitment, its provisions and Title Documents (defined in § 7.2), and if not satisfactory to Buyer,
242 Buyer may exercise Buyer's rights pursuant to § 8.1.
243       **7.2.**    **Copies of Exceptions.** On or before **Record Title Deadline** (§ 3), Seller, at Seller's expense, shall furnish to Buyer
244 and _____, (1) copies of any plats, declarations, covenants, conditions and restrictions burdening
245 the Property, and (2) if a Title Commitment is required to be furnished, and if this box is checked ☐ **Copies of any Other**
246 **Documents** (or, if illegible, summaries of such documents) listed in the schedule of exceptions (Exceptions). Even if the box is not
247 checked, Seller shall have the obligation to furnish these documents pursuant to this section if requested by Buyer any time on or
248 before **Exceptions Request Deadline** (§ 3). This requirement shall pertain only to documents as shown of record in the office of
249 the clerk and recorder in the county where the Property is located. The Abstract or Title Commitment, together with any copies or
250 summaries of such documents furnished pursuant to this section, constitute the title documents (collectively, Title Documents).
251       **7.3.**    **Homeowners' Association Documents.** The term Association Documents consists of all owners' associations
252 (Association) declarations, bylaws, operating agreements, rules and regulations, party wall agreements, minutes of most recent
253 annual owners' meeting and minutes of any directors' or managers' meetings during the six-month period immediately preceding
254 the date of this Contract, if any (Governing Documents), most recent financial documents consisting of (1) annual balance sheet,
255 (2) annual income and expenditures statement, and (3) annual budget (Financial Documents), if any (collectively, Association
256 Documents).
257       **7.3.1.**    **Common Interest Community Disclosure. THE PROPERTY IS LOCATED WITHIN A COMMON
258 INTEREST COMMUNITY AND IS SUBJECT TO THE DECLARATION FOR SUCH COMMUNITY. THE OWNER
259 OF THE PROPERTY WILL BE REQUIRED TO BE A MEMBER OF THE OWNER'S ASSOCIATION FOR THE
260 COMMUNITY AND WILL BE SUBJECT TO THE BYLAWS AND RULES AND REGULATIONS OF THE
261 ASSOCIATION. THE DECLARATION, BYLAWS, AND RULES AND REGULATIONS WILL IMPOSE FINANCIAL
262 OBLIGATIONS UPON THE OWNER OF THE PROPERTY, INCLUDING AN OBLIGATION TO PAY
263 ASSESSMENTS OF THE ASSOCIATION. IF THE OWNER DOES NOT PAY THESE ASSESSMENTS, THE
264 ASSOCIATION COULD PLACE A LIEN ON THE PROPERTY AND POSSIBLY SELL IT TO PAY THE DEBT. THE
265 DECLARATION, BYLAWS, AND RULES AND REGULATIONS OF THE COMMUNITY MAY PROHIBIT THE
266 OWNER FROM MAKING CHANGES TO THE PROPERTY WITHOUT AN ARCHITECTURAL REVIEW BY THE
267 ASSOCIATION (OR A COMMITTEE OF THE ASSOCIATION) AND THE APPROVAL OF THE ASSOCIATION.
268 PURCHASERS OF PROPERTY WITHIN THE COMMON INTEREST COMMUNITY SHOULD INVESTIGATE THE
269 FINANCIAL OBLIGATIONS OF MEMBERS OF THE ASSOCIATION. PURCHASERS SHOULD CAREFULLY
270 READ THE DECLARATION FOR THE COMMUNITY AND THE BYLAWS AND RULES AND REGULATIONS OF
271 THE ASSOCIATION.**
272       **7.3.2.**    **Association Documents to Buyer.**
273 ☐       **7.3.2.1. Seller to Provide Association Documents.** Seller shall cause the Association Documents to be
274 provided to Buyer, at Seller's expense, on or before **Association Documents Deadline** (§ 3).

# Exhibit 7.5 Continued

275   ☐       **7.3.2.2. Seller Authorizes Association.** Seller authorizes the Association to provide the Association
276 Documents to Buyer, at Seller's expense.
277         **7.3.2.3. Seller's Obligation.** Seller's obligation to provide the Association Documents shall be fulfilled
278 upon Buyer's receipt of the Association Documents, regardless of who provides such documents.
279 **Note:** If neither box in this § 7.3.2 is checked, the provisions of § 7.3.2.1 shall apply.
280       **7.3.3.**   **Conditional on Buyer's Review.** If the box in either § 7.3.2.1 or § 7.3.2.2 is checked, the provisions of this
281 § 7.3.3 shall apply. Buyer shall have the Right to Terminate under § 25.1, on or before **Association Documents Objection**
282 **Deadline** (§ 3), based on any unsatisfactory provision in any of the Association Documents, in Buyer's sole subjective discretion.
283 Should Buyer receive the Association Documents after **Association Documents Deadline** (§ 3), Buyer, at Buyer's option, shall
284 have the Right to Terminate under § 25.1 by Buyer's Notice to Terminate received by Seller on or before ten days after Buyer's
285 receipt of the Association Documents. If Buyer does not receive the Association Documents, or if Buyer's Notice to Terminate
286 would otherwise be required to be received by Seller after **Closing Date** (§ 3), Buyer's Notice to Terminate shall be received by
287 Seller on or before three days prior to **Closing Date** (§ 3). If Seller does not receive Buyer's Notice to Terminate within such time,
288 Buyer accepts the provisions of the Association Documents as satisfactory, and Buyer waives any Right to Terminate under this
289 provision, notwithstanding the provisions of § 8.5.

290 **8.   RECORD TITLE AND OFF-RECORD TITLE MATTERS.**
291     **8.1.**   **Record Title Matters.** Buyer has the right to review and object to any of the Title Documents (Right to Object,
292 Resolution) as set forth in § 8.3. Buyer's objection may be based on any unsatisfactory form or content of Title Commitment,
293 notwithstanding § 13, or any other unsatisfactory title condition, in Buyer's sole subjective discretion. If Buyer objects to any of
294 the Title Documents, Buyer shall cause Seller to receive Buyer's Notice to Terminate or Notice of Title Objection on or before
295 **Record Title Objection Deadline** (§ 3). If Title Documents are not received by Buyer, on or before the **Record Title Deadline**
296 (§ 3), or if there is an endorsement to the Title Commitment that adds a new Exception to title, a copy of the new Exception to title
297 and the modified Title Commitment shall be delivered to Buyer. Buyer shall cause Seller to receive Buyer's Notice to Terminate
298 or Notice of Title Objection on or before ten days after receipt by Buyer of the following documents: (1) any required Title
299 Document not timely received by Buyer, (2) any change to the Title Documents, or (3) endorsement to the Title Commitment. If
300 Seller receives Buyer's Notice to Terminate or Notice of Title Objection, pursuant to this § 8.1 (Record Title Matters), any title
301 objection by Buyer and this Contract shall be governed by the provisions set forth in § 8.3 (Right to Object, Resolution). If Seller
302 does not receive Buyer's Notice to Terminate or Notice of Title Objection by the applicable deadline specified above, Buyer
303 accepts the condition of title as disclosed by the Title Documents as satisfactory.
304     **8.2.**   **Off-Record Title Matters.** Seller shall deliver to Buyer, on or before **Off-Record Title Deadline** (§ 3), true copies
305 of all existing surveys in Seller's possession pertaining to the Property and shall disclose to Buyer all easements, liens (including,
306 without limitation, governmental improvements approved, but not yet installed) or other title matters (including, without
307 limitation, rights of first refusal and options) not shown by public records, of which Seller has actual knowledge. Buyer shall have
308 the right to inspect the Property to investigate if any third party has any right in the Property not shown by public records (such as
309 an unrecorded easement, unrecorded lease, boundary line discrepancy or water rights). Buyer's Notice to Terminate or Notice of
310 Title Objection of any unsatisfactory condition (whether disclosed by Seller or revealed by such inspection, notwithstanding § 13),
311 in Buyer's sole subjective discretion, shall be received by Seller on or before **Off-Record Title Objection Deadline** (§ 3). If Seller
312 receives Buyer's Notice to Terminate or Notice of Title Objection pursuant to this § 8.2 (Off-Record Title Matters), any title
313 objection by Buyer and this Contract shall be governed by the provisions set forth in § 8.3 (Right to Object, Resolution). If Seller
314 does not receive Buyer's Notice to Terminate or Notice of Title Objection, on or before **Off-Record Title Objection Deadline**
315 (§ 3), Buyer accepts title subject to such rights, if any, of third parties of which Buyer has actual knowledge.
316     **8.3.**   **Right to Object, Resolution.** Buyer's right to object to any title matters shall include, but not be limited to those
317 matters set forth in §§ 8.1 (Record Title Matters), 8.2 (Off-Record Title Matters) and 13 (Transfer of Title), in Buyer's sole
318 subjective discretion (collectively, Notice of Title Objection). If Buyer objects to any title matter, on or before the applicable
319 deadline, Buyer shall have the choice to either (1) object to the condition of title, or (2) terminate this Contract.
320       **8.3.1.**   **Title Resolution.** If Seller receives Buyer's Notice of Title Objection, as provided in § 8.1 (Record Title
321 Matters) or § 8.2 (Off-Record Title Matters), on or before the applicable deadline, and if Buyer and Seller have not agreed to a
322 written settlement thereof on or before **Title Resolution Deadline** (§ 3), this Contract shall terminate on the expiration of **Title**
323 **Resolution Deadline** (§ 3), unless Seller receives Buyer's written withdrawal of Buyer's Notice of Title Objection (i.e., Buyer's
324 written notice to waive objection to such items and waives the Right to Terminate for that reason), on or before expiration of **Title**
325 **Resolution Deadline** (§ 3).
326       **8.3.2.**   **Right to Terminate – Title Objection.** Buyer shall have the Right to Terminate under § 25.1, on or
327 before the applicable deadline, based on any unsatisfactory title matter, in Buyer's sole subjective discretion.
328     **8.4.**   **Special Taxing Districts.** SPECIAL TAXING DISTRICTS MAY BE SUBJECT TO GENERAL OBLIGATION
329 INDEBTEDNESS THAT IS PAID BY REVENUES PRODUCED FROM ANNUAL TAX LEVIES ON THE TAXABLE
330 PROPERTY WITHIN SUCH DISTRICTS. PROPERTY OWNERS IN SUCH DISTRICTS MAY BE PLACED AT RISK
331 FOR INCREASED MILL LEVIES AND TAX TO SUPPORT THE SERVICING OF SUCH DEBT WHERE
332 CIRCUMSTANCES ARISE RESULTING IN THE INABILITY OF SUCH A DISTRICT TO DISCHARGE SUCH

---

CBS1-10-11. **CONTRACT TO BUY AND SELL REAL ESTATE (RESIDENTIAL)**          **Page 7 of 15**

*(continued)*

# Exhibit 7.5 Continued

333 INDEBTEDNESS WITHOUT SUCH AN INCREASE IN MILL LEVIES. BUYERS SHOULD INVESTIGATE THE
334 SPECIAL TAXING DISTRICTS IN WHICH THE PROPERTY IS LOCATED BY CONTACTING THE COUNTY
335 TREASURER, BY REVIEWING THE CERTIFICATE OF TAXES DUE FOR THE PROPERTY, AND BY OBTAINING
336 FURTHER INFORMATION FROM THE BOARD OF COUNTY COMMISSIONERS, THE COUNTY CLERK AND
337 RECORDER, OR THE COUNTY ASSESSOR.

338     Buyer shall have the Right to Terminate under § 25.1, on or before **Off-Record Title Objection Deadline** (§ 3), based on
339 any unsatisfactory effect of the Property being located within a special taxing district, in Buyer's sole subjective discretion.

340     **8.5.**   **Right of First Refusal or Contract Approval.** If there is a right of first refusal on the Property, or a right to
341 approve this Contract, Seller shall promptly submit this Contract according to the terms and conditions of such right. If the holder
342 of the right of first refusal exercises such right or the holder of a right to approve disapproves this Contract, this Contract shall
343 terminate. If the right of first refusal is waived explicitly or expires, or the Contract is approved, this Contract shall remain in full
344 force and effect. Seller shall promptly notify Buyer in writing of the foregoing. If expiration or waiver of the right of first refusal
345 or Contract approval has not occurred on or before **Right of First Refusal Deadline** (§ 3), this Contract shall then terminate.

346     **8.6.**   **Title Advisory.** The Title Documents affect the title, ownership and use of the Property and should be reviewed
347 carefully. Additionally, other matters not reflected in the Title Documents may affect the title, ownership and use of the Property,
348 including, without limitation, boundary lines and encroachments, area, zoning, unrecorded easements and claims of easements,
349 leases and other unrecorded agreements, and various laws and governmental regulations concerning land use, development and
350 environmental matters. **The surface estate may be owned separately from the underlying mineral estate, and transfer of the**
351 **surface estate does not necessarily include transfer of the mineral rights or water rights. Third parties may hold interests in**
352 **oil, gas, other minerals, geothermal energy or water on or under the Property, which interests may give them rights to**
353 **enter and use the Property.** Such matters may be excluded from or not covered by the title insurance policy. Buyer is advised to
354 timely consult legal counsel with respect to all such matters as there are strict time limits provided in this Contract [e.g., **Record**
355 **Title Objection Deadline** (§ 3) and **Off-Record Title Objection Deadline** (§ 3)].

356 **9.**   **CURRENT SURVEY REVIEW.**
357     **9.1.**   **Current Survey Conditions.** If the box in § 9.1.1 or § 9.1.2 is checked, Buyer, the issuer of the Title Commitment
358 or the provider of the opinion of title if an abstract, and _____ shall receive a Current Survey, i.e.,
359 Improvement Location Certificate, Improvement Survey Plat or other form of survey set forth in § 9.1.2 (collectively, Current
360 Survey), on or before **Current Survey Deadline** (§ 3). The Current Survey shall be certified by the surveyor to all those who are
361 to receive the Current Survey.

362 ☐     **9.1.1.**   **Improvement Location Certificate.** If the box in this § 9.1.1 is checked, ☐ **Seller** ☐ **Buyer** shall order
363 or provide, and pay, on or before Closing, the cost of an **Improvement Location Certificate**.

364 ☐     **9.1.2.**   **Other Survey.** If the box in this § 9.1.2 is checked, a Current Survey, other than an Improvement Location
365 Certificate, shall be an ☐ **Improvement Survey Plat** ☐ _____. The parties agree that payment of the cost of
366 the Current Survey and obligation to order or provide the Current Survey shall be as follows:

367
368
369

370     **9.2.**   **Survey Objection.** Buyer shall have the right to review and object to the Current Survey. Buyer shall have the Right
371 to Terminate under § 25.1, on or before the **Current Survey Objection Deadline** (§ 3), if the Current Survey is not timely
372 received by Buyer or based on any unsatisfactory matter with the Current Survey, notwithstanding § 8.2 or § 13.

373 **DISCLOSURE, INSPECTION AND DUE DILIGENCE**

374 **10.**   **PROPERTY DISCLOSURE, INSPECTION, INDEMNITY, INSURABILITY, DUE DILIGENCE, BUYER**
375 **DISCLOSURE AND SOURCE OF WATER.**
376     **10.1.**   **Seller's Property Disclosure Deadline.** On or before **Seller's Property Disclosure Deadline** (§ 3), Seller agrees to
377 deliver to Buyer the most current version of the applicable Colorado Real Estate Commission's Seller's Property Disclosure form
378 completed by Seller to Seller's actual knowledge, current as of the date of this Contract.
379     **10.2.**   **Inspection Objection Deadline.** Unless otherwise provided in this Contract, Buyer acknowledges that Seller is
380 conveying the Property to Buyer in an "as is" condition, "where is" and "with all faults". Seller shall disclose to Buyer, in writing,
381 any latent defects actually known by Seller. Buyer, acting in good faith, shall have the right to have inspections (by one or more
382 third parties, personally or both) of the Property and Inclusions (Inspection), at Buyer's expense. If (1) the physical condition of
383 the Property, including, but not limited to, the roof, walls, structural integrity of the Property, the electrical, plumbing, HVAC and
384 other mechanical systems of the Property, (2) the physical condition of the Inclusions, (3) service to the Property (including
385 utilities and communication services), systems and components of the Property, e.g. heating and plumbing, (4) any proposed or
386 existing transportation project, road, street or highway, or (5) any other activity, odor or noise (whether on or off the Property) and

# Exhibit 7.5 Continued

387 its effect or expected effect on the Property or its occupants is unsatisfactory, in Buyer's sole subjective discretion, Buyer shall, on
388 or before **Inspection Objection Deadline** (§ 3):
389    **10.2.1. Notice to Terminate.** Notify Seller in writing that this Contract is terminated; or
390    **10.2.2. Inspection Objection.** Deliver to Seller a written description of any unsatisfactory physical condition that
391 Buyer requires Seller to correct.
392   Buyer shall have the Right to Terminate under § 25.1, on or before **Inspection Objection Deadline** (§ 3), based on any
393 unsatisfactory physical condition of the Property or Inclusions, in Buyer's sole subjective discretion.
394   **10.3. Inspection Resolution Deadline.** If an Inspection Objection is received by Seller, on or before **Inspection
395 Objection Deadline** (§ 3), and if Buyer and Seller have not agreed in writing to a settlement thereof on or before **Inspection
396 Resolution Deadline** (§ 3), this Contract shall terminate on **Inspection Resolution Deadline** (§ 3), unless Seller receives Buyer's
397 written withdrawal of the Inspection Objection before such termination, i.e., on or before expiration of **Inspection Resolution
398 Deadline** (§ 3).
399   **10.4. Damage, Liens and Indemnity.** Buyer, except as otherwise provided in this Contract or other written agreement
400 between the parties, is responsible for payment for all inspections, tests, surveys, engineering reports, or any other work performed
401 at Buyer's request (Work) and shall pay for any damage that occurs to the Property and Inclusions as a result of such Work. Buyer
402 shall not permit claims or liens of any kind against the Property for Work performed on the Property at Buyer's request. Buyer
403 agrees to indemnify, protect and hold Seller harmless from and against any liability, damage, cost or expense incurred by Seller
404 and caused by any such Work, claim, or lien. This indemnity includes Seller's right to recover all costs and expenses incurred by
405 Seller to defend against any such liability, damage, cost or expense, or to enforce this section, including Seller's reasonable
406 attorney fees, legal fees and expenses. The provisions of this section shall survive the termination of this Contract.
407   **10.5. Insurability.** Buyer shall have the right to review and object to the availability, terms and conditions of and
408 premium for property insurance (Property Insurance). Buyer shall have the Right to Terminate under § 25.1, on or before **Property
409 Insurance Objection Deadline** (§ 3), based on any unsatisfactory provision of the Property Insurance, in Buyer's sole subjective
410 discretion.
411   **10.6. Due Diligence Documents.** Seller agrees to deliver copies of the following documents and information pertaining to
412 the Property (Due Diligence Documents) to Buyer on or before **Due Diligence Documents Delivery Deadline** (§ 3) to the extent
413 such Due Diligence Documents exist and are in Seller's possession:
414    **10.6.1.** All current leases, including any amendments or other occupancy agreements, pertaining to the Property
415 (Leases).
416    **10.6.2.** Other documents and information:
417
418
419
420
421
422   **10.7. Due Diligence Documents Conditions.** Buyer shall have the right to review and object to Due Diligence Documents,
423 in Buyer's sole subjective discretion, or Seller's failure to deliver to Buyer all Due Diligence Documents. Buyer shall also have the
424 unilateral right to waive any condition herein.
425    **10.7.1. Due Diligence Documents Objection.** Buyer shall have the Right to Terminate under § 25.1, on or before
426 **Due Diligence Documents Objection Deadline** (§ 3), based on any unsatisfactory matter with the Due Diligence Documents, in
427 Buyer's sole subjective discretion. If, however, Due Diligence Documents are not timely delivered under § 10.6, or if Seller fails
428 to deliver all Due Diligence Documents to Buyer, then Buyer shall have the Right to Terminate under § 25.1 on or before the
429 earlier of ten days after **Due Diligence Documents Objection Deadline** (§ 3) or Closing.
430   **10.8. Buyer Disclosure.** Buyer represents that Buyer ☐ **Does** ☐ **Does Not** need to sell and close a property to complete
431 this transaction.
432 **Note:** Any property sale contingency should appear in **Additional Provisions** (§ 30).
433   **10.9. Source of Potable Water (Residential Land and Residential Improvements Only).** Buyer ☐ **Does** ☐ **Does Not**
434 acknowledge receipt of a copy of Seller's Property Disclosure or Source of Water Addendum disclosing the source of potable water
435 for the Property. Buyer ☐ **Does** ☐ **Does Not** acknowledge receipt of a copy of the current well permit. ☐ There is **No Well**.
436 **Note to Buyer: SOME WATER PROVIDERS RELY, TO VARYING DEGREES, ON NONRENEWABLE GROUND
437 WATER. YOU MAY WISH TO CONTACT YOUR PROVIDER (OR INVESTIGATE THE DESCRIBED SOURCE) TO
438 DETERMINE THE LONG-TERM SUFFICIENCY OF THE PROVIDER'S WATER SUPPLIES.**
439   **10.10. Carbon Monoxide Alarms. Note:** If the improvements on the Property have a fuel-fired heater or appliance, a
440 fireplace, or an attached garage and include one or more rooms lawfully used for sleeping purposes (Bedroom), the parties
441 acknowledge that Colorado law requires that Seller assure the Property has an operational carbon monoxide alarm installed within
442 fifteen feet of the entrance to each Bedroom or in a location as required by the applicable building code.
443   **10.11. Lead-Based Paint.** Unless exempt, if the improvements on the Property include one or more residential dwellings
444 for which a building permit was issued prior to January 1, 1978, this Contract shall be void unless (1) a completed Lead-Based
445 Paint Disclosure (Sales) form is signed by Seller, the required real estate licensees and Buyer, and (2) Seller receives the

---

CBS1-10-11. **CONTRACT TO BUY AND SELL REAL ESTATE (RESIDENTIAL)**          **Page 9 of 15**

*(continued)*

## Exhibit 7.5 Continued

446 completed and fully executed form prior to the time when this Contract is signed by all parties. Buyer acknowledges timely receipt
447 of a completed Lead-Based Paint Disclosure (Sales) form signed by Seller and the real estate licensees.
448     **10.12.**  **Methamphetamine Disclosure.** If Seller knows that methamphetamine was ever manufactured, processed, cooked,
449 disposed of, used or stored at the Property, Seller is required to disclose such fact. No disclosure is required if the Property was
450 remediated in accordance with state standards and other requirements are fulfilled pursuant to § 25-18.5-102, C.R.S. Buyer further
451 acknowledges that Buyer has the right to engage a certified hygienist or industrial hygienist to test whether the Property has ever
452 been used as a methamphetamine laboratory. Buyer shall have the Right to Terminate under § 25.1, upon Seller's receipt of
453 Buyer's written notice to terminate, notwithstanding any other provision of this Contract, based on Buyer's test results that indicate
454 the Property has been contaminated with methamphetamine, but has not been remediated to meet the standards established by rules
455 of the State Board of Health promulgated pursuant to § 25-18.5-102, C.R.S. Buyer shall promptly give written notice to Seller of
456 the results of the test.

457 **11.**  **COLORADO FORECLOSURE PROTECTION ACT.** The Colorado Foreclosure Protection Act (Act) generally applies
458 if: (1) the Property is residential, (2) Seller resides in the Property as Seller's principal residence, (3) Buyer's purpose in purchase
459 of the Property is not to use the Property as Buyer's personal residence, and (4) the Property is in foreclosure or Buyer has notice
460 that any loan secured by the Property is at least thirty days delinquent or in default. If the transaction is a Short Sale transaction
461 and a Short Sale Addendum is part of this Contract, the Act does not apply. Each party is further advised to consult an attorney.

462                                      | **CLOSING PROVISIONS** |

463 **12.**  **CLOSING DOCUMENTS, INSTRUCTIONS AND CLOSING.**
464     **12.1.**  **Closing Documents and Closing Information.** Seller and Buyer shall cooperate with the Closing Company to
465 enable the Closing Company to prepare and deliver documents required for Closing to Buyer and Seller and their designees. If
466 Buyer is obtaining a new loan to purchase the Property, Buyer acknowledges Buyer's lender shall be required to provide the
467 Closing Company in a timely manner all required loan documents and financial information concerning Buyer's new loan. Buyer
468 and Seller will furnish any additional information and documents required by Closing Company that will be necessary to complete
469 this transaction. Buyer and Seller shall sign and complete all customary or reasonably required documents at or before Closing.
470     **12.2.**  **Closing Instructions.** Buyer and Seller agree to execute the Colorado Real Estate Commission's Closing Instructions.
471 Such Closing Instructions ☐ **Are** ☐ **Are Not** executed with this Contract. Upon mutual execution, ☐ **Seller** ☐ **Buyer** shall
472 deliver such Closing Instructions to the Closing Company.
473     **12.3.**  **Closing.** Delivery of deed from Seller to Buyer shall be at closing (Closing). Closing shall be on the date specified
474 as the **Closing Date** (§ 3) or by mutual agreement at an earlier date. The hour and place of Closing shall be as designated
475 by_____.
476     **12.4.**  **Disclosure of Settlement Costs.** Buyer and Seller acknowledge that costs, quality, and extent of service vary
477 between different settlement service providers (e.g., attorneys, lenders, inspectors and title companies).

478 **13.**  **TRANSFER OF TITLE.** Subject to tender of payment at Closing as required herein and compliance by Buyer with the
479 other terms and provisions hereof, Seller shall execute and deliver a good and sufficient _____ deed
480 to Buyer, at Closing, conveying the Property free and clear of all taxes except the general taxes for the year of Closing. Except as
481 provided herein, title shall be conveyed free and clear of all liens, including any governmental liens for special improvements
482 installed as of the date of Buyer's signature hereon, whether assessed or not. Title shall be conveyed subject to:
483     **13.1.**  Those specific Exceptions described by reference to recorded documents as reflected in the Title Documents
484 accepted by Buyer in accordance with **Record Title Matters** (§ 8.1),
485     **13.2.**  Distribution utility easements (including cable TV),
486     **13.3.**  Those specifically described rights of third parties not shown by the public records of which Buyer has actual
487 knowledge and which were accepted by Buyer in accordance with **Off-Record Title Matters** (§ 8.2) and **Current Survey Review**
488 (§ 9),
489     **13.4.**  Inclusion of the Property within any special taxing district, and
490     **13.5.**  Other_____.

491 **14.**  **PAYMENT OF ENCUMBRANCES.** Any encumbrance required to be paid shall be paid at or before Closing from the
492 proceeds of this transaction or from any other source.

493 **15.**  **CLOSING COSTS, CLOSING FEE, ASSOCIATION FEES AND TAXES.**
494     **15.1.**  **Closing Costs.** Buyer and Seller shall pay, in Good Funds, their respective closing costs and all other items required
495 to be paid at Closing, except as otherwise provided herein.
496     **15.2.**  **Closing Services Fee.** The fee for real estate closing services shall be paid at Closing by ☐ **Buyer** ☐ **Seller**
497 ☐ **One-Half by Buyer and One-Half by Seller** ☐ **Other**_____.

# Exhibit 7.5 Continued

| 498 | **15.3.** **Status Letter and Transfer Fees.** Any fees incident to the issuance of Association's statement of assessments
| 499 | (Status Letter) shall be paid by ☐ **Buyer** ☐ **Seller** ☐ **One-Half by Buyer and One-Half by Seller** ☐ **None.** Any transfer
| 500 | fees assessed by the Association including, but not limited to, any record change fee, regardless of name or title of such fee
| 501 | (Association's Transfer Fee) shall be paid by ☐ **Buyer** ☐ **Seller** ☐ **One-Half by Buyer and One-Half by Seller** ☐ **None.**
| 502 | **15.4.** **Local Transfer Tax.** ☐ **The Local Transfer Tax** of _____ % of the Purchase Price shall be paid at Closing by
| 503 | ☐ **Buyer** ☐ **Seller** ☐ **One-Half by Buyer and One-Half by Seller** ☐ **None.**
| 504 | **15.5.** **Private Transfer Fee.** Private transfer fees and other fees due to a transfer of the Property, payable at Closing, such
| 505 | as community association fees, developer fees and foundation fees, shall be paid at Closing by ☐ **Buyer** ☐ **Seller** ☐ **One-Half**
| 506 | **by Buyer and One-Half by Seller** ☐ **None.**
| 507 | **15.6.** **Sales and Use Tax.** Any sales and use tax that may accrue because of this transaction shall be paid when due by
| 508 | ☐ **Buyer** ☐ **Seller** ☐ **One-Half by Buyer and One-Half by Seller** ☐ **None.**

509   **16.** **PRORATIONS.** The following shall be prorated to **Closing Date** (§ 3), except as otherwise provided:
510     **16.1.** **Taxes.** Personal property taxes, if any, special taxing district assessments, if any, and general real estate taxes for the
511   year of Closing, based on ☐ **Taxes for the Calendar Year Immediately Preceding Closing** ☐ **Most Recent Mill Levy and**
512   **Most Recent Assessed Valuation**, adjusted by any applicable qualifying seniors property tax exemption, or ☐ **Other** _____.
513     **16.2.** **Rents.** Rents based on ☐ **Rents Actually Received** ☐ **Accrued**. At Closing, Seller shall transfer or credit to
514   Buyer the security deposits for all Leases assigned, or any remainder after lawful deductions, and notify all tenants in writing of
515   such transfer and of the transferee's name and address. Seller shall assign to Buyer all Leases in effect at Closing and Buyer shall
516   assume Seller's obligations under such Leases.
517     **16.3.** **Association Assessments.** Current regular Association assessments and dues (Association Assessments) paid in
518   advance shall be credited to Seller at Closing. Cash reserves held out of the regular Association Assessments for deferred
519   maintenance by the Association shall not be credited to Seller except as may be otherwise provided by the Governing Documents.
520   Buyer acknowledges that Buyer may be obligated to pay the Association, at Closing, an amount for reserves or working capital.
521   Any special assessment assessed prior to **Closing Date** (§ 3) by the Association shall be the obligation of ☐ **Buyer** ☐ **Seller**.
522   Except however, any special assessment by the Association for improvements that have been installed as of the date of Buyer's
523   signature hereon, whether assessed prior to or after Closing, shall be the obligation of Seller. Seller represents that the Association
524   Assessments are currently payable at $_____ per _____ and that there are no unpaid regular or special
525   assessments against the Property except the current regular assessments and _____. Such
526   assessments are subject to change as provided in the Governing Documents. Seller agrees to promptly request the Association to
527   deliver to Buyer before **Closing Date** (§ 3) a current Status Letter.
528     **16.4.** **Other Prorations.** Water and sewer charges, interest on continuing loan, and _____.
529     **16.5.** **Final Settlement.** Unless otherwise agreed in writing, these prorations shall be final.

530   **17.** **POSSESSION.** Possession of the Property shall be delivered to Buyer on **Possession Date** (§ 3) at **Possession Time** (§ 3),
531   subject to the following Leases or tenancies:
532
533
534     If Seller, after Closing, fails to deliver possession as specified, Seller shall be subject to eviction and shall be additionally
535   liable to Buyer for payment of $_____ per day (or any part of a day notwithstanding § 18.1) from **Possession Date**
536   (§ 3) and **Possession Time** (§ 3) until possession is delivered.
537     Buyer ☐ **Does** ☐ **Does Not** represent that Buyer will occupy the Property as Buyer's principal residence.

538             **GENERAL PROVISIONS**

539   **18.** **DAY; COMPUTATION OF PERIOD OF DAYS, DEADLINE.**
540     **18.1.** **Day.** As used in this Contract, the term "day" shall mean the entire day ending at 11:59 p.m., United States
541   Mountain Time (Standard or Daylight Savings as applicable).
542     **18.2.** **Computation of Period of Days, Deadline.** In computing a period of days, when the ending date is not specified,
543   the first day is excluded and the last day is included, e.g., three days after MEC. If any deadline falls on a Saturday, Sunday or
544   federal or Colorado state holiday (Holiday), such deadline ☐ **Shall** ☐ **Shall Not** be extended to the next day that is not a
545   Saturday, Sunday or Holiday. Should neither box be checked, the deadline shall not be extended.

546   **19.** **CAUSES OF LOSS, INSURANCE; CONDITION OF, DAMAGE TO PROPERTY AND INCLUSIONS AND**
547   **WALK-THROUGH.** Except as otherwise provided in this Contract, the Property, Inclusions or both shall be delivered in the
548   condition existing as of the date of this Contract, ordinary wear and tear excepted.
549     **19.1.** **Causes of Loss, Insurance.** In the event the Property or Inclusions are damaged by fire, other perils or causes of
550   loss prior to Closing in an amount of not more than ten percent of the total Purchase Price (Property Damage), Seller shall be

---

*(continued)*

## Exhibit 7.5 Continued

551 obligated to repair the same before **Closing Date** (§ 3). In the event such damage is not repaired within said time or if the damage
552 exceeds such sum, this Contract may be terminated at the option of Buyer. Buyer shall have the Right to Terminate under § 25.1,
553 on or before **Closing Date** (§ 3), based on any Property Damage not repaired before **Closing Date** (§ 3). Should Buyer elect to
554 carry out this Contract despite such Property Damage, Buyer shall be entitled to a credit at Closing for all insurance proceeds that
555 were received by Seller (but not the Association, if any) resulting from such damage to the Property and Inclusions, plus the
556 amount of any deductible provided for in such insurance policy. Such credit shall not exceed the Purchase Price. In the event Seller
557 has not received such insurance proceeds prior to Closing, the parties may agree to extend the **Closing Date** (§ 3) or, at the option
558 of Buyer, Seller shall assign such proceeds at Closing, plus credit Buyer the amount of any deductible provided for in such
559 insurance policy, but not to exceed the total Purchase Price.
560     **19.2. Damage, Inclusions and Services.** Should any Inclusion or service (including utilities and communication
561 services), systems and components of the Property, e.g., heating or plumbing, fail or be damaged between the date of this Contract
562 and Closing or possession, whichever shall be earlier, then Seller shall be liable for the repair or replacement of such Inclusion,
563 service, system, component or fixture of the Property with a unit of similar size, age and quality, or an equivalent credit, but only
564 to the extent that the maintenance or replacement of such Inclusion, service, system, component or fixture is not the responsibility
565 of the Association, if any, less any insurance proceeds received by Buyer covering such repair or replacement. Seller and Buyer
566 are aware of the existence of pre-owned home warranty programs that may be purchased and may cover the repair or replacement
567 of such Inclusions.
568     **19.3. Condemnation.** In the event Seller receives actual notice prior to Closing that a pending condemnation action may
569 result in a taking of all or part of the Property or Inclusions, Seller shall promptly notify Buyer, in writing, of such condemnation
570 action. Buyer shall have the Right to Terminate under § 25.1, on or before **Closing Date** (§ 3), based on such condemnation action,
571 in Buyer's sole subjective discretion. Should Buyer elect to consummate this Contract despite such diminution of value to the
572 Property and Inclusions, Buyer shall be entitled to a credit at Closing for all condemnation proceeds awarded to Seller for the
573 diminution in the value of the Property or Inclusions but such credit shall not include relocation benefits or expenses, or exceed the
574 Purchase Price.
575     **19.4. Walk-Through and Verification of Condition.** Buyer, upon reasonable notice, shall have the right to walk through
576 the Property prior to Closing to verify that the physical condition of the Property and Inclusions complies with this Contract.

577 **20. RECOMMENDATION OF LEGAL AND TAX COUNSEL.** By signing this document, Buyer and Seller acknowledge
578 that the respective broker has advised that this document has important legal consequences and has recommended the examination
579 of title and consultation with legal and tax or other counsel before signing this Contract.

580 **21. TIME OF ESSENCE, DEFAULT AND REMEDIES.** Time is of the essence hereof. If any note or check received as
581 Earnest Money hereunder or any other payment due hereunder is not paid, honored or tendered when due, or if any obligation
582 hereunder is not performed or waived as herein provided, there shall be the following remedies:
583     **21.1. If Buyer is in Default:**
584 ☐     **21.1.1. Specific Performance.** Seller may elect to treat this Contract as canceled, in which case all Earnest Money
585 (whether or not paid by Buyer) shall be paid to Seller and retained by Seller; and Seller may recover such damages as may be
586 proper; or Seller may elect to treat this Contract as being in full force and effect and Seller shall have the right to specific
587 performance or damages, or both.
588     **21.1.2. Liquidated Damages, Applicable. This § 21.1.2 shall apply <u>unless the box in § 21.1.1. is checked</u>.** All
589 Earnest Money (whether or not paid by Buyer) shall be paid to Seller, and retained by Seller. Both parties shall thereafter be
590 released from all obligations hereunder. It is agreed that the Earnest Money specified in § 4.1 is LIQUIDATED DAMAGES, and
591 not a penalty, which amount the parties agree is fair and reasonable and (except as provided in §§ 10.4, 22, 23 and 24), said
592 payment of Earnest Money shall be SELLER'S SOLE AND ONLY REMEDY for Buyer's failure to perform the obligations of
593 this Contract. Seller expressly waives the remedies of specific performance and additional damages.
594     **21.2. If Seller is in Default:** Buyer may elect to treat this Contract as canceled, in which case all Earnest Money received
595 hereunder shall be returned and Buyer may recover such damages as may be proper, or Buyer may elect to treat this Contract as
596 being in full force and effect and Buyer shall have the right to specific performance or damages, or both.

597 **22. LEGAL FEES, COST AND EXPENSES.** Anything to the contrary herein notwithstanding, in the event of any arbitration
598 or litigation relating to this Contract, prior to or after **Closing Date** (§ 3), the arbitrator or court shall award to the prevailing party
599 all reasonable costs and expenses, including attorney fees, legal fees and expenses.

600 **23. MEDIATION.** If a dispute arises relating to this Contract, prior to or after Closing, and is not resolved, the parties shall first
601 proceed in good faith to submit the matter to mediation. Mediation is a process in which the parties meet with an impartial person
602 who helps to resolve the dispute informally and confidentially. Mediators cannot impose binding decisions. The parties to the
603 dispute must agree, in writing, before any settlement is binding. The parties will jointly appoint an acceptable mediator and will
604 share equally in the cost of such mediation. The mediation, unless otherwise agreed, shall terminate in the event the entire dispute

# Exhibit 7.5 Continued

605  is not resolved within thirty days of the date written notice requesting mediation is delivered by one party to the other at the party's
606  last known address. This section shall not alter any date in this Contract, unless otherwise agreed.

607  **24.   EARNEST MONEY DISPUTE.** Except as otherwise provided herein, Earnest Money Holder shall release the Earnest
608  Money as directed by written mutual instructions, signed by both Buyer and Seller. In the event of any controversy regarding the
609  Earnest Money (notwithstanding any termination of this Contract), Earnest Money Holder shall not be required to take any action.
610  Earnest Money Holder, at its option and sole subjective discretion, may (1) await any proceeding, (2) interplead all parties and
611  deposit Earnest Money into a court of competent jurisdiction and shall recover court costs and reasonable attorney and legal fees,
612  or (3) provide notice to Buyer and Seller that unless Earnest Money Holder receives a copy of the Summons and Complaint or
613  Claim (between Buyer and Seller) containing the case number of the lawsuit (Lawsuit) within one hundred twenty days of Earnest
614  Money Holder's notice to the parties, Earnest Money Holder shall be authorized to return the Earnest Money to Buyer. In the event
615  Earnest Money Holder does receive a copy of the Lawsuit, and has not interpled the monies at the time of any Order, Earnest
616  Money Holder shall disburse the Earnest Money pursuant to the Order of the Court. The parties reaffirm the obligation of
617  **Mediation** (§ 23). The provisions of this § 24 apply only if the Earnest Money Holder is one of the Brokerage Firms named in
618  § 33 or § 34.

619  **25.   TERMINATION.**
620      **25.1.   Right to Terminate.** If a party has a right to terminate, as provided in this Contract (Right to Terminate), the
621  termination shall be effective upon the other party's receipt of a written notice to terminate (Notice to Terminate), provided such
622  written notice was received on or before the applicable deadline specified in this Contract. If the Notice to Terminate is not
623  received on or before the specified deadline, the party with the Right to Terminate shall have accepted the specified matter,
624  document or condition as satisfactory and waived the Right to Terminate under such provision.
625      **25.2.   Effect of Termination.** In the event this Contract is terminated, all Earnest Money received hereunder shall be
626  returned and the parties shall be relieved of all obligations hereunder, subject to §§ 10.4, 22, 23 and 24.

627  **26.   ENTIRE AGREEMENT, MODIFICATION, SURVIVAL.** This Contract, its exhibits and specified addenda, constitute
628  the entire agreement between the parties relating to the subject hereof, and any prior agreements pertaining thereto, whether oral or
629  written, have been merged and integrated into this Contract. No subsequent modification of any of the terms of this Contract shall
630  be valid, binding upon the parties, or enforceable unless made in writing and signed by the parties. Any obligation in this Contract
631  that, by its terms, is intended to be performed after termination or Closing shall survive the same.

632  **27.   NOTICE, DELIVERY, AND CHOICE OF LAW.**
633      **27.1.   Physical Delivery.** All notices must be in writing, except as provided in § 27.2. Any document, including a signed
634  document or notice, from or on behalf of Seller, and delivered to Buyer shall be effective when physically received by Buyer, any
635  signatory on behalf of Buyer, any named individual of Buyer, any representative of Buyer, or Brokerage Firm of Broker working
636  with Buyer (except for delivery, after Closing, of the notice requesting mediation described in § 23) and except as provided in
637  § 27.2. Any document, including a signed document or notice, from or on behalf of Buyer, and delivered to Seller shall be
638  effective when physically received by Seller, any signatory on behalf of Seller, any named individual of Seller, any representative
639  of Seller, or Brokerage Firm of Broker working with Seller (except for delivery, after Closing, of the notice requesting mediation
640  described in § 23) and except as provided in § 27.2.
641      **27.2.   Electronic Delivery.** As an alternative to physical delivery, any document, including any signed document or
642  written notice, may be delivered in electronic form only by the following indicated methods: ☐ **Facsimile** ☐ **Email** ☐ **Internet**
643  ☐ **No Electronic Delivery**. If the box "No Electronic Delivery" is checked, this § 27.2 shall not be applicable and § 27.1 shall
644  govern notice and delivery. Documents with original signatures shall be provided upon request of any party.
645      **27.3.   Choice of Law.** This Contract and all disputes arising hereunder shall be governed by and construed in accordance
646  with the laws of the State of Colorado that would be applicable to Colorado residents who sign a contract in Colorado for property
647  located in Colorado.

648  **28.   NOTICE OF ACCEPTANCE, COUNTERPARTS.** This proposal shall expire unless accepted in writing, by Buyer and
649  Seller, as evidenced by their signatures below, and the offering party receives notice of such acceptance pursuant to § 27 on or
650  before **Acceptance Deadline Date** (§ 3) and **Acceptance Deadline Time** (§ 3). If accepted, this document shall become a contract
651  between Seller and Buyer. A copy of this document may be executed by each party, separately, and when each party has executed
652  a copy thereof, such copies taken together shall be deemed to be a full and complete contract between the parties.

653  **29.   GOOD FAITH.** Buyer and Seller acknowledge that each party has an obligation to act in good faith including, but not
654  limited to, exercising the rights and obligations set forth in the provisions of **Financing Conditions and Obligations** (§ 5),
655  **Record Title and Off-Record Title Matters** (§ 8), **Current Survey Review** (§ 9) and **Property Disclosure, Inspection,**
656  **Indemnity, Insurability, Due Diligence, Buyer Disclosure and Source of Water** (§ 10).

---

CBS1-10-11.  **CONTRACT TO BUY AND SELL REAL ESTATE (RESIDENTIAL)**                                    Page 13 of 15

*(continued)*

**Exhibit 7.5** Continued

657 | ADDITIONAL PROVISIONS AND ATTACHMENTS

658 **30. ADDITIONAL PROVISIONS.** (The following additional provisions have not been approved by the Colorado Real Estate
659 Commission.)
660
661
662
663

664 **31. ATTACHMENTS.** The following are a part of this Contract:
665
666
667
668 **Note:** The following disclosure forms **are attached** but are **not** a part of this Contract:
669
670
671

672 | SIGNATURES

673

Buyer's Name: _____                Buyer's Name: _____

_____                              _____
Buyer's Signature                    Date             Buyer's Signature                    Date

Address: _____                     Address: _____

Phone No.: _____                   Phone No.: _____
Fax No.: _____                     Fax No.: _____
Electronic Address: _____          Electronic Address: _____

674 **[NOTE: If this offer is being countered or rejected, do not sign this document. Refer to § 32]**

Seller's Name: _____               Seller's Name: _____

_____                              _____
Seller's Signature                    Date            Seller's Signature                    Date

Address: _____                     Address: _____

Phone No.: _____                   Phone No.: _____
Fax No.: _____                     Fax No.: _____
Electronic Address: _____          Electronic Address: _____

675

676 **32. COUNTER; REJECTION.** This offer is ☐ **Countered** ☐ **Rejected.**
677 **Initials only of party (Buyer or Seller) who countered or rejected offer** _____

678 | **END OF CONTRACT TO BUY AND SELL REAL ESTATE** |

**33. BROKER'S ACKNOWLEDGMENTS AND COMPENSATION DISCLOSURE.**
(To be completed by Broker working with Buyer)

CBS1-10-11. **CONTRACT TO BUY AND SELL REAL ESTATE (RESIDENTIAL)**                **Page 14 of 15**

# Exhibit 7.5 Continued

Broker ☐ **Does** ☐ **Does Not** acknowledge receipt of Earnest Money deposit and, while not a party to the Contract, agrees to cooperate upon request with any mediation concluded under § 23. Broker agrees that if Brokerage Firm is the Earnest Money Holder and, except as provided in § 24, if the Earnest Money has not already been returned following receipt of a Notice to Terminate or other written notice of termination, Earnest Money Holder shall release the Earnest Money as directed by the written mutual instructions. Such release of Earnest Money shall be made within five days of Earnest Money Holder's receipt of the executed written mutual instructions, provided the Earnest Money check has cleared. Broker agrees that if Earnest Money Holder is other than the Brokerage Firm identified in § 33 or § 34, Closing Instructions signed by Buyer, Seller, and Earnest Money Holder must be obtained on or before delivery of Earnest Money to Earnest Money Holder.

Broker is working with Buyer as a ☐ **Buyer's Agent** ☐ **Seller's Agent** ☐ **Transaction-Broker** in this transaction.
☐ This is a **Change of Status**.

Brokerage Firm's compensation or commission is to be paid by ☐ **Listing Brokerage Firm** ☐ **Buyer** ☐ **Other** _____.

Brokerage Firm's Name: _____
Broker's Name: _____

_____
Broker's Signature                              Date

Address: _____
_____
Phone No.: _____
Fax No.: _____
Electronic Address: _____

## 34. BROKER'S ACKNOWLEDGMENTS AND COMPENSATION DISCLOSURE.
(To be completed by Broker working with Seller)

Broker ☐ **Does** ☐ **Does Not** acknowledge receipt of Earnest Money deposit and, while not a party to the Contract, agrees to cooperate upon request with any mediation concluded under § 23. Broker agrees that if Brokerage Firm is the Earnest Money Holder and, except as provided in § 24, if the Earnest Money has not already been returned following receipt of a Notice to Terminate or other written notice of termination, Earnest Money Holder shall release the Earnest Money as directed by the written mutual instructions. Such release of Earnest Money shall be made within five days of Earnest Money Holder's receipt of the executed written mutual instructions, provided the Earnest Money check has cleared. Broker agrees that if Earnest Money Holder is other than the Brokerage Firm identified in § 33 or § 34, Closing Instructions signed by Buyer, Seller, and Earnest Money Holder must be obtained on or before delivery of Earnest Money to Earnest Money Holder.

Broker is working with Seller as a ☐ **Seller's Agent** ☐ **Buyer's Agent** ☐ **Transaction-Broker** in this transaction.
☐ This is a **Change of Status**.

Brokerage Firm's compensation or commission is to be paid by ☐ **Seller** ☐ **Buyer** ☐ **Other** _____.

Brokerage Firm's Name: _____
Broker's Name: _____

_____
Broker's Signature                              Date

Address: _____
_____
Phone No.: _____
Fax No.: _____
Electronic Address: _____

679

**PRACTICE TIP**

Two things are important for the legal team and the real estate professional:

1. To keep track of deadlines
2. When deadlines are approaching that may not be met, a written addendum to the agreement should be signed by the buyer and seller to extend that deadline.

## Time Being of the Essence

Every contract for the sale of real estate has a provision stating that time is of the essence. In Exhibit 7.5 this is in paragraph 21. This phrase has been interpreted to mean that the times, dates, and deadlines set forth in the contract are essential to fulfilling the terms of the contract. For example, many home purchases are contingent upon the buyer providing evidence of a mortgage commitment from a lender by a particular date. If the buyer fails to provide the notice by the deadline, the contract is terminated unless an agreement to extend the deadline is signed by the seller and buyer, as shown in Exhibit 7.6. The seller is relieved of an obligation to sell the property to the buyer in the case of noncompliance.

## Arbitration Clauses

In the last several decades, there has been a rise in the use of alternative means to resolve contract disputes. Contract disputes for breach of contract—that is, failing to satisfy the terms of the contract—can be brought to court with a lawsuit. Lawsuits can take years before a decision is reached. Lawyers' fees can be costly. The parties may be unable to move forward until the dispute is resolved. In the real estate context, a dispute involving an Agreement of Sale can mean the property cannot be sold until the dispute is resolved—a bad result for the seller and buyer.

**arbitration**
a form of alternate dispute resolution where the parties submit their dispute in an informal manner to a panel of arbitrators who render a decision

In an effort to resolve disputes more quickly, most agreement forms contain an arbitration or mediation clause. **Arbitration** is a form of alternate dispute resolution where the parties submit their dispute in an informal manner to a panel of arbitrators. The arbitrators then issue a decision. This procedure is much faster than resorting to the court system and allows the buyer and seller to move forward—either concluding the sale between them or allowing them to move forward individually, with the seller being able to find a new buyer and the buyer being free to look for another property. The agreement in Exhibit 7.5 contains a mediation clause at paragraph 23. Mediation is another method of alternative dispute resolution, where an independent third party assists the seller and buyer in reaching a resolution of their dispute.

**liquidated damages**
an amount the parties agree is adequate compensation for a breach

Along with the arbitration clause, there may be a clause that limits the damages that can be awarded in the event there is a breach of contract. The **liquidated damages** clause in Exhibit 7.5 appears at paragraph 21.1.2 and limits the seller's damages, usually to the amount of the buyer's deposit money. A liquidated damage clause is used to set an amount the parties agree is adequate for a breach. So when a buyer breaches the terms of the agreement, the buyer will lose his or her deposit money. Where the seller is in breach, the buyer's deposit will be refunded.

## Contingency Clauses

**contingencies**
items that must be satisfied in order for the sale to go forward

Each contract will have a number of **contingencies**; these are items that must be satisfied in order for the sale to go forward. Any contingency that is not satisfied will end the contract. Listed below are common contingencies in most Agreements of Sale.

## Exhibit 7.6 Standard extension agreement form

| | |
|---|---|
| 1 | The printed portions of this form, except differentiated additions, have been approved by the Colorado Real Estate Commission. |
| 2 | (AE41-10-11) (Mandatory 1-12) |

3

4 **THIS FORM HAS IMPORTANT LEGAL CONSEQUENCES AND THE PARTIES SHOULD CONSULT LEGAL AND TAX OR**
5 **OTHER COUNSEL BEFORE SIGNING.**

6

7 AGREEMENT TO AMEND/EXTEND CONTRACT

8

9 Date: _____

10

11 1.   This agreement amends the contract dated _____ (Contract), between _____

12 _____ (Seller), and _____

13 (Buyer), relating to the sale and purchase of the following legally described real estate in the County of _____,

14 Colorado:

15

16

17

18 known as No. _____ (Property).

19       Street Address                    City                    State               Zip

20

21 **NOTE: If the table is omitted, or if any item is left blank or is marked in the "No Change" column, it means no change to**
22 **the corresponding provision of the Contract. If any item is marked in the "Deleted" column, it means that the**
23 **corresponding provision of the Contract to which reference is made is deleted.**

24

25 2.   **§ 3. DATES AND DEADLINES.** [Note: This table may be omitted if inapplicable.]

| Item No. | Reference | Event | Date or Deadline | No Change | Deleted |
|---|---|---|---|---|---|
| 1 | § 4.2 | Alternative Earnest Money Deadline | | | |
| | | **Title and Association Documents** | | | |
| 2 | § 7.1 | Record Title Deadline | | | |
| 3 | § 7.2 | Exceptions Request Deadline | | | |
| 4 | § 8.1 | Record Title Objection Deadline | | | |
| 5 | § 8.2 | Off-Record Title Deadline | | | |
| 6 | § 8.2 | Off-Record Title Objection Deadline | | | |
| 7 | § 8.3 | Title Resolution Deadline | | | |
| 8 | § 7.3 | Association Documents Deadline | | | |
| 9 | § 7.3 | Association Documents Objection Deadline | | | |
| 10 | § 8.5 | Right of First Refusal Deadline | | | |
| | | **Seller's Property Disclosure** | | | |
| 11 | § 10.1 | Seller's Property Disclosure Deadline | | | |
| | | **Loan and Credit** | | | |
| 12 | § 5.1 | Loan Application Deadline | | | |
| 13 | § 5.2 | Loan Conditions Deadline | | | |
| 14 | § 5.3 | Buyer's Credit Information Deadline | | | |
| 15 | § 5.3 | Disapproval of Buyer's Credit Information Deadline | | | |
| 16 | § 5.4 | Existing Loan Documents Deadline | | | |
| 17 | § 5.4 | Existing Loan Documents Objection Deadline | | | |
| 18 | § 5.4 | Loan Transfer Approval Deadline | | | |
| | | **Appraisal** | | | |
| 19 | § 6.2 | Appraisal Deadline | | | |
| 20 | § 6.2 | Appraisal Objection Deadline | | | |
| | | **Survey** | | | |
| 21 | § 9.1 | Current Survey Deadline | | | |
| 22 | § 9.2 | Current Survey Objection Deadline | | | |

AE41-10-11.  **AGREEMENT TO AMEND/EXTEND CONTRACT**                              Page 1 of 2

*(continued)*

## Exhibit 7.6 Continued

| | | | Inspection and Due Diligence | | | |
|---|---|---|---|---|---|---|
| 23 | § 10.2 | | Inspection Objection Deadline | | | |
| 24 | § 10.3 | | Inspection Resolution Deadline | | | |
| 25 | § 10.5 | | Property Insurance Objection Deadline | | | |
| 26 | § 10.6 | | Due Diligence Documents Delivery Deadline | | | |
| 27 | § 10.7 | | Due Diligence Documents Objection Deadline | | | |
| 28 | § 10.8 | | Environmental Inspection Objection Deadline CBS2, 3, 4 | | | |
| 29 | § 10.8 | | ADA Evaluation Objection Deadline CBS2, 3, 4 | | | |
| 30 | § 11.1 | | Tenant Estoppel Statements Deadline CBS2, 3, 4 | | | |
| 31 | § 11.2 | | Tenant Estoppel Statements Objection Deadline CBS2, 3, 4 | | | |
| | | | **Closing and Possession** | | | |
| 32 | § 12.3 | | **Closing Date** | | | |
| 33 | § 17 | | Possession Date | | | |
| 34 | § 17 | | Possession Time | | | |
| | | | | | | |
| | | | | | | |

**3.** Other dates or deadlines set forth in the Contract shall be changed as follows:

**4.** Additional amendments:

All other terms and conditions of the Contract shall remain the same.

This proposal shall expire unless accepted in writing by Seller and Buyer as evidenced by their signatures below and the offering party to this document receives notice of such acceptance on or before _____.

Date          Time

Buyer's Name: _____          Buyer's Name: _____

Buyer's Signature          Date          Buyer's Signature          Date

Seller's Name: _____          Seller's Name: _____

Seller's Signature          Date          Seller's Signature          Date

## Mortgage

The mortgage or financing contingency, paragraphs 4 and 5 in Exhibit 7.5, states that the sale will be completed if the buyer is able to obtain a mortgage with particular terms, such as the amount of the loan and interest rate. If the buyer uses his or her best efforts in applying for the loan but does not qualify, the contract ends and the deposit money is refunded.

## Sale of Another Home

Sometimes a buyer must sell another home to have the money available to purchase the new home. In that event, the agreement will be contingent on the sale of the other home.

## Inspections

Many Agreements of Sale include inspection clauses granting the buyer the right to conduct an inspection of certain components of the property and, if there are any deficiencies, to give the seller the opportunity to correct deficiencies. Inspections can be done to

1. determine the present or past infestation by wood-destroying insects such as termites.
2. determine the presence of radon.
3. determine the drinkability of the water.
4. determine the suitability of the septic sewage system.
5. determine the presence of lead paint.
6. determine the structural integrity of the house.
7. determine the suitability of the mechanical components of the house.

> **PRACTICE TIP**
> Additional inspections may be required depending on local custom, such as testing underground heating oil storage tanks in the eastern portion of the United States.

In each instance, the seller must be provided a copy of the report, such as that shown in Exhibit 7.7, and given a chance to correct the deficiency. If the seller does not agree to correct the deficiency, the buyer may terminate the contract or accept the property as is, without correction or adjustment, or accept a reduction in price.

## Exhibit 7.7 Inspection report for presence of mold

---

**OBSERVATIONS**

At the time of the inspection the subject property exhibited the following notable conditions that merit attention.

**Lower Level Spaces**
Previous water intrusion occurred at the north wall of the property (front) due to suspected drain pipe failure. The pipe has been repaired (according to current tenants).

Air sampling collected by World Inspect Net (not affiliated with Environix) returned showing an airborne spore elevation (Penicillium/Aspergillus, Stachybotrys & Chaetomium).

---

*(continued)*

**Exhibit 7.7** Continued

The Environix inspector noted:

- Visible mold growth on overhead wood surfaces located above drop ceiling tiles (throughout).
- Carpet in place throughout the lower level spaces.
  - Carpets will hold mold spores which will aerosolize when walked on. Cleaning of carpets may not effectively remove spores from the space to acceptable clearance levels.
- There were no areas of current hidden or visible moisture intrusion (checked by Infra-red camera and protimeter moisture meter).

  - Witnessed growths are attributed to:

    - Previous water intrusion events creating elevated humidity condition (positive mold growth and proliferation).
    - Improperly remediatied/removed mold contaminated materials.
      - Improperly cleaned mold growths will leave mold spore concentration in the living spaces until properly removed using HEPA filtration.

# ETHICAL Considerations

## CONFLICT OF INTEREST

For those in the legal profession, representing one client whose interests are directly adverse to the interest of another client is a conflict of interest that should be avoided. The rule is founded on the principle that a person cannot be loyal to two masters with opposing interests. In certain limited circumstances, dual representation is permitted. Both clients must be notified of the existence of a conflict, be advised of and understand the consequences of the attorney representing both clients, and be advised that they may seek representation from another attorney. If after receiving this information the clients still wish to be represented by the same attorney, they must waive the conflict of interest by signing a written document. Lawyers frequently represent unmarried couples who are purchasing real estate. One of the individuals may be the primary wage earner who will be making the monthly mortgage payment; the other may be contributing a large sum of money toward the down payment. In the unhappy circumstance that one of them should die or their relationship should end, how would the property be divided between them? The interests of the unmarried individuals may conflict with one another, and the legal professional must be sensitive to those opposing interests at the time the home is purchased rather than when the unfortunate event occurs. Unmarried couples lack the protections that are afforded married individuals under the intestate and divorce statutes. What is best for the person contributing the down payment will not be best for the person contributing the mortgage payments. Here the lawyer may continue to advise both parties so long as there is notification and a signed waiver of the conflict.

## KEY TERMS

## CHAPTER SUMMARY

| | |
|---|---|
| Introduction to Real Estate Sales | Contracts play a major role in real estate transactions. Most sales of residential real estate are completed with the assistance of a real estate broker. |
| Contract Law | In the typical real estate transaction there are two significant contracts: (1) the listing agreement between a seller and a realtor and (2) the agreement of sale between the seller and the purchaser. |
| Contract | Sometimes called a valid contract, a contract is an enforceable agreement between competent parties, supported by consideration for a lawful purpose. |
| Agreement | Every contract starts with an agreement, an offer, and an acceptance of that specific offer. |
| Consideration | Every contract must be accompanied by consideration. Consideration in contract law is anything of value given in exchange for a promise. |
| Capacity | Contracts in which either or both of the parties lacks capacity are called voidable contracts, because the party claiming a lack of capacity may be able to avoid the contract being enforced against them. Capacity is the legal ability to enter into a contract, including being of legal age, called the age of majority. |
| Legality of Purpose | A contract requires that the object or purpose of the contract must be legal. |
| The Relationship Between the Seller and Broker | A seller typically uses a real estate professional to help market and sell the property and will sign a listing agreement or listing contract. The listing contract is an agency relationship contract between the seller (the principal) and the broker (the agent). |

| Creation of the Agency Relationship | An agency relationship is formed by mutual agreement where one party, the principal, agrees that another, the agent, shall act on his or her behalf, at the principal's direction, and under the principal's control. |
|---|---|
| Dual Agency | When a broker/agent represents both the buyer and seller in a real estate transaction. |
| The Listing Contract | Listing contract gives the broker/agent the right, under agreed terms and conditions, to sell a property in exchange for payment in the form of a sales commission.<br>In an open listing, the seller grants the right to market and sell the property to a number of brokers at the same time.<br>In a flat fee listing, the seller and broker/agent agree to a set compensation amount unrelated to the sale price.<br>In a net listing, the broker/agent earns a commission only on the part of the sales price that exceeds a stated price.<br>In an exclusive agency agreement, the broker is the sole, exclusive agent, with the exclusive right to sell the property. |
| Sellers' Disclosure | A detailed statement prepared by the seller concerning the property and its condition. This type of disclosure form has become common is most states. |
| Sales Agreement | The Sales Agreement or Agreement of Sale is the written contract between the seller and the buyer that sets the terms for the purchase and sale of real property. As the agreement affects an interest in land, it must be in writing as required by the Statute of Frauds. |
| Offer to Purchase | The real estate agent for the buyer will draft an Agreement of Sale which is referred to an offer to purchase real estate. This offer is then delivered to the seller's real estate agent who present the offer to the seller. The seller may accept, reject, or prepare a counteroffer. |
| Time Being of the Essence | Every contract for the sale of real estate has a provision stating that time is of the essence. This phrase has been interpreted to mean that the times, dates, and deadlines set forth in the contract are essential to fulfilling the terms of the contract. |
| Arbitration Clauses | Arbitration is a form of alternate dispute resolution where the parties submit their dispute in an informal manner to a panel of arbitrators. The arbitrators then issue a decision. This procedure is much faster than resorting to the court system. |
| Contingency Clauses | Items that must be satisfied in order for the sale to go forward. Any contingency that is not satisfied will end the contract. Common contingencies in most agreements of sale:<br>Mortgage<br>Sale of another home<br>Inspections |

## REVIEW QUESTIONS AND EXERCISES

1. What are the elements of an agreement between two parties that will form a contract?
2. What is consideration? Must it be financial only?
3. What does it mean to have capacity to enter a contract? Who does not have capacity?
4. What is legality of purpose in the terms of a contract?
5. What is an agency relationship, and who are the parties to an agency relationship?
6. What duties does an agent owe a principal in an agency relationship?
7. What is an exlcusive agency? What is a dual agency?
8. What is a listing contract?
9. Describe the ways in which a real estate sales broker may be compensated.
10. How is the listing price determined in a listing contract?
11. What are the methods of marketing that a real estate agent may utilize?
12. What is a Sellers' Disclosure Statement and what purpose does it serve?
13. Is an offer to purchase the same thing as an Agreement of Sale? If not, how is it different? How is it similar?
14. What does it mean for a contract to say time is of the essence?
15. What is the purpose of an arbitration or mediation clause?
16. What is a contingency? List and describe the contingencies found in the typical agreement of sale.

## VIDEO CASE STUDY

Go to www.pearsonhighered.com/careers to view the following videos.

### Author Introduction to Real Estate Sales
Author video introduction to chapter coverage.

### Seller's Second Meeting with Attorney
Seller meets with attorney to discuss inspection reports related to the contingencies in the agreement of sale

## INTERNET AND TECHNOLOGY EXERCISES

1. Using the Internet, determine what inspections are customarily obtained in your community.
2. Using the Internet, determine whether the local board of realtors will permit use of its forms by non-members. And if not, is there a fee that can be paid to use those forms?

## REAL ESTATE PORTFOLIO EXERCISES

**Real Estate Sales**

**To:** Paralegal Intern
**From:** Charles Hart
**Case Name:** Mrs. Taylor
**Re:** Home Sale

Research the standards or levels of mold and radon that are unacceptable under government guidelines.
Prepare a letter to the buyer's lawyer offering to cover the cost over the first $2,500.

Portfolio items produced:
1. Memo on acceptable limits for radon and mold.
2. Letter to buyers' attorney offering $2,500.00

Go to www.pearsonhighered.com/careers to download instructions.

## LEARNING OBJECTIVES

*Upon completion of this chapter, you should be able to*

1. Describe the purpose of recording statutes.

2. Explain the purpose and steps in a title search.

3. Distinguish between title searching, title abstracting, and title examination.

4. Describe the purpose of the title report.

# Title Searching and Pre-Closing Activities

## CHAPTER 8

## ■ INTRODUCTION TO TITLE SEARCHING AND PRE-CLOSING ACTIVITIES

Before completing a real estate transaction, a search of the public records is performed to confirm that the seller has good tile and that there are no claims against the property or against the proceeds of the sale. The search looks at public records such as mortgages, tax liens, easements, covenants, and judgments. The information is reported in the form of a title report. This report lists any items that impair the rights of the seller to freely transfer the real estate. Any items that appear on the title report that would negatively affect the title must be resolved before settlement can be completed. These items include existing mortgages that must be paid in full, real estate and income taxes that have not been paid, or interests of owners that may not be extinguished, such as marital property rights of divorced spouses.

## ■ PUBLIC RECORDS SYSTEM FOR REAL ESTATE

Each state has a public records system for real estate. A real estate **public records system** is a system for registering documents in a government office for public inspection. Generally, any agreement or document that affects any interest in real estate may be recorded.

The government office for recording may be called Recorder of Deeds, Land Registry Office, or Records Clerk. In many states, there are public records of land

**LEARNING OBJECTIVE 1**
Describe the purpose of recording statutes.

**public records system**
system for registering documents in a government office for public inspection

---

### DIGITAL RESOURCES

Author Introduction to Title Searching.

Buyers' Second Meeting with Attorney.

Sample forms and templates.

**chain of title**
the history of the land ownership

ownership dating to the original founding of the state or original land grant from the king, such as that to William Penn for Pennsylvania in 1681. Maintenance of these public records allows a **chain of title,** or history of the land ownership, to be traced to the original recorded landowners.

Public records recording statutes were implemented as a way of preventing disputes over the rightful ownership of property. Prior to the public record systems, evidence of ownership was by possession of a deed. Without a recording system, an owner could prepare additional deeds and sell the property multiple times to unsuspecting buyers. Without a neutral recording system, each buyer was left to prove that he or she was the first to obtain a deed—the same problem the Statute of Frauds was design to prevent—and the courts had to determine whom to believe. Those with the most power and prestige frequently prevailed over the innocent and uneducated. The public records system was developed to prevent this type of fraud and avoid perjured testimony.

### Race Statute

- Delaware, Louisiana, and North Carolina

### Notice Statute

- Alabama, Arizona, Connecticut, Florida, Illinois, Iowa, Kansas, Kentucky, Maine, Massachusetts, Missouri, New Hampshire, New Mexico, Oklahoma, Rhode Island, South Carolina, Tennessee, Vermont, and West Virginia

### Race-Notice Statute

- Alaska, Arkansas, California, Colorado, District of Columbia, Georgia, Hawaii, Idaho, Indiana, Maryland, Michigan, Minnesota, Mississippi, Montana, Nebraska, Nevada, New Jersey, New York, North Dakota, Ohio (regarding mortgages, OH follows race statute), Oregon, Pennsylvania (regarding mortgages, PA follows race statute), South Dakota, Texas, Utah, Washington, Wisconsin, and Wyoming

*Source:* http://www.legalmatch.com/law-library/article/recording-acts.html

**recording statutes**
statutes that do not require, but strongly encourage, all documents affecting ownership or claims against real estate to be filed in a government office

All 50 states have **recording statutes** that do not require, but strongly encourage, all documents affecting ownership or claims against real estate to be filed in a government office. The filed document is notice to anyone interested in the property of the ownership claim and other claims or liens.

## Methods for Determining Priorities

**pure race system**
method for determining the priority of claims, with the first document recorded for a property given priority over a document filed later

Recording statutes use three methods for determining priorities. A few states use a **pure race system** for determining the priority of claims. In these states, the first to record a document is given priority over other documents of the same type. For example, the first deed recorded for a property is given priority over a later filed deed in establishing ownership, even if the second deed was issued first. Similarly, the first recorded mortgage is given priority over a subsequently filed mortgage. It is quite literally a race to record, often referred to as a "first in time, first in right" rule. For example, if Harry gives a deed to John on Monday and another deed to the same property to Charles on Wednesday, even though

Harry had nothing to give or sell to Charles because he already gave or sold his ownership to John, Charles is the owner *if* he records his deed first.

Other states use a **notice system,** which gives the last **good faith purchaser** priority unless a subsequent good faith purchaser records his or her deed first. A good faith purchaser is one who has no knowledge of any prior conveyances; knowledge can be *constructive* because there are no recorded documents or actual because the purchaser has no firsthand knowledge of any transfers. In the previous example, if Charles knew about the prior deed to John, even if Charles records his deed first, John would be the rightful owner of the real estate because Charles had actual knowledge of the other deed and therefore was not a *good faith purchaser*.

Finally, in **race-notice jurisdictions,** priority is given to the first good faith purchaser to record. Thus, those who fail to record their deeds risk their claim of ownership being defeated.

Compliance with the recording statute is voluntary. There is no requirement that one record a document related to property ownership. With potential loss of ownership as the result, however, it is rare that documents affecting real estate are not recorded.

As public records are open to the public and available for review, it is important for someone acquiring an interest in real estate to conduct a search of the records to confirm that the person transferring the interest is the rightful owner and has not made any other transfers that would impair or limit what will be received.

**notice system**
the last good faith purchaser is given priority unless a subsequent good faith purchaser records a deed first

**good faith purchaser**
one who purchases without actual or constructive knowledge of a prior transfer to another

**race-notice jurisdictions**
priority is given to the first good faith purchaser to record

## ■ TITLE SEARCH

Establishing ownership and any defects in ownership is a vital step in the process of the transfer of real estate interests. A **title search** is the process of searching public records to determine the ownership of a property, claims or liens against the property or the owner, and the existence of any other matters that might affect transfer of **good title,** the ability to convey a good ownership interest. The term **title** is used interchangeably with *ownership*.

**LEARNING OBJECTIVE 2**
Explain the purpose and steps in a title search.

**title search**
the process of searching public records to determine the ownership of a property, claims or liens against the property or the owner, and the existence of any other matters that might affect transfer of good title

### Conducting and Abstracting a Title Search

There are three steps in the title search process:

- conducting and abstracting a title search
- examining the abstract of title
- issuing a report of the results

**Conducting a title search** is the physical process of searching the public records for recorded documents that may affect the title to real estate. A **title abstract** is a written listing of all recorded documents and notices of public record. The abstract lists the document, its type (such as judgments, child support records, death notices, etc.), and in some cases, provides copies of those documents. Typically, the search and abstract are done at the same time by the title searcher, who may be an agent or employee of a title company or a lawyer.

A title search begins with the current owner of the real estate and reviews the previous deeds for prior owners and how they passed title to each

**good title**
the ability to convey a good ownership interest

**title**
used interchangeably with *ownership*

**conducting a title search**
the physical process of searching the public records for recorded documents that may affect the title to real estate

**title abstract**
a written listing of all recorded documents and notices of public record that affect a particular piece of property

subsequent owner in the chain of title. A title search reviews the legal description of the property transferred, to confirm that each prior grantor owned all of the property described. In some cases, the search may go back to the original land grant from the king or the federal government transfer in the westward expansion. In some states, that could mean that title searching would need to be completed for 300 or more years. Recognizing the burden this could be, some states have enacted statutes that create a presumption of valid ownership beginning at a certain date.

In states where there is an active title insurance industry, the title search can be ended when the searcher determines the last insured transfer. A transfer is insured when there is a title insurance policy. **Title insurance** is an insurance policy that insures the ownership of the property as of a particular deed transferring ownership. The title insurance company insures that the title is free and clear of any claims against it and agrees to compensate the owner and any insured mortgage lender for any losses if the title insurance company cannot resolve any claims against the property that existed as of the date of the issue of the policy, usually the settlement or closing date.

**title insurance**
insurance policy that insures the ownership of the property as of a particular deed transferring ownership

A title search is a backwards and forwards process. It begins with the current owner of the real estate and looks back to the former owner. It then looks

# STATUTES DECLARING ALL DEEDS VALID

## Michigan: All deeds executed before February 2, 1861, are valid

### 565.601 Deed executed according to law of place of execution; validity.

Sec. 1. *That all deeds* of lands situated within this state, heretofore or hereafter made without this state, and executed according to the laws of the place where made, and acknowledged to be the free act of the grantor or grantors therein named, before any person authorized to take the acknowledgment of deeds by the laws of the place where executed, or of the laws of the territory or state of Michigan, in force at the date of such acknowledgment, *shall be deemed between the parties thereto, and all persons claiming under or through them, as valid and effectual* to convey the legal estate.

**History:** 1861, Act 21, Imd. Eff. Feb. 2, 1861; CL 1871, 4250; How. 5724; CL 1897, 9048; CL 1915, 11781; CL 1929, 13383; CL 1948, 565.601.

## Ohio: All deeds more that 21 years old are valid

### 5301.07 Validating certain deeds-limitations.

*When any instrument conveying real estate, or any interest therein, is of record for more than twenty-one years in the office of the county recorder* of the county

within this state in which such real estate is situated, and the record shows that there is a defect in such instrument, such instrument and the record thereof shall be cured of such defect and *be effective* in all respects as if such instrument had been legally made, executed, and acknowledged, if such defect is due to any one or more of the following:

(A) Such instrument was not properly witnessed.
(B) Such instrument contained no certificate of acknowledgment.
(C) The certificate of acknowledgment was defective in any respect.

*Any person claiming adversely to such instrument, if not already barred by limitation or otherwise, may, at any time within twenty-one years after the time of recording such instrument, bring proceedings to contest the effect of such instrument.*

This section does not affect any suit brought prior to November 9, 1959 in which the validity of the acknowledgment of any such instrument is drawn in question.

Effective date: 01-10-1961

## Exhibit 8.1  Taylor to Schan Deed

BEING THE SAME PREMISES WHICH FELIX J. KNOWLES AND ANNA F. KNOWLES BY DEED DATED SEPTEMBER 11, 1968, AND RECORDED AT DEED BOOK 1673 PAGE 0949 CONVEYED UNTO ROBERT J. TAYLOR AND MOLLY TAYLOR, IN FEE.

forward from the date the current owner took title to the present for anything recorded that would have been a claim or cloud on the title of the former or current owner—for example, a tax lien that was not satisfied when the transfer to the current owner was made that continues as a lien against the property. The process is repeated of looking back at the transfer to each of the prior owners from the date they obtained title and a search forward for claims or clouds on their title.

For example, in the Taylor–Schan deed (Exhibit 8.1), the Taylors received title from Felix J. and Anna F. Knowles in a deed dated September 11, 1968, and recorded in Deed Book 1673, page 0949.

A search would begin at the time the Taylors took title and come forward to the present time. Then a search would be made of all **predecessors in title** prior to the Taylors—all those who held title to the property in the past. Starting with the Knowleses, the searcher will go back to the date they took title and search forward until September 11, 1968, for any document affecting the real estate. The same process could be followed for each prior owner until the initial land grant from the government to the first owner of the real estate.

The records that must be searched are not limited to ownership or chain of title records. Records must also be searched to uncover any encumbrances, restrictions, covenants, easements, mortgages, judgments, or liens. Each may be recorded in a different book or database or in a different office; for example, judgments may be recorded in the clerk of courts or prothonotary's records, tax liens in the tax claim bureau, and mortgages in a separate volume in the same office as the recorder of deeds.

The act of searching public records is changing as more jurisdictions convert to electronic filing. But not all the needed documents in a chain of title may have been converted from paper to electronic form in every jurisdiction. Searchers still must be able to search both electronic and paper records.

For electronic records, searching the records is similar to any database search using a search engine similar to that shown in Exhibit 8.2. First select the correct data—e.g., deed records, mortgage records, or judgments index. In addition to knowing which database, you must know which public office maintains those electronic records, for it is its database that will be searched. Deed and mortgage records are generally maintained by the recorder of deeds or land registry office. Judgment records are kept in the prothonotary's office or the clerk of courts office. Tax lien records will be found in the tax collector or tax assessor's office. A search is conducted by entering the name and searching for the relevant time period. In the case of the Taylors, *Molly Taylor* would be entered in the database search engine for the clerk's office, and the searcher would look for any judgments entered against her from the date she took title—September 11, 1968, forward to the present date. The same process

**predecessors in title**
all those who held title to the property in the past

### PRACTICE TIP

Check your jurisdiction for a statute declaring ownership valid as of a particular date or for the custom to stop the title search at the last insured transfer.

### PRACTICE TIP

When a property is insured, the deed is usually recorded by the title company and will include the name of the title insurance agent or company and the policy or file number. Where a question about prior claims arise, the title agency or company may be contacted for information and their abstract of title.

## Exhibit 8.2 Public access database search window

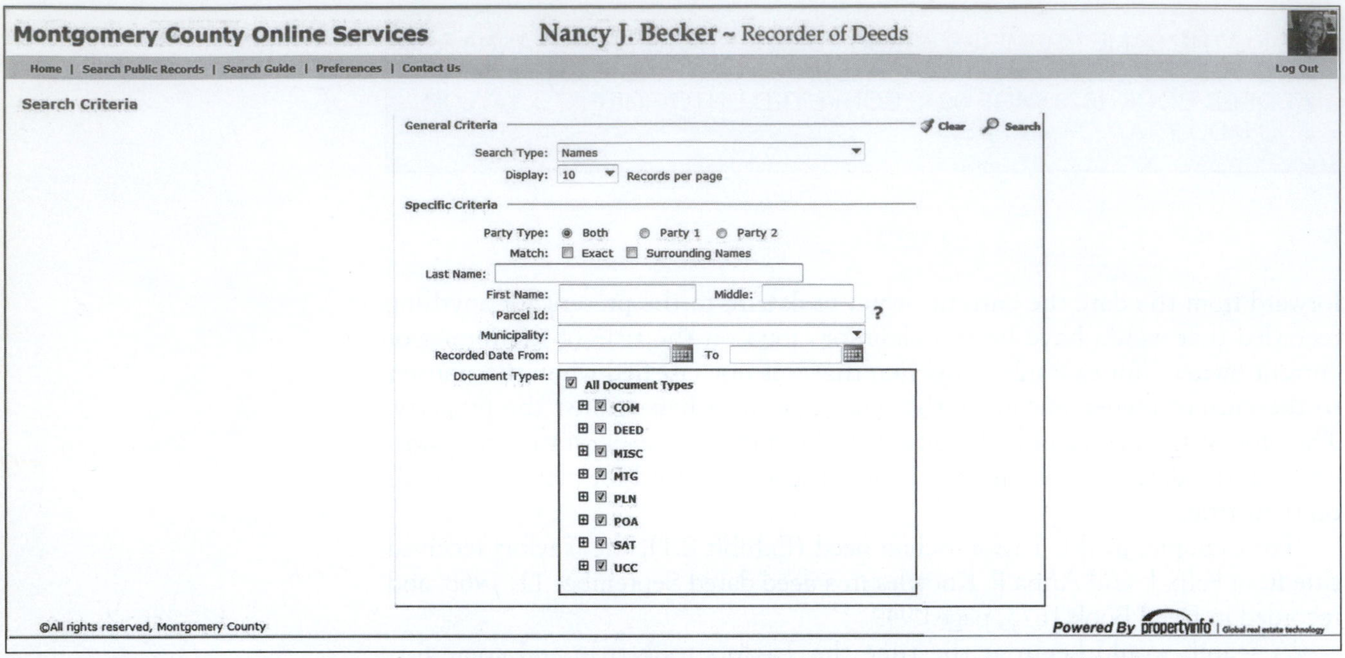


*Source:* Montgomery County Pennsylvania Recorder of Deeds public access service, http://rodviewer.montcopa.org/countyweb/disclaimer.do

### PRACTICE TIP

In jurisdictions where records are maintained electronically, be sure to check the effective date. If you need older records, you will need to check the paper records in addition to the electronic records.

**Grantor/Grantee Index**
the index that shows all documents by grantor name

**Grantee/Grantor Index**
the index that lists all documents by grantee name

would be followed for each database. And in the event that the database only goes back to 1990, the paper records will need to be searched from 1968 through and including 1990. The same process would be followed by a search for *Robert Taylor*.

To search paper records requires a trip to the appropriate location for the documents desired—generally the recorder of deeds office. For paper records, each deed is recorded in two places: the **Grantor/Grantee Index** and the **Grantee/Grantor Index**. The grantor is the one who has transferred property, and theirs is the name searched for in the Grantor/Grantee Index, which lists all documents by grantor name. The grantee is the person who has received an interest in property, and theirs is the name searched for the in Grantee/Grantor Index, which lists all document by grantee name. These two sets of books are maintained to ease some of the burden of the paper search. Once you determine the identity of an owner and the relevant time frame, the searcher is only concerned with transfers made by that individual—that is, transfers where that person was the grantor. By using the grantor index, the searcher knows that any document listed represents some transfer or creation of an interest in real estate.

To find the name of the prior owners, the index showing the current seller as the grantee must be searched for the person, the grantor, who transferred the property to that seller. The indexes are arranged by year or years so that all the deeds for a particular year, say 1989 or the years 1987–89, are in the same volume.

In our example above for the Taylors, the deed they received will appear in the grantor index under the names of Knowles. In the grantee index, the transfer will be located under the name Taylor. Each entry will give the names, the date of the transfer, the property address, and the book and page or electronic reference where the deed is recorded. Using the date of the transfer, the searcher will search the grantor index and look in each index for each year going forward to the present time for any transfer made by the Taylors as grantors. If they have made a transfer, their names will appear, the information will be noted for the title abstract, and, if needed, a copy of the document will be obtained or copied from the deed book. The searcher will look for any easements or other agreements related to the property. It is important to check legal descriptions to be certain that documents are related to the property being searched. For example, the Taylors could own another property that they transferred and that would not impact the title on the property in question.

Deeds can contain more than just the transfer of the property from the seller to the buyer. A deed can contain an easement, a restriction, or a covenant, all of which could affect the ownership of the property and would be noted in the abstract of title. And where the easement, covenant, or restriction is not in the original deed, copies of the other documents would be obtained for the title examination.

The Register of Wills office is searched to determine whether any of the present or prior owners died while they held title. If so, there may be outstanding claims of heirs, beneficiaries, or state or federal estate or inheritance taxes that could represent a lien on the real estate.

Mortgages and judgments must be paid or satisfied for good title to exist. Mortgage and judgment records follow the same method of grantor/grantee indexes and must be searched in the same manner as ownership records.

## Common Search Areas

The most common searches that will need to be conducted with regard to judgments and liens include the following.

**Mortgages** are the documents that use real property as collateral to secure the repayment of a loan. The *Direct Mortgage Index*, usually found in a land records office, is arranged in the same manner as the grantor/grantee index and is searched to find mortgages created by the owner of the property, which must be **satisfied**—paid in full—and marked in the records. The existence of any mortgage and any information regarding its satisfaction will be included in the abstract.

**mortgages**
documents that use real property as collateral to secure the repayment of a loan

**satisfied**
paid in full

**Judgments** are usually the result of a lawsuit with a monetary award being entered in favor of one of the parties. The judgment, when filed in the appropriate office, represents a lien against all real estate owned by the judgment debtor and therefore must be paid in full to transfer good title. The clerk of courts or the Prothonotary's Office maintains a judgment index. A judgment may appear in the judgment index, as follows:

**judgments**
monetary awards entered in favor of one of the parties to a lawsuit

| Defendant | Plaintiff | Court | Term | No. | Atty. | Date | Amount |
|---|---|---|---|---|---|---|---|
| Taylor, Robert | Robinson | 1 | J.58 | 1478 | Smith | 06/09/85 | $2,000 |

If the judgment has been paid, or otherwise satisfied, that fact and its date would be noted on the record in some fashion. Otherwise, the judgment should be noted in the abstract and a copy obtained.

**Federal taxes liens** are judgments obtained by the federal government for unpaid income taxes. They are filed in a separate index in the office of the clerk

**federal taxes liens**
judgments obtained by the federal government for unpaid income taxes

of courts or prothonotary. This index is arranged in the same manner as the judgment index and must be checked. Any listing against a prior owner should be noted in the abstract.

**local real estate taxes and municipal charges**
unpaid taxes and charges that represent a lien against a property

**Local real estate taxes and municipal charges** that are unpaid represent a lien against a property. These records may be maintained in the clerk of courts office or a separate office for the taxing or municipal authority, such as water and sewer authority.

For each of these records, the same search process will be followed. Starting with the date the owners took title and going forward to the present, the searcher looks for any time a mortgage was created or a judgment filed. This information is added to the abstract and, where possible, copies obtained. The process of searching is repeated for each predecessor in title, to determine that there are no outstanding mortgages or liens that remain unsatisfied. Exhibit 8.3 is a Title Abstract Worksheet that contains space for writing down information as it is obtained in the searching process. This would include names, dates, and the location where recorded documents can be found. A notation would be included to indicate which documents have been copied and attached to the abstract.

## Examining a Title Search Abstract

**LEARNING OBJECTIVE 3**
Distinguish between title searching, title abstracting, and title examination.

**title examination**
the process by which someone reviews the chain of title shown in the abstract and all the documents that have been recorded to determine which of those items negatively impact the seller's ability to give good title

Examining a title search abstract, or **title examination,** is the process by which someone reviews the chain of title shown in the abstract and all the documents that have been recorded, to determine what, if any, item represents an impediment to the seller's ownership and therefore being able to give the buyer good title. The title examiner must:

- Review the title abstract, which includes all documents affecting the title to the property.
- Examine each document, including the deeds, mortgages, liens, judgments, easements, plat books, maps, contracts, and agreements, in order to verify the legal description, ownership, existence of restrictions, covenants, easements, mortgages, and judgments.
- Review each restriction, covenant, and easement, determining if they negatively impact title or limit property use.
- Review each mortgage, judgment, and lien, determining whether they have been satisfied and, if not, whether they negatively impact title.

The final step for the examiner is to issue a summary report that lists any matters that negatively impact title and the ability of the seller to transfer good title. This can be a separate report that lists only those items that impact the title, or it can be the title abstract worksheet with items crossed out that are not applicable and items highlighted that are. The remaining or highlighted items are those that will appear in the title report.

## Title Report

**title report**
a summary report that describes ownership, identifies anything impacting that ownership, and lists items that might affect the ability to give good title

**LEARNING OBJECTIVE 4**
Describe the purpose of the title report.

From the report of the title examiner, a title report will be issued. A **title report** is a summary report that provides a legal description of the real estate, describes how the sellers acquired ownership, identifies anything impacting that ownership, and lists items that might affect the ability to give good title to the buyer. In essence, the title report lists any clouds on the title. The typical matters that will appear are mortgages that must be paid off at closing, certification that there are no unpaid taxes or municipal charges that would represent a lien on the title,

## Exhibit 8.3  Title Abstract Worksheet

**DATASEARCH**
PEOPLE.PARTNERS.PIONEERS

**TITLE ABSTRACT WORKSHEET**
Copy Costs: $_____     Report Fee: $_____

**DSI Report Number:** _____

**Address:**_____  **Verified with County?**  Yes   No

**County:** _____  **County Land Records Thru Date:**  _____/_____/_____

**Judgment Records Thru Date:**  _____/_____/_____

---

**DEED INFO**

**Deed Type (Circle One):**  Quit Claim - Tax - Sheriff - Trustee - Warranty - Probate/Estate - Other

**Current Owner:**_____

_____

**Prior Owner):**_____

**Dated:** _____/_____/_____  **Recorded:** _____/_____/_____  **BK:**_____  **PG:**_____  **Instr:**_____

**Tenancy:** T/E - T/C - J/T - Sole - H/W     **(Circle if Applies)**  Survivorship - No Survivorship - Life Estate/Interest

**% of Interest:** _____     First Right of Refusal - Missing Interest

---

**TAX INFO**

**Taxed (Circle One):**  Annual - Biannual - Quarterly - Winter/Summer - Other _____

**Tax / Parcel Number:** _____  Map: _____  District: _____

| Year/Period | Amount | Status (Circle) | Due | Paid | Thru |
|---|---|---|---|---|---|
| _____ | $_____ | Paid - Due - Open - Del | ___/___/___ | ___/___/___ | ___/___/___ |
| _____ | $_____ | Paid - Due - Open - Del | ___/___/___ | ___/___/___ | ___/___/___ |
| _____ | $_____ | Paid - Due - Open - Del | ___/___/___ | ___/___/___ | ___/___/___ |
| _____ | $_____ | Paid - Due - Open - Del | ___/___/___ | ___/___/___ | ___/___/___ |

**Delinquent Tax Year(s):** _____  **Amount(s):** _____

| Other Tax Type | Amount | Status (Circle) | Notes |
|---|---|---|---|
| _____ | $_____ | Paid - Due - Open - Del | _____ |
| _____ | $_____ | Paid - Due - Open - Del | _____ |

**Did you search for Tax Sales?**  Yes   No     **Did you search for delinquent taxes?**  Yes   No

**Manufactured Home?**  Yes   No     **If Yes**, taxed as     Real / Personal Property.

Assessed Value: Land:_____  Improvements:_____  Total: _____

---

**ENCUMBRANCES**

Type: _____  Dated: _____/_____/_____  Recorded: _____/_____/_____

BK:_____  PG:_____  Instr:_____  Amount: $ _____

To: _____

Trustee: _____

Signed: All Parties on Deed - Prior Owner - Other:_____

Assignment: _____

Notice of Default/Foreclosure?  Yes   No     Circle if applicable: Equity Line - Line of Credit - Open Ended

ARE THERE ADDITIONAL ENCUMBRANCES?  YES _____ (SEE ADDITIONAL SHEET)     NO _____

---

**LIENS**

**ARE THERE JUDGMENTS?**  YES _____ (SEE ADDITIONAL SHEET)     NO - JUDGMENTS ARE CLEAR _____

**ESTATE/PROBATE INFORMATION:** YES _____ (SEE ADDITIONAL SHEET) NO _____

**OUT CONVEYANCES:** YES _____ (SEE ADDITIONAL SHEET)  NO _____

**Page _____ of _____**

Web: www.data-search.com • E-Mail: titles@data-search.com • Voice: (800) 817-7730 • Fax: (800) 270-6619

*(continued)*

**Exhibit 8.3** Continued

# DATASEARCH
PEOPLE.PARTNERS.PIONEERS

DSI Report Number: _____

**ADDITIONAL ENCUMBRANCE INFORMATION**

Type: _____ Dated: ____/____/____ Recorded: ____/____/____

BK:_____ PG:_____ Instr:_____ Amount: $ _____

To: _____

Trustee: _____

Signed: All Parties on Deed - Prior Owner - Other:_____

Assignment: _____

Notice of Default/Foreclosure?  Yes   No        Circle if applicable: Equity Line  -  Line of Credit  -  Open Ended

Type: _____ Dated: ____/____/____ Recorded: ____/____/____

BK:_____ PG:_____ Instr:_____ Amount: $ _____

To: _____

Trustee: _____

Signed: All Parties on Deed - Prior Owner - Other:_____

Assignment: _____

Notice of Default/Foreclosure?  Yes   No        Circle if applicable: Equity Line  -  Line of Credit  -  Open Ended

Type: _____ Dated: ____/____/____ Recorded: ____/____/____

BK:_____ PG:_____ Instr:_____ Amount: $ _____

To: _____

Trustee: _____

Signed: All Parties on Deed - Prior Owner - Other:_____

Assignment: _____

Notice of Default/Foreclosure?  Yes   No        Circle if applicable: Equity Line  -  Line of Credit  -  Open Ended

Type: _____ Dated: ____/____/____ Recorded: ____/____/____

BK:_____ PG:_____ Instr:_____ Amount: $ _____

To: _____

Trustee: _____

Signed: All Parties on Deed - Prior Owner - Other:_____

Assignment: _____

Notice of Default/Foreclosure?  Yes   No        Circle if applicable: Equity Line  -  Line of Credit  -  Open Ended

Notes:

ARE THERE ADDITIONAL ENCUMBRANCES?   YES _____ (SEE ADDITIONAL SHEET)        NO _____

**Page _____ of _____**

## Exhibit 8.3  Continued

---

# DATASEARCH
PEOPLE.PARTNERS.PIONEERS

**DSI Report Number:** _____

### JUDGMENT / LIEN INFORMATION

Type: _____  Dated: ____/____/____  Recorded: ____/____/____

Docket:_____  Page:_____  Case #:_____  Amount: $ _____

Plaintiff:_____

Attorney:_____

Defendant:_____

Address: _____  Other Info:_____

Court Filed In:_____  Pending:  Yes   No

---

Type: _____  Dated: ____/____/____  Recorded: ____/____/____

Docket:_____  Page:_____  Case #:_____  Amount: $ _____

Plaintiff:_____

Attorney:_____

Defendant:_____

Address: _____  Other Info:_____

Court Filed In:_____  Pending:  Yes   No

---

Type: _____  Dated: ____/____/____  Recorded: ____/____/____

Docket:_____  Page:_____  Case #:_____  Amount: $ _____

Plaintiff:_____

Attorney:_____

Defendant:_____

Address: _____  Other Info:_____

Court Filed In:_____  Pending:  Yes   No

---

Type: _____  Dated: ____/____/____  Recorded: ____/____/____

Docket:_____  Page:_____  Case #:_____  Amount: $ _____

Plaintiff:_____

Attorney:_____

Defendant:_____

Address: _____  Other Info:_____

Court Filed In:_____  Pending:  Yes   No

---

Notes:




ARE THERE ADDITIONAL JUDGEMENTS / LIENS?   YES _____  (SEE ADDITIONAL SHEET)      NO _____

Page _____ of _____

Web: www.data-search.com • E-Mail: titles@data-search.com • Voice: (800) 817-7730 • Fax: (800) 270-6619

*(continued)*

## Exhibit 8.3 Continued

# DATASEARCH
PEOPLE.PARTNERS.PIONEERS

**DSI Report Number:** _____

**PROBATE / ESTATE INFORMATION**

Decedent:_____ Date of Death:____/____/____ Estate Closed: Yes  No

Died Intestate - No Will Found: _____  Executor of Estate:_____

Book: _____ Page: _____ Dated: ____/____/____ Recorded: ____/____/____

| Heir / Devisee | Relation | Heir / Devisee | Relation |
|---|---|---|---|
| _____ | _____ | _____ | _____ |
| _____ | _____ | _____ | _____ |
| _____ | _____ | _____ | _____ |

Notes:_____
_____
_____

Decedent:_____ Date of Death:____/____/____ Estate Closed: Yes  No

Died Intestate - No Will Found: _____  Executor of Estate:_____

Book: _____ Page: _____ Dated: ____/____/____ Recorded: ____/____/____

| Heir / Devisee | Relation | Heir / Devisee | Relation |
|---|---|---|---|
| _____ | _____ | _____ | _____ |
| _____ | _____ | _____ | _____ |
| _____ | _____ | _____ | _____ |

Notes:_____
_____
_____

**OUT SALES / OUT CONVEYANCES**

Book:_____ Page:_____ Instr#:_____ Dated: ____/____/____ Recorded: ____/____/____

From: _____

To:_____

Description of Parcel conveyed: _____

Book:_____ Page:_____ Instr#:_____ Dated: ____/____/____ Recorded: ____/____/____

From: _____

To:_____

Description of Parcel conveyed: _____

Book:_____ Page:_____ Instr#:_____ Dated: ____/____/____ Recorded: ____/____/____

From: _____

To:_____

Description of Parcel conveyed: _____

**Page _____ of _____**

Web: www.data-search.com • E-Mail: titles@data-search.com • Voice: (800) 817-7730 • Fax: (800) 270-6619

## Exhibit 8.3 Continued

# DATASEARCH
PEOPLE.PARTNERS.PIONEERS

**DSI Report Number:** _____

**CHAIN OF TITLE**

**Deed Type (Circle One):** Quit Claim - Tax - Sheriff - Trustee - Warranty - Probate/Estate - Other

Book:_____ Page:_____ Instr#:_____ Dated: ____/____/____ Recorded: ____/____/____

Grantee: _____

Grantor:_____

Legal Description same as current deed: Yes   No       If no, explain:_____

All interests accounted for: Yes   No       If no, explain: _____

Notes:_____

_____

**Deed Type (Circle One):** Quit Claim - Tax - Sheriff - Trustee - Warranty - Probate/Estate - Other

Book:_____ Page:_____ Instr#:_____ Dated: ____/____/____ Recorded: ____/____/____

Grantee: _____

Grantor:_____

Legal Description same as current deed: Yes   No       If no, explain:_____

All interests accounted for: Yes   No       If no, explain: _____

Notes:_____

_____

**Deed Type (Circle One):** Quit Claim - Tax - Sheriff - Trustee - Warranty - Probate/Estate - Other

Book:_____ Page:_____ Instr#:_____ Dated: ____/____/____ Recorded: ____/____/____

Grantee: _____

Grantor:_____

Legal Description same as current deed: Yes   No       If no, explain:_____

All interests accounted for: Yes   No       If no, explain: _____

Notes:_____

_____

**Deed Type (Circle One):** Quit Claim - Tax - Sheriff - Trustee - Warranty - Probate/Estate - Other

Book:_____ Page:_____ Instr#:_____ Dated: ____/____/____ Recorded: ____/____/____

Grantee: _____

Grantor:_____

Legal Description same as current deed: Yes   No       If no, explain:_____

All interests accounted for: Yes   No       If no, explain: _____

Notes:_____

_____

Page _____ of _____

Web: www.data-search.com • E-Mail: titles@data-search.com • Voice: (800) 817-7730 • Fax: (800) 270-6619

and confirmation related to the marital status of the parties. The existence of easements, restrictions, and covenants will be disclosed, and copies of those documents will be attached to the report, unless they are too large for copying. In the latter case, a notation will be made that they are available for review. In cases where one of the owners has died, there will be questions related to the death of that person: proof of death by way of an original death certificate being presented to the title company and payments of estate and inheritance taxes.

In states where there is an active title insurance industry, the title report represents a **binder for title insurance,** an agreement that the title company insurer will issue title insurance if certain items, or objections, are resolved. The objections are the items that represent potential clouds on the title, such as mortgages and unpaid municipal taxes. Exhibit 8.4 is Schedule A from a title report and lists the standard objections related to the identity of the seller.

Each of the items that appears in the title report must be cleared in order for the seller to be able to transfer good title.

**binder for title insurance**
an agreement that the title company insurer will issue title insurance if certain objections are resolved

**Exhibit 8.4** Schedule A from a title report

| American Land Title Association | Owner's Policy Adopted 6-17-06 |
|---|---|

### SCHEDULE A

Name and Address of Title Insurance Company: Newtown Title Company
1415 Parc Ave

[File No.: 201322200]　　　　　Policy No.: 20130025

Address Reference: 489 Jefferson Street, Newtown

Amount of Insurance: $308,000 [Premium: $ 1933]

Date of Policy: April 30, 2013　　　　　[at 11:59 a.m./p.m.]

1. Name of Insured: Daniel and Sara Schan
2. The estate or interest in the Land that is insured by this policy is: Fee simple
3. Title is vested in: Molly Taylor
4. The Land referred to in this policy is described as follows: See Schedule A Legal Description

AMERICAN
LAND TITLE
ASSOCIATION

*Source:* http://www.positivelyminnesota.com/Government/Shovel_Ready_Site_Certification/PDFs/Supporting_Documents/Title_Commitment.pdf

# ETHICAL Considerations

## DILIGENCE

Under the Model Rules of Professional Conduct, a lawyer, as well as all members of the legal team, is required to act with "diligence and promptness." This rule seeks to avoid procrastination and delay in representing a client's interest. From investigating the client's claim to filing a lawsuit on behalf of the client, the legal team must act without unnecessary delay. With regard to real estate transactions, failure to be prompt and diligent can be fatal when it comes to filing documents that impact an interest in real estate. Failure to promptly file under the Recording Statutes would violate the ethical duty and potentially impact the client's interests.

See the Model Rules of Professional Conduct at www.abanet.org/cpr

## KEY TERMS

Public records system   161
Chain of title   162
Recording statutes   162
Pure race system   162
Conducting a title search   163
Good faith purchaser   163
Notice system   163
Race-notice jurisdiction   163
Title search   163

Title   163
Good title   163
Title abstract   163
Title insurance   164
Claim or cloud   165
Predecessors in title   165
Grantor/Grantee Index   166
Grantee/Grantor Index   166
Satisfied   167

Mortgages   167
Judgments   167
Federal tax liens   167
Local real estate taxes and municipal charges   168
Title examination   168
Title report   168
Objections   174
Binder for title insurance   174

## CHAPTER SUMMARY

| | |
|---|---|
| Introduction to Title Searching and Pre-Closing Activities | Before completing a real estate transaction, a search of the public records is performed to confirm that the seller has good title and that there are no claims against the property or against the proceeds of the sale. |
| Public Records System for Real Estate | Each state has a public records system for real estate. A real estate public records system is a system for registering documents in a government office for public inspection. Generally, any agreement or document that affects any interest in real estate may be recorded. |
| Methods for Determining Priorities | A pure race system is one in which the first to record a document is given priority.<br>A notice system gives the last good faith purchaser priority unless a subsequent good faith purchaser records a deed first. In race-notice jurisdictions, priority is given to the first good faith purchaser to record. |

| | |
|---|---|
| Title Search | A title search is the process of searching public records to determine the ownership of a property, claims or liens against the property or the owner, and the existence of any other matters that might affect transfer of good title, the ability to convey a good ownership interest. |
| Conducting and Abstracting a Title Search | Conducting a title search is the physical process of searching the public records for recorded documents that may affect the title to real estate. <br><br> A title abstract is a written listing of all recorded documents and notices of public record. <br><br> The records that must be searched are not limited to ownership or chain of title records. Records must also be searched to uncover any encumbrances, restrictions, covenants, easements, mortgages, judgments, or liens. |
| Common Search Areas | Mortgages are the documents that use the real property as collateral to secure the repayment of a loan. <br><br> Judgments are usually the result of a lawsuit with a monetary award being entered in favor of one of the parties. <br><br> Federal taxes liens are judgments obtained by the federal government for unpaid income taxes. <br><br> Local real estate taxes and municipal charges that are unpaid represent a lien against a property. |
| Examining a Title Search Abstract | Title examination is the process by which someone reviews the chain of title shown in the abstract and all the documents that have been recorded, to determine what, if any, item represents an impediment to the seller's ownership and therefore being able to give the buyer good title. |
| Title Report | A title report is a summary report that provides a legal description of the real estate, describes how the sellers acquired ownership, identifies anything impacting that ownership, and lists items that might affect the ability to give good title to the buyer. |

## REVIEW QUESTIONS AND EXERCISES

1. What is the benefit of maintaining a public record system?
2. Define and describe the difference between race, notice, and race-notice systems.
3. Distinguish between actual and constructive notice, and give an example of each.
4. What is the purpose of title searching?
5. How is a title search a forward and backward process?
6. Is it necessary to search public records back to the original land grant from the government? Why?
7. What is a title abstract and how is it related to a title search?
8. What is a title examination and how is it different from a title search? How is it different from a title abstract?
9. What is a cloud on the title? How does a cloud on title impact the seller's ability to transfer "good title"?
10. What are predecessors in title?
11. What is a title report and what role does it play in the real estate transaction?

## VIDEO CASE STUDY

Go to www.pearsonhighered.com/careers to view the following videos.

### Author Introduction to Title Searching
Author video introduction to chapter coverage.

### Buyers' Second Meeting With Attorney

Buyer meets with attorney to review discuss options related to correction of radon and mold findings in inspection reports.

## INTERNET AND TECHNOLOGY EXERCISES

1. Use the Internet to determine whether your jurisdiction is a race, notice, or race-notice jurisdiction for the purposes of recording documents in the public record system for real estate.

2. Using the Internet, determine how far back a title search must be conducted in your jurisdiction.

## REAL ESTATE PORTFOLIO EXERCISES

**Title Searching and Pre-Closing Activities**

**To:** Paralegal Intern
**From:** Paul Saunders
**Case Name:** Mr. & Mrs. Schan
**Re:** Home Purchase

Prepare a letter requesting the seller remediate the mold and radon issues as suggested, subject to a re-inspection.

Portfolio item produced:
Letter to seller's attorney requesting seller remediate the mold and radon as suggested, subject to re-inspection

Go to www.pearsonhighered.com/careers to download instructions.

## LEARNING OBJECTIVES

*Upon completion of this chapter, you should be able to*

1. Describe the steps in the mortgage lending process.

2. Explain the different types of mortgage loans and the benefits of each.

# Residential Real Estate Loan Process

## ■ INTRODUCTION TO THE REAL ESTATE LOAN PROCESS

Most buyers require a mortgage to pay for the purchase of real estate. The process may begin with the buyer seeking a pre-approval to determine the mortgage amount for which they qualify. Armed with this information, the buyer can determine the price range of affordable real estate. The loan application process begins with completion of the Uniform Residential Loan Application. Based on review of the loan application, the lender may also require supporting information such as a credit report, a letter of explanation for anything unusual in the credit history, and employment confirmation.

The lender will obtain an independent appraisal to determine the value of the real estate being purchased. Many lenders will not lend more than 80 percent of this value. Lenders use two tools to evaluate the risk of being repaid: the buyers' creditworthiness and the value of the real estate.

## ■ THE MORTGAGE LENDING PROCESS

The cost of purchasing real estate can be in the hundreds of thousands of dollars. The purchase of a home is, for most individuals, the most significant purchase made during their lifetime. Given the cost, it is rare that a purchaser will have sufficient resources to pay cash to complete the purchase, requiring most buyers to borrow funds for this purpose.

**LEARNING OBJECTIVE 1**
Describe the steps in the mortgage lending process.

### DIGITAL RESOURCES

Author Introduction to Residential Real Estate Loan Process.

Sample forms and templates.

**mortgage lending or real estate financing**
the process of borrowing funds to purchase real estate

**Mortgage lending** or **real estate financing** is the process of borrowing funds to purchase real estate. With mortgage financing, the home being purchased is used as collateral to secure repayment of the loan. The mortgage lending process has three phases that culminate in the loan approval: pre-qualification, loan application, and loan qualification.

## Pre-Qualification

**pre-qualification**
determining a potential buyer's financial ability to borrow funds to purchase real estate

The buyers' **pre-qualification** is an effort by real estate professionals and lenders to screen potential buyers to determine their financial ability to purchase real estate. Pre-qualification establishes the loan amount a buyer will likely qualify for when making a formal application for a mortgage. The amount a buyer can borrow will determine the price range of housing the buyer can afford. Real estate agents use a form like the one that appears in Exhibit 9.1 to ascertain information on a buyer's assets and income.

A real estate broker or agent will try to pre-qualify a buyer to determine what they can afford, to avoid wasting time showing properties that they will not be able to qualify to buy. From the buyer's financial information, the real estate agent looks at the assets, liabilities, and income to determine the potential down payment and the maximum monthly mortgage payment the buyer can pay. The down payment will be based on a percentage of the home's value. The rule of thumb is that a down payment should be at least 5 percent of the purchase price, but preferably 20 percent. If the buyer has $15,000 in savings, that would be the equivalent to a 5 percent down payment on a $300,000 house and a 20 percent down payment on a $75,000 house.

**income-to-housing expense ratio**
compares gross monthly income to estimated housing expense

**housing expense**
includes monthly mortgage payment, real estate taxes, and insurance

There is a significant range of purchasing power between $75,000 and $300,000, which can be narrowed by determining the monthly loan payment the buyer can afford. This calculation is estimated based on an **income-to-housing expense ratio**, which compares gross monthly income to estimated housing expense. **Housing expense** includes monthly mortgage payment, real estate taxes, and insurance and, under the real estate agent's rule of thumb, should be less than 40 percent of income. If the buyer has a gross income of $50,000.00 per year, or $4,166.67 per month, then the monthly housing cost should be $1,666 ($4,166 × 40%) or less. From here the real estate professional will consult a mortgage rate and payment chart such as that in Exhibit 9.2, which shows the monthly payment of interest and principal required for a $100,000 loan for a 15-year and a 30-year term. If the current interest rate is 5 percent, the maximum the buyers could afford is a monthly payment for a $300,000 loan, of $1,610 (the monthly amount for a 30-year $100,000 loan at 5% times 3, or $536.82 × 3 = $1,610). This is the mortgage payment only and does not include taxes and insurance, which must be added to calculate the actual monthly housing cost. The real estate professional will feel confident of a potential sale when showing the buyer homes in the price range that the buyer will be able to afford.

Pre-qualification by lenders has become a standard in real estate markets that are active, where there are more buyers competing to purchase fewer properties. The lender pre-qualification process follows many of the same general rules but is more detailed and results in a pre-qualification letter issued to the buyer. The letter states that the lender has reviewed the financial information of the buyer to determine a loan amount the buyer will qualify for under that lender's requirements. Armed with this letter, the buyer is a more desirable

**Exhibit 9.1** Buyer's Financial Information

## BUYER'S FINANCIAL INFORMATION

**BFI**

This form recommended and approved for, but not restricted to use by, the members of the Pennsylvania Association of REALTORS® (PAR).

1 BUYER 1 _____

2 ADDRESS _____

3 _____

4 BUYER 2 _____

5 ADDRESS _____

6 _____

7

8

9 **The following information is requested to determine the buyer's financial ability to purchase the property.**

10

11 1. Will you occupy the premises?  ☐ Yes  ☐ No

12 2. Have you in the last 7 years declared bankruptcy, suffered foreclosure, had an account for collection action, had a history of late pay-

13  ments, or had any legal action affecting ability to finance?  ☐ Yes  ☐ No

14  If yes, explain. _____

15 3. Is any part of purchase price or settlement costs being obtained from a source other than shown below?  ☐ Yes  ☐ No

16  If yes, explain. _____

17 4. Have you at any time on or since January 1, 1998, been obligated to pay support under an order that is on record in any Pennsylvania

18  county?  ☐ Yes  ☐ No

19  If yes, list the county and the Domestic Relations File or Docket Number: _____

20 5. Are there any arrearages for alimony or child/spousal support due in this, or any other, jurisdiction?  ☐ Yes  ☐ No

21  If yes, explain: _____

22

23 **For a purchase involving mortgage financing, disclose at least a minimum net worth of liquid assets in the amount of the down**

24 **payment plus settlement costs. For cash sales, disclose at least a minimum amount equal to the purchase price plus settlement**

25 **costs.**

26

27 **ASSETS (Bank accounts, stocks, etc.)**  **BUYER 1**  **BUYER 2**

28

| | BUYER 1 | BUYER 2 |
|---|---|---|
| 29 | $ _____ | $ _____ |
| 30 | $ _____ | $ _____ |
| 31 | $ _____ | $ _____ |
| 32 | $ _____ | $ _____ |
| 33 | $ _____ | $ _____ |
| 34 | TOTAL $ _____ | $ _____ |

35

36 **The information in this section must be provided if Buyer(s) require a mortgage loan.**

37

38 **LIABILITIES (list all liabilities,**  **BUYER 1**  **BUYER 2**

39 **including alimony or child/spousal support, if any)**  Balance  Per Month  Balance  Per Month

| | Balance | Per Month | Balance | Per Month |
|---|---|---|---|---|
| 40 | $ _____ | $ _____ | $ _____ | $ _____ |
| 41 | $ _____ | $ _____ | $ _____ | $ _____ |
| 42 | $ _____ | $ _____ | $ _____ | $ _____ |
| 43 | $ _____ | $ _____ | $ _____ | $ _____ |
| 44 | $ _____ | $ _____ | $ _____ | $ _____ |
| 45 TOTAL | $ _____ | $ _____ | $ _____ | $ _____ |

46

47 **Real Estate Currently Owned** (First Property)     **Real Estate Currently Owned** (Second Property)

48

49 Address _____     Address _____

50

51 Value $ _____  Mo. Payment $ _____     Value $ _____  Mo. Payment $ _____

52 Mortgage/Equity Loan Balance $ _____     Mortgage/Equity Loan Balance $ _____

53

54 **Buyer Initials:** _____ / _____     BFI Page 1 of 2

**Pennsylvania Association of REALTORS®**

*(continued)*

## Exhibit 9.1 Continued

55 The information in this section must be provided if Buyer(s) require a mortgage loan, but only to the extent necessary to prove
56 the ability to qualify for the mortgage loan.

57

58 **EMPLOYMENT INFORMATION -- BUYER 1**     **EMPLOYMENT INFORMATION -- BUYER 2**

59

60 Current Employer: _____     Current Employer: _____
61 Address: _____     Address: _____
62 _____     _____
63 Occupation: _____     Occupation: _____
64 Years at job: _____     Years at job: _____

65

66 Prior Employer: _____     Prior Employer: _____
67 Address: _____     Address: _____
68 _____     _____
69 Occupation: _____     Occupation: _____
70 Years at job: _____     Years at job: _____

71

72 **ANNUAL INCOME**          **BUYER 1**     **ANNUAL INCOME**          **BUYER 2**

73

74 Basic Salary          $ _____     Basic Salary          $ _____
75 Overtime          $ _____     Overtime          $ _____
76 Bonuses          $ _____     Bonuses          $ _____
77 Commissions          $ _____     Commissions          $ _____
78 Dividends          $ _____     Dividends          $ _____
79 Interest          $ _____     Interest          $ _____
80 _____          $ _____     _____          $ _____
81 _____          $ _____     _____          $ _____
82 TOTAL $ _____     TOTAL $ _____
83 **COMBINED TOTAL INCOME $** _____

84

85 ADDITIONAL  INFORMATION: _____
86 _____
87 _____
88 _____
89 _____

90 Buyer(s) affirm that the above information is true and correct.  Buyer(s) understand that the information may be used as a basis for
91 the acceptance or rejection of an offer by the seller.  Buyer(s) further understand that the information may be provided to a lender in
92 conjunction with the placement of a mortgage loan.  Buyer(s) acknowledge that failure to provide truthful and correct information
93 may result in the forfeiture of any deposits made by Buyer(s) and may subject Buyer(s) to other financial loss or penalties.

94 ☐ If checked, Buyer(s) expressly authorize and direct _____
95 (Broker)  acting as ☐ Broker for Seller  ☐ Broker for Buyer   ☐ Transaction Licensee, to obtain any information or
96 reports from a credit reporting agency including, but not limited to consumer reports, credit reports, criminal histo-
97 ry reports, judgments of record and verification of employment and salary history deemed necessary for furthering
98 the completion of this and any related transactions, and for the evaluation of the information provided by Buyer(s).
99 Upon signing this form, Buyer(s) agree to provide their social security number(s) to the broker identified above for the
100 purposes of obtaining such reports and information.

101 Buyer(s) expressly authorize Broker to provide the information contained in this form and any reports or information obtained by
102 Broker for the purposes stated above, to the seller(s), cooperating broker(s), mortgage broker(s) and lender(s) involved in this trans-
103 action or any related transaction.  BUYER(S) UNDERSTAND THAT BROKER HAS NO CONTROL OVER THE USE OF ANY
104 INFORMATION AFTER IT IS DISCLOSED TO A THIRD PARTY; BUYER(S) AGREE TO RELEASE AND HOLD BROKER
105 HARMLESS FROM ANY AND ALL LIABILITY FOR ANY MISUSE OR SUBSEQUENT DISCLOSURE BY ANY THIRD PARTY
106 OF THE INFORMATION OR REPORTS DISCLOSED BY BROKER PURSUANT TO THE TERMS OF THIS AUTHORIZATION.

107

108 Buyers' signatures serve as an acknowledgement of receipt of a copy of this financial information sheet.

109

110 **BUYER**_____ **DATE** _____
111 **BUYER**_____ **DATE** _____
112 **BUYER**_____ **DATE** _____

**BFI Page 2 of 2**

**Exhibit 9.2** Monthly mortgage payment chart for $100,000 loan

| Rate | 15 Years | 30 Years |
|------|----------|----------|
| 4.0% | $739.69 | $477.42 |
| 4.5% | 764.99 | 506.90 |
| 5.0% | 790.79 | 536.82 |
| 5.5% | 817.08 | 567.79 |
| 6.0% | 843.86 | 599.55 |
| 6.5% | 871.11 | 632.07 |
| 7.0 % | 898.83 | 665.31 |

purchaser. When a seller considers offers from two potential buyers, the one who has the pre-approval letter is more likely to qualify for the mortgage financing required to purchase a home, making that a more attractive offer. The lender's rules in reviewing the financial ability of the buyer are dictated by federal, state, and local lending standards and practices. Most loans are backed through federal government agencies and therefore are subject to federal lending standards that change over time. In recent years, the federal programs have become more stringent, making it difficult for buyers to qualify for loans. The real estate professional's rule of thumb calculations may say that the buyer would qualify for a $300,000 loan, while the federal standards and lender's standards may be entirely different. Lenders are more conservative because of the potential long-term relationship with the borrower and the concern about repayment. Real estate agents are more concerned with the short-term sale. When the lender calculates the **income-to-debt ratio,** the lender includes all monthly debt obligations such as credit cards, car loans, and student loans. These will be combined with the housing expense to determine the loan amount for which the buyer can qualify. The lender's more conservative ratio requirement may be 40 percent for the total income-to-debt ratio and 30 percent for the income-to-housing expense ratio. This is significantly different from the real estate agent's calculation. With the hypothetical buyer having a gross monthly income of $4,166, the *total debt* at 40 percent must not exceed $1,667, and the housing expense at 30 percent should be less than $1,249. That would result in the buyer qualifying for a $200,000 mortgage with a monthly payment of $1,073.64 ($536.82 × 2). Combined with the down payment, the buyer should be looking for housing in the $200,000 to $225,000 price range.

The lender pre-qualification is more rigorous and precise using the most current lending standards and practices, making its pre-qualification letter more accurate. Exhibit 9.3 is a lender's pre-qualification letter.

**WEB EXPLORATION**
Use the link below to calculate the mortgage payment for a specific loan amount and interest rate.
http://homes.yahoo.com/calculators/payment.html

## Loan Application

Once the buyer has found the desired property and the Agreement of Sale contract has been accepted by the seller, the formal mortgage loan application process can begin. The process begins with a meeting with a mortgage lender or

**Exhibit 9.3** Lender's pre-approval letter

January 27, 2013

Bryan and Kerry McNamara
2500 Spring Road
Apartment #D202
OldeCity, Any State

Dear Bryan and Kerry,
We are pleased to notify you that your application for a mortgage pre-approval has been approved. This approval is based on a purchase price of $350,000.00 and a conventional loan amount of $280,000.00 under prevailing rates and terms. This pre-approval is issued based on your current credit history, income, assets and debt assuming that there are no changes in your financial situation. This pre-approval should not be considered a commitment to lend until the following conditions are met:

(X) A valid sales contract is ratified on a property;
(X) A satisfactory appraisal is accomplished on such property;
(X) You select a mortgage program, which causes your mortgage payment to fall within the preapproved amount;
(X) A rate commitment is issued by our company under the above-referenced mortgage program.

We wish you luck in the home buying process, and we thank you for choosing National Bank & Trust Company for your mortgage transaction.

Sincerely,

*National Bank & Trust*

Note: This pre-approval only valid for loan originated with National Bank & Trust.
   This pre-approval expires 60 dates from the date hereof.
   This pre-approval is invalid should a change in the credit report or employment of the borrower occur.

**borrower authorization or release**
written permission to obtain confirmation of the information disclosed in the application

**good faith estimate of closing costs**
statement of the costs required to be paid in conjunction with obtaining a loan

**truth-in-lending disclosure statement**
a statement of the effective or annual percentage rate (APR) of the loan, taking into account the costs of the loan

broker, during which a final loan application is completed, typically using the Uniform Residential Loan Application shown in Exhibit 9.4.

The application is very detailed in seeking information about the borrower and any co-borrower, the type of loan requested, and the property being purchased. Information is also required on employment history, sources of income, assets, and liabilities for each borrower.

As part of the loan application process, certain additional forms and disclosures may be required for submission with the application. The lenders will ask for a **borrower authorization** or **borrower release** that will permit the lender to obtain confirmation of the information disclosed in the application, such as employment and copies of tax returns.

Under federal regulations, lenders must provide the borrowers with a **Good Faith Estimate of Closing Costs** and a **Truth-in-Lending Disclosure Statement** for the potential loan, to allow the borrower to compare different loans and lenders. The example of a good faith estimate of closing costs shown in Exhibit 9.5 lists the costs the borrower will be required to pay

# Exhibit 9.4 Uniform Residential Loan Application

## Uniform Residential Loan Application

This application is designed to be completed by the applicant(s) with the Lender's assistance. Applicants should complete this form as "Borrower" or "Co-Borrower," as applicable. Co-Borrower information must also be provided (and the appropriate box checked) when ☐ the income or assets of a person other than the Borrower (including the Borrower's spouse) will be used as a basis for loan qualification or ☐ the income or assets of the Borrower's spouse or other person who has community property rights pursuant to state law will not be used as a basis for loan qualification, but his or her liabilities must be considered because the spouse or other person has community property rights pursuant to applicable law and Borrower resides in a community property state, the security property is located in a community property state, or the Borrower is relying on other property located in a community property state as a basis for repayment of the loan.

If this is an application for joint credit, Borrower and Co-Borrower each agree that we intend to apply for joint credit (sign below):

Borrower _____    Co-Borrower _____

### I. TYPE OF MORTGAGE AND TERMS OF LOAN

| Mortgage Applied for: | ☐ VA ☐ FHA | ☐ Conventional ☐ USDA/Rural Housing Service | ☐ Other (explain): | Agency Case Number | Lender Case Number |
|---|---|---|---|---|---|

| Amount $ | Interest Rate % | No. of Months | Amortization Type: | ☐ Fixed Rate ☐ GPM | ☐ Other (explain): ☐ ARM (type): |
|---|---|---|---|---|---|

### II. PROPERTY INFORMATION AND PURPOSE OF LOAN

| Subject Property Address (street, city, state & ZIP) | No. of Units |
|---|---|

| Legal Description of Subject Property (attach description if necessary) | Year Built |
|---|---|

| Purpose of Loan | ☐ Purchase ☐ Refinance | ☐ Construction ☐ Construction-Permanent | ☐ Other (explain): | Property will be: ☐ Primary Residence  ☐ Secondary Residence  ☐ Investment |
|---|---|---|---|---|

*Complete this line if construction or construction-permanent loan.*

| Year Lot Acquired | Original Cost $ | Amount Existing Liens $ | (a) Present Value of Lot $ | (b) Cost of Improvements $ | Total (a + b) $ |
|---|---|---|---|---|---|

*Complete this line if this is a refinance loan.*

| Year Acquired | Original Cost $ | Amount Existing Liens $ | Purpose of Refinance | Describe Improvements  ☐ made  ☐ to be made  Cost: $ |
|---|---|---|---|---|

| Title will be held in what Name(s) | Manner in which Title will be held | Estate will be held in: ☐ Fee Simple ☐ Leasehold (show expiration date) |
|---|---|---|

| Source of Down Payment, Settlement Charges, and/or Subordinate Financing (explain) |
|---|

### III. BORROWER INFORMATION

| Borrower | | Co-Borrower | |
|---|---|---|---|

| Borrower's Name (include Jr. or Sr. if applicable) | Co-Borrower's Name (include Jr. or Sr. if applicable) |
|---|---|

| Social Security Number | Home Phone (incl. area code) | DOB (mm/dd/yyyy) | Yrs. School | Social Security Number | Home Phone (incl. area code) | DOB (mm/dd/yyyy) | Yrs. School |
|---|---|---|---|---|---|---|---|

| ☐ Married  ☐ Separated | ☐ Unmarried (include single, divorced, widowed) | Dependents (not listed by Co-Borrower) no.     ages | ☐ Married  ☐ Separated | ☐ Unmarried (include single, divorced, widowed) | Dependents (not listed by Borrower) no.     ages |
|---|---|---|---|---|---|

| Present Address (street, city, state, ZIP)  ☐ Own ☐ Rent ___No. Yrs. | Present Address (street, city, state, ZIP)  ☐ Own ☐ Rent ___No. Yrs. |
|---|---|

| Mailing Address, if different from Present Address | Mailing Address, if different from Present Address |
|---|---|

*If residing at present address for less than two years, complete the following:*

| Former Address (street, city, state, ZIP)  ☐ Own ☐ Rent ___No. Yrs. | Former Address (street, city, state, ZIP)  ☐ Own ☐ Rent ___No. Yrs. |
|---|---|

### IV. EMPLOYMENT INFORMATION

| Borrower | | Co-Borrower | |
|---|---|---|---|

| Name & Address of Employer | ☐ Self Employed | Yrs. on this job | Name & Address of Employer | ☐ Self Employed | Yrs. on this job |
|---|---|---|---|---|---|
| | | Yrs. employed in this line of work/profession | | | Yrs. employed in this line of work/profession |

| Position/Title/Type of Business | Business Phone (incl. area code) | Position/Title/Type of Business | Business Phone (incl. area code) |
|---|---|---|---|

*If employed in current position for less than two years or if currently employed in more than one position, complete the following:*

*(continued)*

# Exhibit 9.4 Continued

| Borrower | | IV. EMPLOYMENT INFORMATION (cont'd) | | Co-Borrower | |
|---|---|---|---|---|---|
| Name & Address of Employer | ☐ Self Employed | Dates (from – to) | Name & Address of Employer | ☐ Self Employed | Dates (from – to) |
| | | Monthly Income $ | | | Monthly Income $ |
| Position/Title/Type of Business | | Business Phone (incl. area code) | Position/Title/Type of Business | | Business Phone (incl. area code) |
| Name & Address of Employer | ☐ Self Employed | Dates (from – to) | Name & Address of Employer | ☐ Self Employed | Dates (from – to) |
| | | Monthly Income $ | | | Monthly Income $ |
| Position/Title/Type of Business | | Business Phone (incl. area code) | Position/Title/Type of Business | | Business Phone (incl. area code) |

## V. MONTHLY INCOME AND COMBINED HOUSING EXPENSE INFORMATION

| Gross Monthly Income | Borrower | Co-Borrower | Total | Combined Monthly Housing Expense | Present | Proposed |
|---|---|---|---|---|---|---|
| Base Empl. Income* | $ | $ | $ | Rent | $ | |
| Overtime | | | | First Mortgage (P&I) | | $ |
| Bonuses | | | | Other Financing (P&I) | | |
| Commissions | | | | Hazard Insurance | | |
| Dividends/Interest | | | | Real Estate Taxes | | |
| Net Rental Income | | | | Mortgage Insurance | | |
| Other (before completing, see the notice in "describe other income," below) | | | | Homeowner Assn. Dues | | |
| | | | | Other: | | |
| Total | $ | $ | $ | Total | $ | $ |

\* Self Employed Borrower(s) may be required to provide additional documentation such as tax returns and financial statements.

**Describe Other Income**      *Notice:* Alimony, child support, or separate maintenance income need not be revealed if the Borrower (B) or Co-Borrower (C) does not choose to have it considered for repaying this loan.

| B/C | | Monthly Amount |
|---|---|---|
| | | $ |
| | | |
| | | |

## VI. ASSETS AND LIABILITIES

This Statement and any applicable supporting schedules may be completed jointly by both married and unmarried Co-Borrowers if their assets and liabilities are sufficiently joined so that the Statement can be meaningfully and fairly presented on a combined basis; otherwise, separate Statements and Schedules are required. If the Co-Borrower section was completed about a non-applicant spouse or other person, this Statement and supporting schedules must be completed about that spouse or other person also.

Completed ☐ Jointly ☐ Not Jointly

| ASSETS Description | Cash or Market Value | **Liabilities and Pledged Assets.** List the creditor's name, address, and account number for all outstanding debts, including automobile loans, revolving charge accounts, real estate loans, alimony, child support, stock pledges, etc. Use continuation sheet, if necessary. Indicate by (*) those liabilities, which will be satisfied upon sale of real estate owned or upon refinancing of the subject property. | | |
|---|---|---|---|---|
| Cash deposit toward purchase held by: | $ | | | |
| *List checking and savings accounts below* | | LIABILITIES | Monthly Payment & Months Left to Pay | Unpaid Balance |
| Name and address of Bank, S&L, or Credit Union | | Name and address of Company | $ Payment/Months | $ |
| Acct. no. | $ | Acct. no. | | |
| Name and address of Bank, S&L, or Credit Union | | Name and address of Company | $ Payment/Months | $ |
| Acct. no. | $ | Acct. no. | | |
| Name and address of Bank, S&L, or Credit Union | | Name and address of Company | $ Payment/Months | $ |
| Acct. no. | $ | Acct. no. | | |

**Uniform Residential Loan Application**
Freddie Mac Form 65  7/05 (rev. 6/09)      Page 2 of 5      Fannie Mae Form 1003   7/05 (rev.6/09)

## Exhibit 9.4 Continued

### VI. ASSETS AND LIABILITIES (cont'd)

| Name and address of Bank, S&L, or Credit Union | Name and address of Company | $ Payment/Months | $ |
|---|---|---|---|
| Acct. no. $ | Acct. no. | | |
| Stocks & Bonds (Company name/ number & description) $ | Name and address of Company | $ Payment/Months | $ |
| | Acct. no. | | |
| Life insurance net cash value $ | Name and address of Company | $ Payment/Months | $ |
| Face amount: $ | | | |
| **Subtotal Liquid Assets** $ | | | |
| Real estate owned (enter market value from schedule of real estate owned) $ | | | |
| Vested interest in retirement fund $ | | | |
| Net worth of business(es) owned (attach financial statement) $ | Acct. no. | | |
| Automobiles owned (make and year) $ | Alimony/Child Support/Separate Maintenance Payments Owed to: $ | | |
| Other Assets (itemize) $ | Job-Related Expense (child care, union dues, etc.) $ | | |
| | **Total Monthly Payments** $ | | |
| **Total Assets a.** $ | Net Worth (a minus b) ▶ $ | **Total Liabilities b.** $ | |

**Schedule of Real Estate Owned** (If additional properties are owned, use continuation sheet.)

| Property Address (enter S if sold, PS if pending sale or R if rental being held for income) ▼ | Type of Property | Present Market Value | Amount of Mortgages & Liens | Gross Rental Income | Mortgage Payments | Insurance, Maintenance, Taxes & Misc. | Net Rental Income |
|---|---|---|---|---|---|---|---|
| | | $ | $ | $ | $ | $ | $ |
| | | | | | | | |
| | | | | | | | |
| Totals | | $ | $ | $ | $ | $ | $ |

**List any additional names under which credit has previously been received and indicate appropriate creditor name(s) and account number(s):**

| Alternate Name | Creditor Name | Account Number |
|---|---|---|
| | | |

### VII. DETAILS OF TRANSACTION

| | | |
|---|---|---|
| a. | Purchase price | $ |
| b. | Alterations, improvements, repairs | |
| c. | Land (if acquired separately) | |
| d. | Refinance (incl. debts to be paid off) | |
| e. | Estimated prepaid items | |
| f. | Estimated closing costs | |
| g. | PMI, MIP, Funding Fee | |
| h. | Discount (if Borrower will pay) | |
| i. | Total costs (add items a through h) | |

### VIII. DECLARATIONS

If you answer "Yes" to any questions a through i, please use continuation sheet for explanation.

| | Borrower Yes No | Co-Borrower Yes No |
|---|---|---|
| a. Are there any outstanding judgments against you? | ☐ ☐ | ☐ ☐ |
| b. Have you been declared bankrupt within the past 7 years? | ☐ ☐ | ☐ ☐ |
| c. Have you had property foreclosed upon or given title or deed in lieu thereof in the last 7 years? | ☐ ☐ | ☐ ☐ |
| d. Are you a party to a lawsuit? | ☐ ☐ | ☐ ☐ |
| e. Have you directly or indirectly been obligated on any loan which resulted in foreclosure, transfer of title in lieu of foreclosure, or judgment? | ☐ ☐ | ☐ ☐ |

(This would include such loans as home mortgage loans, SBA loans, home improvement loans, educational loans, manufactured (mobile) home loans, any mortgage, financial obligation, bond, or loan guarantee. If "Yes," provide details, including date, name, and address of Lender, FHA or VA case number, if any, and reasons for the action.)

**Uniform Residential Loan Application**
**Freddie Mac Form 65   7/05 (rev.6/09)**

**Fannie Mae Form 1003   7/05 (rev.6/09)**

(continued)

# Exhibit 9.4 Continued

| VII. DETAILS OF TRANSACTION | | VIII. DECLARATIONS | | | | |
|---|---|---|---|---|---|---|

| | | | | Borrower | | Co-Borrower | |
|---|---|---|---|---|---|---|---|
| | | If you answer "Yes" to any questions a through i, please use continuation sheet for explanation. | | Yes | No | Yes | No |
| j. | Subordinate financing | f. | Are you presently delinquent or in default on any Federal debt or any other loan, mortgage, financial obligation, bond, or loan guarantee? | ☐ | ☐ | ☐ | ☐ |
| k. | Borrower's closing costs paid by Seller | g. | Are you obligated to pay alimony, child support, or separate maintenance? | ☐ | ☐ | ☐ | ☐ |
| l. | Other Credits (explain) | h. | Is any part of the down payment borrowed? | ☐ | ☐ | ☐ | ☐ |
| | | i. | Are you a co-maker or endorser on a note? | ☐ | ☐ | ☐ | ☐ |
| m. | Loan amount (exclude PMI, MIP, Funding Fee financed) | j. | Are you a U.S. citizen? | ☐ | ☐ | ☐ | ☐ |
| n. | PMI, MIP, Funding Fee financed | k. | Are you a permanent resident alien? | ☐ | ☐ | ☐ | ☐ |
| o. | Loan amount (add m & n) | l. | Do you intend to occupy the property as your primary residence? If Yes," complete question m below. | ☐ | ☐ | ☐ | ☐ |
| p. | Cash from/to Borrower (subtract j, k, l & o from i) | m. | Have you had an ownership interest in a property in the last three years? | ☐ | ☐ | ☐ | ☐ |
| | | | (1) What type of property did you own—principal residence (PR), second home (SH), or investment property (IP)? | _____ | | _____ | |
| | | | (2) How did you hold title to the home— by yourself (S), jointly with your spouse (SP), or jointly with another person (O)? | _____ | | _____ | |

## IX. ACKNOWLEDGEMENT AND AGREEMENT

Each of the undersigned specifically represents to Lender and to Lender's actual or potential agents, brokers, processors, attorneys, insurers, servicers, successors and assigns and agrees and acknowledges that: (1) the information provided in this application is true and correct as of the date set forth opposite my signature and that any intentional or negligent misrepresentation of this information contained in this application may result in civil liability, including monetary damages, to any person who may suffer any loss due to reliance upon any misrepresentation that I have made on this application, and/or criminal penalties including, but not limited to, fine or imprisonment or both under the provisions of Title 18, United States Code, Sec. 1001, et seq.; (2) the loan requested pursuant to this application (the "Loan") will be secured by a mortgage or deed of trust on the property described in this application; (3) the property will not be used for any illegal or prohibited purpose or use; (4) all statements made in this application are made for the purpose of obtaining a residential mortgage loan; (5) the property will be occupied as indicated in this application; (6) the Lender, its servicers, successors or assigns may retain the original and/or an electronic record of this application, whether or not the Loan is approved; (7) the Lender and its agents, brokers, insurers, servicers, successors, and assigns may continuously rely on the information contained in the application, and I am obligated to amend and/or supplement the information provided in this application if any of the material facts that I have represented herein should change prior to closing of the Loan; (8) in the event that my payments on the Loan become delinquent, the Lender, its servicers, successors or assigns may, in addition to any other rights and remedies that it may have relating to such delinquency, report my name and account information to one or more consumer reporting agencies; (9) ownership of the Loan and/or administration of the Loan account may be transferred with such notice as may be required by law; (10) neither Lender nor its agents, brokers, insurers, servicers, successors or assigns has made any representation or warranty, express or implied, to me regarding the property or the condition or value of the property; and (11) my transmission of this application as an "electronic record" containing my "electronic signature," as those terms are defined in applicable federal and/or state laws (excluding audio and video recordings), or my facsimile transmission of this application containing a facsimile of my signature, shall be as effective, enforceable and valid as if a paper version of this application were delivered containing my original written signature.

Acknowledgement. Each of the undersigned hereby acknowledges that any owner of the Loan, its servicers, successors and assigns, may verify or reverify any information contained in this application or obtain any information or data relating to the Loan, for any legitimate business purpose through any source, including a source named in this application or a consumer reporting agency.

| Borrower's Signature X | Date | Co-Borrower's Signature X | Date |
|---|---|---|---|

## X. INFORMATION FOR GOVERNMENT MONITORING PURPOSES

The following information is requested by the Federal Government for certain types of loans related to a dwelling in order to monitor the lender's compliance with equal credit opportunity, fair housing and home mortgage disclosure laws. You are not required to furnish this information, but are encouraged to do so. The law provides that a lender may not discriminate either on the basis of this information, or on whether you choose to furnish it. If you furnish the information, please provide both ethnicity and race. For race, you may check more than one designation. If you do not furnish ethnicity, race, or sex, under Federal regulations, this lender is required to note the information on the basis of visual observation and surname if you have made this application in person. If you do not wish to furnish the information, please check the box below. (Lender must review the above material to assure that the disclosures satisfy all requirements to which the lender is subject under applicable state law for the particular type of loan applied for.)

| BORROWER ☐ I do not wish to furnish this information | | CO-BORROWER ☐ I do not wish to furnish this information | |
|---|---|---|---|
| Ethnicity: ☐ Hispanic or Latino  ☐ Not Hispanic or Latino | | Ethnicity: ☐ Hispanic or Latino  ☐ Not Hispanic or Latino | |
| Race: ☐ American Indian or Alaska Native   ☐ Asian   ☐ Black or African American ☐ Native Hawaiian or Other Pacific Islander   ☐ White | | Race: ☐ American Indian or Alaska Native   ☐ Asian   ☐ Black or African American ☐ Native Hawaiian or Other Pacific Islander   ☐ White | |
| Sex: ☐ Female  ☐ Male | | Sex: ☐ Female  ☐ Male | |

To be Completed by Loan Originator:
This information was provided:
☐ In a face-to-face interview
☐ In a telephone interview
☐ By the applicant and submitted by fax or mail
☐ By the applicant and submitted via e-mail or the Internet

| Loan Originator's Signature X | | Date |
|---|---|---|
| Loan Originator's Name (print or type) | Loan Originator Identifier | Loan Originator's Phone Number (including area code) |
| Loan Origination Company's Name | Loan Origination Company Identifier | Loan Origination Company's Address |

# Exhibit 9.4  Continued

| **CONTINUATION SHEET/RESIDENTIAL LOAN APPLICATION** | | |
|---|---|---|
| Use this continuation sheet if you need more space to complete the Residential Loan Application. Mark **B** f or Borrower or **C** for Co-Borrower. | Borrower: | Agency Case Number: |
| | Co-Borrower: | Lender Case Number: |

I/We fully understand that it is a Federal crime punishable by fine or imprisonment, or both, to knowingly make any false statements concerning any of the above facts as applicable under the provisions of Title 18, United States Code, Section 1001, et seq.

| Borrower's Signature | Date | Co-Borrower's Signature | Date |
|---|---|---|---|
| X | | X | |

**Uniform Residential Loan Application**
Freddie Mac Form 65   7/05 (rev.6/09)                    Page 5 of 5                    Fannie Mae Form 1003   7/05 (rev.6/09)

## Exhibit 9.5 Good Faith Estimate of closing costs

OMB Approval No. 2502-0265

# Good Faith Estimate (GFE)

| Name of Originator | ABC BANK | Borrower | Daniel and Sara Schan |
|---|---|---|---|
| Originator Address | 1 Bank Place | Property Address | 489 Jefferson Street Newtowne, YS |
| Originator Phone Number | 555 322 5804 | | |
| Originator Email | | Date of GFE | |

**Purpose**

This GFE gives you an estimate of your settlement charges and loan terms if you are approved for this loan. For more information, see HUD's *Special Information Booklet* on settlement charges, your *Truth-in-Lending Disclosures*, and other consumer information at www.hud.gov/respa. If you decide you would like to proceed with this loan, contact us.

**Shopping for your loan**

Only you can shop for the best loan for you. Compare this GFE with other loan offers, so you can find the best loan. Use the shopping chart on page 3 to compare all the offers you receive.

**Important dates**

1. The interest rate for this GFE is available through ☐ April 30 ☐. After this time, the interest rate, some of your loan Origination Charges, and the monthly payment shown below can change until you lock your interest rate.

2. This estimate for all other settlement charges is available through ☐ April 30 ☐.

3. After you lock your interest rate, you must go to settlement within ☐ days (your rate lock period) to receive the locked interest rate.

4. You must lock the interest rate at least ☐7☐ days before settlement.

**Summary of your loan**

| | |
|---|---|
| Your initial loan amount is | $ 246,400.00 |
| Your loan term is | 30 years |
| Your initial interest rate is | 6.125 % |
| Your initial monthly amount owed for principal, interest, and any mortgage insurance is | $ 1,497.15 per month |
| Can your interest rate rise? | ☒ No ☐ Yes, it can rise to a maximum of %. The first change will be in . |
| Even if you make payments on time, can your loan balance rise? | ☒ No ☐ Yes, it can rise to a maximum of $ |
| Even if you make payments on time, can your monthly amount owed for principal, interest, and any mortgage insurance rise? | ☒ No ☐ Yes, the first increase can be in and the monthly amount owed can rise to $ . The maximum it can ever rise to is $ . |
| Does your loan have a prepayment penalty? | ☒ No ☐ Yes, your maximum prepayment penalty is $ . |
| Does your loan have a balloon payment? | ☒ No ☐ Yes, you have a balloon payment of $ due in years. |

**Escrow account information**

Some lenders require an escrow account to hold funds for paying property taxes or other property-related charges in addition to your monthly amount owed of $ ☐ 300.00 ☐.

Do we require you to have an escrow account for your loan?

☐ No, you do not have an escrow account. You must pay these charges directly when due.

☒ Yes, you have an escrow account. It may or may not cover all of these charges. Ask us.

**Summary of your settlement charges**

| **A** | Your Adjusted Origination Charges *(See page 2.)* | $ |
|---|---|---|
| **B** | Your Charges for All Other Settlement Services *(See page 2.)* | $ 6378 |
| **A + B** | Total Estimated Settlement Charges | $ 6378 |

**Good Faith Estimate (HUD-GFE)** 1

# Exhibit 9.5 Continued

**Understanding your estimated settlement charges**

*Some of these charges can change at settlement. See the top of page 3 for more information.*

## Your Adjusted Origination Charges

**1. Our origination charge**
This charge is for getting this loan for you.

**2. Your credit or charge (points) for the specific interest rate chosen**

☐ The credit or charge for the interest rate of [      ] % is included in "Our origination charge." (See item 1 above.)

☐ You receive a credit of $[          ] for this interest rate of [      ] %. This credit **reduces** your settlement charges.

☐ You pay a charge of $[          ] for this interest rate of [      ] %. This charge (points) **increases** your total settlement charges.

The tradeoff table on page 3 shows that you can change your total settlement charges by choosing a different interest rate for this loan.

**A** | Your Adjusted Origination Charges | $

## Your Charges for All Other Settlement Services

**3. Required services that we select**
These charges are for services we require to complete your settlement. We will choose the providers of these services.

| Service | Charge |
|---|---|
|  |  |

**4. Title services and lender's title insurance**
This charge includes the services of a title or settlement agent, for example, and title insurance to protect the lender, if required.

**5. Owner's title insurance**
You may purchase an owner's title insurance policy to protect your interest in the property. — 1933

**6. Required services that you can shop for**
These charges are for other services that are required to complete your settlement. We can identify providers of these services or you can shop for them yourself. Our estimates for providing these services are below.

| Service | Charge |
|---|---|
|  |  |

**7. Government recording charges**
These charges are for state and local fees to record your loan and title documents. — 180

**8. Transfer taxes**
These charges are for state and local fees on mortgages and home sales. — 3080

**9. Initial deposit for your escrow account**
This charge is held in an escrow account to pay future recurring charges on your property and includes [x] all property taxes, ☐ all insurance, and ☐ other [          ]. — 1185

**10. Daily interest charges**
This charge is for the daily interest on your loan from the day of your settlement until the first day of the next month or the first day of your normal mortgage payment cycle. This amount is $[ 41.92 ] per day for [ 2 ] days (if your settlement is [11/29 ]).

**11. Homeowner's insurance**
This charge is for the insurance you must buy for the property to protect from a loss, such as fire.

| Policy | Charge |
|---|---|
|  |  |

**B** | Your Charges for All Other Settlement Services | $ 6378

**A + B** | Total Estimated Settlement Charges | $ 6378

Good Faith Estimate (HUD-GFE) 2

*(continued)*

**Exhibit 9.5** Continued

## Instructions

**Understanding which charges can change at settlement**

This GFE estimates your settlement charges. At your settlement, you will receive a HUD-1, a form that lists your actual costs. Compare the charges on the HUD-1 with the charges on this GFE. Charges can change if you select your own provider and do not use the companies we identify. (See below for details.)

| These charges **cannot increase** at settlement: | The total of these charges **can increase up to 10%** at settlement: | These charges **can change** at settlement: |
|---|---|---|
| <ul><li>Our origination charge</li><li>Your credit or charge (points) for the specific interest rate chosen *(after you lock in your interest rate)*</li><li>Your adjusted origination charges *(after you lock in your interest rate)*</li><li>Transfer taxes</li></ul> | <ul><li>Required services that we select</li><li>Title services and lender's title insurance *(if we select them or you use companies we identify)*</li><li>Owner's title insurance *(if you use companies we identify)*</li><li>Required services that you can shop for *(if you use companies we identify)*</li><li>Government recording charges</li></ul> | <ul><li>Required services that you can shop for *(if you do not use companies we identify)*</li><li>Title services and lender's title insurance *(if you do not use companies we identify)*</li><li>Owner's title insurance *(if you do not use companies we identify)*</li><li>Initial deposit for your escrow account</li><li>Daily interest charges</li><li>Homeowner's insurance</li></ul> |

**Using the tradeoff table**

In this GFE, we offered you this loan with a particular interest rate and estimated settlement charges. However:

- If you want to choose this same loan with **lower settlement charges,** then you will have a **higher interest rate.**
- If you want to choose this same loan with a **lower interest rate,** then you will have **higher settlement charges.**

If you would like to choose an available option, you must ask us for a new GFE.

*Loan originators have the option to complete this table. Please ask for additional information if the table is not completed.*

| | The loan in this GFE | The same loan with lower settlement charges | The same loan with a lower interest rate |
|---|---|---|---|
| Your initial loan amount | $ | $ | $ |
| Your initial interest rate[1] | % | % | % |
| Your initial monthly amount owed | $ | $ | $ |
| Change in the monthly amount owed from this GFE | No change | You will pay $ **more** every month | You will pay $ **less** every month |
| Change in the amount you will pay at settlement with this interest rate | No change | Your settlement charges will be **reduced** by $ | Your settlement charges will **increase** by $ |
| How much your total estimated settlement charges will be | $ | $ | $ |

[1] *For an adjustable rate loan, the comparisons above are for the initial interest rate before adjustments are made.*

**Using the shopping chart**

Use this chart to compare GFEs from different loan originators. Fill in the information by using a different column for each GFE you receive. By comparing loan offers, you can shop for the best loan.

| | This loan | Loan 2 | Loan 3 | Loan 4 |
|---|---|---|---|---|
| Loan originator name | | | | |
| Initial loan amount | | | | |
| Loan term | | | | |
| Initial interest rate | | | | |
| Initial monthly amount owed | | | | |
| Rate lock period | | | | |
| Can interest rate rise? | | | | |
| Can loan balance rise? | | | | |
| Can monthly amount owed rise? | | | | |
| Prepayment penalty? | | | | |
| Balloon payment? | | | | |
| **Total Estimated Settlement Charges** | | | | |

**If your loan is sold in the future**

Some lenders may sell your loan after settlement. Any fees lenders receive in the future cannot change the loan you receive or the charges you paid at settlement.

 **Good Faith Estimate (HUD-GFE)** 3

in conjunction with obtaining the loan. These costs can include the loan application fee, the cost of obtaining credit and appraisal reports, loan origination fees (which are usually a percentage of the loan amount), and the amount of any tax escrows, title insurance, notary fees, recording fees, and transfer tax.

The Truth-in-Lending Disclosure Statement shown in Exhibit 9.6 is required by federal law to be prepared by the lender and provided to the borrower, showing the effective or annual percentage rate (APR) of interest on the loan. The APR is calculated by taking into account the charges the lender requires the borrower to pay to obtain the loan and the actual amount of funds lent to the borrower after deducting these costs. The mortgage loan is based on the gross amount borrowed that must be repaid and the interest used to calculate the monthly payments to repay the loan, but the amount of funds actually provided is the net amount after deduction of costs or charges, resulting in a lower net amount. The APR is calculated on the net amount for comparison purposes. Because all lenders are required to prepare this calculation in the same manner and provide it to the borrower, the truth-in-lending disclosure allows borrowers to compare other loan offers on an equal basis. The costs included in this calculation are the application and origination fees.

The lender must also provide notices required under the Fair Credit Reporting Act (FCRA), 15 U.S.C. § 1681 et seq, Equal Credit Opportunity Act, and Right to Financial Privacy Act. The federal Fair Credit Reporting Act promotes the accuracy, fairness, and privacy of information in the files of consumer credit reporting agencies. In the event that there is a negative credit report or a discrepancy in a credit report, the borrower has the right to be advised of the information, request and receive a copy of the information, dispute incomplete or inaccurate information, and request that credit reporting agencies correct or delete inaccurate, incomplete, or unverifiable information.

The Equal Credit Opportunity Act prohibits credit discrimination on the basis of race, color, religion, national origin, sex, marital status, age, or because one receives public assistance. Lenders must advise borrowers of the protection afforded by this act.

The Right to Financial Privacy Act seeks to protect the privacy of financial information. The borrower's financial records may only be released with the signed written authorization of the borrower, which identifies the records that may be released, to whom, and the purpose for which they are requested.

The lender must provide a copy of a pamphlet explaining the Real Estate Settlement Procedures Act (RESPA). The RESPA booklet outlines all the elements of a typical real estate transaction and attempts to explain, in plain English, what buyers and sellers can expect during the transaction. In particular, RESPA covers the buyer's and seller's costs and the kinds of expenses that are likely to be seen in a real estate transaction. It is not a document of legal authority but provides guidance for both the uninitiated and the experienced.

In many states, lenders have subsidiaries that provide services related to real estate transactions, such as title searching, closing and settlement agents, and homeowners or other insurance. Lenders must disclose the existence of these subsidiaries as well as a notify borrowers that they have the right to refuse such services and to select their own agents.

**WEB EXPLORATION**
The Fair Credit Reporting Act (FCRA) requires each of the three nationwide credit reporting companies—Equifax, Experian, and TransUnion—to give you a free copy of your credit report, at your request, once every 12 months. To order your report, visit annualcreditreport.com, call toll free 1-877-322-8228, or complete the annual credit report request form and mail it to: Annual Credit Report Request Service, P.O. Box 105281, Atlanta, GA 30348-5281. http://www.ftc.gov/bcp/edu/pubs/consumer/credit/cre15.shtm

**WEB EXPLORATION**
The Fair Credit Reporting Act can be found on the Federal Trade Commission website at http://www.ftc.gov/os/statutes/fcrajump.shtm
The Equal Credit Opportunity Act can be found at http://www.ftc.gov/bcp/edu/pubs/consumer/credit/cre15.shtm
The Right to Financial Privacy Act information can be reviewed on the Federal Deposit Insurance Corporation website at http://www.fdic.gov/regulations/laws/rules/6500-2550.html

**WEB EXPLORATION**
Effective July 21, 2011, the **Real Estate Settlement Procedures Act (RESPA)** is administered and enforced by the Consumer Financial Protection Bureau (CFPB). Details about RESPA, including current forms, may be viewed at http://portal.hud.gov/hudportal/HUD?src=/program_offices/housing/rmra/res/respa_hm

## Exhibit 9.6 Truth-in-Lending Disclosure Statement

### FEDERAL TRUTH-IN-LENDING DISCLOSURE STATEMENT
(THIS IS NEITHER A CONTRACT NOR A COMMITMENT TO LEND)

Applicants: Daniel Schan & Sara Schan          Prepared By: Jason Moore

Property Address:   489 Jefferson St

Application No:  A456                           Date Prepared:
Check box if applicable:

| ANNUAL PERCENTAGE RATE<br><br>The cost of your credit as a yearly rate | FINANCE CHARGE<br><br>The dollar amount the credit will cost you | Amount Financed<br><br>The amount of credit provided to you or on your behalf | Total of Payments<br><br>The amount you will have paid after making all payments as scheduled |
|---|---|---|---|
| 6.136          % | $  293,303.72 | $  246672.72 | $  538,976.44 |

☐ REQUIRED DEPOSIT:   The annual percentage rate does not take into account your required deposit
PAYMENTS:   Your payment schedule will be:

| Number of Payments | Amount of Payments ** | When Payments Are Due | Number of Payments | Amount of Payments ** | When Payments Are Due | Number of Payments | Amount of Payments ** | When Payments Are Due |
|---|---|---|---|---|---|---|---|---|
| 359 | 1497.15 | December 1 | | | | | | |
| 1 | 1499.59 | November 1 | | | | | | |

☐ DEMAND FEATURE:  This obligation has a demand feature.
☐ VARIABLE RATE FEATURE:  This loan contains a variable rate feature.  A variable rate disclosure has been provided earlier.

CREDIT LIFE/CREDIT DISABILIY:  Credit life insurance and credit disability insurance are not required to obtain credit, and will not be provided unless you sign and agree to pay the additional cost.

| Type | Premium | Signature | |
|---|---|---|---|
| Credit Life | 23. | I want credit life insurance. | X |
| Credit Disability | | I want credit disability insurance. | X |
| Credit Life and Disability | | I want credit life and disability insurance. | X |

INSURANCE:  The following insurance is required to obtain credit:
☐ Credit life insurance  ☐ Credit disability  ☐ Property insurance    ☐ Flood insurance
You may obtain the insurance from anyone you want that is acceptable to creditor
☐ If you purchase     ☐ property     ☐ flood insurance from creditor you will pay $            for a one year term.
SECURITY:  You are giving a security interest in:
☐ The goods or property being purchased        ☐ Real property you already own.
FILING FEES: $  180
LATE CHARGE:  If a payment is more than    5   days late, you will be charged      5      %
PREPAYMENT:  If you pay off early, you
☐ may        ☒ will not   have to pay a penalty.
☐ may        ☒ will not   be entitled to a refund of part of the finance charge.
ASSUMPTION:  Someone buying your property
☐ may        ☐ may, subject to conditions        ☒ may not    assume the remainder of your loan on the original terms.

# ■ TYPES OF MORTGAGE LOANS

As part of the application process, the lender's representative or mortgage broker taking the application will review the various types of mortgage loans. Mortgage loans are competitive products designed to meet the needs of consumers looking for the "best deal." Mortgage loans are available from a wide variety of providers, such as private financiers, banks, savings and loans, credit unions, insurance companies, and other investors. Buyers frequently use **mortgage brokers**, loan specialists who match borrowers with lenders, to find mortgages that meet their needs.

A **fixed-rate mortgage** is a mortgage where the interest is fixed for the duration of the loan. The benefit of a fixed-rate mortgage for a home buyer is that the monthly payment is the same for the loan duration, which assists in monthly household budgeting. Historically, fixed-rate mortgages have been the preferred choice of prospective home buyers. The rate is determined by economic conditions in the marketplace and over the past 50 years has been as low as 3 percent and as high as 21. The loan duration can range from 10 to 40 years. The loan is **self-amortizing**, meaning that the loan balance is paid off over the life of the loan. Each monthly payment is comprised of interest and principal. As each payment is made, the interest portion of the payment gets smaller and the principal portion increases until the loan is repaid in full. Exhibit 9.7 is a portion of an amortization schedule for a $100,000 loan repaid over 30 years at an interest rate of 5 percent.

An **adjustable-rate mortgage (ARM)** is a mortgage where the interest rate can be adjusted over the lifetime of the loan. The primary advantage to borrowers of an ARM is the lower and more enticing rate during the first year or two of the loan. The interest rate will be adjusted based on interest-rate fluctuations in the market. When the interest rate is adjusted, the monthly mortgage payment will also be adjusted. The time for adjustment will be determined in the loan agreement and can be 30 days or a number of years. Some ARMs offer a feature that allows the borrower to convert to a fixed-rate loan after a certain period of time. Adjustable rate mortgages usually have a **rate cap**, or limit on the maximum increase of the interest rate; for example, the interest rate can only increase two percentage points in a given year and have a maximum increase of six percentage points over the life of the loan.

A **balloon mortgage** is a mortgage where the payments are based on a fixed rate over a long-term period, such as 30 years, but the loan balance is due in full at the end of a short term, such as five years. In some instances, the monthly payment is interest only. The primary advantage of a balloon mortgage is to set a low, manageable payment for a fixed period of time. The disadvantage is that payment in full, or a balloon payment, is due at the end of five years, requiring the borrower to refinance with another mortgage company or obtain the funds from other sources at higher interest rates.

A **graduated-payment mortgage (GPM)** has an initial low monthly payment that is below the required self-amortizing amount. Over time, the monthly payment is gradually increased to the point where it exceeds the required self-amortizing payment, to make up the shortfall that occurred in the early years of repayment. This type of loan offers a lower payment to first-time home buyers, who might be struggling to pay a full monthly amount; the expectation is that their earnings will increase as the payments increase over time.

**Assumed mortgages** occur when the purchaser of a home assumes or takes over payment of the seller's existing mortgage. This type of loan is advantageous when the interest rate on the seller's existing mortgage is lower than current rates

**LEARNING OBJECTIVE 2**
Explain the different types of mortgage loans and the benefits of each.

**mortgage brokers**
loan specialists who match borrowers with lenders to find mortgages that meet their needs

 **WEB EXPLORATION**
The Federal Reserve Board publishes guidance on the types and characteristics of the various mortgage loans available. Check the following website: www.federalreserve.gov/pubs/mortgage/mortb_1.htm

**fixed-rate mortgage**
mortgage where the interest is set for the duration of the loan

**self-amortizing**
the loan is paid off with the required payments made over the life of the loan

**adjustable-rate mortgage (ARM)**
mortgage where the interest rate can be adjusted over the lifetime of the loan

**rate cap**
limit on the maximum increase of the interest rate

**balloon mortgage**
mortgage with a lump sum due after a specific period of time, but with regular payments based on a longer period for amortization purposes

**graduated-payment mortgage (GPM)**
mortgage with an initial low periodic payment that is below the required self-amortizing payment

**assumed mortgages**
mortgage of the seller assumed by the buyer

## Exhibit 9.7 Loan amortization schedule

|  | Enter values |
| --- | --- |
| Loan amount | $100,000.00 |
| Annual interest rate | 5.000% |
| Loan period in years | 30 |
| Start date of loan | 1/1/2013 |
|  |  |
| Monthly payment | $ 536.82 |
| Number of payments | 360 |
| Total interest | $ 93,255.78 |
| Total cost of loan | $ 193,255.78 |

| No. | Payment Date | Beginning Balance | Payment | Principal | Interest | Ending Balance |
| --- | --- | --- | --- | --- | --- | --- |
| 1 | 2/1/2013 | $ 100,000.00 | $ 536.82 | $ 120.15 | $ 416.67 | $ 99,879.85 |
| 2 | 3/1/2013 | 99,879.85 | 536.82 | 120.66 | 416.17 | 99,759.19 |
| 3 | 4/1/2013 | 99,759.19 | 536.82 | 121.16 | 415.66 | 99,638.03 |
| 4 | 5/1/2013 | 99,638.03 | 536.82 | 121.66 | 415.16 | 99,516.37 |
| 5 | 6/1/2013 | 99,516.37 | 536.82 | 122.17 | 414.65 | 99,394.20 |
| 6 | 7/1/2013 | 99,394.20 | 536.82 | 122.68 | 414.14 | 99,271.52 |
| 7 | 8/1/2013 | 99,271.52 | 536.82 | 123.19 | 413.63 | 99,148.33 |
| 8 | 9/1/2013 | 99,148.33 | 536.82 | 123.70 | 413.12 | 99,024.62 |
| 9 | 10/1/2013 | 99,024.62 | 536.82 | 124.22 | 412.60 | 98,900.41 |
| 10 | 11/1/2013 | 98,900.41 | 536.82 | 124.74 | 412.09 | 98,775.67 |
| 11 | 12/1/2013 | 98,775.67 | 536.82 | 125.26 | 411.57 | 98,650.41 |
| 12 | 1/1/2014 | 98,650.41 | 536.82 | 125.78 | 411.04 | 98,524.63 |
| 13 | 2/1/2014 | 98,524.63 | 536.82 | 126.30 | 410.52 | 98,398.33 |
| 14 | 3/1/2014 | 98,398.33 | 536.82 | 126.83 | 409.99 | 98,271.50 |
| 15 | 4/1/2014 | 98,271.50 | 536.82 | 127.36 | 409.46 | 98,144.15 |
| 16 | 5/1/2014 | 98,144.15 | 536.82 | 127.89 | 408.93 | 98,016.26 |
| 17 | 6/1/2014 | 98,016.26 | 536.82 | 128.42 | 408.40 | 97,887.84 |
| 18 | 7/1/2014 | 97,887.84 | 536.82 | 128.96 | 407.87 | 97,758.88 |
| 19 | 8/1/2014 | 97,758.88 | 536.82 | 129.49 | 407.33 | 97,629.39 |
| 20 | 9/1/2014 | 97,629.39 | 536.82 | 130.03 | 406.79 | 97,499.36 |
| 21 | 10/1/2014 | 97,499.36 | 536.82 | 130.57 | 406.25 | 97,368.78 |

*(continued)*

**Exhibit 9.7** Continued

| No. | Payment Date | Beginning Balance | Payment | Principal | Interest | Ending Balance |
|-----|-----|-----|-----|-----|-----|-----|
| 22 | 11/1/2014 | 97,368.78 | 536.82 | 131.12 | 405.70 | 97,237.66 |
| 23 | 12/1/2014 | 97,237.66 | 536.82 | 131.66 | 405.16 | 97,106.00 |
| 24 | 1/1/2015 | 97,106.00 | 536.82 | 132.21 | 404.61 | 96,973.79 |
| 25 | 2/1/2015 | 96,973.79 | 536.82 | 132.76 | 404.06 | 96,841.02 |
| 26 | 3/1/2015 | 96,841.02 | 536.82 | 133.32 | 403.50 | 96,707.71 |
| 27 | 4/1/2015 | 96,707.71 | 536.82 | 133.87 | 402.95 | 96,573.83 |
| 28 | 5/1/2015 | 96,573.83 | 536.82 | 134.43 | 402.39 | 96,439.40 |
| 29 | 6/1/2015 | 96,439.40 | 536.82 | 134.99 | 401.83 | 96,304.41 |
| 30 | 7/1/2015 | 96,304.41 | 536.82 | 135.55 | 401.27 | 96,168.86 |
| 31 | 8/1/2015 | 96,168.86 | 536.82 | 136.12 | 400.70 | 96,032.74 |
| 32 | 9/1/2015 | 96,032.74 | 536.82 | 136.69 | 400.14 | 95,896.05 |
| 33 | 10/1/2015 | 95,896.05 | 536.82 | 137.25 | 399.57 | 95,758.80 |
| 34 | 11/1/2015 | 95,758.80 | 536.82 | 137.83 | 398.99 | 95,620.97 |
| 35 | 12/1/2015 | 95,620.97 | 536.82 | 138.40 | 398.42 | 95,482.57 |
| 36 | 1/1/2016 | 95,482.57 | 536.82 | $ 138.98 | 397.84 | 95,343.59 |

in the mortgage marketplace. The terms of the existing mortgage must permit assumption, the lender must agree to the loan being assumed, and the buyer must go through the loan application and qualification process.

A **seller's purchase-money mortgage** is a mortgage that is provided by the seller of the real estate to the buyer. For the buyer, a seller's purchase-money mortgage creates a loan opportunity for a buyer who cannot qualify for a loan with a traditional lender at favorable terms. For the seller, it can provide a steady stream of income in the form of monthly mortgage payments. The money for the mortgage reduces the seller's proceeds from the sale of the property.

**seller's purchase-money mortgage**
mortgage that is provided by the seller

A **reverse mortgage** is a mortgage where the lender pays the homeowner monthly payments. The advantage is that the loan does not have to be repaid until the property is sold, the homeowner dies, or the owner no longer uses the home as his or her primary residence. Reverse mortgages are a new type of mortgage designed for homeowners 62 years of age or older who own and reside in their homes. The primary advantage is to supplement income of retired or elderly homeowners who have significant equity in their home but no other assets or sufficient retirement savings but wish to remain in their home.

**reverse mortgage**
mortgage where the homeowner receives monthly payments from the lender but the loan does not have to be repaid until the property is sold, the homeowner dies, or the owner no longer uses the home as his or her primary residence

**Government-backed mortgages** are those that are insured by a government agency, which guarantees repayment of the loan. Three federal agencies most often involved are the Department of Veterans Affairs (VA), the Federal Housing Administration (FHA), and the Farmers Home Administration (FMHA). Each of these agencies has its own lending requirements, rules, and regulations that can be more burdensome than those of traditional lending. Some of the burdens imposed by these programs are so onerous that a seller will reject any offer that

**government-backed mortgages**
mortgages that are insured by a government agency, which guarantees repayment of the loan

**Exhibit 9.8** Real estate appraisal requirements for FHA and VA loans

1. Properties in industrial, commercial, or main highway areas are not acceptable.

2. Exterior paint must be in good condition.

3. Porches must be in good repair.

4. Stairs must have handrails on one side.

5. All windows must be operable, with no broken or cracked glass.

6. No captive bathrooms or baths off the kitchen allowed.

7. Furnaces must be in good repair; gas conversion furnaces must be inspected and proved energy efficient.

8. The roof must prevent entrance of moisture.

9. Repair of a broken sidewalk will be required.

10. The plumbing should be copper; steel is acceptable if in good condition.

11. Gas water heaters must have relief valves and drains and be of such a size as to provide an adequate supply of hot water.

12. Downspouts must be in good repair, with property drainage or splash blocks.

13. Homes with integral garages must have a firewall with fire-resistant door.

14. Home must have a proper sewage disposal system.

15. The attic window must allow proper ventilation.

16. Home should be free of flood, subsidence, or badly eroded areas.

17. No water seepage is allowed in basement.

18. Knob and tube wiring is not acceptable unless in very good condition.

19. Townhouses should be separated by an adequate firewall to the roof.

is based on FHA, VA, or FMHA financing. Exhibit 9.8 lists the requirements of FHA and VA real estate appraisal requirements—just one example of the additional burdens that are placed on the seller.

The Bureau of Veterans Affairs VA Home Loan program dates back to the Serviceman's Readjustment Act of 1944, amended by the Korean Conflict GI Bill (July 1952), and followed by the Veterans Housing Acts of 1970 and 1974. Under these laws, eligible veterans having served at least 180 days active military service after September 16, 1940, and having been honorably discharged may obtain partially guaranteed loans for the purchase or construction of a home. Additionally, widows or widowers of veterans who died in the service or from service-related causes, who have not remarried, may make use of this privilege. The veteran usually receives the mortgage money from a local lender; however, the VA may lend money directly if no VA-approved lender is available.

The Federal Housing Administration (FHA) was created by the National Housing Act of 1934, for the purposes of assisting first-time homebuyers and stimulating the housing market. The FHA does not lend money directly to the purchaser, but instead serves as a guarantor to the bank for any money lent.

## Loan Qualification

Once the application is complete and the particular mortgage type selected, the lender will begin the loan qualification process. During the **loan qualification process**, the lender evaluates two items to determine whether to approve the

**WEB EXPLORATION**
VA Loan information is available at the Department of Veterans Affairs website at www.benefits. va.gov/homeloans/elig_center.asp

**WEB EXPLORATION**
Current FHA loan requirements information is available on the FHA website at www.benefits.va.gov/ homeloans/elig_center.asp

**loan qualification process**
process wherein the lender evaluates the buyer's creditworthiness and the value of the real estate to determine whether to approve a loan

loan. First, a review is conducted of the loan application to verify the information contained in the application to determine whether the borrower is creditworthy—that is, whether the borrower is more likely than not to repay the loan. Copies of credit reports are obtained to confirm the debts and obligations disclosed by the borrower on the application. The credit report also reveals the borrower's payment history with regard to those obligations: if payments have been made on time, were late, or were missed. A history of late or missed payments reflects poorly on a borrower's likelihood to repay the mortgage loan. A letter may be sent to the borrower's employer to confirm employment, length of employment, and wages. The lender may require the borrower to provide copies of prior years' income tax returns, or the lender may obtain those directly from the IRS. Copies of bank and brokerage statements for six months to three years may be reviewed to confirm the borrower's assets. Those statements will also be reviewed for unusual transactions, such as a large deposit. The borrower may have to explain where those funds came from: a bonus from employment, an inheritance, lottery winnings, a cash advance on a credit card, or a gift. In the event of a gift, the donor of the gift may be required to provide a letter to the lender confirming the gift and stating that there is no expectation of being repaid. All of these factors determine whether the borrower has the financial ability and likelihood to repay the mortgage loan.

The second portion of the loan qualification process relates to the real estate that is being purchased and pledged as the collateral for the loan. In the unfortunate event of the borrower's default or failure to repay the loan, the lender wants to be certain that the value of the real estate will cover the unpaid amount of the loan. Two items assist the lender in making this determination: a real estate appraisal and a title report. The **real estate appraisal** establishes a value of the real estate, independent of the price set forth in the Agreement of Sale. A licensed real estate appraiser inspects the property, investigates and reports sales of similar properties in the same community (called comparable sales), and determines the fair market value of the property. The appraiser issues a written report that contains an evaluation of the property, the community in which it is located, and the physical characteristics and the amenities of the home. The report may include the estimated cost to rebuild the home—the replacement cost excluding land value. The comparable sales are chosen based on being in the same community and having similar characteristics such as house style, bedroom and bath count, and square footage. The appraisal may also include information on similar homes currently listed for sale. Based on all this information, the appraiser states an estimate of fair market value. It is this value the lender will rely on to determine the amount of the loan. In many instances, the lender will loan 80 percent of the value of the real estate. The buyer may have signed an agreement of sale with a sale price of $200,000, thinking he or she can borrow $160,000, or 80 percent, of the purchase price. However, the real estate appraisal may determine that the value of the real estate is $180,000, and a loan at 80 percent of that value would be $144,000. This could significantly impact the ability of the borrower to conclude the transaction, requiring the buyer to make an additional down payment of $16,000. Alternatively, the seller could agree to reduce the sales price to the appraised value.

In addition to the real estate appraisal for determining value, the lender will initially require a title report, to confirm that there are no impediments to the seller transferring good title, and title insurance for the amount of the loan, as insurance that there are no claims against the property. The lender wants to be

**PRACTICE TIP**

As a result of the financial problems of the mortgage industry, most mortgage loans are covered under some form of federal mortgage insurance. As a result, any falsification on an application or supporting document potentially comes under the federal law for false swearing, including supporting documents supporting gifts to borrowers.

**real estate appraisal**
determining the fair market value of real estate, independent of the price set forth in the Agreement of Sale

certain that the mortgage loan will be the first lien in priority on the property. That is, should the borrower default and fail to pay the mortgage and the property needs to be sold to pay off the loan, there are no other creditors or claims that will be entitled to payment before the lender. Once the lender is satisfied that the borrower is financially qualified to repay the loan and that the real estate represents sufficient collateral, the loan will be approved.

## PRACTICE TIP

### SUBPRIME MORTGAGE CRISIS

Lenders' relaxed qualification standards for borrowers during a period of increasing real estate sales prices resulted in what is call the *subprime mortgage crisis of 2007*. In the period leading up to the crisis, sometimes loans were approved without verification of income, assets, and liabilities and sometimes for an amount that exceeded the value of the property. The result was many borrowers could not afford the loans granted them. The heart of the crisis occurred when real estate prices fell as the real estate bubble burst, and the properties given as collateral could not be sold for enough to pay off the loans. Instead of owning loans with the right to receive monthly mortgage payments, banks became the owners of millions of homes through the mortgage foreclosure process.

There have been several legislative enactments to assist the lending industry and homeowners during the crisis. For lenders, the Troubled Asset Relief Program (TARP) infused the lending industry with federal funds to make up the money lost on bad loans. Borrowers now face increased scrutiny of their qualifications to repay loans requested and increased review of the appraisals of the values of the properties. For new borrowers, those purchasing homes now, the loan qualification requirements are being stringently enforced. This strict adherence to tests related to creditworthiness has made it more difficult for borrowers to qualify for mortgage loans.

# ETHICAL Considerations

## COMPETENCY

Competency requires use of legal knowledge and skill to provide representation to the client. A key component of competence is staying up to date on changes in the law, particularly in the area of law in which one practices. For the real estate lawyer and the members of the legal team, it means understanding all the changes that are taking place in the real estate lending industry and how those changes will affect the client. The federal and state governments continue to act in response to the subprime mortgage crisis, making available favorable programs for borrowers. A lawyer who fails to know and advise the client of an opportunity to save the client's home from mortgage foreclosure proceedings has failed in his or her ethical obligation.

## KEY TERMS

## CHAPTER SUMMARY

| | |
|---|---|
| Introduction to the Real Estate Loan Process | Most buyers require a mortgage to pay for the purchase of real estate. The process may begin with the buyer seeking pre-approval to determine the mortgage amount for which the buyer qualifies. |
| The Mortgage Lending Process | Given the cost, it is rare that a purchaser will have sufficient resources to pay cash to complete the purchase, requiring most buyers to borrow funds for this purpose. Mortgage lending or real estate financing is the process of borrowing funds to purchase real estate. |
| Pre-Qualification | The buyers' pre-qualification is an effort by real estate professionals and lenders to screen potential buyers to determine their financial ability to purchase real estate. |
| Loan Application | The process begins with a meeting with a mortgage lender or broker, during which a formal loan application will be completed. The application is very detailed in seeking information about the borrower, the type of loan requested, and the property being purchased. Information is also required on employment history, sources of income, assets, and liabilities for each borrower. |

| Types of Mortgage Loans | Mortgage loans are competitive products designed to meet the needs of consumers looking for the "best deal." Mortgage loans are available from a wide variety of providers, such as private financiers, banks, savings and loans, credit unions, insurance companies, and other investors. A number of solutions are offered to meet the borrowers' needs: fixed-rate mortgage, a mortgage where the interest is set for the duration of the loan; an adjustable-rate mortgage (ARM), a mortgage where the interest rate can be adjusted over the lifetime of the loan; a balloon mortgage, a mortgage where the payments are based on a fixed rate over a long-term period, such as 30 years, but the loan balance is due in full at the end of a short term; a graduated-payment mortgage (GPM), a mortgage with an initial low periodic payment that is below the required self-amortizing payment.<br><br>Additionally, sellers may help the buyer by having the buyer assume the seller's mortgage or taking back a mortgage, referred to as a purchase-money mortgage.<br><br>For senior citizens who wish to stay in their own home but obtain funds based on the home collateral, some lenders provide a reverse mortgage; the homeowner receives monthly payments from the lender, but the loan does not have to be repaid until the property is sold, the homeowner dies, or the owner no longer uses the home as his or her primary residence. |
| --- | --- |
| Loan Qualification | During the loan qualification process, the lender evaluates two items to determine whether to approve the loan. First is a review of the loan application, verifying the information contained in the application to determine whether the borrower is creditworthy—that is, more likely than not to repay the loan. The second part relates to the use of the real estate as collateral for the loan: its value and any clouds on the title. |

## REVIEW QUESTIONS AND EXERCISES

1. What is a fixed-rate mortgage and what are its advantages?
2. What is an adjustable-rate mortgage? What are the advantages and disadvantages?
3. How does a balloon mortgage assist a first-time home buyer? Describe the disadvantages, if any.
4. How does a graduated-payment mortgage assist a first-time home buyer? Describe the disadvantages, if any.

5. What are the advantages of assuming a seller's existing mortgage?
6. Under what circumstances would a seller offer a purchase-money mortgage to the buyer?
7. What is a reverse mortgage? Describe the advantages and the individuals this mortgage is designed to assist.

8. What is loan pre-qualification? How does the pre-qualification a real estate agent performs differ from the lender's pre-qualification?
9. What is the benefit to the buyer of having a pre-qualification letter?
10. Describe the loan application process.

11. What is the purpose of the loan qualification process?
12. Describe the tools utilized in determining a buyer's creditworthiness.
13. Describe the tools utilized to confirm the value and status of the real estate as collateral for a loan.

## VIDEO CASE STUDY

Go to www.pearsonhighered.com/careers to view the following videos.

**Author Introduction to Residential Real Estate Loan Process**
Author video introduction to chapter coverage.

## INTERNET AND TECHNOLOGY EXERCISES

1. Use a mortgage calculator to determine the monthly payment for a $275,000 mortgage at 3.5 percent for 20 years, 25 years, and 30 years.
2. Use the debt-to-loan and living-expense ratios currently in effect as shown on the VA or FHA website to determine the allowable amounts for someone making $3,000 a month.

3. Download a copy of the truth-in-lending form from the HUD website for your portfolio.
4. Obtain a copy of the Uniform Residential Loan Application.

## REAL ESTATE PORTFOLIO EXERCISES

**Real Estate Loan Process**

**To:** Paralegal Intern
**From:** Paul Saunders
**Case Name:** Mr. & Mrs. Schan
**Re:** Home Purchase

I received a call from Mr. Schan. His mortgage company is concerned that he does not have enough money for the down payment and may have borrowed the funds for the down payment from his uncle. Please prepare a letter from the uncle indicating that the money was an unconditional gift and not a loan.

Since this is a federally-insured mortgage, I need to caution him that there are severe penalties for lying on any documents in the mortgage process.

Please check the HUD web site for language on the penalties for making false statements on an application that we can incorporate into the letter.

Portfolio items produced:
1. Memo on making false statements on federal loan applications
2. Letter for acknowledging unconditional gift
3. Cover letter

Go to www.pearsonhighered.com/careers to download instructions.

# UNIT III   Real Estate Closing Process

## OVERVIEW OF THE REAL ESTATE CLOSING PROCESS

Before the seller and buyer can finalize the real estate transaction, a number of critical functions must be completed. Mortgage lenders must complete their determination of the creditworthiness of the borrower and that the property being offered as collateral for the loan is of sufficient value to support the recovery of the amounts lent if there is a default.

Depending on local custom or practice, a title or closing company, lawyer, or escrow agent will be hired to check on the title, or ownership, of the property and any claims that may impact the buyer obtaining good, or full, title.

After the loan issues and title search are completed, the documents must be prepared to properly reflect the terms of the loan or mortgage and to convey the transfer of the interest in the property to be transferred.

The final step in the process is the payment of the purchase price and a transfer of the property by deed from seller to buyer. The final meeting of the parties is called the settlement or closing, depending on the jurisdiction. It is a final chance for the closing attorney or title agent to verify that all obligations that may impact ownership are satisfied, including paying off the seller's mortgages and lien, taxes due, and any other potential claims. For the buyer, this is when the final mortgage papers are executed. The loan proceeds provided by the lender are submitted to the neutral closing or settlement agent, which acts as a clearinghouse, collecting all funds, paying all claims and costs associated with the sale, and distributing the proceeds to the seller.

## LEARNING OBJECTIVES

*Upon completion of this chapter, you should be able to*

1. Describe the purpose and required clauses of a deed.

2. Describe and explain the uses of the different types of deeds.

3. Distinguish between title and lien theory jurisdictions.

4. Describe and explain the documents used in creating mortgages in residential real estate loans.

# Deeds, Promissory Notes, and Mortgages

## CHAPTER 10

## ■ INTRODUCTION TO DEEDS, PROMISSORY NOTES, AND MORTGAGES

The three most important documents in a real estate sale are the deed, promissory note, and mortgage or deed of trust. A deed is a document which conveys an ownership interest in real property and provides evidence of title to that property. A promissory note is a written personal obligation to repay the sum of money borrowed. A mortgage or deed of trust is the document used to pledge the real property to secure the promise to repay the amount borrowed under the terms of the promissory note. The mortgage pledges the real estate as the collateral for the amount borrowed. If the borrower fails to make payments, the real estate can be taken through the mortgage foreclosure process. If the proceeds from the foreclosure sale of the real estate do not pay off the outstanding loan balance, the borrower remains personally responsible for the loan amount under the terms of the promissory note.

## ■ DEED

A **deed** is a document that conveys an ownership interest in real property and is evidence of title to that property. The required clauses of the deed reflect the rights conveyed and the warranties made by the grantor to the grantee. The grantor can use the deed to expand or restrict certain rights regarding the use of

**LEARNING OBJECTIVE 1**
Describe the purpose and required clauses of a deed.

**deed**
a document that conveys an ownership interest in real property and is evidence of title to that property

## DIGITAL RESOURCES

Author Introduction to Deeds, Promissory Notes and Mortgages.

Sample forms and templates.

land or to impose obligations upon the grantee. The deed may be used to describe specific rights to use easements, riparian or water rights, air rights, mineral rights, and party walls or fences.

## Parts of a Deed

The deed is a document signed by the grantor, with several distinct parts or clauses.

Some items in the document are not of legal consequence but are included to satisfy local recording requirements or process. These may vary based on the local method of processing recorded documents manually or electronically. Blank space is usually required at the top for the recorder's office use, to allow staff to enter the recording, filing, or document identification information. Most documents include information on who prepared the deed and to whom the recorded deed should be returned, which may be the lawyer for the buyer or the title insurance agent or company. This information assists the Recorder of Deeds in returning the recorded deed to the proper party or the representative after processing. The information is also of assistance to title searchers in the title-searching process. It provides them with details about the existence of potential title insurance and the availability of a prior title abstract or report as well as help if there is some error in the deed that must be corrected.

**Parts of a deed.** A deed has four major parts or clauses: the premises, the habendum, the covenants, and the execution clause.

### Premises

**premises**
the first of four portions of a deed, containing the date and identification of the parties, the granting clause, the legal description, the recital, the under and subject clause, and the appurtenances clause

The **premises** is the first required clause or portion of the deed and includes the date and identification of the parties, the granting clause, the legal description, the recital, the under and subject clause, and the appurtenances clause as shown in Exhibit 10.1 in the labeled portion of the premises section and explained in further detail below.

**PRACTICE TIP**

It is important to check local rules for format and other filing requirements for deeds and mortgages. Many jurisdictions require a specific format, including accepted margins and other standards.

## Exhibit 10.1 Deed

| | |
|---|---|
| | **THIS INDENTURE,** MADE this day _____ of 2013 |
| | **BETWEEN** |
| **1. Date and identification of the parties** | MOLLY TAYLOR (HEREINAFTER CALLED THE GRANTEES), AND DANIEL SCHAN and SARA SCHAN, H/W (HEREINAFTER CALLED THE GRANTEES), |
| **2. Granting clause** | **WITNESSETH** That the said Grantor for and in consideration of the sum of THREE HUNDRED AND EIGHT THOUSAND ($308,000.00) Dollars lawful money of the United States of America, unto her well and truly paid by the Grantees, at or before the sealing and delivery hereof, the receipt whereof is hereby acknowledged, hath granted, bargained and sold, released and confirmed, and by these presents doth grant, bargain and sell, release and confirm unto the said Grantess, their heirs and assigns, in fee as tenants by the entireties. |

**Exhibit 10.1** Continued

| | |
|---|---|
| **3. Legal description, of the property conveyed** | ALL THAT PARCEL OF LAND IN THE TOWNSHIP OF NEWTOWNE, AS MORE FULLY DESCRIBED IN DEED BOOK 1673, PAGE 0949, ID# 55-24-157, BEING KNOWN AND DESIGNATED AS:<br><br>BEGINNING AT A POINT ON THE NORTHWESTERLY SIDE OF JEFFERSON STREET (50 FEET WIDE), A CORNER OF LOT #166 ON AFOREMENTIONED PLAN, SAID POINT BEING MEASURED THE FOUR FOLLOWING COURSES AND DISTANCES FROM A POINT OF CURVE ON THE NORTH-EASTERLY SIDE OF LIBERTY STREET (60 FEET WIDE), (1) LEAVING SAID SIDE OF LIBERTY STREET ON THE ARC OF A CIRCLE CURVING TO THE LEFT, NORTH-EASTWARDLY, HAVING A RADIUS OF 20.00 FEET THE ARC DISTANCE OF 31.42 FEET TO A POINT OF TANGENT ON AFORESAID SIDE OF JEFFERSON STREET, (2) ALONG SAID SIDE OF JEFFERSON STREET NORTH 19 DEGREES 40 MINUTES 45 SECONDS EAST 61.90 FEET TO A POINT OF CURVE, (3) ON THE ARC OF A CIRCLE CURVING TO THE RIGHT, NORTHEASTWARDLY, HAVING A RADIUS OF 175.00 FEET THE ARC DISTANCE OF 176.77 FEET TO A POINT OF TANGENT AND (4) NORTH 77 DEGREES 33 MINUTES 15 SECONDS EAST 284.34 FEET TO POINT OF BEGINNING.<br>BEING LOT #489. |
| **4. Recital, how the property was acquired by the grantor** | BEING THE SAME PREMISES WHICH FELIX J. KNOWLES AND ANNA F. KNOWLES BY DEED DATED SEPTEMBER 11, 1968, AND RECORDED AT DEED BOOK 1673 PAGE 0949 CONVEYED UNTO ROBERT J. TAYLOR AND MOLLY TAYLOR, IN FEE. AND THE SAID ROBERT J. TAYLOR DEPARTED THIS LIFE ON _____. |
| **5. Under and subject clause describing any restrictions on the use of the property** | UNDER AND SUBJECT TO an easement of record allowing the adjacent parcel known as Lot #490 use of a certain five (5') foot wide driveway at and for a driveway for access to the said Liberty Street. |
| **6. Appurtenances clause** | **TOGETHER** with all land singular the buildings, improvements, ways, streets, alleys, driveways, passages, water, water-courses, rights, liberties, privileges, hereditaments and appurtenances, whatsoever unto the hereby granted premises belonging or in any wise appertaining, and the reversions and remainders, rents, issues, and profits thereof; and all the estate, right, title, interest, property, claim and demand whatsoever of the said Grantor, as well at law as in equity, of, in and to the same. |

1. **Date and identification of the parties.** The date is the date the deed was signed by the grantor, usually the same date the deed is delivered to the grantee. Under common law, the transfer of the deed was not effective unless the deed was physically handed or delivered to the grantee. The parties should be identified by their legal names, and it is important to check for middle names, initials, suffixes such as *Jr.*, and of course, correct spelling.

---

THIS INDENTURE, MADE this day of 2013

BETWEEN                  MOLLY TAYLOR
                            (hereinafter called the Grantor),

                            AND

                            DANIEL SCHAN and SARA SCHAN, H/W
                            (hereinafter called the Grantees),

---

**granting clause**
states that the grantors have granted and conveyed the property to the grantees in exchange for the consideration paid to the grantor by the grantee

2. The **granting clause** states that the grantors have granted and conveyed the property to the grantees in exchange for the consideration paid to the grantor by the grantee. The granting clause concludes with the identification of the quality of the title, usually in fee simple. When there is more than one grantee, the granting clause ends by identifying how the grantees will hold title, such as tenants in common, joint tenants with right of survivorship, or tenants by the entireties.

---

**WITNESSETH** that the said Grantors for and in consideration of the sum of Three Hundred and Eight Thousand ($308,000.00) Dollars lawful money of the United States of America, unto her well and truly paid by the Grantees, at or before the sealing and delivery hereof, the receipt whereof is hereby acknowledged, hath granted, bargained and sold, released and confirmed, and by these presents doth grant, bargain and sell, release and confirm unto the said Grantees, their heirs and assigns, infee as tenants by the entireties.

---

**legal description**
describes the property being transferred

3. The **legal description** describes the property being transferred.

---

ALL THAT PARCEL OF LAND IN THE TOWNSHIP OF NEWTOWNE, AS MORE FULLY DESCRIBED IN DEED BOOK 1673, PAGE 0949, ID# 55-24-157, BEING KNOWN AND DESIGNATED AS:
    BEGINNING AT A POINT ON THE NORTHWESTERLY SIDE OF JEFFERSON STREET (50 FEET WIDE), A CORNER OF LOT #166 ON AFOREMENTIONED PLAN, SAID POINT BEING MEASURED THE FOUR FOLLOWING COURSES AND DISTANCES FROM A POINT OF CURVE ON THE NORTHEASTERLY SIDE OF LIBERTY STREET (60 FEET WIDE), (1) LEAVING SAID SIDE OF LIBERTY STREET ON THE ARC OF A CIRCLE CURVING TO THE LEFT, NORTHEASTWARDLY, HAVING A RADIUS OF 20.00 FEET THE ARC DISTANCE OF 31.42 FEET TO A POINT OF TANGENT ON AFORESAID SIDE OF JEFFERSON STREET, (2) ALONG SAID SIDE OF JEFFERSON STREET NORTH 19 DEGREES 40 MINUTES 45 SECONDS EAST 61.90 FEET TO A POINT OF CURVE, (3) ON THE ARC OF A CIRCLE CURVING TO THE RIGHT, NORTHEASTWARDLY, HAVING A RADIUS OF 175.00 FEET THE ARC DISTANCE OF 176.77 FEET TO

A POINT OF TANGENT AND (4) NORTH 77 DEGREES 33 MINUTES 15 SECONDS EAST 284.34 FEET TO POINT OF BEGINNING.

BEING LOT #489.

4. The **recital,** which describes how the grantor of the deed obtained title.

**recital**
describes how the grantor of the deed obtained title

BEING THE SAME PREMISES WHICH FELIX J. KNOWLES AND ANNA F. KNOWLES BY DEED DATED SEPTEMBER 11, 1968, AND RECORDED AT DEED BOOK 1673 PAGE 0949 CONVEYED UNTO ROBERT J. TAYLOR AND MOLLY TAYLOR, IN FEE.

AND THE SAID ROBERT J. TAYLOR DEPARTED THIS LIFE ON _____.

5. **Under and subject clause** lists encumbrances, covenants, and easements or restrictions.

**under and subject clause**
lists encumbrances, covenants, and easements or restrictions

UNDER AND SUBJECT TO an easement of record allowing the adjacent parcel known as Lot #490 use of a certain five-foot (5') wide driveway as and for a driveway for access to the said Liberty Street.

6. The **appurtenances clause,** which states that the grantor transfers not only the land, but also all the buildings, improvements, and rights associated with the ownership, possession, and use of the land.

**appurtenances clause**
states that the grantor transfers not only the land, but also all the buildings, improvements, and rights associated with the ownership, possession, and use of the land

**TOGETHER** with all land singular the buildings, improvements, ways, streets, alleys, driveways, passages, water, watercourses, rights, liberties, privileges, hereditaments and appurtenances, whatsoever unto the hereby granted premises belonging or in any wise appertaining, and the reversions and remainders, rents, issues, and profits thereof; and all the estate, right, title, interest, property, claim and demand whatsoever of the said Grantor, as well at law as in equity, of, in and to the same.

Habendum, covenants, and execution clauses. The concluding portion of the deed includes the habendum, covenants, and execution clauses as shown in Exhibit 10.2 and described below.

## Exhibit 10.2 Annotated concluding portions of deed

**Habendum** clause, defines the nature of the estate that it being transfened.

**TO HAVE AND TO HOLD** the said lot or piece of ground above described with the buildings and improvements thereon erected, the hereditaments and premises hereby granted, or mentioned and intended so to be, with the appurtenances, unto the said Grantees, their heirs and assigns, to and for the only proper use and behoof of the said Grantees, their heirs and assigns forever, in fee as tenants by the entireties.

*(continued)*

**Exhibit 10.2** Continued

| | |
|---|---|
| **Covenants** clause contains promises made by the grantor | **AND** the said Grantor, for herself, her heirs and assigns does, by these presents, covenant, grant and agree to and with the said Grantees, their heirs and assigns, that she the said Grantor, her heirs and assigns all and singular the hereditaments and premises herein above described and granted or mentioned and intended so to be with the appurtenances, unto the said Grantees, their heirs and assigns against them, the said Grantor, her heirs and assigns and against all and every person or persons whomsoever lawfully claiming the same or any part thereof, by, from or under him, her, them, or any of them shall and will by these presents WARRANT and forever DEFEND. |
| **Execution clause** | **IN WITNESS WHEREOF,** The said Grantor has caused these presents to be duly executed the day and year first herein above written.<br><br>SEATED AND DELIVERED<br>IN THE PRESENCE OF US:<br><br>_____    _____(SEAL)<br>MOLLY TAYLOR |
| **Acknowledgement clause** | STATE OF _____<br>COUNTY OF _____<br><br>    On this, the day of 2013, before me, the undersigned officer, personally appeared MOLLY TAYLOR, known to me (or satisfactorily proven) to be the person whose name is subscribed to the within instrument, and acknowledged that she executed the same for the purposes therein contained.<br><br>    IN WITNESS WHEREOF, I hereunto set my hand and official seal.<br><br>_____<br>NOTARY PUBLIC |

## Habendum

**habendum clause**
defines the nature of the estate that is being transferred

The **habendum clause** defines the nature of the estate that is being transferred.

> **TO HAVE AND TO HOLD** the said lot or piece of ground above described with the buildings and improvements thereon erected, the hereditaments and premises hereby granted, or mentioned and intended so to be, with the appurtenances, unto the said Grantees, their heirs and assigns, to and for the only proper use and behoof of the said Grantees, their heirs and assigns forever, in fee as tenants by the entireties.

## Covenants

**covenants clause**
contains promises made by the grantor with regard to the title that has been transferred

The **covenants clause** contains promises made by the grantor with regard to the title that has been transferred. The grantor is affirming that she is in title and there are no encumbrances on her right to freely transfer the property to the grantee. The grantor then promises to defend against any claims that may be brought in the future that would challenge her right to transfer the property.

> AND the said Grantor, for herself, her heirs and assigns does, by these presents, covenant, grant and agree to and with the said Grantees, their heirs and assigns, that she the said Grantor, her heirs and assigns all and singular the hereditaments and premises herein above described and granted or mentioned and intended so to be with the appurtenances, unto the said Grantees, their heirs and assigns against them, the said Grantor, her heirs and assigns and against all and every person or persons whomsoever lawfully claiming the same or any part thereof, by, from or under him, her, them, or any of them shall and will by these presents WARRANT and forever DEFEND.

## Execution Clause

The final section of the deed includes the **execution clause,** which precedes the grantor's signature, and the **acknowledgement clause,** which is evidence that the deed was signed in the presence of an official who has the authority to take oaths.

> IN WITNESS WHEREOF, the said Grantor has caused these presents to be duly executed the day and year first herein above written.
>
> SEALED AND DELIVERED
> IN THE PRESENCE OF US:
>
> _____     _____ (SEAL)
>                                            MOLLY TAYLOR
>
>
> STATE OF _____
> COUNTY OF _____
>
>     On this, the day of 2013, before me, the undersigned officer, personally appeared MOLLY TAYLOR, known to me (or satisfactorily proven) to be the person whose name is subscribed to the within instrument, and acknowledged that she executed the same for the purposes therein contained.
>
> IN WITNESS WHEREOF, I hereunto set my hand and official seal.
>
> _____
>                          NOTARY PUBLIC

## Types of Deeds

Deeds are classified based on the warranties that are included or on the identity of the grantor.

A **general warranty deed** is the highest level of assurance to a buyer. The grantor warrants or guarantees to the grantees that the property is being transferred and conveyed without any reservation and is free and clear of any

**execution clause**
statement that precedes the grantor's signature

**acknowledgement clause**
evidence that the deed was signed in the presence of an official who has the authority to take oaths

**LEARNING OBJECTIVE 2**
Describe and explain the uses of the different types of deeds.

**general warranty deed**
the grantor warrants or guarantees to the grantees that the property is being transferred and conveyed without any reservation and is free and clear of any encumbrances or defects, including those from prior owners

**covenant of quiet enjoyment**
the grantor promises that the grantees' ownership, use, and possession will not be challenged by anyone past, present, or future

**special warranty deed**
the grantor assures the grantee only of his or her interest in the property—there is no assurance with respect to previous owners in the chain of title

**quitclaim deed**
the grantor makes no assurances concerning the quality and content of title

**sheriff's deed**
used to transfer property sold at a judicial sale

**fiduciary's deed**
used when real estate has been in the possession of a trustee, guardian, executor, or administrator

**fiduciary**
one who holds or controls assets for the benefit of another

**corporate deed**
a special form of deed used when a corporation transfers real estate

### PRACTICE TIP

A properly executed resolution from the granting corporation authorizing the sale and confirming the authority of the corporate officers to execute the documents is generally required by title companies. In the absence of title insurance companies, the grantee should require a certified copy for his or her records and potential use in future transfers.

**LEARNING OBJECTIVE 3**
Distinguish between title and lien theory jurisdictions.

**title theory state**
(also called an escrow jurisdiction) the lender or a third party holds equitable title to the real estate in the name of the borrower under the terms of a deed of trust

encumbrances or defects, including those from prior owners. This is sometimes referred to as the **covenant of quiet enjoyment,** meaning the grantor promises that the grantees' ownership, use, and possession will not be challenged by anyone past, present, or future. In effect, the grantor gives a warranty relative to the whole world, assuring the buyer that any and all claims will be defended.

In a **special warranty deed,** the grantor gives a limited warranty, which extends to the grantor's interest only. The grantor assures the grantee only of his or her interest in the property—there is no assurance with respect to previous owners in the chain of title.

In a **quitclaim deed,** the grantor makes no assurances concerning the quality and content of title. There is no assurance or warranty regarding ownership, predecessors in title, liens, remaining tax obligations, judgments attached to the interest, or holdover lessees. The quitclaim deed is used when the interest of the grantor may be in doubt. By signing the deed, the grantor says, "I'm not certain what interest I have, but whatever I have I now transfer to the grantee." These deeds may be used in a decedent's estate where there is a beneficiary whose rights have not been clearly identified and represent a cloud on the title.

A **sheriff's deed** is used to transfer property sold at a judicial sale. It represents the official act of the sheriff following the local procedure to sell real estate and use the proceeds to satisfy liens against the owner of the real estate. Whether the lien is for a mortgage, real estate taxes, or judgment obtained in litigation, the procedure to sell the real estate to satisfy the lien is concluded with a sheriff's deed confirming ownership by the individual who purchases the property at the judicial sale.

A **fiduciary's deed** is used when real estate has been in the possession of a trustee, guardian, executor, or administrator. A **fiduciary** is one who holds or controls assets for the benefit of another: A guardian possesses and controls the assets of a minor or a person declared incapacitated; an executor or administrator possesses and controls the assets of a deceased person's estate; and a trustee possesses and controls assets placed into a trust for the benefit of a beneficiary. A fiduciary's deed guarantees that the fiduciary has the authority to make the transfer and warrants against any claims that might arise during the period of time he or she serves as fiduciary.

A **corporate deed** is a special form of deed used when a corporation transfers real estate. Increased attention to execution and signature requirements for corporations is mandatory. The deed requires certain formalities with regard to its signing; it must be signed by a corporate officer with authority to act for the corporation board of directors; the corporate officer's signature must be attested to by the corporate secretary, who also signs the deed document, and the corporate seal may need to be affixed.

## ■ TITLE AND LIEN THEORY JURISDICTIONS

A mortgage is a lien on real property, created by the owner and using the property as collateral for the loan. Mortgage law is determined by the existing laws in the state where the real estate used as collateral is located. There are two theories of mortgage lien used by the different state jurisdictions: title theory and lien theory. In a **title theory state,** also called an **escrow jurisdiction,** the lender or a third party holds equitable title to the real estate in the name of the borrower under the terms of a deed of trust. The borrower is the owner, but the deed of trust

**Exhibit 10.3**  Title and lien theory states

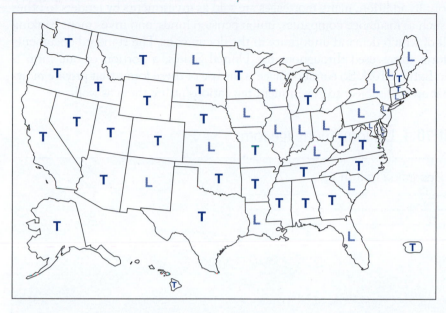

*Source:* http://title.grabois.com/

represents a claim against that ownership, or cloud on the title. In a **lien theory state**, the borrower holds title to the property and the lender places a lien on the property through use of the mortgage document. Exhibit 10.3 identifies title and lien theory states in the United States.

In title theory states, if a third party is involved in the transaction, a trustee holds title for the benefit of the lender and the borrower until the loan is paid in full. A **deed of trust** is used to define the terms and relationships of the parties to the loan agreement. Once the loan is paid, the trustee prepares and records a **release of deed of trust**, a document used to release ownership to the borrower, thereby removing any cloud from the borrower's title. The ownership is said to be "in escrow" until the loan is paid and the deed of trust is released.

In a lien theory state, a mortgage is used to define the terms and relationships of the parties: the borrower is the mortgagor, and the lender is the mortgagee. The mortgage is the document file of record, giving notice of the claim of the lender. When the mortgage is paid off, a Mortgage Satisfaction is prepared and filed to release the lien on record on the property.

Note that the term *mortgage loan* will be used below, but the information is equally applicable to deeds of trust.

**lien theory state**
the borrower holds title to the property, and the lender places a lien on the property through use of the mortgage document

**deed of trust**
used to define the terms and relationships of the parties to the loan agreement in a title theory state

**release of deed of trust**
a document used to release ownership to the borrower, thereby removing any cloud on the borrower's title

## ■ RESIDENTIAL MORTGAGE LOAN DOCUMENTS

Two documents are used in mortgage financing:

- a promissory note, which is the personal promise to repay a debt
- a mortgage or deed of trust, which secures the repayment promise by using the real estate as collateral

The mortgage lending industry is heavily controlled by state and federal regulation. Many of the provisions required in mortgage documents—particularly

**LEARNING OBJECTIVE 4**
Describe and explain the documents used in creating mortgages in residential real estate loans.

in federally insured mortgages typical of most home mortgages—are a result of this regulation. In addition, many mortgages are sold as investments by lenders to other lenders such as insurance companies, union pension funds, and investment banking firms, all of which demand uniformity in the documents. The standard documents are uniform forms used throughout the United States; a portion of one form is shown in Exhibit 10.4. So commonplace is the use of these forms that private mortgages that are not subject to government regulations utilize them as well.

**WEB EXPLORATION**
State-specific forms for first liens are available from the Federal National Mortgage Corporation at http://www.freddiemac.com/uniform/unifsecurity.html

## Exhibit 10.4 Uniform mortgage form

After Recording Return To:

_____

_____

_____

_____

_____ **[Space Above This Line For Recording Data]** _____

**MORTGAGE**

**WORDS USED OFTEN IN THIS DOCUMENT**

**(A)** **"Security Instrument."** This document, which is dated _____, _____, together with all Riders to this document, will be called the "Security Instrument."

**(B)** **"Borrower."** _____, whose address is _____ _____ sometimes will be called "Borrower" and sometimes simply "I" or "me."

**(C)** **"Lender."** _____ will be called "Lender." Lender is a corporation or association which exists under the laws of _____. Lender's address is _____.

**(D)** **"Note."** The note signed by Borrower and dated _____, _____, will be called the "Note." The Note shows that I owe Lender _____ _____ Dollars (U.S. $_____) plus interest and other amounts that may be payable. I have promised to pay this debt in Periodic Payments and to pay the debt in full by _____, _____.

**(E)** **"Property."** The property that is described below in the section titled "Description of the Property," will be called the "Property."

**(F)** **"Loan."** The "Loan" means the debt evidenced by the Note, plus interest, any prepayment charges and late charges due under the Note, and all sums due under this Security Instrument, plus interest.

**(G)** **"Sums Secured."** The amounts described below in the section titled "Borrower's Transfer to Lender of Rights in the Property" sometimes will be called the "Sums Secured."

## Promissory Note

A **promissory note** is a personal obligation in writing to repay the sum of money that has been borrowed. Whether in a title or lien theory jurisdiction, the loan documentation begins with the borrower's personal promise to repay the money borrowed. Exhibit 10.5 is a Promissory Note for the Schan mortgage loan.

**promissory note**
a personal obligation in writing to repay the sum of money that has been borrowed

**Exhibit 10.5**  Schan promissory note

---

### NOTE

**1. BORROWER'S PROMISE TO PAY**

In return for a loan that I have received, I promise to pay U.S. $246,400.00 (this amount is called "Principal"), plus interest, to the order of the Lender. The Lender is Bank Mortgage Company. I will make all payments under this Note in the form of cash, check or money order.

I understand that the Lender may transfer this Note. The Lender or anyone who takes this Note by transfer and who is entitled to receive payments under this Note is called the "Note Holder."

**2. INTEREST**

Interest will be charged on unpaid principal until the full amount of Principal has been paid. I will pay interest at a yearly rate of 6.125%.

The interest rate required by this Section 2 is the rate I will pay both before and after any default described in Section 6(B) of this Note.

**3. PAYMENTS**

**(A) Time and Place of Payments**

I will pay principal and interest by making a payment every month.

I will make my monthly payment on the First day of each month beginning on March 1. I will make these payments every month until I have paid all of the principal and interest and any other charges described below that I may owe under this Note. Each monthly payment will be applied as of its scheduled due date and will be applied to interest before Principal. If I still owe amounts under this Note, I will pay those amounts in full on that "Maturity Date."

I will make my monthly payments at 1 Bank Place or at a different place if required by the Note Holder.

**(B) Amount of Monthly Payments**

My monthly payment will be in the amount of U.S. $ 1,497.15.

**4. BORROWER'S RIGHT TO PREPAY**

I have the right to make payments of Principal at any time before they are due. A payment of Principal only is known as a "Prepayment." When I make a Prepayment, I will tell the Note Holder in writing that I am doing so. I may not designate a payment as a Prepayment if I have not made all the monthly payments due under the Note.

I may make a full Prepayment or partial Prepayments without paying a Prepayment charge. The Note Holder will use my Prepayments to reduce the amount of Principal that I owe under this Note. However, the Note Holder may apply my Prepayment to the accrued and unpaid interest on the Prepayment amount, before applying my Prepayment to reduce the Principal amount of the Note. If I make a partial Prepayment, there will be no changes in the due date or in the amount of my monthly payment unless the Note Holder agrees in writing to those changes.

**5. LOAN CHARGES**

If a law, which applies to this loan and which sets maximum loan charges, is finally interpreted so that the interest or other loan charges collected or to be collected in connection with this loan exceed the permitted limits, then: (a) any such loan charge shall be reduced by the amount necessary to reduce the charge to the permitted limit; and (b) any sums already collected from me which exceeded permitted limits will be refunded to me. The Note Holder may choose to make this refund by reducing the Principal I owe under this Note or by making a direct payment to me. If a refund reduces Principal, the reduction will be treated as a partial Prepayment.

---

*(continued)*

**Exhibit 10.5** Continued

### 6. BORROWER'S FAILURE TO PAY AS REQUIRED

#### (A) Late Charge for Overdue Payments

If the Note Holder has not received the full amount of any monthly payment by the end of 15 calendar days after the date it is due, I will pay a late charge to the Note Holder. The amount of the charge will be 5% of my overdue payment of principal and interest. I will pay this late charge promptly but only once on each late payment.

#### (B) Default

If I do not pay the full amount of each monthly payment on the date it is due, I will be in default.

#### (C) Notice of Default

If I am in default, the Note Holder may send me a written notice telling me that if I do not pay the overdue amount by a certain date, the Note Holder may require me to pay immediately the full amount of Principal which has not been paid and all the interest that I owe on that amount. That date must be at least 30 days after the date on which the notice is mailed to me or delivered by other means.

#### (D) No Waiver By Note Holder

Even if, at a time when I am in default, the Note Holder does not require me to pay immediately in full as described above, the Note Holder will still have the right to do so if I am in default at a later time.

#### (E) Payment of Note Holder's Costs and Expenses

If the Note Holder has required me to pay immediately in full as described above, the Note Holder will have the right to be paid back by me for all of its costs and expenses in enforcing this Note to the extent not prohibited by applicable law. Those expenses include, for example, reasonable attorneys' fees.

### 7. GIVING OF NOTICES

Unless applicable law requires a different method, any notice that must be given to me under this Note will be given by delivering it or by mailing it by first class mail to me at the Property Address above or at a different address if I give the Note Holder a notice of my different address.

Any notice that must be given to the Note Holder under this Note will be given by delivering it or by mailing it by first class mail to the Note Holder at the address stated in Section 3(A) above or at a different address if I am given a notice of that different address.

### 8. OBLIGATIONS OF PERSONS UNDER THIS NOTE

If more than one person signs this Note, each person is fully and personally obligated to keep all of the promises made in this Note, including the promise to pay the full amount owed. Any person who is a guarantor, surety or endorser of this Note is also obligated to do these things. Any person who takes over these obligations, including the obligations of a guarantor, surety or endorser of this Note, is also obligated to keep all of the promises made in this Note. The Note Holder may enforce its rights under this Note against each person individually or against all of us together. This means that any one of us may be required to pay all of the amounts owed under this Note.

### 9. WAIVERS

I and any other person who has obligations under this Note waive the rights of Presentment and Notice of Dishonor. "Presentment" means the right to require the Note Holder to demand payment of amounts due. "Notice of Dishonor" means the right to require the Note Holder to give notice to other persons that amounts due have not been paid.

### 10. UNIFORM SECURED NOTE

This Note is a uniform instrument with limited variations in some jurisdictions. In addition to the protections given to the Note Holder under this Note, a Mortgage, Deed of Trust, or Security Deed (the "Security Instrument"), dated the same date as this Note, protects the Note Holder from possible losses which might result if I do not keep the promises which I make in this Note. That Security Instrument describes how and under what conditions I may be required to make immediate payment in full of all amounts I owe under this Note. Some of those conditions are described as follows:

If all or any part of the Property or any Interest in the Property is sold or transferred (or if Borrower is not a natural person and a beneficial interest in Borrower is sold or transferred) without Lender's prior written consent, Lender may require immediate payment in full of all sums secured by this Security Instrument. However, this option shall not be exercised by Lender if such exercise is prohibited by Applicable Law.

## Exhibit 10.5 Continued

If Lender exercises this option, Lender shall give Borrower notice of acceleration. The notice shall provide a period of not less than 30 days from the date the notice is given in accordance with Section 15 within which Borrower must pay all sums secured by this Security Instrument. If Borrower fails to pay these sums prior to the expiration of this period, Lender may invoke any remedies permitted by this Security Instrument without further notice or demand on Borrower.

WITNESS THE HAND(S) AND SEAL(S) OF THE UNDERSIGNED.

_____ (Seal)
**DANIEL SCHAN**- Borrower

_____ (Seal)
**SARA SCHAN**- Borrower

*[Sign Original Only]*

In paragraph 1, the borrower promises to repay the funds borrowed to purchase the home. The promissory note defines the repayment terms, including the interest rate charged (paragraph 2), the monthly payment and when it is due (paragraph 3), and the penalties for failure to make payment (paragraph 6).

Paragraph 4 permits the borrower to pay the loan off earlier than set forth in paragraph 3 without imposition of any penalty.

Paragraph 5 is a statement that the lender's charges are only those that are allowable by federal law.

Paragraph 6 states that failure to make a regular payment when due results in default and that when the borrower defaults, the entire loan balance becomes due. This language is known as an **acceleration clause**; the due date is moved up, or accelerated. The lender is obligated to provide a notice to the borrower of the default. Notably, under paragraph 6D, if the lender does not act immediately upon the default, that does not change the fact of default, and the lender retains the right to accelerate the debt.

**acceleration clause**
clause in a promissory note that declares the entire amount owed due upon default

Paragraph 7 describes how notices are to be given to the lender and to the borrower. Paragraph 8 states that each person who signs the note is personally liable for the debt, and if two people sign the note, they are jointly and individually liable. In the event of default, this clause gives the lender the power to seek payment from assets owned jointly and individually by the borrowers. Finally, a paragraph that identifies this as a uniform form, and any items that follow that paragraph, are specific to the local jurisdiction's lending requirements.

## Mortgage/Deed of Trust

A mortgage or deed of trust is the document that pledges the real property to secure the promise to repay the amount borrowed under the terms of the promissory note. In lien theory states, the mortgage pledges the real estate as the collateral for the amount borrowed. The mortgage becomes a lien against the real estate. Exhibit 10.6 is the Schan mortgage. In title theory states, the

**Exhibit 10.6** Schan mortgage

After Recording Return To:

ABC Bank Mortgage Company

1 Bank Place

———————————— [Space Above This Line For Recording Data] ————————————

**MORTGAGE**

DEFINITIONS

Words used in multiple sections of this document are defined below and other words are defined in Sections 3, 11, 13, 18, 20 and 21. Certain rules regarding the usage of words used in this document are also provided in Section 16.

**(A)** **"Security Instrument"** means this document, which is dated ———————————, ———————————, together with all Riders to this document.

**(B)** **"Borrower"** is **DANIEL SCHAN AND SARA SCHAN**. Borrower is the mortgagor under this Security Instrument.

**"Lender"** is Bank Mortgage Company. Lender is a Corporation organized and existing under the laws of North Dakota. Lender's address is 1 Bank Place. Lender is the mortgagee under this Security Instrument.

**(C)** **"Note"** means the promissory note signed by Borrower and dated ———————————, ———————————. The Note states that Borrower owes Lender Two Hundred Twenty Six thousand four hundred Dollars (U.S. $246,400) plus interest. Borrower has promised to pay this debt in regular Periodic Payments and to pay the debt in full not later than March 31 2031.

**(D)** **"Property"** means the property that is described below under the heading "Transfer of Rights in the Property."

**(E)** **"Loan"** means the debt evidenced by the Note, plus interest, any prepayment charges and late charges due under the Note, and all sums due under this Security Instrument, plus interest.

**(F)** **"Riders"** means all Riders to this Security Instrument that are executed by Borrower. The following Riders are to be executed by Borrower [check box as applicable]:

☐ Adjustable Rate Rider ☐ Condominium Rider ☐ Second Home Rider
☐ Balloon Rider ☐ Planned Unit Development Rider ☐ Other(s) [specify] ———————
☐ 1-4 Family Rider ☐ Biweekly Payment Rider

**(H)** **"Applicable Law"** means all controlling applicable federal, state and local statutes, regulations, ordinances and administrative rules and orders (that have the effect of law) as well as all applicable final, non-appealable judicial opinions.

**(I)** **"Community Association Dues, Fees, and Assessments"** means all dues, fees, assessments and other charges that are imposed on Borrower or the Property by a condominium association, homeowners association or similar organization.

**(J)** **"Electronic Funds Transfer"** means any transfer of funds, other than a transaction originated by check, draft, or similar paper instrument, which is initiated through an electronic terminal, telephonic instrument, computer, or magnetic tape so as to order, instruct, or authorize a financial institution to debit or credit an account. Such term includes, but is not limited to, point-of-sale transfers, automated teller machine transactions, transfers initiated by telephone, wire transfers, and automated clearinghouse transfers.

**Exhibit 10.6** Continued

**(K)** **"Escrow Items"** means those items that are described in Section 3.

**(L)** **"Miscellaneous Proceeds"** means any compensation, settlement, award of damages, or proceeds paid by any third party (other than insurance proceeds paid under the coverages described in Section 5) for: (i) damage to, or destruction of, the Property; (ii) condemnation or other taking of all or any part of the Property; (iii) conveyance in lieu of condemnation; or (iv) misrepresentations of, or omissions as to, the value and/or condition of the Property.

**(M)** **"Mortgage Insurance"** means insurance protecting Lender against the nonpayment of, or default on, the Loan.

**(N)** **"Periodic Payment"** means the regularly scheduled amount due for (i) principal and interest under the Note, plus (ii) any amounts under Section 3 of this Security Instrument.

**(O)** **"RESPA"** means the Real Estate Settlement Procedures Act (12 U.S.C. §2601 et seq.) and its implementing regulation, Regulation X (24 C.F.R. Part 3500), as they might be amended from time to time, or any additional or successor legislation or regulation that governs the same subject matter. As used in this Security Instrument, "RESPA" refers to all requirements and restrictions that are imposed in regard to a "federally related mortgage loan" even if the Loan does not qualify as a "federally related mortgage loan" under RESPA.

**(P)** **"Successor in Interest of Borrower"** means any party that has taken title to the Property, whether or not that party has assumed Borrower's obligations under the Note and/or this Security Instrument.

TRANSFER OF RIGHTS IN THE PROPERTY

This Security Instrument secures to Lender: (i) the repayment of the Loan, and all renewals, extensions and modifications of the Note; and (ii) the performance of Borrower's covenants and agreements under this Security Instrument and the Note. For this purpose, Borrower does hereby mortgage, grant and convey to Lender the following described property located in the

_County                                          of                          Bucks:

[Type of Recording Jurisdiction]                                    [Name of Recording Jurisdiction]

which currently has the address of _                    489 Jefferson Street _____

                                                        [Street]

Newtowne_____, Your State _____ ("Property Address"):

          [City]                                                [Zip Code]

TOGETHER WITH all the improvements now or hereafter erected on the property, and all easements, appurtenances, and fixtures now or hereafter a part of the property. All replacements and additions shall also be covered by this Security Instrument. All of the foregoing is referred to in this Security Instrument as the "Property."

BORROWER COVENANTS that Borrower is lawfully seised of the estate hereby conveyed and has the right to mortgage, grant and convey the Property and that the Property is unencumbered, except for encumbrances of record. Borrower warrants and will defend generally the title to the Property against all claims and demands, subject to any encumbrances of record.

THIS SECURITY INSTRUMENT combines uniform covenants for national use and non-uniform covenants with limited variations by jurisdiction to constitute a uniform security instrument covering real property.

*(continued)*

**Exhibit 10.6** Continued

UNIFORM COVENANTS. Borrower and Lender covenant and agree as follows:

1. **Payment of Principal, Interest, Escrow Items, Prepayment Charges, and Late Charges.** Borrower shall pay when due the principal of, and interest on, the debt evidenced by the Note and any prepayment charges and late charges due under the Note. Borrower shall also pay funds for Escrow Items pursuant to Section 3. Payments due under the Note and this Security Instrument shall be made in U.S. currency. However, if any check or other instrument received by Lender as payment under the Note or this Security Instrument is returned to Lender unpaid, Lender may require that any or all subsequent payments due under the Note and this Security Instrument be made in one or more of the following forms, as selected by Lender: (a) cash; (b) money order; (c) certified check, bank check, treasurer's check or cashier's check, provided any such check is drawn upon an institution whose deposits are insured by a federal agency, instrumentality, or entity; or (d) Electronic Funds Transfer.

   Payments are deemed received by Lender when received at the location designated in the Note or at such other location as may be designated by Lender in accordance with the notice provisions in Section 15. Lender may return any payment or partial payment if the payment or partial payments are insufficient to bring the Loan current. Lender may accept any payment or partial payment insufficient to bring the Loan current, without waiver of any rights hereunder or prejudice to its rights to refuse such payment or partial payments in the future, but Lender is not obligated to apply such payments at the time such payments are accepted. If each Periodic Payment is applied as of its scheduled due date, then Lender need not pay interest on unapplied funds. Lender may hold such unapplied funds until Borrower makes payment to bring the Loan current. If Borrower does not do so within a reasonable period of time, Lender shall either apply such funds or return them to Borrower. If not applied earlier, such funds will be applied to the outstanding principal balance under the Note immediately prior to foreclosure. No offset or claim which Borrower might have now or in the future against Lender shall relieve Borrower from making payments due under the Note and this Security Instrument or performing the covenants and agreements secured by this Security Instrument.

2. **Application of Payments or Proceeds.** Except as otherwise described in this Section 2, all payments accepted and applied by Lender shall be applied in the following order of priority: (a) interest due under the Note; (b) principal due under the Note; (c) amounts due under Section 3. Such payments shall be applied to each Periodic Payment in the order in which it became due. Any remaining amounts shall be applied first to late charges, second to any other amounts due under this Security Instrument, and then to reduce the principal balance of the Note.

   If Lender receives a payment from Borrower for a delinquent Periodic Payment which includes a sufficient amount to pay any late charge due, the payment may be applied to the delinquent payment and the late charge. If more than one Periodic Payment is outstanding, Lender may apply any payment received from Borrower to the repayment of the Periodic Payments if, and to the extent that, each payment can be paid in full. To the extent that any excess exists after the payment is applied to the full payment of one or more Periodic Payments, such excess may be applied to any late charges due. Voluntary prepayments shall be applied first to any prepayment charges and then as described in the Note.

   Any application of payments, insurance proceeds, or Miscellaneous Proceeds to principal due under the Note shall not extend or postpone the due date, or change the amount, of the Periodic Payments.

3. **Funds for Escrow Items.** Borrower shall pay to Lender on the day Periodic Payments are due under the Note, until the Note is paid in full, a sum (the "Funds") to provide for payment of amounts due for: (a) taxes and assessments and other items which can attain priority over this Security Instrument as a lien or encumbrance on the Property; (b) leasehold payments or ground rents on the Property, if any; (c) premiums for any and all insurance required by Lender under Section 5; and (d) Mortgage Insurance premiums, if any, or any sums payable by Borrower to Lender in lieu of the payment of Mortgage Insurance premiums in accordance with the provisions of Section 10. These items are called "Escrow Items." At origination or at any time during the term of the Loan, Lender may require that Community Association Dues, Fees, and Assessments, if any, be escrowed by Borrower, and such dues, fees and assessments shall be an Escrow Item. Borrower shall promptly furnish to Lender all notices of amounts to be paid under this Section. Borrower shall pay Lender the Funds for Escrow Items unless Lender waives Borrower's obligation to pay the Funds for any or all Escrow Items. Lender may waive Borrower's obligation to pay to Lender Funds for any or all Escrow Items at any time. Any such waiver may only be in writing. In the event of such waiver, Borrower shall pay directly, when and where payable, the amounts due for any Escrow

## Exhibit 10.6 Continued

Items for which payment of Funds has been waived by Lender and, if Lender requires, shall furnish to Lender receipts evidencing such payment within such time period as Lender may require. Borrower's obligation to make such payments and to provide receipts shall for all purposes be deemed to be a covenant and agreement contained in this Security Instrument, as the phrase "covenant and agreement" is used in Section 9. If Borrower is obligated to pay Escrow Items directly, pursuant to a waiver, and Borrower fails to pay the amount due for an Escrow Item, Lender may exercise its rights under Section 9 and pay such amount and Borrower shall then be obligated under Section 9 to repay to Lender any such amount. Lender may revoke the waiver as to any or all Escrow Items at any time by a notice given in accordance with Section 15 and, upon such revocation, Borrower shall pay to Lender all Funds, and in such amounts, that are then required under this Section 3.

Lender may, at any time, collect and hold Funds in an amount (a) sufficient to permit Lender to apply the Funds at the time specified under RESPA, and (b) not to exceed the maximum amount a lender can require under RESPA. Lender shall estimate the amount of Funds due on the basis of current data and reasonable estimates of expenditures of future Escrow Items or otherwise in accordance with Applicable Law.

The Funds shall be held in an institution whose deposits are insured by a federal agency, instrumentality, or entity (including Lender, if Lender is an institution whose deposits are so insured) or in any Federal Home Loan Bank. Lender shall apply the Funds to pay the Escrow Items no later than the time specified under RESPA. Lender shall not charge Borrower for holding and applying the Funds, annually analyzing the escrow account, or verifying the Escrow Items, unless Lender pays Borrower interest on the Funds and Applicable Law permits Lender to make such a charge. Unless an agreement is made in writing or Applicable Law requires interest to be paid on the Funds, Lender shall not be required to pay Borrower any interest or earnings on the Funds. Borrower and Lender can agree in writing, however, that interest shall be paid on the Funds. Lender shall give to Borrower, without charge, an annual accounting of the Funds as required by RESPA.

If there is a surplus of Funds held in escrow, as defined under RESPA, Lender shall account to Borrower for the excess funds in accordance with RESPA. If there is a shortage of Funds held in escrow, as defined under RESPA, Lender shall notify Borrower as required by RESPA, and Borrower shall pay to Lender the amount necessary to make up the shortage in accordance with RESPA, but in no more than 12 monthly payments. If there is a deficiency of Funds held in escrow, as defined under RESPA, Lender shall notify Borrower as required by RESPA, and Borrower shall pay to Lender the amount necessary to make up the deficiency in accordance with RESPA, but in no more than 12 monthly payments.

Upon payment in full of all sums secured by this Security Instrument, Lender shall promptly refund to Borrower any Funds held by Lender.

4. **Charges; Liens.** Borrower shall pay all taxes, assessments, charges, fines, and impositions attributable to the Property which can attain priority over this Security Instrument, leasehold payments or ground rents on the Property, if any, and Community Association Dues, Fees, and Assessments, if any. To the extent that these items are Escrow Items, Borrower shall pay them in the manner provided in Section 3.

Borrower shall promptly discharge any lien which has priority over this Security Instrument unless Borrower: (a) agrees in writing to the payment of the obligation secured by the lien in a manner acceptable to Lender, but only so long as Borrower is performing such agreement; (b) contests the lien in good faith by, or defends against enforcement of the lien in, legal proceedings which in Lender's opinion operate to prevent the enforcement of the lien while those proceedings are pending, but only until such proceedings are concluded; or (c) secures from the holder of the lien an agreement satisfactory to Lender subordinating the lien to this Security Instrument. If Lender determines that any part of the Property is subject to a lien which can attain priority over this Security Instrument, Lender may give Borrower a notice identifying the lien. Within 10 days of the date on which that notice is given, Borrower shall satisfy the lien or take one or more of the actions set forth above in this Section 4.

Lender may require Borrower to pay a one-time charge for a real estate tax verification and/or reporting service used by Lender in connection with this Loan.

5. **Property Insurance.** Borrower shall keep the improvements now existing or hereafter erected on the Property insured against loss by fire, hazards included within the term "extended coverage," and any other hazards including, but not limited to, earthquakes and floods, for which Lender requires insurance. This

*(continued)*

**Exhibit 10.6** Continued

insurance shall be maintained in the amounts (including deductible levels) and for the periods that Lender requires. What Lender requires pursuant to the preceding sentences can change during the term of the Loan. The insurance carrier providing the insurance shall be chosen by Borrower subject to Lender's right to disapprove Borrower's choice, which right shall not be exercised unreasonably. Lender may require Borrower to pay, in connection with this Loan, either: (a) a one-time charge for flood zone determination, certification and tracking services; or (b) a one-time charge for flood zone determination and certification services and subsequent charges each time remappings or similar changes occur which reasonably might affect such determination or certification. Borrower shall also be responsible for the payment of any fees imposed by the Federal Emergency Management Agency in connection with the review of any flood zone determination resulting from an objection by Borrower.

If Borrower fails to maintain any of the coverages described above, Lender may obtain insurance coverage, at Lender's option and Borrower's expense. Lender is under no obligation to purchase any particular type or amount of coverage. Therefore, such coverage shall cover Lender, but might or might not protect Borrower, Borrower's equity in the Property, or the contents of the Property, against any risk, hazard or liability and might provide greater or lesser coverage than was previously in effect. Borrower acknowledges that the cost of the insurance coverage so obtained might significantly exceed the cost of insurance that Borrower could have obtained. Any amounts disbursed by Lender under this Section 5 shall become additional debt of Borrower secured by this Security Instrument. These amounts shall bear interest at the Note rate from the date of disbursement and shall be payable, with such interest, upon notice from Lender to Borrower requesting payment.

All insurance policies required by Lender and renewals of such policies shall be subject to Lender's right to disapprove such policies, shall include a standard mortgage clause, and shall name Lender as mortgagee and/or as an additional loss payee. Lender shall have the right to hold the policies and renewal certificates. If Lender requires, Borrower shall promptly give to Lender all receipts of paid premiums and renewal notices. If Borrower obtains any form of insurance coverage, not otherwise required by Lender, for damage to, or destruction of, the Property, such policy shall include a standard mortgage clause and shall name Lender as mortgagee and/or as an additional loss payee.

In the event of loss, Borrower shall give prompt notice to the insurance carrier and Lender. Lender may make proof of loss if not made promptly by Borrower. Unless Lender and Borrower otherwise agree in writing, any insurance proceeds, whether or not the underlying insurance was required by Lender, shall be applied to restoration or repair of the Property, if the restoration or repair is economically feasible and Lender's security is not lessened. During such repair and restoration period, Lender shall have the right to hold such insurance proceeds until Lender has had an opportunity to inspect such Property to ensure the work has been completed to Lender's satisfaction, provided that such inspection shall be undertaken promptly. Lender may disburse proceeds for the repairs and restoration in a single payment or in a series of progress payments as the work is completed. Unless an agreement is made in writing or Applicable Law requires interest to be paid on such insurance proceeds, Lender shall not be required to pay Borrower any interest or earnings on such proceeds. Fees for public adjusters, or other third parties, retained by Borrower shall not be paid out of the insurance proceeds and shall be the sole obligation of Borrower. If the restoration or repair is not economically feasible or Lender's security would be lessened, the insurance proceeds shall be applied to the sums secured by this Security Instrument, whether or not then due, with the excess, if any, paid to Borrower. Such insurance proceeds shall be applied in the order provided for in Section 2.

If Borrower abandons the Property, Lender may file, negotiate and settle any available insurance claim and related matters. If Borrower does not respond within 30 days to a notice from Lender that the insurance carrier has offered to settle a claim, then Lender may negotiate and settle the claim. The 30-day period will begin when the notice is given. In either event, or if Lender acquires the Property under Section 22 or otherwise, Borrower hereby assigns to Lender (a) Borrower's rights to any insurance proceeds in an amount not to exceed the amounts unpaid under the Note or this Security Instrument, and (b) any other of Borrower's rights (other than the right to any refund of unearned premiums paid by Borrower) under all insurance policies covering the Property, insofar as such rights are applicable to the coverage of the Property. Lender may use the insurance proceeds either to repair or restore the Property or to pay amounts unpaid under the Note or this Security Instrument, whether or not then due.

## Exhibit 10.6 Continued

6. **Occupancy.** Borrower shall occupy, establish, and use the Property as Borrower's principal residence within 60 days after the execution of this Security Instrument and shall continue to occupy the Property as Borrower's principal residence for at least one year after the date of occupancy, unless Lender otherwise agrees in writing, which consent shall not be unreasonably withheld, or unless extenuating circumstances exist which are beyond Borrower's control.

7. **Preservation, Maintenance and Protection of the Property; Inspections.** Borrower shall not destroy, damage or impair the Property, allow the Property to deteriorate or commit waste on the Property. Whether or not Borrower is residing in the Property, Borrower shall maintain the Property in order to prevent the Property from deteriorating or decreasing in value due to its condition. Unless it is determined pursuant to Section 5 that repair or restoration is not economically feasible, Borrower shall promptly repair the Property if damaged to avoid further deterioration or damage. If insurance or condemnation proceeds are paid in connection with damage to, or the taking of, the Property, Borrower shall be responsible for repairing or restoring the Property only if Lender has released proceeds for such purposes. Lender may disburse proceeds for the repairs and restoration in a single payment or in a series of progress payments as the work is completed. If the insurance or condemnation proceeds are not sufficient to repair or restore the Property, Borrower is not relieved of Borrower's obligation for the completion of such repair or restoration.

   Lender or its agent may make reasonable entries upon and inspections of the Property. If it has reasonable cause, Lender may inspect the interior of the improvements on the Property. Lender shall give Borrower notice at the time of or prior to such an interior inspection specifying such reasonable cause.

8. **Borrower's Loan Application.** Borrower shall be in default if, during the Loan application process, Borrower or any persons or entities acting at the direction of Borrower or with Borrower's knowledge or consent gave materially false, misleading, or inaccurate information or statements to Lender (or failed to provide Lender with material information) in connection with the Loan. Material representations include, but are not limited to, representations concerning Borrower's occupancy of the Property as Borrower's principal residence.

9. **Protection of Lender's Interest in the Property and Rights Under this Security Instrument.** If (a) Borrower fails to perform the covenants and agreements contained in this Security Instrument, (b) there is a legal proceeding that might significantly affect Lender's interest in the Property and/or rights under this Security Instrument (such as a proceeding in bankruptcy, probate, for condemnation or forfeiture, for enforcement of a lien which may attain priority over this Security Instrument or to enforce laws or regulations), or (c) Borrower has abandoned the Property, then Lender may do and pay for whatever is reasonable or appropriate to protect Lender's interest in the Property and rights under this Security Instrument, including protecting and/or assessing the value of the Property, and securing and/or repairing the Property. Lender's actions can include, but are not limited to: (a) paying any sums secured by a lien which has priority over this Security Instrument; (b) appearing in court; and (c) paying reasonable attorneys' fees to protect its interest in the Property and/or rights under this Security Instrument, including its secured position in a bankruptcy proceeding. Securing the Property includes, but is not limited to, entering the Property to make repairs, change locks, replace or board up doors and windows, drain water from pipes, eliminate building or other code violations or dangerous conditions, and have utilities turned on or off. Although Lender may take action under this Section 9, Lender does not have to do so and is not under any duty or obligation to do so. It is agreed that Lender incurs no liability for not taking any or all actions authorized under this Section 9.

   Any amounts disbursed by Lender under this Section 9 shall become additional debt of Borrower secured by this Security Instrument. These amounts shall bear interest at the Note rate from the date of disbursement and shall be payable, with such interest, upon notice from Lender to Borrower requesting payment.

   If this Security Instrument is on a leasehold, Borrower shall comply with all the provisions of the lease. If Borrower acquires fee title to the Property, the leasehold and the fee title shall not merge unless Lender agrees to the merger in writing.

10. **Mortgage Insurance.** If Lender required Mortgage Insurance as a condition of making the Loan, Borrower shall pay the premiums required to maintain the Mortgage Insurance in effect. If, for any reason, the Mortgage Insurance coverage required by Lender ceases to be available from the mortgage insurer that previously provided such insurance and Borrower was required to make separately designated

*(continued)*

**Exhibit 10.6** Continued

payments toward the premiums for Mortgage Insurance, Borrower shall pay the premiums required to obtain coverage substantially equivalent to the Mortgage Insurance previously in effect, at a cost substantially equivalent to the cost to Borrower of the Mortgage Insurance previously in effect, from an alternate mortgage insurer selected by Lender. If substantially equivalent Mortgage Insurance coverage is not available, Borrower shall continue to pay to Lender the amount of the separately designated payments that were due when the insurance coverage ceased to be in effect. Lender will accept, use and retain these payments as a non-refundable loss reserve in lieu of Mortgage Insurance. Such loss reserve shall be non-refundable, notwithstanding the fact that the Loan is ultimately paid in full, and Lender shall not be required to pay Borrower any interest or earnings on such loss reserve. Lender can no longer require loss reserve payments if Mortgage Insurance coverage (in the amount and for the period that Lender requires) provided by an insurer selected by Lender again becomes available, is obtained, and Lender requires separately designated payments toward the premiums for Mortgage Insurance. If Lender required Mortgage Insurance as a condition of making the Loan and Borrower was required to make separately designated payments toward the premiums for Mortgage Insurance, Borrower shall pay the premiums required to maintain Mortgage Insurance in effect, or to provide a non-refundable loss reserve, until Lender's requirement for Mortgage Insurance ends in accordance with any written agreement between Borrower and Lender providing for such termination or until termination is required by Applicable Law. Nothing in this Section 10 affects Borrower's obligation to pay interest at the rate provided in the Note.

Mortgage Insurance reimburses Lender (or any entity that purchases the Note) for certain losses it may incur if Borrower does not repay the Loan as agreed. Borrower is not a party to the Mortgage Insurance.

Mortgage insurers evaluate their total risk on all such insurance in force from time to time, and may enter into agreements with other parties that share or modify their risk, or reduce losses. These agreements are on terms and conditions that are satisfactory to the mortgage insurer and the other party (or parties) to these agreements. These agreements may require the mortgage insurer to make payments using any source of funds that the mortgage insurer may have available (which may include funds obtained from Mortgage Insurance premiums).

As a result of these agreements, Lender, any purchaser of the Note, another insurer, any reinsurer, any other entity, or any affiliate of any of the foregoing, may receive (directly or indirectly) amounts that derive from (or might be characterized as) a portion of Borrower's payments for Mortgage Insurance, in exchange for sharing or modifying the mortgage insurer's risk, or reducing losses. If such agreement provides that an affiliate of Lender takes a share of the insurer's risk in exchange for a share of the premiums paid to the insurer, the arrangement is often termed "captive reinsurance." Further:

(a) **Any such agreements will not affect the amounts that Borrower has agreed to pay for Mortgage Insurance, or any other terms of the Loan. Such agreements will not increase the amount Borrower will owe for Mortgage Insurance, and they will not entitle Borrower to any refund.**

(b) **Any such agreements will not affect the rights Borrower has - if any - with respect to the Mortgage Insurance under the Homeowners Protection Act of 1998 or any other law. These rights may include the right to receive certain disclosures, to request and obtain cancellation of the Mortgage Insurance, to have the Mortgage Insurance terminated automatically, and/or to receive a refund of any Mortgage Insurance premiums that were unearned at the time of such cancellation or termination.**

11. **Assignment of Miscellaneous Proceeds; Forfeiture.** All Miscellaneous Proceeds are hereby assigned to and shall be paid to Lender.

If the Property is damaged, such Miscellaneous Proceeds shall be applied to restoration or repair of the Property, if the restoration or repair is economically feasible and Lender's security is not lessened. During such repair and restoration period, Lender shall have the right to hold such Miscellaneous Proceeds until Lender has had an opportunity to inspect such Property to ensure the work has been completed to Lender's satisfaction, provided that such inspection shall be undertaken promptly. Lender may pay for the repairs and restoration in a single disbursement or in a series of progress payments as the work is completed. Unless an agreement is made in writing or Applicable Law requires interest to be paid on such Miscellaneous Proceeds, Lender shall not be required to pay Borrower any interest or earnings on such Miscellaneous Proceeds. If the restoration or repair is not economically feasible or Lender's security would be lessened, the Miscellaneous Proceeds shall be applied to the sums secured by this Security Instrument, whether or not then due, with the excess, if any, paid to Borrower. Such Miscellaneous Proceeds shall be applied in the order provided for in Section 2.

# Exhibit 10.6  Continued

In the event of a total taking, destruction, or loss in value of the Property, the Miscellaneous Proceeds shall be applied to the sums secured by this Security Instrument, whether or not then due, with the excess, if any, paid to Borrower.

In the event of a partial taking, destruction, or loss in value of the Property in which the fair market value of the Property immediately before the partial taking, destruction, or loss in value is equal to or greater than the amount of the sums secured by this Security Instrument immediately before the partial taking, destruction, or loss in value, unless Borrower and Lender otherwise agree in writing, the sums secured by this Security Instrument shall be reduced by the amount of the Miscellaneous Proceeds multiplied by the following fraction: (a) the total amount of the sums secured immediately before the partial taking, destruction, or loss in value divided by (b) the fair market value of the Property immediately before the partial taking, destruction, or loss in value. Any balance shall be paid to Borrower.

In the event of a partial taking, destruction, or loss in value of the Property in which the fair market value of the Property immediately before the partial taking, destruction, or loss in value is less than the amount of the sums secured immediately before the partial taking, destruction, or loss in value, unless Borrower and Lender otherwise agree in writing, the Miscellaneous Proceeds shall be applied to the sums secured by this Security Instrument whether or not the sums are then due.

If the Property is abandoned by Borrower, or if, after notice by Lender to Borrower that the Opposing Party (as defined in the next sentence) offers to make an award to settle a claim for damages, Borrower fails to respond to Lender within 30 days after the date the notice is given, Lender is authorized to collect and apply the Miscellaneous Proceeds either to restoration or repair of the Property or to the sums secured by this Security Instrument, whether or not then due. "Opposing Party" means the third party that owes Borrower Miscellaneous Proceeds or the party against whom Borrower has a right of action in regard to Miscellaneous Proceeds.

Borrower shall be in default if any action or proceeding, whether civil or criminal, is begun that, in Lender's judgment, could result in forfeiture of the Property or other material impairment of Lender's interest in the Property or rights under this Security Instrument. Borrower can cure such a default and, if acceleration has occurred, reinstate as provided in Section 19, by causing the action or proceeding to be dismissed with a ruling that, in Lender's judgment, precludes forfeiture of the Property or other material impairment of Lender's interest in the Property or rights under this Security Instrument. The proceeds of any award or claim for damages that are attributable to the impairment of Lender's interest in the Property are hereby assigned and shall be paid to Lender.

All Miscellaneous Proceeds that are not applied to restoration or repair of the Property shall be applied in the order provided for in Section 2.

12. **Borrower Not Released; Forbearance By Lender Not a Waiver.** Extension of the time for payment or modification of amortization of the sums secured by this Security Instrument granted by Lender to Borrower or any Successor in Interest of Borrower shall not operate to release the liability of Borrower or any Successors in Interest of Borrower. Lender shall not be required to commence proceedings against any Successor in Interest of Borrower or to refuse to extend time for payment or otherwise modify amortization of the sums secured by this Security Instrument by reason of any demand made by the original Borrower or any Successors in Interest of Borrower. Any forbearance by Lender in exercising any right or remedy including, without limitation, Lender's acceptance of payments from third persons, entities or Successors in Interest of Borrower or in amounts less than the amount then due, shall not be a waiver of or preclude the exercise of any right or remedy.

13. **Joint and Several Liability; Co-signers; Successors and Assigns Bound.** Borrower covenants and agrees that Borrower's obligations and liability shall be joint and several. However, any Borrower who co-signs this Security Instrument but does not execute the Note (a "co-signer"): (a) is co-signing this Security Instrument only to mortgage, grant and convey the co-signer's interest in the Property under the terms of this Security Instrument; (b) is not personally obligated to pay the sums secured by this Security Instrument; and (c) agrees that Lender and any other Borrower can agree to extend, modify, forbear or make any accommodations with regard to the terms of this Security Instrument or the Note without the co-signer's consent.

Subject to the provisions of Section 18, any Successor in Interest of Borrower who assumes Borrower's obligations under this Security Instrument in writing, and is approved by Lender, shall obtain all of Borrower's rights and benefits under this Security Instrument. Borrower shall not be released from

*(continued)*

**Exhibit 10.6** Continued

Borrower's obligations and liability under this Security Instrument unless Lender agrees to such release in writing. The covenants and agreements of this Security Instrument shall bind (except as provided in Section 20) and benefit the successors and assigns of Lender.

14. **Loan Charges.** Lender may charge Borrower fees for services performed in connection with Borrower's default, for the purpose of protecting Lender's interest in the Property and rights under this Security Instrument, including, but not limited to, attorneys' fees, property inspection and valuation fees. In regard to any other fees, the absence of express authority in this Security Instrument to charge a specific fee to Borrower shall not be construed as a prohibition on the charging of such fee. Lender may not charge fees that are expressly prohibited by this Security Instrument or by Applicable Law.

    If the Loan is subject to a law which sets maximum loan charges, and that law is finally interpreted so that the interest or other loan charges collected or to be collected in connection with the Loan exceed the permitted limits, then: (a) any such loan charge shall be reduced by the amount necessary to reduce the charge to the permitted limit; and (b) any sums already collected from Borrower which exceeded permitted limits will be refunded to Borrower. Lender may choose to make this refund by reducing the principal owed under the Note or by making a direct payment to Borrower. If a refund reduces principal, the reduction will be treated as a partial prepayment without any prepayment charge (whether or not a prepayment charge is provided for under the Note). Borrower's acceptance of any such refund made by direct payment to Borrower will constitute a waiver of any right of action Borrower might have arising out of such overcharge.

15. **Notices.** All notices given by Borrower or Lender in connection with this Security Instrument must be in writing. Any notice to Borrower in connection with this Security Instrument shall be deemed to have been given to Borrower when mailed by first class mail or when actually delivered to Borrower's notice address if sent by other means. Notice to any one Borrower shall constitute notice to all Borrowers unless Applicable Law expressly requires otherwise. The notice address shall be the Property Address unless Borrower has designated a substitute notice address by notice to Lender. Borrower shall promptly notify Lender of Borrower's change of address. If Lender specifies a procedure for reporting Borrower's change of address, then Borrower shall only report a change of address through that specified procedure. There may be only one designated notice address under this Security Instrument at any one time. Any notice to Lender shall be given by delivering it or by mailing it by first class mail to Lender's address stated herein unless Lender has designated another address by notice to Borrower. Any notice in connection with this Security Instrument shall not be deemed to have been given to Lender until actually received by Lender. If any notice required by this Security Instrument is also required under Applicable Law, the Applicable Law requirement will satisfy the corresponding requirement under this Security Instrument.

16. **Governing Law; Severability; Rules of Construction.** This Security Instrument shall be governed by federal law and the law of the jurisdiction in which the Property is located. All rights and obligations contained in this Security Instrument are subject to any requirements and limitations of Applicable Law. Applicable Law might explicitly or implicitly allow the parties to agree by contract or it might be silent, but such silence shall not be construed as a prohibition against agreement by contract. In the event that any provision or clause of this Security Instrument or the Note conflicts with Applicable Law, such conflict shall not affect other provisions of this Security Instrument or the Note which can be given effect without the conflicting provision.

    As used in this Security Instrument: (a) words of the masculine gender shall mean and include corresponding neuter words or words of the feminine gender; (b) words in the singular shall mean and include the plural and vice versa; and (c) the word "may" gives sole discretion without any obligation to take any action.

17. **Borrower's Copy.** Borrower shall be given one copy of the Note and of this Security Instrument.

18. **Transfer of the Property or a Beneficial Interest in Borrower.** As used in this Section 18, "Interest in the Property" means any legal or beneficial interest in the Property, including, but not limited to, those beneficial interests transferred in a bond for deed, contract for deed, installment sales contract or escrow agreement, the intent of which is the transfer of title by Borrower at a future date to a purchaser.

    If all or any part of the Property or any Interest in the Property is sold or transferred (or if Borrower is not a natural person and a beneficial interest in Borrower is sold or transferred) without Lender's prior

**Exhibit 10.6** Continued

written consent, Lender may require immediate payment in full of all sums secured by this Security Instrument. However, this option shall not be exercised by Lender if such exercise is prohibited by Applicable Law.

   If Lender exercises this option, Lender shall give Borrower notice of acceleration. The notice shall provide a period of not less than 30 days from the date the notice is given in accordance with Section 15 within which Borrower must pay all sums secured by this Security Instrument. If Borrower fails to pay these sums prior to the expiration of this period, Lender may invoke any remedies permitted by this Security Instrument without further notice or demand on Borrower.

19. **Borrower's Right to Reinstate After Acceleration.** If Borrower meets certain conditions, Borrower shall have the right to have enforcement of this Security Instrument discontinued at any time prior to the earliest of: (a) five days before sale of the Property pursuant to any power of sale contained in this Security Instrument; (b) such other period as Applicable Law might specify for the termination of Borrower's right to reinstate; or (c) entry of a judgment enforcing this Security Instrument. Those conditions are that Borrower: (a) pays Lender all sums which then would be due under this Security Instrument and the Note as if no acceleration had occurred; (b) cures any default of any other covenants or agreements; (c) pays all expenses incurred in enforcing this Security Instrument, including, but not limited to, reasonable attorneys' fees, property inspection and valuation fees, and other fees incurred for the purpose of protecting Lender's interest in the Property and rights under this Security Instrument; and (d) takes such action as Lender may reasonably require to assure that Lender's interest in the Property and rights under this Security Instrument, and Borrower's obligation to pay the sums secured by this Security Instrument, shall continue unchanged. Lender may require that Borrower pay such reinstatement sums and expenses in one or more of the following forms, as selected by Lender: (a) cash; (b) money order; (c) certified check, bank check, treasurer's check or cashier's check, provided any such check is drawn upon an institution whose deposits are insured by a federal agency, instrumentality or entity; or (d) Electronic Funds Transfer. Upon reinstatement by Borrower, this Security Instrument and obligations secured hereby shall remain fully effective as if no acceleration had occurred. However, this right to reinstate shall not apply in the case of acceleration under Section 18.

20. **Sale of Note; Change of Loan Servicer; Notice of Grievance.** The Note or a partial interest in the Note (together with this Security Instrument) can be sold one or more times without prior notice to Borrower. A sale might result in a change in the entity (known as the "Loan Servicer") that collects Periodic Payments due under the Note and this Security Instrument and performs other mortgage loan servicing obligations under the Note, this Security Instrument, and Applicable Law. There also might be one or more changes of the Loan Servicer unrelated to a sale of the Note. If there is a change of the Loan Servicer, Borrower will be given written notice of the change which will state the name and address of the new Loan Servicer, the address to which payments should be made and any other information RESPA requires in connection with a notice of transfer of servicing. If the Note is sold and thereafter the Loan is serviced by a Loan Servicer other than the purchaser of the Note, the mortgage loan servicing obligations to Borrower will remain with the Loan Servicer or be transferred to a successor Loan Servicer and are not assumed by the Note purchaser unless otherwise provided by the Note purchaser.

   Neither Borrower nor Lender may commence, join, or be joined to any judicial action (as either an individual litigant or the member of a class) that arises from the other party's actions pursuant to this Security Instrument or that alleges that the other party has breached any provision of, or any duty owed by reason of, this Security Instrument, until such Borrower or Lender has notified the other party (with such notice given in compliance with the requirements of Section 15) of such alleged breach and afforded the other party hereto a reasonable period after the giving of such notice to take corrective action. If Applicable Law provides a time period which must elapse before certain action can be taken, that time period will be deemed to be reasonable for purposes of this paragraph. The notice of acceleration and opportunity to cure given to Borrower pursuant to Section 22 and the notice of acceleration given to Borrower pursuant to Section 18 shall be deemed to satisfy the notice and opportunity to take corrective action provisions of this Section 20.

21. **Hazardous Substances.** As used in this Section 21: (a) "Hazardous Substances" are those substances defined as toxic or hazardous substances, pollutants, or wastes by Environmental Law and

*(continued)*

**Exhibit 10.6** Continued

the following substances: gasoline, kerosene, other flammable or toxic petroleum products, toxic pesticides and herbicides, volatile solvents, materials containing asbestos or formaldehyde, and radioactive materials; (b) "Environmental Law" means federal laws and laws of the jurisdiction where the Property is located that relate to health, safety or environmental protection; (c) "Environmental Cleanup" includes any response action, remedial action, or removal action, as defined in Environmental Law; and (d) an "Environmental Condition" means a condition that can cause, contribute to, or otherwise trigger an Environmental Cleanup.

Borrower shall not cause or permit the presence, use, disposal, storage, or release of any Hazardous Substances, or threaten to release any Hazardous Substances, on or in the Property. Borrower shall not do, nor allow anyone else to do, anything affecting the Property (a) that is in violation of any Environmental Law, (b) which creates an Environmental Condition, or (c) which, due to the presence, use, or release of a Hazardous Substance, creates a condition that adversely affects the value of the Property. The preceding two sentences shall not apply to the presence, use, or storage on the Property of small quantities of Hazardous Substances that are generally recognized to be appropriate to normal residential uses and to maintenance of the Property (including, but not limited to, hazardous substances in consumer products).

Borrower shall promptly give Lender written notice of (a) any investigation, claim, demand, lawsuit or other action by any governmental or regulatory agency or private party involving the Property and any Hazardous Substance or Environmental Law of which Borrower has actual knowledge, (b) any Environmental Condition, including but not limited to, any spilling, leaking, discharge, release or threat of release of any Hazardous Substance, and (c) any condition caused by the presence, use or release of a Hazardous Substance which adversely affects the value of the Property. If Borrower learns, or is notified by any governmental or regulatory authority, or any private party, that any removal or other remediation of any Hazardous Substance affecting the Property is necessary, Borrower shall promptly take all necessary remedial actions in accordance with Environmental Law. Nothing herein shall create any obligation on Lender for an Environmental Cleanup.

NON-UNIFORM COVENANTS. Borrower and Lender further covenant and agree as follows:

22. **Acceleration; Remedies. Lender shall give notice to Borrower prior to acceleration following Borrower's breach of any covenant or agreement in this Security Instrument (but not prior to acceleration under Section 18 unless Applicable Law provides otherwise). Lender shall notify Borrower of, among other things: (a) the default; (b) the action required to cure the default; (c) when the default must be cured; and (d) that failure to cure the default as specified may result in acceleration of the sums secured by this Security Instrument, foreclosure by judicial proceeding and sale of the Property. Lender shall further inform Borrower of the right to reinstate after acceleration and the right to assert in the foreclosure proceeding the non-existence of a default or any other defense of Borrower to acceleration and foreclosure. If the default is not cured as specified, Lender at its option may require immediate payment in full of all sums secured by this Security Instrument without further demand and may foreclose this Security Instrument by judicial proceeding. Lender shall be entitled to collect all expenses incurred in pursuing the remedies provided in this Section 22, including, but not limited to, attorneys' fees and costs of title evidence to the extent permitted by Applicable Law.**

23. **Release.** Upon payment of all sums secured by this Security Instrument, this Security Instrument and the estate conveyed shall terminate and become void. After such occurrence, Lender shall discharge and satisfy this Security Instrument. Borrower shall pay any recordation costs. Lender may charge Borrower a fee for releasing this Security Instrument, but only if the fee is paid to a third party for services rendered and the charging of the fee is permitted under Applicable Law.

24. **Waivers.** Borrower, to the extent permitted by Applicable Law, waives and releases any error or defects in proceedings to enforce this Security Instrument, and hereby waives the benefit of any present or future laws providing for stay of execution, extension of time, exemption from attachment, levy and sale, and homestead exemption.

25. **Reinstatement Period.** Borrower's time to reinstate provided in Section 19 shall extend to one hour prior to the commencement of bidding at a sheriff's sale or other sale pursuant to this Security Instrument.

## Exhibit 10.6 Continued

26. **Purchase Money Mortgage.** If any of the debt secured by this Security Instrument is lent to Borrower to acquire title to the Property, this Security Instrument shall be a purchase money mortgage.

27. **Interest Rate After Judgment.** Borrower agrees that the interest rate payable after a judgment is entered on the Note or in an action of mortgage foreclosure shall be the rate payable from time to time under the Note.

BY SIGNING BELOW, Borrower accepts and agrees to the terms and covenants contained in this Security Instrument and in any Rider executed by Borrower and recorded with it.

Witnesses:

_____          _____ (Seal)
                                          **DANIEL SCHAN- BORROWER**

_____          _____ (Seal)
                                          **SARA SCHAN- BORROWER**

_____ **[Space Below This Line For Acknowledgment]** _____

deed of trust transfers title to the real estate to the lender or a third party who holds title in trust for the benefit of the borrower until the loan is paid in full. Exhibit 10.7 is a deed of trust.

Both the mortgage and deed of trust contain terms and conditions to which both borrower (mortgagor) and lender (mortgagee) agree, including:

- Reference to the promissory note
- Payment of principal and interest
- Prepayment without penalty and late charges
- Funds escrowed for real estate taxes and homeowner's or hazard insurance
- Application of mortgage payments first to interest charges then to principal
- Charges unpaid become additional liens
- Requirement of owner occupancy of the property
- Preservation, maintenance, and protection of the property
- Leaseholds
- Lender's rights in the property
- Mortgage insurance
- Lender's right to inspect the property
- Rights and obligations in event of condemnation
- Release and forbearance
- Successors and assigns
- Loan charges, including points
- Borrower's right to reinstate the loan in the event of default
- Loan is due upon transfer of the property to another
- Lender's right to sell the loan to another
- Environmental consideration
- Default and acceleration of the loan balance

## Exhibit 10.7 Deed of trust

| | |
|---|---|
| 1 | The printed portions of this form, except differentiated additions, have been approved by the Colorado Real Estate Commission |
| 2 | (TD72-9-08) (Mandatory 1-09) |

**IF THIS FORM IS USED IN A CONSUMER CREDIT TRANSACTION, CONSULT LEGAL COUNSEL.**
**THIS IS A LEGAL INSTRUMENT. IF NOT UNDERSTOOD, LEGAL, TAX OR OTHER COUNSEL SHOULD BE**
**CONSULTED BEFORE SIGNING.**

**DEED OF TRUST**
(Due on Transfer - Strict)

THIS DEED OF TRUST is made this _____ day of _____, 20 __, between _____
_____ (Borrower), whose address is _____;
and the Public Trustee of the County in which the Property (see paragraph 1) is situated (Trustee); for the benefit of
_____ (Lender), whose address is
_____.

Borrower and Lender covenant and agree as follows:

    **1.**    **Property in Trust.** Borrower, in consideration of the indebtedness herein recited and the trust herein created, hereby grants and conveys to Trustee in trust, with power of sale, the following legally described property located in the _____ County of _____, State of Colorado:

known as No. _____ (Property Address),
                Street Address             City       State       Zip
together with all its appurtenances (Property).

    **2.**    **Note: Other Obligations Secured.** This Deed of Trust is given to secure to Lender:

        A. the repayment of the indebtedness evidenced by Borrower's note (Note) dated _____ in the principal sum of _____ Dollars (U.S. $_____), with interest on the unpaid principal balance from _____ until paid, at the rate of _____ percent rate per annum, with principal and interest payable at _____
or such other place as Lender may designate, in _____ payments of _____ Dollars (U.S. $ _____), due on the ____ day of each _____ beginning _____; such payments to continue until the entire indebtedness evidenced by said Note is fully paid; however, if not sooner paid, the entire principal amount outstanding and accrued interest thereon shall be due and payable on _____; and Borrower is to pay to Lender a late charge of _____ % of any payment not received by Lender within _____ days after payment is due; and Borrower has the right to prepay the principal amount outstanding under said Note, in whole or in part, at any time without penalty except
_____.

        B. the payment of all other sums, with interest thereon at _____ % per annum, disbursed by Lender in accordance with this Deed of Trust to protect the security of this Deed of Trust; and

        C. the performance of the covenants and agreements of Borrower herein contained.

    **3.**    **Title.** Borrower covenants that Borrower owns and has the right to grant and convey the Property, and warrants title to the same, subject to general real estate taxes for the current year, easements of record or in existence, and recorded declarations, restrictions, reservations and covenants, if any, as of this date; and subject to _____.

    **4.**    **Payment of Principal and Interest.** Borrower shall promptly pay when due the principal of and interest on the indebtedness evidenced by the Note, and late charges as provided in the Note and shall perform all of Borrower's other covenants contained in the Note.

    **5.**    **Application of Payments.** All payments received by Lender under the terms hereof shall be applied by Lender first in payment of amounts due pursuant to paragraph 23 (Escrow Funds for Taxes and Insurance), then to amounts disbursed by Lender pursuant to paragraph 9 (Protection of Lender's Security), and the balance in accordance with the terms and conditions of the Note.

    **6.**    **Prior Mortgages and Deeds of Trust; Charges; Liens.** Borrower shall perform all of Borrower's obligations under any prior deed of trust and any other prior liens. Borrower shall pay all taxes, assessments and other charges, fines and impositions attributable to the Property which may have or attain a priority over this Deed of Trust, and leasehold payments or ground rents, if any, in the manner set out in paragraph 23 (Escrow Funds for Taxes and Insurance) or, if not required to be paid in such manner, by Borrower making payment when due, directly to the payee thereof. Despite the foregoing, Borrower shall not be required to make payments otherwise required by this paragraph if Borrower, after notice to Lender, shall in good faith contest such obligation by, or defend enforcement of such obligation in, legal proceedings which operate to prevent the enforcement of the obligation or forfeiture of the Property or any part thereof, only upon Borrower making all such contested payments and other payments as ordered by the court to the registry of the court in which such proceedings are filed.

    **7.**    **Property Insurance.** Borrower shall keep the improvements now existing or hereafter erected on the Property insured against loss by fire or hazards included within the term "extended coverage" in an amount at least equal to the lesser of (a) the insurable value of the Property or (b) an amount sufficient to pay the sums secured by this Deed of Trust as well as any prior encumbrances on the Property. All of the foregoing shall be known as "Property Insurance."

    The insurance carrier providing the insurance shall be qualified to write Property Insurance in Colorado and shall be chosen by Borrower subject to Lender's right to reject the chosen carrier for reasonable cause. All insurance policies and renewals thereof

# Exhibit 10.7 Continued

shall include a standard mortgage clause in favor of Lender, and shall provide that the insurance carrier shall notify Lender at least ten (10) days before cancellation, termination or any material change of coverage. Insurance policies shall be furnished to Lender at or before closing. Lender shall have the right to hold the policies and renewals thereof.

In the event of loss, Borrower shall give prompt notice to the insurance carrier and Lender. Lender may make proof of loss if not made promptly by Borrower.

Insurance proceeds shall be applied to restoration or repair of the Property damaged, provided said restoration or repair is economically feasible and the security of this Deed of Trust is not thereby impaired. If such restoration or repair is not economically feasible or if the security of this Deed of Trust would be impaired, the insurance proceeds shall be applied to the sums secured by this Deed of Trust, with the excess, if any, paid to Borrower. If the Property is abandoned by Borrower, or if Borrower fails to respond to Lender within 30 days from the date notice is given in accordance with paragraph 16 (Notice) by Lender to Borrower that the insurance carrier offers to settle a claim for insurance benefits, Lender is authorized to collect and apply the insurance proceeds, at Lender's option, either to restoration or repair of the Property or to the sums secured by this Deed of Trust.

Any such application of proceeds to principal shall not extend or postpone the due date of the installments referred to in paragraphs 4 (Payment of Principal and Interest) and 23 (Escrow Funds for Taxes and Insurance) or change the amount of such installments. Notwithstanding anything herein to the contrary, if under paragraph 18 (Acceleration; Foreclosure; Other Remedies) the Property is acquired by Lender, all right, title and interest of Borrower in and to any insurance policies and in and to the proceeds thereof resulting from damage to the Property prior to the sale or acquisition shall pass to Lender to the extent of the sums secured by this Deed of Trust immediately prior to such sale or acquisition.

All of the rights of Borrower and Lender hereunder with respect to insurance carriers, insurance policies and insurance proceeds are subject to the rights of any holder of a prior deed of trust with respect to said insurance carriers, policies and proceeds.

**8. Preservation and Maintenance of Property.** Borrower shall keep the Property in good repair and shall not commit waste or permit impairment or deterioration of the Property and shall comply with the provisions of any lease if this Deed of Trust is on a leasehold. Borrower shall perform all of Borrower's obligations under any declarations, covenants, by-laws, rules, or other documents governing the use, ownership or occupancy of the Property.

**9. Protection of Lender's Security.** Except when Borrower has exercised Borrower's rights under paragraph 6 above, if Borrower fails to perform the covenants and agreements contained in this Deed of Trust, or if a default occurs in a prior lien, or if any action or proceeding is commenced which materially affects Lender's interest in the Property, then Lender, at Lender's option, with notice to Borrower if required by law, may make such appearances, disburse such sums and take such action as is necessary to protect Lender's interest, including, but not limited to:

(a) any general or special taxes or ditch or water assessments levied or accruing against the Property;

(b) the premiums on any insurance necessary to protect any improvements comprising a part of the Property;

(c) sums due on any prior lien or encumbrance on the Property;

(d) if the Property is a leasehold or is subject to a lease, all sums due under such lease;

(e) the reasonable costs and expenses of defending, protecting, and maintaining the Property and Lender's interest in the Property, including repair and maintenance costs and expenses, costs and expenses of protecting and securing the Property, receiver's fees and expenses, inspection fees, appraisal fees, court costs, attorney fees and costs, and fees and costs of an attorney in the employment of Lender or holder of the certificate of purchase;

(f) all other costs and expenses allowable by the evidence of debt or this Deed of Trust; and

(g) such other costs and expenses which may be authorized by a court of competent jurisdiction.

Borrower hereby assigns to Lender any right Borrower may have by reason of any prior encumbrance on the Property or by law or otherwise to cure any default under said prior encumbrance.

Any amounts disbursed by Lender pursuant to this paragraph 9, with interest thereon, shall become additional indebtedness of Borrower secured by this Deed of Trust. Such amounts shall be payable upon notice from Lender to Borrower requesting payment thereof, and Lender may bring suit to collect any amounts so disbursed plus interest specified in paragraph 2B (Note; Other Obligations Secured). Nothing contained in this paragraph 9 shall require Lender to incur any expense or take any action hereunder.

**10. Inspection.** Lender may make or cause to be made reasonable entries upon and inspection of the Property, provided that Lender shall give Borrower notice prior to any such inspection specifying reasonable cause therefore related to Lender's interest in the Property.

**11. Condemnation.** The proceeds of any award or claim for damages, direct or consequential, in connection with any condemnation or other taking of the Property, or part thereof, or for conveyance in lieu of condemnation, are hereby assigned and shall be paid to Lender as herein provided. However, all of the rights of Borrower and Lender hereunder with respect to such proceeds are subject to the rights of any holder of a prior deed of trust.

In the event of a total taking of the Property, the proceeds shall be applied to the sums secured by this Deed of Trust, with the excess, if any, paid to Borrower. In the event of a partial taking of the Property, the proceeds remaining after taking out any part of the award due any prior lien holder (net award) shall be divided between Lender and Borrower, in the same ratio as the amount of the sums secured by this Deed of Trust immediately prior to the date of taking bears to Borrower's equity in the Property immediately prior to the date of taking. Borrower's equity in the Property means the fair market value of the Property less the amount of sums secured by both this Deed of Trust and all prior liens (except taxes) that are to receive any of the award, all at the value immediately prior to the date of taking.

If the Property is abandoned by Borrower or if, after notice by Lender to Borrower that the condemnor offers to make an award or settle a claim for damages, Borrower fails to respond to Lender within 30 days after the date such notice is given, Lender is

*(continued)*

## Exhibit 10.7 Continued

authorized to collect and apply the proceeds, at Lender's option, either to restoration or repair of the Property or to the sums secured by this Deed of Trust.

Any such application of proceeds to principal shall not extend or postpone the due date of the installments referred to in paragraphs 4 (Payment of Principal and Interest) and 23 (Escrow Funds for Taxes and Insurance) nor change the amount of such installments.

**12.    Borrower not Released.** Extension of the time for payment or modification of amortization of the sums secured by this Deed of Trust granted by Lender to any successor in interest of Borrower shall not operate to release, in any manner, the liability of the original Borrower, nor Borrower's successors in interest, from the original terms of this Deed of Trust. Lender shall not be required to commence proceedings against such successor or refuse to extend time for payment or otherwise modify amortization of the sums secured by this Deed of Trust by reason of any demand made by the original Borrower nor Borrower's successors in interest.

**13.    Forbearance by Lender Not a Waiver.** Any forbearance by Lender in exercising any right or remedy hereunder, or otherwise afforded by law, shall not be a waiver or preclude the exercise of any such right or remedy.

**14.    Remedies Cumulative.** Each remedy provided in the Note and this Deed of Trust is distinct from and cumulative to all other rights or remedies under the Note and this Deed of Trust or afforded by law or equity, and may be exercised concurrently, independently or successively.

**15.    Successors and Assigns Bound; Joint and Several Liability; Captions.** The covenants and agreements herein contained shall bind, and the rights hereunder shall inure to, the respective successors and assigns of Lender and Borrower, subject to the provisions of paragraph 24 (Transfer of the Property; Assumption). All covenants and agreements of Borrower shall be joint and several. The captions and headings of the paragraphs in this Deed of Trust are for convenience only and are not to be used to interpret or define the provisions hereof.

**16.    Notice.** Except for any notice required by law to be given in another manner, (a) any notice to Borrower provided for in this Deed of Trust shall be in writing and shall be given and be effective upon (1) delivery to Borrower or (2) mailing such notice by first class U.S. mail, addressed to Borrower at Borrower's address stated herein or at such other address as Borrower may designate by notice to Lender as provided herein, and (b) any notice to Lender shall be in writing and shall be given and be effective upon (1) delivery to Lender or (2) mailing such notice by first class U.S. mail, to Lender's address stated herein or to such other address as Lender may designate by notice to Borrower as provided herein. Any notice provided for in this Deed of Trust shall be deemed to have been given to Borrower or Lender when given in any manner designated herein.

**17.    Governing Law; Severability.** The Note and this Deed of Trust shall be governed by the law of Colorado. In the event that any provision or clause of this Deed of Trust or the Note conflicts with the law, such conflict shall not affect other provisions of this Deed of Trust or the Note which can be given effect without the conflicting provision, and to this end the provisions of the Deed of Trust and Note are declared to be severable.

**18.    Acceleration; Foreclosure; Other Remedies.** Except as provided in paragraph 24 (Transfer of the Property; Assumption), upon Borrower's breach of any covenant or agreement of Borrower in this Deed of Trust, or upon any default in a prior lien upon the Property, (unless Borrower has exercised Borrower's rights under paragraph 6 above), at Lender's option, all of the sums secured by this Deed of Trust shall be immediately due and payable (Acceleration). To exercise this option, Lender may invoke the power of sale and any other remedies permitted by law. Lender shall be entitled to collect all reasonable costs and expenses incurred in pursuing the remedies provided in this Deed of Trust, including, but not limited to, reasonable attorney's fees.

If Lender invokes the power of sale, Lender shall give written notice to Trustee of such election. Trustee shall give such notice to Borrower of Borrower's rights as is provided by law. Trustee shall record a copy of such notice as required by law. Trustee shall advertise the time and place of the sale of the Property, for not less than four weeks in a newspaper of general circulation in each county in which the Property is situated, and shall mail copies of such notice of sale to Borrower and other persons as prescribed by law. After the lapse of such time as may be required by law, Trustee, without demand on Borrower, shall sell the Property at public auction to the highest bidder for cash at the time and place (which may be on the Property or any part thereof as permitted by law) in one or more parcels as Trustee may think best and in such order as Trustee may determine. Lender or Lender's designee may purchase the Property at any sale. It shall not be obligatory upon the purchaser at any such sale to see to the application of the purchase money.

Trustee shall apply the proceeds of the sale in the following order: (a) to all reasonable costs and expenses of the sale, including, but not limited to, reasonable Trustee's and attorney's fees and costs of title evidence; (b) to all sums secured by this Deed of Trust; and (c) the excess, if any, to the person or persons legally entitled thereto.

**19.    Borrower's Right to Cure Default.** Whenever foreclosure is commenced for nonpayment of any sums due hereunder, the owners of the Property or parties liable hereon shall be entitled to cure said defaults by paying all delinquent principal and interest payments due as of the date of cure, costs, expenses, late charges, attorney's fees and other fees all in the manner provided by law. Upon such payment, this Deed of Trust and the obligations secured hereby shall remain in full force and effect as though no Acceleration had occurred, and the foreclosure proceedings shall be discontinued.

**20.    Assignment of Rents; Appointment of Receiver; Lender in Possession.** As additional security hereunder, Borrower hereby assigns to Lender the rents of the Property; however, Borrower shall, prior to Acceleration under paragraph 18 (Acceleration; Foreclosure; Other Remedies) or abandonment of the Property, have the right to collect and retain such rents as they become due and payable.

# Exhibit 10.7  Continued

Lender or the holder of the Trustee's certificate of purchase shall be entitled to a receiver for the Property after Acceleration under paragraph 18 (Acceleration; Foreclosure; Other Remedies), and shall also be so entitled during the time covered by foreclosure proceedings and the period of redemption, if any; and shall be entitled thereto as a matter of right without regard to the solvency or insolvency of Borrower or of the then owner of the Property, and without regard to the value thereof. Such receiver may be appointed by any Court of competent jurisdiction upon ex parte application and without notice; notice being hereby expressly waived.

Upon Acceleration under paragraph 18 (Acceleration; Foreclosure; Other Remedies) or abandonment of the Property, Lender, in person, by agent or by judicially-appointed receiver, shall be entitled to enter upon, take possession of and manage the Property and to collect the rents of the Property including those past due. All rents collected by Lender or the receiver shall be applied, first to payment of the costs of preservation and management of the Property, second to payments due upon prior liens, and then to the sums secured by this Deed of Trust. Lender and the receiver shall be liable to account only for those rents actually received.

**21.**   **Release.**   Upon payment of all sums secured by this Deed of Trust, Lender shall cause Trustee to release this Deed of Trust and shall produce for Trustee the Note. Borrower shall pay all costs of recordation and shall pay the statutory Trustee's fees. If Lender shall not produce the Note as aforesaid, then Lender, upon notice in accordance with paragraph 16 (Notice) from Borrower to Lender, shall obtain, at Lender's expense, and file any lost instrument bond required by Trustee or pay the cost thereof to effect the release of this Deed of Trust.

**22.**   **Waiver of Exemptions.**   Borrower hereby waives all right of homestead and any other exemption in the Property under state or federal law presently existing or hereafter enacted.

**23.**   **Escrow Funds for Taxes and Insurance.**   This paragraph 23 is not applicable if Funds, as defined below, are being paid pursuant to a prior encumbrance. Subject to applicable law, Borrower shall pay to Lender, on each day installments of principal and interest are payable under the Note, until the Note is paid in full, a sum (herein referred to as "Funds") equal to _____ of the yearly taxes and assessments which may attain priority over this Deed of Trust, plus _____ of yearly premium installments for Property Insurance, all as reasonably estimated initially and from time to time by Lender on the basis of assessments and bills and reasonable estimates thereof, taking into account any excess Funds not used or shortages.

The principal of the Funds shall be held in a separate account by Lender in trust for the benefit of Borrower and deposited in an institution, the deposits or accounts of which are insured or guaranteed by a federal or state agency. Lender shall apply the Funds to pay said taxes, assessments and insurance premiums. Lender may not charge for so holding and applying the Funds, analyzing said account or verifying and compiling said assessments and bills. Lender shall not be required to pay Borrower any interest or earnings on the Funds. Lender shall give to Borrower, without charge, an annual accounting of the Funds showing credits and debits to the Funds and the purpose for which each debit to the Funds was made. The Funds are pledged as additional security for the sums secured by this Deed of Trust.

If the amount of the Funds held by Lender shall not be sufficient to pay taxes, assessments and insurance premiums as they fall due, Borrower shall pay to Lender any amount necessary to make up the deficiency within 30 days from the date notice is given in accordance with paragraph 16 (Notice) by Lender to Borrower requesting payment thereof. Provided however, if the loan secured by this Deed of Trust is subject to RESPA or other laws regulating Escrow Accounts, such deficiency, surplus or any other required adjustment shall be paid, credited or adjusted in compliance with such applicable laws.

Upon payment in full of all sums secured by this Deed of Trust, Lender shall simultaneously refund to Borrower any Funds held by Lender. If under paragraph 18 (Acceleration; Foreclosure; Other Remedies) the Property is sold or the Property is otherwise acquired by Lender, Lender shall apply, no later than immediately prior to the sale of the Property or its acquisition by Lender, whichever occurs first, any Funds held by Lender at the time of application as a credit against the sums secured by this Deed of Trust.

**24.**   **Transfer of the Property; Assumption.**   The following events shall be referred to herein as a "Transfer": (i) a transfer or conveyance of title (or any portion thereof, legal or equitable) of the Property (or any part thereof or interest therein), (ii) the execution of a contract or agreement creating a right to title (or any portion thereof, legal or equitable) in the Property (or any part thereof or interest therein), (iii) or an agreement granting a possessory right in the Property (or any portion thereof), in excess of 3 years, (iv) a sale or transfer of, or the execution of a contract or agreement creating a right to acquire or receive, more than fifty percent (50%) of the controlling interest or more than fifty percent (50%) of the beneficial interest in Borrower, (v) the reorganization, liquidation or dissolution of Borrower. Not to be included as a Transfer are (i) the creation of a lien or encumbrance subordinate to this Deed of Trust, (ii) the creation of a purchase money security interest for household appliances, or (iii) a transfer by devise, descent or by operation of the law upon the death of a joint tenant. At the election of Lender, in the event of each and every Transfer:

(a)   All sums secured by this Deed of Trust shall become immediately due and payable (Acceleration).

(b)   If a Transfer occurs and should Lender not exercise Lender's option pursuant to this paragraph 24 to Accelerate, Transferee shall be deemed to have assumed all of the obligations of Borrower under this Deed of Trust including all sums secured hereby whether or not the instrument evidencing such conveyance, contract or grant expressly so provides. This covenant shall run with the Property and remain in full force and effect until said sums are paid in full. Lender may without notice to Borrower deal with Transferee in the same manner as with Borrower with reference to said sums including the payment or credit to Transferee of undisbursed reserve Funds on payment in full of said sums, without in any way altering or discharging Borrower's liability hereunder for the obligations hereby secured.

(c)   Should Lender not elect to Accelerate upon the occurrence of such Transfer then, subject to (b) above, the mere fact of a lapse of time or the acceptance of payment subsequent to any of such events, whether or not Lender had actual or constructive notice of such Transfer, shall not be deemed a waiver of Lender's right to make such election nor shall Lender be estopped therefrom

---

**TD72-9-08.   DEED OF TRUST (DUE ON TRANSFER - STRICT)**                                    Page 4 of 5

*(continued)*

# Exhibit 10.7 Continued

by virtue thereof. The issuance on behalf of Lender of a routine statement showing the status of the loan, whether or not Lender had actual or constructive notice of such Transfer, shall not be a waiver or estoppel of Lender's said rights.

25. **Borrower's Copy.** Borrower acknowledges receipt of a copy of the Note and this Deed of Trust.

EXECUTED BY BORROWER.

IF BORROWER IS NATURAL PERSON(s):

_____

_____ doing business as _____

IF BORROWER IS CORPORATION:

ATTEST:                                              _____
                                                                    Name of Corporation

_____        By _____
            Secretary                                              President

    (SEAL)

IF BORROWER IS PARTNERSHIP:                          _____
                                                                    Name of Partnership

                                                     By _____
                                                                    A General Partner

IF BORROWER IS LIMITED LIABILITY COMPANY:            _____
                                                                    Name of Limited Liability Company

                                                     By _____
                                                                    Its authorized representative

                                                        _____
                                                                    Title of authorized representative

STATE OF COLORADO                    ⎤
                                     ⎬ ss.
_____ COUNTY OF _____      ⎦

    The foregoing instrument was acknowledged before me this _____ day of _____, 20 ___, by*
_____.

    Witness my hand and official seal.
    My commission expires: _____.

                                                        _____
                                                                    Notary Public

*If a natural person or persons, insert the name(s) of such person(s). If a corporation, insert, for example, "John Doe as President and Jane Doe as Secretary of Doe & Co., a Colorado corporation." If a partnership, insert, for example, "Sam Smith as general partner in and for Smith & Smith, a general partnership." A Statement of Authority may be required if borrower is a limited liability company or other entity (38-30-172, C.R.S.).

**TD72-9-08. DEED OF TRUST (DUE ON TRANSFER - STRICT)**                    Page 5 of 5

Under either of these documents, if the borrower fails to make payments, the real estate can be taken through the mortgage foreclosure process. If the proceeds from the foreclosure sale of the real estate do not pay off the outstanding loan balance, the borrower remains personally responsible for the loan amount under the terms of the promissory note.

## FNMA AND FHLMC

Home ownership has long been a treasured goal in the United States. Since the Great Depression of the last century, the federal government has actively participated in making funds available to banks, which banks in turn use to create mortgages.

The **Federal National Mortgage Association (FNMA)**, commonly referred to as "Fannie Mae," was founded in 1938 with the original purpose of directly infusing federal funds into banks to enhance their ability to make mortgage loans. Over time, the methods FNMA has used have changed and become almost identical to the process utilized by the **Federal Home Loan Mortgage Corporation (FHLMC)**, commonly referred to as "Freddie Mac." Banks create loans, which represent an asset on their balance sheet, and the right to receive a stream of monthly payments over the life of the loan. "Fannie Mae" and "Freddie Mac" agree to purchase the right to receive those monthly payments, and the loan is sold by the bank to them. The bank has converted a stream of monthly payments to a lump sum that can now be used to create another loan. Generally, every loan created by the bank is subject to this process so the bank can continue to make loans.

So loans from Texas can be compared on an equal basis with loans from Illinois and any other state, Fannie and Freddie have instituted uniform standards applicable to all 50 states. The standards control the forms used for the promissory note, mortgage, deed of trust, truth-in-lending disclosure statement, mortgage application, and loan qualification requirements. These standards account for the uniform lending process in the United States.

# ETHICAL Considerations

## CONFLICT OF INTEREST

Lawyers' ethical obligation requires them to avoid a conflict of interest or a potential conflict of interest. Representation of the lender and of the borrower presents a potential conflict of interest, even where the forms used are standard form documents. Any explanation of the terms and conditions by a lender's counsel may be biased in presenting information that is not clearly representative of the rights of the individual borrower—for example, grace periods for late payments.

In foreclosure proceedings, the bank counsel must avoid self-dealing in buying or acquiring property being foreclosed on by the bank client.

Lawyers for co-borrowers may also have a potential conflict representing cosigning parties such as family or friends cosigning to obtain a loan.

**WEB EXPLORATION**
To review standard forms of FNMA and FHLMC, check the website below: https://www.efanniemae.com/sf/formsdocs/documents/notes/index.jsp

## KEY TERMS

## CHAPTER SUMMARY

| | |
|---|---|
| Introduction to Deeds, Promissory Notes, and Mortgages | The three most important documents in a real estate sale are the deed, promissory note, and mortgage or deed of trust. A deed is a document which conveys an ownership interest in real property and provides evidence of title to that property. A promissory note is a written personal obligation to repay the sum of money owed. A mortgage or deed of trust is the document used to pledge the real property to secure the promise to repay the amount borrowed under the terms of the promissory note. |
| Deed | A deed is a document that conveys an ownership interest in real property and is evidence of title to that property. The required clauses of the deed reflect the rights conveyed and the warranties made by the grantor to the grantee. The grantor can use the deed to expand or restrict certain rights regarding the use of land or to impose obligations upon the grantee. |
| Parts of a Deed | A deed has four major parts or clauses: the premises, the habendum, the covenants, and the execution clause. The premises is the first required clause or portion of the deed and includes the date and identification of the parties, the granting clause, the legal description, the recital, the under and subject clause, and the appurtenances clause The concluding portion of the deed includes the habendum, covenants, and execution clauses. |

| Types of Deeds | Deeds are classified based on the warranties that are included or on the identity of the grantor.<br>A general warranty deed is the highest level of assurance to a buyer.<br>In a special warranty deed, the grantor gives a limited warranty, which extends to the grantor's interest only.<br>In a quitclaim deed, the grantor makes no assurances concerning the quality and content of title.<br>A sheriff's deed is used to transfer property sold at a judicial sale.<br>A fiduciary's deed is used when real estate has been in the possession of a trustee, guardian, executor, or administrator.<br>A corporate deed is a special form of deed used when a corporation transfers real estate. Increased attention to execution and signature requirements for corporations is mandatory. |
|---|---|
| Title and Lien Theory Jurisdictions | In a title theory state, also called an escrow jurisdiction, the lender or a third party holds equitable title to the real estate in the name of the borrower under the terms of a deed of trust.<br>In a lien theory state, the borrower holds title to the property, and the lender places a lien on the property through use of the mortgage document. |
| Residential Mortgage Loan Documents | Two documents are used in mortgage financing:<br>■ a promissory note, which is the personal promise to repay a debt<br>■ a mortgage or deed of trust, which secures the repayment promise by using the real estate as collateral |
| Promissory Note | Whether in a title or lien theory jurisdiction, the loan documentation begins with the borrower's personal promise to repay the money borrowed. |
| Mortgage/Deed of Trust | A mortgage or deed of trust is the document that pledges the real property to secure the promise to repay the amount borrowed under the terms of the promissory note. In lien theory states, the mortgage pledges the real estate as the collateral for the amount borrowed. The mortgage becomes a lien against the real estate. |
| FNMA and FHLMC | The Federal National Mortgage Association (FNMA), commonly referred to as "Fannie Mae," was founded in 1938 with the original purpose of directly infusing federal funds into banks to enhance their ability to make mortgage loans.<br>Over time, the methods FNMA has used have changed and become almost identical to the process utilized by the Federal Home Loan Mortgage Corporation (FHLMC), commonly referred to as "Freddie Mac." |

## REVIEW QUESTIONS AND EXERCISES

1. Describe the purpose of a deed.
2. Identify and describe the required clauses in a deed.
3. List and describe the components of the premises clause of a deed.
4. Why is it good practice to include the identification of the preparer of the deed on the first page of the deed?
5. What is the purpose of including the identification of title insurance on the first page of the deed?

6. What is the difference between a general warranty deed, a special warranty deed, and a quitclaim deed?
7. Under what circumstances is a fiduciary's deed used?
8. What is a title theory jurisdiction and how does it differ from a lien theory jurisdiction?
9. What is the purpose of the promissory note in a mortgage loan transaction?
10. What is a mortgage? What is a deed of trust? How are these documents similar and how are they different?

## VIDEO CASE STUDY

Go to www.pearsonhighered.com/careers to view the following videos.

**Author Introduction to Deeds, Promissory Notes and Mortgages**
Author video introduction to chapter coverage.

## INTERNET AND TECHNOLOGY EXERCISES

A. Deed
1. Using the fact pattern from the Appendix selected by your instructor, prepare a deed in the proper format for recording in your jurisdiction.
2. Obtain and prepare any additional cover sheets or forms necessary to record the deed in your jurisdiction.

B. Using the fact pattern from the Appendix selected by your instructor, prepare the note and mortgage for the buyers and property.
1. Use a mortgage calculator to compute the monthly payment.

## REAL ESTATE PORTFOLIO EXERCISES

**Deed, Mortgages and Promissory Notes**

| | |
|---|---|
| **To:** | Paralegal Intern |
| **From:** | Bank Counsel |
| **Case Name:** | Schan Mortgage |
| **Re:** | Preparation of documents for mortgage closing |

Using the standard single family home purchase forms, please complete the promissory note and mortgage for this transaction using the information in the file.

Portfolio items produced:
1. Promissory Note
2. Mortgage

| | |
|---|---|
| **To:** | Paralegal Intern |
| **From:** | Charles Hart |
| **Case Name:** | Mrs. Taylor |
| **Re:** | Seller's Deed |

Please prepare the deed for Mrs. Taylor's transfer of the property to the buyers.

The original deed is in the client file. The buyer information is on the agreement of sale.

Prepare a cover letter to the client for my signature, with a copy of the deed. The letter should explain the purpose of the deed and ask her to bring to settlement her husband's death certificate and her photo ID.

Portfolio Items produced:
1. Deed
2. Letter to client

Go to www.pearsonhighered.com/careers to download instructions.

## LEARNING OBJECTIVES

*Upon completion of this chapter, you should be able to*

1. Describe the process and procedures for preparing the documents necessary for the real estate closing.

2. Describe the process of and prepare the documents related to the residential real estate closing/settlement.

## ■ INTRODUCTION TO CLOSING

The culmination of the sale and purchase process is the closing, or settlement. To convey good title, any issues raised in the title report must be resolved. By the closing, all the contingencies in the Agreement of Sale must have been satisfied or must be removed. The final step in the process is the execution by buyers and sellers of the required documents: The sellers sign the deed to convey ownership to the buyers, and buyers execute the documents to secure the mortgage loan and pay the seller.

Closing finalizes the financial components of the transaction as well. The settlement or disbursement sheet in mortgage-based sales, the HUD-1 Settlement Statement, is completed, listing and describing the financial details, including the sale price, the buyer's cost to complete the sale, the source of the funds including the amount of any mortgage financing, the seller's costs to sell, and the net proceeds to the seller.

An independent party, in many states the title search or title insurance company, handles the processing of the documents and the exchange of funds. This neutral party may also be an escrow agent or an attorney specializing in the closing process.

## ■ PREPARING FOR CLOSING

A real estate closing, or a settlement, as it is called in some locales, can be a disorganized nightmare or a well-planned and organized transaction, depending on the preparation of the real estate and legal professionals involved. Preparing for

**LEARNING OBJECTIVE 1**
Describe the process and procedures for preparing the documents necessary for the real estate closing.

## DIGITAL RESOURCES

Author Introduction to Closing.

Real Estate Closing - Overview.

Real Estate Closing - Buyers' Attorney Explains Documents.

Real Estate Closing - Seller's Attorney Explains Documents.

Sample forms and templates.

**contingencies**
items that must be completed by the buyer or seller for the agreement of sale contract to become binding

**mortgage contingency**
clause in the agreement of sale that provides a period of time to apply for and obtain a mortgage for a specific amount and with specific terms (rate and time)

closing requires managing deadlines, communication, and cooperation between the various parties involved in the transaction—sellers, buyers, real estate brokers and agents, mortgage lenders, and title companies. Each plays a role in obtaining and providing needed information and documentation for clearing title issues, handling contingencies in the Agreement of Sale, and providing information and documentation to obtain the mortgage funds on time.

## Agreement of Sale Contingencies

In each Agreement of Sale there are certain **contingencies**, items that must be completed by the buyer or seller for the Agreement of Sale contract to become binding. Most of the contingencies are tied to a deadline for completion, such as the time period to obtain a mortgage, make an inspection, or complete a repair. The goal is to satisfy all of the contingencies prior to the closing date. Uncompleted contingencies create uncertainty and can result in the transaction falling apart or an extension of time to complete settlement. The difficulty is that each side has issues and commitments that any failure of the transaction or extension can exacerbate. Sellers may be purchasing another property and depend on the funds from the current sale to complete the next purchase. Buyers and sellers may have firm contracts with movers to move household goods from other properties or to new homes. If the transaction does not close or settle, the new issue is the demands of the movers of where to store the goods as they must clear their trucks for the next job they have scheduled.

The most significant contingency, after home inspection reports that call for repairs before closing, is the buyers obtaining the needed mortgage financing. The number and types of contingencies in the agreement of sale are part of the negotiation between the seller and the buyer. Each is free to agree or not agree to each contingency.

### Mortgage Contingency

The most commonly agreed-to contingency is the mortgage contingency, a recognition that buyers will usually require some amount of mortgage to be able to complete the transaction. The **mortgage contingency** is a clause in the agreement of sale that provides a period of time to apply and obtain a mortgage for a specific amount and with specific terms (rate and time). The first deadline in a mortgage contingency is for the buyer to make a completed mortgage application by a certain date. A second deadline is usually a date by which the buyer must have a written approval from the mortgage lender. The deadline for the mortgage commitment is usually 30 days prior to the closing date. Generally, where the buyer is unable to qualify for a mortgage loan, the contract will be terminated and the deposit money will be refunded to the buyer. Most buyers are encouraged by the real estate brokers and agents to obtain a pre-qualification letter from a lender, indicating that they are capable of obtaining the desired financing and completing the purchase. Complying with the lender's requests for information during the loan qualification process can be frustrating for buyers, who may need to locate, copy, and provide years of financial records to the lender. The real estate and legal professionals can assist the buyer in this process, by explaining the process and the reasons for the needed information.

## Inspections Contingencies

**Inspections contingencies** are provisions that allow the buyer to have the property inspected to determine if there are any issues related to maintenance, structural integrity, or habitability. Buyers on a tight budget want to be certain that there are no issues with the property that will require immediate repairs or present a health hazard. Contingency clauses frequently provide an amount of expected normal repair cost that the buyer will absorb, but beyond that limit require the seller to fix the items as a contingency for completion of the purchase. Inspection clauses present time management issues that must be considered, including time to engage the inspectors, obtain the reports, and make any needed corrections. More than any other clause in the agreement of sale, inspection issues are one of the main reasons for the termination of contracts. Managing the number of inspections—structural, water, radon, mold, roof, heating, and the like—can be a difficult task and requires cooperation to assure access. When reports indicate there is a problem, there is a need for cooperative negotiation of calm professionals to assist the parties in determining a solution and the impact on the completion of the purchase and sale. With a set price in mind, sellers frequently are reluctant to make concessions that will reduce the amount of the proceeds they will receive, and the buyers may feel they have offered the maximum they are willing to pay.

All inspection contingencies have similar features:

1. The buyer has the right to obtain, at buyer's own cost, an inspection within a certain number of days, usually 10 days, following the Agreement of Sale being signed by both parties.
2. As the buyer receives reports of the results of the inspections, those reports must be provided to the seller within a certain number of days following their receipt, usually five days.
3. If the report has a negative result, such as the presence of termites, water that is contaminated, or a sewage septic system that is not properly functioning, the seller has these options: correct the item at his or her own cost; not correct the item but adjust the sale price or give the buyer a lump sum that would represent the cost of repair; or do nothing. Whatever the seller's proposal to correct or not correct the item, that must be communicated to the buyer with in a certain number of days following receipt of the report, usually five days.
4. The buyer then must decide how to proceed. Where the seller agrees to make the repair at his or her own expense or agrees to give the buyer a sum of money to take care of the item, it is likely the buyer will be satisfied and the sale will more forward. If the seller decides not to correct or contribute to the items being corrected, the buyer can accept the property as is, without repair, or terminate the Agreement of Sale. The buyer's decision must be communicated to the seller within a certain time—again, usually five days.
5. Where corrective work is performed, the buyer will have the right to a second inspection to confirm that the item is indeed corrected, such as another test to make sure water is drinkable.

The timeline for completing the inspections may be short, 10 to 30 days. Where repairs that were not contemplated must be made due to the findings of the inspection, such as installing a new well or remediating the presence

**inspections contingencies** are provisions that allow the buyer to have the property inspected to determine if there are any issues related to maintenance, structural integrity, or habitability

List of possible inspections:

- Infestation by wood-destroying insects such as termites
- Acceptable levels of radon
- Drinkability of the water
- Capacity and suitability of the septic sewage system
- Presence of lead-based paint
- Structural integrity of the house
- Suitability of the mechanical components of the house

**PRACTICE TIP**

Additional inspections may be required, depending on the local custom, such as testing underground heating oil tanks for leaks in the eastern portion of the United States or earthquake retrofit in parts of the western states.

of radon or mold, additional time will be required to complete the repairs and a second inspection upon completion to ensure acceptable remediation. This delay is beyond the control of the parties and requires patience and flexibility. It may also require the parties to enter an agreement to extend the time for settlement.

A problem can arise when the buyer is not properly counseled on potential issues shown in the inspection report that are not of immediate concern. These are the component lifetime items. Buyers—particularly first-time buyers—may not have any thought about how long a component of a house lasts or the cost to replace it. For example, water heaters have a useful life of 8 to 10 years, or a roof has a 20- to 25-year life. Most inspection reports list these items, note the age, and may indicate that the remaining useful life is short and that replacement may be required within a year or so. For the buyer, this represents a potential major expense not in the budget. It is rare that any seller would agree to this as a contingency that he or she must satisfy. If the contingencies clause does not specify anything about this issue, the buyer must accept the property or be in default.

This is precisely the type of matter that will require the real estate and legal professionals to work together to find a resolution that both the buyer and seller can accept so the sale can be concluded. The personal desires of the seller and buyer may be an important component to how the matter is resolved. The buyer needs housing and does not have time to find another more suitable home. For the seller, there may be a need to conclude settlement to have funds to purchase another home. And while it may be legal for the seller to say, "I have no obligation to do anything about the old roof" from a practical standpoint, to get the sale to go through, the seller may offer something to the buyer, such as paying one-half of the cost of a new roof.

**pre-settlement inspection**
inspection by buyer just prior to settlement

Under the Agreement of Sale, the buyer is permitted to conduct a **pre-settlement inspection** just prior to settlement, to make sure the home is in the same condition and has been cleaned out by the seller. Many times it is discovered that appliances, heating, air conditioning, and other items are not functioning properly. Damage may have occurred to the flooring or walls as a result of the seller removing personal belongings. All of these items will need to be addressed and perhaps adjusted for at settlement. This is one of the items that cannot be prepared for in advance and requires a solution at the closing.

## Conveying Good Title

The Agreement of Sale requires the seller to convey good title, and the lender requires that there be no other liens against the real estate that prevent the mortgage from being in first-priority position following the settlement. The title search and report provide the information necessary to evaluate and satisfy these two requirements. Exhibit 11.1 is a title report.

The objections raised on the title report represent potential clouds on the title that, if unresolved at or before closing, will prevent the seller from conveying good title as required by the Agreement of Sale. These may include unpaid liens, taxes, mortgages and judgments, or proof of the death of a person named as the owner of the property on the last deed, such as the deceased husband of the seller.

The closing agent, whether an attorney or title company, will require written documentation, such as proof of the payoff of a previous mortgage or tax payment

**Exhibit 11.1** Title report

---

**American Land Title Association**

**Owner's Policy**
**Adopted 6-17-06**

---

### OWNER'S POLICY OF TITLE INSURANCE

Issued by

### BLANK TITLE INSURANCE COMPANY

**Any notice of claim and any other notice or statement in writing required to be given to the Company under this Policy must be given to the Company at the address shown in Section 18 of the Conditions.**

COVERED RISKS

SUBJECT TO THE EXCLUSIONS FROM COVERAGE, THE EXCEPTIONS FROM COVERAGE CONTAINED IN SCHEDULE B, AND THE CONDITIONS, BLANK TITLE INSURANCE COMPANY, a Blank corporation (the "Company") insures, as of Date of Policy and, to the extent stated in Covered Risks 9 and 10, after Date of Policy, against loss or damage, not exceeding the Amount of Insurance, sustained or incurred by the Insured by reason of:

1. Title being vested other than as stated in Schedule A.

2. Any defect in or lien or encumbrance on the Title. This Covered Risk includes but is not limited to insurance against loss from

   (a) A defect in the Title caused by

       (i)   forgery, fraud, undue influence, duress, incompetency, incapacity, or impersonation;

       (ii)  failure of any person or Entity to have authorized a transfer or conveyance;

       (iii) a document affecting Title not properly created, executed, witnessed, sealed, acknowledged, notarized, or delivered;

       (iv) failure to perform those acts necessary to create a document by electronic means authorized by law;

       (v)  a document executed under a falsified, expired, or otherwise invalid power of attorney;

       (vi) a document not properly filed, recorded, or indexed in the Public Records including failure to perform those acts by electronic means authorized by law; or

       (vii) a defective judicial or administrative proceeding.

   (b) The lien of real estate taxes or assessments imposed on the Title by a governmental authority due or payable, but unpaid.

   (c) Any encroachment, encumbrance, violation, variation, or adverse circumstance affecting the Title that would be disclosed by an accurate and complete land survey of the Land. The term "encroachment" includes encroachments of existing improvements located on the Land onto adjoining land, and encroachments onto the Land of existing improvements located on adjoining land.

3. Unmarketable Title.

4. No right of access to and from the Land.

---

AMERICAN
LAND TITLE
ASSOCIATION

(continued)

**Exhibit 11.1** Continued

5. The violation or enforcement of any law, ordinance, permit, or governmental regulation (including those relating to building and zoning) restricting, regulating, prohibiting, or relating to

   (a) the occupancy, use, or enjoyment of the Land;
   (b) the character, dimensions, or location of any improvement erected on the Land;
   (c) the subdivision of land; or
   (d) environmental protection

   if a notice, describing any part of the Land, is recorded in the Public Records setting forth the violation or intention to enforce, but only to the extent of the violation or enforcement referred to in that notice.

6. An enforcement action based on the exercise of a governmental police power not covered by Covered Risk 5 if a notice of the enforcement action, describing any part of the Land, is recorded in the Public Records, but only to the extent of the enforcement referred to in that notice.

7. The exercise of the rights of eminent domain if a notice of the exercise, describing any part of the Land, is recorded in the Public Records.

8. Any taking by a governmental body that has occurred and is binding on the rights of a purchaser for value without Knowledge.

9. Title being vested other than as stated in Schedule A or being defective

   (a) as a result of the avoidance in whole or in part, or from a court order providing an alternative remedy, of a transfer of all or any part of the title to or any interest in the Land occurring prior to the transaction vesting Title as shown in Schedule A because that prior transfer constituted a fraudulent or preferential transfer under federal bankruptcy, state insolvency, or similar creditors' rights laws; or

   (b) because the instrument of transfer vesting Title as shown in Schedule A constitutes a preferential transfer under federal bankruptcy, state insolvency, or similar creditors' rights laws by reason of the failure of its recording in the Public Records

      (i) to be timely, or
      (ii) to impart notice of its existence to a purchaser for value or to a judgment or lien creditor.

10. Any defect in or lien or encumbrance on the Title or other matter included in Covered Risks 1 through 9 that has been created or attached or has been filed or recorded in the Public Records subsequent to Date of Policy and prior to the recording of the deed or other instrument of transfer in the Public Records that vests Title as shown in Schedule A.

The Company will also pay the costs, attorneys' fees, and expenses incurred in defense of any matter insured against by this Policy, but only to the extent provided in the Conditions.

[Witness clause optional]

**BLANK TITLE INSURANCE COMPANY**

**BY:**                                      **PRESIDENT**

**BY:**                                      **SECRETARY**

---

AMERICAN
LAND TITLE
ASSOCIATION

**Exhibit 11.1** Continued

| American Land Title Association | Owner's Policy<br>Adopted 6-17-06 |
|---|---|

## EXCLUSIONS FROM COVERAGE

The following matters are expressly excluded from the coverage of this policy, and the Company will not pay loss or damage, costs, attorneys' fees, or expenses that arise by reason of:

1. (a) Any law, ordinance, permit, or governmental regulation (including those relating to building and zoning) restricting, regulating, prohibiting, or relating to

   (i)   the occupancy, use, or enjoyment of the Land;
   (ii)  the character, dimensions, or location of any improvement erected on the Land;
   (iii) the subdivision of land; or
   (iv) environmental protection;

   or the effect of any violation of these laws, ordinances, or governmental regulations. This Exclusion 1(a) does not modify or limit the coverage provided under Covered Risk 5.

   (b) Any governmental police power. This Exclusion 1(b) does not modify or limit the coverage provided under Covered Risk 6.

2. Rights of eminent domain. This Exclusion does not modify or limit the coverage provided under Covered Risk 7 or 8.

3. Defects, liens, encumbrances, adverse claims, or other matters

   (a) created, suffered, assumed, or agreed to by the Insured Claimant;
   (b) not Known to the Company, not recorded in the Public Records at Date of Policy, but Known to the Insured Claimant and not disclosed in writing to the Company by the Insured Claimant prior to the date the Insured Claimant became an Insured under this policy;
   (c) resulting in no loss or damage to the Insured Claimant;
   (d) attaching or created subsequent to Date of Policy (however, this does not modify or limit the coverage provided under Covered Risk 9 and 10); or
   (e) resulting in loss or damage that would not have been sustained if the Insured Claimant had paid value for the Title.

4. Any claim, by reason of the operation of federal bankruptcy, state insolvency, or similar creditors' rights laws, that the transaction vesting the Title as shown in Schedule A, is

   (a) a fraudulent conveyance or fraudulent transfer; or
   (b) a preferential transfer for any reason not stated in Covered Risk 9 of this policy.

5. Any lien on the Title for real estate taxes or assessments imposed by governmental authority and created or attaching between Date of Policy and the date of recording of the deed or other instrument of transfer in the Public Records that vests Title as shown in Schedule A.

AMERICAN
LAND TITLE
ASSOCIATION

receipts, to remove the objections raised in the title report. In many jurisdictions, this is a service that can be provided by the title agency, the real estate office, or the legal office.

The paralegal in a law firm or the conveyancer in a real estate office is typically responsible for obtaining the required documentation to satisfy the items on the title report. It is important to determine at the earliest time who will handle the task. Duplication of efforts is bad, but it is worse for everyone to arrive at settlement only to find that no one has taken care of obtaining these items because each thought the other was responsible.

Typically, there is a form letter that is used to request a mortgage payoff amount, judgment payoff, and certification regarding municipal charges such as tax, sewer rent, and water usage. Exhibits 11.2 and 11.3 contain samples of each. It is important to issue these requests early enough so the payoff information is received prior to closing. If the information is not available at closing, the closing agent may not be able to ensure good title for the buyers and meet requirements of the new mortgage lender by ensuring that it has first priority.

**Exhibit 11.2** Sample letter used for requesting a mortgage or lien payoff

[date]

[lender name and address]


Re:       Seller name
          Mortgage Loan Account #

Dear Lady or Gentleman:

This office is assisting the above captioned seller, [insert name], with the sale of her home at [insert address].

Settlement is scheduled for [insert date].

We require your statement of the amount necessary to payoff your loan at settlement. Please include your per diem charges and instructions for forwarding the payoff amount by wire funds transfer.

We have enclosed the Seller's Authorization, which allows you to release this information to our office.

Should you have any questions, please feel free to contact the undersigned.

Thank you for your prompt attention to this matter.

Very truly yours,




/s
Enclosure

**Exhibit 11.3** Sample letter used for requesting certifications from municipalities

[date]

[municipality office and address]

Re:     Seller name
        Property Address
        Tax Account # or Water/Sewer Account #

Dear Lady or Gentleman:

This office is assisting the above captioned seller, [insert name], with the sale of her home at [insert address].

Settlement is scheduled for [insert date].

We require your certification of payment of taxes for the last three years. Please be sure to include taxes that are due but not yet payable for the current year. A check is enclosed in the amount of $ _____, which represents your fee to provide this certification.

We have enclosed the Sellers Authorization, which allows you to release this information to our office.

Should you have any questions, please feel free to contact the undersigned.

Thank you for your prompt attention to this matter.

Very truly yours,



/s
Enclosure

There may be items in the title report related to the ownership of the property. Frequent matters that need to be resolved include the death of an owner and any inheritance or estate taxes due as a result, divorce of the owners and proof that one or the other is entitled to the proceeds of sale, and judgments against someone with a similar name.

Particularly with regard to estates and divorces, these matters should be resolved as soon as possible. The legal team is likely to have this information in its file. Contacting the closing agent and providing the required documentation well before attending settlement can make things go smoother. The closing agent will have a chance to review the items to determine whether they sufficiently resolve the objections or if additional information is required. If additional information is required, there is still time to obtain and provide it prior to closing rather than coming to settlement unprepared.

**PRACTICE TIP**

Review the title abstract as soon as received to determine what documentation may be required, even if the responsibility is with a conveyancer or title agent. Some items may be in the lawyer's files, such as death certificates. Confirm who is obtaining the needed documents. Some may require an extended time frame and certification, such as obtaining death certificates.

**PRACTICE TIP**

Deed preparation is controlled by custom and sometimes statute within the jurisdiction. In some jurisdictions, the title or closing agent prepares the deed as part of the title search and abstract services. In other jurisdictions, only an attorney may prepare the deed.

**PRACTICE TIP**

Check with the closing agent in advance of closing to determine the acceptable methods of payment from the buyer. Most will require wire transfer of funds if they are required to issue immediate payment of proceeds. Under bank clearing regulations, even certified checks may be held for three days before the funds will be disbursed. If wired funds are required, obtain the wiring instruction in writing for transmittal to the buyer and the mortgage company, to avoid issues at the closing.

Part of preparing for closing includes preparation of the deed that the seller will sign, conveying title to the buyer. Once again, communication is key to determine which professional will be responsible for preparing the deed.

## Estimate of Closing Costs

A good faith estimate of closing costs should be prepared for the parties; the seller will want to know how much the proceeds of sale will be, and the buyer wants to know how much money will be needed to complete the transaction.

### Seller's Closing Costs

For the seller, the costs related to the sale of the real estate include the real estate sales commission, realty transfer taxes, title insurance and survey, and payoff of judgments and existing loans. The sales commission will be determined from the provision in the listing contract and the sale price. Typically, the commission will be six percent of the sales price. Realty transfer taxes are taxes collected by the municipality and state and are usually a percentage of the sale price. Title insurance and survey costs will be available from the closing agent and in some jurisdictions are the responsibility of the buyer rather than the seller. The amount to pay off any judgment or mortgage will be determined from the responses received to the payoff request letters.

   **Proration.** Of particular interest to the seller is reimbursement for taxes and municipal charges paid in advance of closing. Certain expenses related to home ownership will be paid on an annual or quarterly basis by the seller. Real estate taxes are usually billed on a calendar-year basis. Many municipalities also impose a school tax on real estate, which is typically billed on a fiscal year from July 1 of one year to June 30 of the following year. Public water, sewer, and trash collection are often billed on a quarterly basis by the municipality. Where the seller has paid an item in full, the seller will be entitled to reimbursement from the buyer, which effectively increases the funds the seller will receive at settlement. Where a bill is unpaid and the buyer will be charged for that item at closing, the seller will reimburse the buyer for a portion of the bill (this is a cost of closing for the seller). Three examples follow.

1. County and municipal real estate taxes for the period 1/1 to 12/31 were paid in full by the seller in the amount of $3,578.45. Settlement is on July 15. The seller needs to be reimbursed for the time the buyer will be the owner of the property, from July 15 to December 31. The seller will receive reimbursement from the buyer for 16 days in July and the 5 months to the end of the year.

   $3,578.45/yr ÷ 12 months = $298.20/mo × 5 months = $1,491.00
   $298.20/mo ÷ 31 days     =    $9.62/day × 16 days   = $  153.92
   TOTAL REIMBURSEMENT TO SELLER            $1,644.92

2. School district real estate taxes for the period from 7/1 to 6/30 in the amount of $7,258.25 are due and have not been paid. Settlement is July 15. The buyer will pay the taxes at settlement, and the seller will reimburse the buyer for the 15 days in July.

   $7,258.25/yr ÷ 365 days = $19.88/day × 15 days = $298.20
   TOTAL REIMBURSEMENT TO BUYER            $298.20

**Exhibit 11.4** Seller's estimate of closing costs

**Seller's Estimate of Closing Costs**

| | |
|---|---|
| **Seller(s):** | Jane Adams |
| **Buyer(s):** | Gerald Burnett |
| **Property Address:** | 568 Everest Drive, Olde City |
| **Settlement Date:** | July 15 |

| | |
|---|---|
| Sale Price: | $350,000.00 |
| PLUS Adjustments to Sale Price: | |
| County & Town Tax 7/15 to 12/31 | $    1,644.92 |
| School Tax | |
| Sewer Rent | |
| Adjusted Gross Proceeds | $351,644.92 |
| | |
| LESS: | |
| Existing Mortgage Payoff | None known |
| Closing Costs | |
| Realtors Commission @ 6% of $350,000.00 | $ 21,000.00 |
| Realty Transfer Tax @ 1% of $350,000.00 | $   3,500.00 |
| Miscellaneous Costs – notary | $      100.00 |
| Adjustments for items not paid by Seller | |
| County & Town Tax | |
| School Tax 7/1 to 7/15 | $      298.20 |
| Sewer Rent 7/1 to 7/15 | $        29.25 |
| | |
| Total Deductions | $ 24,927.45 |
| | |
| Adjusted Gross Proceeds | $351,644.92 |
| LESS: Deductions | 24,927.45 |
| **NET PROCEEDS TO SELLER:** | **$ 326,717.47** |

3. Sewer rent is billed on a quarterly basis from 1/1 to 3/31, 4/1 to 6/30, 7/1 to 9/30, and 10/1 to 12/31. It is a flat fee of $180.00 per quarter. The seller has paid the bill through June 30, and the third-quarter bill will be paid by the buyer at settlement. The seller will need to reimburse the buyer for 15 days in July.

$180.00/quarter ÷ 92 days = $1.95/day × 15 days = $29.25

TOTAL REIMBURSEMENT TO BUYER          $29.25

Exhibit 11.4 is the estimate of seller's closing costs and net proceeds where the sale price is $350,000.00, the sales commission is six percent of the sale price, and transfer tax is one percent.

### Buyer's Closing Costs

For the buyer, an estimate of closing costs is required so the buyer can determine the additional funds required to complete purchase of the property and make arrangements for those funds to be deposited with the closing agent. The buyer's closing costs include the sale price, the tax and municipal charges that must be reimbursed to the seller, the costs associated with the mortgage loan, costs of title insurance, realty transfer taxes, recording fees to record the deed and mortgage,

**PRACTICE TIP**

The memory aid "30 days has September, April, June, and November; all the rest have 31, except February has 28, leap year gives it 29" is a helpful reminder when calculating the number of days for proration.

### Exhibit 11.5  Buyer's estimate of closing costs

**Buyers' Estimate of Closing Costs**

| | | |
|---|---|---|
| **Seller(s):** | Jane Adams | |
| **Buyer(s):** | Gerald Burnett | |
| **Property Address:** | 568 Everest Drive, Olde City | |
| **Settlement Date:** | July 15 | |

| | | |
|---|---|---|
| Sales Price: | | $350,000.00 |
| PLUS: | | |
| Closing Costs: | | |
| Loan Origination Fee | $2,800.00 | |
| Appraisal & Credit Reports | 475.00 | |
| Title Insurance | 2,600.00 | |
| Recording Fees | 250.00 | |
| Realty Transfer Tax | 3,000.00 | |
| Funds necessary for escrow | 2,998.90 | |
| Interest to end of month | 613.70 | |
| Homeowners Insurance | 895.00 | |
| Real estate taxes due or adjustment | | |
| For tax paid by seller in advance | 8,500.00 | $ 22,132.60 |
| Adjusted Sales Price | | $372,132.60 |
| | | |
| LESS: | | |
| Deposit Money | | $ 20,000.00 |
| Mortgage | | $280,000.00 |
| Adjustments for items not paid by Seller | | |
| County & Town Tax | | |
| School Tax 7/1 to 7/15 | | $     298.20 |
| Sewer Rent 7/1 to 7/15 | | $      29.25 |
| Total Deductions | | $ 300,327.45 |
| | | |
| Adjusted Sale Price | | $372,132.60 |
| LESS: Deductions | | 300,327.45 |
| **ADDITIONAL FUNDS TO COMPLETE PURCHASE:** | | **$ 71,805.15** |

and costs of any inspection reports. From the total of these expenses will be deducted the mortgage loan amount and the buyer's deposit monies, to determine an amount the buyer will be required to bring to settlement to complete the purchase. Using the same example sale price of $350,000, a deposit of $20,000, a mortgage loan of $280,000, and the same prorations, an estimate of the buyer's closing costs appears in Exhibit 11.5.

**LEARNING OBJECTIVE 2**
Describe the process of and prepare the documents related to the residential real estate closing/settlement.

## ■ REAL ESTATE CLOSING

The real estate closing is the culmination of the real estate transaction. The parties gather, the buyer signs the loan documents, the seller signs the deed, and the closing agent collects any information required to clear the title report of objections. The closing agent will also act as a financial clearinghouse, accepting all the funds, preparing the HUD-1 settlement sheet, and disbursing checks for payment of all the expenses and the seller's proceeds of sale.

## Clearing Title

The most common items resolved at the settlement table are related to the identity of the parties; payment of any judgments or mortgages, outstanding taxes, and other outstanding municipal charges; and obtaining the original documents related to clearing clouds on the seller's title.

For the buyer, this will require signing a buyer's affidavit of title, shown in Exhibit 11.6. Here, the buyers confirm that they are the purchasers of the

## Exhibit 11.6 Buyer's affidavit of title

**PURCHASER'S AFFIDAVIT**

COMMONWEALTH OF YOUR STATE :

COUNTY OF BUCKS                    :

On the _____ day of _____, 201__, before me a Notary Public for the Commonwealth of Your State appeared: **Daniel Schan and Sara Schan,** who being duly sworn according to law, do(es) depose(s) and say(s) that he/she is/are the purchaser(s) of the premises known as: **489 Jefferson Street,** and further described in the title report of the issuing title insurance company under the above file number and that (I)(We) are eighteen years and upward of age and under no legal disability.

THAT (I) (WE) CERFITY THAT (I) (WE) HAVE NOT BORROWED ANY MONEY FOR THE PURPOSE OF BUYING THIS PROPERTY OR EQUIPMENT, OR FOR ANY OTHER PURPOSE EXCEPTING MORTGAGE BEING CREATED IN THIS SETTLEMENT, NOR HAVE (I) (WE) SIGNED ANY JUDGMENT NOTES.

_____

_____

FURTHER, that this affidavit is given to the title insurance company to certify that on this date settlement was made on the premises at which time the appropriate adjustments, if any, were made for municipal minimum water and sewer rents.

FURTHER, that (I) (We) understand that (I) (We) am/are responsible for the payment of the 20 _____ cycle water and sewer rents and possible excess from _____

_____.

This affidavit is made for the purpose of inducing the issuing title insurance company to remove the obligations noted on its Title Report aforesaid.

Sworn and subscribed before me
this day of 20  .

_____
DANIEL SCHAN- BUYER

_____
Notary Public

_____
SARA SCHAN- BUYER
489 Jefferson Street, Newtowne
Address

property, are over 18 years of age, are under no legal disability that would prevent them from entering a contract, and that they have not created any debt other than the mortgage being created at closing. In some instances, where judgments against either of the borrowers have appeared on the title report, those, too, will need to be resolved. In some instances, where a judgment represents a claim against the borrower, it must be paid. In other instances, the judgment may be against someone with the same or similar name but is not the buyer. In that event, the judgment would be included on the buyer's affidavit, with the buyer stating that the judgment is not against him or her but against someone else.

For the seller, clearing title will include providing the payoff statements for any mortgage or judgments. The seller will provide documents related to clearing title that may be related to the death of a co-owner or a divorce. Ideally, copies of these items would be provided prior to closing and originals presented at closing. The seller will sign a seller's affidavit of title like the one that appears in Exhibit 11.7.

The seller's affidavit states that the seller is over 18 and not suffering from any condition that would impact his or her mental faculties; that all taxes, water, sewer, and other municipal charges have been paid; that there are no repairs to the house that haven't been paid for; and that no notices have been received from the municipality for building code or zoning violations or notices for improvements such as sidewalks or sewer lines.

**Exhibit 11.7** Seller's affidavit of title

All Questions in this Affidavit must be answered
*Question (1) and (2) do not apply to Philadelphia

PREMISES: **489 Jefferson Street**
DATE:

On the above date before me a Notary Public, personally appeared **Molly Taylor,** who being duly sworn according to law, and intending to be legally bound, depose and says that the answers and statements are true.

(1)* Has a bill been received or notice served for additional taxes assessed for new construction or major improvements? _____

(2)* Are water, sewer services or electricity supplied by Municipality or Municipal Authority? _____

(3) Has any building construction, alterations, additions been done on the above premises within the four month period preceding the above date? _____

_____

(4) Has any work for sewer construction, water pipe, paving of street, driveway, curb or sidewalk been done or ordered to be done abutting or upon the premises? _____

_____

(5) Are there any mortgages, judgments or pending court suits affecting the said premises other than those shown on above numbered Title Report? _____

## Exhibit 11.7  Continued

(6)  Who is in possession of the premises? _____

(7)  Are there any Agreements of Sale outstanding other than relating to the present transaction?
_____

(8)  Are all taxes, water and sewer rents assessed against above premises up to and including the year 20__ fully paid? _____

FURTHER, that the Grantor, Mortgagor(s) in the present transaction are of full age and under no legal disability to execute the proposed conveyance-mortgage.

FURTHER, that the deponent(s) named herein is/are the same person(s) so named in the Recital set forth in the above-numbered title report, and that the facts of identity relating to any other person(s) named in the said recital are true and correct.

FURTHER, that the Grantee in the last deed of record as set forth in said Recital, if shown to be husband and wife, have not been divorced after the acquisition of title on the date set forth herein.

Deponent(s) make this affidavit for the purpose of inducing the issuing title insurance company to hold settlement for the above premises, and to issue its Title Insurance Policy insuring the title thereto.

Sworn to and subscribed
and subscribed before
me this day                                          _____
of, 201 .                                                Molly Taylor

_____                   _____
Notary Public

Finally, the seller is required to complete a tax information reporting form for the Internal Revenue Service, such as the one that appears in Exhibit 11.8. Under IRS regulations, closing agents are obligated to report the sale and the gross proceeds of sale received by the seller in any real estate sales transaction. From this information form, the closing agent will prepare the tax document,

## Exhibit 11.8  Seller's disclosure for income tax purposes

**CERTIFICATION FOR NO INFORMATION REPORTING
ON THE SALE OR EXCHANGE OF A PRINCIPAL RESIDENCE**

This form may be completed by the seller of a principal residence. This information is necessary to determine whether the sale or exchange should be reported to the seller, and to the Internal Revenue Service on Form 1099-S, Proceeds from Real Estate Transactions. If the seller properly completes Parts I and II, and make a "yes" response to assurances (1) though (4) in Part II, no information reporting to the seller or to the Service will be required for that seller. The term "seller" includes each owner of the residence that is sold or exchanged. Thus, if a residence has more than one owner, a real estate reporting person must either obtain a certification from each owner (whether married or not) or file an information return and furnish a payee statement for any owner that does not make the certification.

(continued)

## Exhibit 11.8 Continued

PART I - Seller Information

1. Name: **Molly Taylor**

2. Address or legal description (including city, state and zip code) of residence being sold or exchanged: **489 Jefferson Street, Newtowne, YS**

3. Forwarding Address: Barclay Court Center
   4 Barclay Street, Newtowne, YS

4. Taxpayer Identification Number: 555-44-3333

PART II – Seller Assurances

Check "yes" or "no" for assurances (1) through (4)

| Yes | No | |
|-----|-----|-----|
| [ X ] | [ ] | 1. I owned and used the residence as my principal residence for periods Aggregating 2 years or more during the 5-year period ending on the date of the sale or exchange of the residence. |
| [ X ] | [ ] | 2. I have not sold or exchanged another principal residence during the 2 year period ending on the date of the sale or exchange of the residence (not taking into account any sale or exchange before May 7, 1997). |
| [ X ] | [ ] | 3. No portion of the residence has been used for business or rentalpurposes by me (or my spouse if I am married) after May 6, 1997. |
| [ ] | [ X ] | 4. At least one of the following three statements applies: The sale or exchange is of the entire residence for $250,000 or less. |

**OR**

I am married, the sale or exchange is of the entire residence for $500,000 or less, and the gain on the sale or exchange of the entire residence is $250,000 or less.

**OR**

I am married, the sale or exchange of the entire residence for $500,00 or less and (a) I intend to file a joint return for the year of the sale or exchange, (b) my spouse also used the residence as his or her principal residence for periods aggregating 2 years or more during the 5-year period ending on the date of the sale or exchange of the residence and (c) my spouse also has not sold or exchanged another principal residence during the 2-year period ending on the date of the sale or exchange of the residence (not taking into account any sale or exchange before May 7, 1997).

## Exhibit 11.8 Continued

**PART III – Seller Certification**

Under penalties of perjury, I certify that all of the above information is true as of the end of the day of the sale or exchange.

Signature of Seller:

_____                        Date:_____

MOLLY TAYLOR

_____

Settlement Date:
Sale Price: $308,000
Seller Names: Molly Taylor
TAX CREDIT:

1099-S Proceeds from Real Estate Transactions, to report the sale to the Internal Revenue Service and the seller at the end of the year. Exhibit 11.9 contains the 1099-S reporting form.

## Loan Documents

The processing of the loan documents at settlement is controlled by the lender. In some instances, the lender will send a representative to review the documents with the buyer/borrower and to make sure all the lender's requirements are

## Exhibit 11.9 Form 1099-S Proceeds from Real Estate Transactions

| 7575 ☐ VOID ☐ CORRECTED | | |
|---|---|---|
| FILER'S name, street address, city, state, ZIP code, and telephone no. | **1** Date of closing | OMB No. 1545-0997 |
| | **2** Gross proceeds $ | 20**12** Form **1099-S** — Proceeds From Real Estate Transactions |
| FILER'S federal identification number    TRANSFEROR'S identification number | **3** Address or legal description (including city, state, and ZIP code) | **Copy A** For **Internal Revenue Service Center** File with Form 1096. |
| TRANSFEROR'S name | | For Privacy Act and Paperwork Reduction Act Notice, see the |
| Street address (including apt. no.) | | |
| City, state, and ZIP code | **4** Check here if the transferor received or will receive property or services as part of the consideration ▶ ☐ | **2012 General Instructions for Certain Information Returns.** |
| Account or escrow number (see instructions) | **5** Buyer's part of real estate tax $ | |

Form **1099-S**       Cat. No. 64292E      Department of the Treasury - Internal Revenue Service

**Do Not Cut or Separate Forms on This Page — Do Not Cut or Separate Forms on This Page**

complied with. It is more likely, however, that the responsibility for compliance with the lender's requirements will be placed on the closing agent. Lenders issue a detailed instruction letter to the closing agent, such as the one that appears in Exhibit 11.10. All the conditions must be met before the closing agent may release funds.

At closing, buyers sign the promissory note, mortgage, and other documents required by the lender. Some of the documents will be familiar, as they were part of the loan application process. The forms prepared at the time of

**Exhibit 11.10** Lender's closing instructions letter

The documents necessary for closing this loan are attached. Some of these documents may be partially completed. Prior to execution and before we obtain the closing package, please make certain all documents are fully completed. All copies must conform to signature, dates, notary acknowledgement, and certified by you to be true and correct copies of the original instruments. You are to close the loan and disburse our check **ONLY** after you have secured a Funding Number and/or complied with items listed in these Loan Closing Instructions, our General Instructions, the Fee Schedule (241139), the Sales Contract, and any addendum (if applicable), and are prepared to file your final certificate for title policy.

X  1. TRUTH IN LENDING Disclosure - Before signing closing documents, each borrower (and owner occupant title holder on a refinance transaction) must date and sign. Original to Borrower, signed original to Wachovia; copies to all signers.

___  2. Notice of Right to Cancel (Two for each borrower/owner occupant title holder).

X  3. **Note-** Signed original.
   ( ) Addendum to Note for _____
   _____

X  4. *Security Instrument - Original or 1 certified copy of original instrument including Rider(s) and/or Attachment(s) if specified below:

   ( ) VA Assumption Rider      *( ) Condominium      *(X) PUD      ( ) 2nd Home Rider
   *( ) 1-4 Family Rider      *( ) Adjustable Rate Rider      *( ) Graduated Payment Rider
   *( ) Addendum to Adjustable Rate/Graduated Payment Rider (Fixed Rate Conversion Option)
   ( ) Balloon Rider
   ( ) Non-Owner Occupancy Rider (FHA refinances)
   ( ) _____

X  5. Receipt from Recorder's Office showing original Security Instrument filed for recording or original recorded Security Instrument.

X  6. ☒ (A). Hazard Insurance Policy in minimum amount of $ ___**340,000.00**___ with receipt attached for payment of first annual premium.

   ☐ (B). Hazard Insurance Binder in minimum amount of $ _____ with receipt attached for payment of first annual premium. Minimum Binder term is 60 days unless prohibited by State law.

   ☐ (C). Master Policy is required for Condominiums with a Certificate of Insurance for the individual unit.

   ☐      If marked, Certified True Copy of Master Insurance Policy is needed.

The "Standard" Mortgagee Clause is "**Wachovia Mortgage Corporation, its Successors and/or Assigns, Post Office Box 57664, Jacksonville, FL 32241-7664**." For construction loans only, the clause is "Wachovia Mortgage Corporation, its Successors and/or Assigns, 3563 Phillips Highway, Suite 400C, 2nd Floor, Jacksonville, FL 32207."

## Exhibit 11.10 Continued

___ 7. Flood Insurance - Original policy in die amount of $ _____ (or for the maximum amount available) or Copy of Application for Flood Insurance and receipt indicating first annual premium is paid.

_X_ 8. Mortgage title insurance policy in the amount of the loan (or the peak amount in the event of a Graduated Payment Mortgage) and must be issued by the company specified above. (If company is not specified, policy must be issued by a company on Wachovia's list of approved title insurance companies, copy attached.)

    a. (X) Title Policy may need additional affirmative coverage if Condominium or PUD Project. See Item 32, Title Insurance, in our General Closing Instructions.

    b. (X) Final Title Policy must include the following endorsement forms and also any others required because of property or loan type as listed in the General Instructions: ALTA 8.1 or T-36 in Texas (Environmental lien); ALTA 9 or CLTA 100 in CA (Restrictions); Form 9 in FL **ALTA 5, ALTA 100, ALTA 300**

    c. ( ) See General Instructions for special wording needed for Extendable Term Balloon loans.

    **d. (X) ALTA Short Form Title Contract (Revised 10-17-92) with no addendum attached is acceptable. Contact Wachovia prior to closing if you are unable to issue an ALTA Short Form.**

    **e. ( ) ALTA Mortgage Title Contract (Revised 10-17-92) is required.**

    **See attached form 240363 for acceptable Title Companies (except states that receive a title policy prior to** closing.)

_X_ 9. HUD-1 Settlement Statement - Completed and signed original or 1 certified copy (must include correct names and address of Borrower(s) and Seller(s) in Sections D & E.) Line 201 must match Earnest Money figure on sales contract.

_X_ 10. Buyer(s), Seller(s), and Closing Agent must execute the Addendum to HUD-1 Settlement Statement (243128).

_X_ 11. The completed Initial Escrow Account Disclosure Statement (243134) must be signed by the Borrower(s).

_X_ 12. First Payment Notice (242110) or (242115).

_X_ 13. (X) Settlement Acknowledgement and Certification (241045) in duplicate to be signed by all parties as indicated.

**IF LENDER'S DISBURSEMENT DATES FOR TAXES OR ASSESSMENTS ARE PRIOR TO THE FIRST PAYMENT DUE DATE, THE CLOSING AGENT IS RESPONSIBLE FOR PAYMENT OF THOSE BILLS.**

_X_ 15. Borrower Certifications - 242836 must be signed by borrower(s) and notarized.

_X_ 16. Copy of recorded restrictions (if violated) and copy of any recorded joint agreements, i.e. driveways, garages, etc.

___ 17. Compliance with FHA Addendum to Closing Instructions (243106) is required.

_X_ 18. Signed and dated FNMA-1003/240122 Residential Loan Application.

___ 19. Direct Endorsement Approval (HUD-92900A pp.3&4) (243289) executed by Mortgagors named in Commitment.

___ 20. Closing Agent must complete Form 26-1820 in triplicate and have signed by veteran, and if spouse is to take title, veteran and spouse must sign.

___ 21. VA Form 26-1847 (243382) signed by veteran in duplicate re: escrow for completion.

___ 22. VA Form 26-1849 (243383) signed by Lender and Seller re: escrow for completion.

___ 23. Escrow Agreement (Conventional Loan) ( ) 240359 ( ) Other _____

*(continued)*

## Exhibit 11.10 Continued

___ 24. 10 Year Protection Warranty - Builder must be in good standing within 15 days prior to closing.

___ 25. Warranty of Completion (HUD-92544/VA-26-1859) (243325), signed by Borrower(s) and Builder.

___ 26. Buy down Escrow Agreement - Original - 24 _____ signed by Borrower(s) & provider of funds.

     **IMPORTANT:** The Note and Security Instrument **must not** make reference to the buydown arrangement. The Note must include the interest rate and payment required to amortize the loan as if there were no buydown arrangement.

___ 27. Illinois ONLY-Escrow Account Disclosure Agreement (242581) to be signed by borrower(s).

___ 28. Maryland Only - Certification of Closing Attorney and Borrower's Acknowledgement (241995).

_X_ 29. See attached Addendum to Closing Instructions which is incorporated and made a part of these instructions.

___ 30. This loan is closing in Power of Attorney. Please see General Closing instructions (240896) for further instruction.

___ 31. **ON TEXAS LOANS - Delete Paragraph 13 of Schedule B of Mortgagee Policy (Arbitration Provision).**

___ 32. _____

___ 33. _____

___ 34. _____

___ 35. _____

___ 36. _____

___ 37. _____

___ 38. _____

___ 39. _____

___ 40. _____

_X_ 41. Provide Privacy Notice (244271) to borrowers.

___ 42. Closing agent/attorney to confirm title holders and execute Certification of Ownership.

**\*IMPORTANT:** On the Security Instrument, appropriate boxes preceding Borrower(s) signature(s) must be checked. Information on Riders must conform wide Note. Original Rider(s) must be dated and signed the same as Note and Security Instrument. Rider forms must be attached to and recorded with Security Instrument. If Note forms are revised prior to closing, Rider forms must be revised accordingly.

A copy of the completed Note, Security Instrument and Rider(s), if applicable, should be given to the Borrower(s) at closing.

**IMPORTANT: TORRENS REGISTRATION.** On loans where property is registered with Torrens system, 3 original Mortgages must be signed by Borrower(s) and presented to office Registrar of Titles. We must be furnished with a duplicate Mortgage showing Torrens Registrar stamp and filing receipt.

application may have been handwritten or estimates. At closing, the forms are no longer estimates, but final and are all typewritten. The forms including the following:

- Final Loan Application
- Final Truth-in-Lending Disclosure Statement
- Tax authorization notice for real estate tax bills to be sent to the lender, who is collecting monthly payments toward the tax bill
- Homeowner's authorization for insurance bills to be sent to the lender, who is collecting monthly payments toward the insurance bill
- Initial disclosure revealing how the monthly escrow amounts for taxes and insurance is calculated, including a statement of how the amount on the settlement sheet for escrows is calculated
- Compliance Agreement that both the buyer and seller sign, agreeing to cooperate in the event there is a clerical error requiring forms to be corrected and re-signed after closing
- Buyer's statement that no other funds have been borrowed from any other source to complete the purchase
- Certification of federal tax identification or social security number
- Authorization for the lender to obtain the borrower's income tax records from the IRS
- Signature and name affidavit, to include middle initials or other names
- First payment letter
- Affidavit of intention to occupy the home

## HUD-1 Settlement Sheet

The HUD-1 settlement sheet is a summary of the financial transaction for the purchase and sale of the real estate. Typically, it is prepared by the closing agent, but all parties to the transaction have some statutory responsibility to provide the seller or the buyer with an estimate of closing costs during the pendency of the sale. Thus, mortgage lenders, real estate agents, and lawyers must be able to prepare and explain the HUD-1.

Exhibit 11.11 is the current HUD-1 form, approved for use in 2011.

Page 1 represents a summary of the sales transaction, including purchase price, deposits, mortgage loan amount, mortgage payoffs, settlement costs, and reimbursements.

Page 2 is the listing of the costs related to the real estate settlement and mortgage loan.

Page 3 is a comparison of the estimated costs and the actual costs and the deviation, if any. Page 1 cannot be completed until page 2 itemizing the costs is completed. For both pages 1 and 2, the right side represents the seller's portion of the transaction, while the left side represents the buyer's side.

Briefly, page 2 includes the following:

*Lines 700–704: Total Real Estate Broker Fees.* The commission is calculated and entered on line 703. The specific realtors and the split of the commission will appear on lines 701 and 702. This calculation is made based on a percentage of the purchase price, usually six or seven percent.
*Lines 800–808: Items Payable in Connection with Loan* includes all charges relating to financing of the purchase price and are listed as follows:
801–803: Points and up-front charges (loan origination and loan discount fees) are calculated here. The borrower is always responsible for points

# Exhibit 11.11 HUD-1 real estate settlement sheet

## A. **Settlement Statement (HUD-1)**

### B. Type of Loan

| 1. ☐ FHA | 2. ☐ RHS | 3. ☐ Conv. Unins. | 6. File Number: | 7. Loan Number: | 8. Mortgage Insurance Case Number: |
|---|---|---|---|---|---|
| 4. ☐ VA | 5. ☐ Conv. Ins. | | | | |

C. Note:  This form is furnished to give you a statement of actual settlement costs. Amounts paid to and by the settlement agent are shown. Items marked "(p.o.c.)" were paid outside the closing; they are shown here for informational purposes and are not included in the totals.

| D. Name & Address of Borrower: | E. Name & Address of Seller: | F. Name & Address of Lender: |
|---|---|---|
| G. Property Location: | H. Settlement Agent: | I. Settlement Date: |
| | Place of Settlement: | |

| J. Summary of Borrower's Transaction | | K. Summary of Seller's Transaction | |
|---|---|---|---|
| **100. Gross Amount Due from Borrower** | | **400. Gross Amount Due to Seller** | |
| 101. Contract sales price | | 401. Contract sales price | |
| 102. Personal property | | 402. Personal property | |
| 103. Settlement charges to borrower (line 1400) | | 403. | |
| 104. | | 404. | |
| 105. | | 405. | |
| Adjustment for items paid by seller in advance | | Adjustment for items paid by seller in advance | |
| 106. City/town taxes          to | | 406. City/town taxes          to | |
| 107. County taxes          to | | 407. County taxes          to | |
| 108. Assessments          to | | 408. Assessments          to | |
| 109. | | 409. | |
| 110. | | 410. | |
| 111. | | 411. | |
| 112. | | 412. | |
| **120. Gross Amount Due from Borrower** | | **420. Gross Amount Due to Seller** | |
| **200. Amount Paid by or in Behalf of Borrower** | | **500. Reductions In Amount Due to seller** | |
| 201. Deposit or earnest money | | 501. Excess deposit (see instructions) | |
| 202. Principal amount of new loan(s) | | 502. Settlement charges to seller (line 1400) | |
| 203. Existing loan(s) taken subject to | | 503. Existing loan(s) taken subject to | |
| 204. | | 504. Payoff of first mortgage loan | |
| 205. | | 505. Payoff of second mortgage loan | |
| 206. | | 506. | |
| 207. | | 507. | |
| 208. | | 508. | |
| 209. | | 509. | |
| Adjustments for items unpaid by seller | | Adjustments for items unpaid by seller | |
| 210. City/town taxes          to | | 510. City/town taxes          to | |
| 211. County taxes          to | | 511. County taxes          to | |
| 212. Assessments          to | | 512. Assessments          to | |
| 213. | | 513. | |
| 214. | | 514. | |
| 215. | | 515. | |
| 216. | | 516. | |
| 217. | | 517. | |
| 218. | | 518. | |
| 219. | | 519. | |
| **220. Total Paid by/for Borrower** | | **520. Total Reduction Amount Due Seller** | |
| **300. Cash at Settlement from/to Borrower** | | **600. Cash at Settlement to/from Seller** | |
| 301. Gross amount due from borrower (line 120) | | 601. Gross amount due to seller (line 420) | |
| 302. Less amounts paid by/for borrower (line 220) | (          ) | 602. Less reductions in amounts due seller (line 520) | (          ) |
| **303. Cash** ☐ From ☐ To Borrower | | **603. Cash** ☐ To ☐ From Seller | |

The Public Reporting Burden for this collection of information is estimated at 35 minutes per response for collecting, reviewing, and reporting the data. This agency may not collect this information, and you are not required to complete this form, unless it displays a currently valid OMB control number. No confidentiality is assured; this disclosure is mandatory. This is designed to provide the parties to a RESPA covered transaction with information during the settlement process.

# Exhibit 11.11 Continued

## L. Settlement Charges

| | Paid From Borrower's Funds at Settlement | Paid From Seller's Funds at Settlement |
|---|---|---|
| **700. Total Real Estate Broker Fees** | | |
| Division of commission (line 700) as follows : | | |
| 701. $ ___ to ___ | | |
| 702. $ ___ to ___ | | |
| 703. Commission paid at settlement | | |
| 704. | | |
| **800. Items Payable in Connection with Loan** | | |
| 801. Our origination charge $ ___ (from GFE #1) | | |
| 802. Your credit or charge (points) for the specific interest rate chosen $ ___ (from GFE #2) | | |
| 803. Your adjusted origination charges (from GFE #A) | | |
| 804. Appraisal fee to (from GFE #3) | | |
| 805. Credit report to (from GFE #3) | | |
| 806. Tax service to (from GFE #3) | | |
| 807. Flood certification to (from GFE #3) | | |
| 808. | | |
| 809. | | |
| 810. | | |
| 811. | | |
| **900. Items Required by Lender to be Paid in Advance** | | |
| 901. Daily interest charges from ___ to ___ @ $ ___ /day (from GFE #10) | | |
| 902. Mortgage insurance premium for ___ months to ___ (from GFE #3) | | |
| 903. Homeowner's insurance for ___ years to ___ (from GFE #11) | | |
| 904. | | |
| **1000. Reserves Deposited with Lender** | | |
| 1001. Initial deposit for your escrow account (from GFE #9) | | |
| 1002. Homeowner's insurance ___ months @ $ ___ per month $ ___ | | |
| 1003. Mortgage insurance ___ months @ $ ___ per month $ ___ | | |
| 1004. Property Taxes ___ months @ $ ___ per month $ ___ | | |
| 1005. ___ months @ $ ___ per month $ ___ | | |
| 1006. ___ months @ $ ___ per month $ ___ | | |
| 1007. Aggregate Adjustment -$ ___ | | |
| **1100. Title Charges** | | |
| 1101. Title services and lender's title insurance (from GFE #4) | | |
| 1102. Settlement or closing fee $ ___ | | |
| 1103. Owner's title insurance (from GFE #5) | | |
| 1104. Lender's title insurance $ ___ | | |
| 1105. Lender's title policy limit $ ___ | | |
| 1106. Owner's title policy limit $ ___ | | |
| 1107. Agent's portion of the total title insurance premium to $ ___ | | |
| 1108. Underwriter's portion of the total title insurance premium to $ ___ | | |
| 1109. | | |
| 1110. | | |
| 1111. | | |
| **1200. Government Recording and Transfer Charges** | | |
| 1201. Government recording charges (from GFE #7) | | |
| 1202. Deed $ ___ Mortgage $ ___ Release $ ___ | | |
| 1203. Transfer taxes (from GFE #8) | | |
| 1204. City/County tax/stamps Deed $ ___ Mortgage $ ___ | | |
| 1205. State tax/stamps Deed $ ___ Mortgage $ ___ | | |
| 1206. | | |
| **1300. Additional Settlement Charges** | | |
| 1301. Required services that you can shop for (from GFE #6) | | |
| 1302. $ ___ | | |
| 1303. $ ___ | | |
| 1304. | | |
| 1305. | | |
| **1400. Total Settlement Charges (enter on lines 103, Section J and 502, Section K)** | | |

*(continued)*

## Exhibit 11.11 Continued

| Comparison of Good Faith Estimate (GFE) and HUD-1 Charrges | | Good Faith Estimate | HUD-1 |
|---|---|---|---|
| Charges That Cannot Increase | HUD-1 Line Number | | |
| Our origination charge | # 801 | | |
| Your credit or charge (points) for the specific interest rate chosen | # 802 | | |
| Your adjusted origination charges | # 803 | | |
| Transfer taxes | # 1203 | | |

| Charges That In Total Cannot Increase More Than 10% | | Good Faith Estimate | HUD-1 |
|---|---|---|---|
| Government recording charges | # 1201 | | |
| | # | | |
| | # | | |
| | # | | |
| | # | | |
| | # | | |
| | # | | |
| | # | | |
| Total | | | |
| Increase between GFE and HUD-1 Charges | | $          or          % | |

| Charges That Can Change | | Good Faith Estimate | HUD-1 |
|---|---|---|---|
| Initial deposit for your escrow account | # 1001 | | |
| Daily interest charges  $          /day | # 901 | | |
| Homeowner's insurance | # 903 | | |
| | # | | |
| | # | | |
| | # | | |

**Loan Terms**

| | |
|---|---|
| Your initial loan amount is | $ |
| Your loan term is | years |
| Your initial interest rate is | % |
| Your initial monthly amount owed for principal, interest, and any mortgage insurance is | $          includes ☐ Principal ☐ Interest ☐ Mortgage Insurance |
| Can your interest rate rise? | ☐ No ☐ Yes, it can rise to a maximum of          %. The first change will be on          and can change again every          after          . Every change date, your interest rate can increase or decrease by          %. Over the life of the loan, your interest rate is guaranteed to never be **lower** than          % or **higher** than          %. |
| Even if you make payments on time, can your loan balance rise? | ☐ No ☐ Yes, it can rise to a maximum of $ |
| Even if you make payments on time, can your monthly amount owed for principal, interest, and mortgage insurance rise? | ☐ No ☐ Yes, the first increase can be on          and the monthly amount owed can rise to $          . The maximum it can ever rise to is $          . |
| Does your loan have a prepayment penalty? | ☐ No ☐ Yes, your maximum prepayment penalty is $ |
| Does your loan have a balloon payment? | ☐ No ☐ Yes, you have a balloon payment of $          due in          years on          . |
| Total monthly amount owed including escrow account payments | ☐ You do not have a monthly escrow payment for items, such as property taxes and homeowner's insurance. You must pay these items directly yourself. ☐ You have an additional monthly escrow payment of $          that results in a total initial monthly amount owed of $          . This includes principal, interest, any mortgage insurance and any items checked below: ☐ Property taxes   ☐ Homeowner's insurance   ☐ Flood insurance   ☐   ☐   ☐ |

**Note:** If you have any questions about the Settlement Charges and Loan Terms listed on this form, please contact your lender.

under a real estate contract, unless another arrangement has previously been agreed upon. Certain governmental programs, such as FHA, defer the point expense to the seller.

*804:* The borrower usually pays a real estate appraisal fee. This expense can range from $150 to $400 for a typical residential appraisal.

*805:* The borrower also pays for a credit report, required for all mortgage applications, ranging from $25 to $100.

*806–807:* Listed here are any tax service fees or flood certifications necessary to obtain the loan. Usually, these amounts are payable by the borrower.

*Lines 900–904: Items Required by Lender to be Paid in Advance.* All lenders require certain items to be prepaid to ensure the economic viability of the loan. Interest is required to be paid in advance of the settlement at the borrower's expense.

*Lines 1000–1007: Reserves Deposited with Lender.* A lender will require certain reserves to be deposited—such as hazard insurance, mortgage insurance, city and county taxes, and assessments. The number of months calculated is based on the date of settlement, when the borrower's first payment will begin, and when the taxes are next due. The goal for the lender is to receive 12 months of tax payments so there are sufficient funds to pay the tax when due. If settlement is in July and the first payment is in September and the taxes are due in April, the borrower will make eight monthly payments from September to April, leaving a shortfall of four payments. The lender will collect a minimum of four months' taxes to fund the escrow account. Under the law, the lender is entitled to collect an additional two months' as a cushion to account for tax increases.

*Lines 1100–1108: Title Charges.* In this section, settlement closing fees, abstract searches, title searches, title binders, document preparation, notary fees, and title insurance acquisition are all calculated. These are typically the buyer's expenses.

*Lines 1200–1206: Government Recording and Transfer Charges.* This section includes recordation expenses for deeds, mortgages, and releases; the custom of the community will determine who has the responsibility to pay each. The realty transfer is a percentage of the sales price and is usually assessed against both the buyer and the seller. Local custom will dictate who must pay the transfer tax.

*Lines 1300–1305: Additional Settlement Charges.* Additional settlement charges may be either the buyer's or the seller's responsibility. Survey costs, pest inspection, water and sewer assessments, and other extraordinary charges are listed in this section. Once all of the charges are calculated, the total settlement charges for both the buyer and seller are entered in lines 103 and 502, respectively, on page 1 of the settlement sheet.

Personal property the buyer may be purchasing from the seller and settlement charges are added to the sales price at lines 102 and 402. Sometimes, when a seller is downsizing from a large to a smaller home, large items of furniture, such as a grand piano, may be purchased by the buyer as part of buying the house. They are not part of the purchase price but instead represent personal property. City, town, and county taxes and other assessments are always prorated across the board. On lines 201 to 209, deposit or earnest money, new loans or existing loans, and so forth are listed. At line 220, the total paid by or for the borrower is subtracted from the total due, resulting in an outstanding balance or refund for the borrower at line 303.

The sales price, plus any purchase price for personal property due to the seller, subtracted from any adjustments from line 420, is then listed. At lines 501 to 509, the seller has to meet any existing cash obligations that are unpaid up to the settlement. A total reduction amount due the seller is at line 520. At line 600, the cash at settlement due to or from the seller is listed. The gross amount due to seller is listed at line 601. Line 603 lists the net cash due to or from the seller.

The revised HUD-1 includes a third page, where a comparison is made between the settlement statement completed at closing and the Good Faith Estimate of Closing Costs. The first section includes charges that cannot increase between the time the estimate was prepared and closing. Section 2 lists charges that cannot increase by more than 10 percent. Charges that can change are listed in section 3. There is also a section with loan specifics, such as the loan amount, term, interest rate and type, pre-payment penalties, and balloon payment options.

## Proceeds Escrows

Sometimes there are issues related to the contingencies in the agreement of sale or the objections raised on the title report that cannot be resolved prior to settlement. In an effort to complete the sale, the closing agent may agree to withhold a portion of the seller's proceeds and place those funds in an escrow account. The funds are released to pay for the item, and any balance is refunded to the seller.

Many municipalities take a final reading for utilities such as sewer and water usage and issue a bill to the seller after closing. These municipal charges are required to be paid in full under the terms of the Agreement of Sale and, if unpaid, can become a lien on the property. But the bill is not immediately available at the time of settlement. The closing agent will withhold a sum equal to the average of the prior water usage to cover the final bill. Once the bill is received, the closing agent will pay it in full from the escrow account and refund the balance to the seller.

**Real Estate Settlement and Procedures Act (RESPA)**
federal law to regulate and reform lending practices as well as closing and settlement procedures

**WEB EXPLORATION**

For more information on the cost savings, see the HUD press release at http://archives.hud.gov/news/2008/pr08-175.cfm

# REAL ESTATE SETTLEMENT PROCEDURES ACT (RESPA)

Congress enacted the **Real Estate Settlement and Procedures Act (RESPA)** to regulate and reform lending practices as well as closing and settlement procedures. The goal was to ensure that consumers are advised of all costs related to the real estate transaction in easily understandable terms. RESPA attempts to give regularity to the settlement process and to thwart unfair and fraudulent practices. Any loan that has a federal connection or is federally insured is subject to the RESPA requirements. Although cash transactions and mortgages provided by the seller are not subject to RESPA requirements, they often use the same forms.

In 2011, Housing and Urban Development promulgated a new format for the Settlement Statement. For the first time in more than 30 years, the U.S. Department of Housing and Urban Development (HUD) issued long-anticipated mortgage reforms to help consumers shop for the lowest-cost mortgage and avoid costly and potentially harmful loan offers. Lenders and mortgage brokers must provide consumers with a standard Good Faith Estimate (GFE) that clearly discloses key loan terms and closing costs. HUD estimates that its new regulation will save consumers nearly $700 at the closing. The entire RESPA process is guided by new statutory provisions, administrative regulations, and the promulgation of new standards for the closing process.

Another typical example where funds may be withheld is where the owner of the property has died and the Estate is selling the property. In many jurisdictions, there is an inheritance or estate tax on the value of all assets owned at the time of death. And if the tax is not paid, it becomes a lien on the real estate. Thus, the title report will include an objection that those taxes be paid or some provision be made to pay the inheritance tax. Where an estate has not paid the tax, the closing agent will withhold from the proceeds of sale an amount that will sufficiently cover the inheritance tax due on the real estate plus a cushion of 25 to 50 percent for additional inheritance tax due on other estate assets, interest, and any penalty that may be due. For example, the real estate sale price is $200,000.00 and the inheritance tax rate is 12 percent. The closing agent may hold between $24,000 ($200,000 × 12%) to $36,000. When the estate has the tax return prepared, the closing agent may issue a check from the escrow account to pay the tax. The balance of the escrow, if any, will be released to the seller when the inheritance tax return is approved.

Finally, unexpected things sometimes occur on the eve of closing that require the seller to make a repair that cannot be accomplished before settlement occurs. Appliances included with the purchase can and do break on the day of closing. To ensure that the buyer receives a home with the required repair or working dishwasher, the closing agent may agree to withhold a reasonable sum of money to cover the cost of the repair or to obtain a replacement dishwasher.

No matter which event generates the requirement to withhold a portion of the proceeds, there will be a written agreement between the closing agent and the seller that governs the manner in which the funds are held and may be disbursed. Exhibit 11.12 is a typical escrow agreement from a closing agent.

## Exhibit 11.12 Closing agent's escrow agreement

**ESCROW AGREEMENT**

The undersigned hereby agree that _____ as Escrow Agents, shall hold the sum of $ _____ from the Seller's net proceeds of the sale of _____ to secure the _____ for such property. Seller shall proceed with due diligence to complete such work on or before _____, 20_, weather permitting.

Upon completion of the work and a satisfactory inspection report by _____, Escrow Agent shall disburse the escrowed funds to seller. In the event the required work is not completed as set forth in this agreement, purchaser and the first mortgage lender may use the escrowed funds to obtain such completion.

THIS THE _____ DAY OF _____, 20 _____.

_____
CLOSING AGENT, AS ECROW AGENT

_____
SELLER

_____
SELLER

# ETHICAL Considerations

## DILIGENCE

Nowhere in the real estate transaction is diligence more important than in the time between signing the Agreement of Sale and settlement. The entire time is controlled by deadlines that must be managed and met. Failure to meet deadlines can have devastating consequences. For example, should the buyer miss the date to provide the inspection reports to the seller, under the terms of the Agreement, the seller is relieved of any obligation to correct items contained in the report. Diligence requires the legal team to act promptly in the representation of the client's interests. In real estate, that means awareness of the upcoming deadlines and, when it is anticipated that there may be difficulty in complying with the deadline, obtaining an extension of time under the Agreement of Sale.

## KEY TERMS

## CHAPTER SUMMARY

| | |
|---|---|
| Introduction to Closing | The culmination of the sale and purchase process is the closing, or settlement. |
| Preparing for Closing | Preparing for closing requires managing deadlines, communication, and cooperation between the various parties involved in the transaction—sellers, buyers, real estate brokers and agents, mortgage lenders, and title companies. |
| Agreement of Sale Contingencies | In each Agreement of Sale there are certain contingencies, items that must be completed by the buyer or seller for the agreement of sale contract to become binding. Most of the contingencies are tied to a deadline for completion, such as the time period to obtain a mortgage, make an inspection, or complete a repair. The goal is to satisfy all of the contingencies prior to the closing date. |
| Mortgage Contingency | The most commonly agreed-to contingency is the mortgage contingency, a recognition that buyers will usually require some amount of mortgage to be able to complete the transaction. The mortgage contingency is a clause in the agreement of sale that provides a period of time to apply and obtain a mortgage for a specific amount and with specific terms (rate and time). |

| Inspections Contingencies | Inspections contingencies are provisions that allow the buyer to have the property inspected to determine if there are any issues related to maintenance, structural integrity, or habitability. Buyers on a tight budget want to be certain that there are no issues with the property that will require immediate repairs or present a health hazard. |
|---|---|
| Conveying Good Title | The Agreement of Sale requires the seller to convey good title, and the lender requires that there be no other liens against the real estate that prevent the mortgage from being in first-priority position following the settlement. The title search and report provide the information necessary to evaluate and satisfy these two requirements. |
| Estimate of Closing Costs | A good faith estimate of closing costs should be prepared for the parties; the seller will want to know how much the proceeds of sale will be, and the buyer wants to know how much money will be needed to complete the transaction. |
| Seller's Closing Costs | For the seller, the costs related to the sale of the real estate include the real estate sales commission, realty transfer taxes, title insurance and survey, and payoff of judgments and existing loans. |
| Buyer's Closing Costs | For the buyer, an estimate of closing costs is required so the buyer can determine the additional funds required to complete purchase of the property and make arrangements for those funds to be deposited with the closing agent. |
| Real Estate Closing | The real estate closing is the culmination of the real estate transaction. The parties gather, the buyer signs the loan documents, the seller signs the deed, and the closing agent collects any information required to clear the title report of objections. The closing agent will also act as a financial clearinghouse, accepting all the funds, preparing the HUD-1 settlement sheet, and disbursing checks for payment of all the expenses and the seller's proceeds of sale. |
| Clearing Title | The most common items resolved at the settlement table are related to the identity of the parties; payment of any judgments or mortgages, outstanding taxes, and other outstanding municipal charges; and obtaining the original documents related to clearing clouds on the seller's title. |
| Loan Documents | At closing, buyers sign the promissory note, mortgage, and other documents required by the lender. |

| HUD-1 Settlement Sheet | The HUD-1 settlement sheet is a summary of the financial transaction for the purchase and sale of the real estate. Typically, it is prepared by the closing agent, but all parties to the transaction have some statutory responsibility to provide the seller or the buyer with an estimate of closing costs during the pendency of the sale. |
|---|---|
| Proceeds Escrows | Sometimes there are issues related to the contingencies in the agreement of sale or the objections raised on the title report that cannot be resolved prior to settlement. In an effort to complete the sale, the closing agent may agree to withhold a portion of the seller's proceeds and place those funds in an escrow account. |

## REVIEW QUESTIONS AND EXERCISES

1. Describe the components of the pre-closing process.
2. What items in the pre-closing process relate to satisfying the terms of the Agreement of Sale?
3. Describe the components in the process of clearing title.
4. Discuss the importance of communication in completing the tasks related to pre-closing.
5. What is the purpose of the pre-settlement inspection?
6. Describe the components that affect the seller at closing.
7. Describe the components that affect the buyer at closing.
8. What is the purpose of the HUD-1 settlement statement?
9. What were the goals of the Real Estate Settlement Procedures Act?
10. What is the purpose of withholding funds from the seller's proceeds of sale?

## VIDEO CASE STUDY

Go to www.pearsonhighered.com/careers to view the following videos.

### Author Introduction to Closing
Author video introduction to chapter coverage.

### Real Estate Closing – Overview
An overview of the Closing/Settlement.

### Real Estate Closing - Buyers' Attorney Explains Documents
Buyers' attorney explains the documents the Buyers are required to sign at the real estate closing.

### Real Estate Closing - Seller's Attorney Explains Documents
Sellers Lawyer explains the document the Seller is required to sign at the real estate closing.

## INTERNET AND TECHNOLOGY EXERCISES

Using the Internet, determine the realty transfer tax in your jurisdiction and whether the seller, the buyer, or both are obligated to pay it.

## REAL ESTATE PORTFOLIO EXERCISES

**Closing**

**To:**        Paralegal Intern
**From:**      Mr. Saunders
**Case Name:** Mr. & Mrs. Schan
**Re:**        Preliminary HUD-1

Our clients have asked me to calculate how much money they need to bring to the closing on their new home purchase.
      From the information in the file, please prepare a preliminary estimate suing the HUD-1 form.
      Draft a cover letter to the clients for my signature  reminding them to bring the funds in a certified check, and to bring photo ids.

Portfolio items produced:
1. Preliminary HUD-1 settlement statement.
2. Letter to client


**To:**        Paralegal
**From:**      Mr. Saunders
**Case Name:** Mr. & Mrs. Schan
**Re:**        Preliminary HUD-1

Research the costs to record a deeds and a mortgage in your jurisdiction.
      What are the requirements and the process for filing documents?
      Are there any cover documents, size limits or other physical specifications.
      Prepare a checklist for the person filing the documents on where to go, what to take with them and how much is required for filing fees.

Portfolio items produced:
Checklist for recording documents in your jurisdiction.

Go to www.pearsonhighered.com/careers to download instructions.

# UNIT IV   Special Real Estate

# REAL ESTATE AS AN INVESTMENT

In addition to real estate purchased for personal or business use, it is also a popular investment for individuals and businesses. Renting and managing residential, commercial and industrial property is an area within the industry in which many legal and real estate professionals specialize. Professionals in this area of practice have ongoing relationships tied to the length of the leases or rental agreements. This may include finding tenants, drafting leases, collecting rents, arranging repairs and maintenance and sometimes instituting litigation to collect rents or evict tenants.

Numerous efforts have been made to make home ownership a reality. One way to make real estate ownership more affordable is through common ownership which results in shared expenses and costs. Among the first efforts was co-operative ownership of apartments for workers, who owned shares in the corporation that owned the property. The co-operative form of ownership permits occupancy of the apartment as a benefit of stock ownership, but stock ownership is subject to approval from the members of the co-operative. The concept was changed and refined by legislation in the 1960's allowing the conversion of apartments to and development of condominiums. Unlike the cooperative, the condominium form of ownership allowed individual ownership of apartments with the right to freely sell units without approval.

The condominium has been a popular form of real estate investment for landlords and developers.

Real estate development is also an area of specialization for the real estate and legal professional. It may involve the location of appropriate raw land or suitable structures for development or conversion. Working in this area of specialty may include acting as a straw party for the developer during the assembly of a number of tracts of land to negotiate a better price where the developer is a well-known successful business from whom sellers would demand a higher price. Typically legal professionals for developers spend time in public meetings before local governmental agencies and follow up where necessary with the litigation for appeals.

APARTMENT
FOR
RENT
267-454-7070

## LEARNING OBJECTIVES

*Upon completion of this chapter, you should be able to*

1. Describe the types of leasehold interests.

2. Describe the components of a lease agreement.

3. Describe the rights and obligations of lessors and lessees.

4. Describe the process of enforcing landlords' and tenants' rights.

5. Explain the use of lease agreements in the real estate purchase transaction.

# Landlord–Tenant Law | CHAPTER 12

## ■ INTRODUCTION TO LANDLORD–TENANT LAW

Landlord–tenant law defines the relationship between owners of real estate and their tenants. Like many areas of law, the foundations of landlord–tenant law developed over a long time and can be found in the common law. Many states have moved to replace their common law governing residential landlord–tenant relations with statutory law. Common law tended to favor the landlord. As the consumer protection movement gained national prominence in the 1960s, the tenant—as a "consumer"—received greater protection under case law and statutory law.

## ■ LEASEHOLD INTERESTS

Leases are a form of interest in real property known as a non-freehold or less-than-freehold estate. A **non-freehold estate**, also referred to as the **leasehold estate,** is an estate in real property that has a definite time period and is limited to present possessory rights. The owner of the freehold estate, known as the **lessor** or **landlord**, transfers the right of possession, usually by way of a written lease agreement, to the owner of the non-freehold estate in exchange for some consideration, usually monthly rental payments. The owner of the non-freehold estate is the **lessee** or **tenant.** Renters of apartments and office space are examples of owners of non-freehold estates. There are four types of leasehold estates: tenancy for years, periodic tenancy, tenancy at will, and tenancy by sufferance.

> **LEARNING OBJECTIVE 1**
> Describe the types of leasehold interests.
>
> **non-freehold estate**
> (**leasehold estate**) an estate in real property that has a definite time period and is limited to present possessory rights
>
> **lessor or landlord**
> the owner of the freehold estate
>
> **lessee or tenant**
> the owner of the non-freehold estate

## DIGITAL RESOURCES

Author Introduction to Landlord Tenant Law.

Sample forms and templates.

## Tenancy for Years

A **tenancy for years** is any leasehold interest of a specific duration, no matter how long or short. The leasehold terminates automatically upon expiration of the specific duration, even if the term is less than one (1) year. Because the term is certain, even a term of less than one (1) year is a tenancy for years.

## Periodic Tenancy

A **periodic tenancy** is any leasehold interest with no stated duration or lease period, but with rental payments due at particular intervals. A periodic tenancy may be terminated by giving notice of termination at the end of a payment interval. Most periodic tenancies are month-to-month leases, where possession continues from month to month for so long as the tenant continues to pay the rent. Either the tenants or the landlord can give notice to terminate the tenancy at the end of the next periodic payment period.

## Tenancy at Will

A **tenancy at will**, also called an **estate at will**, is an informal lease arrangement where the landlord allows a tenant to stay on a month-to-month basis and which may be terminated at any time by the landlord or the tenant. This is the typical situation following a tenancy for years, where the specific term in the lease has ended but the landlord allows the tenancy to continue so long as the tenant pays the rent.

## Tenancy at Sufferance

A **tenancy at sufferance** is a tenancy created when a tenant retains possession after the end of a valid tenancy. The tenant–lessee is also called a **holdover tenant**, a tenant who stays beyond the end of the lease period. Tenancy at

# THE STATUTE OF FRAUDS

A lease is a contract expressly entered into by the landlord/lessor and the tenant/lessee. Depending on the provisions enacted within the individual states, a lease may be required to be in writing because the lease affects an interest in real estate, the duration of the lease exceeds some time period, and/or the total of the rent payments exceeds some dollar amount. If one of the parties asserts a claim or right under a lease, the lease must be in writing or the lack of a written document will be used as an affirmative defense to bar the claim. For example, see the Ohio codification of the Statute of Frauds below.

A.  A lease contract is not enforceable by way of action or defense unless one of the following applies:

1.  The total payments to be made under the lease contract, excluding payments for options to renew or buy, are less than $1,000.

2.  There is a writing, signed by the party against whom enforcement is sought or by that party's authorized agent, sufficient to indicate that a lease contract has been made between the parties and to describe the goods leased and the lease term.

B.  Any description of leased goods or of the lease term is sufficient and satisfies division (A)(2) of this section, whether or not it is specific, if it reasonably identifies what is described.

C.  A writing is not insufficient because it omits or incorrectly states a term agreed upon, but the lease contract is not enforceable under division (A)(2) of this section beyond the lease term and the quantity of goods shown in the writing.

Ohio Rev. Code §1310.08.

sufferance commences only when the tenant had an original right to possess, the right to possess has ended, and the tenant remains in possession without the agreement of the landlord. The lessee remains responsible for rent payment during the extended period, called an estate at sufferance.

## COMPONENTS OF A LEASE

A lease is a written contract, and in many jurisdictions, form leases have been developed similar to the lease form that appears in Exhibit 12.1.

Each lease should have certain information, such as:

- Identification of the parties, the lessor and lessee
- Description of the leased property
- Specific beginning date, the duration of the period of tenancy, and the ending date
- Amount of rent, when due, the acceptable method of payment, and where to make the payment
- Requirement and amount of security deposit, its purposes, and how it will be returned to the lessee
- Right to and terms of renewal periods
- Terms of the use and occupancy
- Covenants and obligations of the landlord and the tenant, including maintenance and repairs
- Remedies in the event of breach, including eviction and self-help

Statutory enactments in some locales may impact tenant–landlord agreements. **Plain English lease provisions** represent such an enactment, requiring landlords to use lease forms written in understandable, non-legal language. Pennsylvania has been in the forefront of this movement toward clarity in lease documents, as shown in a portion of the Pennsylvania statute that provides this protection:

> § 2201. Short title
> This act shall be known and may be cited as the Plain Language Consumer Contract Act.
> § 2202. Legislative findings and intent
> (a) LEGISLATIVE FINDINGS.– The General Assembly finds that many consumer contracts are writ- ten, arranged, and designed in a way that makes them hard for consumers to understand. Competi-tion would be aided if these contracts were easier to understand.
> (b) LEGISLATIVE INTENT.– By passing this act, the General Assembly wants to promote the writing of consumer contracts in plain language. This act will protect consumers from making contracts that they do not understand. It will help consumers know better their rights and duties under those contracts.
>
> § 2203. Definitions
> The following words and phrases when used in this act shall have the meanings given to them in this section unless the context clearly indicates otherwise:
> "CONSUMER." Any individual who borrows, buys, leases, or obtains credit, money, services, or property under a consumer contract.
> "CONSUMER CONTRACT" or "CONTRACT." A written agreement between a consumer and a party acting in the usual course of business,

**PRACTICE TIP**

To avoid misunderstandings and have proof if a civil action is filed by either the landlord or the tenant, every lease should be in writing, regardless of its duration.

**LEARNING OBJECTIVE 2**
Describe the components of a lease agreement.

**plain English lease provisions**
requirements that lease forms be written in understandable, non-legal language

## Exhibit 12.1 Residential lease agreement

# Lease

This Lease is made on
**BETWEEN** the Tenant(s)

whose address is

referred to as the "Tenant,"
**AND** the Landlord

whose address is

referred to as the "Landlord."
The word "Tenant" means each Tenant named above.

**1. Property.**    The Tenant agrees to rent from the Landlord and the Landlord agrees to lease to the Tenant the property known as

referred to as the "Property."

**2. Term.**    The term of this Lease is for                              starting on                              and ending                              . The Landlord is not responsible if the Landlord cannot give the Tenant possession of the Property at the start of this Lease. However, rent will only be charged from the date on which possession of the Property is made available to the Tenant. If the Landlord cannot give possession within 30 days after the starting date, the Tenant may cancel this Lease.

**3. Rent.**    The Tenant agrees to pay $                  as rent, to be paid as follows: $                  per month, due on the                  day of each month. The first payment of rent and any security deposit is due upon the signing of this Lease by the Tenant. The Tenant must pay a late charge of $                  for each payment that is more than 10 days late. This late charge is due with the monthly rent payment. All rent and other payments due Landlord hereunder shall be made at the address given above or such other address as Landlord shall specify in writing.

**4. Use of Property.**    The Tenant may use the Property only for the following purpose(s):

**5. Eviction.**    If the Tenant does not pay the rent within           days after it is due, the Tenant may be evicted. The Landlord may also evict the Tenant if the Tenant does not comply with all of the terms of this Lease and for all other causes allowed by law. If evicted, the Tenant must continue to pay the rent for the rest of the term. The Tenant must also pay all costs, including reasonable attorney fees, related to the eviction and the collection of any moneys owed the Landlord, along with the cost of re-entering, re-renting, cleaning and repairing the Property. Rent received from any new tenant will reduce the amount owed the Landlord.

**6. Payments by the Landlord.**    If the Tenant fails to comply with the terms of this Lease, the Landlord may take any required action and charge the cost, including reasonable attorney fees, to the Tenant as additional rent. Failure to pay such additional rent upon demand is a violation of this Lease.

**7. Care of the Property.**    The Tenant has examined the Property, including all facilities, furniture and appliances, and is satisfied with its present condition. The Tenant agrees to maintain the property in as good condition as it is at the start of this Lease except for ordinary wear and tear. The Tenant must pay for all repairs, replacements and damages caused by the act or neglect of the Tenant or the Tenant's visitors. The Tenant will remove all of the Tenant's property at the end of this Lease. Any property that is left becomes the property of the Landlord and may be thrown out.

**8. Quiet Enjoyment.**    The Tenant may remain in and use the Property without interference by Landlord or anyone claiming through Landlord, subject to the terms of this Lease.

**9. Validity of Lease.**    If a clause or provision of this Lease is legally invalid, the rest of this Lease remains in effect.

251 - Lease - General
Ind. or Corp. Plain Language
Rev. 9/02   P11/07

©2002 by ALL-STATE LEGAL®
A Division of ALL-STATE International, Inc.
www.aslegal.com   800.222.0510        Page 1

# Exhibit 12.1 Continued

**10. Lead Paint Lease Disclosure.** The Landlord, Tenant and Agent (if any), have signed the "Disclosure to Tenants" form for lease of residential property (if the housing was built before 1978). For all such above leases the tenant has also been provided with a copy of the EPA pamphlet, "Protect Your Family from Lead in Your Home." 42 U.S.C. 4852d; 24 C.F.R. 35.88; 40 C.F.R. 745.107.

**11. Private Well Testing Act (N.J.S.A. 58:12A-26 et seq.)** In accordance with the Private Well Testing Act (the "Act"), if potable water for the Property is supplied by a private well, and testing of the water supply is not required pursuant to any other State law, Landlord is required to test the water (i) by March 14, 2004, and (ii) every five years thereafter, in the manner established under the Act and to provide a copy of the results thereof to each tenant. If such testing has been done prior to the date hereof, upon signing this Lease, Landlord shall provide Tenant with a written copy of the most recent test results.

**12. Parties.** The Landlord and each of the Tenants is bound by this Lease. All parties who lawfully succeed to their rights and responsibilities are also bound.

**13. Entire Lease.** All promises the Landlord has made are contained in this written lease. This Lease can only be changed by an agreement in writing by both the Tenant and the Landlord.

**14. Signatures.** The Landlord and the Tenant agree to the terms of this Lease. If this Lease is made by a corporation, its proper corporate officers sign and its corporate seal is affixed.

Witnessed or Attested by:

_____     _____ (Seal)
                                                                          *Landlord*

_____     _____ (Seal)
                                                                          *Tenant*

                                              _____ (Seal)
                                                                          *Tenant*

**LEASE**                          Dated:

                                   Expires on

                       Landlord

        TO                         Rent $

                       Tenant

251 - Lease - General
Ind. or Corp. Plain Language
Rev. 9/02  P11/07

©2002 by ALL-STATE LEGAL®
A Division of ALL-STATE International, Inc.
www.aslegal.com  800.222.0510  Page 2

made primarily for personal, family, or household purposes in which a consumer does any of the following:

(1) Borrows money

(2) Buys, leases, or rents personal property, real property, or services for cash or on credit

(3) Obtains credit

§ 2204. Application of act and interpretation

(a) GENERAL RULE.– This act applies to all contracts that are made, solicited, or intended to be performed in this Commonwealth after the effective date of this act.

(b) EXCLUSIONS.– This act does not apply to the following:

(1) Real estate conveyance documents and contracts, deeds and mortgages, real estate certificates of title, and title insurance contracts.

(2) Consumer contracts involving amounts of more than $50,000.

(3) Marital agreements.

(4) Contracts to buy securities.

(5) Documents used by financial institutions, which financial institutions are subject to examination or other supervision by Federal or State regulatory authorities, or documents used by affiliates, subsidiaries, or service corporations of such financial institutions.

(6) Contracts for insurance or insurance policies.

(7) Contracts subject to examination or other supervision by the Pennsylvania Public Utility Commission or by the Federal Energy Regulatory Commission.

(8) Commercial leases.

(c) INTERPRETATION.– This act shall be liberally interpreted to protect consumers.[4]

*Source:* 73 Pa. Cons. Stat. §§2201-2204 (2009).

## ■ RIGHTS AND DUTIES OF LESSORS AND LESSEES

**LEARNING OBJECTIVE 3**
Describe the rights and obligations of lessors and lessees.

The rights and duties of a landlord and tenant will depend in great part on the negotiated terms of the written lease agreement and on general legal principals. For example, the landlord agrees to provide the space and the tenant agrees to pay a rental amount, and in the case of a residential property and based on general legal principles or statutory law, the landlord guarantees that the premises will be in a habitable condition.

A **residential lease** is a contract to lease a specific property for the sole purpose of occupying it as the tenant's home. **Habitability** is a minimum standard of suitability for human living and has been interpreted to require certain safety, sanitary, and living conditions. For example, locks on doors and installation of smoke detectors represent safety concerns; garbage removal, working toilets, heat, and cooking appliances represent sanitary living conditions. In some jurisdictions, such as in the City of Philadelphia, a certification or license is required. In 2006, Philadelphia passed an ordinance requiring a landlord, prior to renting a residential property, to obtain from the Department of Licenses and Inspections a certificate stating that there are no building code violations and that all fire protection and smoke detection equipment is in working order and free of anything that affects habitability (Title 4 of the Philadelphia Code, Subcode PM, Section 102.6.4.1).

The tenant has the right to occupy the property and use it in any way that is permissible under the terms of the lease agreement so long as the use is not illegal and does not interfere with the rights of adjoining owners and occupiers. The tenant

**residential lease**
contract to lease a specific property for the sole purpose of occupying it as the tenant's home

**habitability**
a minimum standard of suitability for human living

**WEB EXPLORATION**

According to the 2009 U.S. Census Bureau American Housing Survey, roughly one third of Americans rent their homes. For the latest data, see the HUD website at http://www.huduser.org/portal/datasets/ahs/ahsdata11.html

must return the property at the end of the lease term in the same condition as at the beginning of the term, subject to damages associated with only normal wear and tear.

In exchange, the tenant is obligated to pay the agreed rental payment. Lease agreements may also have provisions that indicate who is responsible for maintenance and repair of common areas such as parking lots, sidewalks, and hallways.

## Rights and Duties of Landlords

In renting or leasing property, the landlord is concerned with the ability of the tenant to pay the rent. In order to make a decision on the financial ability of the tenant to pay the rent, the landlord may use a screening process that includes a rental application such as the one that appears in Exhibit 12.2. The landlord may also conduct a tenant-authorized credit and employment background check and review the tenant's tax returns.

In most jurisdictions, the landlord has the right to collect a security deposit from the tenant to apply against damages; this can be from one to two months' rent, and in some cases, the last month's rent in advance, in addition to the first month's rent. Depending on local requirements, the security deposit and in some cases, the unearned last month's rent may have to be deposited in a separate escrow account for the benefit of the tenant, with an accounting of interest earned and deductions made from the account when returning the funds within a fixed period, usually 30 to 60 days, after the end of the lease and return of the property to the landlord.

Other duties of landlords are specified in the lease. This may include the obligation to provide utilities or other building services such snow removal or grounds maintenance. However, some leases may make these expenses the obligation of the tenant.

In commercial leases, including retail- and warehouse-type uses, landlords typically provide bare-walls premises—that is, the existing empty space with little or no improvements. The terms of the lease may permit the retail or warehouse user to improve the space in whatever way is required for its business purpose, at its own expense. This may include the installation of divider walls, display cases, and shelving, as well as the running of lines for utilities and computer systems. The terms of the lease will give the retail or warehouse tenant the right to remove those improvements, but more likely they will be left behind for the benefit of subsequent tenants. In commercial leases, it is generally accepted that the tenant will pay rent, utilities, taxes, and insurance on the leased area; this is sometimes referred to as a triple net lease.

In residential leases, it is more typical for the landlord and tenant to negotiate whether basic utilities will or will not be included—such as cable, water, electric, and heat. The landlord and tenant may also negotiate the responsibilities related to repairs and maintenance.

## Rights and Duties of Tenants

Tenants have a right to **quiet enjoyment** of the rented property. This is the right to peaceful possession of the property. Landlords may not enter the property during the period of tenancy, except in the event of an emergency or by agreement in the lease terms for purposes of performing repairs. In exchange, the tenant has the obligation to pay rent, to avoid creating any damage to the property, and to refrain from behavior that interferes with the right of quiet enjoyment of other tenants.

Tenants are obligated to **surrender** or return the property peacefully at the end of the term of the lease in the same condition as when the tenancy commenced,

**PRACTICE TIP**

One of the main issues in the termination of leases is a determination of what is permissible wear and tear. Normal wear and tear is the deterioration consistent with the normal reduction in the useful life of the item; for example, a water heater wears out after 10 to 12 years, which is normal, but holes in walls and broken pipes are not normal.

To avoid some issues, advise clients, whether representing the landlord or the tenant, to document the condition of the property before move-in and at the time of move-out. Photographing all walls, floors, and built-in items will serve to document abnormal wear at the end of the lease.

**surrender**
return the property

**Exhibit 12.2** Rental application

**RENTAL APPLICATION**

**NOTICE:**         Co-Applicant must complete a separate Rental Application Form.
The undersigned hereby makes application to rent _____ located at beginning on
_____, 20_____, at a monthly rent of $_____.

PLEASE TELL US ABOUT YOURSELF

FULL NAME _____ Phone (_____) _____
Date of Birth _____ Social Security No. _____
Name of Co-Applicant _____
Number of Dependents (excluding Co-Applicant) _____
Ages of Dependents _____
Other Occupants and their Relationship _____
Pets (Number and Kind) _____

PLEASE GIVE YOUR RESIDENCE HISTORY FOR THE PAST 3 YEARS
(Beginning with the most current)

CURRENT ADDRESS _____
Month & Year moved in _____
Reason for Leaving _____
Owner or Agent _____ Phone (_____) _____
PREVIOUS ADDRESS (if within 3 years) _____
Month & Year moved in _____ Moved out _____
Reason for Leaving _____
Owner or Agent _____ Phone (_____) _____

PLEASE GIVE YOUR EMPLOYMENT INFORMATION

YOUR STATUS         [ ] Employed Full-Time      [ ] Employed Part-Time
                    [ ] Student      [ ] Retired         [ ] Unemployed

EMPLOYER _____
Dates Employed _____ Employed as _____
Supervisor _____ Phone (____) _____
Address _____
Salary $_____per _____

If employed by above less than six months, give name and address of previous employer or school.
_____

## Exhibit 12.2 Continued

PLEASE LIST YOUR BANK AND CREDIT REFERENCE

Your Bank(s)    City-State    Branch  Type of Acct.    Acct. #

1. _____

2. _____

3. _____

Your Driver's License Number _____ State _____

Your Vehicle Make/Model _____ Year _____ Tag No. _____ State _____

Second Vehicle Make/Model _____ Year _____ Tag No. _____ State _____

I hereby deposit $_____ in earnest money to be refunded to me if this application is not accepted within ____ business banking days, plus a $25.00 NONREFUNDABLE credit investigation fee. Upon acceptance of this application, this deposit shall be retained as part of the security deposit. When so approved and accepted I agree to execute a lease for _____ months and agree to pay the balance of the security deposit within ____ business banking days after being notified of acceptance, or the deposit will be forfeited as liquidated damages in payment for the agent's time and effort in processing my inquiry and application, including making necessary investigation of my credit, character, and reputation. If this application is not approved and accepted by the owner or agent, the deposit will be refunded, the applicant thereby waiving any claim for damages by reason of nonacceptance which the owner or his agent may reject without stating any reason for so doing.

The above information, to the best of my knowledge, is true and correct.

APPLICANT'S SIGNATURE _____ DATE _____

---

normal wear and tear excepted. Normal wear and tear is usually the wear of a property or appliance consistent with the gradual wearing out over a normal useful life of the item, not the result of abuse and damage requiring extraordinary repairs.

Where a dispute arises between landlords and tenants, the courts provide a neutral place for resolution if the parties cannot otherwise resolve the issue. In many areas, arbitration and mediation are available to resolve the issues without court intervention. A substantial body of statutory and case law has developed in recent years, specifying the legal rights and duties of both the tenant and the landlord.

## ■ REMEDIES FOR LANDLORDS AND TENANTS

The primary interest of most landlords is receiving the prompt payment of rent from tenants who do not physically damage the property. At times, this may conflict with tenants who feel that the landlord is not providing the agreed services, such as heat and water, or is not maintaining the property, such as not repairing leaking roofs and broken plumbing. Tenants with a grievance may threaten or actually withhold rent to attempt to get the landlord to cure a problem.

**LEARNING OBJECTIVE 4**
Describe the process of enforcing landlords' and tenants' rights.

### Eviction

**Eviction** is a legal proceeding brought by the landlord to remove the tenant for breach of any of the terms of the lease, but generally for failure to make rent payments or surrender the premises at the end of the term of the lease. Eviction may be actual or constructive. **Actual eviction** is the actual removal or physical barring of the tenant from the premises or other physical dispossession of the tenant.

**eviction**
legal proceeding brought by the landlord to remove the tenant for breach of any of the terms of the lease

**actual eviction**
the actual removal or physical barring of the tenant from the premises or other physical dispossession of the tenant

Actual eviction may be the result of a judicial order granting the landlord or other designated party, such as the sheriff or constable, the authority to remove the tenant and their property.

**Constructive eviction** is when the premises are substantially unavailable for the tenant's use. Landlords in some cases may take steps to cut off utilities to pressure a tenant to pay rent. Constructive eviction is when the landlord withholds essential services such as heat in the winter or water and sewer utilities. Constructive eviction may be an actionable wrong for which the tenant may bring action against the landlord. A landlord's failure to properly maintain a property, making it unsuitable or uninhabitable, would be a constructive eviction.

A California court addressed the issues of constructive eviction, saying:

> …The Cause of Action for Constructive Eviction
>
> [13a] The cause of action for constructive eviction seeks compensatory and punitive damages and alleges: "Due to the continuing intolerable conditions of the [subject premises], plaintiff and her family were compelled to abandon the premises, which they did, on or about August 19, 1977." [14] "A constructive eviction occurs when the acts or omissions…of a landlord, or any disturbance or interference with [101 Cal.App.3d 926] the tenant's possession by the landlord, renders the premises, or a substantial portion thereof, unfit for the purposes for which they were leased, or has the effect of depriving the tenant for a substantial period of time of the beneficial enjoyment or use of the premises." (Groh v. Kover's Bull Pen, Inc. (1963) 221 Cal.App.2d 611, 614 [34 Cal.Rptr. 637]; see also 42 Cal.Jur.3d, § 124, pp. 143–144.) Abandonment of premises by the tenant within a reasonable time after the wrongful act of the landlord is essential to enable the tenant to claim a constructive eviction (id, at § 125, p. 144). Failure to repair and keep the premises in a condition suitable for the purposes for which they were leased has been held to constitute eviction (id, at § 126, p. 145). [13b] Appellant has stated a cause of action for constructive eviction. She was forced to abandon the premises after the Kern County Health Department ordered the premises be vacated and destroyed. Whether she abandoned within a reasonable time would constitute a jury question….Stoiber v. Honeychuck (1980) 101 Cal. App.3d 903, 925-26 , 162 Cal.Rptr. 194.

Constructive eviction is not always the result of the landlord failure to provide services. Constructive eviction can result from a natural disaster such as Superstorm Sandy, which devasted a large section of metropolitan New York and the entire New Jersey coast in October 2012. In any location where an apartment was rendered uninhabitable by the storm or its aftereffects, such as no electric or heat, the tenants were constructively evicted and the obligation to pay rents was relieved. This was particularly troublesome for tenants of high-rise apartment buildings where there was no damage to their upper floor apartments but the utility services, housed in the basement or first floor of the building were inoperable rendering the apartment uninhabitable.

A **judicial eviction process** is the practice and procedure for eviction, which varies widely from state to state. However, certain fundamentals are common. **Notice to quit**, a notice to vacate the premises or face eviction proceedings, must be given to the tenant (in some cases by personal service, in others by mail or certified mail) and must have proof of that service attached to any complaint filed with the court or presented at the court hearing. A hearing must be held to give the tenant an opportunity to appear and present a defense. It may be in a small claims court, a trial court, or a special landlord–tenant court. Only after a judgment is entered and the necessary appeal time expires may a court order to evict be used to remove the tenant.

**constructive eviction**
when the premises are substantially unavailable for the tenant's use

**PRACTICE TIP**

In some jurisdictions, landlords may not evict tenants during certain periods of the year. For example, in regions that experience cold, snowy winter months, evictions are prohibited during those months.

**judicial eviction process**
the practice and procedure for eviction

**notice to quit**
notice to vacate the premises or face eviction proceedings

## Self-Help

**Self-help** is a catchall expression for attempting to resolve an issue without use of legal process—for example, a tenant withholding rent or a landlord cutting off services. In some jurisdictions, statutes or regulations may permit a limited form of self-help. In these jurisdictions, residential tenants may be authorized to withhold rent, conditioned on the withheld rent being deposited into a separate or escrow account, notice provided to the landlord of rent deposited to that account and its location, and the landlord given a list of complaints, generally related to habitability or safety. Once those issues are addressed by the landlord, the escrow should be released to the landlord. For example, California offers a rent and deduct remedy in Civil Code Section 1942: The "repair and deduct" remedy allows a tenant to deduct money from the rent, up to the amount of one month's rent, to pay for repair of defects in the rental unit. This remedy covers substandard conditions that affect the tenant's health and safety, and that substantially breach the implied warranty of habitability. Examples might include a leak in the roof during the rainy season, no hot running water, or a gas leak.

As a practical matter, the repair and deduct remedy allows a tenant to make needed repairs of serious conditions without filing a lawsuit against the landlord. Because this remedy involves legal technicalities, it's a good idea for the tenant to talk to a lawyer, legal aid organization, or tenants' association before proceeding.

The basic requirements and steps for using the repair and deduct remedy are as follows:

1. The defects must be serious and directly related to the tenant's health and safety.
2. The repairs cannot cost more than one month's rent.
3. The tenant cannot use the repair and deduct remedy more than twice in any 12-month period.
4. The tenant or the tenant's family, guests, or pets must not have caused the defects that require repair.
5. The tenant must inform the landlord, either orally or in writing, of the repairs that are needed.
6. The tenant must give the landlord a reasonable period of time to make the needed repairs.

*Source:* http://www.dca.ca.gov/publications/landlordbook/repairs.shtml#footnote156

## ■ LEASES IN PURCHASE AND SALE OF REAL ESTATE

There are times when leases are used as a component of a real estate purchase and sale. The lease may represent a creative vehicle for purchasing a home. The lease may also be used to permit the purchaser of real estate to gain possession when the scheduled settlement date must be delayed or to allow the seller to remain in possession beyond the closing date.

**LEARNING OBJECTIVE 5**
Explain the use of lease agreements in the real estate purchase transaction.

## Lease Purchase Agreement

There are times when a lessee may wish to test or try out a specific property before making an outright purchase. Other times, a prospective buyer lacks current financial resources to purchase. To prevent the owner from selling the property to another, the prospective buyer promises to purchase in the future. In either of these cases, a lease purchase agreement may be used.

The landlord/seller may decide to enter into a temporary lease, without an obligation to sell the property. In that event, the prospective buyer wishes to occupy the rental property without a binding commitment, and the lease will contain an **option** to purchase at the end of the term. An option is a right to purchase, exercisable solely by purchaser, with no legal liability for failure to do so. Exhibit 12.3 shows a Lease Agreement and Option to Purchase contract.

The landlord may also enter a lease–purchase agreement where the commitment to purchase the property is included in the terms of the lease. The rental payment may be a slightly greater amount, with a portion of the payment being deemed rent and the other portion being credited toward the purchase price. In effect, the portion assigned to the purchase price represents a deposit against the ultimate purchase price. The terms may vary, and at the end of the term, the tenant/buyer is expected to arrange financing so that the sale can be concluded. The financing can be a traditional mortgage loan, or the seller may agree to provide the mortgage.

**option**
a right to purchase, exercisable solely by purchaser, with no legal liability for failure to do so

**PRACTICE TIP**

The prospective tenant/ purchaser should be screened, as any other tenant would be when entering into a lease. However, that screening would also address long-term financial abilities, similar to a loan qualification process.

## Leases for Sellers in Real Estate Transactions

If the seller is unable to vacate the premises at the time of the scheduled settlement, the seller's occupancy of the property may be extended through a short-term lease such as the one found in Exhibit 12.4.

A short-term lease protects the buyer who allows the seller to remain in a leasehold capacity. The seller agrees to pay a reasonable rental—usually equal to the amount of the buyer's monthly mortgage payment—pay the utilities, and peacefully surrender the premises at the end of the term. The seller will also be responsible for any damage to the property while he or she remains in possession. It should be noted that the buyer's lender, if any, may oppose this transaction. As part of the standard clauses in the mortgage, the buyer certifies that the property will be owner occupied. If the seller remains in possession following the settlement, the property is not owner occupied. The requirements of the lender may eliminate the ability to accommodate the seller's needs and instead force the settlement to be delayed until the seller can move out. This can be a great risk for the buyer, as mortgage underwriting rules and the availability of loan funds may change and the mortgage lender may not make the loan in the future.

## Leases for Buyers in Real Estate Transactions

**PRACTICE TIP**

From the seller's viewpoint, it may not be desirable to allow the buyer to occupy the property before purchase. Like a test-drive, occupancy may reveal issues that are only obvious when living in a property, such as uneven heating or air conditioning, excessive noise, sticking windows, and the like.

Witnessed with less regularity is the lease granted to a buyer. In this case, the seller has vacated the premises in advance of the closing date and, at the same time, has no objection to the buyer taking early possession of the property.

As in the event of a seller remaining after a closing date, leasehold principles apply, and a written lease agreement must be prepared.

A short-term lease much like the one in Exhibit 12.4 can be used. If buyers take early possession, a liability release clause protecting sellers should be drafted. See Exhibit 12.5. See another version of a buyer's Early Possession Agreement in Exhibit 12.6.

These types of advance agreements are sometimes employed in construction loan agreements of sale. Buyers, anxious to have the job done right, prefer to take possession in advance of the completed construction.

**Exhibit 12.3** Lease agreement and option to purchase contract

**LEASE AGREEMENT AND OPTION TO PURCHASE**

THIS LEASE AGREEMENT ("Agreement" or "Lease"), made this ___ day of
_____.

BY AND BETWEEN:

1. PARTIES: _____ and _____, his wife, hereinafter referred to as "Lessor";

AND

_____ and _____, his wife, hereinafter referred to as "Lessee."

2. LEASE. In consideration of the covenants and promises hereby mutually undertaken to be kept and performed by the parties hereto, Lessor hereby leases to Lessee and Lessee hereby rents and takes the condominium unit located at _____, _____, State of _____, (hereinafter the "Demised Premises"). (For legal description see attached Exhibit "A").

3. TERMS. This lease shall be for a maximum of _____ (__) months commencing on the ____ day of _____, year__, and ending on the ____ day of _____.

4. TERMINATION OF LEASE. This Lease shall automatically terminate if the option set forth in paragraph 15 if not exercised by Lessee prior to _____, ___ or, if there has been an unremedied default in accordance with paragraph 20 of this Lease.

5. RENT. Lessee hereby covenant and agree to pay Lessor, without notice, demand, or setoff at the address to be specified by Lessor, in equal monthly installments in advance, on or before the first day of each and every month during said term, and sum of _____ ($_____). Also due and payable shall be an option payment of _____ ($_____) as outlined in paragraph 15 hereof.

    A. Further, Lessee agrees that if such rent and option payment are not paid on or by the tenth day of every month, Lessee shall be subject to a late charge of _____ ($_____) per month.

    B. Lessee is aware that the current condominium fee of _____ ($_____) is due and payable by Lessee to the Condominium Association on or before the first of each month. Furthermore, a late fee is imposed currently of $_____ for any fee paid after the ___ day of the month. All current and future condominium fees due during the term of special amounts and assessments which shall become due and payable or which are issued against or levied upon the Demised Premises during the term of this Lease.

7. UTILITIES. It shall be the Lessees' responsibility and expense to obtain the transfer of all utility accounts into the Lessee's name. Lessee shall pay all charges for gas, water, sewage, electricity, light, heat or power, telephone used or supplied in connection with the Demised Premises, and all other utility services used or supplied in connection with the Demised Premises during the term of this Lease. Lessee shall supply proof of payment of the utilities upon request by the Lessor during the term of the Lease. Upon vacating the Demised Premises, Lessee shall submit proof of payment of all utilities used in connection with the Demised Premises.

*(continued)*

## Exhibit 12.3 Continued

8. INSURANCE. Lessee agrees to hold harmless Lessor from any loss due to theft or other criminal act during the term of this Agreement. During the term of this Lease, the Lessor agrees to maintain and keep in force a residential dwelling policy with $_____ of liability coverage and $_____ in medical payment coverage.

Lessee, during the term of this Agreement, agrees to maintain and keep in force a renters' insurance policy with a minimum amount of $_____ in public liability insurance and $_____ in medical payment coverage. Lessee, at the time of the signing of this Agreement, will provide proof of such coverage to the Lessor and shall subsequently provide proof to the Lessor of such coverage upon every anniversary date of this Agreement thereafter.

The cost of all insurance coverage carried by Lessor during the term of this Agreement and required by this Agreement on the Demised Premises, shall be reimbursed to the Lessor within _____ (__) days after notice is given to Lessee of the premium then due and owing.

9. FURNITURE & APPLIANCES. Any appliance, furniture, draperies, or the like, left on the Demised Premises by the Lessor are left in an "as is" condition and as a convenience to the Lessee and they shall not be repaired or replaced by the Lessor during the term of the Lease. Regardless of the foregoing, Lessee shall be liable for any damages to any property on the Demised Premises which damage is the fault of the Lessee, their agents and invitees.

A. Lessee specifically acknowledges that the Demised Premises were equipped with the following items, in good working order, upon their occupancy: [list items]
[list any items removed by the Lessor prior to Lessees' occupancy]

10. REPAIRS. The Lessee acknowledges that the Demised Premises and all appliances are being accepted by the Lessee "as is" without any warranties or representations of any kind from the Lessor or their agents. The responsibility for repair of all appliances and the routine and normal repairs to the Demised Premises are the responsibility of the Lessee during the term of this Lease Agreement. If any repairs remain unfinished in whole or in part, the Lessor, after _____ (__) days written notice to the Lessee of the need of such repair, the Lessor may make such repair and charge the cost of the repair as rent due and owing to Lessor with the next month's rent.

11. DESTRUCTION OF PREMISES. Should the Demised Premises be destroyed or rendered unfit for use and occupancy by fire or other casualty, in whole or in part, Lessor shall, at his option replace or repair the same, or terminate the Lease. In the event this Lease is terminated for this reason, the option payments shall be retained by Lessor.

At the option of the Lessee, if the property or the building of which it is a part, shall be damaged by fire or other peril or casualty during the term of this Lease Agreement, the Lessee may repair such damage, at Lessee's cost and expense. Such repairs by Lessee, Lessor shall assign to Lessee the proceeds of the insurance policy maintained by Lessor. Damage to the property of the building by fire or other casualty shall not automatically cause a termination of this Agreement.

12. DEFECTS. Lessee agrees that the Demised Premises have been inspected prior to the execution of this Lease and Lessee has found the Demised Premises to be habitable and in good repair. Lessor shall not be liable to Lessee or any other person for any loss suffered during the term of this Lease on account of any defective condition of the Demised Premises. In this regard, Lessee shall indemnify Lessor against all suits, actions or claims made on account of the condition of the Demised Premises.

13. ALTERATIONS AND IMPROVEMENTS. Lessee shall not structurally alter nor substantially repair the Demised Premises or any item therein without the consent of the Lessor. Such consent shall not be unreasonably withheld by Lessor. Upon vacating the Demised Premises, Lessee shall make "broom clean" all carpeting, appliances and all other areas of the Demised Premises.

## Exhibit 12.3 Continued

14. USE OF PREMISES. The Demised Premises shall be used and occupied by Lessee exclusively as a private single family residence, and neither the premises nor any part thereof shall be used at any time during the term of this Lease by Lessee for the purpose of carrying on any business, profession, or trade of any kind, or for any purpose other than as a private single family residence. Lessee shall comply with all the sanitary laws, ordinances, rules and orders of appropriate governmental authorities and the Homeowners' Association affecting the cleanliness, occupancy and preservation of the Demised Premises, and the sidewalks connected thereto, during the term of this Lease. The only pet permitted on the Demised Premises shall be one dog.

15. OPTION TO PURCHASE. Lessor hereby grants to Lessee the option to purchase, at the time, for the consideration and upon the terms and conditions set forth hereafter:

A. Lessee may purchase the Demised Premises at any time after the effective date of the Lease Agreement and prior to the 15th month of the Lease Agreement by giving _____ (__) days written notice to the Lessor of their intent to purchase the Demised Premises. Such notice shall also be accompanied with a signed, standard multi-list sales agreement which shall incorporate all terms of the purchase set forth herein and provide a closing date within _____ (__) days of the mailing of the notice and sales agreement. The sales agreement will be reviewed by the Lessor and if it contains the terms and conditions of sale accurately set forth as herein, Lessor shall sign said agreement and return it to the Lessee.

The terms of purchase shall be as follows:

A. Sales price to be _____ DOLLARS ($_____) and shall include all appliances and drapes left on the Demised Premises. The closing costs shall be divided as outlined on a standard multi-list condominium sales agreement and as is the custom of buyers and sellers in the area of _____ at the time of this closing. Lessor acknowledges receipt of one note for _____ DOLLARS ($_____) to be redeemed for cash on or before _____,year____. Said note will be held by the Broker until the option is exercised by the Lessee. This note with interest will be forfeited if the option is not exercised by Lessee or his assigns. Any interest accumulating prior to closing will be the sole property of the Lessor.

B. The monthly option payment of _____ DOLLARS ($_____) shall be paid along with the rent due to the Lessor. If the option is not exercised by Lessee, all option payments shall be forfeited and become the exclusive sole property of the Lessor.

C. In addition to the monthly rent and option payment due Lessor from Lessee, there shall also be due and owing during the term of this Lease Agreement, quarterly option payments of _____ DOLLARS ($_____) which shall be due to Lessor on: [list dates]_____

D. In the event that Lessee properly exercises the option during the term of the Lease Agreement, full credit of all option payments shall be given to Lessee toward the purchase price of the Demised Premises.

E. The Demised Premises shall be conveyed by the Lessor to the Lessee free and clear of all liens or encumbrances and the transfer of the Demised Premises by the Lessor to Lessee shall be by a general warranty deed.

F. The right to exercise this option is conditioned upon the faithful performance by the Lessee of all the covenants, conditions and agreements required to be performed by it as Lessee under this Lease, and the payment by the Lessee of all rent and any other payments as provided in this Lease Agreement to the closing date.

G. Adjustments and proration of taxes, insurance premiums and similar items shall be made as of the closing date.

## Exhibit 12.4 Short-term lease

---

**SHORT-TERM LEASE**

Address: _____

Seller: _____

Buyer: _____

Date: _____

This short-term lease is to be read in conjunction with and be made part of the Agreement of Sale dated _____, year ___ by and between the same parties.

Whereas the sellers are desirous of remaining in possession of said property after delivery of the deed and in consideration whereof the sellers covenant to pay $____ without demand in advance for a term of _____ commencing on _____ and ending _____.
In addition, the parties agree as follows:

1.      That a settlement on the above-mentioned property shall take place on _____, _____, wherein buyer shall purchase from seller said property at the stipulated amount for consideration.

2.      Sellers' Fire & Liability Insurance will remain in effect to coincide with lease term. And a rider will be attached to their existing policy protecting the buyers (proof of said property to be given to buyers prior to settlement).

3.      Sellers shall be liable for all utilities (gas, electric, water and sewage) for the term of this lease.

4.      Sellers agree to hold harmless and release the buyers from any liability as a result of their possession.

5.      Sellers agree to escrow with buyer $_____ as security against any damage and/or maintenance and/or litigation that may result in their occupancy.

6.      Time is of the essence with respect to the dates and terms mentioned in this Lease. In the event the seller does not vacate the property as indicated above, sellers shall be liable for additional rent in the amount of $_____per day, and buyer may take possession according to the terms stipulated in Paragraph #_____ of the Agreement of Sale and apply escrow monies towards any damages and/or legal expenses incurred.

_____          _____
Witness                                                       Seller

_____          _____
Witness                                                       Seller

_____          _____
Witness                                                       Buyer

_____          _____
Witness                                                       Buyer

---

Closely aligned to the construction scenario is when a buyer needs to make extensive repairs to the property being purchased before the official settlement or closing transfer.

**Exhibit 12.5** Release of liability

---

**LIABILITY RELEASE**

This addendum is attached to and made a part of the agreement of sale dated _____ by and between _____ (seller) and _____ (buyers) for the property located AT _____.

We grant permission for you to remain at _____ until _____.
We therefore request that in consideration of our granting permission for you to stay at the property, after closing date of _____ , you agree to the following:

1.  Release the record owner of the property from any and all liabilities for loss of property, or for personal injury which you may sustain in and about the property.
2.  Indemnify and hold harmless the record owner of the property from liability on account of loss or damage to the property of any person or persons, or on account of any injury sustained by, or the death of any person or persons resulting from the condition of the property, or caused in any manner by your acts or the acts of your agents.
3.  Maintain Homeowner Insurance policy up to and including the day of scheduled vacancy.
4.  Pay to the owner of record a rental charge of $_____dollars per day up to and including the last day of your possession at said premises.

If the foregoing is acceptable to you, please indicate your agreement by signing.

| | |
|---|---|
| WITNESS | BUYER |
| DATE | BUYER |
| WITNESS | SELLER |
| DATE | SELLER |

---

# ETHICAL Considerations

## UPL—GIVING ADVICE TO FRIEND WITH A LEASE ISSUE

Paralegals are seen by most friends and relatives as legal experts and a source of help and advice. A paralegal may be asked for free advice by a friend about issues with a lease or dispute with a landlord. The friend may be upset with the landlord's position on having a pet dog in an apartment. The request for a little free advice may be posed in an informal way and not even appear to be a request for legal advice. *I have this problem. What do I do?* The paralegal may want to help. But the offer of any advice that may impact the legal right of the paralegal's friend may constitute the unauthorized practice of law. Only a lawyer may offer legal advice, and as difficult as it may be, the paralegal must advise the friend to consult a lawyer. However, the paralegal may suggest non-legal remedies, like suggesting that the friend discuss the issue with the landlord to determine why the landlord has a restriction on pets. It may be that the landlord may allow some pets or some dogs of a limited size.

**Exhibit 12.6** Early possession agreement

---

**EARLY POSSESSION AGREEMENT**

PROPERTY ADDRESS: _____

SELLERS: _____

BUYERS: _____

1.  WHEREAS: The buyers are desirous of having possession of the above-captioned property prior to delivery of deed and full payment of purchase price, the sellers hereby in consideration of the sum of $_____ permit the buyers to enter into possession of said property for the sole purpose of:

2.  Buyers hereby agree to make no material changes or to use said property except as stated above without prior written consent of the sellers.
    a.
    b.
    c.

3.  Buyers have hereby obtained adequate fire, casualty and liability (but not limited to) insurance. Sellers assume no liability or responsibility for buyers' possessions or for anyone allowed to enter on and in said property by reason of the buyers having possession, and buyers assume said liability and responsibility.

4.  Buyers have made final inspection of above-captioned property prior to the signing of this addendum and are purchasing the same solely upon that inspection and not by promises or guarantees of any person whomsoever. Buyers are purchasing the property in as is condition.

5.  Sellers will pay all utilities until the time of settlement and buyers will have the utilities changed to their names prior to settlement.

6.  If for any reason whatsoever the buyers are not able to close due to whatever reason on or before _____then either party may extend the terms of this agreement for an additional 30 days. Buyers will pay an additional $_____.

7.  Should settlement not occur on or before _____ due to default by the buyers then the sellers may take all legal remedies as stated in the sales agreement. Buyers waive all rights against eviction in the State of _____ and will relinquish possession immediately. Time is of the essence in this agreement. In such case the Sellers shall receive the $ in hard money.

8.  Buyers do hereby release and forever hold harmless the sellers and the listing broker, _____ and the selling broker, _____ and their agents, against all judgments, claims and/or actions arising from the above-captioned sale, purchase and early possession.

9.  All other terms of the sale and purchase agreement remain in full force and effect.

10. Buyers intend to take possession on the following date for the above purpose: _____.

IN WITNESS WHEREOF the sellers and buyers have hereunto set their hands and seals, intending to be legally bound thereby this _____ day of, year.

Witness:_____          Seller:_____

                                         Seller:_____

Witness:_____          Buyer:_____

                                         Buyer:_____

## KEY TERMS

## CHAPTER SUMMARY

| | |
|---|---|
| Introduction to Landlord–Tenant Law | Landlord–tenant law defines the relationship between owners of real estate and their tenants. |
| Leasehold Interests | Leases are a form of interest in real property known as a non-freehold or less-than-freehold estate. A non-freehold estate, also referred to as the leasehold estate, is an estate in real property that has a definite time period and is limited to present possessory rights. There are four types of leasehold estates: tenancy for years, periodic tenancy, tenancy at will, and tenancy at sufferance. |
| Tenancy for Years | A tenancy for years is any leasehold interest of a specific duration, no matter how long or short. |
| Periodic Tenancy | A periodic tenancy is any leasehold interest with no stated duration or lease period, but with rental payments due at particular intervals. |
| Tenancy at Will | A tenancy at will is a tenancy created when a tenant retains possession after the end of a valid tenancy, with the landlord's consent and the continued payment of rent. |
| Tenancy at Sufferance | A tenancy at sufferance is a tenancy created when a tenant, without the landlord's consent, retains possession after the end of a valid tenancy. |
| Components of a Lease | Each lease should have certain information, such as: <br><br>■ Identification of the parties, the lessor and lessee <br>■ Description of the leased property <br>■ Specific beginning date, the duration of the period of tenancy, and the ending date <br>■ Amount of rent, when due, the acceptable method of payment, and where to make the payment <br>■ Requirement and amount of security deposit, its purposes, and how it will be returned to the lessee <br>■ Right to and terms of renewal periods <br>■ Terms of the use and occupancy <br>■ Covenants and obligations of the landlord and the tenant, including maintenance and repairs <br>■ Remedies in the event of breach, including eviction and self-help |

| | |
|---|---|
| Rights and Duties of Lessors and Lessees | The rights and duties of a landlord and tenant will depend in great part on the negotiated terms of the written lease agreement and on general legal principals. A residential lease is a contract to lease a specific property for the sole purpose of occupying it as the tenant's home. Habitability is a minimum standard of suitability for human living. |
| Rights and Duties of Landlords | In renting or leasing property, the landlord is concerned with the ability of the tenant to pay the rent. In most jurisdictions, the landlord has the right to collect a security deposit from the tenant to apply against damages. Other duties of landlords are specified in the lease. This may include the obligation to provide utilities or other building services such snow removal or grounds maintenance. |
| Rights and Duties of Tenants | Tenants have a right to quiet enjoyment of the rented property. Tenants are obligated to surrender or return the property peacefully at the end of the term of the lease, in the same condition as when the tenancy commenced, normal wear and tear excepted. |
| Remedies for Landlords and Tenants | Eviction is a legal proceeding brought by the landlord to remove the tenant for breach of any of the terms of the lease, but generally for failure to make rent payments or surrender the premises at the end of the term of the lease. Actual eviction is the actual removal or physical barring of the tenant from the premises or other physical dispossession of the tenant. Constructive eviction is when the premises are substantially unavailable for the tenant's use. A judicial eviction process is the practice and procedure for eviction, which varies widely from state to state. Self-help is a catchall expression for attempting to resolve an issue without use of legal process—for example, a tenant withholding rent or a landlord cutting off services. |
| Leases in Purchase and Sale of Real Estate | The lease may represent a creative vehicle for permitting the purchase of real estate or for permitting possession in advance of the settlement date or after settlement. |
| Lease Purchase Agreement | There are times when a lessee may wish to test or try out a specific property before making an outright purchase. Other times, a prospective buyer lacks current financial resources to purchase and will enter a lease purchase agreement. |
| Leases for Sellers in Real Estate Transactions | When the seller is unable to vacate the premises before the scheduled settlement, a lease extending the seller's occupany a lease will be used. |
| Leases for Buyers in Real Estate Transactions | In this case, if the seller has vacated the premises in advance of the closing date and, at the same time, has no objection, the buyer may taking early possession of the property. |

## REVIEW QUESTIONS AND EXERCISES

1. Describe the types of leasehold estates.
2. List the components of the lease agreement.
3. Describe the warranty of quiet enjoyment with respect to a lease. Does the tenant have any obligations with regard to this warranty?
4. What obligations does a landlord have under the terms of the lease?
5. What rights does the landlord have under the terms of the lease?

6. What obligations does the tenant have under the terms of the lease?

7. What rights does the tenant have under the terms of the lease?

8. Compare and contrast actual eviction, constructive eviction, and the judicial eviction process.

9. What rights of self-help do the landlord and tenant have?

10. How are leases used in the purchase of real estate?

## VIDEO CASE STUDY

Go to www.pearsonhighered.com/careers to view the following videos.

**Author Introduction to Landlord Tenant Law**
Author video introduction to chapter coverage.

## INTERNET AND TECHNOLOGY EXERCISES

1. Using the Internet, determine what leases, if any, your jurisdiction requires be put in writing. What leases, if any, must be prepared in plain English?

2. Using the Internet, determine what requirements, if any, are imposed on the landlord's right to collect, maintain, and refund a security deposit for residential leases.

3. Using the Internet, determine if your jurisdiction stays eviction proceedings during a particular time of the year.

## REAL ESTATE PORTFOLIO EXERCISES

**Landlord–Tenant Law**

**To:**    Paralegal Intern
**From:** Supervising Attorney
**Re:**    Tenant eviction

We are representing a family referred to us by a legal aid organization, on a pro bono basis.

They admit they are four months behind on the payment of rent. Their electricity has already been shut off by the electric utility for non-payment. The landlord is threatening them with eviction. They tell me they have nowhere to go.

I am not aware of the current rules on this since we don't normally do this type of work. But, I want to meet my responsibilities. Research the law and procedure in our jurisdiction on the rights of landlords and tenants in rent disputes. What is the court process and time line? Are there any remedies that the tenant might use to delay or avoid eviction?

Portfolio item produced:
Memorandum on law and procedure in our jurisdiction on the rights of landlords and tenants in rent disputes

**To:**    Paralegal Intern
**From:** Supervising Attorney
**Re:**    Tenant eviction

The seller, Mrs. Taylor, is selling her house to move into a retirement community. Unfortunately, she has just learned that her unit in the community will not be ready for her to move into until three months after the closing date on the sale of her home. The buyers, Daniel and Sara Schan, are living in an apartment on a month-to-month basis and do not need to move into the property immediately. The buyers' mortgage company has agreed to allow a short-term lease. The Schans' out-of-pocket costs for the three month will be $2,000 per month. Draft a short-term lease to be signed by the Schans and Mrs. Taylor at settlement.

Portfolio item produced:
Short term lease agreement.

Go to www.pearsonhighered.com/careers to download instructions.

## LEARNING OBJECTIVES

*Upon completion of this chapter, you should be able to*

1. Explain the concept of common interest communities in real estate.

2. Describe the differences between different forms of common interest communities.

# Common Interest Communities | CHAPTER 13

## ■ INTRODUCTION TO COMMON INTEREST COMMUNITIES

A **common interest community,** or CIC, is one in which individuals share ownership and expenses of real property in the same development. It may be the ownership of one's dwelling unit and shared ownership of common areas, such as playgrounds, pools, parking areas, sidewalks, and open spaces. Or it could be a share of ownership in the property and a right to use a dwelling, with fees assessed to pay for the maintenance, upkeep, and insurance on the common areas.

Common interest communities are based on state statutory schemes that determine the requirements for development, operation, and ultimate dissolution of the CIC.

## ■ COMMON INTEREST COMMUNITIES

The security of home ownership is an ideal that most people of the world desire. Achieving the goal has not always been easy because of the cost to purchase and maintain real estate. One way to achieve the ownership goal is to share with others the ownership and the related costs for upkeep and taxes. Traditional ownership forms, such as ownership as tenants in common or as joint tenants, is one method. These traditional forms of ownership are frequently used by family members, trusted friends, or business partners to acquire individual parcels of properties, with the common law and some statutes providing methods for resolving issues of ownership transfer and deadlocks in decision making.

**LEARNING OBJECTIVE 1**
Explain the concept of common interest communities in real estate.

**common interest community**
shared ownership of real estate

## DIGITAL RESOURCES

Author Introduction to Common Interest Communities.

Sample forms and templates.

Where the parties are not well known to each other, and in the absence of other common law forms to define and protect interests, two relatively new forms of common interest ownership have arisen: cooperatives and condominiums.

A **cooperative,** or **co-op,** is a modern form of ownership based on statute. The modern co-op is patterned after corporate stock ownership, reported to have first been used in the 1920s by workers who wanted to achieve some form of home ownership. A group of workers pooled their resources and built the first cooperative apartments in New York City.

The idea was that people would buy shares in the corporation that owned the building. Those shares came with the right to occupy but not own individual apartments. The shares could only be sold back to the corporation and not to the general public.

Until the condominium legislation of the 1960s, the co-op offered the only method of common interest ownership. Contemporary co-ops may allow the owners to sell their shares to anyone, but that buyer must be approved as a member of the co-op by a vote of the entire membership or an elected board of directors or special committee. This potential for rejection of potential residents has resulted in numerous lawsuits, some claiming discrimination against the buyer and others economic hardship against the sellers who are unable to obtain approval for a buyer.

The co-op concept has spread over the years to specific-purpose real estate ownership, such as specialized housing for the elderly, for students, and for small businesses. The common thread is a common ownership interest with shared expenses. Typically, nonprofit agencies are involved in many of the specialized co-op residences.

In some areas, the co-op model is used in agriculture. With the high cost of farming equipment, many farms have pooled their resources to create a cooperative that allows them to share the cost of expensive equipment needed only part of the year. Harvesting and processing equipment is owned cooperatively, with the cost to purchase shared among many farmers, who have the right to use the equipment, such as that employed in some apple- and cranberry-growing areas. The distinctive characteristic of the cooperative is shared user ownership, control, and benefit.

Some examples of co-ops are as follows:

> The California Canning Peach Association is a cooperative bargaining association based in Lafayette. Peach growers contract their production to processors.
>
> St. Mary's General Hospital in Lewiston, a 230-bed rural health care facility, is a member of Synernet, a cooperative that serves 20 hospitals.
>
> Tillamook County Creamery Association was organized in 1909 as a quality control organization for 25 cheese factories operating in Tillamook County, an area 30 miles wide and 60 miles long between the Pacific Ocean and the Coastal Range Mountains.

*Source:* http://www.rurdev.usda.gov/rbs/pub/cir7/cir7rpt.htm

Typically, co-ops are managed by an elected board of directors that serves without pay. In the larger co-ops, the board of directors may employ administrative and operations personnel to run the day-to-day operations.

In this regard, they are similar to condominiums that typically have a board of directors and employee staff.

Like the co-op, a **condominium** is a method of ownership based on statute. Unlike co-op owners, condominium owners own their individual units in fee simple and own a percentage of the common areas (parking lot, hallways, and

**cooperative or co-op**
modern form of property ownership based on statute and patterned after corporate stock ownership; identified by the right to occupy but not own individual apartments or property

**WEB EXPLORATION**
The creation of the first co-op is attributed to the director of the Amalgamated Clothing Workers Credit Union, Abraham Kazan.

For more insight into the creation of co-ops in New York, see the website http://www.athomeinutopia.com/ about the film *At Home in Utopia.*

One of the most famous cooperatives is the Dakota co-op apartment in New York City. Home to many celebrities and politicians, it was originally built between 1882 to 1884, contains 10 floors, and has units that sell for an average of over $2,400 per square foot.

**condominium**
modern form of ownership based on statute where owners own their individual units in fee simple and own a percentage of the common areas

recreation areas) as tenants in common with other unit owners. With the passage of condominium legislation, developers and large apartment complexes saw an opportunity to sell home ownership with the ability to freely transfer ownership, unlike the co-op restricted sale of stock. Condominium owners automatically become members of the condominium or homeowners' association that is the governing body for the condominium. Members may elect a board of directors or, in smaller condominiums, act collectively as a board. The board acts as the governing body, hiring staff to handle the day-to-day operation of the condominium, including the repair and maintenance of the common areas. The governing body also establishes budgets and replacement schedules for major components of the condo such as the roofing system, the siding, and the parking areas. Once established, the budget then determines the fees assessed on the individual units in the condominium, generally based on a percentage of ownership. This percentage of ownership is, in turn, based on the total individual apartment or condominium square footage in comparison to the square footage of the entire condominium project.

For example, a 1,000-square-foot unit in a building with 10 similar-sized units, or a total of 10,000 square feet, would pay 10 percent of the common area shared costs. A 2,000-square-foot unit in the same building would pay 20 percent of the shared costs. Exhibit 13.1 is an Allocation of Condominium Expenses and Real Estate Taxes for a property known as the Warwick.

## ■ CONDOMINIUMS

Condominium creation, like the corporation used in early co-op creation, is one of statute. Condominium statutes vary by state but have common elements, including the requirement of preparing and filing a Declaration of Condominium describing the proposed condominium, such as that prescribed in the Illinois Condominium Property Act shown below:

**LEARNING OBJECTIVE 2**
Describe the differences between different forms of common interest communities.

    (765 ILCS 605/4) (from Ch. 30, par. 304)

        Sec. 4. Declaration - Contents. The declaration shall set forth the following particulars:

        (a) The legal description of the parcel.

        (b) The legal description of each unit, which may consist of the identifying number or symbol of such unit as shown on the plat.

        (c) The name of the condominium, which name shall include the word "Condominium" or be followed by the words "a Condominium."

        (d) The name of the city and county or counties in which the condominium is located.

        (e) The percentage of ownership interest in the common elements allocated to each unit. Such percentages shall be computed by taking as a basis the value of each unit in relation to the value of the property as a whole, and having once been determined and set forth as herein provided, such percentages shall remain constant unless otherwise provided in this Act or thereafter changed by agreement of all unit owners.

        (f) If applicable, all matters required by this Act in connection with an add-on condominium.

        (g) A description of both the common and limited common elements, if any, indicating the manner of their assignment to a unit or units.

        (h) If applicable, all matters required by this Act in connection with a conversion condominium.

## Exhibit 13.1 Allocation of common expenses

Warwick Residential Condominium
Allocation of Master and Residential Condominium Expenses and Real Estate Taxes

| | | | | Estimated Annual Cost | | Estimated Monthly Cost | |
| --- | --- | --- | --- | --- | --- | --- | --- |
| UNIT | SF | Percentage Interest | Type | $746,029 Common Expense Allocation | $316,083 Real Estate & CCD Tax Expense Allocation | Common Expense Allocation | Real Estate & CCD Tax Expense Allocation |
| 1901 | 678 | 0.58279% | 1 BR | 4,199.58 | 1,778.88 | 349.88 | 148.24 |
| 1902 | 1,200 | 0.89608% | 2 BR | 7,431.05 | 3,148.44 | 618.25 | 262.37 |
| 1903 | 422 | 0.35029% | Efficiency | 2,613.26 | 1,107.21 | 217.77 | 92.27 |
| 1904 | 1,986 | 1.64852% | 3 BR | 12,298.44 | 5,210.69 | 1,024.87 | 434.22 |
| 1905 | 1,096 | 0.80975% | 2 BR | 6,787.00 | 2,875.57 | 565.58 | 239.63 |
| 1906 | 331 | 0.27475% | Efficiency | 2,049.71 | 858.44 | 170.81 | 72.37 |
| 1907 | 514 | 0.42688% | Efficiency | 3,183.01 | 1,348.60 | 265.25 | 112.38 |
| 1909 | 1,992 | 1.65350% | 3 BR | 12,335.59 | 5,226.43 | 1,027.97 | 435.54 |
| 1910 | 1,321 | 1.09652% | 2 BR | 6,180.36 | 3,465.91 | 681.70 | 288 83 |
| 1912 | 1,582 | 1.31317% | 2 BR/Den | 9,796.63 | 4,150.71 | 816.39 | 345.89 |
| 1914 | 2,417 | 2.00628% | 3 BR/Den | 14,967.43 | 6,341.51 | 1,247.29 | 528.46 |
| 1915 | 710 | 0.58935% | 1 BR | 4,396.72 | 1,962.84 | 366.39 | 155.24 |
| 1916 | 387 | 0.30464% | Efficiency | 2,272.70 | 962.92 | 189.39 | 80.24 |
| 1917 | 412 | 0.34199% | Efficiency | 2,551.34 | 1,080.97 | 212.61 | 90.06 |
| 2001 | 678 | 0.56279% | 1 BR | 4,198.58 | 1,778.88 | 349.89 | 148.24 |
| 2002 | 1,200 | 0.95008% | 2 BR | 7,431.06 | 3,148.44 | 619.25 | 262.37 |
| 3003 | 422 | 0.35029% | Efficiency | 2,613.26 | 1,107.21 | 217.77 | 92.27 |
| 2004 | 1,986 | 1.64852% | 3 BR | 12,298.44 | 5,210-69 | 1,024.87 | 434.22 |
| 2005 | 1,096 | 0.90975% | 2 BR | 6,787.00 | 2,875.57 | 565.58 | 239.83 |
| 2006 | 331 | 0.27475% | Efficiency | 2,049.71 | 868.44 | 170.81 | 72.37 |
| 2007 | 514 | 0.42888% | Efficiency | 3,183.01 | 1,348.60 | 265.25 | 112.38 |
| 2009 | 1,992 | 1.65350% | 3 BR | 12,335.58 | 5,226.43 | 1,027.87 | 435.54 |
| 2010 | 1,318 | 1.09403% | 2 BR | 8,161.78 | 3,458.04 | 680.15 | 288.17 |
| 2012 | 774 | 0.64247% | 1 BR | 4,793.01 | 2,030.74 | 389.42 | 169.23 |
| 2014 | 2,914 | 2.41882% | 3 BR/Den | 18,045.10 | 7,645.48 | 1,503.78 | 637 12 |
| 2015 | 905 | 0.75121% | 1 BR | 5,604.24 | 2,374.46 | 467.02 | 197.67 |
| 2016 | 367 | 0.30464% | Efficiency | 2,272.70 | 962.92 | 169.39 | 80.24 |
| 2017 | 412 | 0.34199% | Efficiency | 2,551.34 | 1,080.97 | 212.61 | 90.08 |
| 2101 | 678 | 0.56279% | 1 BR | 4,198.58 | 1,778.88 | 349.88 | 148.24 |

**Exhibit 13.1** Continued

| UNIT | SF | Percentage Interest | Type | Estimated Annual Cost | | Estimated Monthly Cost | |
|------|-----|------|------|------|------|------|------|
| | | | | $746,029 Common Expense Allocation | $316,083 Real Estate & CCD Tax Expense Allocation | Common Expense Allocation | Real Estate & CCD Tax Expense Allocation |
| 2102 | 811 | 0.67319% | 1 BR | 5,022.19 | 2.127.84 | 418.52 | 177.32 |
| 2104 | 2,443 | 2.02785% | 3 8R | 15,128.42 | 6,409.72 | 1,260.70 | 534.14 |
| 2105 | 1,041 | 0.86410% | 2BR | 6,446.44 | 2,731.27 | 537.20 | 227.61 |
| 2106 | 331 | 0.27475% | Efficiency | 2,049.71 | 868.44 | 170.61 | 72.37 |
| 2107 | 487 | 0.40424% | Efficiency | 3,016.75 | 1,277.73 | 251.31 | 106.48 |
| 2109 | 2,881 | 2.38143% | 3 BR | 17,840.76 | 7,558.80 | 1,486.73 | 629.91 |
| 2110 | 644 | 0.53456% | 1 BR | 3,987.97 | 1,669.66 | 332.33 | 140.80 |
| 2112 | 1,037 | 0.86078% | 2 BR | 6,421.67 | 2,720.78 | 535.14 | 225.73 |
| 2112-loft | 414 | 0.34365% | | 2,583.73 | 1,088.22 | 213.64 | 90.52 |
| 2114 | 3,849 | 3.19476% | 3 BR | 23,833.99 | 10,098.15 | 1,986.17 | 841.61 |
| 2116 | 387 | 0.30484% | Efficiency | 2,272.70 | 962.92 | 189.39 | 80.24 |
| 2117 | 412 | 0 34199% | Efficiency | 2,551.34 | 1,080.97 | 212.61 | 90.08 |
| | | | | 746.029 00 | 316.083.00 | | |
| | | | | Coat per Square Foot | | $6.19 | $2.82 |

Common Expense Allocation is based on the estimated Residential Condominium Budget including the residential share ot the Master Condominium Budget subsequent to the Ramp Up Period which ends in 2009.

Real Estate and CCD Tax Expense Allocation Is based upon the estimated residential portion of the real estate tax for the entire property prior to Improvement of the residential units and the related center

(h-5) If the condominium is a leasehold condominium, then:
   (1) The date of recording and recording document number for the lease creating a leasehold interest as described in item (x) of Section 2;
   (2) The date on which the lease is scheduled to expire;
   (3) The legal description of the property subject to the lease;
   (4) Any right of the unit owners to redeem the reversion and the manner whereby those rights may be exercised, or a statement that the unit owners do not have such rights;
   (5) Any right of the unit owners to remove any improvements within a reasonable time after the expiration or termination of the lease, or a statement that the unit owners do not have such rights;

(6) Any rights of the unit owners to renew the lease and the conditions of any renewal, or a statement that the unit owners do not have such rights; and

(7) A requirement that any sale of the property pursuant to Section 15 of this Act, or any removal of the property pursuant to Section 16 of this Act, must be approved by the lessor under the lease.

(i) Such other lawful provisions not inconsistent with the provisions of this Act as the owner or owners may deem desirable in order to promote and preserve the co-operative aspect of ownership of the property and to facilitate the proper administration thereof.

(*Source:* P.A. 89-89, eff. 6-30-95.)

*Source:* http://ilga.gov/legislation/ilcs/ilcs3.asp?ActID=2200&ChapAct=765%26nbsp%3BILCS%26nbsp%3B605%2F&ChapterID=62&ChapterName=PROPERTY&ActName=Condominium+Property+Act

As the Illinois statute indicates, condominium legislation can be complex in the manner in which it is written. Some states have a legislative counsel's office that will provide an outline or summary of the law to convert the concepts that are covered by a statute to plain language. Below is the statement from the California Office of Legislative Counsel describing the rules which govern the use of common elements:

RULES GOVERNING USE OF COMMON ELEMENTS

**14.** (1) The bylaws may provide for the making of rules by members of the corporation who together own a majority of the units respecting the use of the common elements for the purpose of preventing unreasonable interference with the use and enjoyment of the units and common elements.

(2) The rules shall be reasonable and consistent with this Act, the declaration and the bylaws.

(3) The rules shall be complied with and enforced in the same manner as the bylaws. (1977,c.6,s.14)

The elected board, or governing body, enforces the rules, such as payment of monthly assessments, setting those assessments, and rules on the use of common areas. Condominiums may be developed as part of the construction process from raw land or the conversion of existing property. Depending on the location and market, it may be on land purchased outright or obtained under a long-term lease, such as waterfront property built on long-term leased piers owned by a municipal government or private pier operator. Conversion of existing apartments and hotels has been popular in large cities such as Chicago, Philadelphia, and New York. Each method presents additional issues that may be addressed in local statues, such as those in the Florida Condominium Statute that appears below. There are specific provisions for the topics listed, including the rights of existing tenants when a property is converted to condominium:

Florida Condominium Statutes (Chapter 718)

Leaseholds.
Condominium leases; escalation clauses.
Conversion of existing improvements to condominium.
Phase condominiums.
Mixed-use condominiums.
Multicondominiums; multicondominium associations.

**WEB EXPLORATION**

Compare The California Condominium Act of 1976 found at at http://www.cga.ct.gov/2011/pub/chap825.htm#TOC with the Report of Legislative Counsel concerning the Condominium Act found at http://www.gov.pe.ca/law/statutes/pdf/c-16.pdf

**PRACTICE TIP**

Always check the source of the materials you are relying on. In some instances, the simple statement of the law may come from a secondary source, such as legislative counsel's office. And while the material may be easier to understand, only a primary source of the law, such as the statute itself, can be relied on in legal writings.

718.612 Right of first refusal.—

(1) Each tenant, who for the 180 days preceding a notice of intended conversion has been a residential tenant of the existing improvements, shall have the right of first refusal to purchase the unit in which he or she resides on the date of the notice, under the following terms and conditions:

(a) Within 90 days following the written notice of the intended conversion, the developer shall deliver to the tenant the following purchase materials: an offer to sell stating the price and terms of purchase, the economic information required by s. 718.614, and the disclosure documents required by ss. 718.503 and 718.504. The failure by the developer to deliver such purchase materials within 90 days following the written notice of the intended conversion will automatically extend the rental agreement, any extension of the rental agreement provided for in s. 718.606, or any other extension of the rental agreement. The extension shall be for that number of days in excess of 90 days that has elapsed from the date of the written notice of the intended conversion to the date when the purchase materials are delivered.

**WEB EXPLORATION**

The Florida Condominium Statutes may be viewed at http://www.leg.state.fl.us/Statutes/index.cfm?App_mode=Display_Statute&URL=0700-0799/0718/0718ContentsIndex.html

In the condominium, common areas and facilities are shared. The cost of maintaining these could be a matter of concern if not spelled out in the Declaration of Condominium, in the bylaws, or by legislation as shown in the Minnesota statute:

### 515.06 COMMON AREAS AND FACILITIES.

(a) Each apartment owner shall be entitled to an undivided interest in the common areas and facilities in the percentage expressed in the declaration. Such percentage shall be computed by taking as a basis the value of the apartment in relation to the value of the property.

(b) The percentage of the undivided interest of each apartment owner in the common areas and facilities as expressed in the declaration shall have a permanent character and shall not be altered without the consent of all of the apartment owners expressed in an amended declaration duly recorded. The percentage of the undivided interest in the common areas and facilities shall not be separated from the apartment to which it appertains and shall be deemed to be conveyed or encumbered with the apartment even though such interest is not expressly mentioned or described in the conveyance or other instrument.

(c) The common areas and facilities shall remain undivided and no apartment owner or any other person shall bring any action for partition or division of any part thereof, unless the property has been removed from the provisions of sections 515.01 to 515.29 as provided in sections 515.16 and 515.26. Any covenant to the contrary shall be null and void.

(d) Each apartment owner may use the common areas and facilities in accordance with the purpose for which they were intended without hindering or encroaching upon the lawful rights of the other apartment owners.

(e) The necessary work of maintenance, repair, and replacement of the common areas and facilities and the making of any additions or improvements thereto shall be carried out only as provided herein and in the bylaws.

(f) The association of apartment owners shall have the irrevocable right, to be exercised by the manager or board of directors, to have access to each apartment from time to time during reasonable hours as may be necessary for the maintenance, repair, or replacement of any of the common areas and facilities therein or accessible therefrom, or for making emergency repairs therein necessary to prevent damage to the common areas and facilities or to another apartment or apartments.

**WEB EXPLORATION**

The Minnesota statutes are available at https://www.revisor.mn.gov/statutes/?id=515.06

## ■ COOPERATIVE

Technically, the individual does not own a real estate interest. Rather, the real estate is owned by a corporation; individuals purchase stock in the corporation. Stock ownership includes the right to use and occupy a portion of the real estate owned by the corporation. Stock ownership includes the right to participate in the decision making of the corporation with regard to the operation, maintenance, and upkeep of the property, and sale of additional shares in the corporation.

Through stock ownership and voting, the existing residents have the power to permit or deny someone access to their building by agreeing or refusing to sell them shares of stock and have the power to deny modification and improvements. The extent of the control of modifications and improvements is illustrated in the New York case of *Matter of Levandusky*.

# IN THE WORDS OF THE COURT

### *Matter of Levandusky v. One Fifth Ave. Apt. Corp*, 75 NY2d 530

As cooperative and condominium home ownership has grown increasingly popular, courts confronting disputes between tenant–owners and governing boards have fashioned a variety of rules for adjudicating such claims (*see generally*, Goldberg, *Community Association Use Restrictions: Applying the Business Judgment Doctrine*, 64 Chi-Kent L Rev 653 [1988] [hereinafter *Goldberg, Community Association Use Restrictions*]; Note, *Judicial Review of Condominium Rulemaking*, 94 Harv L Rev 647 [1981]). In the process, several salient characteristics of the governing board–homeowner relationship have been identified as relevant to the judicial inquiry.

As courts and commentators have noted, the cooperative or condominium association is a quasi-government—"a little democratic sub society of necessity" (*Hidden Harbour Estates v Norman*, 309 So 2d 180, 182 [Fla Dist Ct App]). The proprietary lessees or condominium owners consent to be governed, in certain respects, by the decisions of a board. Like a municipal government, such governing boards are responsible for running the day-to-day affairs of the cooperative and to that end, often have broad powers in areas that range from financial decisionmaking to promulgating regulations regarding pets and parking spaces (*see generally*, Note, *Promulgation and Enforcement of House Rules*, 48 St John's L Rev 1132 [1974]). Authority to approve or disapprove structural alterations, as in this case, is commonly given to the governing board. (*See*, Siegler, *Apartment Alterations*, NYLJ, May 4, 1988, at 1, col 1.)

Through the exercise of this authority, to which would-be apartment owners must generally acquiesce, a governing board may significantly restrict the bundle of rights a property owner normally enjoys. Moreover, as with any authority to govern, the broad powers of a cooperative board hold potential for abuse through arbitrary and malicious decisionmaking, favoritism, discrimination and the like.

On the other hand, agreement to submit to the decisionmaking authority of a cooperative board is voluntary in a sense that submission to government authority is not; there is always the freedom not to purchase the apartment. The stability offered by community control, through a board, has its own economic and social benefits, and purchase of a cooperative apartment represents a voluntary choice to cede certain of the privileges of single ownership to a governing body, often made up of fellow tenants who volunteer their time, without

(*continued*)

### WEB EXPLORATION

Read the following articles to learn about alleged discrimination against celebrities in the issuance of shares in a co-op and denial of approval to make modification.

http://lawblog.legalmatch.com/2011/02/11/housing-discrimination-can-happen-to-celebrities-and-also-to-antonio-banderas/

http://www.habitatmag.com/Publication-Content/Habitat-s-Purchasing-Primer-News-for-New-Buyers/Admissions

compensation. The board, in return, takes on the burden of managing the property for the benefit of the proprietary lessees. As one court observed: "Every man may justly consider his home his castle and himself as the king thereof; nonetheless his sovereign fiat to use his property as he pleases must yield, at least in degree, where ownership is in common or co-operation with others. The benefits of condominium living and ownership demand no less." *(Sterling Vil. Condominium v Breitenbach,* 251 So 2d 685, 688, n 6 [Fla Dist Ct App].)

## ■ TIME SHARE

**Time shares** are fractional ownership of property, usually based on a time factor, such as a particular week or month every year. Variations of the concept have become popular for vacation properties where the time of year is factored into the ownership based on the popularity of the time of year and location. For example, a week at a Caribbean resort in the winter is more valuable than one in the summer, and a similar interest may only be good for four days in the peak season and seven days in the low-demand season. One of the most popular time shares is that of the Disney Vacation Club, which offers a variety of accommodation types and destinations based on a points approach; more popular times and locations and sizes of units require more points.

The time share is a special kind of common interest community but not a true ownership interest in real estate. Rather, the time share interest represents the right to occupy and use a place for a specific time period.

**time shares**
fractional ownership of property, usually based on a time factor, such as a particular week or month every year

**WEB EXPLORATION**

For more information on the Disney Vacation Club, see http:// disneyvacationclub.disney.go.com

## ■ RETIREMENT COMMUNITIES

Some retirement communities are common interest properties. These generally include ownership based on the cooperative model, where an interest is purchased that may be resold. Some offer a variation that requires an initial deposit, some or all of which is returned, but do not offer any other attributes of real estate ownership. In most cases, in addition to the upfront fee is a monthly fee for services such as food, medical care, and maintenance.

Some retirement communities are true cooperatives or are in condominium form. For older individuals, these forms of ownership give them the comfort of home ownership without the burdens related to repairs and maintenance. The shares in retirement co-ops and the deeds for retirement condominiums will contain restrictions limiting resale to anyone over a certain age or prohibiting occupancy by anyone under a certain age, such as school-age children. The restrictions have in some cases been required as part of obtaining zoning approval. In an effort to reduce the impact on residential support services, municipalities have approved developments as long as no additional costs are incurred for schools or the type of services required to support younger residents (such as the increased costs of police or refuse removal).

While not technically real estate ownership, for many senior citizens entry into a **Continuing Care Retirement Community (CCRC)** is like buying into a home. CCRCs offer a variety of housing and health care options. These range from skilled care down to independent living.

According to the Government Accountability Office:

> CCRCs typically offer one of three general types of contracts that involve different combinations of entrance and monthly fee payments. Some CCRCs may offer residents a choice of the following contract types, while others may choose to offer only one.

**Continuing Care Retirement Community (CCRC)**
for senior citizens, a type of housing option that may include a defined level of health care services, meals, and amenities in addition to the housing unit

Type A, extensive or Life Care contracts, include housing, residential services, and amenities—including unlimited use of health care services—at little or no increase in monthly fees as a resident moves from independent living to assisted living, and, if needed, to nursing care. Type A contracts generally feature substantial entrance fees but may be attractive because monthly payments do not increase substantially as residents move through the different levels of care. As a result, CCRCs absorb the risk of any increases in the cost of providing health and long-term care to residents with these contracts.

Type B, or modified contracts, often have lower monthly fees than Type A contracts, and include the same housing and residential amenities as Type A contracts. However, only some health care services are included in the initial monthly fee. When a resident's needs exceed those services, the fees increase to market rates. For example, a resident may receive 30, 60, or 90 days of assisted living or nursing care without an increased charge. Thereafter, residents would pay the market daily rate or a discounted daily rate—as determined by the CCRC—for all assisted living or nursing care required and face the risk of having to pay high costs for needed care.

Type C, or fee-for-service contracts, include the same housing, residential services, and amenities as Type A and B arrangements but require residents to pay market rates for all health-related services on an as-needed basis. Type C contracts may involve lower entrance and monthly fees while a resident resides in independent living, but the risk of higher long-term care expenses rests with the resident.

| | **Range of CCRC Fees by Contract Type** | | | |
|---|---|---|---|---|
| | **A–Life Care** | **B–Modified** | **C–Fee for Service** | **D–Rental** |
| Entry fee | $160,000 to $600,000 | $80,000 to $750,000 | $100,000 to $500,000 | $1,800 to $30,000 |
| Independent living monthly fee | $2,500 to $5,400 | $1,500 to $2,500 | $1,300 to $4,300 | $900 to $2,700 |
| Assisted living monthly fee | $2,500 to $5,400 | $1,500 to $2,500 | $3,700 to $5,800 | $4,700 to $6,500 |
| Nursing care monthly fee | $2,500 to $5,400 | $1,500 to $2,500 | $8,100 to $10,000 | $8,100 to $10,700 |

**Table 1: 2009 Entrance and Monthly Fees for Selected CCRCs by Contract Type**
*Source:* GAO analysis of information obtained from eight selected CCRCs.

Some CCRCs offer a fourth type of contract, Type D or rental agreements, which generally require no entrance fee but guarantee access to CCRC services and health care. Type D contracts are essentially pay-as-you-go:

CCRCs charge monthly fees of residents based on the size of the living unit and the services and care provided.

*Source:* Report to the Chairman, Special Committee on Aging, U.S. Senate "June 2010 OLDER AMERICANS Continuing Care Retirement Communities Can Provide Benefits, but Not Without Some Risk"

**WEB EXPLORATION**

The complete GAO report on CCRC is available at the Government Accountability Office website at http://www.gao.gov/assets/310/305752.pdf

For the purchaser of a common interest property, there is much to be concerned about from statutory control, to the declaration of the condominium, to the bylaws, rules and regulation. Exhibit 13.2 is a Common Interest Community checklist to be used in making sure that all relevant information is obtained from the seller and provided to the purchaser.

## Exhibit 13.2  CIC checklist

**COMMON INTEREST COMMUNITY CHECKLIST FOR BROKERAGE FIRM**

**NOTE:** Any recipient of this form is advised to independently verify information listed below.

Property Address: _____          Date: _____

| Item | Yes | No | Don't Know | Amount | Comments |
|------|-----|----|-----------|--------|----------|
| 1.  Are there any unpaid expenses or assessments on the property? | | | | | |
| 2.  Are there any unpaid special assessments on the property? | | | | | |
| 3.  Are there any unpaid liens on the property? | | | | | |
| 4.  Are any special assessments being contemplated on the property? | | | | | |
| 5.  Are any increases being contemplated to the periodic fee? | | | | | |
| 6.  Is there a monthly association fee? | | | | | |
| 7.  Is there a quarterly association fee? | | | | | |
| 8.  Is there a semi-annual association fee? | | | | | |
| 9.  Is there an annual association fee? | | | | | |
| 10.  Is the property subject to more than one association fee? | | | | | |
| 11.  Must a buyer prepay monthly association dues at time of closing?  If so, how many months? _____ | | | | | |
| 12.  Is a working capital reserve deposit required from the buyer? | | | | | |
| 13.  Is a transfer fee imposed by the association upon sale of the property? | | | | | |
| 14.  Is a fee imposed by the association for providing a status letter? | | | | | |
| 15.  Is there a charge for common area access devices?  (pool keys, common hallway keys, etc.) | | | | | |
| 16.  Are any other fees imposed by the association upon sale of the property? | | | | | |
| 17.  Are there any violations of covenants that the seller has been advised of? | | | | | |
| 18.  Are there any existing or pending law suits against the association and/or the property? | | | | | |
| 19.  Is the association still under the control of the developer? | | | | | |
| 20.  Is there any damage to this property, any common areas, any adjacent properties, or violations of the covenants or rules and regulations that could cause a lien against the property? | | | | | |
| 21.  Is the sale of this property subject to a right of first refusal by the association or a member? | | | | | |
| 22.  Does this property include the use of? | | | | | |

|  | Deeded | Exclusive use |
|--|--------|---------------|
| Storage unit(s) | ☐ | ☐ |
| Parking space(s) | ☐ | ☐ |
| Carport(s | ☐ | ☐ |
| Garage(s) | ☐ | ☐ |

| Item | Yes | No | Don't Know | Amount | Comments |
|------|-----|----|-----------|--------|----------|
| 23.  The regular association dues includes the following: | | | | | |
| Management | | | | | |

**COMMON INTEREST COMMUNITY CHECKLIST FOR BROKERAGE FIRM**                    **Page 1**

*(continued)*

## Exhibit 13.2 Continued

| | | | | | |
|---|---|---|---|---|---|
| Insurance premiums<br>    a.   Structure(s)<br>    b.   Common area liability | | | | | |
| Common area/element repair, maintenance or replacement | | | | | |
| Trash collection | | | | | |
| Water | | | | | |
| Sewer | | | | | |
| Heat | | | | | |
| Hot water | | | | | |
| Snow removal | | | | | |
| Roof | | | | | |
| Indoor swimming pool | | | | | |
| Outdoor swimming pool | | | | | |
| Hot tub | | | | | |
| Tennis court(s) | | | | | |
| Club house | | | | | |
| Perimeter fencing | | | | | |
| Cable/satellite TV | | | | | |
| Gas service | | | | | |
| Electric service | | | | | |
| Road maintenance | | | | | |
| Common area utilities | | | | | |
| Exterior maintenance | | | | | |
| Other _____ | | | | | |

Explain any "Yes" answers to the above questions:

_____

_____

_____

Association Name: _____

Association Address: _____

Association Phone: _____ Association President: _____

Association e-mail address: _____

Association website: _____

Association Management Company: _____

Management Company Address: _____

Management Company Phone: _____ Fax: _____

Management Company e-mail address: _____

Management Company Website: _____

Is there a Sub-Association?  If so, the above information for the Sub-Association:

_____

_____

_____

## KEY TERMS

Common interest community    300          Condominium    300          Continuing Care Retirement
Cooperative or co-op    300               Time share    307            Community (CCRC)    307

## CHAPTER SUMMARY

| Introduction to Common Interest Communities | A common interest community, or CIC, is one in which individuals share ownership and expenses of real property in the same development. |
|---|---|
| Common Interest Communities | Achieving the goal of home ownership has not always been easy because of the cost to purchase and maintain real estate. One way to achieve the ownership goal is to share with others the ownership and the related costs for upkeep and taxes. |
| Condominiums | A method of ownership based on statute. Unlike co-op owners, condominium owners own their individual unit in fee simple and own a percentage of the common areas (parking lot, hallways, and recreation areas) as tenants in common with other unit owners. |
| Cooperative | Technically, the individual does not own a real estate interest in a cooperative. Rather, the real estate is owned by a corporation; individuals purchase stock in the corporation. Stock ownership includes the right to use and occupy a portion of the real estate owned by the corporation. Stock ownership includes the right to participate in the decision making of the corporation with regard to the operation, maintenance, upkeep, and sale of additional shares in the corporation. |
| Time Share | Time shares are fractional ownership of property, usually based on a time factor, such as a particular week or month every year. Variations of the concept have become popular for vacation properties where the time of year is factored into the ownership based on the popularity of the time of year and location. |

| Retirement Communities | Some retirement communities are common interest properties. These generally include ownership based on the cooperative model, where an interest is purchased that may be resold. Some offer a variation that requires an initial deposit, some or all of which is returned, but do not offer any other attributes of real estate ownership. In most cases, in addition to the upfront fee is a monthly fee for services such as food, medical care, and maintenance. |
| --- | --- |

## REVIEW QUESTIONS AND EXERCISES

1. What is a common interest community?
2. How do common interest communities make home ownership more affordable?
3. How is the co-op a form of real estate ownership?
4. What are the benefits of co-op ownership?
5. How is the condominium a form of real estate ownership?
6. What are the benefits of condominium ownership?
7. Describe the disadvantages of co-op and condominium ownership.
8. How are these forms of ownership created?
9. What unique advantages do co-op and condominium ownership provide to retirees?
10. What is a time share? Is it a form of real estate ownership? Why or why not?
11. What is a CCRC? Is it a form of real estate ownership? Why or why not?

## VIDEO CASE STUDY

Go to www.pearsonhighered.com/careers to view the following videos.

**Author Introduction to Common Interest Communities**
Author video introduction to chapter coverage.

## INTERNET AND TECHNOLOGY EXERCISES

1. Using the Internet, determine whether your jurisdiction permits the co-operative form of ownership.

2. Using the Internet, locate your jurisdiction's statute on condominium creation and obtain the provision on maintenance of common areas.

## REAL ESTATE PORTFOLIO EXERCISES

**Common Interest Communities**

**To:**        Paralegal Intern
**From:**      Charles Hart
**Case Name:** Mrs. Taylor
**Re:**         Retirement Housing Options

Mrs. Taylor has been looking at different retirement housing options. She has looked at a ground floor apartment in a new condominium building that has a pool and health spa where she says most owners are in their 40s-50s.

Across the street is an older building of older wealthy residents that is a cooperative.

She has also looked at a small townhome in a small development near her children that is managed by a homeowners association.

She would like to know what the pros and cons are of each types of management.

Portfolio items produced:
1. Memo on the differences between the three forms of property ownership
2. Letter to client explaining the pros and cons of each type of ownership

Go to www.pearsonhighered.com/careers to download instructions.

## LEARNING OBJECTIVES

*Upon completion of this chapter, you should be able to*

1. Describe the process of real estate development.

# Real Estate Development and Investment

CHAPTER **14**

## ■ INTRODUCTION TO REAL ESTATE DEVELOPMENT AND INVESTMENT

Real estate development is the process of acquiring land, determining the best and most profitable use for that land, making those improvements, and selling or leasing it in order to make a profit.

With many stages from start to completion, real estate development can be a long and difficult process. Real estate development is a highly risky endeavor, but with high risks can come high rewards.

The process is made risky by the unknowns and uncontrollable elements the developer frequently encounters. For example, a developer may determine that a parcel of land is just the spot for a mixed use of offices and retail space. During the process, the developer may encounter a contaminated site that must be cleaned up before proceeding, zoning requirements that are difficult to comply with, and, worst of all, a community that does not want more shops and offices.

## ■ REAL ESTATE DEVELOPMENT

For many, the term *real estate development* brings up an image of farmland being plowed under for the construction of large tracts of homes, as in the development of the Levittown projects of Long Island, New York, and Bucks County, Pennsylvania.

**LEARNING OBJECTIVE 1**
Describe the process of real estate development.

## DIGITAL RESOURCES

Author Introduction to Real Estate Land Development and Investment.

These massive land developments were among the first developments of whole communities including housing, schools, shopping areas, recreation facilities, and public works.

Real estate development also includes smaller-scale development of tracts with as few as two to ten units on a small tract of farm or forested land. But in contemporary development, it often includes reclaiming inner-city land, renovating older historic homes, or building new communities.

Developers are returning to inner cities and towns and developing or redeveloping areas—including residential, office, retail, and industrial areas—bringing back from economic collapse many areas in large cities such as New York, Philadelphia, and Chicago and smaller cities such as Lancaster, Pennsylvania, and Portland, Oregon.

Except for some nonprofit organizations, most real estate developers are investors looking for opportunity. All real estate development has some common issues: finding a suitable property for development, arranging the needed financing, and obtaining the needed government approvals.

## Property Acquisition

Before property is acquired, a determination must be made that the final project will be economically viable; the resulting property can be sold, rented, or leased. In a practical sense, the project must return enough revenue to pay off all the financing and result in a profit for the developer. Even with the best planning, this is not always the case. Billion-dollar casinos have been built in Atlantic City with the expectation by very sophisticated investors, lenders, and operators that these would be successful, only to have many of the projects teeter on the brink of bankruptcy. Similarly, large-scale home developments have been built but then face economic ruin, as in Las Vegas when the home sales market collapsed.

Whether the developer plans a residential development, office complex, or warehouse space, large tracts of land are required. Typically, large single tracts of just the right size and location are difficult to locate and purchase.

One way is to purchase large farming tracts. Old family farms are sold to generate cash for the family farmer. Developers find these large parcels attractive when they are located in rural and suburban areas with good access to roads where people work and with the availability of utilities. The developer then devises a plan to generate the greatest profit from the land. However, there are not a lot of farms for sale.

In other instances, the developer may identify a desirable area or community in which it appears that the project will be successful. Over time, the developer may purchase lots in a particular location, with the idea that this is an area that would be good for development. The process is one that requires a great deal of patience on the part of the developer, for it may take many years to acquire all the necessary land. It also requires a commitment to the success of the project. This process may include communicating with the local real estate community, watching for properties to be listed for sale, and soliciting property owners to get them to sell.

Sometimes the developer may use a **straw party** to acquire the land. A straw party is someone who stands in the shoes of the purchaser, purchases, and takes title to the real estate. The straw party has an agreement with the developer, acknowledging that the land is being purchased for the benefit of

**straw party**
someone who stands in the shoes of the purchaser, purchases, and takes title to the real estate

the developer and agreeing to keep the identity of the developer confidential. There are times when word spreads through a community that a developer is "snatching up land." Some owners of land may try to take advantage of that fact and seek a higher selling price; others may try to stop the process by refusing to sell and influencing public opinion about the project.

The most important component to selecting the targeted land for acquisition is location, location, location. The developer will want a community that has access to roadways that lead to employment centers; access to roadways and railways for shipment of goods; availability of utilities such as electric, public water and sewer, gas, telephone, and Internet services; school districts with a good reputation; and a community with a reputation for supporting development.

**WEB EXPLORATION**

The development of Disney World in Florida shows the time involved and some of the issues in large-scale development. See the timeline at http://kpolsson.com/wdworld

### Economics of Development

With any business enterprise, there is a benefit known as the economy of scale. In development, increasing the number of units built on the same parcel of land reduces the cost per unit because the overhead costs are spread over more units. For example, building 10 units rather than 5 on the same parcel of land that was acquired at $100,000 reduces the land cost per unit from $20,000 per unit for 5 units to $10,000 per unit for 10 units. The developer's desire for higher density, or more units per acre, is a desire to spread the cost over more units. In addition to the cost of the land is the cost of obtaining the approval for development. In some cases, this involves obtaining multiple levels of government approval from zoning boards, land development committees, and town councils or boards of supervisors. Occasionally, the approval process will require court proceedings to obtain a court order compelling the issuance of the necessary approvals and permits. In each of these hearings, it is common for the developer to have subdivision plans and occasionally models of the project presented by teams of lawyers, architects, and engineers, all of which represents a significant expense even before the project can be started.

Typically, agreements to purchase land are subject to obtaining the necessary approvals. Developers will frequently enter into to a contract with the landowner that is contingent on getting approval before the transaction is finalized. In many cases, this includes a nonrefundable down payment or option payment to the seller to cover the seller's cost for keeping the property off the market.

## Government Approvals

The ability to develop real estate in most jurisdictions will be controlled by some form of government oversight. In most cases, land development is controlled by a local **zoning code**. Zoning codes establish criteria for different land uses and a plan for multiple uses within a community. The purpose of zoning is to control the "look and feel" of a community. People do not want an industrial building erected next to their homes. Zoning codes seek to group similar uses in the same areas, as shown in the zoning map in Exhibit 14.1.

Within these zoned areas, additional requirements may be imposed, setting limits on minimum lot sizes and the heights of buildings, requirements for off-street parking, setbacks from property lines, and in many communities, conformance to a certain look, such as the historical appearance of other structures in

**zoning code**
statutory criteria for allowable land uses and a plan for multiple uses within a community

**Exhibit 14.1** Zoning map

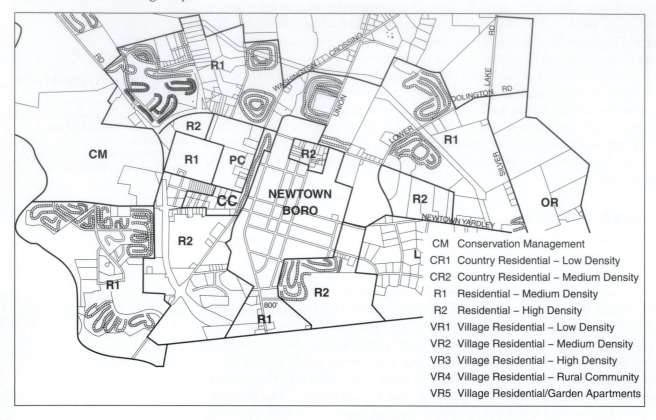

| | |
|---|---|
| CM | Conservation Management |
| CR1 | Country Residential – Low Density |
| CR2 | Country Residential – Medium Density |
| R1 | Residential – Medium Density |
| R2 | Residential – High Density |
| VR1 | Village Residential – Low Density |
| VR2 | Village Residential – Medium Density |
| VR3 | Village Residential – High Density |
| VR4 | Village Residential – Rural Community |
| VR5 | Village Residential/Garden Apartments |

**subdivision**
the development of one parcel of land into multiple parcels, literally dividing one parcel into many

the area. Exhibit 14.2 is a portion of the zoning code for Hamilton, Massachusetts, specifying the permitted uses in their zoning code for the Building District.

### Subdivision

A **subdivision** is the development of one parcel of land into multiple parcels, literally dividing one parcel into many. Where multiple parcels are going to be sold out of the original land, a subdivision plan may need to be prepared and approved by the local government. The subdivision plan approval generally requires a showing that each individual lot meets the zoning minimum requirements and that each property will have proper access to and from public roads. The public access is not required just for the convenience of the potential owner, but also for access by emergency vehicles such as fire trucks, and may require an approval from the fire department as part of the final approval process.

The subdivision process may include requests for variances, exemptions from certain requirements of the zoning code. In many communities, the issue of on- and off-street parking can be the stumbling block to approval for a building of a particular size, which in turn limits the space available for on-site parking, and causes a failure to meet the minimum requirement. The developer will request permission to vary or be exempted from that requirement so the project can move forward. Depending on the political climate in the community, pro- or anti-development, the request will be granted or denied. For communities on the rise, prodevelopment attitudes tend to freely grant these exemptions and variances to encourage economic development. For communities that have reached their limit, antidevelopment forces will be at work, looking for ways to control overburdened infrastructure such as roads, schools, and water and sewer facilities.

## Exhibit 14.2 Business district permitted uses

B. **Business District** is intended for retail and local neighborhood shopping, for offices, and for other business uses.

Permitted Uses:

1. All residence, agricultural and other uses permitted in the R-1a and R-1b districts subject to the same restrictions (Ed. Note: including Special Permit requirements) as prescribed for such uses in said Districts.

2. Retail store or service establishment. This use requires Site Plan Review; see section VI.H.

3. Business or professional office, or bank. These uses require Site Plan Review; see section VI.H.

4. Restaurant or other place for serving food. This use requires Site Plan Review; see section VI.H.

5. Municipal, State or Federal governmental buildings. This use requires Site Plan Review; see section VI.H.

6. Nonprofit civic and fraternal building. This use requires Site Plan Review; see section VI.H.

7. Use of land for a public utility.

8. Parking area or garage for use of employees, customers or visitors under the conditions specified in Paragraphs D and H of Section VI for approval of site plan, etc. This use requires Site Plan Review; see section VI.H.

9. Signs or display advertising goods or services available on the lot as provided in Paragraph E of Section VI.

10. Accessory buildings and uses customarily incidental to permitted uses. These uses may require Site Plan Review; see section VI.H.

11. Subject to Special Permit by the Board of Appeals as provided for in Section IX.D below, the following:

   a. Gasoline Service Station provided that repairs shall be limited to minor changes and adjustments and that gasoline pumps and equipment shall be so located that vehicles to be serviced are entirely upon the service station lot.

This use requires Site Plan Review; see section VI.H.

*Source:* http://www.hamiltonma.gov/pages/HamiltonMA_Planning/ZBLOct2010.pdf

Subdivision approval is also based on a showing that basic utilities are provided. Critical are those of water and sewer. In areas serviced by public water and sewer, there must be a demonstration that the new development will not overburden the existing system and its capacity. In some rural areas where public water and sewer are not available, alternate methods of providing them must be shown and approved. This may include proof that there is available well water on each property and that sufficient alternate sewage treatment is available that will not interfere with other users or the existing water wells.

Exhibit 14.3 is a small subdivision plan for four lots, showing access and building placement for a property in Hawaii.

**WEB EXPLORATION**

The entire Hamilton Zoning Bylaw can be read at http://www.hamiltonma .gov/pages/HamiltonMA_ Planning/ZBLOct2010.pdf

## Financing

It is rare for a developer to finance a development project without outside financing. Depending on the scale of the development, this may come from local banks and credit unions or larger regional or national banks, and in some cases, insurance companies and labor unions or public retirement funds.

Depending on the type and scope of development, the normal financing plan provides for initial or construction funding and final or permanent financing. **Construction funding** represents the funds provided to cover the out-of-pocket costs of construction, which are usually released by the lender based on a

**construction funding**
represents the funds provided to cover the out-of-pocket costs of construction, which are usually released by the lender based on a percentage of completion of the project

## Exhibit 14.3 Subdivision plan

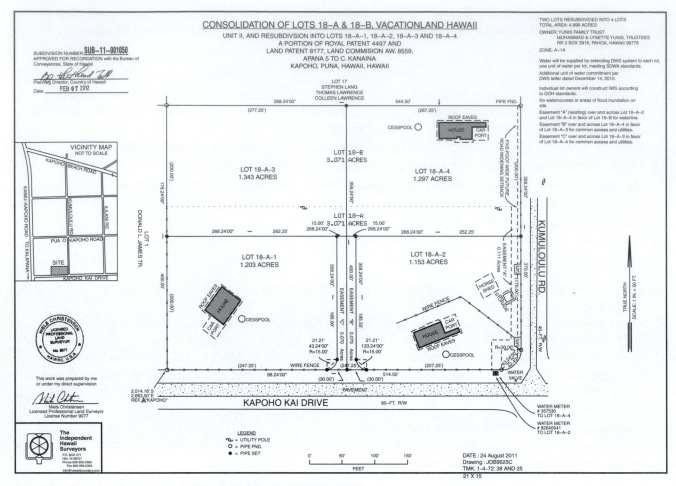

Source: http://www.hawaiicounty.gov/subdivision-maps/after-6-1-05/2011-to-2015/

percentage of completion of the project. Lenders will commit to a certain amount of funding to be released over the duration of the construction process. To release funds, lenders require proof of payment to the contractors and suppliers or, alternatively, pay the contractors and suppliers directly. Other lenders release funds based on percentage of completion. In this case, the lender will hire an independent inspector to provide a report on the percentage of completion of the project as a requirement for the release of the funds. Some lenders specialize in this form of short-term or temporary financing. These lenders expect to be repaid in full when the project is complete and will require proof that a permanent source of funds is available on completion to repay them.

**permanent lenders**
those lenders who do not want the risk inherent in financing a construction project that may never be completed or may encounter escalating costs

**Permanent lenders** are those lenders who do not want the risk inherent in financing a construction project that may never be completed or may encounter escalating costs. Permanent lenders will only fund the completed project, but will agree to pay off the construction lender on completion. Permanent lenders usually charge a fee, sometimes called a stand-by fee, for committing and holding the funds necessary for use in paying off the construction loans.

In some projects, the lender is interested in providing mortgages to the ultimate purchasers. In the case of the development of a tract of homes near a local bank or credit union, the construction financing is a way to obtain the new customers, and for the developers, a way to offer the end buyer a financing source.

In commercial development, such as shopping centers or commercial rental property, the lender may require the developer to assign to the lender all of the future rents from tenants as additional security in addition to the traditional mortgage. This additional security provides the lender with an immediate source of funds if a default occurs.

## Marketing

The marketing effort for most development begins as soon as there is an option to purchase or an agreement of sale signed. Ultimately, the success of any development depends on a good marketing effort to generate interest, which results in sales or rentals. Scale models and architect's renderings prepared for governmental hearings are frequently used in marketing efforts. These may be released as part of a public relations campaign for publication in newspapers and media at the time of the hearings, in advertisements, or on websites created for the project. Most projects will have signs erected on the property describing the project features, depicting the project, and giving contact information. Sale signs (example shown in Exhibit 14.4) are promptly posted as properties are sold, to create concern in potential buyers that they may miss a chance to purchase their desired lot or property.

In commercial development, the developer may have already secured a commitment from tenants expressing an interest or a firm commitment to rent if the project is completed. Firm commitments from major tenants, such as national chains and department stores, are used to convince lenders of the viability of the project, to advise the local government of the potential tax revenue that will be generated, to attract other tenants, and to advise the community of the overall benefit of the project to the community.

In residential projects, an on-site trailer may be set up for potential buyers to meet with a representative to obtain information about the project and, if

## Exhibit 14.4 New development sale notice

interested, to sign a prebuilding agreement to purchase. In larger-scale development, the trailer will be replaced when the first home constructed is converted to a sample house and office.

A contemporary area of development is of retirement communities and specifically continuing care retirement communities (CCRC). The development of a CCRC follows the same pattern and has many of the same issues as any other real estate development.

The Government Accountability Office has reported the following to Congress in its report on CCRCs.

According to industry participants, building and operating a CCRC is a complex process that typically begins with an initial planning phase. During this phase, the company assembles a development team, makes financial projections, assesses market demand, and determines the kinds of housing and services to be offered....Initial and longer-term planning also entails assessing funding sources and seeking funding commitments from investors and lenders, particularly construction loans and state tax-exempt bond proceeds, where applicable. During the developmental phase, developers will presell units to begin building capital to fund construction of CCRC housing and other facilities and begin construction. Once the initial phases of construction are complete, CCRC providers have move-in periods for new residents, continue marketing efforts to build toward full occupancy, complete construction, and begin making long-term debt service payments.

CCRCs, like other businesses, face a number of risks during the start-up phase. First, actual construction costs and consumer demand may not match developers' forecasts. To attract financing from lenders and ensure adequate underwriting for CCRC projects, developers need to generate sufficient presales and deposits prior to construction to show a tangible commitment from prospective residents. In addition, facilities in the start-up stage need to reach full occupancy as quickly as possible in order to generate income that will not only cover operational costs once built but also help pay down construction loans. As a result, accurate projections of future revenues and costs are important as a CCRC becomes operational.

Second, entrance fees and monthly fees may ultimately prove to be inadequate to cover the CCRC's costs. CCRCs generally have to keep prices low enough to attract residents and stay competitive but high enough to meet short- and long-term costs. Determining appropriate fees can, in itself, be a complex process because it involves projecting a number of variables into the future, including occupancy levels, mortality rates, medical and labor costs, and capital improvement costs. For this reason, many CCRCs use actuarial consultants to help in these determinations. CCRCs that set fees too low may have to significantly raise entrance and other fees to meet the costs of care and future capital improvements. Fee increases can take the form of larger-than-projected monthly fees for assisted living or nursing care and fees on other miscellaneous services, both of which can affect residents' long-term ability to pay and the competitive position of the CCRC in the marketplace.

CCRCs may face other financial risks, including unforeseen events that lead to higher-than-expected costs. For example, many nonprofit CCRCs rely on property tax exemptions when estimating CCRC costs and developing CCRC projects. According to industry associations and a state regulator, however, difficult economic times are causing some municipalities to look for new sources of revenue, and some may be reevaluating property tax exemptions previously granted to CCRCs. Loss of these exemptions can be very costly; for example, industry participants attributed one recent CCRC failure in Pennsylvania in part to the loss of its property tax exemption.

**PRACTICE TIP**

Specialty programs of study are offered to those interested in real estate development by schools such as Columbia University in its graduate school, providing a Masters of Science in Real Estate Development (http://www.arch.columbia.edu/programs/real-estate-development), and the Arizona State University certificate program, which is a sampler of real estate topics including real estate fundamentals, law, investments, and land development (https://webapp4.asu.edu/programs/t5/majorinfo/ASU00/BAREAMIN/undergrad/true).

# ETHICAL Considerations

## CONFIDENTIALITY

Frequently, the large tracts of land that are acquired for development have interesting prior uses that in today's world could represent problems for ultimate purchasers. We tend to think of farmland as pristine and uncontaminated, but the farmer may have used pesticides and fertilizers that are now considered hazardous or repaired vehicles and dumped petroleum waste products in the ground. These materials may remain in the soil or water found on the land. A lumberyard, while not pristine, regardless of specific uses, may also have been used to construct and finish furniture on the site with stripping and refinishing chemicals that are considered hazardous. Under state and federal guidelines, these types of hazardous materials must be cleaned up before the project can move forward. The cost to remediate some sites can be more than the potential value of the completed project. Failure to clean up the site has serious financial penalties. Covering up or paving over hazardous sites has criminal penalties and may constitute a clear and present danger to the health of the community. The ethical duty of confidentiality is not absolute. The lawyer who knows of the potential commission of a crime or the potential of danger to the public may have a duty to disclose the information.

## KEY TERMS

| | |
|---|---|
| Straw party   316 | Construction funding   319 |
| Zoning code   317 | Permanent lenders   320 |
| Subdivision   318 | |

## CHAPTER SUMMARY

| | |
|---|---|
| Introduction to Real Estate Development and Investment | Real estate development is the process of acquiring land, determining the best and most profitable use for that land, making those improvements, and selling or leasing it in order to make a profit. With many stages from start to completion, real estate development can be a long and difficult process. |
| Real Estate Development | Real estate development includes the construction of large tracts of homes as well as smaller-scale development of tracts with as few as two to ten units on a small tract of farm or forested land. But in contemporary development, it also includes reclaiming inner-city land, renovating older historic homes, or building new communities. |
| Property Acquisition | Before property is acquired, a determination must be made that the final project will be economically viable; the resulting property can be sold, rented, or leased. In a practical sense, the project must return enough revenue to pay off all the financing and result in a profit for the developer. |

| Economics of Development | In development, increasing the number of units built on the same parcel of land reduces the cost per unit because the overhead costs are spread over more units. |
|---|---|
| Government Approvals | The ability to develop real estate in most jurisdictions will be controlled by some form of government oversight. In most cases, land development is controlled by a local zoning code. |
| Subdivision | A subdivision is the development of one parcel of land into multiple parcels, literally dividing one parcel into many. Where multiple parcels are going to be sold out of the original land, a subdivision plan may need to be prepared and approved by the local government. |
| Financing | It is rare for a developer to finance a development project without outside financing. Depending on the scale of the development, this may come from local banks and credit unions or larger regional or national banks, and in some cases, insurance companies and labor unions or public retirement funds. <br><br>Construction funding represents the funds provided to cover the out-of-pocket costs of construction, which are usually released by the lender based on a percentage of completion of the project. <br><br>Permanent lenders will only fund the completed project, but will agree to pay off the construction lender on completion. |
| Marketing | The marketing effort for most development begins as soon as there is an option to purchase or an agreement of sale signed. Ultimately, the success of any development depends on a good marketing effort to generate interest, which results in sales or rentals. |

## REVIEW QUESTIONS AND EXERCISES

1. Describe the process of real estate development.
2. What are the risks that real estate developers face?
3. Describe some of the forms of projects that real estate developers create.
4. Why do real estate developers take risks? Explain.
5. What initial determinations do developers have to make before acquiring properties?
6. Is real estate development a certainty for profitability? Explain.
7. Explain some of the types of properties developers may acquire.
8. What is a straw party? Why would a developer use a straw party as part of the development process?
9. What are the advantages of large-scale development over smaller-scale development?
10. How do local governments control development?
11. What is the role of a zoning code?
12. What is a subdivision plan?
13. What is the difference between construction and permanent financing?
14. How important is the marketing effort in the development process?
15. What is a continuing care retirement community?
16. What are some of the issues in developing a continuing care retirement community?
17. What are the ethical implications for the legal team that is aware of hazardous materials on a site that a client proposes to develop?

## VIDEO CASE STUDY

Go to www.pearsonhighered.com/careers to view the following videos.

**Author Introduction to Real Estate Land Development and Investment**
Author video introduction to chapter coverage.

## INTERNET AND TECHNOLOGY EXERCISES

1. Using the Internet, locate your jurisdiction's requirement for subdivision of land.

2. Using the Internet, investigate the interest rates and terms for construction loans and compare to the interest rates and terms for a traditional purchase money mortgage.

## REAL ESTATE PORTFOLIO EXERCISES

**Real Estate Development and Investment**

**To:** Paralegal Intern
**From:** Charles Hart
**Case Name:** Thomas Aaron
**Re:** Subdivision

Our client wants to divide his 30 acres farmette into three separate lots and build houses on the two vacant lots for his children to live in.
   He would like to know the formalities and time line for doing this in our local area.
   Please research the steps and the required paperwork to subdivide the property into three lots. Where possible obtain copies of the blank forms.
   Research the filing fees required and the documentation that must be submitted and the costs and timeline.

Portfolio items produced:
1. Memo on the subdivision process in your area
2. Letter to client explaining the process to subdivide and build the two houses

**To:** Paralegal Intern
**From:** Human Resources Director
**Re:** Time Records

We have enjoyed having you with us. You have been a big help in a number of cases.
   Before you leave, please prepare a summary of all your time in this internship and print out a copy I can use to report your internship activity.
   To enable us to bill for your time where allowed, print out a separate billing report for each matter you worked on.

Portfolio items produced:
1. Summary of time spent showing cumulative total hours
2. Separate billing summary for each matter worked on

Go to www.pearsonhighered.com/careers to download instructions.

# APPENDIX A – FORMS

# FORM 1 – UNIFORM RESIDENTIAL MORTGAGE

After Recording Return To:

_____

_____

_____

_____

_____ [Space Above This Line For Recording Data] _____

## MORTGAGE

## DEFINITIONS

Words used in multiple sections of this document are defined below and other words are defined in Sections 3, 11, 13, 18, 20 and 21. Certain rules regarding the usage of words used in this document are also provided in Section 16.

**(A)** **"Security Instrument"** means this document, which is dated _____, _____, together with all Riders to this document.

**(B)** **"Borrower"** is _____.
Borrower is the mortgagor under this Security Instrument.

**(C)** **"Lender"** is _____. Lender is a _____ organized and existing under the laws of _____. Lender's address is _____ _____ Lender is the mortgagee under this Security Instrument.

**(D)** **"Note"** means the promissory note signed by Borrower and dated _____, _____. The Note states that Borrower owes Lender _____ _____ Dollars (U.S. $_____) plus interest. Borrower has promised to pay this debt in regular Periodic Payments and to pay the debt in full not later than _____ _____.

**(E)** **"Property"** means the property that is described below under the heading "Transfer of Rights in the Property."

**(F)** **"Loan"** means the debt evidenced by the Note, plus interest, any prepayment charges and late charges due under the Note, and all sums due under this Security Instrument, plus interest.

**(G) "Riders"** means all Riders to this Security Instrument that are executed by Borrower. The following Riders are to be executed by Borrower [check box as applicable]:

☐ Adjustable Rate Rider     ☐ Condominium Rider     ☐ Second Home Rider

☐ Balloon Rider     ☐ Planned Unit Development Rider     ☐ Other(s) [specify] _____

☐ 1-4 Family Rider     ☐ Biweekly Payment Rider

**(H) "Applicable Law"** means all controlling applicable federal, state and local statutes, regulations, ordinances and administrative rules and orders (that have the effect of law) as well as all applicable final, non-appealable judicial opinions.

**(I) "Community Association Dues, Fees, and Assessments"** means all dues, fees, assessments and other charges that are imposed on Borrower or the Property by a condominium association, homeowners association or similar organization.

**(J) "Electronic Funds Transfer"** means any transfer of funds, other than a transaction originated by check, draft, or similar paper instrument, which is initiated through an electronic terminal, telephonic instrument, computer, or magnetic tape so as to order, instruct, or authorize a financial institution to debit or credit an account. Such term includes, but is not limited to, point-of-sale transfers, automated teller machine transactions, transfers initiated by telephone, wire transfers, and automated clearinghouse transfers.

**(K) "Escrow Items"** means those items that are described in Section 3.

**(L) "Miscellaneous Proceeds"** means any compensation, settlement, award of damages, or proceeds paid by any third party (other than insurance proceeds paid under the coverages described in Section 5) for: (i) damage to, or destruction of, the Property; (ii) condemnation or other taking of all or any part of the Property; (iii) conveyance in lieu of condemnation; or (iv) misrepresentations of, or omissions as to, the value and/or condition of the Property.

**(M) "Mortgage Insurance"** means insurance protecting Lender against the non-payment of, or default on, the Loan.

**(N) "Periodic Payment"** means the regularly scheduled amount due for (i) principal and interest under the Note, plus (ii) any amounts under Section 3 of this Security Instrument.

**(O) "RESPA"** means the Real Estate Settlement Procedures Act (12 U.S.C. §2601 et seq.) and its implementing regulation, Regulation X (24 C.F.R. Part 3500), as they might be amended from time to time, or any additional or successor legislation or regulation that governs the same subject matter. As used in this Security Instrument, "RESPA" refers to all requirements and restrictions that are imposed in regard to a "federally related mortgage loan" even if the Loan does not qualify as a "federally related mortgage loan" under RESPA.

**(P) "Successor in Interest of Borrower"** means any party that has taken title to the Property, whether or not that party has assumed Borrower's obligations under the Note and/or this Security Instrument.

TRANSFER OF RIGHTS IN THE PROPERTY

This Security Instrument secures to Lender: (i) the repayment of the Loan, and all renewals, extensions and modifications of the Note; and (ii) the performance of Borrower's covenants and agreements under this Security Instrument and the Note. For this purpose, Borrower does hereby mortgage, grant and convey to Lender the following described property located in the

_____ of _____:

   [Type of Recording Jurisdiction]    [Name of Recording Jurisdiction]

which currently has the address of _____

                                           [Street]

_____, Pennsylvania _____ ("Property Address"):

   [City]                    [Zip Code]

TOGETHER WITH all the improvements now or hereafter erected on the property, and all easements, appurtenances, and fixtures now or hereafter a part of the property. All replacements and additions shall also be covered by this Security Instrument. All of the foregoing is referred to in this Security Instrument as the "Property."

BORROWER COVENANTS that Borrower is lawfully seised of the estate hereby conveyed and has the right to mortgage, grant and convey the Property and that the Property is unencumbered, except for encumbrances of record. Borrower warrants and will defend generally the title to the Property against all claims and demands, subject to any encumbrances of record.

THIS SECURITY INSTRUMENT combines uniform covenants for national use and non-uniform covenants with limited variations by jurisdiction to constitute a uniform security instrument covering real property.

UNIFORM COVENANTS. Borrower and Lender covenant and agree as follows:

**1. Payment of Principal, Interest, Escrow Items, Prepayment Charges, and Late Charges.** Borrower shall pay when due the principal of, and interest on, the debt evidenced by the Note and any prepayment charges and late charges due under the Note. Borrower shall also pay funds for Escrow Items pursuant to Section 3. Payments due under the Note and this Security Instrument shall be made in U.S. currency. However, if any check or other instrument received by Lender as payment under the Note or this Security Instrument is returned to Lender unpaid, Lender may require that any or all subsequent payments due under the Note and this Security Instrument be made in one or more of the following forms, as selected by Lender: (a) cash; (b) money order; (c) certified check, bank check, treasurer's check or cashier's check, provided any such check is drawn upon an institution whose deposits are insured by a federal agency, instrumentality, or entity; or (d) Electronic Funds Transfer.

Payments are deemed received by Lender when received at the location designated in the Note or at such other location as may be designated by Lender in accordance with the notice provisions in Section 15. Lender may return any payment or partial payment if the payment or partial payments are insufficient to bring the Loan current. Lender may accept any payment or partial payment insufficient to bring the Loan current, without waiver of any rights hereunder or prejudice to its rights to refuse such payment or partial payments in the future, but Lender is not obligated to apply such payments at the time such payments are accepted. If each Periodic Payment is applied as of its scheduled due date, then Lender need not pay interest on unapplied funds. Lender may hold such unapplied funds until Borrower makes payment to bring the Loan current. If Borrower does not do so within a reasonable period of time, Lender shall either apply such funds or return them to Borrower. If not applied earlier, such funds will be applied to the outstanding principal balance under the Note immediately prior to foreclosure. No offset or claim which Borrower might have now or in the future against Lender shall relieve Borrower from making payments due under the Note and this Security Instrument or performing the covenants and agreements secured by this Security Instrument.

**2. Application of Payments or Proceeds.** Except as otherwise described in this Section 2, all payments accepted and applied by Lender shall be applied in the following order of priority: (a) interest due under the Note; (b) principal due under the Note; (c) amounts due under Section 3. Such payments shall be applied to each Periodic Payment in the order in which it became due. Any remaining amounts shall be applied first to late charges, second to any other amounts due under this Security Instrument, and then to reduce the principal balance of the Note.

If Lender receives a payment from Borrower for a delinquent Periodic Payment which includes a sufficient amount to pay any late charge due, the payment may be applied to the delinquent payment and the late charge. If more than one Periodic Payment is outstanding, Lender may apply any payment received from Borrower to the repayment of the Periodic Payments if, and to the extent that, each payment can be paid in full. To the extent that any excess exists after the payment is applied to the full payment of one or more Periodic Payments, such excess may be applied to any late charges due. Voluntary prepayments shall be applied first to any prepayment charges and then as described in the Note.

Any application of payments, insurance proceeds, or Miscellaneous Proceeds to principal due under the Note shall not extend or postpone the due date, or change the amount, of the Periodic Payments.

**3. Funds for Escrow Items.** Borrower shall pay to Lender on the day Periodic Payments are due under the Note, until the Note is paid in full, a sum (the "Funds") to provide for payment of amounts due for: (a) taxes and assessments and other items which can attain priority over this Security Instrument as a lien or encumbrance on the Property; (b) leasehold payments or ground rents on the Property, if any; (c) premiums for any and all insurance required by Lender under Section 5; and (d) Mortgage Insurance premiums, if any, or any sums payable by Borrower to Lender in lieu of the payment of Mortgage Insurance premiums in accordance with the provisions of Section 10. These items are called "Escrow Items." At origination or at any time during the term of the Loan, Lender may require that Community Association Dues, Fees, and Assessments, if any, be escrowed by Borrower, and such dues, fees and assessments shall be an Escrow Item. Borrower shall promptly furnish to Lender all notices of amounts to be paid under this Section. Borrower shall pay Lender the Funds for Escrow Items unless Lender waives Borrower's obligation to pay the Funds for any or all Escrow Items. Lender may waive Borrower's obligation to pay to Lender Funds for any or all Escrow Items at any time. Any such waiver may only be in writing. In the event of such waiver, Borrower shall pay directly, when and where payable, the amounts due for any Escrow Items for which payment of Funds has been waived by Lender and, if Lender requires, shall furnish to Lender receipts evidencing such payment within such time period as Lender may require. Borrower's obligation to make such payments and to provide receipts shall for all purposes be deemed to be a covenant and agreement contained in this Security Instrument, as the phrase "covenant and agreement" is used in Section 9. If Borrower is obligated to pay Escrow Items directly, pursuant to a waiver, and Borrower fails to pay the amount due for an Escrow Item, Lender may exercise its rights under Section 9 and pay such amount and Borrower shall then be obligated under Section 9 to repay to Lender any such amount. Lender may revoke the waiver as to any or all Escrow Items at any time by a notice given in accordance with Section 15 and, upon such revocation, Borrower shall pay to Lender all Funds, and in such amounts, that are then required under this Section 3.

Lender may, at any time, collect and hold Funds in an amount (a) sufficient to permit Lender to apply the Funds at the time specified under RESPA, and (b) not to exceed the maximum amount a lender can require under RESPA. Lender shall estimate the amount of Funds due on the basis of current data and reasonable estimates of expenditures of future Escrow Items or otherwise in accordance with Applicable Law.

The Funds shall be held in an institution whose deposits are insured by a federal agency, instrumentality, or entity (including Lender, if Lender is an institution whose deposits are so insured) or in any Federal Home Loan Bank. Lender shall apply the Funds to pay the Escrow Items no later than the time specified under RESPA. Lender shall not charge Borrower for holding and applying the Funds, annually analyzing the escrow account, or verifying the Escrow Items, unless Lender pays Borrower interest on the Funds and Applicable Law permits Lender to make such a charge. Unless an agreement is made in writing or Applicable Law requires interest to be paid on the Funds, Lender shall not be required to pay Borrower any interest or earnings on the Funds. Borrower and Lender can agree in writing, however, that interest shall be paid on the Funds. Lender shall give to Borrower, without charge, an annual accounting of the Funds as required by RESPA.

If there is a surplus of Funds held in escrow, as defined under RESPA, Lender shall account to Borrower for the excess funds in accordance with RESPA. If there is a shortage of Funds held in escrow, as defined under RESPA, Lender shall notify Borrower as required by RESPA, and Borrower shall pay to Lender the amount necessary to make up the shortage in accordance with RESPA, but in no more than 12 monthly payments. If there is a deficiency of Funds held in escrow, as defined under RESPA, Lender shall notify Borrower as required by RESPA, and Borrower shall pay to Lender the amount necessary to make up the deficiency in accordance with RESPA, but in no more than 12 monthly payments.

Upon payment in full of all sums secured by this Security Instrument, Lender shall promptly refund to Borrower any Funds held by Lender.

**4. Charges; Liens.** Borrower shall pay all taxes, assessments, charges, fines, and impositions attributable to the Property which can attain priority over this Security Instrument, leasehold payments or ground rents on the Property, if any, and Community Association Dues, Fees, and Assessments, if any. To the extent that these items are Escrow Items, Borrower shall pay them in the manner provided in Section 3.

Borrower shall promptly discharge any lien which has priority over this Security Instrument unless Borrower: (a) agrees in writing to the payment of the obligation secured by the lien in a manner acceptable to Lender, but only so long as Borrower is performing such agreement; (b) contests the lien in good faith by, or defends against enforcement of the lien in, legal proceedings which in Lender's opinion operate to prevent the enforcement of the lien while those proceedings are pending, but only until such proceedings are concluded; or (c) secures from the holder of the lien an agreement satisfactory to Lender subordinating the lien to this Security Instrument. If Lender determines that any part of the Property is subject to a lien which can attain priority over this Security Instrument, Lender may give Borrower a notice identifying the lien. Within 10 days of the date on which that notice is given, Borrower shall satisfy the lien or take one or more of the actions set forth above in this Section 4.

Lender may require Borrower to pay a one-time charge for a real estate tax verification and/or reporting service used by Lender in connection with this Loan.

**5. Property Insurance.** Borrower shall keep the improvements now existing or hereafter erected on the Property insured against loss by fire, hazards included within the term "extended coverage," and any other hazards including, but not limited to, earthquakes and floods, for which Lender requires insurance. This insurance shall be maintained in the amounts (including deductible levels) and for the periods that Lender requires. What Lender requires pursuant to the preceding sentences can change during the term of the Loan. The insurance carrier providing the insurance shall be chosen by Borrower subject to Lender's right to disapprove Borrower's choice, which right shall not be exercised unreasonably. Lender may require Borrower to pay, in connection with this Loan, either: (a) a one-time charge for flood zone determination, certification and tracking services; or (b) a one-time charge for flood zone determination and certification services and subsequent charges each time remappings or similar changes occur which reasonably might affect such determination or certification. Borrower shall also be responsible for the payment of any fees imposed by the Federal Emergency Management Agency in connection with the review of any flood zone determination resulting from an objection by Borrower.

If Borrower fails to maintain any of the coverages described above, Lender may obtain insurance coverage, at Lender's option and Borrower's expense. Lender is under no obligation to purchase any particular type or amount of coverage. Therefore, such coverage shall cover Lender, but might or might not protect Borrower, Borrower's equity in the Property, or the contents of the Property, against any risk, hazard or liability and might provide greater or lesser coverage than was previously in effect. Borrower acknowledges that the cost of the insurance coverage so obtained might significantly exceed the cost of insurance that Borrower could have obtained. Any amounts disbursed by Lender under this Section 5 shall become additional debt of Borrower secured by this Security Instrument. These amounts shall bear interest at the Note rate from the date of disbursement and shall be payable, with such interest, upon notice from Lender to Borrower requesting payment.

All insurance policies required by Lender and renewals of such policies shall be subject to Lender's right to disapprove such policies, shall include a standard mortgage clause, and shall name Lender as mortgagee and/or as an additional loss payee. Lender shall have the right to hold the policies and renewal certificates. If Lender requires, Borrower shall promptly give to Lender all receipts of paid premiums and renewal notices. If Borrower obtains any form of insurance coverage, not otherwise required by Lender, for damage to, or destruction of, the Property, such policy shall include a standard mortgage clause and shall name Lender as mortgagee and/or as an additional loss payee.

In the event of loss, Borrower shall give prompt notice to the insurance carrier and Lender. Lender may make proof of loss if not made promptly by Borrower. Unless Lender and Borrower otherwise agree in writing, any insurance proceeds, whether or not the underlying insurance was required by Lender, shall be applied to restoration or repair of the Property, if the restoration or repair is economically feasible and Lender's security is not lessened. During such repair and restoration period, Lender shall have the right to hold such insurance proceeds until Lender has had an opportunity to inspect such Property to ensure the work has been completed to Lender's satisfaction, provided that such inspection shall be undertaken promptly. Lender may disburse proceeds for the repairs and restoration in a single payment or in a series of progress payments as the work is completed. Unless an agreement is made in writing or Applicable Law requires interest to be paid on such insurance proceeds, Lender shall not be required to pay Borrower any interest or earnings on such proceeds. Fees for public adjusters, or other third parties, retained by Borrower shall not be paid out of the insurance proceeds and shall be the sole obligation of Borrower. If the restoration or repair is not economically feasible or Lender's security would be lessened, the insurance proceeds shall be applied to the sums secured by this Security Instrument, whether or not then due, with the excess, if any, paid to Borrower. Such insurance proceeds shall be applied in the order provided for in Section 2.

If Borrower abandons the Property, Lender may file, negotiate and settle any available insurance claim and related matters. If Borrower does not respond within 30 days to a notice from Lender that the insurance carrier has offered to settle a claim, then Lender may negotiate and settle the claim. The 30-day period will begin when the notice is given. In either event, or if Lender acquires the Property under Section 22 or otherwise, Borrower hereby assigns to Lender (a) Borrower's rights to any insurance proceeds in an amount not to exceed the amounts unpaid under the Note or this Security Instrument, and (b) any other of Borrower's rights (other than the right to any refund of unearned premiums paid by Borrower) under all insurance policies covering the Property, insofar as such rights are applicable to the coverage of the Property. Lender may use the insurance proceeds either to repair or restore the Property or to pay amounts unpaid under the Note or this Security Instrument, whether or not then due.

**6. Occupancy.** Borrower shall occupy, establish, and use the Property as Borrower's principal residence within 60 days after the execution of this Security Instrument and shall continue to occupy the Property as Borrower's principal residence for at least one year after the date of occupancy, unless Lender otherwise agrees in writing, which consent shall not be unreasonably withheld, or unless extenuating circumstances exist which are beyond Borrower's control.

**7. Preservation, Maintenance and Protection of the Property; Inspections.** Borrower shall not destroy, damage or impair the Property, allow the Property to deteriorate or commit waste on the Property. Whether or not Borrower is residing in the Property, Borrower shall maintain the Property in order to prevent the Property from deteriorating or decreasing in value due to its condition. Unless it is determined pursuant to Section 5 that repair or restoration is not economically feasible, Borrower shall promptly repair the Property if damaged to avoid further deterioration or damage. If insurance or condemnation proceeds are paid in connection with damage to, or the taking of, the Property, Borrower shall be responsible for repairing or restoring the Property only if Lender has released proceeds for such purposes. Lender may disburse proceeds for the repairs and restoration in a single payment or in a series of progress payments as the work is completed. If the insurance or condemnation proceeds are not sufficient to repair or restore the Property, Borrower is not relieved of Borrower's obligation for the completion of such repair or restoration.

Lender or its agent may make reasonable entries upon and inspections of the Property. If it has reasonable cause, Lender may inspect the interior of the improvements on the Property. Lender shall give Borrower notice at the time of or prior to such an interior inspection specifying such reasonable cause.

**8. Borrower's Loan Application.** Borrower shall be in default if, during the Loan application process, Borrower or any persons or entities acting at the direction of Borrower or with Borrower's knowledge or consent gave materially false, misleading, or inaccurate information or statements to Lender (or failed to provide Lender with material information) in connection with the Loan. Material representations include, but are not limited to, representations concerning Borrower's occupancy of the Property as Borrower's principal residence.

**9. Protection of Lender's Interest in the Property and Rights Under this Security Instrument.** If (a) Borrower fails to perform the covenants and agreements contained in this Security Instrument, (b) there is a legal proceeding that might significantly affect Lender's interest in the Property and/or rights under this Security Instrument (such as a proceeding in bankruptcy, probate, for condemnation or forfeiture, for enforcement of a lien which may attain priority over this Security Instrument or to enforce laws or regulations), or (c) Borrower has abandoned the Property, then Lender may do and pay for whatever is reasonable or appropriate to protect Lender's interest in the Property and rights under this Security Instrument, including protecting and/or assessing the value of the Property, and securing and/or repairing the Property. Lender's actions can include, but are not limited to: (a) paying any sums secured by a lien which has priority over this Security Instrument; (b) appearing in court; and (c) paying reasonable attorneys' fees to protect its interest in the Property and/or rights under this Security Instrument, including its secured position in a bankruptcy proceeding. Securing the Property includes, but is not limited to, entering the Property to make repairs, change locks, replace or board up doors and windows, drain water from pipes, eliminate building or other code violations or dangerous conditions, and have utilities turned on or off. Although Lender may take action under this Section 9, Lender does not have to do so and is not under any duty or obligation to do so. It is agreed that Lender incurs no liability for not taking any or all actions authorized under this Section 9.

Any amounts disbursed by Lender under this Section 9 shall become additional debt of Borrower secured by this Security Instrument. These amounts shall bear interest at the Note rate from the date of disbursement and shall be payable, with such interest, upon notice from Lender to Borrower requesting payment.

If this Security Instrument is on a leasehold, Borrower shall comply with all the provisions of the lease. If Borrower acquires fee title to the Property, the leasehold and the fee title shall not merge unless Lender agrees to the merger in writing.

**10. Mortgage Insurance.** If Lender required Mortgage Insurance as a condition of making the Loan, Borrower shall pay the premiums required to maintain the Mortgage Insurance in effect. If, for any reason, the Mortgage Insurance coverage required by Lender ceases to be available from the mortgage insurer that previously provided such insurance and Borrower was required to make separately designated payments toward the premiums for Mortgage Insurance, Borrower shall pay the premiums required to obtain coverage substantially equivalent to the Mortgage Insurance previously in effect, at a cost substantially equivalent to the cost to Borrower of the Mortgage Insurance previously in effect, from an alternate mortgage insurer selected by Lender. If substantially equivalent Mortgage Insurance coverage is not available, Borrower shall continue to pay to Lender the amount of the separately designated payments that were due when the insurance coverage ceased to be in effect. Lender will accept, use and retain these payments as a non-refundable loss reserve in lieu of Mortgage Insurance. Such loss reserve shall be non-refundable, notwithstanding the fact that the Loan is ultimately paid in full, and Lender shall not be required to pay Borrower any interest or earnings on such loss reserve. Lender can no longer require loss reserve payments if Mortgage Insurance coverage (in the amount and for the period that Lender requires) provided by an insurer selected by Lender again becomes available, is obtained, and Lender requires separately designated payments toward the premiums for Mortgage Insurance. If Lender required Mortgage Insurance as a condition of making the Loan and Borrower was required to make separately designated payments toward the premiums for Mortgage Insurance, Borrower shall pay the premiums required to maintain Mortgage Insurance in effect, or to provide a non-refundable loss reserve, until Lender's requirement for Mortgage Insurance ends in accordance with any written agreement between Borrower and Lender providing for such termination or until termination is required by Applicable Law. Nothing in this Section 10 affects Borrower's obligation to pay interest at the rate provided in the Note.

Mortgage Insurance reimburses Lender (or any entity that purchases the Note) for certain losses it may incur if Borrower does not repay the Loan as agreed. Borrower is not a party to the Mortgage Insurance.

Mortgage insurers evaluate their total risk on all such insurance in force from time to time, and may enter into agreements with other parties that share or modify their risk, or reduce losses. These agreements are on terms and conditions that are satisfactory to the mortgage insurer and the other party (or parties) to these agreements. These agreements may require the mortgage insurer to make payments using any source of funds that the mortgage insurer may have available (which may include funds obtained from Mortgage Insurance premiums).

As a result of these agreements, Lender, any purchaser of the Note, another insurer, any reinsurer, any other entity, or any affiliate of any of the foregoing, may receive (directly or indirectly) amounts that derive from (or might be characterized as) a portion of Borrower's payments for Mortgage Insurance, in exchange for sharing or modifying the mortgage insurer's risk, or reducing losses. If such agreement provides that an affiliate of Lender takes a share of the insurer's risk in exchange for a share of the premiums paid to the insurer, the arrangement is often termed "captive reinsurance." Further:

**(a) Any such agreements will not affect the amounts that Borrower has agreed to pay for Mortgage Insurance, or any other terms of the Loan. Such agreements will not increase the amount Borrower will owe for Mortgage Insurance, and they will not entitle Borrower to any refund.**

(b) Any such agreements will not affect the rights Borrower has - if any - with respect to the Mortgage Insurance under the Homeowners Protection Act of 1998 or any other law. These rights may include the right to receive certain disclosures, to request and obtain cancellation of the Mortgage Insurance, to have the Mortgage Insurance terminated automatically, and/or to receive a refund of any Mortgage Insurance premiums that were unearned at the time of such cancellation or termination.

11. Assignment of Miscellaneous Proceeds; Forfeiture. All Miscellaneous Proceeds are hereby assigned to and shall be paid to Lender.

If the Property is damaged, such Miscellaneous Proceeds shall be applied to restoration or repair of the Property, if the restoration or repair is economically feasible and Lender's security is not lessened. During such repair and restoration period, Lender shall have the right to hold such Miscellaneous Proceeds until Lender has had an opportunity to inspect such Property to ensure the work has been completed to Lender's satisfaction, provided that such inspection shall be undertaken promptly. Lender may pay for the repairs and restoration in a single disbursement or in a series of progress payments as the work is completed. Unless an agreement is made in writing or Applicable Law requires interest to be paid on such Miscellaneous Proceeds, Lender shall not be required to pay Borrower any interest or earnings on such Miscellaneous Proceeds. If the restoration or repair is not economically feasible or Lender's security would be lessened, the Miscellaneous Proceeds shall be applied to the sums secured by this Security Instrument, whether or not then due, with the excess, if any, paid to Borrower. Such Miscellaneous Proceeds shall be applied in the order provided for in Section 2.

In the event of a total taking, destruction, or loss in value of the Property, the Miscellaneous Proceeds shall be applied to the sums secured by this Security Instrument, whether or not then due, with the excess, if any, paid to Borrower.

In the event of a partial taking, destruction, or loss in value of the Property in which the fair market value of the Property immediately before the partial taking, destruction, or loss in value is equal to or greater than the amount of the sums secured by this Security Instrument immediately before the partial taking, destruction, or loss in value, unless Borrower and Lender otherwise agree in writing, the sums secured by this Security Instrument shall be reduced by the amount of the Miscellaneous Proceeds multiplied by the following fraction: (a) the total amount of the sums secured immediately before the partial taking, destruction, or loss in value divided by (b) the fair market value of the Property immediately before the partial taking, destruction, or loss in value. Any balance shall be paid to Borrower.

In the event of a partial taking, destruction, or loss in value of the Property in which the fair market value of the Property immediately before the partial taking, destruction, or loss in value is less than the amount of the sums secured immediately before the partial taking, destruction, or loss in value, unless Borrower and Lender otherwise agree in writing, the Miscellaneous Proceeds shall be applied to the sums secured by this Security Instrument whether or not the sums are then due.

If the Property is abandoned by Borrower, or if, after notice by Lender to Borrower that the Opposing Party (as defined in the next sentence) offers to make an award to settle a claim for damages, Borrower fails to respond to Lender within 30 days after the date the notice is given, Lender is authorized to collect and apply the Miscellaneous Proceeds either to restoration or repair of the Property or to the sums secured by this Security Instrument, whether or not then due. "Opposing Party" means the third party that owes Borrower Miscellaneous Proceeds or the party against whom Borrower has a right of action in regard to Miscellaneous Proceeds.

Borrower shall be in default if any action or proceeding, whether civil or criminal, is begun that, in Lender's judgment, could result in forfeiture of the Property or other material impairment of Lender's interest in the Property or rights under this Security Instrument. Borrower can cure such a default and, if acceleration has occurred, reinstate as provided in Section 19, by causing the action or proceeding to be dismissed with a ruling that, in Lender's judgment, precludes forfeiture of the Property or other material impairment of Lender's interest in the Property or rights under this Security Instrument. The proceeds of any award or claim for damages that are attributable to the impairment of Lender's interest in the Property are hereby assigned and shall be paid to Lender.

All Miscellaneous Proceeds that are not applied to restoration or repair of the Property shall be applied in the order provided for in Section 2.

**12. Borrower Not Released; Forbearance By Lender Not a Waiver.** Extension of the time for payment or modification of amortization of the sums secured by this Security Instrument granted by Lender to Borrower or any Successor in Interest of Borrower shall not operate to release the liability of Borrower or any Successors in Interest of Borrower. Lender shall not be required to commence proceedings against any Successor in Interest of Borrower or to refuse to extend time for payment or otherwise modify amortization of the sums secured by this Security Instrument by reason of any demand made by the original Borrower or any Successors in Interest of Borrower. Any forbearance by Lender in exercising any right or remedy including, without limitation, Lender's acceptance of payments from third persons, entities or Successors in Interest of Borrower or in amounts less than the amount then due, shall not be a waiver of or preclude the exercise of any right or remedy.

**13. Joint and Several Liability; Co-signers; Successors and Assigns Bound.** Borrower covenants and agrees that Borrower's obligations and liability shall be joint and several. However, any Borrower who co-signs this Security Instrument but does not execute the Note (a "co-signer"): (a) is co-signing this Security Instrument only to mortgage, grant and convey the co-signer's interest in the Property under the terms of this Security Instrument; (b) is not personally obligated to pay the sums secured by this Security Instrument; and (c) agrees that Lender and any other Borrower can agree to extend, modify, forbear or make any accommodations with regard to the terms of this Security Instrument or the Note without the co-signer's consent.

Subject to the provisions of Section 18, any Successor in Interest of Borrower who assumes Borrower's obligations under this Security Instrument in writing, and is approved by Lender, shall obtain all of Borrower's rights and benefits under this Security Instrument. Borrower shall not be released from Borrower's obligations and liability under this Security Instrument unless Lender agrees to such release in writing. The covenants and agreements of this Security Instrument shall bind (except as provided in Section 20) and benefit the successors and assigns of Lender.

**14. Loan Charges.** Lender may charge Borrower fees for services performed in connection with Borrower's default, for the purpose of protecting Lender's interest in the Property and rights under this Security Instrument, including, but not limited to, attorneys' fees, property inspection and valuation fees. In regard to any other fees, the absence of express authority in this Security Instrument to charge a specific fee to Borrower shall not be construed as a prohibition on the charging of such fee. Lender may not charge fees that are expressly prohibited by this Security Instrument or by Applicable Law.

If the Loan is subject to a law which sets maximum loan charges, and that law is finally interpreted so that the interest or other loan charges collected or to be collected in connection with the Loan exceed the permitted limits, then: (a) any such loan charge shall be reduced by the amount necessary to reduce the charge to the permitted limit; and (b) any sums already collected from Borrower which exceeded permitted limits will be refunded to Borrower. Lender may choose to make this refund by reducing the principal owed under the Note or by making a direct payment to Borrower. If a refund reduces principal, the reduction will be treated as a partial prepayment without any prepayment charge (whether or not a prepayment charge is provided for under the Note). Borrower's acceptance of any such refund made by direct payment to Borrower will constitute a waiver of any right of action Borrower might have arising out of such overcharge.

**15. Notices.** All notices given by Borrower or Lender in connection with this Security Instrument must be in writing. Any notice to Borrower in connection with this Security Instrument shall be deemed to have been given to Borrower when mailed by first class mail or when actually delivered to Borrower's notice address if sent by other means. Notice to any one Borrower shall constitute notice to all Borrowers unless Applicable Law expressly requires otherwise. The notice address shall be the Property Address unless Borrower has designated a substitute notice address by notice to Lender. Borrower shall promptly notify Lender of Borrower's change of address. If Lender specifies a procedure for reporting Borrower's change of address, then Borrower shall only report a change of address through that specified procedure. There may be only one designated notice address under this Security Instrument at any one time. Any notice to Lender shall be given by delivering it or by mailing it by first class mail to Lender's address stated herein unless Lender has designated another address by notice to Borrower. Any notice in connection with this Security Instrument shall not be deemed to have been given to Lender until actually received by Lender. If any notice required by this Security Instrument is also required under Applicable Law, the Applicable Law requirement will satisfy the corresponding requirement under this Security Instrument.

**16. Governing Law; Severability; Rules of Construction.** This Security Instrument shall be governed by federal law and the law of the jurisdiction in which the Property is located. All rights and obligations contained in this Security Instrument are subject to any requirements and limitations of Applicable Law. Applicable Law might explicitly or implicitly allow the parties to agree by contract or it might be silent, but such silence shall not be construed as a prohibition against agreement by contract. In the event that any provision or clause of this Security Instrument or the Note conflicts with Applicable Law, such conflict shall not affect other provisions of this Security Instrument or the Note which can be given effect without the conflicting provision.

As used in this Security Instrument: (a) words of the masculine gender shall mean and include corresponding neuter words or words of the feminine gender; (b) words in the singular shall mean and include the plural and vice versa; and (c) the word "may" gives sole discretion without any obligation to take any action.

**17. Borrower's Copy.** Borrower shall be given one copy of the Note and of this Security Instrument.

**18. Transfer of the Property or a Beneficial Interest in Borrower.** As used in this Section 18, "Interest in the Property" means any legal or beneficial interest in the Property, including, but not limited to, those beneficial interests transferred in a bond for deed, contract for deed, installment sales contract or escrow agreement, the intent of which is the transfer of title by Borrower at a future date to a purchaser.

If all or any part of the Property or any Interest in the Property is sold or transferred (or if Borrower is not a natural person and a beneficial interest in Borrower is sold or transferred) without Lender's prior written consent, Lender may require immediate payment in full of all sums secured by this Security Instrument. However, this option shall not be exercised by Lender if such exercise is prohibited by Applicable Law.

If Lender exercises this option, Lender shall give Borrower notice of acceleration. The notice shall provide a period of not less than 30 days from the date the notice is given in accordance with Section 15 within which Borrower must pay all sums secured by this Security Instrument. If Borrower fails to pay these sums prior to the expiration of this period, Lender may invoke any remedies permitted by this Security Instrument without further notice or demand on Borrower.

**19. Borrower's Right to Reinstate After Acceleration.** If Borrower meets certain conditions, Borrower shall have the right to have enforcement of this Security Instrument discontinued at any time prior to the earliest of: (a) five days before sale of the Property pursuant to any power of sale contained in this Security Instrument; (b) such other period as Applicable Law might specify for the termination of Borrower's right to reinstate; or (c) entry of a judgment enforcing this Security Instrument. Those conditions are that Borrower: (a) pays Lender all sums which then would be due under this Security Instrument and the Note as if no acceleration had occurred; (b) cures any default of any other covenants or agreements; (c) pays all expenses incurred in enforcing this Security Instrument, including, but not limited to, reasonable attorneys' fees, property inspection and valuation fees, and other fees incurred for the purpose of protecting Lender's interest in the Property and rights under this Security Instrument; and (d) takes such action as Lender may reasonably require to assure that Lender's interest in the Property and rights under this Security Instrument, and Borrower's obligation to pay the sums secured by this Security Instrument, shall continue unchanged. Lender may require that Borrower pay such reinstatement sums and expenses in one or more of the following forms, as selected by Lender: (a) cash; (b) money order; (c) certified check, bank check, treasurer's check or cashier's check, provided any such check is drawn upon an institution whose deposits are insured by a federal agency, instrumentality or entity; or (d) Electronic Funds Transfer. Upon reinstatement by Borrower, this Security Instrument and obligations secured hereby shall remain fully effective as if no acceleration had occurred. However, this right to reinstate shall not apply in the case of acceleration under Section 18.

**20. Sale of Note; Change of Loan Servicer; Notice of Grievance.** The Note or a partial interest in the Note (together with this Security Instrument) can be sold one or more times without prior notice to Borrower. A sale might result in a change in the entity (known as the "Loan Servicer") that collects Periodic Payments due under the Note and this Security Instrument and performs other mortgage loan servicing obligations under the Note, this Security Instrument, and Applicable Law. There also might be one or more changes of the Loan Servicer unrelated to a sale of the Note. If there is a change of the Loan Servicer,

Borrower will be given written notice of the change which will state the name and address of the new Loan Servicer, the address to which payments should be made and any other information RESPA requires in connection with a notice of transfer of servicing. If the Note is sold and thereafter the Loan is serviced by a Loan Servicer other than the purchaser of the Note, the mortgage loan servicing obligations to Borrower will remain with the Loan Servicer or be transferred to a successor Loan Servicer and are not assumed by the Note purchaser unless otherwise provided by the Note purchaser.

Neither Borrower nor Lender may commence, join, or be joined to any judicial action (as either an individual litigant or the member of a class) that arises from the other party's actions pursuant to this Security Instrument or that alleges that the other party has breached any provision of, or any duty owed by reason of, this Security Instrument, until such Borrower or Lender has notified the other party (with such notice given in compliance with the requirements of Section 15) of such alleged breach and afforded the other party hereto a reasonable period after the giving of such notice to take corrective action. If Applicable Law provides a time period which must elapse before certain action can be taken, that time period will be deemed to be reasonable for purposes of this paragraph. The notice of acceleration and opportunity to cure given to Borrower pursuant to Section 22 and the notice of acceleration given to Borrower pursuant to Section 18 shall be deemed to satisfy the notice and opportunity to take corrective action provisions of this Section 20.

**21. Hazardous Substances.** As used in this Section 21: (a) "Hazardous Substances" are those substances defined as toxic or hazardous substances, pollutants, or wastes by Environmental Law and the following substances: gasoline, kerosene, other flammable or toxic petroleum products, toxic pesticides and herbicides, volatile solvents, materials containing asbestos or formaldehyde, and radioactive materials; (b) "Environmental Law" means federal laws and laws of the jurisdiction where the Property is located that relate to health, safety or environmental protection; (c) "Environmental Cleanup" includes any response action, remedial action, or removal action, as defined in Environmental Law; and (d) an "Environmental Condition" means a condition that can cause, contribute to, or otherwise trigger an Environmental Cleanup.

Borrower shall not cause or permit the presence, use, disposal, storage, or release of any Hazardous Substances, or threaten to release any Hazardous Substances, on or in the Property. Borrower shall not do, nor allow anyone else to do, anything affecting the Property (a) that is in violation of any Environmental Law, (b) which creates an Environmental Condition, or (c) which, due to the presence, use, or release of a Hazardous Substance, creates a condition that adversely affects the value of the Property. The preceding two sentences shall not apply to the presence, use, or storage on the Property of small quantities of Hazardous Substances that are generally recognized to be appropriate to normal residential uses and to maintenance of the Property (including, but not limited to, hazardous substances in consumer products).

Borrower shall promptly give Lender written notice of (a) any investigation, claim, demand, lawsuit or other action by any governmental or regulatory agency or private party involving the Property and any Hazardous Substance or Environmental Law of which Borrower has actual knowledge, (b) any Environmental Condition, including but not limited to, any spilling, leaking, discharge, release or threat of release of any Hazardous Substance, and (c) any condition caused by the presence, use or release of a Hazardous Substance which adversely affects the value of the Property. If Borrower learns, or is notified by any governmental or regulatory authority, or any private party, that any removal or other remediation of any Hazardous Substance affecting the Property is necessary, Borrower shall promptly take all necessary remedial actions in accordance with Environmental Law. Nothing herein shall create any obligation on Lender for an Environmental Cleanup.

NON-UNIFORM COVENANTS. Borrower and Lender further covenant and agree as follows:

**22. Acceleration; Remedies. Lender shall give notice to Borrower prior to acceleration following Borrower's breach of any covenant or agreement in this Security Instrument (but not prior to acceleration under Section 18 unless Applicable Law provides otherwise). Lender shall notify Borrower of, among other things: (a) the default; (b) the action required to cure the default; (c) when the default must be cured; and (d) that failure to cure the default as specified may result in acceleration of the sums secured by this Security Instrument, foreclosure by judicial proceeding and sale of the Property. Lender shall further inform Borrower of the right to reinstate after acceleration and the right to assert in the foreclosure proceeding the non-existence of a default or any other defense of Borrower to acceleration and foreclosure. If the default is not cured as specified, Lender at its option may require immediate payment in full of all sums secured by this Security Instrument without further demand and may foreclose this Security Instrument by judicial proceeding. Lender shall be entitled to collect all expenses incurred in pursuing the remedies provided in this Section 22, including, but not limited to, attorneys' fees and costs of title evidence to the extent permitted by Applicable Law.**

**23. Release.** Upon payment of all sums secured by this Security Instrument, this Security Instrument and the estate conveyed shall terminate and become void. After such occurrence, Lender shall discharge and satisfy this Security Instrument. Borrower shall pay any recordation costs. Lender may charge Borrower a fee for releasing this Security Instrument, but only if the fee is paid to a third party for services rendered and the charging of the fee is permitted under Applicable Law.

**24. Waivers.** Borrower, to the extent permitted by Applicable Law, waives and releases any error or defects in proceedings to enforce this Security Instrument, and hereby waives the benefit of any present or future laws providing for stay of execution, extension of time, exemption from attachment, levy and sale, and homestead exemption.

**25. Reinstatement Period.** Borrower's time to reinstate provided in Section 19 shall extend to one hour prior to the commencement of bidding at a sheriff's sale or other sale pursuant to this Security Instrument.

**26. Purchase Money Mortgage.** If any of the debt secured by this Security Instrument is lent to Borrower to acquire title to the Property, this Security Instrument shall be a purchase money mortgage.

**27. Interest Rate After Judgment.** Borrower agrees that the interest rate payable after a judgment is entered on the Note or in an action of mortgage foreclosure shall be the rate payable from time to time under the Note.

BY SIGNING BELOW, Borrower accepts and agrees to the terms and covenants contained in this Security Instrument and in any Rider executed by Borrower and recorded with it.

Witnesses:

_____     _____ (Seal)
                                                                                        - Borrower

_____     _____ (Seal)
                                                                                        - Borrower

_____ **[Space Below This Line For Acknowledgment]**_____

# FORM 2 – UNIFORM RESIDENTIAL PROMISSORY NOTE FIXED RATE

## NOTE

_____, _____   _____  _____
[Date]                    [City]          [State]

_____
[Property Address]

### 1. BORROWER'S PROMISE TO PAY

In return for a loan that I have received, I promise to pay U.S. $_____ (this amount is called "Principal"), plus interest, to the order of the Lender. The Lender is _____. I will make all payments under this Note in the form of cash, check or money order.

I understand that the Lender may transfer this Note. The Lender or anyone who takes this Note by transfer and who is entitled to receive payments under this Note is called the "Note Holder."

### 2. INTEREST

Interest will be charged on unpaid principal until the full amount of Principal has been paid. I will pay interest at a yearly rate of _____%.

The interest rate required by this Section 2 is the rate I will pay both before and after any default described in Section 6(B) of this Note.

### 3. PAYMENTS

#### (A) Time and Place of Payments

I will pay principal and interest by making a payment every month.

I will make my monthly payment on the _____ day of each month beginning on _____, _____. I will make these payments every month until I have paid all of the principal and interest and any other charges described below that I may owe under this Note. Each monthly payment will be applied as of its scheduled due date and will be applied to interest before Principal. If, on _____, 20%, _____, I still owe amounts under this Note, I will pay those amounts in full on that date, which is called the "Maturity Date."

I will make my monthly payments at _____ or at a different place if required by the Note Holder.

#### (B) Amount of Monthly Payments

My monthly payment will be in the amount of U.S. $ _____.

### 4. BORROWER'S RIGHT TO PREPAY

I have the right to make payments of Principal at any time before they are due. A payment of Principal only is known as a "Prepayment." When I make a

Prepayment, I will tell the Note Holder in writing that I am doing so. I may not designate a payment as a Prepayment if I have not made all the monthly payments due under the Note.

I may make a full Prepayment or partial Prepayments without paying a Prepayment charge. The Note Holder will use my Prepayments to reduce the amount of Principal that I owe under this Note. However, the Note Holder may apply my Prepayment to the accrued and unpaid interest on the Prepayment amount, before applying my Prepayment to reduce the Principal amount of the Note. If I make a partial Prepayment, there will be no changes in the due date or in the amount of my monthly payment unless the Note Holder agrees in writing to those changes.

## 5.  LOAN CHARGES

If a law, which applies to this loan and which sets maximum loan charges, is finally interpreted so that the interest or other loan charges collected or to be collected in connection with this loan exceed the permitted limits, then: (a) any such loan charge shall be reduced by the amount necessary to reduce the charge to the permitted limit; and (b) any sums already collected from me which exceeded permitted limits will be refunded to me. The Note Holder may choose to make this refund by reducing the Principal I owe under this Note or by making a direct payment to me. If a refund reduces Principal, the reduction will be treated as a partial Prepayment.

## 6.  BORROWER'S FAILURE TO PAY AS REQUIRED

### (A) Late Charge for Overdue Payments
If the Note Holder has not received the full amount of any monthly payment by the end of _____ calendar days after the date it is due, I will pay a late charge to the Note Holder. The amount of the charge will be _____% of my overdue payment of principal and interest. I will pay this late charge promptly but only once on each late payment.

### (B) Default
If I do not pay the full amount of each monthly payment on the date it is due, I will be in default.

### (C) Notice of Default
If I am in default, the Note Holder may send me a written notice telling me that if I do not pay the overdue amount by a certain date, the Note Holder may require me to pay immediately the full amount of Principal which has not been paid and all the interest that I owe on that amount. That date must be at least 30 days after the date on which the notice is mailed to me or delivered by other means.

### (D) No Waiver By Note Holder
Even if, at a time when I am in default, the Note Holder does not require me to pay immediately in full as described above, the Note Holder will still have the right to do so if I am in default at a later time.

### (E) Payment of Note Holder's Costs and Expenses
If the Note Holder has required me to pay immediately in full as described above, the Note Holder will have the right to be paid back by me for all of its costs and expenses in enforcing this Note to the extent not prohibited by applicable law. Those expenses include, for example, reasonable attorneys' fees.

## 7.  GIVING OF NOTICES

Unless applicable law requires a different method, any notice that must be given to me under this Note will be given by delivering it or by mailing it by first class mail to me at the Property Address above or at a different address if I give the Note Holder a notice of my different address.

Any notice that must be given to the Note Holder under this Note will be given by delivering it or by mailing it by first class mail to the Note Holder at the address stated in Section 3(A) above or at a different address if I am given a notice of that different address.

## 8.  OBLIGATIONS OF PERSONS UNDER THIS NOTE

If more than one person signs this Note, each person is fully and personally obligated to keep all of the promises made in this Note, including the promise to pay the full amount owed. Any person who is a guarantor, surety or endorser of this Note is also obligated to do these things. Any person who takes over these obligations, including the obligations of a guarantor, surety or endorser of this Note, is also obligated to keep all of the promises made in this Note. The Note Holder may enforce its rights under this Note against each person individually or against all of us together. This means that any one of us may be required to pay all of the amounts owed under this Note.

## 9.  WAIVERS

I and any other person who has obligations under this Note waive the rights of Presentment and Notice of Dishonor. "Presentment" means the right to require the Note Holder to demand payment of amounts due. "Notice of Dishonor" means the right to require the Note Holder to give notice to other persons that amounts due have not been paid.

## 10. UNIFORM SECURED NOTE

This Note is a uniform instrument with limited variations in some jurisdictions. In addition to the protections given to the Note Holder under this Note, a Mortgage, Deed of Trust, or Security Deed (the "Security Instrument"), dated the same date as this Note, protects the Note Holder from possible losses which might result if I do not keep the promises which I make in this Note. That Security Instrument describes how and under what conditions I may be required to make immediate payment in full of all amounts I owe under this Note. Some of those conditions are described as follows:

If all or any part of the Property or any Interest in the Property is sold or transferred (or if Borrower is not a natural person and a beneficial interest in Borrower is sold or transferred) without Lender's prior written consent, Lender may require immediate payment in full of all sums secured by this Security Instrument. However, this option shall not be exercised by Lender if such exercise is prohibited by Applicable Law.

If Lender exercises this option, Lender shall give Borrower notice of acceleration. The notice shall provide a period of not less than 30 days from the date the notice is given in accordance with Section 15 within which Borrower must pay all sums secured by this Security Instrument. If Borrower fails to pay these sums prior to the expiration of this period, Lender may invoke any remedies permitted by this Security Instrument without further notice or demand on Borrower.

## WITNESS THE HAND(S) AND SEAL(S) OF THE UNDERSIGNED.

_____ (Seal)
- Borrower

_____ (Seal)
- Borrower

_____ (Seal)
- Borrower

_[Sign Original Only]_

# FORM 3 – UNIFORM RESIDENTIAL PROMISSARY NOTE BALLOON RATE

## BALLOON NOTE
### (FIXED RATE)

**THIS LOAN IS PAYABLE IN FULL AT MATURITY. YOU MUST REPAY THE ENTIRE PRINCIPAL BALANCE OF THE LOAN AND UNPAID INTEREST THEN DUE. THE LENDER IS UNDER NO OBLIGATION TO REFINANCE THE LOAN AT THAT TIME. YOU WILL, THEREFORE, BE REQUIRED TO MAKE PAYMENT OUT OF OTHER ASSETS THAT YOU MAY OWN, OR YOU WILL HAVE TO FIND A LENDER, WHICH MAY BE THE LENDER YOU HAVE THIS LOAN WITH, WILLING TO LEND YOU THE MONEY. IF YOU REFINANCE THIS LOAN AT MATURITY, YOU MAY HAVE TO PAY SOME OR ALL OF THE CLOSING COSTS NORMALLY ASSOCIATED WITH A NEW LOAN EVEN IF YOU OBTAIN REFINANCING FROM THE SAME LENDER.**

_____, _____    _____, _____
[Date]                            [City]              [State]

_____
[Property Address]

## 1.  BORROWER'S PROMISE TO PAY

In return for a loan that I have received, I promise to pay U.S. $_____ (this amount is called "Principal"), plus interest, to the order of the Lender. The Lender is _____ _____. I will make all payments under this Note in the form of cash, check or money order.

I understand that the Lender may transfer this Note. The Lender or anyone who takes this Note by transfer and who is entitled to receive payments under this Note is called the "Note Holder."

## 2.  INTEREST

Interest will be charged on unpaid principal until the full amount of Principal has been paid. I will pay interest at a yearly rate of _____%.

The interest rate required by this Section 2 is the rate I will pay both before and after any default described in Section 6(B) of this Note.

## 3.  PAYMENTS

### (A) Time and Place of Payments

I will pay principal and interest by making a payment every month.

I will make my monthly payment on the _____ day of each month beginning on _____, _____. I will make these payments every month until I have paid all of the principal and interest and any other charges described below that I may owe under this Note. Each monthly payment will be applied as of its scheduled due date and will be applied to interest before Principal. If, on _____, _____, I still owe amounts under this Note, I will pay those amounts in full on that date, which is called the "Maturity Date."

I will make my monthly payments at _____ _____ or at a different place if required by the Note Holder.

**(B) Amount of Monthly Payments**
My monthly payment will be in the amount of U.S. $ _____ _____.

### 4. BORROWER'S RIGHT TO PREPAY

I have the right to make payments of Principal at any time before they are due. A payment of Principal only is known as a "Prepayment." When I make a Prepayment, I will tell the Note Holder in writing that I am doing so. I may not designate a payment as a Prepayment if I have not made all the monthly payments due under the Note.

I may make a full Prepayment or partial Prepayments without paying any Prepayment charge. The Note Holder will use my Prepayments to reduce the amount of Principal that I owe under this Note. However, the Note Holder may apply my Prepayment to the accrued and unpaid interest on the Prepayment amount before applying my Prepayment to reduce the Principal amount of the Note. If I make a partial Prepayment, there will be no changes in the due date or in the amount of my monthly payment unless the Note Holder agrees in writing to those changes.

### 5. LOAN CHARGES

If a law, which applies to this loan and which sets maximum loan charges, is finally interpreted so that the interest or other loan charges collected or to be collected in connection with this loan exceed the permitted limits, then: (a) any such loan charge shall be reduced by the amount necessary to reduce the charge to the permitted limit; and (b) any sum already collected from me which exceeded permitted limits will be refunded to me. The Note Holder may choose to make this refund by reducing the Principal I owe under this Note or by making a direct payment to me. If a refund reduces Principal, the reduction will be treated as a partial Prepayment.

### 6. BORROWER'S FAILURE TO PAY AS REQUIRED

**(A) Late Charges for Overdue Payments**
If the Note Holder has not received the full amount of any monthly payment by the end of _____ calendar days after the date it is due, I will pay a late charge to the Note Holder. The amount of the charge will be _____% of my overdue payment of principal and interest. I will pay this late charge promptly but only once on each late payment.

**(B) Default**
If I do not pay the full amount of each monthly payment on the date it is due, I will be in default.

**(C) Notice of Default**

If I am in default, the Note Holder may send me a written notice telling me that if I do not pay the overdue amount by a certain date, the Note Holder may require me to pay immediately the full amount of Principal which has not been paid and all the interest that I owe on that amount. That date must be at least 30 days after the date on which the notice is mailed to me or delivered by other means.

**(D) No Waiver By Note Holder**

Even if, at a time when I am in default, the Note Holder does not require me to pay immediately in full as described above, the Note Holder will still have the right to do so if I am in default at a later time.

**(E) Payment of Note Holder's Costs and Expenses**

If the Note Holder has required me to pay immediately in full as described above, the Note Holder will have the right to be paid back by me for all of its costs and expenses in enforcing this Note to the extent not prohibited by applicable law. Those expenses include, for example, reasonable attorneys' fees.

## 7.  GIVING OF NOTICES

Unless applicable law requires a different method, any notice that must be given to me under this Note will be given by delivering it or by mailing it by first class mail to me at the Property Address above or at a different address if I give the Note Holder a notice of my different address.

Any notice that must be given to the Note Holder under this Note will be given by delivering it or by mailing it by first class mail to the Note Holder at the address stated in Section 3(A) above or at a different address if I am given a notice of that different address.

## 8.  OBLIGATIONS OF PERSONS UNDER THIS NOTE

If more than one person signs this Note, each person is fully and personally obligated to keep all of the promises made in this Note, including the promise to pay the full amount owed. Any person who is a guarantor, surety or endorser of this Note is also obligated to do these things. Any person who takes over these obligations, including the obligations of a guarantor, surety or endorser of the Note, is also obligated to keep all of the promises made in this Note. The Note Holder may enforce its rights under this Note against each person individually or against all of us together. This means that anyone of us maybe required to pay all of the amounts owed under this Note.

## 9.  WAIVERS

I and any other person who has obligations under this Note waive the rights of Presentment and Notice of Dishonor. "Presentment" means the rights to require the Note Holder to demand payment of amounts due. "Notice of Dishonor" means the right to require the Note Holder to give notice to other persons that amounts due have not been paid.

## 10. UNIFORM SECURED NOTE

This Note is a uniform instrument with limited variations in some jurisdictions. In addition to the protections given to the Note Holder under this Note, a Mortgage, Deed of Trust, or Security Deed (the "Security Instrument"), dated the same date as this Note, protects the Note Holder from possible losses which might result if I do not keep the promises which I make in this Note. That Security Instrument describes how and under what conditions I may be required to make immediate payment in full of all amounts I owe under the Note. Some of those conditions are described as follows:

**Transfer of the Property or a Beneficial Interest in Borrower.** If all or any part of the Property or any Interest in the Property is sold or transferred (or if Borrower is not a natural person and a beneficial interest in Borrower is sold or transferred) without Lender's prior written consent, Lender may require immediate payment in full of all sums secured by this Security Instrument. However, this option shall not be exercised by Lender if such exercise is prohibited by Applicable Law.

If Lender exercises this option, Lender shall give Borrower notice of acceleration. The notice shall provide a period of not less than 30 days from the date the notice is given in accordance with Section 15 within which Borrower must pay all sums secured by this Security Instrument. If Borrower fails to pay these sums prior to the expiration of this period, Lender may invoke any remedies permitted by this Security Instrument without further notice or demand on Borrower.

WITNESS THE HAND(S) AND SEAL(S) OF THE UNDERSIGNED.

_____ (Seal)
- Borrower

_____ (Seal)
- Borrower

_____ (Seal)
- Borrower

*[Sign Original Only]*

# FORM 4 – UNIFORM RESIDENTIAL PROMISSORY NOTE CONVERTIBLE ARM

### ADJUSTABLE RATE NOTE

(1-Year Treasury Index - Rate Caps - Fixed Rate Conversion Option)

(Assumable after Initial Period unless Converted - Convertible 1st, 2nd or 3rd Change Date)

THIS NOTE CONTAINS PROVISIONS ALLOWING FOR CHANGES IN MY INTEREST RATE AND MY MONTHLY PAYMENT. THIS NOTE LIMITS THE AMOUNT MY INTEREST RATE CAN CHANGE AT ANY ONE TIME AND THE MAXIMUM RATE I MUST PAY. THIS NOTE ALSO CONTAINS AN OPTION TO CONVERT MY ADJUSTABLE INTEREST RATE TO A FIXED RATE.

_____, _____    _____, _____
[Date]                        [City]              [State]

_____
[Property Address]

## 1.  BORROWER'S PROMISE TO PAY

In return for a loan that I have received, I promise to pay U.S. $_____ (this amount is called "Principal"), plus interest, to the order of the Lender. The Lender is _____ _____. I will make all payments under this Note in the form of cash, check or money order.

I understand that the Lender may transfer this Note. The Lender or anyone who takes this Note by transfer and who is entitled to receive payments under this Note is called the "Note Holder."

## 2.  INTEREST

Interest will be charged on unpaid principal until the full amount of Principal has been paid. I will pay interest at a yearly rate of _____%. The interest rate I will pay will change in accordance with Sections 4 or 5 of this Note.

The interest rate required by this Section 2 and Sections 4 or 5 of this Note is the rate I will pay both before and after any default described in Section 8(B) of this Note.

## 3.  PAYMENTS

### (A) Time and Place of Payments

I will pay principal and interest by making a payment every month.

I will make my monthly payment on the first day of each month beginning on _____, _____. I will make these payments every month until I have paid all of the principal and interest and any other charges described below that I may owe under this Note. Each monthly payment will be applied as of its scheduled due date and will be applied to interest before Principal. If, on _____, _____, I still owe amounts under this Note, I will pay those amounts in full on that date, which is called the "Maturity Date."

I will make my monthly payments at ———————————————— ———————————————————— or at a different place if required by the Note Holder.

**(B) Amount of My Initial Monthly Payments**
Each of my initial monthly payments will be in the amount of U.S. $————————————————. This amount may change.

**(C) Monthly Payment Changes**
Changes in my monthly payment will reflect changes in the unpaid principal of my loan and in the interest rate that I must pay. The Note Holder will determine my new interest rate and the changed amount of my monthly payment in accordance with Sections 4 or 5 of this Note.

4. **INTEREST RATE AND MONTHLY PAYMENT CHANGES**

**(A) Change Dates**
The interest rate I will pay may change on the first day of ———————— ————————————, ————————————, and may change on that day every 12th month thereafter. Each date on which my interest rate could change is called a "Change Date."

**(B) The Index**
Beginning with the first Change Date, my interest rate will be based on an Index. The "Index" is the weekly average yield on United States Treasury securities adjusted to a constant maturity of one year, as made available by the Federal Reserve Board. The most recent Index figure available as of the date 45 days before each Change Date is called the "Current Index."

If the Index is no longer available, the Note Holder will choose a new index which is based upon comparable information. The Note Holder will give me notice of this choice.

**(C) Calculation of Changes**
Before each Change Date, the Note Holder will calculate my new interest rate by adding ———————————————————————— percentage point(s) (————————————————%) to the Current Index. The Note Holder will then round the result of this addition to the nearest one-eighth of one percentage point (0.125%). Subject to the limits stated in Section 4(D) below, this rounded amount will be my new interest rate until the next Change Date.

The Note Holder will then determine the amount of the monthly payment that would be sufficient to repay the unpaid principal that I am expected to owe at the Change Date in full on the Maturity Date at my new interest rate in substantially equal payments. The result of this calculation will be the new amount of my monthly payment.

**(D) Limits on Interest Rate Changes**
The interest rate I am required to pay at the first Change Date will not be greater than ————————————% or less than ——————————%. Thereafter, my interest rate will never be increased or decreased on any single Change Date by more than ———————————————————— percentage point(s) (————————————%) from the rate of interest I have been paying for the preceding 12 months. My interest rate will never be greater than ——————————% (the "Maximum Rate").

### (E) Effective Date of Changes

My new interest rate will become effective on each Change Date. I will pay the amount of my new monthly payment beginning on the first monthly payment date after the Change Date until the amount of my monthly payment changes again.

### (F) Notice of Changes

The Note Holder will deliver or mail to me a notice of any changes in my interest rate and the amount of my monthly payment before the effective date of any change. The notice will include information required by law to be given to me and also the title and telephone number of a person who will answer any question I may have regarding the notice.

## 5.  FIXED INTEREST RATE CONVERSION OPTION

### (A) Option to Convert to Fixed Rate

I have a Conversion Option which I can exercise unless I am in default or this Section 5(A) will not permit me to do so. The "Conversion Option" is my option to convert the interest rate I am required to pay by this Note from an adjustable rate with interest rate limits to the fixed rate calculated under Section 5(B) below.

The conversion can only take place on the first, second or third Change Date. Each date on which my adjustable interest rate can convert to the new fixed rate is called the "Conversion Date."

If I want to exercise the Conversion Option, I must first meet certain conditions. Those conditions are that: (i) I must give the Note Holder notice that I want to do so; (ii) on the Conversion Date, I must not be in default under the Note or the Security Instrument; (iii) by a date specified by the Note Holder, I must pay the Note Holder a conversion fee of U.S. $_____; and (iv) I must sign and give the Note Holder any documents the Note Holder requires to effect the conversion.

### (B) Calculation of Fixed Rate

My new, fixed interest rate will be equal to the Federal Home Loan Mortgage Corporation's required net yield as of a date and time of day specified by the Note Holder for (i) if the original term of this Note is greater than 15 years, 30-year fixed rate mortgages covered by applicable 60-day mandatory delivery commitments, plus three-eighths of one percentage point (0.375%), or (ii) if the original term of this Note is 15 years or less, 15-year fixed rate mortgages covered by applicable 60-day mandatory delivery commitments, plus three-eighths of one percentage point (0.375%). If this required net yield cannot be determined because the applicable commitments are not available, the Note Holder will determine my interest rate by using comparable information. My new rate calculated under this Section 5(B) will not be greater than the Maximum Rate stated in Section 4(D) above.

### (C) New Payment Amount and Effective Date

If I choose to exercise the Conversion Option, the Note Holder will determine the amount of the monthly payment that would be sufficient to repay the unpaid principal I am expected to owe on the Conversion Date in full on the Maturity Date at my new fixed interest rate in substantially equal payments. The result of this calculation will be the new amount of my monthly payment. Beginning with my first monthly payment after the Conversion Date, I will pay the new amount as my monthly payment until the Maturity Date.

### 6. BORROWER'S RIGHT TO PREPAY

I have the right to make payments of Principal at any time before they are due. A payment of Principal only is known as a "Prepayment." When I make a Prepayment, I will tell the Note Holder in writing that I am doing so. I may not designate a payment as a Prepayment if I have not made all the monthly payments due under the Note.

I may make a full Prepayment or partial Prepayments without paying a Prepayment charge. The Note Holder will use my Prepayments to reduce the amount of Principal that I owe under this Note. However, the Note Holder may apply my Prepayment to the accrued and unpaid interest on the Prepayment amount before applying my Prepayment to reduce the Principal amount of the Note. If I make a partial Prepayment, there will be no changes in the due dates of my monthly payment unless the Note Holder agrees in writing to those changes. My partial Prepayment may reduce the amount of my monthly payments after the first Change Date following my partial Prepayment. However, any reduction due to my partial Prepayment may be offset by an interest rate increase.

### 7. LOAN CHARGES

If a law, which applies to this loan and which sets maximum loan charges, is finally interpreted so that the interest or other loan charges collected or to be collected in connection with this loan exceed the permitted limits, then: (a) any such loan charge shall be reduced by the amount necessary to reduce the charge to the permitted limit; and (b) any sums already collected from me which exceeded permitted limits will be refunded to me. The Note Holder may choose to make this refund by reducing the Principal I owe under this Note or by making a direct payment to me. If a refund reduces Principal, the reduction will be treated as a partial Prepayment.

### 8. BORROWER'S FAILURE TO PAY AS REQUIRED

**(A) Late Charges for Overdue Payments**
If the Note Holder has not received the full amount of any monthly payment by the end of _____ calendar days after the date it is due, I will pay a late charge to the Note Holder. The amount of the charge will be _____% of my overdue payment of principal and interest. I will pay this late charge promptly but only once on each late payment.

**(B) Default**
If I do not pay the full amount of each monthly payment on the date it is due, I will be in default.

### (C) Notice of Default

If I am in default, the Note Holder may send me a written notice telling me that if I do not pay the overdue amount by a certain date, the Note Holder may require me to pay immediately the full amount of Principal which has not been paid and all the interest that I owe on that amount. That date must be at least 30 days after the date on which the notice is mailed to me or delivered by other means.

### (D) No Waiver By Note Holder

Even if, at a time when I am in default, the Note Holder does not require me to pay immediately in full as described above, the Note Holder will still have the right to do so if I am in default at a later time.

### (E) Payment of Note Holder's Costs and Expenses

If the Note Holder has required me to pay immediately in full as described above, the Note Holder will have the right to be paid back by me for all of its costs and expenses in enforcing this Note to the extent not prohibited by applicable law. Those expenses include, for example, reasonable attorneys' fees.

## 9.  GIVING OF NOTICES

Unless applicable law requires a different method, any notice that must be given to me under this Note will be given by delivering it or by mailing it by first class mail to me at the Property Address above or at a different address if I give the Note Holder a notice of my different address.

Any notice that must be given to the Note Holder under this Note will be given by delivering it or by mailing it by first class mail to the Note Holder at the address stated in Section 3(A) above or at a different address if I am given a notice of that different address.

## 10. OBLIGATIONS OF PERSONS UNDER THIS NOTE

If more than one person signs this Note, each person is fully and personally obligated to keep all of the promises made in this Note, including the promise to pay the full amount owed. Any person who is a guarantor, surety or endorser of this Note is also obligated to do these things. Any person who takes over these obligations, including the obligations of a guarantor, surety or endorser of this Note, is also obligated to keep all of the promises made in this Note. The Note Holder may enforce its rights under this Note against each person individually or against all of us together. This means that any one of us may be required to pay all of the amounts owed under this Note.

## 11. WAIVERS

I and any other person who has obligations under this Note waive the rights of Presentment and Notice of Dishonor. "Presentment" means the right to require the Note Holder to demand payment of amounts due. "Notice of Dishonor" means the right to require the Note Holder to give notice to other persons that amounts due have not been paid.

### 12. UNIFORM SECURED NOTE

This Note is a uniform instrument with limited variations in some jurisdictions. In addition to the protections given to the Note Holder under this Note, a Mortgage, Deed of Trust, or Security Deed (the "Security Instrument"), dated the same date as this Note, protects the Note Holder from possible losses which might result if I do not keep the promises which I make in this Note. That Security Instrument describes how and under what conditions I may be required to make immediate payment in full of all amounts I owe under this Note. Some of those conditions are described as follows:

**(A) UNTIL MY INITIAL INTEREST RATE CHANGES UNDER THE TERMS STATED IN SECTION 4 ABOVE AND AFTER I EXERCISE MY CONVERSION OPTION UNDER THE CONDITIONS STATED IN SECTION 5 ABOVE, UNIFORM COVENANT 18 OF THE SECURITY INSTRUMENT IS DESCRIBED AS FOLLOWS:**

**Transfer of the Property or a Beneficial Interest in Borrower.** As used in this Section 18, "Interest in the Property" means any legal or beneficial interest in the Property, including, but not limited to, those beneficial interests transferred in a bond for deed, contract for deed, installment sales contract or escrow agreement, the intent of which is the transfer of title by Borrower at a future date to a purchaser.

If all or any part of the Property or any Interest in the Property is sold or transferred (or if Borrower is not a natural person and a beneficial interest in Borrower is sold or transferred) without Lender's prior written consent, Lender may require immediate payment in full of all sums secured by this Security Instrument. However, this option shall not be exercised by Lender if such exercise is prohibited by Applicable Law.

If Lender exercises this option, Lender shall give Borrower notice of acceleration. The notice shall provide a period of not less than 30 days from the date the notice is given in accordance with Section 15 within which Borrower must pay all sums secured by this Security Instrument. If Borrower fails to pay these sums prior to the expiration of this period, Lender may invoke any remedies permitted by this Security Instrument without further notice or demand on Borrower.

**(B) AFTER MY INITIAL INTEREST RATE CHANGES UNDER THE TERMS STATED IN SECTION 4 ABOVE, UNLESS I EXERCISE MY CONVERSION OPTION UNDER THE CONDITIONS STATED IN SECTION 5 ABOVE, UNIFORM COVENANT 18 OF THE SECURITY INSTRUMENT DESCRIBED IN SECTION 12(A) ABOVE SHALL THEN CEASE TO BE IN EFFECT, AND UNIFORM COVENANT 18 OF THE SECURITY INSTRUMENT SHALL INSTEAD BE DESCRIBED AS FOLLOWS:**

**Transfer of the Property or a Beneficial Interest in Borrower.** As used in this Section 18, "Interest in the Property" means any legal or beneficial interest in the Property, including, but not limited to, those beneficial interests transferred in a bond for deed, contract for deed, installment sales contract or escrow agreement, the intent of which is the transfer of title by Borrower at a future date to a purchaser.

If all or any part of the Property or any Interest in the Property is sold or transferred (or if Borrower is not a natural person and a beneficial interest in Borrower is sold or transferred) without Lender's prior written consent, Lender may require immediate payment in full of all sums secured by this Security Instrument. However, this option shall not be exercised by Lender if such exercise is prohibited by Applicable Law. Lender also shall not exercise this option if: (a) Borrower causes to be submitted to Lender information required by Lender to evaluate the intended transferee as if a new loan were being made to the transferee; and (b) Lender reasonably determines that Lender's security will not be impaired by the loan assumption and that the risk of a breach of any covenant or agreement in this Security Instrument is acceptable to Lender.

To the extent permitted by Applicable Law, Lender may charge a reasonable fee as a condition to Lender's consent to the loan assumption. Lender may also require the transferee to sign an assumption agreement that is acceptable to Lender and that obligates the transferee to keep all the promises and agreements made in the Note and in this Security Instrument. Borrower will continue to be obligated under the Note and this Security Instrument unless Lender releases Borrower in writing.

If Lender exercises the option to require immediate payment in full, Lender shall give Borrower notice of acceleration. The notice shall provide a period of not less than 30 days from the date the notice is given in accordance with Section 15 within which Borrower must pay all sums secured by this Security Instrument. If Borrower fails to pay these sums prior to the expiration of this period, Lender may invoke any remedies permitted by this Security Instrument without further notice or demand on Borrower.

WITNESS THE HAND(S) AND SEAL(S) OF THE UNDERSIGNED.

_____ (Seal)
                                                - Borrower

_____ (Seal)
                                                - Borrower

_____ (Seal)
                                                - Borrower

*[Sign Original Only]*

# FORM 5 – STANDARD FORM EXTENSION/ADDENDUM TO AGREEMENT OF SALE

| 1 | The printed portions of this form, except differentiated additions, have been approved by the Colorado Real Estate Commission. (AE41-10-11) (Mandatory 1-12) |
| 2 | |

3

4 **THIS FORM HAS IMPORTANT LEGAL CONSEQUENCES AND THE PARTIES SHOULD CONSULT LEGAL AND TAX OR**
5 **OTHER COUNSEL BEFORE SIGNING.**

6

7 ## AGREEMENT TO AMEND/EXTEND CONTRACT

8

9 Date: _____

10

11 **1.** This agreement amends the contract dated _____ (Contract), between _____
12 _____ (Seller), and _____
13 (Buyer), relating to the sale and purchase of the following legally described real estate in the County of _____,
14 Colorado:

15

16

17

18 known as No. _____ (Property).
19       Street Address             City           State       Zip

20

21 **NOTE: If the table is omitted, or if any item is left blank or is marked in the "No Change" column, it means no change to**
22 **the corresponding provision of the Contract. If any item is marked in the "Deleted" column, it means that the**
23 **corresponding provision of the Contract to which reference is made is deleted.**

24

25 **2.** **§ 3. DATES AND DEADLINES.** [Note: This table may be omitted if inapplicable.]

| Item No. | Reference | Event | Date or Deadline | No Change | Deleted |
|---|---|---|---|---|---|
| 1 | § 4.2 | Alternative Earnest Money Deadline | | | |
| | | **Title and Association Documents** | | | |
| 2 | § 7.1 | Record Title Deadline | | | |
| 3 | § 7.2 | Exceptions Request Deadline | | | |
| 4 | § 8.1 | Record Title Objection Deadline | | | |
| 5 | § 8.2 | Off-Record Title Deadline | | | |
| 6 | § 8.2 | Off-Record Title Objection Deadline | | | |
| 7 | § 8.3 | Title Resolution Deadline | | | |
| 8 | § 7.3 | Association Documents Deadline | | | |
| 9 | § 7.3 | Association Documents Objection Deadline | | | |
| 10 | § 8.5 | Right of First Refusal Deadline | | | |
| | | **Seller's Property Disclosure** | | | |
| 11 | § 10.1 | Seller's Property Disclosure Deadline | | | |
| | | **Loan and Credit** | | | |
| 12 | § 5.1 | Loan Application Deadline | | | |
| 13 | § 5.2 | Loan Conditions Deadline | | | |
| 14 | § 5.3 | Buyer's Credit Information Deadline | | | |
| 15 | § 5.3 | Disapproval of Buyer's Credit Information Deadline | | | |
| 16 | § 5.4 | Existing Loan Documents Deadline | | | |
| 17 | § 5.4 | Existing Loan Documents Objection Deadline | | | |
| 18 | § 5.4 | Loan Transfer Approval Deadline | | | |
| | | **Appraisal** | | | |
| 19 | § 6.2 | Appraisal Deadline | | | |
| 20 | § 6.2 | Appraisal Objection Deadline | | | |
| | | **Survey** | | | |
| 21 | § 9.1 | Current Survey Deadline | | | |
| 22 | § 9.2 | Current Survey Objection Deadline | | | |

| | | Inspection and Due Diligence | | | |
|---|---|---|---|---|---|
| 23 | § 10.2 | Inspection Objection Deadline | | | |
| 24 | § 10.3 | Inspection Resolution Deadline | | | |
| 25 | § 10.5 | Property Insurance Objection Deadline | | | |
| 26 | § 10.6 | Due Diligence Documents Delivery Deadline | | | |
| 27 | § 10.7 | Due Diligence Documents Objection Deadline | | | |
| 28 | § 10.8 | Environmental Inspection Objection Deadline CBS2, 3, 4 | | | |
| 29 | § 10.8 | ADA Evaluation Objection Deadline CBS2, 3, 4 | | | |
| 30 | § 11.1 | Tenant Estoppel Statements Deadline CBS2, 3, 4 | | | |
| 31 | § 11.2 | Tenant Estoppel Statements Objection Deadline CBS2, 3, 4 | | | |
| | | **Closing and Possession** | | | |
| 32 | § 12.3 | **Closing Date** | | | |
| 33 | § 17 | Possession Date | | | |
| 34 | § 17 | Possession Time | | | |
| | | | | | |
| | | | | | |

26
27   **3.**   Other dates or deadlines set forth in the Contract shall be changed as follows:
28
29
30
31   **4.**   Additional amendments:
32
33
34
35   All other terms and conditions of the Contract shall remain the same.
36
37
38   This proposal shall expire unless accepted in writing by Seller and Buyer as evidenced by their signatures below and the offering
39   party to this document receives notice of such acceptance on or before _____.
40                                                                        Date                    Time
41
42

Buyer's Name: _____          Buyer's Name: _____


_____          _____          _____          _____
Buyer's Signature                         Date          Buyer's Signature                         Date


Seller's Name: _____          Seller's Name: _____


_____          _____          _____          _____
Seller's Signature                         Date          Seller's Signature                         Date
43

# FORM 6 – BROKERAGE DUTIES ADDENDUM

| 1 | The printed portions of this form have been approved, except differentiated additions, by the Colorado Real Estate Commission. |
| 2 | (BDA55-5-09) (Mandatory 7-09) |

3

4 **THIS FORM HAS IMPORTANT LEGAL CONSEQUENCES AND THE PARTIES SHOULD CONSULT LEGAL AND TAX**
5 **OR OTHER COUNSEL BEFORE SIGNING.**

6

7 **DIFFERENT BROKERAGE RELATIONSHIPS ARE AVAILABLE WHICH INCLUDE LANDLORD AGENCY, TENANT**
8 **AGENCY, BUYER AGENCY, SELLER AGENCY OR TRANSACTION-BROKERAGE.**

9

10 

**BROKERAGE DUTIES ADDENDUM**
11 **TO PROPERTY MANAGEMENT AGREEMENT**
12 **(Leasing Activities)**

13

14 ☐ **LANDLORD AGENCY**   ☐ **TRANSACTION-BROKERAGE**

15

16 This Brokerage Duties Addendum (Addendum) is made a part of the agreement for the management and leasing of the Property known
17 as _____ (Property),
18 which is dated _____, between Brokerage Firm and Landlord (Agreement). This Addendum supplements
19 the Agreement.

20

21 **1.   BROKER AND BROKERAGE FIRM.**

22 ☐   **1.1.   Multiple-Person Firm.** If this box is checked, the individual designated by Brokerage Firm to perform leasing services
23 for Landlord is called Broker. If more than one individual is so designated, then references in this Addendum to Broker shall include all
24 persons so designated, including substitute or additional brokers. The brokerage relationship exists only with Broker and does not extend
25 to the employing broker, Brokerage Firm or to any other brokers employed or engaged by Brokerage Firm who are not so designated.

26 ☐   **1.2.   One-Person Firm.** If this box is checked, Broker is a real estate brokerage firm with only one licensed natural person.
27 References to Broker or Brokerage Firm mean both the licensed natural person and brokerage firm who shall perform leasing services for
28 Landlord.

29

30 **2.   DEFINED TERMS.**

31    **2.1.   Landlord:** _____

32    **2.2.   Brokerage Firm:** _____

33    **2.3.   Broker:** _____
34 shall act for or assist Landlord when performing leasing activities in the capacity as shown by the box checked at the top of this page 1.

35

36 **3.   BROKERAGE RELATIONSHIP.**
37    **3.1.**   If the Landlord Agency box at the top of page 1 is checked, Broker shall represent Landlord as a limited agent
38 (Landlord's Agent). If the Transaction-Brokerage box at the top of page 1 is checked, Broker shall act as a Transaction-Broker.
39    **3.2.   In-Company Transaction – Different Brokers.** When Landlord and tenant in a transaction are working with different
40 brokers, those brokers continue to conduct themselves consistent with the brokerage relationships they have established. Landlord
41 acknowledges that Brokerage Firm is allowed to offer and pay compensation to brokers within Brokerage Firm working with a tenant.
42    **3.3.   In-Company Transaction – One Broker.** If Landlord and tenant are both working with the same broker, the parties
43 agree the following applies:
44       **3.3.1.   Landlord's Agent.** If the Landlord Agency box at the top of page 1 is checked, the parties agree the following
45 applies:
46          **3.3.1.1.   Landlord Agency Only.** Unless the box in § 3.3.1.2 **(Landlord Agency Unless Brokerage**
47 **Relationship with Both)** is checked, Broker shall represent Landlord as Landlord's Agent and shall treat the tenant as a customer. A
48 customer is a party to a transaction with whom Broker has no brokerage relationship. Broker shall disclose to such customer Broker's
49 relationship with Landlord.
50 ☐          **3.3.1.2.   Landlord Agency Unless Brokerage Relationship with Both.** If this box is checked, Broker shall
51 represent Landlord as Landlord's Agent and shall treat the tenant as a customer, unless Broker currently has or enters into an agency or
52 Transaction-Brokerage relationship with the tenant, in which case Broker shall act as a Transaction-Broker.
53       **3.3.2.   Transaction-Broker.** If the Transaction-Brokerage box at the top of page 1 is checked, or in the event neither
54 box is checked, Broker shall work with Landlord as a Transaction-Broker. A Transaction-Broker shall perform the duties described in §
55 4 and facilitate lease transactions without being an advocate or agent for either party. If Landlord and tenant are working with the same
56 broker, Broker shall continue to function as a Transaction-Broker.

57

58 **4.   BROKERAGE DUTIES.** Brokerage Firm, acting through Broker, as either a Transaction-Broker or a Landlord's Agent, shall
59 perform the following **Uniform Duties** when working with Landlord:
60    **4.1.**   Broker will exercise reasonable skill and care for Landlord, including, but not limited to the following:
61       **4.1.1.**   Performing the terms of any written or oral agreement with Landlord;
62       **4.1.2.**   Presenting all offers to and from Landlord in a timely manner regardless of whether the Property is subject to a
63 lease or letter of intent to lease;
64       **4.1.3.**   Disclosing to Landlord adverse material facts actually known by Broker;
65       **4.1.4.**   Advising Landlord regarding the transaction and advising Landlord to obtain expert advice as to material

66    matters about which Broker knows but the specifics of which are beyond the expertise of Broker;

67    **4.1.5.**    Accounting in a timely manner for all money and property received; and

68    **4.1.6.**    Keeping Landlord fully informed regarding the transaction.

69    **4.2.**    Broker shall not disclose the following information without the informed consent of Landlord:

70    **4.2.1.**    That Landlord is willing to accept less than the asking lease rate for the Property;

71    **4.2.2.**    What Landlord's motivating factors are to lease the Property;

72    **4.2.3.**    That Landlord will agree to lease terms other than those offered;

73    **4.2.4.**    Any material information about Landlord unless disclosure is required by law or failure to disclose such

74    information would constitute fraud or dishonest dealing; or

75    **4.2.5.**    Any facts or suspicions regarding circumstances that could psychologically impact or stigmatize the Property.

76    **4.3.**    Landlord consents to Broker's disclosure of Landlord's confidential information to the supervising broker or designee for

77    the purpose of proper supervision, provided such supervising broker or designee shall not further disclose such information without

78    consent of Landlord, or use such information to the detriment of Landlord.

79    **4.4.**    Brokerage Firm may have agreements with other landlords to market and lease their property.  Broker may show

80    alternative properties not owned by Landlord to other prospective tenants and list competing properties for lease.

81    **4.5.**    If all or a portion of the Property is subject to a lease, or letter of intent to Lease, obtained by Broker, Broker shall not be

82    obligated to seek additional offers to lease such portion of the Property.

83    **4.6.**    Broker has no duty to conduct an independent inspection of the Property for the benefit of tenant and has no duty to

84    independently verify the accuracy or completeness of statements made by Landlord or independent inspectors.

85    **4.7.**    Landlord understands that Landlord shall not be liable for Broker's acts or omissions that have not been approved,

86    directed, or ratified by Landlord.

87

88    **5.    ADDITIONAL DUTIES OF LANDLORD'S AGENT.**  If the Landlord Agency box is checked, Broker is Landlord's Agent,

89    with the following additional duties:

90    **5.1.**    Promoting the interests of Landlord with the utmost good faith, loyalty and fidelity.

91    **5.2.**    Seeking rental rates and terms that are acceptable to Landlord.

92    **5.3.**    Counseling Landlord as to any material benefits or risks of a transaction that are actually known to Broker.

93

94    **6.    MATERIAL DEFECTS, DISCLOSURES AND INSPECTION.**

95    **6.1.    Broker's Obligations.**  Colorado law requires a broker to disclose to any prospective tenant all adverse material facts

96    actually known by such broker including but not limited to adverse material facts pertaining to the title to the Property, the physical

97    condition of the Property, any material defects in the Property, and any environmental hazards affecting the Property required by law to

98    be disclosed.  These types of disclosures may include such matters as structural defects, soil conditions, violations of health, zoning or

99    building laws, and nonconforming uses and zoning variances.  Landlord agrees that any tenant may have the Property and Inclusions

100   inspected and authorizes Broker to disclose any facts actually known by Broker about the Property.  Broker shall not be obligated to

101   conduct an independent investigation of the tenant's financial condition except as otherwise provided in the Agreement.

102   **6.1.1.    Required Information to County Assessor.**  Landlord consents that Broker may supply certain information to

103   the county assessor if the Property is residential and is furnished.

104   **6.2.    Landlord's Obligations.**

105   **6.2.1.    Landlord's Property Disclosure Form.**  A landlord is not required by law to provide any particular disclosure

106   form.  However, disclosure of known material latent (not obvious) defects is required by law.  Landlord ☐ **Agrees** ☐ **Does Not Agree**

107   to provide a written disclosure of adverse matters regarding the Property completed to the best of Landlord's current, actual knowledge.

108   **6.2.2.    Lead-Based Paint.**  Unless exempt, if the improvements on the Property include one or more residential

109   dwellings for which a building permit was issued prior to January 1, 1978, a completed Lead-Based Paint Disclosure (Rental) form must

110   be signed by Landlord and the real estate licensees, and given to any potential tenant in a timely manner.

111   **6.2.3.    Carbon Monoxide Alarms.**  Landlord acknowledges that, unless exempt, if the Premises includes one or more

112   rooms lawfully used for sleeping purposes (Bedroom), an operational carbon monoxide alarm must be installed within fifteen feet of the

113   entrance to each Bedroom or in a location as required by the applicable building code, prior to offering the Property for sale or lease.

114

115   **7.    ADDITIONAL AMENDMENTS:**

116

117

118

119   Date: _____    Date: _____

120

121

122   _____    _____

123   Landlord    Landlord

124

125

126   Date: _____    _____

127   Broker

128

129   Brokerage Firm's Name: _____

130

# FORM 7 – STANDARD FORM AGREEMENT OF SALE

1  The printed portions of this form, except differentiated additions, have been approved by the Colorado Real Estate Commission.
2  (CBS1-10-11) (Mandatory 1-12)
3
4  **THIS FORM HAS IMPORTANT LEGAL CONSEQUENCES AND THE PARTIES SHOULD CONSULT LEGAL AND TAX OR**
5  **OTHER COUNSEL BEFORE SIGNING.**
6
7  ## CONTRACT TO BUY AND SELL REAL ESTATE
   ## (RESIDENTIAL)
8
9
10  Date: _____

11  | AGREEMENT |

12  **1.  AGREEMENT.** Buyer, identified in § 2.1, agrees to buy, and Seller, identified in § 2.3, agrees to sell, the Property
13  described below on the terms and conditions set forth in this contract (Contract).

14  **2.  PARTIES AND PROPERTY.**
15      **2.1.  Buyer.** Buyer, _____, will take title to the Property
16  described below as ☐ **Joint Tenants** ☐ **Tenants In Common** ☐ **Other** _____.
17      **2.2.  Assignability and Inurement.** This Contract ☐ **Shall** ☐ **Shall Not** be assignable by Buyer without Seller's prior
18  written consent. Except as so restricted, this Contract shall inure to the benefit of and be binding upon the heirs, personal
19  representatives, successors and assigns of the parties.
20      **2.3.  Seller.** Seller, _____, is the current owner of the
21  Property described below.
22      **2.4.  Property.** The Property is the following legally described real estate in the County of _____, Colorado:
23
24
25
26
27  known as No. _____,
28        Street Address             City       State       Zip
29  together with the interests, easements, rights, benefits, improvements and attached fixtures appurtenant thereto, and all interest of
30  Seller in vacated streets and alleys adjacent thereto, except as herein excluded (Property).
31      **2.5.  Inclusions.** The Purchase Price includes the following items (Inclusions):
32          **2.5.1.  Fixtures.** If attached to the Property on the date of this Contract: lighting, heating, plumbing, ventilating
33  and air conditioning fixtures, TV antennas, inside telephone, network and coaxial (cable) wiring and connecting blocks/jacks,
34  plants, mirrors, floor coverings, intercom systems, built-in kitchen appliances, sprinkler systems and controls, built-in vacuum
35  systems (including accessories), garage door openers including _____ remote controls.
36  **Other Fixtures:**
37
38
39  If any fixtures are attached to the Property after the date of this Contract, such additional fixtures are also included in the Purchase
40  Price.
41          **2.5.2.  Personal Property.** If on the Property whether attached or not on the date of this Contract: storm windows,
42  storm doors, window and porch shades, awnings, blinds, screens, window coverings, curtain rods, drapery rods, fireplace inserts,
43  fireplace screens, fireplace grates, heating stoves, storage sheds, and all keys. If checked, the following are included: ☐ **Water**
44  **Softeners** ☐ **Smoke/Fire Detectors** ☐ **Security Systems** ☐ **Satellite Systems** (including satellite dishes).
45  **Other Personal Property:**
46
47
48      The Personal Property to be conveyed at Closing shall be conveyed by Seller free and clear of all taxes (except
49  personal property taxes for the year of Closing), liens and encumbrances, except _____.
50  Conveyance shall be by bill of sale or other applicable legal instrument.
51          **2.5.3.  Parking and Storage Facilities.** ☐ **Use Only** ☐ **Ownership** of the following parking facilities:
52  _____; and ☐ **Use Only** ☐ **Ownership** of the following storage facilities: _____.

| | |
|---|---|
| 53 | **2.5.4.  Water Rights, Water and Sewer Taps.** |
| 54 | **2.5.4.1.  Deeded Water Rights.** The following legally described water rights: |
| 55 | |
| 56 | |
| 57 | Any water rights shall be conveyed by ☐ _____ **Deed** ☐ **Other** applicable legal instrument. |

58 ☐        **2.5.4.2.  Well Rights.** If any water well is to be transferred to Buyer, Seller agrees to supply required
59 information about such well to Buyer. Buyer understands that if the well to be transferred is a Small Capacity Well or a Domestic
60 Exempt Water Well used for ordinary household purposes, Buyer shall, prior to or at Closing, complete a Change in Ownership
61 form for the well. If an existing well has not been registered with the Colorado Division of Water Resources in the Department of
62 Natural Resources (Division), Buyer shall complete a registration of existing well form for the well and pay the cost of
63 registration. If no person will be providing a closing service in connection with the transaction, Buyer shall file the form with the
64 Division within sixty days after Closing. The Well Permit # is _____.

65        **2.5.4.3.** ☐ **Water Stock Certificates:**
66
67
68        **2.5.4.4.** ☐ **Water Tap**       ☐ **Sewer Tap**

69 **Note: Buyer is advised to obtain, from the provider, written confirmation of the amount remaining to be paid, if any, time**
70 **and other restrictions for transfer and use of the tap.**
71        **2.5.4.5.  Other Rights:**
72
73

74     **2.6.**    **Exclusions.** The following items are excluded (Exclusions):
75
76

77 **3.**    **DATES AND DEADLINES.**

| Item No. | Reference | Event | Date or Deadline |
|---|---|---|---|
| 1 | § 4.2 | Alternative Earnest Money Deadline | |
| | | **Title and Association** | |
| 2 | § 7.1 | Record Title Deadline | |
| 3 | § 7.2 | Exceptions Request Deadline | |
| 4 | § 8.1 | Record Title Objection Deadline | |
| 5 | § 8.2 | Off-Record Title Deadline | |
| 6 | § 8.2 | Off-Record Title Objection Deadline | |
| 7 | § 8.3 | Title Resolution Deadline | |
| 8 | § 7.3 | Association Documents Deadline | |
| 9 | § 7.3 | Association Documents Objection Deadline | |
| 10 | § 8.5 | Right of First Refusal Deadline | |
| | | **Seller's Property Disclosure** | |
| 11 | § 10.1 | Seller's Property Disclosure Deadline | |
| | | **Loan and Credit** | |
| 12 | § 5.1 | Loan Application Deadline | |
| 13 | § 5.2 | Loan Conditions Deadline | |
| 14 | § 5.3 | Buyer's Credit Information Deadline | |
| 15 | § 5.3 | Disapproval of Buyer's Credit Information Deadline | |
| 16 | § 5.4 | Existing Loan Documents Deadline | |
| 17 | § 5.4 | Existing Loan Documents Objection Deadline | |
| 18 | § 5.4 | Loan Transfer Approval Deadline | |
| | | **Appraisal** | |
| 19 | § 6.2 | Appraisal Deadline | |
| 20 | § 6.2 | Appraisal Objection Deadline | |
| | | **Survey** | |
| 21 | § 9.1 | Current Survey Deadline | |
| 22 | § 9.2 | Current Survey Objection Deadline | |
| | | **Inspection and Due Diligence** | |
| 23 | § 10.2 | Inspection Objection Deadline | |
| 24 | § 10.3 | Inspection Resolution Deadline | |

| | | | |
|---|---|---|---|
| 25 | § 10.5 | Property Insurance Objection Deadline | |
| 26 | § 10.6 | Due Diligence Documents Delivery Deadline | |
| 27 | § 10.7 | Due Diligence Documents Objection Deadline | |
| | | **Closing and Possession** | |
| 28 | § 12.3 | **Closing Date** | |
| 29 | § 17 | Possession Date | |
| 30 | § 17 | Possession Time | |
| 31 | § 28 | **Acceptance Deadline Date** | |
| 32 | § 28 | **Acceptance Deadline Time** | |
| | | | |
| | | | |

78 **Note: Applicability of Terms.**
79 Any box, blank or line in this Contract left blank or completed with the abbreviation "N/A", or the word "Deleted" means such
80 provision in **Dates and Deadlines** (§ 3), including any deadline, is not applicable and the corresponding provision of this Contract
81 to which reference is made is deleted.

82 The abbreviation "MEC" (mutual execution of this Contract) means the date upon which both parties have signed this Contract.

83 **Note:** If **FHA** or **VA** loan boxes are checked in § 4.5.3 (Loan Limitations), the **Appraisal Deadline** (§ 3) does **Not** apply to **FHA**
84 insured or **VA** guaranteed loans.

85 **4. PURCHASE PRICE AND TERMS.**
86     **4.1. Price and Terms.** The Purchase Price set forth below shall be payable in U.S. Dollars by Buyer as follows:

| Item No. | Reference | Item | Amount | Amount |
|---|---|---|---|---|
| 1 | § 4.1 | Purchase Price | $ | |
| 2 | § 4.2 | Earnest Money | | $ |
| 3 | § 4.5 | New Loan | | |
| 4 | § 4.6 | Assumption Balance | | |
| 5 | § 4.7 | Seller or Private Financing | | |
| 6 | | | | |
| 7 | | | | |
| 8 | § 4.3 | Cash at Closing | | |
| 9 | | **TOTAL** | $ | $ |

87     **4.2. Earnest Money.** The Earnest Money set forth in this section, in the form of _____, shall be
88 payable to and held by _____ (Earnest Money Holder), in its trust account, on behalf of
89 both Seller and Buyer. The Earnest Money deposit shall be tendered with this Contract unless the parties mutually agree to an
90 **Alternative Earnest Money Deadline** (§ 3) for its payment. If Earnest Money Holder is other than the Brokerage Firm identified
91 in § 33 or § 34, Closing Instructions signed by Buyer, Seller and Earnest Money Holder must be obtained on or before delivery of
92 Earnest Money to Earnest Money Holder. The parties authorize delivery of the Earnest Money deposit to the company conducting
93 the Closing (Closing Company), if any, at or before Closing. In the event Earnest Money Holder has agreed to have interest on
94 Earnest Money deposits transferred to a fund established for the purpose of providing affordable housing to Colorado residents,
95 Seller and Buyer acknowledge and agree that any interest accruing on the Earnest Money deposited with the Earnest Money
96 Holder in this transaction shall be transferred to such fund.
97     **4.2.1. Alternative Earnest Money Deadline.** The deadline for delivering the Earnest Money, if other than at the
98 time of tender of this Contract is as set forth as the **Alternative Earnest Money Deadline** (§ 3).
99     **4.2.2. Return of Earnest Money.** If Buyer has a Right to Terminate and timely terminates, Buyer shall be
100 entitled to the return of Earnest Money as provided in this Contract. If this Contract is terminated as set forth in § 25 and, except as
101 provided in § 24, if the Earnest Money has not already been returned following receipt of a Notice to Terminate, Seller agrees to
102 execute and return to Buyer or Broker working with Buyer, written mutual instructions, i.e., Earnest Money Release form, within
103 three days of Seller's receipt of such form.
104     **4.3. Form of Funds; Time of Payment; Funds Available.**
105     **4.3.1. Good Funds.** All amounts payable by the parties at Closing, including any loan proceeds, Cash at Closing
106 and closing costs, shall be in funds that comply with all applicable Colorado laws, including electronic transfer funds, certified
107 check, savings and loan teller's check and cashier's check (Good Funds).
108     **4.3.2. Available Funds.** All funds required to be paid at Closing or as otherwise agreed in writing between the
109 parties shall be timely paid to allow disbursement by Closing Company at Closing **OR SUCH PARTY SHALL BE IN DEFAULT**.

110   Buyer represents that Buyer, as of the date of this Contract, ☐ **Does** ☐ **Does Not** have funds that are immediately verifiable and
111   available in an amount not less than the amount stated as Cash at Closing in § 4.1.

112       **4.4.**    **Seller Concession.** Seller, at Closing, shall credit, as directed by Buyer, an amount of $_____ to assist
113   with Buyer's closing costs, loan discount points, loan origination fees, prepaid items (including any amounts that Seller agrees to
114   pay because Buyer is not allowed to pay due to FHA, CHFA, VA, etc.), and any other fee, cost, charge, expense or expenditure
115   related to Buyer's New Loan or other allowable Seller concession (collectively, Seller Concession). Seller Concession is in
116   addition to any sum Seller has agreed to pay or credit Buyer elsewhere in this Contract. Seller Concession shall be reduced to the
117   extent it exceeds the amount allowed by Buyer's lender as set forth in the Closing Statement or HUD-1, at Closing.

118       **4.5.**    **New Loan.**

119           **4.5.1.**    **Buyer to Pay Loan Costs.** Buyer, except as provided in § 4.4, if applicable, shall timely pay Buyer's loan
120   costs, loan discount points, prepaid items and loan origination fees, as required by lender.

121           **4.5.2.**    **Buyer May Select Financing.** Buyer may pay in cash or select financing appropriate and acceptable to
122   Buyer, including a different loan than initially sought, except as restricted in § 4.5.3 or § 30 (Additional Provisions).

123           **4.5.3.**    **Loan Limitations.** Buyer may purchase the Property using any of the following types of loan:
124   ☐ **Conventional** ☐ **FHA** ☐ **VA** ☐ **Bond** ☐ **Other** _____.

125           **4.5.4.**    **Good Faith Estimate – Monthly Payment and Loan Costs.** Buyer is advised to review the terms, conditions
126   and costs of Buyer's New Loan carefully. If Buyer is applying for a residential loan, the lender generally must provide Buyer with
127   a good faith estimate of Buyer's closing costs within three days after Buyer completes a loan application. Buyer should also obtain
128   an estimate of the amount of Buyer's monthly mortgage payment. If the New Loan is unsatisfactory to Buyer, Buyer shall have the
129   Right to Terminate under § 25.1, on or before **Loan Conditions Deadline** (§ 3).

130       **4.6.**    **Assumption.** Buyer agrees to assume and pay an existing loan in the approximate amount of the Assumption
131   Balance set forth in § 4.1, presently payable at $_____ per _____ including principal and interest
132   presently at the rate of _____% per annum, and also including escrow for the following as indicated: ☐ **Real Estate Taxes**
133   ☐ **Property Insurance Premium** ☐ **Mortgage Insurance Premium** and ☐ _____.
134   Buyer agrees to pay a loan transfer fee not to exceed $_____. At the time of assumption, the new interest rate shall
135   not exceed _____% per annum and the new payment shall not exceed $_____ per _____ principal and
136   interest, plus escrow, if any. If the actual principal balance of the existing loan at Closing is less than the Assumption Balance,
137   which causes the amount of cash required from Buyer at Closing to be increased by more than $_____, then Buyer shall
138   have the Right to Terminate under § 25.1, on or before **Closing Date** (§ 3), based on the reduced amount of the actual principal
139   balance.
140       Seller ☐ **Shall** ☐ **Shall Not** be released from liability on said loan. If applicable, compliance with the requirements for
141   release from liability shall be evidenced by delivery ☐ **on or before Loan Transfer Approval Deadline** (§ 3) ☐ **at Closing** of
142   an appropriate letter of commitment from lender. Any cost payable for release of liability shall be paid by _____
143   in an amount not to exceed $_____.

144       **4.7.**    **Seller or Private Financing.** Buyer agrees to execute a promissory note payable to _____,
145   as ☐ **Joint Tenants** ☐ **Tenants In Common** ☐ **Other** _____, on the note form as indicated:
146   ☐ **(Default Rate)** NTD81-10-06 ☐ **Other** _____ secured by a _____
147   (1st, 2nd, etc.) deed of trust encumbering the Property, using the form as indicated:
148   ☐ **Due on Transfer – Strict** (TD72-8-10) ☐ **Due on Transfer – Creditworthy** (TD73-8-10) ☐ **Assumable – Not Due on**
149   **Transfer** (TD74-8-10) ☐ **Other** _____.
150       The promissory note shall be amortized on the basis of _____ ☐ **Years** ☐ **Months**, payable at $_____
151   per _____ including principal and interest at the rate of _____% per annum. Payments shall commence
152   _____ and shall be due on the _____ day of each succeeding _____. If not sooner
153   paid, the balance of principal and accrued interest shall be due and payable _____ after Closing.
154   Payments ☐ **Shall** ☐ **Shall Not** be increased by _____ of estimated annual real estate taxes, and ☐ **Shall** ☐ **Shall**
155   **Not** be increased by _____ of estimated annual property insurance premium. The loan shall also contain the following
156   terms: (1) if any payment is not received within _____ days after its due date, a late charge of _____% of such payment
157   shall be due; (2) interest on lender disbursements under the deed of trust shall be _____% per annum; (3) default interest rate
158   shall be _____% per annum; (4) Buyer may prepay without a penalty except _____;
159   and (5) Buyer ☐ **Shall** ☐ **Shall Not** execute and deliver, at Closing, a Security Agreement and UCC-1 Financing Statement
160   granting the holder of the promissory note a _____ (1st, 2nd, etc.) lien on the personal property included in this sale.
161       Buyer ☐ **Shall** ☐ **Shall Not** provide a mortgagee's title insurance policy, at Buyer's expense.

---

162

| TRANSACTION PROVISIONS |

163 **5. FINANCING CONDITIONS AND OBLIGATIONS.**

164     **5.1. Loan Application.** If Buyer is to pay all or part of the Purchase Price by obtaining one or more new loans (New
165 Loan), or if an existing loan is not to be released at Closing, Buyer, if required by such lender, shall make an application verifiable
166 by such lender, on or before **Loan Application Deadline** (§ 3) and exercise reasonable efforts to obtain such loan or approval.

167     **5.2. Loan Conditions.** If Buyer is to pay all or part of the Purchase Price with a New Loan, this Contract is conditional
168 upon Buyer determining, in Buyer's sole subjective discretion, whether the New Loan is satisfactory to Buyer, including its
169 availability, payments, interest rate, terms, conditions, and cost of such New Loan. This condition is for the benefit of Buyer.
170 Buyer shall have the Right to Terminate under § 25.1, on or before **Loan Conditions Deadline** (§ 3), if the New Loan is not
171 satisfactory to Buyer, in Buyer's sole subjective discretion. **IF SELLER DOES NOT TIMELY RECEIVE WRITTEN NOTICE**
172 **TO TERMINATE, BUYER'S EARNEST MONEY SHALL BE NONREFUNDABLE,** except as otherwise provided in this
173 Contract (e.g., Appraisal, Title, Survey).

174     **5.3. Credit Information and Buyer's New Senior Loan.** If Buyer is to pay all or part of the Purchase Price by
175 executing a promissory note in favor of Seller, or if an existing loan is not to be released at Closing, this Contract is conditional
176 (for the benefit of Seller) upon Seller's approval of Buyer's financial ability and creditworthiness, which approval shall be at
177 Seller's sole subjective discretion. In such case: (1) Buyer shall supply to Seller by **Buyer's Credit Information Deadline** (§ 3),
178 at Buyer's expense, information and documents (including a current credit report) concerning Buyer's financial, employment and
179 credit condition and Buyer's New Senior Loan, defined below, if any; (2) Buyer consents that Seller may verify Buyer's financial
180 ability and creditworthiness; (3) any such information and documents received by Seller shall be held by Seller in confidence, and
181 not released to others except to protect Seller's interest in this transaction; and (4) in the event Buyer is to execute a promissory
182 note secured by a deed of trust in favor of Seller, this Contract is conditional (for the benefit of Seller) upon Seller's approval of
183 the terms and conditions of any New Loan to be obtained by Buyer if the deed of trust to Seller is to be subordinate to Buyer's
184 New Loan (Buyer's New Senior Loan). If the Cash at Closing is less than as set forth in § 4.1 of this Contract or Buyer's New
185 Senior Loan changes from that approved by Seller, Seller shall have the Right to Terminate under § 25.1, at or before Closing. If
186 Seller disapproves of Buyer's financial ability, creditworthiness or Buyer's New Senior Loan, in Seller's sole subjective discretion,
187 Seller shall have the Right to Terminate under § 25.1, on or before **Disapproval of Buyer's Credit Information Deadline** (§ 3).

188     **5.4. Existing Loan Review.** If an existing loan is not to be released at Closing, Seller shall deliver copies of the loan
189 documents (including note, deed of trust, and any modifications) to Buyer by **Existing Loan Documents Deadline** (§ 3). For the
190 benefit of Buyer, this Contract is conditional upon Buyer's review and approval of the provisions of such loan documents. Buyer
191 shall have the Right to Terminate under § 25.1, on or before **Existing Loan Documents Objection Deadline** (§ 3), based on any
192 unsatisfactory provision of such loan documents, in Buyer's sole subjective discretion. If the lender's approval of a transfer of the
193 Property is required, this Contract is conditional upon Buyer's obtaining such approval without change in the terms of such loan,
194 except as set forth in § 4.6. If lender's approval is not obtained by **Loan Transfer Approval Deadline** (§ 3), this Contract shall
195 terminate on such deadline. Seller shall have the Right to Terminate under § 25.1, on or before Closing, in Seller's sole subjective
196 discretion, if Seller is to be released from liability under such existing loan and Buyer does not obtain such compliance as set forth
197 in § 4.6.

198 **6. APPRAISAL PROVISIONS.**

199     **6.1. Lender Property Requirements.** If the lender imposes any requirements or repairs (Requirements) to be made to
200 the Property (e.g., roof repair, repainting), beyond those matters already agreed to by Seller in this Contract, Seller shall have the
201 Right to Terminate under § 25.1, (notwithstanding § 10 of this Contract), on or before three days following Seller's receipt of the
202 Requirements, based on any unsatisfactory Requirements, in Seller's sole subjective discretion. Seller's Right to Terminate in this
203 § 6.1 shall not apply if, on or before any termination by Seller pursuant to this § 6.1: (1) the parties enter into a written agreement
204 regarding the Requirements; or (2) the Requirements have been completed; or (3) the satisfaction of the Requirements is waived in
205 writing by Buyer.

206     **6.2. Appraisal Condition.** The applicable Appraisal provision set forth below shall apply to the respective loan type set
207 forth in § 4.5.3, or if a cash transaction, i.e. no financing, § 6.2.1 shall apply.

208       **6.2.1. Conventional/Other.** Buyer shall have the sole option and election to terminate this Contract if the
209 Property's valuation is less than the Purchase Price determined by an appraiser engaged on behalf of _____.
210 The appraisal shall be received by Buyer or Buyer's lender on or before **Appraisal Deadline** (§ 3). Buyer shall have the Right to
211 Terminate under § 25.1, on or before **Appraisal Objection Deadline** (§ 3), if the Property's valuation is less than the Purchase
212 Price and Seller's receipt of either a copy of such appraisal or written notice from lender that confirms the Property's valuation is
213 less than the Purchase Price.

214       **6.2.2. FHA.** It is expressly agreed that, notwithstanding any other provisions of this Contract, the Purchaser
215 (Buyer) shall not be obligated to complete the purchase of the Property described herein or to incur any penalty by forfeiture of
216 Earnest Money deposits or otherwise unless the Purchaser (Buyer) has been given in accordance with HUD/FHA or VA
217 requirements a written statement issued by the Federal Housing Commissioner, Department of Veterans Affairs, or a Direct

218   Endorsement lender, setting forth the appraised value of the Property of not less than $\$$_____. The Purchaser (Buyer)
219   shall have the privilege and option of proceeding with the consummation of this Contract without regard to the amount of the
220   appraised valuation. The appraised valuation is arrived at to determine the maximum mortgage the Department of Housing and
221   Urban Development will insure. HUD does not warrant the value nor the condition of the Property. The Purchaser (Buyer) should
222   satisfy himself/herself that the price and condition of the Property are acceptable.

223          **6.2.3.**   **VA.** It is expressly agreed that, notwithstanding any other provisions of this Contract, the purchaser (Buyer)
224   shall not incur any penalty by forfeiture of Earnest Money or otherwise or be obligated to complete the purchase of the Property
225   described herein, if the Contract Purchase Price or cost exceeds the reasonable value of the Property established by the Department
226   of Veterans Affairs. The purchaser (Buyer) shall, however, have the privilege and option of proceeding with the consummation of
227   this Contract without regard to the amount of the reasonable value established by the Department of Veterans Affairs.

228          **6.3.**   **Cost of Appraisal.** Cost of any appraisal to be obtained after the date of this Contract shall be timely paid by
229   ☐ **Buyer** ☐ **Seller.**

230   **7.   EVIDENCE OF TITLE AND ASSOCIATION DOCUMENTS.**

231          **7.1.**   **Evidence of Title.** On or before **Record Title Deadline** (§ 3), Seller shall cause to be furnished to Buyer, at Seller's
232   expense, a current commitment for owner's title insurance policy (Title Commitment) in an amount equal to the Purchase Price, or
233   if this box is checked, ☐ **An Abstract** of title certified to a current date. If title insurance is furnished, Seller shall also deliver to
234   Buyer copies of any abstracts of title covering all or any portion of the Property (Abstract) in Seller's possession. At Seller's
235   expense, Seller shall cause the title insurance policy to be issued and delivered to Buyer as soon as practicable at or after Closing.
236   The title insurance commitment ☐ **Shall** ☐ **Shall Not** commit to delete or insure over the standard exceptions which relate to:
237   (1) parties in possession, (2) unrecorded easements, (3) survey matters, (4) unrecorded mechanics' liens, (5) gap period (effective
238   date of commitment to date deed is recorded), and (6) unpaid taxes, assessments and unredeemed tax sales prior to the year of
239   Closing. Any additional premium expense to obtain this additional coverage shall be paid by ☐ **Buyer** ☐ **Seller.**
240   **Note:** The title insurance company may not agree to delete or insure over any or all of the standard exceptions. Buyer shall have
241   the right to review the Title Commitment, its provisions and Title Documents (defined in § 7.2), and if not satisfactory to Buyer,
242   Buyer may exercise Buyer's rights pursuant to § 8.1.

243          **7.2.**   **Copies of Exceptions.** On or before **Record Title Deadline** (§ 3), Seller, at Seller's expense, shall furnish to Buyer
244   and _____, (1) copies of any plats, declarations, covenants, conditions and restrictions burdening
245   the Property, and (2) if a Title Commitment is required to be furnished, and if this box is checked ☐ **Copies of any Other**
246   **Documents** (or, if illegible, summaries of such documents) listed in the schedule of exceptions (Exceptions). Even if the box is not
247   checked, Seller shall have the obligation to furnish these documents pursuant to this section if requested by Buyer any time on or
248   before **Exceptions Request Deadline** (§ 3). This requirement shall pertain only to documents as shown of record in the office of
249   the clerk and recorder in the county where the Property is located. The Abstract or Title Commitment, together with any copies or
250   summaries of such documents furnished pursuant to this section, constitute the title documents (collectively, Title Documents).

251          **7.3.**   **Homeowners' Association Documents.** The term Association Documents consists of all owners' associations
252   (Association) declarations, bylaws, operating agreements, rules and regulations, party wall agreements, minutes of most recent
253   annual owners' meeting and minutes of any directors' or managers' meetings during the six-month period immediately preceding
254   the date of this Contract, if any (Governing Documents), most recent financial documents consisting of (1) annual balance sheet,
255   (2) annual income and expenditures statement, and (3) annual budget (Financial Documents), if any (collectively, Association
256   Documents).

257          **7.3.1.**   **Common Interest Community Disclosure. THE PROPERTY IS LOCATED WITHIN A COMMON**
258   **INTEREST COMMUNITY AND IS SUBJECT TO THE DECLARATION FOR SUCH COMMUNITY. THE OWNER**
259   **OF THE PROPERTY WILL BE REQUIRED TO BE A MEMBER OF THE OWNER'S ASSOCIATION FOR THE**
260   **COMMUNITY AND WILL BE SUBJECT TO THE BYLAWS AND RULES AND REGULATIONS OF THE**
261   **ASSOCIATION. THE DECLARATION, BYLAWS, AND RULES AND REGULATIONS WILL IMPOSE FINANCIAL**
262   **OBLIGATIONS UPON THE OWNER OF THE PROPERTY, INCLUDING AN OBLIGATION TO PAY**
263   **ASSESSMENTS OF THE ASSOCIATION. IF THE OWNER DOES NOT PAY THESE ASSESSMENTS, THE**
264   **ASSOCIATION COULD PLACE A LIEN ON THE PROPERTY AND POSSIBLY SELL IT TO PAY THE DEBT. THE**
265   **DECLARATION, BYLAWS, AND RULES AND REGULATIONS OF THE COMMUNITY MAY PROHIBIT THE**
266   **OWNER FROM MAKING CHANGES TO THE PROPERTY WITHOUT AN ARCHITECTURAL REVIEW BY THE**
267   **ASSOCIATION (OR A COMMITTEE OF THE ASSOCIATION) AND THE APPROVAL OF THE ASSOCIATION.**
268   **PURCHASERS OF PROPERTY WITHIN THE COMMON INTEREST COMMUNITY SHOULD INVESTIGATE THE**
269   **FINANCIAL OBLIGATIONS OF MEMBERS OF THE ASSOCIATION. PURCHASERS SHOULD CAREFULLY**
270   **READ THE DECLARATION FOR THE COMMUNITY AND THE BYLAWS AND RULES AND REGULATIONS OF**
271   **THE ASSOCIATION.**

272          **7.3.2.**   **Association Documents to Buyer.**
273   ☐          **7.3.2.1. Seller to Provide Association Documents.** Seller shall cause the Association Documents to be
274   provided to Buyer, at Seller's expense, on or before **Association Documents Deadline** (§ 3).

275   ☐     **7.3.2.2. Seller Authorizes Association.** Seller authorizes the Association to provide the Association
276 Documents to Buyer, at Seller's expense.
277         **7.3.2.3. Seller's Obligation.** Seller's obligation to provide the Association Documents shall be fulfilled
278 upon Buyer's receipt of the Association Documents, regardless of who provides such documents.
279 **Note:** If neither box in this § 7.3.2 is checked, the provisions of § 7.3.2.1 shall apply.
280       **7.3.3. Conditional on Buyer's Review.** If the box in either § 7.3.2.1 or § 7.3.2.2 is checked, the provisions of this
281 § 7.3.3 shall apply. Buyer shall have the Right to Terminate under § 25.1, on or before **Association Documents Objection**
282 **Deadline** (§ 3), based on any unsatisfactory provision in any of the Association Documents, in Buyer's sole subjective discretion.
283 Should Buyer receive the Association Documents after **Association Documents Deadline** (§ 3), Buyer, at Buyer's option, shall
284 have the Right to Terminate under § 25.1 by Buyer's Notice to Terminate received by Seller on or before ten days after Buyer's
285 receipt of the Association Documents. If Buyer does not receive the Association Documents, or if Buyer's Notice to Terminate
286 would otherwise be required to be received by Seller after **Closing Date** (§ 3), Buyer's Notice to Terminate shall be received by
287 Seller on or before three days prior to **Closing Date** (§ 3). If Seller does not receive Buyer's Notice to Terminate within such time,
288 Buyer accepts the provisions of the Association Documents as satisfactory, and Buyer waives any Right to Terminate under this
289 provision, notwithstanding the provisions of § 8.5.

290 **8. RECORD TITLE AND OFF-RECORD TITLE MATTERS.**
291     **8.1. Record Title Matters.** Buyer has the right to review and object to any of the Title Documents (Right to Object,
292 Resolution) as set forth in § 8.3. Buyer's objection may be based on any unsatisfactory form or content of Title Commitment,
293 notwithstanding § 13, or any other unsatisfactory title condition, in Buyer's sole subjective discretion. If Buyer objects to any of
294 the Title Documents, Buyer shall cause Seller to receive Buyer's Notice to Terminate or Notice of Title Objection on or before
295 **Record Title Objection Deadline** (§ 3). If Title Documents are not received by Buyer, on or before the **Record Title Deadline**
296 (§ 3), or if there is an endorsement to the Title Commitment that adds a new Exception to title, a copy of the new Exception to title
297 and the modified Title Commitment shall be delivered to Buyer. Buyer shall cause Seller to receive Buyer's Notice to Terminate
298 or Notice of Title Objection on or before ten days after receipt by Buyer of the following documents: (1) any required Title
299 Document not timely received by Buyer, (2) any change to the Title Documents, or (3) endorsement to the Title Commitment. If
300 Seller receives Buyer's Notice to Terminate or Notice of Title Objection, pursuant to this § 8.1 (Record Title Matters), any title
301 objection by Buyer and this Contract shall be governed by the provisions set forth in § 8.3 (Right to Object, Resolution). If Seller
302 does not receive Buyer's Notice to Terminate or Notice of Title Objection by the applicable deadline specified above, Buyer
303 accepts the condition of title as disclosed by the Title Documents as satisfactory.
304     **8.2. Off-Record Title Matters.** Seller shall deliver to Buyer, on or before **Off-Record Title Deadline** (§ 3), true copies
305 of all existing surveys in Seller's possession pertaining to the Property and shall disclose to Buyer all easements, liens (including,
306 without limitation, governmental improvements approved, but not yet installed) or other matters (including, without
307 limitation, rights of first refusal and options) not shown by public records, of which Seller has actual knowledge. Buyer shall have
308 the right to inspect the Property to investigate if any third party has any right in the Property not shown by public records (such as
309 an unrecorded easement, unrecorded lease, boundary line discrepancy or water rights). Buyer's Notice to Terminate or Notice of
310 Title Objection of any unsatisfactory condition (whether disclosed by Seller or revealed by such inspection, notwithstanding § 13),
311 in Buyer's sole subjective discretion, shall be received by Seller on or before **Off-Record Title Objection Deadline** (§ 3). If Seller
312 receives Buyer's Notice to Terminate or Notice of Title Objection pursuant to this § 8.2 (Off-Record Title Matters), any title
313 objection by Buyer and this Contract shall be governed by the provisions set forth in § 8.3 (Right to Object, Resolution). If Seller
314 does not receive Buyer's Notice to Terminate or Notice of Title Objection, on or before **Off-Record Title Objection Deadline**
315 (§ 3), Buyer accepts title subject to such rights, if any, of third parties of which Buyer has actual knowledge.
316     **8.3. Right to Object, Resolution.** Buyer's right to object to any title matters shall include, but not be limited to those
317 matters set forth in §§ 8.1 (Record Title Matters), 8.2 (Off-Record Title Matters) and 13 (Transfer of Title), in Buyer's sole
318 subjective discretion (collectively, Notice of Title Objection). If Buyer objects to any title matter, on or before the applicable
319 deadline, Buyer shall have the choice to either (1) object to the condition of title, or (2) terminate this Contract.
320       **8.3.1. Title Resolution.** If Seller receives Buyer's Notice of Title Objection, as provided in § 8.1 (Record Title
321 Matters) or § 8.2 (Off-Record Title Matters), on or before the applicable deadline, and if Buyer and Seller have not agreed to a
322 written settlement thereof on or before **Title Resolution Deadline** (§ 3), this Contract shall terminate on the expiration of **Title**
323 **Resolution Deadline** (§ 3), unless Seller receives Buyer's written withdrawal of Buyer's Notice of Title Objection (i.e., Buyer's
324 written notice to waive objection to such items and waives the Right to Terminate for that reason), on or before expiration of **Title**
325 **Resolution Deadline** (§ 3).
326       **8.3.2. Right to Terminate – Title Objection.** Buyer shall have the Right to Terminate under § 25.1, on or
327 before the applicable deadline, based on any unsatisfactory title matter, in Buyer's sole subjective discretion.
328     **8.4. Special Taxing Districts. SPECIAL TAXING DISTRICTS MAY BE SUBJECT TO GENERAL OBLIGATION**
329 **INDEBTEDNESS THAT IS PAID BY REVENUES PRODUCED FROM ANNUAL TAX LEVIES ON THE TAXABLE**
330 **PROPERTY WITHIN SUCH DISTRICTS. PROPERTY OWNERS IN SUCH DISTRICTS MAY BE PLACED AT RISK**
331 **FOR INCREASED MILL LEVIES AND TAX TO SUPPORT THE SERVICING OF SUCH DEBT WHERE**
332 **CIRCUMSTANCES ARISE RESULTING IN THE INABILITY OF SUCH A DISTRICT TO DISCHARGE SUCH**

333   INDEBTEDNESS WITHOUT SUCH AN INCREASE IN MILL LEVIES. BUYERS SHOULD INVESTIGATE THE
334   SPECIAL TAXING DISTRICTS IN WHICH THE PROPERTY IS LOCATED BY CONTACTING THE COUNTY
335   TREASURER, BY REVIEWING THE CERTIFICATE OF TAXES DUE FOR THE PROPERTY, AND BY OBTAINING
336   FURTHER INFORMATION FROM THE BOARD OF COUNTY COMMISSIONERS, THE COUNTY CLERK AND
337   RECORDER, OR THE COUNTY ASSESSOR.

338       Buyer shall have the Right to Terminate under § 25.1, on or before **Off-Record Title Objection Deadline** (§ 3), based on
339   any unsatisfactory effect of the Property being located within a special taxing district, in Buyer's sole subjective discretion.

340       **8.5.**    **Right of First Refusal or Contract Approval.** If there is a right of first refusal on the Property, or a right to
341   approve this Contract, Seller shall promptly submit this Contract according to the terms and conditions of such right. If the holder
342   of the right of first refusal exercises such right or the holder of a right to approve disapproves this Contract, this Contract shall
343   terminate. If the right of first refusal is waived explicitly or expires, or the Contract is approved, this Contract shall remain in full
344   force and effect. Seller shall promptly notify Buyer in writing of the foregoing. If expiration or waiver of the right of first refusal
345   or Contract approval has not occurred on or before **Right of First Refusal Deadline** (§ 3), this Contract shall then terminate.

346       **8.6.**    **Title Advisory.** The Title Documents affect the title, ownership and use of the Property and should be reviewed
347   carefully. Additionally, other matters not reflected in the Title Documents may affect the title, ownership and use of the Property,
348   including, without limitation, boundary lines and encroachments, area, zoning, unrecorded easements and claims of easements,
349   leases and other unrecorded agreements, and various laws and governmental regulations concerning land use, development and
350   environmental matters. **The surface estate may be owned separately from the underlying mineral estate, and transfer of the
351   surface estate does not necessarily include transfer of the mineral rights or water rights. Third parties may hold interests in
352   oil, gas, other minerals, geothermal energy or water on or under the Property, which interests may give them rights to
353   enter and use the Property.** Such matters may be excluded from or not covered by the title insurance policy. Buyer is advised to
354   timely consult legal counsel with respect to all such matters as there are strict time limits provided in this Contract [e.g., **Record
355   Title Objection Deadline** (§ 3) and **Off-Record Title Objection Deadline** (§ 3)].

356   **9.**    **CURRENT SURVEY REVIEW.**
357       **9.1.**    **Current Survey Conditions.** If the box in § 9.1.1 or § 9.1.2 is checked, Buyer, the issuer of the Title Commitment
358   or the provider of the opinion of title if an abstract, and _____ shall receive a Current Survey, i.e.,
359   Improvement Location Certificate, Improvement Survey Plat or other form of survey set forth in § 9.1.2 (collectively, Current
360   Survey), on or before **Current Survey Deadline** (§ 3). The Current Survey shall be certified by the surveyor to all those who are
361   to receive the Current Survey.

362   ☐    **9.1.1.**    **Improvement Location Certificate.** If the box in this § 9.1.1 is checked, ☐ **Seller** ☐ **Buyer** shall order
363   or provide, and pay, on or before Closing, the cost of an **Improvement Location Certificate**.

364   ☐    **9.1.2.**    **Other Survey.** If the box in this § 9.1.2 is checked, a Current Survey, other than an Improvement Location
365   Certificate, shall be an ☐ **Improvement Survey Plat** ☐ _____. The parties agree that payment of the cost of
366   the Current Survey and obligation to order or provide the Current Survey shall be as follows:

367
368
369

370       **9.2.**    **Survey Objection.** Buyer shall have the right to review and object to the Current Survey. Buyer shall have the Right
371   to Terminate under § 25.1, on or before the **Current Survey Objection Deadline** (§ 3), if the Current Survey is not timely
372   received by Buyer or based on any unsatisfactory matter with the Current Survey, notwithstanding § 8.2 or § 13.

373   | **DISCLOSURE, INSPECTION AND DUE DILIGENCE** |
   | --- |

374   **10.**    **PROPERTY DISCLOSURE, INSPECTION, INDEMNITY, INSURABILITY, DUE DILIGENCE, BUYER
375   DISCLOSURE AND SOURCE OF WATER.**

376       **10.1.**    **Seller's Property Disclosure Deadline.** On or before **Seller's Property Disclosure Deadline** (§ 3), Seller agrees to
377   deliver to Buyer the most current version of the applicable Colorado Real Estate Commission's Seller's Property Disclosure form
378   completed by Seller to Seller's actual knowledge, current as of the date of this Contract.

379       **10.2.**    **Inspection Objection Deadline.** Unless otherwise provided in this Contract, Buyer acknowledges that Seller is
380   conveying the Property to Buyer in an "as is" condition, "where is" and "with all faults". Seller shall disclose to Buyer, in writing,
381   any latent defects actually known by Seller. Buyer, acting in good faith, shall have the right to have inspections (by one or more
382   third parties, personally or both) of the Property and Inclusions (Inspection), at Buyer's expense. If (1) the physical condition of
383   the Property, including, but not limited to, the roof, walls, structural integrity of the Property, the electrical, plumbing, HVAC and
384   other mechanical systems of the Property, (2) the physical condition of the Inclusions, (3) service to the Property (including
385   utilities and communication services), systems and components of the Property, e.g. heating and plumbing, (4) any proposed or
386   existing transportation project, road, street or highway, or (5) any other activity, odor or noise (whether on or off the Property) and

387   its effect or expected effect on the Property or its occupants is unsatisfactory, in Buyer's sole subjective discretion, Buyer shall, on
388   or before **Inspection Objection Deadline** (§ 3):

    **10.2.1.   Notice to Terminate.** Notify Seller in writing that this Contract is terminated; or

    **10.2.2.   Inspection Objection.** Deliver to Seller a written description of any unsatisfactory physical condition that
Buyer requires Seller to correct.

    Buyer shall have the Right to Terminate under § 25.1, on or before **Inspection Objection Deadline** (§ 3), based on any
unsatisfactory physical condition of the Property or Inclusions, in Buyer's sole subjective discretion.

    **10.3.   Inspection Resolution Deadline.** If an Inspection Objection is received by Seller, on or before **Inspection
Objection Deadline** (§ 3), and if Buyer and Seller have not agreed in writing to a settlement thereof on or before **Inspection
Resolution Deadline** (§ 3), this Contract shall terminate on **Inspection Resolution Deadline** (§ 3), unless Seller receives Buyer's
written withdrawal of the Inspection Objection before such termination, i.e., on or before expiration of **Inspection Resolution
Deadline** (§ 3).

    **10.4.   Damage, Liens and Indemnity.** Buyer, except as otherwise provided in this Contract or other written agreement
between the parties, is responsible for payment for all inspections, tests, surveys, engineering reports, or any other work performed
at Buyer's request (Work) and shall pay for any damage that occurs to the Property and Inclusions as a result of such Work. Buyer
shall not permit claims or liens of any kind against the Property for Work performed on the Property at Buyer's request. Buyer
agrees to indemnify, protect and hold Seller harmless from and against any liability, damage, cost or expense incurred by Seller
and caused by any such Work, claim, or lien. This indemnity includes Seller's right to recover all costs and expenses incurred by
Seller to defend against any such liability, damage, cost or expense, or to enforce this section, including Seller's reasonable
attorney fees, legal fees and expenses. The provisions of this section shall survive the termination of this Contract.

    **10.5.   Insurability.** Buyer shall have the right to review and object to the availability, terms and conditions of and
premium for property insurance (Property Insurance). Buyer shall have the Right to Terminate under § 25.1, on or before **Property
Insurance Objection Deadline** (§ 3), based on any unsatisfactory provision of the Property Insurance, in Buyer's sole subjective
discretion.

    **10.6.   Due Diligence Documents.** Seller agrees to deliver copies of the following documents and information pertaining to
the Property (Due Diligence Documents) to Buyer on or before **Due Diligence Documents Delivery Deadline** (§ 3) to the extent
such Due Diligence Documents exist and are in Seller's possession:

    **10.6.1.** All current leases, including any amendments or other occupancy agreements, pertaining to the Property
(Leases).

    **10.6.2.** Other documents and information:

    **10.7.   Due Diligence Documents Conditions.** Buyer shall have the right to review and object to Due Diligence Documents,
in Buyer's sole subjective discretion, or Seller's failure to deliver to Buyer all Due Diligence Documents. Buyer shall also have the
unilateral right to waive any condition herein.

    **10.7.1.   Due Diligence Documents Objection.** Buyer shall have the Right to Terminate under § 25.1, on or before
**Due Diligence Documents Objection Deadline** (§ 3), based on any unsatisfactory matter with the Due Diligence Documents, in
Buyer's sole subjective discretion. If, however, Due Diligence Documents are not timely delivered under § 10.6, or if Seller fails
to deliver all Due Diligence Documents to Buyer, then Buyer shall have the Right to Terminate under § 25.1 on or before the
earlier of ten days after **Due Diligence Documents Objection Deadline** (§ 3) or Closing.

    **10.8.   Buyer Disclosure.** Buyer represents that Buyer ☐ **Does** ☐ **Does Not** need to sell and close a property to complete
this transaction.

**Note:** Any property sale contingency should appear in **Additional Provisions** (§ 30).

    **10.9.   Source of Potable Water (Residential Land and Residential Improvements Only).** Buyer ☐ **Does** ☐ **Does Not**
acknowledge receipt of a copy of Seller's Property Disclosure or Source of Water Addendum disclosing the source of potable water
for the Property. Buyer ☐ **Does** ☐ **Does Not** acknowledge receipt of a copy of the current well permit. ☐ There is **No Well**.

**Note to Buyer: SOME WATER PROVIDERS RELY, TO VARYING DEGREES, ON NONRENEWABLE GROUND
WATER. YOU MAY WISH TO CONTACT YOUR PROVIDER (OR INVESTIGATE THE DESCRIBED SOURCE) TO
DETERMINE THE LONG-TERM SUFFICIENCY OF THE PROVIDER'S WATER SUPPLIES.**

    **10.10.   Carbon Monoxide Alarms. Note:** If the improvements on the Property have a fuel-fired heater or appliance, a
fireplace, or an attached garage and include one or more rooms lawfully used for sleeping purposes (Bedroom), the parties
acknowledge that Colorado law requires that Seller assure the Property has an operational carbon monoxide alarm installed within
fifteen feet of the entrance to each Bedroom or in a location as required by the applicable building code.

    **10.11.   Lead-Based Paint.** Unless exempt, if the improvements on the Property include one or more residential dwellings
for which a building permit was issued prior to January 1, 1978, this Contract shall be void unless (1) a completed Lead-Based
Paint Disclosure (Sales) form is signed by Seller, the required real estate licensees and Buyer, and (2) Seller receives the

446 completed and fully executed form prior to the time when this Contract is signed by all parties. Buyer acknowledges timely receipt
447 of a completed Lead-Based Paint Disclosure (Sales) form signed by Seller and the real estate licensees.

448     **10.12.  Methamphetamine Disclosure.**  If Seller knows that methamphetamine was ever manufactured, processed, cooked,
449 disposed of, used or stored at the Property, Seller is required to disclose such fact. No disclosure is required if the Property was
450 remediated in accordance with state standards and other requirements are fulfilled pursuant to § 25-18.5-102, C.R.S. Buyer further
451 acknowledges that Buyer has the right to engage a certified hygienist or industrial hygienist to test whether the Property has ever
452 been used as a methamphetamine laboratory. Buyer shall have the Right to Terminate under § 25.1, upon Seller's receipt of
453 Buyer's written notice to terminate, notwithstanding any other provision of this Contract, based on Buyer's test results that indicate
454 the Property has been contaminated with methamphetamine, but has not been remediated to meet the standards established by rules
455 of the State Board of Health promulgated pursuant to § 25-18.5-102, C.R.S. Buyer shall promptly give written notice to Seller of
456 the results of the test.

457 **11.  COLORADO FORECLOSURE PROTECTION ACT.**  The Colorado Foreclosure Protection Act (Act) generally applies
458 if: (1) the Property is residential, (2) Seller resides in the Property as Seller's principal residence, (3) Buyer's purpose in purchase
459 of the Property is not to use the Property as Buyer's personal residence, and (4) the Property is in foreclosure or Buyer has notice
460 that any loan secured by the Property is at least thirty days delinquent or in default. If the transaction is a Short Sale transaction
461 and a Short Sale Addendum is part of this Contract, the Act does not apply. Each party is further advised to consult an attorney.

462
**CLOSING PROVISIONS**

463 **12.  CLOSING DOCUMENTS, INSTRUCTIONS AND CLOSING.**
464     **12.1.  Closing Documents and Closing Information.**  Seller and Buyer shall cooperate with the Closing Company to
465 enable the Closing Company to prepare and deliver documents required for Closing to Buyer and Seller and their designees. If
466 Buyer is obtaining a new loan to purchase the Property, Buyer acknowledges Buyer's lender shall be required to provide the
467 Closing Company in a timely manner all required loan documents and financial information concerning Buyer's new loan. Buyer
468 and Seller will furnish any additional information and documents required by Closing Company that will be necessary to complete
469 this transaction. Buyer and Seller shall sign and complete all customary or reasonably required documents at or before Closing.
470     **12.2.  Closing Instructions.**  Buyer and Seller agree to execute the Colorado Real Estate Commission's Closing Instructions.
471 Such Closing Instructions ☐ **Are** ☐ **Are Not** executed with this Contract. Upon mutual execution, ☐ **Seller** ☐ **Buyer** shall
472 deliver such Closing Instructions to the Closing Company.
473     **12.3.  Closing.**  Delivery of deed from Seller to Buyer shall be at closing (Closing). Closing shall be on the date specified
474 as the **Closing Date** (§ 3) or by mutual agreement at an earlier date. The hour and place of Closing shall be as designated
475 by_____.
476     **12.4.  Disclosure of Settlement Costs.**  Buyer and Seller acknowledge that costs, quality, and extent of service vary
477 between different settlement service providers (e.g., attorneys, lenders, inspectors and title companies).

478 **13.  TRANSFER OF TITLE.**  Subject to tender of payment at Closing as required herein and compliance by Buyer with the
479 other terms and provisions hereof, Seller shall execute and deliver a good and sufficient _____ deed
480 to Buyer, at Closing, conveying the Property free and clear of all taxes except the general taxes for the year of Closing. Except as
481 provided herein, title shall be conveyed free and clear of all liens, including any governmental liens for special improvements
482 installed as of the date of Buyer's signature hereon, whether assessed or not. Title shall be conveyed subject to:
483     **13.1.**  Those specific Exceptions described by reference to recorded documents as reflected in the Title Documents
484 accepted by Buyer in accordance with **Record Title Matters** (§ 8.1),
485     **13.2.**  Distribution utility easements (including cable TV),
486     **13.3.**  Those specifically described rights of third parties not shown by the public records of which Buyer has actual
487 knowledge and which were accepted by Buyer in accordance with **Off-Record Title Matters** (§ 8.2) and **Current Survey Review**
488 (§ 9),
489     **13.4.**  Inclusion of the Property within any special taxing district, and
490     **13.5.**  Other_____.

491 **14.  PAYMENT OF ENCUMBRANCES.**  Any encumbrance required to be paid shall be paid at or before Closing from the
492 proceeds of this transaction or from any other source.

493 **15.  CLOSING COSTS, CLOSING FEE, ASSOCIATION FEES AND TAXES.**
494     **15.1.  Closing Costs.**  Buyer and Seller shall pay, in Good Funds, their respective closing costs and all other items required
495 to be paid at Closing, except as otherwise provided herein.
496     **15.2.  Closing Services Fee.**  The fee for real estate closing services shall be paid at Closing by ☐ **Buyer** ☐ **Seller**
497 ☐ **One-Half by Buyer and One-Half by Seller** ☐ **Other**_____.

498    **15.3.   Status Letter and Transfer Fees.** Any fees incident to the issuance of Association's statement of assessments
499    (Status Letter) shall be paid by ☐ **Buyer** ☐ **Seller** ☐ **One-Half by Buyer and One-Half by Seller** ☐ **None.** Any transfer
500    fees assessed by the Association including, but not limited to, any record change fee, regardless of name or title of such fee
501    (Association's Transfer Fee) shall be paid by ☐ **Buyer** ☐ **Seller** ☐ **One-Half by Buyer and One-Half by Seller** ☐ **None.**
502    **15.4.   Local Transfer Tax.** ☐ **The Local Transfer Tax** of _____% of the Purchase Price shall be paid at Closing by
503    ☐ **Buyer** ☐ **Seller** ☐ **One-Half by Buyer and One-Half by Seller** ☐ **None.**
504    **15.5.   Private Transfer Fee.** Private transfer fees and other fees due to a transfer of the Property, payable at Closing, such
505    as community association fees, developer fees and foundation fees, shall be paid at Closing by ☐ **Buyer** ☐ **Seller** ☐ **One-Half**
506    **by Buyer and One-Half by Seller** ☐ **None.**
507    **15.6.   Sales and Use Tax.** Any sales and use tax that may accrue because of this transaction shall be paid when due by
508    ☐ **Buyer** ☐ **Seller** ☐ **One-Half by Buyer and One-Half by Seller** ☐ **None.**

509    **16.   PRORATIONS.** The following shall be prorated to **Closing Date** (§ 3), except as otherwise provided:
510    **16.1.   Taxes.** Personal property taxes, if any, special taxing district assessments, if any, and general real estate taxes for the
511    year of Closing, based on ☐ **Taxes for the Calendar Year Immediately Preceding Closing** ☐ **Most Recent Mill Levy and**
512    **Most Recent Assessed Valuation**, adjusted by any applicable qualifying seniors property tax exemption, or ☐ **Other** _____.
513    **16.2.   Rents.** Rents based on ☐ **Rents Actually Received** ☐ **Accrued.** At Closing, Seller shall transfer or credit to
514    Buyer the security deposits for all Leases assigned, or any remainder after lawful deductions, and notify all tenants in writing of
515    such transfer and of the transferee's name and address. Seller shall assign to Buyer all Leases in effect at Closing and Buyer shall
516    assume Seller's obligations under such Leases.
517    **16.3.   Association Assessments.** Current regular Association assessments and dues (Association Assessments) paid in
518    advance shall be credited to Seller at Closing. Cash reserves held out of the regular Association Assessments for deferred
519    maintenance by the Association shall not be credited to Seller except as may be otherwise provided by the Governing Documents.
520    Buyer acknowledges that Buyer may be obligated to pay the Association, at Closing, an amount for reserves or working capital.
521    Any special assessment assessed prior to **Closing Date** (§ 3) by the Association shall be the obligation of ☐ **Buyer** ☐ **Seller.**
522    Except however, any special assessment by the Association for improvements that have been installed as of the date of Buyer's
523    signature hereon, whether assessed prior to or after Closing, shall be the obligation of Seller. Seller represents that the Association
524    Assessments are currently payable at $_____ per _____ and that there are no unpaid regular or special
525    assessments against the Property except the current regular assessments and _____. Such
526    assessments are subject to change as provided in the Governing Documents. Seller agrees to promptly request the Association to
527    deliver to Buyer before **Closing Date** (§ 3) a current Status Letter.
528    **16.4.   Other Prorations.** Water and sewer charges, interest on continuing loan, and _____.
529    **16.5.   Final Settlement.** Unless otherwise agreed in writing, these prorations shall be final.

530    **17.   POSSESSION.** Possession of the Property shall be delivered to Buyer on **Possession Date** (§ 3) at **Possession Time** (§ 3),
531    subject to the following Leases or tenancies:
532
533
534    If Seller, after Closing, fails to deliver possession as specified, Seller shall be subject to eviction and shall be additionally
535    liable to Buyer for payment of $_____ per day (or any part of a day notwithstanding § 18.1) from **Possession Date**
536    (§ 3) and **Possession Time** (§ 3) until possession is delivered.
537    Buyer ☐ **Does** ☐ **Does Not** represent that Buyer will occupy the Property as Buyer's principal residence.

538    
┌─────────────────────────────┐
│     **GENERAL PROVISIONS**      │
└─────────────────────────────┘

539    **18.   DAY; COMPUTATION OF PERIOD OF DAYS, DEADLINE.**
540    **18.1.   Day.** As used in this Contract, the term "day" shall mean the entire day ending at 11:59 p.m., United States
541    Mountain Time (Standard or Daylight Savings as applicable).
542    **18.2.   Computation of Period of Days, Deadline.** In computing a period of days, when the ending date is not specified,
543    the first day is excluded and the last day is included, e.g., three days after MEC. If any deadline falls on a Saturday, Sunday or
544    federal or Colorado state holiday (Holiday), such deadline ☐ **Shall** ☐ **Shall Not** be extended to the next day that is not a
545    Saturday, Sunday or Holiday. Should neither box be checked, the deadline shall not be extended.

546    **19.   CAUSES OF LOSS, INSURANCE; CONDITION OF, DAMAGE TO PROPERTY AND INCLUSIONS AND**
547    **WALK-THROUGH.** Except as otherwise provided in this Contract, the Property, Inclusions or both shall be delivered in the
548    condition existing as of the date of this Contract, ordinary wear and tear excepted.
549    **19.1.   Causes of Loss, Insurance.** In the event the Property or Inclusions are damaged by fire, other perils or causes of
550    loss prior to Closing in an amount of not more than ten percent of the total Purchase Price (Property Damage), Seller shall be

551 obligated to repair the same before **Closing Date** (§ 3). In the event such damage is not repaired within said time or if the damage
552 exceeds such sum, this Contract may be terminated at the option of Buyer. Buyer shall have the Right to Terminate under § 25.1,
553 on or before **Closing Date** (§ 3), based on any Property Damage not repaired before **Closing Date** (§ 3). Should Buyer elect to
554 carry out this Contract despite such Property Damage, Buyer shall be entitled to a credit at Closing for all insurance proceeds that
555 were received by Seller (but not the Association, if any) resulting from such damage to the Property and Inclusions, plus the
556 amount of any deductible provided for in such insurance policy. Such credit shall not exceed the Purchase Price. In the event Seller
557 has not received such insurance proceeds prior to Closing, the parties may agree to extend the **Closing Date** (§ 3) or, at the option
558 of Buyer, Seller shall assign such proceeds at Closing, plus credit Buyer the amount of any deductible provided for in such
559 insurance policy, but not to exceed the total Purchase Price.
560     **19.2. Damage, Inclusions and Services.** Should any Inclusion or service (including utilities and communication
561 services), systems and components of the Property, e.g., heating or plumbing, fail or be damaged between the date of this Contract
562 and Closing or possession, whichever shall be earlier, then Seller shall be liable for the repair or replacement of such Inclusion,
563 service, system, component or fixture of the Property with a unit of similar size, age and quality, or an equivalent credit, but only
564 to the extent that the maintenance or replacement of such Inclusion, service, system, component or fixture is not the responsibility
565 of the Association, if any, less any insurance proceeds received by Buyer covering such repair or replacement. Seller and Buyer
566 are aware of the existence of pre-owned home warranty programs that may be purchased and may cover the repair or replacement
567 of such Inclusions.
568     **19.3. Condemnation.** In the event Seller receives actual notice prior to Closing that a pending condemnation action may
569 result in a taking of all or part of the Property or Inclusions, Seller shall promptly notify Buyer, in writing, of such condemnation
570 action. Buyer shall have the Right to Terminate under § 25.1, on or before **Closing Date** (§ 3), based on such condemnation action,
571 in Buyer's sole subjective discretion. Should Buyer elect to consummate this Contract despite such diminution of value to the
572 Property and Inclusions, Buyer shall be entitled to a credit at Closing for all condemnation proceeds awarded to Seller for the
573 diminution in the value of the Property or Inclusions but such credit shall not include relocation benefits or expenses, or exceed the
574 Purchase Price.
575     **19.4. Walk-Through and Verification of Condition.** Buyer, upon reasonable notice, shall have the right to walk through
576 the Property prior to Closing to verify that the physical condition of the Property and Inclusions complies with this Contract.

577 **20. RECOMMENDATION OF LEGAL AND TAX COUNSEL.** By signing this document, Buyer and Seller acknowledge
578 that the respective broker has advised that this document has important legal consequences and has recommended the examination
579 of title and consultation with legal and tax or other counsel before signing this Contract.

580 **21. TIME OF ESSENCE, DEFAULT AND REMEDIES.** Time is of the essence hereof. If any note or check received as
581 Earnest Money hereunder or any other payment due hereunder is not paid, honored or tendered when due, or if any obligation
582 hereunder is not performed or waived as herein provided, there shall be the following remedies:
583     **21.1. If Buyer is in Default:**
584 ☐     **21.1.1. Specific Performance.** Seller may elect to treat this Contract as canceled, in which case all Earnest Money
585 (whether or not paid by Buyer) shall be paid to Seller and retained by Seller; and Seller may recover such damages as may be
586 proper; or Seller may elect to treat this Contract as being in full force and effect and Seller shall have the right to specific
587 performance or damages, or both.
588     **21.1.2. Liquidated Damages, Applicable. This § 21.1.2 shall apply <u>unless the box in § 21.1.1. is checked</u>.** All
589 Earnest Money (whether or not paid by Buyer) shall be paid to Seller, and retained by Seller. Both parties shall thereafter be
590 released from all obligations hereunder. It is agreed that the Earnest Money specified in § 4.1 is LIQUIDATED DAMAGES, and
591 not a penalty, which amount the parties agree is fair and reasonable and (except as provided in §§ 10.4, 22, 23 and 24), said
592 payment of Earnest Money shall be SELLER'S SOLE AND ONLY REMEDY for Buyer's failure to perform the obligations of
593 this Contract. Seller expressly waives the remedies of specific performance and additional damages.
594     **21.2. If Seller is in Default:** Buyer may elect to treat this Contract as canceled, in which case all Earnest Money received
595 hereunder shall be returned and Buyer may recover such damages as may be proper, or Buyer may elect to treat this Contract as
596 being in full force and effect and Buyer shall have the right to specific performance or damages, or both.

597 **22. LEGAL FEES, COST AND EXPENSES.** Anything to the contrary herein notwithstanding, in the event of any arbitration
598 or litigation relating to this Contract, prior to or after **Closing Date** (§ 3), the arbitrator or court shall award to the prevailing party
599 all reasonable costs and expenses, including attorney fees, legal fees and expenses.

600 **23. MEDIATION.** If a dispute arises relating to this Contract, prior to or after Closing, and is not resolved, the parties shall first
601 proceed in good faith to submit the matter to mediation. Mediation is a process in which the parties meet with an impartial person
602 who helps to resolve the dispute informally and confidentially. Mediators cannot impose binding decisions. The parties to the
603 dispute must agree, in writing, before any settlement is binding. The parties will jointly appoint an acceptable mediator and will
604 share equally in the cost of such mediation. The mediation, unless otherwise agreed, shall terminate in the event the entire dispute

605 is not resolved within thirty days of the date written notice requesting mediation is delivered by one party to the other at the party's
606 last known address. This section shall not alter any date in this Contract, unless otherwise agreed.

607 **24. EARNEST MONEY DISPUTE.** Except as otherwise provided herein, Earnest Money Holder shall release the Earnest
608 Money as directed by written mutual instructions, signed by both Buyer and Seller. In the event of any controversy regarding the
609 Earnest Money (notwithstanding any termination of this Contract), Earnest Money Holder shall not be required to take any action.
610 Earnest Money Holder, at its option and sole subjective discretion, may (1) await any proceeding, (2) interplead all parties and
611 deposit Earnest Money into a court of competent jurisdiction and shall recover court costs and reasonable attorney and legal fees,
612 or (3) provide notice to Buyer and Seller that unless Earnest Money Holder receives a copy of the Summons and Complaint or
613 Claim (between Buyer and Seller) containing the case number of the lawsuit (Lawsuit) within one hundred twenty days of Earnest
614 Money Holder's notice to the parties, Earnest Money Holder shall be authorized to return the Earnest Money to Buyer. In the event
615 Earnest Money Holder does receive a copy of the Lawsuit, and has not interpled the monies at the time of any Order, Earnest
616 Money Holder shall disburse the Earnest Money pursuant to the Order of the Court. The parties reaffirm the obligation of
617 **Mediation** (§ 23). The provisions of this § 24 apply only if the Earnest Money Holder is one of the Brokerage Firms named in
618 § 33 or § 34.

619 **25. TERMINATION.**
620     **25.1. Right to Terminate.** If a party has a right to terminate, as provided in this Contract (Right to Terminate), the
621 termination shall be effective upon the other party's receipt of a written notice to terminate (Notice to Terminate), provided such
622 written notice was received on or before the applicable deadline specified in this Contract. If the Notice to Terminate is not
623 received on or before the specified deadline, the party with the Right to Terminate shall have accepted the specified matter,
624 document or condition as satisfactory and waived the Right to Terminate under such provision.
625     **25.2. Effect of Termination.** In the event this Contract is terminated, all Earnest Money received hereunder shall be
626 returned and the parties shall be relieved of all obligations hereunder, subject to §§ 10.4, 22, 23 and 24.

627 **26. ENTIRE AGREEMENT, MODIFICATION, SURVIVAL.** This Contract, its exhibits and specified addenda, constitute
628 the entire agreement between the parties relating to the subject hereof, and any prior agreements pertaining thereto, whether oral or
629 written, have been merged and integrated into this Contract. No subsequent modification of any of the terms of this Contract shall
630 be valid, binding upon the parties, or enforceable unless made in writing and signed by the parties. Any obligation in this Contract
631 that, by its terms, is intended to be performed after termination or Closing shall survive the same.

632 **27. NOTICE, DELIVERY, AND CHOICE OF LAW.**
633     **27.1. Physical Delivery.** All notices must be in writing, except as provided in § 27.2. Any document, including a signed
634 document or notice, from or on behalf of Seller, and delivered to Buyer shall be effective when physically received by Buyer, any
635 signatory on behalf of Buyer, any named individual of Buyer, any representative of Buyer, or Brokerage Firm of Broker working
636 with Buyer (except for delivery, after Closing, of the notice requesting mediation described in § 23) and except as provided in
637 § 27.2. Any document, including a signed document or notice, from or on behalf of Buyer, and delivered to Seller shall be
638 effective when physically received by Seller, any signatory on behalf of Seller, any named individual of Seller, any representative
639 of Seller, or Brokerage Firm of Broker working with Seller (except for delivery, after Closing, of the notice requesting mediation
640 described in § 23) and except as provided in § 27.2.
641     **27.2. Electronic Delivery.** As an alternative to physical delivery, any document, including any signed document or
642 written notice, may be delivered in electronic form only by the following indicated methods: ☐ **Facsimile** ☐ **Email** ☐ **Internet**
643 ☐ **No Electronic Delivery**. If the box "No Electronic Delivery" is checked, this § 27.2 shall not be applicable and § 27.1 shall
644 govern notice and delivery. Documents with original signatures shall be provided upon request of any party.
645     **27.3. Choice of Law.** This Contract and all disputes arising hereunder shall be governed by and construed in accordance
646 with the laws of the State of Colorado that would be applicable to Colorado residents who sign a contract in Colorado for property
647 located in Colorado.

648 **28. NOTICE OF ACCEPTANCE, COUNTERPARTS.** This proposal shall expire unless accepted in writing, by Buyer and
649 Seller, as evidenced by their signatures below, and the offering party receives notice of such acceptance pursuant to § 27 on or
650 before **Acceptance Deadline Date** (§ 3) and **Acceptance Deadline Time** (§ 3). If accepted, this document shall become a contract
651 between Seller and Buyer. A copy of this document may be executed by each party, separately, and when each party has executed
652 a copy thereof, such copies taken together shall be deemed to be a full and complete contract between the parties.

653 **29. GOOD FAITH.** Buyer and Seller acknowledge that each party has an obligation to act in good faith including, but not
654 limited to, exercising the rights and obligations set forth in the provisions of **Financing Conditions and Obligations** (§ 5),
655 **Record Title and Off-Record Title Matters** (§ 8), **Current Survey Review** (§ 9) and **Property Disclosure, Inspection,**
656 **Indemnity, Insurability, Due Diligence, Buyer Disclosure and Source of Water** (§ 10).

---

| | |
|---|---|

**ADDITIONAL PROVISIONS AND ATTACHMENTS**

657

**30. ADDITIONAL PROVISIONS.** (The following additional provisions have not been approved by the Colorado Real Estate Commission.)

658
659
660
661
662
663

**31. ATTACHMENTS.** The following are a part of this Contract:

664
665
666
667

668 **Note:** The following disclosure forms **are attached** but are **not** a part of this Contract:
669
670
671

672

**SIGNATURES**

673

Buyer's Name: _____    Buyer's Name: _____

Buyer's Signature _____ Date ____    Buyer's Signature _____ Date ____

Address: _____    Address: _____

Phone No.: _____    Phone No.: _____
Fax No.: _____    Fax No.: _____
Electronic Address: _____    Electronic Address: _____

674 **[NOTE: If this offer is being countered or rejected, do not sign this document. Refer to § 32]**

Seller's Name: _____    Seller's Name: _____

Seller's Signature _____ Date ____    Seller's Signature _____ Date ____

Address: _____    Address: _____

Phone No.: _____    Phone No.: _____
Fax No.: _____    Fax No.: _____
Electronic Address: _____    Electronic Address: _____

675

676 **32. COUNTER; REJECTION.** This offer is ☐ **Countered** ☐ **Rejected**.
677 **Initials only of party (Buyer or Seller) who countered or rejected offer** _____

678

**END OF CONTRACT TO BUY AND SELL REAL ESTATE**

**33. BROKER'S ACKNOWLEDGMENTS AND COMPENSATION DISCLOSURE.**
(To be completed by Broker working with Buyer)

Broker ☐ **Does** ☐ **Does Not** acknowledge receipt of Earnest Money deposit and, while not a party to the Contract, agrees to cooperate upon request with any mediation concluded under § 23. Broker agrees that if Brokerage Firm is the Earnest Money Holder and, except as provided in § 24, if the Earnest Money has not already been returned following receipt of a Notice to Terminate or other written notice of termination, Earnest Money Holder shall release the Earnest Money as directed by the written mutual instructions. Such release of Earnest Money shall be made within five days of Earnest Money Holder's receipt of the executed written mutual instructions, provided the Earnest Money check has cleared. Broker agrees that if Earnest Money Holder is other than the Brokerage Firm identified in § 33 or § 34, Closing Instructions signed by Buyer, Seller, and Earnest Money Holder must be obtained on or before delivery of Earnest Money to Earnest Money Holder.

Broker is working with Buyer as a ☐ **Buyer's Agent** ☐ **Seller's Agent** ☐ **Transaction-Broker** in this transaction.
☐ This is a **Change of Status**.

Brokerage Firm's compensation or commission is to be paid by ☐ **Listing Brokerage Firm** ☐ **Buyer** ☐ **Other** _____.

Brokerage Firm's Name: _____
Broker's Name: _____

_____
Broker's Signature                              Date

Address: _____
_____
Phone No.: _____
Fax No.: _____
Electronic Address: _____

## 34. BROKER'S ACKNOWLEDGMENTS AND COMPENSATION DISCLOSURE.
(To be completed by Broker working with Seller)

Broker ☐ **Does** ☐ **Does Not** acknowledge receipt of Earnest Money deposit and, while not a party to the Contract, agrees to cooperate upon request with any mediation concluded under § 23. Broker agrees that if Brokerage Firm is the Earnest Money Holder and, except as provided in § 24, if the Earnest Money has not already been returned following receipt of a Notice to Terminate or other written notice of termination, Earnest Money Holder shall release the Earnest Money as directed by the written mutual instructions. Such release of Earnest Money shall be made within five days of Earnest Money Holder's receipt of the executed written mutual instructions, provided the Earnest Money check has cleared. Broker agrees that if Earnest Money Holder is other than the Brokerage Firm identified in § 33 or § 34, Closing Instructions signed by Buyer, Seller, and Earnest Money Holder must be obtained on or before delivery of Earnest Money to Earnest Money Holder.

Broker is working with Seller as a ☐ **Seller's Agent** ☐ **Buyer's Agent** ☐ **Transaction-Broker** in this transaction.
☐ This is a **Change of Status**.

Brokerage Firm's compensation or commission is to be paid by ☐ **Seller** ☐ **Buyer** ☐ **Other** _____.

Brokerage Firm's Name: _____
Broker's Name: _____

_____
Broker's Signature                              Date

Address: _____
_____
Phone No.: _____
Fax No.: _____
Electronic Address: _____

679

# FORM 8 – FEE SIMPLE ABSOLUTE DEED TEMPLATE

Prepared by:

        , Esquire

Return to:

        , Esquire


County Parcel Number:
Fee Simple Deed

THIS INDENTURE, MADE this          day of          20 ,

BETWEEN

        (hereinafter called the Grantor),


        (hereinafter called the Grantee),

WITNESSETH That the said Grantors for and in consideration of the sum of
        ($.00) Dollars
lawful money of the United States of America, unto them well and truly paid by
the Grantee(s), at or before the sealing and delivery hereof, the receipt whereof is
hereby acknowledged, hath granted, bargained and sold, released and confirmed,
and by these presents doth grant, bargain and sell, release and confirm unto the
said Grantee(s), (His), (Her),(their) heirs and assigns.

**ALL THAT CERTAIN** tract of land with the buildings and improvements
thereon erected **SITUATE** in:

**BEGINNING.**

**BEING** known as,

**BEING County Parcel Number.**

BEING the same premises which         , conveyed,
by deed dated, and recorded in the Recorder of Deeds of         ,
Book page on, , to.

TOGETHER with all land singular the buildings, improvements, ways, streets,
alleys, driveways, passages, water, water-courses, rights, liberties, privileges, hereditaments and appurtenances, whatsoever unto the hereby granted premises belonging
or in any wise appertaining, and the reversions and remainders, rents, issues, and
profits thereof; and all the estate, right, title, interest, property, claim and demand
whatsoever of the said Grantor, as well at law as in equity, of, in and to the same.

TO HAVE AND TO HOLD the said lot or piece of ground above described with
the buildings and improvements thereon erected, hereditaments and premises
hereby granted, or mentioned and intended so to be, with the appurtenances,

unto the said Grantees, their heirs and assigns, to and for the only proper use and behoof of the said Grantees, their heirs and assigns forever.

AND the said Grantor, for herself, her heirs and assigns does, by these presents, covenant, grant and agree to and with the said Grantees, their heirs and assigns, that she he said Grantor, her heirs and assigns all and singular the hereditaments and premises herein above described and granted or mentioned and intended so to be with the appurtenances, unto the said Grantees, their heirs and assigns against her, the said Grantor, her heirs and assigns and against all and every person or persons whomsoever lawfully claiming the same or any part thereof, by, from or under him, her, them, or any of them shall and will by these presents WARRANT and forever DEFEND.

IN WITNESS WHEREOF, The said Grantor has caused these presents to be duly executed the day and year first herein above written.

SEALED AND DELIVERED
IN THE PRESENCE OF US:

_____          _____(SEAL)
Witness

_____          _____(SEAL)
Witness

STATE OF

COUNTY OF

On this, the          day of          20  , before me, the under-signed officer, personally appeared          , known to me (or satisfactorily proven) to be the person whose name is subscribed to the within instrument, and acknowledged that he executed the same for the purposes therein contained.

IN WITNESS WHEREOF, I hereunto set my hand and official seal.

_____

NOTARY PUBLIC

The address of the above-named Grantees is

_____

On behalf of the Grantee

# FORM 9 – FEE SIMPLE ABSOLUTE DEED

Prepared by:
Charles Hart, Esquire
138 N. State Street
Newtowne, YS

Return to:
Charles Hart, Esquire
138 N. State Street
Newtowne, YS

CPN: 55-24-157

Fee Simple Deed

**THIS INDENTURE**, MADE this day of 201 ,

| | |
|---|---|
| **BETWEEN** | MOLLY TAYLOR<br>(hereinafter called the grantor), |
| | AND |
| | DANIEL SCHAN<br>(hereinafter called the grantee), |

**WITNESSETH** That the said Grantor for and in consideration of the sum of THREE HUNDRED AND EIGHT THOUSAND ($308,000.00) Dollars lawful money of the United States of America, unto her well and truly paid by the Grantee, at or before the sealing and delivery hereof, the receipt whereof is hereby acknowledged, hath granted, bargained and sold, released and confirmed, and by these presents doth grant, bargain and sell, release and confirm unto the said Grantee, his heirs and assigns, in fee.

ALL THAT PARCEL OF LAND IN THE TOWNSHIP OF NEWTOWNE, AS MORE FULLY DESCRIBED IN DEED BOOK 1673, PAGE 0949, ID# 55-24-157, BEING KNOWN AND DESIGNATED AS:

BEGINNING AT A POINT ON THE NORTHWESTERLY SIDE OF JEFFERSON STREET(50 FEET WIDE), A CORNER OF LOT #166 ON AFOREMENTIONED PLAN, SAID POINT BEING MEASURED THE FOUR FOLLOWING COURSES AND DISTANCES FROM A POINT OF CURVE ON THE NORTHEASTERLY SIDE OF LIBERTY STREET (60 FEET WIDE), (1) LEAVING SAID SIDE OF LIBERTY STREET ON THE ARC OF A CIRCLE CURVING TO THE LEFT, NORTHEASTWARDLY, HAVING A RADIUS OF 20.00 FEET THE ARC DISTANCE OF 31.42 FEET TO A POINT OF TANGENT ON AFORESAID SIDE OF JEFFERSON STREET, (2) ALONG SAID SIDE OF JEFFERSON STREET NORTH 19 DEGREES 40 MINUTES 45 SECONDS EAST 61.90 FEET TO A POINT OF CURVE, (3) ON THE ARC OF A CIRCLE CURVING TO THE RIGHT, NORTHEASTWARDLY, HAVING A RADIUS OF 175.00 FEET THE ARC

DISTANCE OF 176.77 FEET TO A POINT OF TANGENT AND (4) NORTH 77 DEGREES 33 MINUTES 15 SECONDS EAST 284.34 FEET TO POINT OF BEGINNING.
BEING LOT #489.

BEING THE SAME PREMISES WHICH FELIX J. KNOWLES AND ANNA F. KNOWLES BY DEED DATED SEPTEMBER 11, 1968, AND RECORDED AT DEED BOOK 1673 PAGE 0949 CONVEYED UNTO ROBERT J. TAYLOR AND MOLLY TAYLOR, IN FEE.

AND THE SAID ROBERT J. TAYLOR DEPARTED THIS LIFE ON

**TOGETHER** with all land singular the buildings, improvements, ways, streets, alleys, driveways, passages, water, water-courses, rights, liberties, privileges, hereditaments and appurtenances, whatsoever unto the hereby granted premises belonging or in any wise appertaining, and the reversions and remainders, rents, issues, and profits thereof; and all the estate, right, title, interest, property, claim and demand whatsoever of the said Grantor, as well at law as in equity, of, in and to the same.

**TO HAVE AND TO HOLD** the said lot or piece of ground above described with the buildings and improvements thereon erected, hereditaments and premises hereby granted, or mentioned and intended so to be, with the appurtenances, unto the said Grantee, his heirs and assigns, to and for the only proper use and behoof of the said Grantee, his heirs and assigns forever.

AND the said Grantor, for herself, her heirs and assigns do , by these presents, covenant, grant and agree to and with the said Grantee, his heirs and assigns, that she the said Grantor, her heirs and assigns all and singular the hereditaments and premises herein above described and granted or mentioned and intended so to be with the appurtenances, unto the said Grantee, his heirs and assigns against her, the said Grantor, her heirs and assigns and against all and every person or persons whomsoever lawfully claiming the same or any part thereof, by, from or under him, her, them, or any of them shall and will by these presents WARRANT and forever DEFEND.

**IN WITNESS WHEREOF,** The said Grantor has caused these presents to be duly executed the day and year first herein above written.

SEALED AND DELIVERED
IN THE PRESENCE OF US:

_____          _____ (SEAL)
                                        MOLLY TAYLOR

STATE OF

COUNTY OF

On this, the _____ day of 201_, before me, the undersigned officer, personally appeared MOLLY TAYLOR, known to me (or satisfactorily proven) to be the person whose name is subscribed to the within instrument, and acknowledged that he executed the same for the purposes therein contained.

IN WITNESS WHEREOF, I hereunto set my hand and official seal.

_____

NOTARY PUBLIC

The address of the above-named Grantee is:
489 Jefferson Street
Newtowne, YS

_____

On behalf of the Grantee

## FORM 10 – LAWYER'S HOURLY FEE AGREEMENT FOR REAL ESTATE PURCHASE

April 15, 2013

Mr. & Mrs. Daniel Schan
12 Centre Street New Towne,
Your State 99999

Re:     Real Estate Purchase
        4890 Jefferson Street

Dear Mr. & Mrs. Schan:

Pursuant to our initial client conference of April 12, 2013, I have agreed to represent you in connection with your real estate purchase of 4890 Jefferson Street, New Towne.

I want to thank you for placing your trust in me and selecting my law firm to represent you in this matter.

I also wish to set forth our agreement as to payment of legal fees and costs. My fees for legal services are $200.00 per hour. In addition you will be responsible for any costs or expenses that may be incurred, such as filing fees, copying costs, postage, and related expenses. You will be billed on a monthly basis depending upon the amount of work that was done on your file during that period of time. At this point in the case, it is difficult to estimate the amount of time and expense that will be necessary to adequately represent you in this case.

This agreement is limited to matters related to the purchase of real estate. It is not intended to cover representation in the event of litigation. Should a dispute arise and the parties proceed to litigation, arbitration, mediation or other means of dispute resolution, a new fee agreement must be prepared.

I have agreed to waive the customary requirement of a retainer.

I will send you pleadings, documents, correspondence, and other information throughout your representation to keep you advised of the progress in your purchase of the property. These copies will be your file copies. Please retain them. I will also keep the information in a file in my office, which will be my file. Please bring your copy of the file to all of our meetings so that we both have all the necessary information in front of us. When I have completed all the legal work necessary for your case, I will close my file and return original documents to you. I will then store the file for approximately two years. I will destroy the file after that period of time unless you instruct me in writing now to keep your file longer.

A copy of this letter is enclosed for your review, signature, and return to me in the postage-paid envelope. If any of the information in this letter is not consistent with your understanding of our agreement, please contact me before signing the letter. Otherwise, please sign the enclosed copy of this letter and return it to me.

If you have any questions, please contact me at your convenience.

Very truly yours,


I have read this letter and agree to the terms set forth herein.

_____                    _____

Daniel Schan                                        Date

_____                    _____

Sara Schan                                          Date

# FORM 11 – DEED OF CONSERVATION EASEMENT

## DEED OF CONSERVATION EASEMENT

**THIS DEED OF CONSERVATION EASEMENT** ("Conservation Easement") made this _____ day of _____, 200_, by and between _____, ("Grantor(s)"), and The State of Maryland to the use of the Department of Natural Resources ("Grantee"),

**WITNESSETH**

**WHEREAS**, by Contract of Sale approved by the Board of Public Works on February 9, 2000, the Pennsylvania Electric Company agreed to sell and the State of Maryland agreed to buy the bed of Deep Creek Lake and certain surrounding parcels of property, known collectively as Parcel 2, subject to the imposition of a conservation easement upon the State's resale of certain portions of the property;

**WHEREAS**, of the property purchased from Pennsylvania Electric Company, the State has determined to retain a portion of Parcel 2 contiguous to Deep Creek Lake to be reserved for public use and additional land as necessary to protect the Lake's natural, recreational, scenic, and aesthetic resources, and to delineate boundary lines, or to provide for public access to the Lake;

**WHEREAS**, of the remaining portions of Parcel 2, the State has determined to resell to contiguous property owners, certain parcels, subject to this Conservation Easement;

**WHEREAS**, Grantors herein own in fee simple real property situate, lying and being in Garrett County, Maryland, contiguous to Deep Creek Lake, thereby making them eligible to purchase a portion of Parcel 2 subject to this Conservation Easement; and

**WHEREAS**, the within Grantors have availed themselves of the opportunity to purchase property ("Property") and are willing to grant this Conservation Easement on the Property, thereby restricting and limiting the use of the Property as hereinafter provided in this Conservation Easement for the purposes set forth below.

**WHEREAS**, the purpose of the Conservation Easement is to prevent development and maintain the beauty and recreational purpose and to conserve the natural and scenic qualities of the environment of Deep Creek Lake and the surrounding area;

**NOW, THEREFORE**, in consideration of the facts stated in the above paragraphs and the covenants, terms, conditions and restrictions (the "Terms") hereinafter set forth, the receipt and sufficiency of which are hereby acknowledged by the parties, the Grantors unconditionally and irrevocably hereby grant and convey unto the Grantee, its successors and assigns, forever and in perpetuity a Conservation Easement of the nature and character and to the extent hereinafter set forth, with respect to the Property:

## ARTICLE I. DURATION OF EASEMENT

This Conservation Easement shall be perpetual. It is an easement in gross and runs with the land as an incorporeal interest in the Property, enforceable with respect to the Property by the Grantee against the Grantors and their personal representatives, heirs, successors and assigns.

## ARTICLE II. PROHIBITED AND RESTRICTED ACTIVITIES

### A. *Industrial or Commercial Activities on the Property*

Industrial or commercial activities are prohibited on the Property, except, with the approval of the Grantee, for activities necessary to support and gain access to lake-related, commercial and recreational uses permitted by the State of Maryland on immediately contiguous State land or on Deep Creek Lake, at the time of the proposed activity.

### B. *Construction and Improvements*

No building, facility, means of access, fence or other structure shall be permitted on the Property, except: (1) pedestrian pathways or stairways constructed with wood, stone or permeable surfaces of natural materials to provide access to the lake or improvements on the Property from the contiguous property; (2) with the approval of the Grantee, utilities to serve commercial or recreational facilities on the contiguous State land; (3) structures identified on a plat of Parcel 2 as recorded among the Land Records of Garrett County, Maryland in Plat Drawer P, File 134 or in the records of the Department of Natural Resources and those structures identified on the individual plats prepared by the surveyor and recorded with each conveyance, provided that such structures were permitted by the Department or its predecessor in title prior to the Grantor's ownership of the Property; and (4) as subject to the approval of the Grantee, temporary structures with a footprint no greater than 120 square feet.

### C. *Transferable, Cluster and Other Development Rights*

The Grantors hereby grant to the Grantee all transferable, cluster or other development rights under any present or future law that are now or hereafter allocated to, implied, reserved or inherent in the Property, and the parties agree that such rights are terminated and extinguished, and may not be used or transferred to any portion of the Property, or to any other property, nor used for the purpose of calculating permissible size or lot yield of the Property or any other property.

### D. *Trees*

There shall be no burning, cutting, removal or destruction of trees, shrubs and other woody vegetation (collectively "Vegetation"), except: subject to the approval of the Grantee (1) Vegetation that is dead, infested or diseased; (2) Vegetation necessary to control erosion; (3) Vegetation necessary to provide reasonable access to Deep Creek Lake; and (4) Vegetation cut, maintained, or removed pursuant to a forest management plan that has been approved by the Grantee and prepared by a professional forester registered in Maryland. Trimming and maintenance of Vegetation that has been planted by the Grantor or a predecessor in title to the Grantor on the Property is permitted; provided, that the Grantor or the Grantor's predecessor provides written documentation to the Grantee of the type and location of the Vegetation prior to maintenance or trimming.

### E. *Dumping, Placement or Storage of Materials*

No materials may be dumped or stored on the Property, including, but not limited to, ashes, trash, garbage, rubbish, abandoned vehicles, abandoned vessels, abandoned appliances, and abandoned machinery.

### F. *Excavation of Materials*

Excavation or mining of the Property is prohibited, including, but not limited to, removal of soil or sand, except, with the approval of the Grantee, for temporary excavation: (1) to maintain access to Deep Creek Lake; or (2) to repair and extend a septic system or well that has failed on a contiguous property, so long as the failure is not due to increased use, occupancy, or size of the contiguous dwelling that the septic system or well serves, in violation of any health laws, ordinances, regulations or permits.

### G. *Wetlands*

No diking, draining, filling, dredging or removal of any wetland or wetlands is permitted. "Wetland" or "wetlands" means portions of the Property defined by any State or federal laws as a wetland or wetlands at the time of the proposed activity.

**H.** *Signs and Billboards*

No signs, billboards, or outdoor advertising displays may be erected, displayed, placed or maintained on the Property except temporary signs not exceeding six square feet to advertise the property's sale or rental.

**I.** *Public Access*

This Conservation Easement does not grant the public any right to access or any right of use of the Property.

**J.** *Reserved Rights*

Except to the extent that prior written approval of the Grantee is required by any paragraph of this Article, all rights not prohibited by this Conservation Easement are considered to be consistent with the Terms of this Conservation Easement and require no prior notification or approval. If the Grantors have any doubt with respect to whether or not any particular use of the Property is prohibited by the Terms of this Conservation Easement, the Grantors may submit a written request to the Grantee for consideration and approval of such use.

## ARTICLE III. ENFORCEMENT AND REMEDIES

**A.** *Remedies*

Upon any breach of the Terms of this Conservation Easement by the Grantors, the Grantee may exercise any or all of the following remedies:

1. institute suits to enjoin any breach or enforce any covenant by temporary and/or permanent injunction either prohibitive or mandatory; and

2. require that the Property be restored promptly to the condition required by this Conservation Easement.

The Grantee's remedies shall be cumulative and shall be in addition to any other rights and remedies available to the Grantee at law or equity. If the Grantors are found to have breached any of the Terms under this Conservation Easement, the Grantors shall reimburse the Grantee for any costs or expenses incurred by the Grantee, including court costs and reasonable attorney's fees.

**B.** *Effect of Failure to Enforce*

No failure on the part of the Grantee to enforce any Term hereof shall discharge or invalidate such Term or any other Term hereof or affect the right of the Grantee to enforce the same in the event of a subsequent breach or default.

**C.** *Right of Inspection*

The State of Maryland, acting by and through the Department of Natural Resources, the Grantee, their respective employees and agents, have the right, with reasonable notice to the Grantors, to enter the Property at reasonable times for the purpose of inspecting the Property to determine whether the Grantors are complying with the Terms of this Conservation Easement.

## ARTICLE IV. MISCELLANEOUS

**A.** *Future Transfers*

By executing this Conservation Easement, the Grantors acknowledge that this Conservation Easement is permanent and is binding on their heirs, personal representatives, successors or assigns.

**B.** *Effect of Laws Imposing Affirmative Obligations on the Grantors*

In the event that any applicable State or federal law imposes affirmative obligations on owners of land which if complied with by the Grantors would be a violation of a Term of this Conservation Easement, the Grantors shall: (i) if said law requires a specific act without any discretion on the part of the Grantors, comply with said law and give the Grantee written notice of the Grantors' compliance as soon as reasonably possible, but in no event more than thirty (30) days from the time the Grantors begin to comply; or (ii) if said law leaves to the Grantors discretion over how to comply with said law, use the method most protective of the purpose of this Conservation Easement set forth in the recitals herein.

**C.** *Notices to the Grantee*

Any notices by the Grantors to the Grantee pursuant to any Term hereof shall be sent by registered or certified mail, return receipt requested, addressed to the current address of the Secretary, Department of Natural Resources, with a copy to Manager, Deep Creek Lake Natural Resources Management Area.

**D.** *Approval of the Grantee*

In any case where the terms of this Conservation Easement require the approval of the Grantee, such approval shall be requested by written notice to the Grantee. After consultation with the Deep Creek Lake Policy Review Board, approval or disapproval shall be given promptly and in writing; in the event the request is disapproved, a statement of the reasons for the disapproval shall be given.

**E.** *Condemnation*

Whenever all or part of the Property is taken in the exercise of eminent domain, so as to abrogate, in whole or in part, the restrictions imposed by this Conservation Easement, or this Conservation Easement is extinguished, in whole or in part, by other judicial proceeding, the Grantors and the Grantee shall be entitled to proceeds payable in connection with the condemnation or other judicial proceedings in any amount equal to the current fair market value of their relative real estate interests. Any costs of a judicial proceeding allocated by a court to the Grantors and the Grantee shall be allocated in the same manner as the proceeds are allocated.

**F.** *Construction*

This Conservation Easement shall be construed pursuant to the purpose of this Conservation Easement and the purposes of Section 2-118 of the Real Property Article of the Annotated Code of Maryland, and to the laws of the State of Maryland generally.

**G.** *Effect of Laws and Other Restrictions on the Property*

The Terms of this Conservation Easement shall be in addition to any local, State or federal laws imposing restrictions on the Property and any real estate interests imposing restrictions on the Property.

**H.** *Entire Agreement and Severability of the Terms*

This instrument sets forth the entire agreement of the parties with respect to the Conservation Easement and supersedes all prior discussions, negotiations, understanding or agreements relating to the Conservation Easement. If any Term is found to be invalid, the remainder of the Terms of this Conservation Easement, and the application of such Term to persons or circumstances other than those as to which it is found to be invalid, shall not be affected thereby.

**I.** *Successors*

The terms "Grantors" and "Grantee" wherever used herein, and any pronouns used in place thereof, shall include, respectively, the above-named Grantors and their personal representatives, heirs, successors, and assigns and the above-named Grantee and their successors and assigns.

**J.** *Real Property Taxes*

Except to the extent provided for by State or local law, nothing herein contained shall relieve the Grantors of the obligation to pay taxes in connection with the ownership of the Property.

**K.** *Captions*

The captions in this Conservation Easement have been inserted solely for convenience of reference and are not a part of this instrument. Accordingly, the captions shall have no effect upon the construction or interpretation of the Terms of this Conservation Easement.

**IN WITNESS THEREOF**, the Grantors have hereunto set their hands and seals in the day and year above written.

**WITNESS/ATTEST:**                                              **GRANTORS:**

_____                          _____(SEAL)

_____                          _____(SEAL)

**STATE OF MARYLAND,**

_____ of _____ **TO WIT:**

**I HEREBY CERTIFY**, that on this _____ day of _____, 200__, before me the subscriber, a Notary Public of the State aforesaid, personally appeared _____, known to me (or satisfactorily proven) to be a Grantor of the foregoing Deed of Conservation Easement and acknowledged that he/she executed the same for the purposes therein contained and in my presence signed and sealed the same.

WITNESS my hand and Notarial Seal.

Notary Public

My Commission Expires: _____

(Use a separate notary for each Grantor's signature and modify the above certificate if any entity, such as a corporation, is a Grantor.)

I hereby certify that this Deed of Conservation Easement was prepared and reviewed for legal form and sufficiency by _____, an attorney admitted to practice before the Court of Appeals of Maryland.

_____

ASSISTANT ATTORNEY GENERAL

# FORM 12 – LAST WILL AND TESTAMENT

## LAST WILL AND TESTAMENT

I, **AMY BALDWIN**, a resident of Bucks County in the Commonwealth of Virginia, being of sound and disposing mind, memory and understanding, do hereby make, publish and declare this to be my Last Will and Testament. I revoke any and all wills and codicils that I have previously made.

**ARTICLE ONE:** I direct the expenses of my last illness and funeral, the expense of the administration of my estate, and all estate, inheritance and similar taxes payable with respect to the property included in my estate, whether or not passing under this will, and any interest or penalties thereon, shall be paid out of the residue of my estate, without apportionment and with no rights of reimbursement from any recipient of any such property (including reimbursement under Section 2207B of the Internal Revenue Code).

**ARTICLE TWO:** I give all my articles of personal and household use, including automobiles, and all insurance on that property, to my Executor, to be retained or distributed by him in accordance with my wishes which I have made known to him during my lifetime.

**ARTICLE THREE:** I give, devise and bequeath my real estate known as 17 Ocean Avenue, Virginia Beach, Virginia to my children, Joseph Gaitner and Rebecca Gaitner, as joint tenants with the rights of survivorship and not as tenants in common.

**ARTICLE FOUR:** I give, devise and bequeath my real estate known as 3224 University Avenue, State College, Virginia to the University of Virginia.

**ARTICLE FIVE:** All the rest of the real estate that I may own at the time of my death I give to my Executor and direct that each parcel be sold and the proceeds distributed in accordance with Article Six of this my last will and testament.

**ARTICLE SIX:** All the rest, residue and remainder of my estate, real and personal and wheresoever situated I give, devise and bequeath in equal shares to my beloved granddaughter, SUZANNE SHIELDS and my beloved grandson, DAVID BINGHAM, or to the survivor of them.

**ARTICLE SEVEN:** The interests of the beneficiaries hereunder shall not be subject to anticipation or to voluntary or involuntary alienation until distribution is actually made.

**ARTICLE EIGHT:** In addition to the powers granted by law, my fiduciaries, executors, administrator and trustees appointed herein shall have the following powers, exercisable at their discretion from time to time without court approval, with respect to both principal and accumulated income, and such powers shall continue until distribution is actually made:

A. To sell at public or private sale, exchange or lease for any period of time any real or personal property and to give options for sales or leases.
B. To compromise claims, and to disclaim any interest which I may have in an estate or trust.
C. To accept in kind, retain and invest in any form of property without regard to any principal of diversification as to any property owned by me at my death.
D. To make distributions in kind or in cash.
E. If any interest created hereunder vests in a minor or incompetent, my fiduciaries, without court authorization, may distribute the interest in whole or in part to the guardian of the said minor or incompetent.
F. To exercise any options available in determining and paying death taxes in my estate as my executor deems appropriate without requiring adjustments between income and principal.
G. The determination of my fiduciaries as to the amount or advisability of any discretionary payment shall be final and conclusive on all persons, whether or not then in being, having or claiming any interest.

**ARTICLE NINE:** I appoint my grandson DAVID BINGHAM, Executor of this my last will and testament. In the event my grandson DAVID BINGHAM shall predecease me, or should fail or be unable to qualify or having qualified should resign or die, then I appoint my granddaughter SUZANNE SHIELDS, alternate Executrix in his place and stead with all of the rights and powers as though originally appointed.
No Executor appointed hereunder shall be required to furnish bond.

**IN WITNESS WHEREOF,** I have hereunto written my name in the margin of the foregoing two pages of this my last will and testament and set my hand and seal at the end hereof this _____ day of _____, 2013.

_____
AMY BALDWIN

**SIGNED, SEALED, PUBLISHED and DECLARED** by the above named Testatrix, AMY BALDWIN, as and for her last will and testament, in the presence of us, who in her presence and in the presence of each other, all being present at the same time and at her request, have subscribed our names as witnesses hereto.

_____        _____
Sign above and print name                              Sign above and print name
And address below:                                          And address below:

_____        _____
_____        _____
_____        _____


COMMONWEALTH OF VIRGINIA                )
                                                                   ) ss:
COUNTY OF                                                  )

I, AMY BALDWIN, Testatrix, whose name is signed to the attached or foregoing instrument, having been duly qualified according to law, do hereby acknowledge that I have signed and executed the instrument as my last will; that I signed it willingly; and that I signed it as my free and voluntary act for the purposes therein expressed.

_____
AMY BALDWIN

SWORN TO AND SUBSCRIBED:
Before me this _____ day of
_____, 2013:

_____
NOTARY PUBLIC


COMMONWEALTH OF VIRGINIA                )
                                                                   ) ss:
COUNTY OF                                                  )

We, _____ and _____, the witnesses whose names are signed to the attached or foregoing instrument, being duly qualified according to law, do depose and say that we were present and saw the Testatrix sign and execute the instrument as her last will; that the said Testatrix, AMY BALDWIN, signed willingly and that the Testatrix executed it as her sole and voluntary act for the purposes therein expressed; that each of us in the hearing and sight of the Testatrix signed the Will as witnesses; and that to the best of our knowledge the Testatrix was at the time eighteen or more years of age, of sound mind and under no constraint or undue influence.

_____

_____

SWORN TO AND SUBSCRIBED:
Before me this _____ day of
_____, 2013:

_____
NOTARY PUBLIC

# FORM 13 – CLIENT INTERVIEW FORM

## CLIENT INTERVIEW CHECKLIST

**CLIENT PERSONAL INFORMATION**

Name _____

Address _____

City _____ State _____ Zip _____

Phone (hm) _____ (wk) _____ (cell) _____

How long at this address _____

Date of birth _____ Place of birth _____

Social Security No. _____

Prior address _____

City _____ State _____ Zip _____

Dates at this address _____

Employer: _____

Job description _____

Marital status _____ Maiden name _____

Spouse's name _____ Date of birth _____

Child's name _____ Date of birth _____

Child's name _____ Date of birth _____

Child's name _____ Date of birth _____

**CASE INFORMATION**

Case referred by _____

Case type:  ☐ Appeal  ☐ Business  ☐ Corporate  ☐ Estate  ☐ Litigation
            ☐ Municipal  ☐ Real Estate  ☐ Tax  ☐ Trust  ☐ Other

Opposing party(ies) _____

Opposing party _____

Address _____

Opposing attorney _____

Address _____

Date of incident _____ Statute of limitation date _____

Summary of facts _____

_____

_____

_____

# FORM 14 – REAL ESTATE AGENT'S EXCLUSIVE RIGHT TO SELL LISTING CONTRACT

1  | The printed portions of this form, except differentiated additions, have been approved by the Colorado Real Estate Commission.
2  | (LC50-8-10) (Mandatory 1-11)
3

4  **THIS IS A BINDING CONTRACT. THIS FORM HAS IMPORTANT LEGAL CONSEQUENCES AND THE PARTIES SHOULD**
5  **CONSULT LEGAL AND TAX OR OTHER COUNSEL BEFORE SIGNING.**

6  **Compensation charged by brokerage firms is not set by law. Such charges are established by each real estate**
7  **brokerage firm.**

8  **DIFFERENT BROKERAGE RELATIONSHIPS ARE AVAILABLE WHICH INCLUDE BUYER AGENCY, SELLER AGENCY, OR**
9  **TRANSACTION-BROKERAGE.**
10

11  ## EXCLUSIVE RIGHT-TO-SELL LISTING CONTRACT

12  ☐ **SELLER AGENCY**   ☐ **TRANSACTION-BROKERAGE**
13

14  Date: _____

15  **1.   AGREEMENT.** Seller and Brokerage Firm enter into this exclusive, irrevocable contract (Seller Listing Contract) as of the
16  date set forth above.

17  **2.   BROKER AND BROKERAGE FIRM.**
18  ☐ **2.1.   Multiple-Person Firm.** If this box is checked, the individual designated by Brokerage Firm to serve as the broker of
19  Seller and to perform the services for Seller required by this Seller Listing Contract is called Broker. If more than one individual is
20  so designated, then references in this Seller Listing Contract to Broker shall include all persons so designated, including substitute
21  or additional brokers. The brokerage relationship exists only with Broker and does not extend to the employing broker, Brokerage
22  Firm or to any other brokers employed or engaged by Brokerage Firm who are not so designated.
23  ☐ **2.2.   One-Person Firm.** If this box is checked, Broker is a real estate brokerage firm with only one licensed natural person.
24  References in this Seller Listing Contract to Broker or Brokerage Firm mean both the licensed natural person and brokerage firm
25  who shall serve as the broker of Seller and perform the services for Seller required by this Seller Listing Contract.

26  **3.   DEFINED TERMS.**
27  **3.1.   Seller:** _____
28  **3.2.   Brokerage Firm:** _____
29  **3.3.   Broker:** _____
30  **3.4.   Property.** The Property is the following legally described real estate in the County of _____, Colorado:
31
32
33
34  known as No. _____,
35        Street Address                           City                          State                    Zip
36  together with the interests, easements, rights, benefits, improvements and attached fixtures appurtenant thereto, and all interest of
37  Seller in vacated streets and alleys adjacent thereto, except as herein excluded.
38  **3.5.   Sale.**
39  **3.5.1.**   A Sale is the voluntary transfer or exchange of any interest in the Property or the voluntary creation of the
40  obligation to convey any interest in the Property, including a contract or lease. It also includes an agreement to transfer any
41  ownership interest in an entity which owns the Property.
42  ☐   **3.5.2.**   If this box is checked, Seller authorizes Broker to negotiate leasing the Property. Lease of the Property or
43  Lease means any lease of an interest in the Property.
44  **3.6.   Listing Period.** The Listing Period of this Seller Listing Contract shall begin on _____, and
45  shall continue through the earlier of (1) completion of the Sale of the Property or (2) _____.
46  Broker shall continue to assist in the completion of any sale or lease for which compensation is payable to Brokerage Firm under
47  § 7 of this Seller Listing Contract.
48  **3.7.   Applicability of Terms.** A check or similar mark in a box means that such provision is applicable. The abbreviation
49  "N/A" or the word "Deleted" means not applicable. The abbreviation "MEC" (mutual execution of this contract) means the date upon
50  which both parties have signed this Seller Listing Contract.

51 **3.8. Day; Computation of Period of Days, Deadline.**
52     **3.8.1. Day.** As used in this Seller Listing Contract, the term "day" shall mean the entire day ending at 11:59 p.m.,
53 United States Mountain Time (Standard or Daylight Savings as applicable).
54     **3.8.2. Computation of Period of Days, Deadline.** In computing a period of days, when the ending date is not
55 specified, the first day is excluded and the last day is included, e.g., three days after MEC. If any deadline falls on a Saturday,
56 Sunday or federal or Colorado state holiday (Holiday), such deadline ☐ **Shall** ☐ **Shall Not** be extended to the next day that is
57 not a Saturday, Sunday or Holiday. Should neither box be checked, the deadline shall not be extended.

58 **4. BROKERAGE RELATIONSHIP.**
59     **4.1.** If the Seller Agency box at the top of page 1 is checked, Broker shall represent Seller as a Seller's limited agent
60 (Seller's Agent). If the Transaction-Brokerage box at the top of page 1 is checked, Broker shall act as a Transaction-Broker.
61     **4.2. In-Company Transaction – Different Brokers.** When Seller and buyer in a transaction are working with different
62 brokers, those brokers continue to conduct themselves consistent with the brokerage relationships they have established. Seller
63 acknowledges that Brokerage Firm is allowed to offer and pay compensation to brokers within Brokerage Firm working with a
64 buyer.
65     **4.3. In-Company Transaction – One Broker.** If Seller and buyer are both working with the same broker, Broker shall
66 function as:
67     **4.3.1. Seller's Agent.** If the Seller Agency box at the top of page 1 is checked, the parties agree the following applies:
68     **4.3.1.1. Seller Agency Only.** Unless the box in § 4.3.1.2 (**Seller Agency Unless Brokerage Relationship**
69 **with Both**) is checked, Broker shall represent Seller as Seller's Agent and shall treat the buyer as a customer. A customer is a
70 party to a transaction with whom Broker has no brokerage relationship. Broker shall disclose to such customer Broker's
71 relationship with Seller.
72     ☐ **4.3.1.2. Seller Agency Unless Brokerage Relationship with Both.** If this box is checked, Broker shall
73 represent Seller as Seller's Agent and shall treat the buyer as a customer, unless Broker currently has or enters into an agency or
74 Transaction-Brokerage relationship with the buyer, in which case Broker shall act as a Transaction-Broker.
75     **4.3.2. Transaction-Broker.** If the Transaction-Brokerage box at the top of page 1 is checked, or in the event neither
76 box is checked, Broker shall work with Seller as a Transaction-Broker. A Transaction-Broker shall perform the duties described in
77 § 5 and facilitate sales transactions without being an advocate or agent for either party. If Seller and buyer are working with the
78 same broker, Broker shall continue to function as a Transaction-Broker.

79 **5. BROKERAGE DUTIES.** Brokerage Firm, acting through Broker, as either a Transaction-Broker or a Seller's Agent, shall
80 perform the following **Uniform Duties** when working with Seller:
81     **5.1.** Broker shall exercise reasonable skill and care for Seller, including, but not limited to the following:
82     **5.1.1.** Performing the terms of any written or oral agreement with Seller;
83     **5.1.2.** Presenting all offers to and from Seller in a timely manner regardless of whether the Property is subject to a
84 contract for Sale;
85     **5.1.3.** Disclosing to Seller adverse material facts actually known by Broker;
86     **5.1.4.** Advising Seller regarding the transaction and advising Seller to obtain expert advice as to material matters
87 about which Broker knows but the specifics of which are beyond the expertise of Broker;
88     **5.1.5.** Accounting in a timely manner for all money and property received; and
89     **5.1.6.** Keeping Seller fully informed regarding the transaction.
90     **5.2.** Broker shall not disclose the following information without the informed consent of Seller:
91     **5.2.1.** That Seller is willing to accept less than the asking price for the Property;
92     **5.2.2.** What the motivating factors are for Seller to sell the Property;
93     **5.2.3.** That Seller will agree to financing terms other than those offered;
94     **5.2.4.** Any material information about Seller unless disclosure is required by law or failure to disclose such
95 information would constitute fraud or dishonest dealing; or
96     **5.2.5.** Any facts or suspicions regarding circumstances that could psychologically impact or stigmatize the Property.
97     **5.3.** Seller consents to Broker's disclosure of Seller's confidential information to the supervising broker or designee for the
98 purpose of proper supervision, provided such supervising broker or designee shall not further disclose such information without
99 consent of Seller, or use such information to the detriment of Seller.
100     **5.4.** Brokerage Firm may have agreements with other sellers to market and sell their property. Broker may show alternative
101 properties not owned by Seller to other prospective buyers and list competing properties for sale.
102     **5.5.** Broker shall not be obligated to seek additional offers to purchase the Property while the Property is subject to a
103 contract for Sale.
104     **5.6.** Broker has no duty to conduct an independent inspection of the Property for the benefit of a buyer and has no duty to
105 independently verify the accuracy or completeness of statements made by Seller or independent inspectors. Broker has no duty to
106 conduct an independent investigation of a buyer's financial condition or to verify the accuracy or completeness of any statement
107 made by a buyer.

108     **5.7.**   Seller understands that Seller shall not be liable for Broker's acts or omissions that have not been approved, directed, or
109 ratified by Seller.

110     **5.8.**   When asked, Broker ☐ **Shall** ☐ **Shall Not** disclose to prospective buyers and cooperating brokers the existence of
111 offers on the Property and whether the offers were obtained by Broker, a broker within Brokerage Firm or by another broker.

112   **6.**   **ADDITIONAL DUTIES OF SELLER'S AGENT.** If the Seller Agency box at the top of page 1 is checked, Broker is
113 Seller's Agent, with the following additional duties:

114     **6.1.**   Promoting the interests of Seller with the utmost good faith, loyalty and fidelity;

115     **6.2.**   Seeking a price and terms that are set forth in this Seller Listing Contract; and

116     **6.3.**   Counseling Seller as to any material benefits or risks of a transaction that are actually known by Broker.

117   **7.**   **COMPENSATION TO BROKERAGE FIRM; COMPENSATION TO COOPERATIVE BROKER.** Seller agrees that
118 any Brokerage Firm compensation that is conditioned upon the Sale of the Property shall be earned by Brokerage Firm as set forth
119 herein without any discount or allowance for any efforts made by Seller or by any other person in connection with the Sale of the
120 Property.

121     **7.1.**   **Amount.** In consideration of the services to be performed by Broker, Seller agrees to pay Brokerage Firm as follows:

122         **7.1.1.**   **Sale Commission.** (1) _____% of the gross purchase price or (2) _____,
123 in U.S. dollars.

124         **7.1.2.**   **Lease Commission.** If the box in § 3.5.2 is checked, Brokerage Firm shall be paid a fee equal to (1) _____%
125 of the gross rent under the lease, or (2) _____, in U.S. dollars, payable
126 as follows: _____.

127     **7.2.**   **When Earned.** Such commission shall be earned upon the occurrence of any of the following:

128         **7.2.1.**   Any Sale of the Property within the Listing Period by Seller, by Broker or by any other person;

129         **7.2.2.**   Broker finding a buyer who is ready, willing and able to complete the sale or lease as specified in this Seller
130 Listing Contract; or

131         **7.2.3.**   Any Sale (or Lease if § 3.5.2 is checked) of the Property within _____ calendar days subsequent to the
132 expiration of the Listing Period (Holdover Period) (1) to anyone with whom Broker negotiated and (2) whose name was submitted,
133 in writing, to Seller by Broker during the Listing Period, including any extensions thereof, (Submitted Prospect). Provided,
134 however, Seller ☐ **Shall** ☐ **Shall Not** owe the commission to Brokerage Firm under this § 7.2.3 if a commission is earned by
135 another licensed real estate brokerage firm acting pursuant to an exclusive agreement entered into during the Holdover Period and
136 a Sale or Lease to a Submitted Prospect is consummated. If no box is checked above in this § 7.2.3, then Seller shall not owe the
137 commission to Brokerage Firm.

138     **7.3.**   **When Applicable and Payable.** The commission obligation shall apply to a Sale made during the Listing Period or
139 any extension of such original or extended term. The commission described in § 7.1.1 shall be payable at the time of the closing of
140 the Sale, or, if there is no closing (due to the refusal or neglect of Seller) then on the contracted date of closing, as contemplated by
141 § 7.2.1 or § 7.2.3, or upon fulfillment of § 7.2.2 where the offer made by such buyer is not accepted by Seller.

142     **7.4.**   **Other Compensation.** _____

143     **7.5.**   **Cooperative Broker Compensation.** Broker shall seek assistance from, and Brokerage Firm offers compensation to,
144 outside brokerage firms, whose brokers are acting as:

145         ☐ **Buyer Agents:** _____% of the gross sales price or _____, in U.S. dollars.

146         ☐ **Transaction-Brokers:** _____% of the gross sales price or _____, in U.S. dollars.

147   **8.**   **LIMITATION ON THIRD-PARTY COMPENSATION.** Neither Broker nor the Brokerage Firm, except as set forth in
148 § 7, shall accept compensation from any other person or entity in connection with the Property without the written consent of
149 Seller. Additionally, neither Broker nor Brokerage Firm shall assess or receive mark-ups or other compensation for services
150 performed by any third party or affiliated business entity unless Seller signs a separate written consent.

151   **9.**   **OTHER BROKERS' ASSISTANCE, MULTIPLE LISTING SERVICES AND MARKETING.** Seller has been advised
152 by Broker of the advantages and disadvantages of various marketing methods, including advertising and the use of multiple listing
153 services (MLS) and various methods of making the Property accessible by other brokerage firms (e.g., using lock boxes, by-
154 appointment-only showings, etc.), and whether some methods may limit the ability of another broker to show the Property. After
155 having been so advised, Seller has chosen the following (check all that apply):

156     **9.1.**   **MLS/Information Exchange.**

157         **9.1.1.**   The Property ☐ **Shall** ☐ **Shall Not** be submitted to one or more MLS and ☐ **Shall** ☐ **Shall Not** be
158 submitted to one or more property information exchanges. If submitted, Seller authorizes Broker to provide timely notice of any
159 status change to such MLS and information exchanges. Upon transfer of deed from Seller to buyer, Seller authorizes Broker to
160 provide sales information to such MLS and information exchanges.

161         **9.1.2.**   Seller authorizes the use of electronic and all other marketing methods except: _____.

162         **9.1.3.**   Seller further authorizes use of the data by MLS and property information exchanges, if any.

163   **9.1.4.**   The Property Address ☐ **Shall** ☐ **Shall Not** be displayed on the Internet.
164   **9.1.5.**   The Property Listing ☐ **Shall** ☐ **Shall Not** be displayed on the Internet.
165   **9.2.**   **Property Access.** Access to the Property may be by:
166   ☐ Lock Box
167   ☐ _____
168   Other instructions: _____
169   **9.3.**   **Broker Marketing.** The following specific marketing tasks shall be performed by Broker:
170
171
172   **9.4.**   **Brokerage Services.** The Broker shall provide brokerage services to Seller.

173   **10. SELLER'S OBLIGATIONS TO BROKER; DISCLOSURES AND CONSENT.**
174   **10.1. Negotiations and Communication.** Seller agrees to conduct all negotiations for the Sale of the Property only through
175   Broker, and to refer to Broker all communications received in any form from real estate brokers, prospective buyers, tenants or any
176   other source during the Listing Period of this Seller Listing Contract.
177   **10.2. Advertising.** Seller agrees that any advertising of the Property by Seller (e.g., Internet, print and signage) shall first be
178   approved by Broker.
179   **10.3. No Existing Listing Agreement.** Seller represents that Seller ☐ **Is** ☐ **Is Not** currently a party to any listing
180   agreement with any other broker to sell the Property.
181   **10.4. Ownership of Materials and Consent.** Seller represents that all materials (including all photographs, renderings,
182   images or other creative items) supplied to Broker by or on behalf of Seller are owned by Seller, except as Seller has disclosed in
183   writing to Broker. Seller is authorized to and grants to Broker, Brokerage Firm and any MLS (that Broker submits the Property to)
184   a nonexclusive irrevocable, royalty-free license to use such material for marketing of the Property, reporting as required and the
185   publishing, display and reproduction of such material, compilation and data. This license shall survive the termination of this
186   Seller Listing Contract.
187   **10.5. Colorado Foreclosure Protection Act.** The Colorado Foreclosure Protection Act (Act) generally applies if (1) the
188   Property is residential (2) Seller resides in the Property as Seller's principal residence (3) Buyer's purpose in purchase of the
189   Property is not to use the Property as Buyer's personal residence and (4) the Property is in foreclosure or Buyer has notice that any
190   loan secured by the Property is at least thirty days delinquent or in default. If all requirements 1, 2, 3 and 4 are met and the Act
191   otherwise applies, then a contract, between Buyer and Seller for the sale of the Property, that complies with the provisions of the
192   Act is required. If the transaction is a Short Sale transaction and a Short Sale Addendum is part of the Contract between Seller and
193   Buyer, the Act does not apply. It is recommended that Seller consult with an attorney.

194   **11. PRICE AND TERMS.** The following Price and Terms are acceptable to Seller:
195   **11.1. Price.** U.S. $_____
196   **11.2. Terms.** ☐ **Cash** ☐ **Conventional** ☐ **FHA** ☐ **VA** ☐ **Other:** _____
197   **11.3. Loan Discount Points.** _____
198   **11.4. Buyer's Closing Costs (FHA/VA).** Seller shall pay closing costs and fees, not to exceed $_____, that Buyer
199   is not allowed by law to pay, for tax service and _____.
200   **11.5. Earnest Money.** Minimum amount of earnest money deposit U.S. $_____ in the form of _____
201   **11.6. Seller Proceeds.** Seller will receive net proceeds of closing as indicated: ☐ **Cashier's Check** at Seller's expense;
202   ☐ **Funds Electronically Transferred (Wire Transfer)** to an account specified by Seller, at Seller's expense; or ☐ **Closing**
203   **Company's Trust Account Check.**
204   **11.7. Advisory: Tax Withholding.** The Internal Revenue Service and the Colorado Department of Revenue may require
205   closing company to withhold a substantial portion of the proceeds of this Sale when Seller either (1) is a foreign person or (2) will
206   not be a Colorado resident after closing. Seller should inquire of Seller's tax advisor to determine if withholding applies or if an
207   exemption exists.

208   **12. DEPOSITS.** Brokerage Firm is authorized to accept earnest money deposits received by Broker pursuant to a proposed Sale
209   contract. Brokerage Firm is authorized to deliver the earnest money deposit to the closing agent, if any, at or before the closing of
210   the Sale contract.

211   **13. INCLUSIONS AND EXCLUSIONS.**
212   **13.1. Inclusions.** The Purchase Price includes the following items (Inclusions):
213   **13.1.1. Fixtures.** If attached to the Property on the date of this Seller Listing Contract, lighting, heating, plumbing,
214   ventilating, and air conditioning fixtures, TV antennas, inside telephone, network and coaxial (cable) wiring and connecting
215   blocks/jacks, plants, mirrors, floor coverings, intercom systems, built-in kitchen appliances, sprinkler systems and controls, built-in
216   vacuum systems (including accessories), garage door openers including _____ remote controls; and
217

218       **13.1.2. Personal Property.** If on the Property whether attached or not on the date of this Seller Listing Contract:
219 storm windows, storm doors, window and porch shades, awnings, blinds, screens, window coverings, curtain rods, drapery rods,
220 fireplace inserts, fireplace screens, fireplace grates, heating stoves, storage sheds, and all keys. If checked, the following are
221 included: ☐ **Water Softeners**   ☐ **Smoke/Fire Detectors**   ☐ **Security Systems**   ☐ **Satellite Systems** (including satellite
222 dishes); and

223
224
225     The Personal Property to be conveyed at closing shall be conveyed by Seller free and clear of all taxes (except personal
226 property taxes for the year of closing), liens and encumbrances, except _____.
227 Conveyance shall be by bill of sale or other applicable legal instrument.
228       **13.1.3. Trade Fixtures.** The following trade fixtures: _____
229     The Trade Fixtures to be conveyed at closing shall be conveyed by Seller, free and clear of all taxes (except personal property
230 taxes for the year of closing), liens and encumbrances, except _____.
231 Conveyance shall be by bill of sale or other applicable legal instrument.
232       **13.1.4. Parking and Storage Facilities.** ☐ **Use Only** ☐ **Ownership** of the following parking facilities: _____
233 _____; and ☐ **Use Only** ☐ **Ownership** of the following storage facilities: _____.
234       **13.1.5. Water Rights.** The following legally described water rights:

235
236
237     Any water rights shall be conveyed by _____ deed or other applicable legal instrument. The Well
238 Permit # is _____.
239       **13.1.6. Growing Crops.** The following growing crops:

240
241
242    **13.2. Exclusions.** The following are excluded (Exclusions): _____

243 **14. TITLE AND ENCUMBRANCES.** Seller represents to Broker that title to the Property is solely in Seller's name. Seller shall
244 deliver to Broker true copies of all relevant title materials, leases, improvement location certificates and surveys in Seller's
245 possession and shall disclose to Broker all easements, liens and other encumbrances, if any, on the Property, of which Seller has
246 knowledge. Seller authorizes the holder of any obligation secured by an encumbrance on the Property to disclose to Broker the
247 amount owing on said encumbrance and the terms thereof. In case of Sale, Seller agrees to convey, by a _____
248 deed, only that title Seller has in the Property. Property shall be conveyed free and clear of all taxes, except the general taxes for
249 the year of closing.
250     All monetary encumbrances (such as mortgages, deeds of trust, liens, financing statements) shall be paid by Seller and released
251 except as Seller and buyer may otherwise agree. Existing monetary encumbrances are as follows: _____.
252     The Property is subject to the following leases and tenancies: _____.
253     If the Property has been or will be subject to any governmental liens for special improvements installed at the time of signing
254 a Sale contract, Seller shall be responsible for payment of same, unless otherwise agreed. Brokerage Firm may terminate this Seller
255 Listing Contract upon written notice to Seller that title is not satisfactory to Brokerage Firm.

256 **15. EVIDENCE OF TITLE.** Seller agrees to furnish buyer, at Seller's expense, a current commitment and an owner's title
257 insurance policy in an amount equal to the Purchase Price in the form specified in the Sale contract, or if this box is checked,
258 ☐ **An Abstract of Title** certified to a current date.

259 **16. ASSOCIATION ASSESSMENTS.** Seller represents that the amount of the regular owners' association assessment is
260 currently payable at $_____ per _____ and that there are no unpaid regular or special assessments against
261 the Property except the current regular assessments and except _____. Seller agrees to promptly
262 request the owners' association to deliver to buyer before date of closing a current statement of assessments against the Property.

263 **17. POSSESSION.** Possession of the Property shall be delivered to buyer as follows: _____,
264 subject to leases and tenancies as described in § 14.

265 **18. MATERIAL DEFECTS, DISCLOSURES AND INSPECTION.**
266    **18.1. Broker's Obligations.** Colorado law requires a broker to disclose to any prospective buyer all adverse material facts
267 actually known by such broker including but not limited to adverse material facts pertaining to the title to the Property and the
268 physical condition of the Property, any material defects in the Property, and any environmental hazards affecting the Property which
269 are required by law to be disclosed. These types of disclosures may include such matters as structural defects, soil conditions,
270 violations of health, zoning or building laws, and nonconforming uses and zoning variances. Seller agrees that any buyer may have
271 the Property and Inclusions inspected and authorizes Broker to disclose any facts actually known by Broker about the Property.

---

272     **18.2. Seller's Obligations.**
273         **18.2.1. Seller's Property Disclosure Form.** A seller is not required by law to provide a written disclosure of adverse
274     matters regarding the Property. However, disclosure of known material latent (not obvious) defects is required by law. Seller
275     ☐ **Agrees** ☐ **Does Not Agree** to provide a Seller's Property Disclosure form completed to Seller's current, actual knowledge.
276         **18.2.2. Lead-Based Paint.** Unless exempt, if the improvements on the Property include one or more residential
277     dwellings for which a building permit was issued prior to January 1, 1978, a completed Lead-Based Paint Disclosure (Sales) form
278     must be signed by Seller and the real estate licensees, and given to any potential buyer in a timely manner.
279         **18.2.3. Carbon Monoxide Alarms.** Note: If the improvements on the Property have a fuel-fired heater or appliance, a
280     fireplace, or an attached garage and one or more rooms lawfully used for sleeping purposes (Bedroom), Seller understands that
281     Colorado law requires that Seller assure the Property has an operational carbon monoxide alarm installed within fifteen feet of the
282     entrance to each Bedroom or in a location as required by the applicable building code, prior to offering the Property for sale or lease.
283     **18.3. Right of Broker to Terminate.** Although Broker has no obligation to investigate or inspect the Property, and no duty
284     to verify statements made, Broker shall have the right to terminate this Seller Listing Contract if the physical condition of the
285     Property, Inclusions, any proposed or existing transportation project, road, street or highway, or any other activity, odor or noise
286     (whether on or off the Property) and its effect or expected effect on the Property or its occupants, or if any facts or suspicions
287     regarding circumstances that could psychologically impact or stigmatize the Property are unsatisfactory to Broker.

288     **19. FORFEITURE OF PAYMENTS.** In the event of a forfeiture of payments made by a buyer, the sums received shall be
289     divided between Brokerage Firm and Seller, one-half thereof to Brokerage Firm but not to exceed the Brokerage Firm
290     compensation agreed upon herein, and the balance to Seller. Any forfeiture of payment under this section shall not reduce any
291     Brokerage Firm compensation owed, earned and payable under § 7.

292     **20. COST OF SERVICES AND REIMBURSEMENT.** Unless otherwise agreed upon in writing, Brokerage Firm shall bear all
293     expenses incurred by Brokerage Firm, if any, to market the Property and to compensate cooperating brokerage firms, if any.
294     Neither Broker nor Brokerage Firm shall obtain or order any other products or services unless Seller agrees in writing to pay for
295     them promptly when due (examples: surveys, radon tests, soil tests, title reports, engineering studies). Unless otherwise agreed,
296     neither Broker nor Brokerage Firm shall be obligated to advance funds for the benefit of Seller in order to complete a closing.
297     Seller shall reimburse Brokerage Firm for payments made by Brokerage Firm for such products or services authorized by Seller.

298     **21. DISCLOSURE OF SETTLEMENT COSTS.** Seller acknowledges that costs, quality, and extent of service vary between
299     different settlement service providers (e.g., attorneys, lenders, inspectors and title companies).

300     **22. MAINTENANCE OF THE PROPERTY.** Neither Broker nor Brokerage Firm shall be responsible for maintenance of the
301     Property nor shall they be liable for damage of any kind occurring to the Property, unless such damage shall be caused by their
302     negligence or intentional misconduct.

303     **23. NONDISCRIMINATION.** The parties agree not to discriminate unlawfully against any prospective buyer because of the
304     race, creed, color, sex, sexual orientation, marital status, familial status, physical or mental disability, handicap, religion, national
305     origin or ancestry of such person.

306     **24. RECOMMENDATION OF LEGAL AND TAX COUNSEL.** By signing this document, Seller acknowledges that Broker
307     has advised that this document has important legal consequences and has recommended consultation with legal and tax or other
308     counsel before signing this Seller Listing Contract.

309     **25. MEDIATION.** If a dispute arises relating to this Seller Listing Contract, prior to or after closing, and is not resolved, the
310     parties shall first proceed in good faith to submit the matter to mediation. Mediation is a process in which the parties meet with an
311     impartial person who helps to resolve the dispute informally and confidentially. Mediators cannot impose binding decisions. The
312     parties to the dispute must agree, in writing, before any settlement is binding. The parties will jointly appoint an acceptable
313     mediator and will share equally in the cost of such mediation. The mediation, unless otherwise agreed, shall terminate in the event
314     the entire dispute is not resolved within 30 calendar days of the date written notice requesting mediation is delivered by one party
315     to the other at the party's last known address.

316     **26. ATTORNEY FEES.** In the event of any arbitration or litigation relating to this Seller Listing Contract, the arbitrator or court
317     shall award to the prevailing party all reasonable costs and expenses, including attorney and legal fees.

318     **27. ADDITIONAL PROVISIONS.** (The following additional provisions have not been approved by the Colorado Real Estate Commission.)
319
320
321

---

322 **28. ATTACHMENTS.** The following are a part of this Seller Listing Contract:

323

324

325 **29. NO OTHER PARTY OR INTENDED BENEFICIARIES.** Nothing in this Seller Listing Contract shall be deemed to inure
326 to the benefit of any person other than Seller, Broker and Brokerage Firm.

327 **30. NOTICE, DELIVERY AND CHOICE OF LAW.**
328     **30.1. Physical Delivery.** All notices must be in writing, except as provided in § 30.2. Any document, including a signed
329 document or notice, delivered to the other party to this Seller Listing Contract, is effective upon physical receipt. Delivery to Seller
330 shall be effective when physically received by Seller, any signator on behalf of Seller, any named individual of Seller or
331 representative of Seller.
332     **30.2. Electronic Delivery.** As an alternative to physical delivery, any document, including any signed document or written
333 notice may be delivered in electronic form only by the following indicated methods: ☐ **Facsimile** ☐ **Email** ☐ **Internet** ☐ **No**
334 **Electronic Delivery.** Documents with original signatures shall be provided upon request of any party.
335     **30.3. Choice of Law.** This Seller Listing Contract and all disputes arising hereunder shall be governed by and construed in
336 accordance with the laws of the State of Colorado that would be applicable to Colorado residents who sign a contract in this state
337 for property located in Colorado.

338 **31. MODIFICATION OF THIS SELLER LISTING CONTRACT.** No subsequent modification of any of the terms of this
339 Seller Listing Contract shall be valid, binding upon the parties, or enforceable unless made in writing and signed by the parties.

340 **32. COUNTERPARTS.** If more than one person is named as a Seller herein, this Seller Listing Contract may be executed by
341 each Seller, separately, and when so executed, such copies taken together with one executed by Broker on behalf of Brokerage
342 Firm shall be deemed to be a full and complete contract between the parties.

343 **33. ENTIRE AGREEMENT.** This agreement constitutes the entire contract between the parties, and any prior agreements,
344 whether oral or written, have been merged and integrated into this Seller Listing Contract.

345 **34. COPY OF CONTRACT.** Seller acknowledges receipt of a copy of this Seller Listing Contract signed by Broker, including
346 all attachments.

347 Brokerage Firm authorizes Broker to execute this Seller Listing Contract on behalf of Brokerage Firm.

Seller's Name: _____  Broker's Name: _____

_____  _____
Seller's Signature         Date       Broker's Signature         Date
Address: _____  Address: _____

Phone No.: _____  Phone No.: _____
Fax No: _____  Fax No: _____
Electronic Address: _____  Electronic Address: _____

Brokerage
Firm's Name: _____
Address: _____
_____

Phone No.: _____
Fax No.: _____
Electronic Address: _____

348

# FORM 15 – HUD-1 SETTLEMENT STATEMENT

OMB Approval No. 2502-0265

## A. **Settlement Statement (HUD-1)**

| 1. ☐ FHA  2. ☐ RHS  3. ☐ Conv. Unins. | 6. File Number: | 7. Loan Number: | 8. Mortgage Insurance Case Number: |
| 4. ☐ VA  5. ☐ Conv. Ins. | | | |

**C. Note:** This form is furnished to give you a statement of actual settlement costs. Amounts paid to and by the settlement agent are shown. Items marked "(p.o.c.)" were paid outside the closing; they are shown here for informational purposes and are not included in the totals.

| D. Name & Address of Borrower: | E. Name & Address of Seller: | F. Name & Address of Lender: |
| --- | --- | --- |

| G. Property Location: | H. Settlement Agent: | I. Settlement Date: |
| --- | --- | --- |
| | Place of Settlement: | |

**J. Summary of Borrower's Transaction**

**100. Gross Amount Due from Borrower**

| 101. Contract sales price | |
| --- | --- |
| 102. Personal property | |
| 103. Settlement charges to borrower (line 1400) | |
| 104. | |
| 105. | |

Adjustment for items paid by seller in advance

| 106. City/town taxes       to | |
| --- | --- |
| 107. County taxes       to | |
| 108. Assessments       to | |
| 109. | |
| 110. | |
| 111. | |
| 112. | |

**120. Gross Amount Due from Borrower**

**200. Amount Paid by or in Behalf of Borrower**

| 201. Deposit or earnest money | |
| --- | --- |
| 202. Principal amount of new loan(s) | |
| 203. Existing loan(s) taken subject to | |
| 204. | |
| 205. | |
| 206. | |
| 207. | |
| 208. | |
| 209. | |

Adjustments for items unpaid by seller

| 210. City/town taxes       to | |
| --- | --- |
| 211. County taxes       to | |
| 212. Assessments       to | |
| 213. | |
| 214. | |
| 215. | |
| 216. | |
| 217. | |
| 218. | |
| 219. | |

**220. Total Paid by/for Borrower**

**300. Cash at Settlement from/to Borrower**

| 301. Gross amount due from borrower (line 120) | |
| --- | --- |
| 302. Less amounts paid by/for borrower (line 220) | ( ) |

**303. Cash ☐ From ☐ To Borrower**

**K. Summary of Seller's Transaction**

**400. Gross Amount Due to Seller**

| 401. Contract sales price | |
| --- | --- |
| 402. Personal property | |
| 403. | |
| 404. | |
| 405. | |

Adjustment for items paid by seller in advance

| 406. City/town taxes       to | |
| --- | --- |
| 407. County taxes       to | |
| 408. Assessments       to | |
| 409. | |
| 410. | |
| 411. | |
| 412. | |

**420. Gross Amount Due to Seller**

**500. Reductions In Amount Due to seller**

| 501. Excess deposit (see instructions) | |
| --- | --- |
| 502. Settlement charges to seller (line 1400) | |
| 503. Existing loan(s) taken subject to | |
| 504. Payoff of first mortgage loan | |
| 505. Payoff of second mortgage loan | |
| 506. | |
| 507. | |
| 508. | |
| 509. | |

Adjustments for items unpaid by seller

| 510. City/town taxes       to | |
| --- | --- |
| 511. County taxes       to | |
| 512. Assessments       to | |
| 513. | |
| 514. | |
| 515. | |
| 516. | |
| 517. | |
| 518. | |
| 519. | |

**520. Total Reduction Amount Due Seller**

**600. Cash at Settlement to/from Seller**

| 601. Gross amount due to seller (line 420) | |
| --- | --- |
| 602. Less reductions in amounts due seller (line 520) | ( ) |

**603. Cash ☐ To ☐ From Seller**

The Public Reporting Burden for this collection of information is estimated at 35 minutes per response for collecting, reviewing, and reporting the data. This agency may not collect this information, and you are not required to complete this form, unless it displays a currently valid OMB control number. No confidentiality is assured; this disclosure is mandatory. This is designed to provide the parties to a RESPA covered transaction with information during the settlement process.

**L. Settlement Charges**

| **700. Total Real Estate Broker Fees** | | Paid From Borrower's Funds at Settlement | Paid From Seller's Funds at Settlement |
|---|---|---|---|
| Division of commission (line 700) as follows : | | | |
| 701. $ to | | | |
| 702. $ to | | | |
| 703. Commission paid at settlement | | | |
| 704. | | | |

| **800. Items Payable in Connection with Loan** | | | |
|---|---|---|---|
| 801. Our origination charge | $ (from GFE #1) | | |
| 802. Your credit or charge (points) for the specific interest rate chosen | $ (from GFE #2) | | |
| 803. Your adjusted origination charges | (from GFE #A) | | |
| 804. Appraisal fee to | (from GFE #3) | | |
| 805. Credit report to | (from GFE #3) | | |
| 806. Tax service to | (from GFE #3) | | |
| 807. Flood certification to | (from GFE #3) | | |
| 808. | | | |
| 809. | | | |
| 810. | | | |
| 811. | | | |

| **900. Items Required by Lender to be Paid in Advance** | | | |
|---|---|---|---|
| 901. Daily interest charges from to @ $ /day | (from GFE #10) | | |
| 902. Mortgage insurance premium for months to | (from GFE #3) | | |
| 903. Homeowner's insurance for years to | (from GFE #11) | | |
| 904. | | | |

| **1000. Reserves Deposited with Lender** | | | |
|---|---|---|---|
| 1001. Initial deposit for your escrow account | (from GFE #9) | | |
| 1002. Homeowner's insurance months @ $ per month $ | | | |
| 1003. Mortgage insurance months @ $ per month $ | | | |
| 1004. Property Taxes months @ $ per month $ | | | |
| 1005. months @ $ per month $ | | | |
| 1006. months @ $ per month $ | | | |
| 1007. Aggregate Adjustment -$ | | | |

| **1100. Title Charges** | | | |
|---|---|---|---|
| 1101. Title services and lender's title insurance | (from GFE #4) | | |
| 1102. Settlement or closing fee | $ | | |
| 1103. Owner's title insurance | (from GFE #5) | | |
| 1104. Lender's title insurance | $ | | |
| 1105. Lender's title policy limit $ | | | |
| 1106. Owner's title policy limit $ | | | |
| 1107. Agent's portion of the total title insurance premium to | $ | | |
| 1108. Underwriter's portion of the total title insurance premium to | $ | | |
| 1109. | | | |
| 1110. | | | |
| 1111. | | | |

| **1200. Government Recording and Transfer Charges** | | | |
|---|---|---|---|
| 1201. Government recording charges | (from GFE #7) | | |
| 1202. Deed $ Mortgage $ Release $ | | | |
| 1203. Transfer taxes | (from GFE #8) | | |
| 1204. City/County tax/stamps Deed $ Mortgage $ | | | |
| 1205. State tax/stamps Deed $ Mortgage $ | | | |
| 1206. | | | |

| **1300. Additional Settlement Charges** | | | |
|---|---|---|---|
| 1301. Required services that you can shop for | (from GFE #6) | | |
| 1302. | $ | | |
| 1303. | $ | | |
| 1304. | | | |
| 1305. | | | |

| **1400. Total Settlement Charges (enter on lines 103, Section J and 502, Section K)** | | | |
|---|---|---|---|

| Comparison of Good Faith Estimate (GFE) and HUD-1 Charrges | | Good Faith Estimate | HUD-1 |
|---|---|---|---|
| **Charges That Cannot Increase** | **HUD-1 Line Number** | | |
| Our origination charge | # 801 | | |
| Your credit or charge (points) for the specific interest rate chosen | # 802 | | |
| Your adjusted origination charges | # 803 | | |
| Transfer taxes | # 1203 | | |

| Charges That In Total Cannot Increase More Than 10% | | Good Faith Estimate | HUD-1 |
|---|---|---|---|
| Government recording charges | # 1201 | | |
| | # | | |
| | # | | |
| | # | | |
| | # | | |
| | # | | |
| | # | | |
| | # | | |
| | **Total** | | |
| | **Increase between GFE and HUD-1 Charges** | $          or | % |

| Charges That Can Change | | Good Faith Estimate | HUD-1 |
|---|---|---|---|
| Initial deposit for your escrow account | # 1001 | | |
| Daily interest charges          $          /day | # 901 | | |
| Homeowner's insurance | # 903 | | |
| | # | | |
| | # | | |
| | # | | |

**Loan Terms**

| | |
|---|---|
| Your initial loan amount is | $ |
| Your loan term is | years |
| Your initial interest rate is | % |
| Your initial monthly amount owed for principal, interest, and any mortgage insurance is | $          includes<br>☐ Principal<br>☐ Interest<br>☐ Mortgage Insurance |
| Can your interest rate rise? | ☐ No  ☐ Yes, it can rise to a maximum of          %. The first change will be on and can change again every          after          . Every change date, your interest rate can increase or decrease by          %. Over the life of the loan, your interest rate is guaranteed to never be **lower** than          % or **higher** than          %. |
| Even if you make payments on time, can your loan balance rise? | ☐ No  ☐ Yes, it can rise to a maximum of $ |
| Even if you make payments on time, can your monthly amount owed for principal, interest, and mortgage insurance rise? | ☐ No  ☐ Yes, the first increase can be on          and the monthly amount owed can rise to $          . The maximum it can ever rise to is $          . |
| Does your loan have a prepayment penalty? | ☐ No  ☐ Yes, your maximum prepayment penalty is $ |
| Does your loan have a balloon payment? | ☐ No  ☐ Yes, you have a balloon payment of $          due in          years on          . |
| Total monthly amount owed including escrow account payments | ☐ You do not have a monthly escrow payment for items, such as property taxes and homeowner's insurance. You must pay these items directly yourself.<br>☐ You have an additional monthly escrow payment of $          that results in a total initial monthly amount owed of $          . This includes principal, interest, any mortgage insurance and any items checked below:<br>☐ Property taxes          ☐ Homeowner's insurance<br>☐ Flood insurance          ☐<br>☐          ☐ |

**Note:** If you have any questions about the Settlement Charges and Loan Terms listed on this form, please contact your lender.

# FORM 16 – UNIFORM RESIDENTIAL LOAN APPLICATION

## Uniform Residential Loan Application

This application is designed to be completed by the applicant(s) with the Lender's assistance. Applicants should complete this form as "Borrower" or "Co-Borrower," as applicable. Co-Borrower information must also be provided (and the appropriate box checked) when ☐ the income or assets of a person other than the Borrower (including the Borrower's spouse) will be used as a basis for loan qualification or ☐ the income or assets of the Borrower's spouse or other person who has community property rights pursuant to state law will not be used as a basis for loan qualification, but his or her liabilities must be considered because the spouse or other person has community property rights pursuant to applicable law and Borrower resides in a community property state, the security property is located in a community property state, or the Borrower is relying on other property located in a community property state as a basis for repayment of the loan.

If this is an application for joint credit, Borrower and Co-Borrower each agree that we intend to apply for joint credit (sign below):

Borrower _____    Co-Borrower _____

## I. TYPE OF MORTGAGE AND TERMS OF LOAN

| Mortgage Applied for: | ☐ VA<br>☐ FHA | ☐ Conventional<br>☐ USDA/Rural Housing Service | ☐ Other (explain): | Agency Case Number | Lender Case Number |
|---|---|---|---|---|---|

| Amount<br>$ | Interest Rate<br>% | No. of Months | Amortization Type: | ☐ Fixed Rate<br>☐ GPM | ☐ Other (explain):<br>☐ ARM (type): |
|---|---|---|---|---|---|

## II. PROPERTY INFORMATION AND PURPOSE OF LOAN

| Subject Property Address (street, city, state & ZIP) | No. of Units |
|---|---|

| Legal Description of Subject Property (attach description if necessary) | Year Built |
|---|---|

| Purpose of Loan | ☐ Purchase  ☐ Construction  ☐ Other (explain):<br>☐ Refinance  ☐ Construction-Permanent | Property will be:<br>☐ Primary Residence     ☐ Secondary Residence     ☐ Investment |
|---|---|---|

*Complete this line if construction or construction-permanent loan.*

| Year Lot Acquired | Original Cost<br>$ | Amount Existing Liens<br>$ | (a) Present Value of Lot<br>$ | (b) Cost of Improvements<br>$ | Total (a + b)<br>$ |
|---|---|---|---|---|---|

*Complete this line if this is a refinance loan.*

| Year Acquired | Original Cost<br>$ | Amount Existing Liens<br>$ | Purpose of Refinance | Describe Improvements  ☐ made  ☐ to be made<br>Cost: $ |
|---|---|---|---|---|

| Title will be held in what Name(s) | Manner in which Title will be held | Estate will be held in:<br>☐ Fee Simple<br>☐ Leasehold (show expiration date) |
|---|---|---|

| Source of Down Payment, Settlement Charges, and/or Subordinate Financing (explain) |
|---|

## III. BORROWER INFORMATION

| Borrower | Co-Borrower |
|---|---|

| Borrower's Name (include Jr. or Sr. if applicable) | Co-Borrower's Name (include Jr. or Sr. if applicable) |
|---|---|

| Social Security Number | Home Phone (incl. area code) | DOB (mm/dd/yyyy) | Yrs. School | Social Security Number | Home Phone (incl. area code) | DOB (mm/dd/yyyy) | Yrs. School |
|---|---|---|---|---|---|---|---|

| ☐ Married  ☐ Unmarried (include single, divorced, widowed)<br>☐ Separated | Dependents (not listed by Co-Borrower)<br>no.        ages | ☐ Married  ☐ Unmarried (include single, divorced, widowed)<br>☐ Separated | Dependents (not listed by Borrower)<br>no.        ages |
|---|---|---|---|

| Present Address (street, city, state, ZIP)  ☐ Own  ☐ Rent ____ No. Yrs. | Present Address (street, city, state, ZIP)  ☐ Own  ☐ Rent ____ No. Yrs. |
|---|---|

| Mailing Address, if different from Present Address | Mailing Address, if different from Present Address |
|---|---|

*If residing at present address for less than two years, complete the following:*

| Former Address (street, city, state, ZIP)  ☐ Own  ☐ Rent ____ No. Yrs. | Former Address (street, city, state, ZIP)  ☐ Own  ☐ Rent ____ No. Yrs. |
|---|---|

## IV. EMPLOYMENT INFORMATION

| Borrower | Co-Borrower |
|---|---|

| Name & Address of Employer  ☐ Self Employed | Yrs. on this job | Name & Address of Employer  ☐ Self Employed | Yrs. on this job |
|---|---|---|---|
| | Yrs. employed in this line of work/profession | | Yrs. employed in this line of work/profession |

| Position/Title/Type of Business | Business Phone (incl. area code) | Position/Title/Type of Business | Business Phone (incl. area code) |
|---|---|---|---|

*If employed in current position for less than two years or if currently employed in more than one position, complete the following:*

| Borrower | | | IV. EMPLOYMENT INFORMATION (cont'd) | Co-Borrower | | |
|---|---|---|---|---|---|---|
| Name & Address of Employer | ☐ Self Employed | Dates (from – to) | Name & Address of Employer | ☐ Self Employed | Dates (from – to) |
| | | Monthly Income $ | | | Monthly Income $ |
| Position/Title/Type of Business | | Business Phone (incl. area code) | Position/Title/Type of Business | | Business Phone (incl. area code) |
| Name & Address of Employer | ☐ Self Employed | Dates (from – to) | Name & Address of Employer | ☐ Self Employed | Dates (from – to) |
| | | Monthly Income $ | | | Monthly Income $ |
| Position/Title/Type of Business | | Business Phone (incl. area code) | Position/Title/Type of Business | | Business Phone (incl. area code) |

## V. MONTHLY INCOME AND COMBINED HOUSING EXPENSE INFORMATION

| Gross Monthly Income | Borrower | Co-Borrower | Total | Combined Monthly Housing Expense | Present | Proposed |
|---|---|---|---|---|---|---|
| Base Empl. Income* | $ | $ | $ | Rent | $ | |
| Overtime | | | | First Mortgage (P&I) | | $ |
| Bonuses | | | | Other Financing (P&I) | | |
| Commissions | | | | Hazard Insurance | | |
| Dividends/Interest | | | | Real Estate Taxes | | |
| Net Rental Income | | | | Mortgage Insurance | | |
| Other (before completing, see the notice in "describe other income," below) | | | | Homeowner Assn. Dues | | |
| | | | | Other: | | |
| Total | $ | $ | $ | Total | $ | $ |

\* Self Employed Borrower(s) may be required to provide additional documentation such as tax returns and financial statements.

**Describe Other Income**   *Notice:* Alimony, child support, or separate maintenance income need not be revealed if the Borrower (B) or Co-Borrower (C) does not choose to have it considered for repaying this loan.

| B/C | | Monthly Amount |
|---|---|---|
| | | $ |
| | | |
| | | |

## VI. ASSETS AND LIABILITIES

This Statement and any applicable supporting schedules may be completed jointly by both married and unmarried Co-Borrowers if their assets and liabilities are sufficiently joined so that the Statement can be meaningfully and fairly presented on a combined basis; otherwise, separate Statements and Schedules are required. If the Co-Borrower section was completed about a non-applicant spouse or other person, this Statement and supporting schedules must be completed about that spouse or other person also.

Completed ☐ Jointly ☐ Not Jointly

| ASSETS  Description | Cash or Market Value | Liabilities and Pledged Assets. List the creditor's name, address, and account number for all outstanding debts, including automobile loans, revolving charge accounts, real estate loans, alimony, child support, stock pledges, etc. Use continuation sheet, if necessary. Indicate by (*) those liabilities, which will be satisfied upon sale of real estate owned or upon refinancing of the subject property. | | |
|---|---|---|---|---|
| Cash deposit toward purchase held by: | $ | | | |
| **List checking and savings accounts below** | | **LIABILITIES** | Monthly Payment & Months Left to Pay | Unpaid Balance |
| Name and address of Bank, S&L, or Credit Union | | Name and address of Company | $ Payment/Months | $ |
| Acct. no. | $ | Acct. no. | | |
| Name and address of Bank, S&L, or Credit Union | | Name and address of Company | $ Payment/Months | $ |
| Acct. no. | $ | Acct. no. | | |
| Name and address of Bank, S&L, or Credit Union | | Name and address of Company | $ Payment/Months | $ |
| Acct. no. | $ | Acct. no. | | |

| VI. ASSETS AND LIABILITIES (cont'd) | | | |
|---|---|---|---|
| Name and address of Bank, S&L, or Credit Union | Name and address of Company | $ Payment/Months | $ |
| Acct. no. $ | Acct. no. | | |
| Stocks & Bonds (Company name/ number & description) $ | Name and address of Company | $ Payment/Months | $ |
| | Acct. no. | | |
| Life insurance net cash value $ | Name and address of Company | $ Payment/Months | $ |
| Face amount: $ | | | |
| **Subtotal Liquid Assets** $ | | | |
| Real estate owned (enter market value from schedule of real estate owned) $ | | | |
| Vested interest in retirement fund $ | | | |
| Net worth of business(es) owned (attach financial statement) $ | Acct. no. | | |
| Automobiles owned (make and year) $ | Alimony/Child Support/Separate Maintenance Payments Owed to: | $ | |
| Other Assets (itemize) $ | Job-Related Expense (child care, union dues, etc.) | $ | |
| | **Total Monthly Payments** | $ | |
| **Total Assets a.** $ | **Net Worth** (a minus b) ▶ $ | **Total Liabilities b.** | $ |

**Schedule of Real Estate Owned** (If additional properties are owned, use continuation sheet.)

| Property Address (enter S if sold, PS if pending sale or R if rental being held for income) ▼ | Type of Property | Present Market Value | Amount of Mortgages & Liens | Gross Rental Income | Mortgage Payments | Insurance, Maintenance, Taxes & Misc. | Net Rental Income |
|---|---|---|---|---|---|---|---|
| | | $ | $ | $ | $ | $ | $ |
| | | | | | | | |
| | | | | | | | |
| | Totals | $ | $ | $ | $ | $ | $ |

List any additional names under which credit has previously been received and indicate appropriate creditor name(s) and account number(s):

| Alternate Name | Creditor Name | Account Number |
|---|---|---|
| | | |
| | | |

| VII. DETAILS OF TRANSACTION | | VIII. DECLARATIONS | | | | |
|---|---|---|---|---|---|---|
| a. Purchase price | $ | If you answer "Yes" to any questions a through i, please use continuation sheet for explanation. | **Borrower** | | **Co-Borrower** | |
| | | | **Yes** **No** | | **Yes** **No** | |
| b. Alterations, improvements, repairs | | a. Are there any outstanding judgments against you? | ☐ ☐ | | ☐ ☐ | |
| c. Land (if acquired separately) | | b. Have you been declared bankrupt within the past 7 years? | ☐ ☐ | | ☐ ☐ | |
| d. Refinance (incl. debts to be paid off) | | c. Have you had property foreclosed upon or given title or deed in lieu thereof in the last 7 years? | ☐ ☐ | | ☐ ☐ | |
| e. Estimated prepaid items | | d. Are you a party to a lawsuit? | ☐ ☐ | | ☐ ☐ | |
| f. Estimated closing costs | | e. Have you directly or indirectly been obligated on any loan which resulted in foreclosure, transfer of title in lieu of foreclosure, or judgment? | ☐ ☐ | | ☐ ☐ | |
| g. PMI, MIP, Funding Fee | | (This would include such loans as home mortgage loans, SBA loans, home improvement loans, educational loans, manufactured (mobile) home loans, any mortgage, financial obligation, bond, or loan guarantee. If "Yes," provide details, including date, name, and address of Lender, FHA or VA case number, if any, and reasons for the action.) | | | | |
| h. Discount (if Borrower will pay) | | | | | | |
| i. Total costs (add items a through h) | | | | | | |

**Uniform Residential Loan Application**
Freddie Mac Form 65   7/05 (rev.6/09)          Page 3 of 5          Fannie Mae Form 1003   7/05 (rev.6/09)

| VII. DETAILS OF TRANSACTION | | | VIII. DECLARATIONS | | | | |
|---|---|---|---|---|---|---|---|

| | | | | | Borrower | | Co-Borrower | |
|---|---|---|---|---|---|---|---|
| | | | If you answer "Yes" to any questions a through i, please use continuation sheet for explanation. | | Yes | No | Yes | No |
| j. | Subordinate financing | | | | | | | |
| k. | Borrower's closing costs paid by Seller | | f. Are you presently delinquent or in default on any Federal debt or any other loan, mortgage, financial obligation, bond, or loan guarantee? | | ☐ | ☐ | ☐ | ☐ |
| | | | g. Are you obligated to pay alimony, child support, or separate maintenance? | | ☐ | ☐ | ☐ | ☐ |
| l. | Other Credits (explain) | | h. Is any part of the down payment borrowed? | | ☐ | ☐ | ☐ | ☐ |
| | | | i. Are you a co-maker or endorser on a note? | | ☐ | ☐ | ☐ | ☐ |
| m. | Loan amount (exclude PMI, MIP, Funding Fee financed) | | ------------------------------------------------- | | | | | |
| | | | j. Are you a U.S. citizen? | | ☐ | ☐ | ☐ | ☐ |
| n. | PMI, MIP, Funding Fee financed | | k. Are you a permanent resident alien? | | ☐ | ☐ | ☐ | ☐ |
| o. | Loan amount (add m & n) | | l. **Do you intend to occupy the property as your primary residence?** If Yes," complete question m below. | | ☐ | ☐ | ☐ | ☐ |
| p. | Cash from/to Borrower (subtract j, k, l & o from i) | | m. Have you had an ownership interest in a property in the last three years? | | ☐ | ☐ | ☐ | ☐ |
| | | | (1) What type of property did you own—principal residence (PR), second home (SH), or investment property (IP)? | | _____ | | _____ | |
| | | | (2) How did you hold title to the home— by yourself (S), jointly with your spouse (SP), or jointly with another person (O)? | | _____ | | _____ | |

| IX. ACKNOWLEDGEMENT AND AGREEMENT |
|---|

Each of the undersigned specifically represents to Lender and to Lender's actual or potential agents, brokers, processors, attorneys, insurers, servicers, successors and assigns and agrees and acknowledges that: (1) the information provided in this application is true and correct as of the date set forth opposite my signature and that any intentional or negligent misrepresentation of this information contained in this application may result in civil liability, including monetary damages, to any person who may suffer any loss due to reliance upon any misrepresentation that I have made on this application, and/or in criminal penalties including, but not limited to, fine or imprisonment or both under the provisions of Title 18, United States Code, Sec. 1001, et seq.; (2) the loan requested pursuant to this application (the "Loan") will be secured by a mortgage or deed of trust on the property described in this application; (3) the property will not be used for any illegal or prohibited purpose or use; (4) all statements made in this application are made for the purpose of obtaining a residential mortgage loan; (5) the property will be occupied as indicated in this application; (6) the Lender, its servicers, successors or assigns may retain the original and/or an electronic record of this application, whether or not the Loan is approved; (7) the Lender and its agents, brokers, insurers, servicers, successors, and assigns may continuously rely on the information contained in the application, and I am obligated to amend and/or supplement the information provided in this application if any of the material facts that I have represented herein should change prior to closing of the Loan; (8) in the event that my payments on the Loan become delinquent, the Lender, its servicers, successors or assigns may, in addition to any other rights and remedies that it may have relating to such delinquency, report my name and account information to one or more consumer reporting agencies; (9) ownership of the Loan and/or administration of the Loan account may be transferred with such notice as may be required by law; (10) neither Lender nor its agents, brokers, insurers, servicers, successors or assigns has made any representation or warranty, express or implied, to me regarding the property or the condition or value of the property; and (11) my transmission of this application as an "electronic record" containing my "electronic signature," as those terms are defined in applicable federal and/or state laws (excluding audio and video recordings), or my facsimile transmission of this application containing a facsimile of my signature, shall be as effective, enforceable and valid as if a paper version of this application were delivered containing my original written signature.

Acknowledgement. Each of the undersigned hereby acknowledges that any owner of the Loan, its servicers, successors and assigns, may verify or reverify any information contained in this application or obtain any information or data relating to the Loan, for any legitimate business purpose through any source, including a source named in this application or a consumer reporting agency.

| Borrower's Signature<br>X | Date | Co-Borrower's Signature<br>X | Date |
|---|---|---|---|

| X. INFORMATION FOR GOVERNMENT MONITORING PURPOSES |
|---|

The following information is requested by the Federal Government for certain types of loans related to a dwelling in order to monitor the lender's compliance with equal credit opportunity, fair housing and home mortgage disclosure laws. You are not required to furnish this information, but are encouraged to do so. The law provides that a lender may not discriminate either on the basis of this information, or on whether you choose to furnish it. If you furnish the information, please provide both ethnicity and race. For race, you may check more than one designation. If you do not furnish ethnicity, race, or sex, under Federal regulations, this lender is required to note the information on the basis of visual observation and surname if you have made this application in person. If you do not wish to furnish the information, please check the box below. (Lender must review the above material to assure that the disclosures satisfy all requirements to which the lender is subject under applicable state law for the particular type of loan applied for.)

| **BORROWER** ☐ I do not wish to furnish this information | **CO-BORROWER** ☐ I do not wish to furnish this information |
|---|---|
| **Ethnicity:** ☐ Hispanic or Latino ☐ Not Hispanic or Latino | **Ethnicity:** ☐ Hispanic or Latino ☐ Not Hispanic or Latino |
| **Race:** ☐ American Indian or Alaska Native  ☐ Asian  ☐ Black or African American  ☐ Native Hawaiian or Other Pacific Islander  ☐ White | **Race:** ☐ American Indian or Alaska Native  ☐ Asian  ☐ Black or African American  ☐ Native Hawaiian or Other Pacific Islander  ☐ White |
| **Sex:** ☐ Female  ☐ Male | **Sex:** ☐ Female  ☐ Male |

To be Completed by Loan Originator:
This information was provided:
☐ In a face-to-face interview
☐ In a telephone interview
☐ By the applicant and submitted by fax or mail
☐ By the applicant and submitted via e-mail or the Internet

| Loan Originator's Signature<br>X | Date |
|---|---|
| Loan Originator's Name (print or type) | Loan Originator Identifier | Loan Originator's Phone Number (including area code) |
| Loan Origination Company's Name | Loan Origination Company Identifier | Loan Origination Company's Address |

**CONTINUATION SHEET/RESIDENTIAL LOAN APPLICATION**

| Use this continuation sheet if you need more space to complete the Residential Loan Application. Mark **B** f or Borrower or **C** for Co-Borrower. | Borrower: | Agency Case Number: |
|---|---|---|
| | Co-Borrower: | Lender Case Number: |

I/We fully understand that it is a Federal crime punishable by fine or imprisonment, or both, to knowingly make any false statements concerning any of the above facts as applicable under the provisions of Title 18, United States Code, Section 1001, et seq.

| Borrower's Signature | Date | Co-Borrower's Signature | Date |
|---|---|---|---|
| X | | X | |

**Uniform Residential Loan Application**
Freddie Mac Form 65   7/05 (rev.6/09)                    Page 5 of 5                    Fannie Mae Form 1003   7/05 (rev.6/09)

# FORM 17 – GOOD FAITH ESTIMATE OF CLOSING COSTS

OMB Approval No. 2502-0265

## Good Faith Estimate (GFE)

| Name of Originator | ABC BANK | | Borrower | Daniel and Sara Schan |
|---|---|---|---|---|
| Originator Address | 1 Bank Place | | Property Address | 489 Jefferson Street Newtowne, YS |
| Originator Phone Number | 555 322 5804 | | | |
| Originator Email | | | Date of GFE | |

**Purpose**

This GFE gives you an estimate of your settlement charges and loan terms if you are approved for this loan. For more information, see HUD's *Special Information Booklet* on settlement charges, your *Truth-in-Lending Disclosures*, and other consumer information at www.hud.gov/respa. If you decide you would like to proceed with this loan, contact us.

**Shopping for your loan**

Only you can shop for the best loan for you. Compare this GFE with other loan offers, so you can find the best loan. Use the shopping chart on page 3 to compare all the offers you receive.

**Important dates**

1. The interest rate for this GFE is available through ⬚ April 30 ⬚. After this time, the interest rate, some of your loan Origination Charges, and the monthly payment shown below can change until you lock your interest rate.

2. This estimate for all other settlement charges is available through ⬚ April 30 ⬚.

3. After you lock your interest rate, you must go to settlement within ⬚ days (your rate lock period) to receive the locked interest rate.

4. You must lock the interest rate at least ⬚7⬚ days before settlement.

**Summary of your loan**

| | |
|---|---|
| Your initial loan amount is | $ 246,400.00 |
| Your loan term is | 30 years |
| Your initial interest rate is | 6.125 % |
| Your initial monthly amount owed for principal, interest, and any mortgage insurance is | $ 1,497.15 per month |
| Can your interest rate rise? | ☒ No ☐ Yes, it can rise to a maximum of      %. The first change will be in |
| Even if you make payments on time, can your loan balance rise? | ☒ No ☐ Yes, it can rise to a maximum of $ |
| Even if you make payments on time, can your monthly amount owed for principal, interest, and any mortgage insurance rise? | ☒ No ☐ Yes, the first increase can be in       and the monthly amount owed can rise to $      . The maximum it can ever rise to is $       . |
| Does your loan have a prepayment penalty? | ☒ No ☐ Yes, your maximum prepayment penalty is $       . |
| Does your loan have a balloon payment? | ☒ No ☐ Yes, you have a balloon payment of $       due in      years. |

**Escrow account information**

Some lenders require an escrow account to hold funds for paying property taxes or other property-related charges in addition to your monthly amount owed of $ ⬚ 300.00 ⬚.
Do we require you to have an escrow account for your loan?
☐ No, you do not have an escrow account. You must pay these charges directly when due.
☒ Yes, you have an escrow account. It may or may not cover all of these charges. Ask us.

**Summary of your settlement charges**

| | | |
|---|---|---|
| **A** | Your Adjusted Origination Charges *(See page 2.)* | $ |
| **B** | Your Charges for All Other Settlement Services *(See page 2.)* | $ 6378 |
| **A + B** | Total Estimated Settlement Charges | $ 6378 |

**Understanding your estimated settlement charges**

*Some of these charges can change at settlement. See the top of page 3 for more information.*

## Your Adjusted Origination Charges

| | |
|---|---|
| **1. Our origination charge**<br>This charge is for getting this loan for you. | |
| **2. Your credit or charge (points) for the specific interest rate chosen**<br>☐ The credit or charge for the interest rate of [      ] % is included in "Our origination charge." (See item 1 above.)<br>☐ You receive a credit of $ [      ] for this interest rate of [      ] %. This credit **reduces** your settlement charges.<br>☐ You pay a charge of $ [      ] for this interest rate of [      ] %. This charge (points) **increases** your total settlement charges.<br>The tradeoff table on page 3 shows that you can change your total settlement charges by choosing a different interest rate for this loan. | |
| **A**  Your Adjusted Origination Charges | $ |

## Your Charges for All Other Settlement Services

| | |
|---|---|
| **3. Required services that we select**<br>These charges are for services we require to complete your settlement. We will choose the providers of these services.<br>*Service*                      *Charge* | |
| **4. Title services and lender's title insurance**<br>This charge includes the services of a title or settlement agent, for example, and title insurance to protect the lender, if required. | |
| **5. Owner's title insurance**<br>You may purchase an owner's title insurance policy to protect your interest in the property. | 1933 |
| **6. Required services that you can shop for**<br>These charges are for other services that are required to complete your settlement. We can identify providers of these services or you can shop for them yourself. Our estimates for providing these services are below.<br>*Service*                      *Charge* | |
| **7. Government recording charges**<br>These charges are for state and local fees to record your loan and title documents. | 180 |
| **8. Transfer taxes**<br>These charges are for state and local fees on mortgages and home sales. | 3080 |
| **9. Initial deposit for your escrow account**<br>This charge is held in an escrow account to pay future recurring charges on your property and includes [x] all property taxes, ☐ all insurance, and ☐ other [          ]. | 1185 |
| **10. Daily interest charges**<br>This charge is for the daily interest on your loan from the day of your settlement until the first day of the next month or the first day of your normal mortgage payment cycle. This amount is $[ 41.92 ] per day for [ 2 ] days (if your settlement is [11/29] ). | |
| **11. Homeowner's insurance**<br>This charge is for the insurance you must buy for the property to protect from a loss, such as fire.<br>*Policy*                      *Charge* | |
| **B**  Your Charges for All Other Settlement Services | $  6378 |
| **A + B**  Total Estimated Settlement Charges | $  6378 |

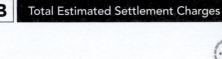

**Good Faith Estimate (HUD-GFE)** 2

# Instructions

### Understanding which charges can change at settlement

This GFE estimates your settlement charges. At your settlement, you will receive a HUD-1, a form that lists your actual costs. Compare the charges on the HUD-1 with the charges on this GFE. Charges can change if you select your own provider and do not use the companies we identify. (See below for details.)

| These charges **cannot increase** at settlement: | The total of these charges **can increase up to 10%** at settlement: | These charges **can change** at settlement: |
|---|---|---|
| ■ Our origination charge<br><br>■ Your credit or charge (points) for the specific interest rate chosen *(after you lock in your interest rate)*<br><br>■ Your adjusted origination charges *(after you lock in your interest rate)*<br><br>■ Transfer taxes | ■ Required services that we select<br><br>■ Title services and lender's title insurance *(if we select them or you use companies we identify)*<br><br>■ Owner's title insurance *(if you use companies we identify)*<br><br>■ Required services that you can shop for *(if you use companies we identify)*<br><br>■ Government recording charges | ■ Required services that you can shop for *(if you do not use companies we identify)*<br><br>■ Title services and lender's title insurance *(if you do not use companies we identify)*<br><br>■ Owner's title insurance *(if you do not use companies we identify)*<br><br>■ Initial deposit for your escrow account<br><br>■ Daily interest charges<br><br>■ Homeowner's insurance |

### Using the tradeoff table

In this GFE, we offered you this loan with a particular interest rate and estimated settlement charges. However:

■ If you want to choose this same loan with **lower settlement charges,** then you will have a **higher interest rate.**
■ If you want to choose this same loan with a **lower interest rate,** then you will have **higher settlement charges.**

If you would like to choose an available option, you must ask us for a new GFE.

*Loan originators have the option to complete this table. Please ask for additional information if the table is not completed.*

|  | The loan in this GFE | The same loan with lower settlement charges | The same loan with a lower interest rate |
|---|---|---|---|
| Your initial loan amount | $ | $ | $ |
| Your initial interest rate[1] | % | % | % |
| Your initial monthly amount owed | $ | $ | $ |
| Change in the monthly amount owed from this GFE | No change | You will pay $ **more** every month | You will pay $ **less** every month |
| Change in the amount you will pay at settlement with this interest rate | No change | Your settlement charges will be **reduced** by $ | Your settlement charges will **increase** by $ |
| How much your total estimated settlement charges will be | $ | $ | $ |

[1] For an adjustable rate loan, the comparisons above are for the initial interest rate before adjustments are made.

### Using the shopping chart

Use this chart to compare GFEs from different loan originators. Fill in the information by using a different column for each GFE you receive. By comparing loan offers, you can shop for the best loan.

|  | This loan | Loan 2 | Loan 3 | Loan 4 |
|---|---|---|---|---|
| Loan originator name |  |  |  |  |
| Initial loan amount |  |  |  |  |
| Loan term |  |  |  |  |
| Initial interest rate |  |  |  |  |
| Initial monthly amount owed |  |  |  |  |
| Rate lock period |  |  |  |  |
| Can interest rate rise? |  |  |  |  |
| Can loan balance rise? |  |  |  |  |
| Can monthly amount owed rise? |  |  |  |  |
| Prepayment penalty? |  |  |  |  |
| Balloon payment? |  |  |  |  |
| **Total Estimated Settlement Charges** |  |  |  |  |

### If your loan is sold in the future

Some lenders may sell your loan after settlement. Any fees lenders receive in the future cannot change the loan you receive or the charges you paid at settlement.

 **Good Faith Estimate (HUD-GFE)** 3

# FORM 18 – REAL ESTATE AGENT'S DUAL AGENCY NOTICE

# AGENCY DISCLOSURE STATEMENT

EQUAL HOUSING OPPORTUNITY

**The real estate agent who is providing you with this form is required to do so by Ohio law. You will not be bound to pay the agent or the agent's brokerage by merely signing this form.** Instead, the purpose of this form is to confirm that you have been advised of the role of the agent(s) in the transaction proposed below. (For purposes of this form, the term "seller" includes a landlord and the term "buyer" includes a tenant.)

Property Address: _____

Buyer(s): _____

Seller(s): _____

## I. TRANSACTION INVOLVING TWO AGENTS IN TWO DIFFERENT BROKERAGES

The buyer will be represented by _____, and _____.
AGENT(S)                                                          BROKERAGE

The seller will be represented by _____, and _____.
AGENT(S)                                                          BROKERAGE

## II. TRANSACTION INVOLVING TWO AGENTS IN THE SAME BROKERAGE

If two agents in the real estate brokerage _____
represent both the buyer and the seller, check the following relationship that will apply:

☐ Agent(s)_____ work(s) for the buyer and
   Agent(s)_____ work(s) for the seller. Unless personally involved in the transaction, the broker and managers will be "dual agents", which is further explained on the back of this form. As dual agents they will maintain a neutral position in the transaction and they will protect all parties' confidential information.

☐ Every agent in the brokerage represents every "client" of the brokerage. Therefore, agents _____
   and _____ will be working for both the buyer and seller as "dual agents". Dual agency is explained on the back of this form. As dual agents they will maintain a neutral position in the transaction and they will protect all parties' confidential information. Unless indicated below, neither the agent(s) nor the brokerage acting as a dual agent in this transaction has a personal, family or business relationship with either the buyer or seller. *If such a relationship does exist, explain:*
   _____.

## III. TRANSACTION INVOLVING ONLY ONE REAL ESTATE AGENT

Agent(s) _____ and real estate brokerage _____ will

☐ be "dual agents" representing both parties in this transaction in a neutral capacity. Dual agency is further explained on the back of this form. As dual agents they will maintain a neutral position in the transaction and they will protect all parties' confidential information. Unless indicated below, neither the agent(s) nor the brokerage acting as a dual agent in this transaction has a personal, family or business relationship with either the buyer or seller. *If such a relationship does exist, explain:* _____
   _____.

☐ represent only the (*check one*) ☐ **seller** or ☐ **buyer** in this transaction as a client. The other party is not represented and agrees to represent his/her own best interest. Any information provided the agent may be disclosed to the agent's client.

### CONSENT

I (we) consent to the above relationships as we enter into this real estate transaction. If there is a dual agency in this transaction, I (we) acknowledge reading the information regarding dual agency explained on the back of this form.

_____    _____    _____    _____
BUYER/TENANT                DATE          SELLER/LANDLORD             DATE

_____    _____    _____    _____
BUYER/TENANT                DATE          SELLER/LANDLORD             DATE

# DUAL AGENCY

Ohio law permits a real estate agent and brokerage to represent both the seller and buyer in a real estate transaction as long as this is disclosed to both parties and they both agree. This is known as dual agency. As a dual agent, a real estate agent and brokerage represent two clients whose interests are, or at times could be, different or adverse. For this reason, the dual agent(s) may not be able to advocate on behalf of the client to the same extent the agent may have if the agent represented only one client.

**As a dual agent, the agent(s) and brokerage shall:**
- Treat both clients honestly;
- Disclose latent (not readily observable) material defects to the purchaser, if known by the agent(s) or brokerage;
- Provide information regarding lenders, inspectors and other professionals, if requested;
- Provide market information available from a property listing service or public records, if requested;
- Prepare and present all offers and counteroffers at the direction of the parties;
- Assist both parties in completing the steps necessary to fulfill the terms of any contract, if requested.

**As a dual agent, the agent(s) and brokerage shall not:**
- Disclose information that is confidential, or that would have an adverse effect on one party's position in the transaction, unless such disclosure is authorized by the client or required by law;
- Advocate or negotiate on behalf of either the buyer or seller;
- Suggest or recommend specific terms, including price, or disclose the terms or price a buyer is willing to offer or that a seller is willing to accept;
- Engage in conduct that is contrary to the instructions of either party and may not act in a biased manner on behalf of one party.

**Compensation:** Unless agreed otherwise, the brokerage will be compensated per the agency agreement.

**Management Level Licensees:** Generally the broker and managers in a brokerage also represent the interests of any buyer or seller represented by an agent affiliated with that brokerage. Therefore, if both buyer and seller are represented by agents in the same brokerage, the broker and manager are dual agents. There are two exceptions to this. The first is where the broker or manager is personally representing one of the parties. The second is where the broker or manager is selling or buying his own real estate. These exceptions only apply if there is another broker or manager to supervise the other agent involved in the transaction.

**Responsibilities of the Parties:** The duties of the agent and brokerage in a real estate transaction do not relieve the buyer and seller from the responsibility to protect their own interests. The buyer and seller are advised to carefully read all agreements to assure that they adequately express their understanding of the transaction. The agent and brokerage are qualified to advise on real estate matters. IF LEGAL OR TAX ADVICE IS DESIRED, YOU SHOULD CONSULT THE APPROPRIATE PROFESSIONAL.

**Consent:** By signing on the reverse side, you acknowledge that you have read and understand this form and are giving your voluntary, informed consent to the agency relationship disclosed. If you do not agree to the agent(s) and/or brokerage acting as a dual agent, you are not required to consent to this agreement and you may either request a separate agent in the brokerage to be appointed to represent your interests or you may terminate your agency relationship and obtain representation from another brokerage.

Any questions regarding the role or responsibilities of the brokerage or its agents should be directed to an attorney or to:
Ohio Department of Commerce
Division of Real Estate & Professional Licensing
77 S. High Street, 20th Floor
Columbus, OH 43215-6133
(614) 466-4100

EQUAL HOUSING
OPPORTUNITY

Effective 01/01/05

# APPENDIX B – REAL ESTATE EXERCISE INFORMATION

| | Exercise A | B | C | D |
|---|---|---|---|---|
| | Property 2009 Washington | Property 642 Osborne | Property 17 Holland Rd | Property 204 Bucks Road |
| Purchase Price | 499,000.00 | $162,000.00 | 429,900.00 | 340,000.00 |
| Cash Deposit at signing of Agreement of Sale | 10,000.00 | 2.000.00 | 5,000.00 | 1,000.00 |
| Additional Cash Deposit | | 6,100.00 | 15,000.00 | 14,013.57 |
| Financing | $399,200 Conventional Mortgage | None Cash Transaction | $340,000 Conventional Mortgage | $323,000 Seller Purchase Money Mortgage |
| School Tax-July 1 to June 30 | 5227.64 | 2565.45 | 2949.08 | 3138.26 |
| County/Parishtax Jan. 1 to Dec 31 | 1750.92 | 1258.38 | 1036.69 | 766.51 |
| Seller Mortgage Payoff | 250,223.01 | 150.304.28 | 39,81300 | None |
| Sellers Mortgage additional interest per day after closing date | 38.46 | 32.1103 | 8.12 | |
| Sale/Broker Commission Rate | 4.50 | 6.00 | 5.00 | 6.00 |
| Seller Realtor share of commission | 2.50 | 4.00 | 2.5 | 3.00 |
| Buyer Realtor share of commission | 2.00 | 2.00 | 2.5 | 3.00 |
| BUYER MORTGAGE | | | | |
| Mortgage | 399,200.00 | N/A - Cash | 340,000.00 | 323,000.00 |
| Interest rate | 4.625 | | 6.50 | 5.375 |
| Number of months | 360 | | 360 | 360 |
| Truth in Lending | | | | |
| APR rate | 4.8813 | | 6.593 | 5.378 |
| Finance Charge | 352,207.06 | | 436,910.63 | 328,229.68 |
| Amount Financed | 386,675.08 | | 337,710.05 | 322,904.88 |
| Total Payments | 738,882.14 | | 774,620.98 | 651,229.68 |
| Appraisal Fee | 300 | | 325.00 | 350 |

*(continued)*

| | Exercise A | B | C | D |
|---|---|---|---|---|
| | Property 2009 Washington | Property 642 Osborne | Property 17 Holland Rd | Property 204 Bucks Road |
| Credit Report | 30. | | 15.00 | 25.00 |
| Flood Certification | 11.00 | | 8.00 | 17.00 |
| Tax Service Fee | 70.00 | | 78.00 | |
| Interest per day to first of Month | 50.5836 | | 60.55 | 95.12 |
| Hazard Insurance | 888.09 | 603 | 1,265.30 | |
| ESCROWS | | | | |
| Hazard # of months required | 3 | | 3 | |
| School tax escrow # of months | 2 | | 6 | 4 |
| County/Parish tax escrow # of months | 6 | | 11 | 8 |
| Title Insurance | Per local rate | Per local rate | Per local rate | Per local rate |
| Recording fee deed | Per local rate | Per local rate | Per local rate | Per local rate |
| Recording fee mortgage | Per local rate | Per local rate | Per local rate | Per local rate |
| State Tax on transfer/ recording | Per local rate | Per local rate | Per local rate | Per local rate |
| Local Tax on transfer/ recording | Per local rate | Per local rate | Per local rate | Per local rate |
| Notary Fee | 50.00 | 25. | 50.00 | 50 |
| Unpaid Water and Sewer | 65 | 250 | 40 | 102.48 |

## ■ LEGAL DESCRIPTION EXERCISE A

**BEGINNING** at a point on the Northeasterly side of Washington Street (unnamed on said Plan) (50 feet wide not shown on said Plan) which point is the common corner of Lots Nos. 139 and 140 on said Plan; thence extending along said Lot No. 140 North 44 degrees 02 minutes 26 seconds East a distance of 161.02 feet to a point a corner in line of lands now or late of Julius Lojeski; thence extending along said lands South 12 degrees 02 minutes 00 seconds East a distance of 36.15 feet to a point a corner of Lot No. 138; thence extending along said Lot No. 138 South 44 degrees 02 minutes 26 seconds West a distance of 143.49 feet to a point of the Northeasterly side of Washington Street aforesaid; thence extending along the same on the arc of a circle curving to the left with a radius of 125.00 feet the arc distance of 30.19 feet to a point a corner of Lot No. 140 aforesaid being the first mentioned point and place of beginning.

**BEING** Lot No. 139 on said Plan.

**BEING** 2009 Washington Street.

**BEING COUNTY PARCEL NUMBER** 22-23-178.

## ■ LEGAL DESCRIPTION EXERCISE B

BEGINNING AT A POINT AT THE INTERSECTION OF THE NORTHERLY SIDE OF OSBORN DRIVE (50 FEET WIDE) AND THE WESTERLY SIDE OF WALTON DRIVE (60 FEET WIDE); THENCE EXTENDING FROM SAID BEGINNING POINT; ALONG THE NORTHERLY SIDE OF OSBORN DRIVE, SOUTH EIGHTY-ONE (81) DEGREES FIFTY-NINE (59') MINUTES FORTY-TWO (42") SECONDS WEST, ONE HUNDRED TWENTY (120.0') FEET TO A POINT; THENCE EXTENDING ALONG THE EASTERLY LINE OF LOT 190, NORTH SEVEN (07) DEGREES FOUR (04') MINUTES WEST, ONE HUNDRED TWENTY-THREE AND FOURTEEN ONE-HUNDREDTHS (123.14') FEET TO A POINT; THENCE EXTENDING ALONG THE SOUTHERLY LINE OF LOT 188, NORTH EIGHTY-THREE (83) DEGREES TWENTY-NINE (29') MINUTES TEN (10") SECONDS EAST, ONE HUNDRED TWENTY-ONE AND FIFTEEN ONE-HUNDREDTHS (121.15') FEET TO A POINT ON THE WESTERLY SIDE OF SAID WALTON DRIVE; THENCE EXTENDING ALONG THE WESTERLY SIDE OF THE SAID WALTON DRIVE, SOUTH SIX (06) DEGREES THIRTY (30') MINUTES FIFTY (50") SECONDS EAST, ONE HUNDRED TWENTY (120.0') FEET TO THE FIRST MENTIONED POINT AND PLACE OF BEGINNING.

BEING LOT 189 AS SHOWN ON SAID PLAN.

BEING KNOWN AS 642 OSBORN DRIVE.

## ■ LEGAL DESCRIPTION EXERCISE C

BEGINNING AT A POINT ON THE NORTHEASTERLY SIDE OF CUL-DE-SAC AT THE TERMINUS OF HOLLAND ROAD (50.00 FEET WIDE) SAID POINT BEING A COMMON CORNER OF LOTS 10 AND 11, THENCE EXTENDING FROM SIDE POINT OF BEGINNING ALONG THE NORTHEASTERLY SIDE OF A CUL-DE-SAC AT THE TERMINUS OF HOLLAND ROAD ON THE ARC OF A CIRCLE CURVING TO THE LEFT HAVING A RADIUS OF 62.00 FEET, THE ARC DISTANCE OF 76.53 FEET TO A POINT, A CORNER OF LOT 9; THENCE EXTENDING ALONG SAME, NORTH 67 DEGREES, 47 MINUTES, 58 SECONDS WEST, 288.75 FEET TO A POINT IN LINE OF LAND, SHOWN AS FLOWAGE EASEMENT NESHAMINY WATER RESOURCES AUTHORITY); THENCE EXTENDING ALONG SAME, THE (4) FOLLOWING COURSES AND DISTANCE (1) NORTH 61 DEGREES, 333 MINUTES, 23 SECONDS EAST, 144.08 FEET TO A POINT; (2) NORTH 42 DEGREES, MINUTES, 02 SECONDS EAST, 40.63 FEET TO A POINT; (3) NORTH 58 DEGREES, 07 MINUTES, 43 SECONDS EAST, 198.33 FEET TO A POINT AND (4) NORTH 65 DEGREES, 01 MINUTES, 58 SECONDS EAST, 22.12 FEET TO A POINT, A CORNER OF LOT 11, AFORESAID; THENCE EXTENDING ALONG SAME, SOUTH 02 DEGREES, 56 MINUTES, 17 SECONDS WEST, 283.75 FEET TO THE FIRST MENTIONED POINT AND PLACE OF BEGINNING.

BEING LOT 10 AS SHOWN ON THE ABOVE MENTIONED PLAN.

BEING KNOWN AS 17 HOLLAND ROAD.

ALSO, UNDER AND SUBJECT TO THE EASEMENTS AND CONDITIONS SET FORTH IN FINAL SUBDIVISION PLAN OF HIDDEN LAKE, DATED 01/13/1989 AND LAST REVISED 05/24/1990.

## ■ LEGAL DESCRIPTION EXERCISE D

BEGINNING AT AN INTERIOR POINT A CORNER OF LOT 24, SAID POINT BEING MEASURED THE FIVE FOLLOWING COURSES AND DISTANCES FROM THE NORTHERLY POINT OF REVERSE CURVE OF THE NORTHWESTERLY RADIUS CORNER AT THE INTERSECTION OF BUCKS ROAD (50 FEET WIDE) AND RITTENHOUSE CIRCLE (50 FEET WIDE) VIZ: (1) ALONG THE NORTHERLY SIDE OF SAID BUCKS ROAD BY A CURVE TO THE RIGHT IN A SOUTHWESTERLY DIRECTION HAVING A RADIUS OF 110.00 FEET AND FOR THE ARC DISTANCE OF 135.41 FEET TO A POINT OF TANGENCY; THENCE (2) CONTINUING ALONG THE NORTHERLY SIDE OF THE SAID BUCKS ROAD NORTH 89 DEGREES 46 MINUTES 25 SECONDS WEST 116.50 FEET TO A POINT A CORNER; THENCE (3) LEAVING THE SAID BUCKS ROAD NORTH 00 DEGREES 13 MINUTES 35 SECONDS EAST 177.00 FEET TO A POINT A CORNER; THENCE (4) NORTH 21 DEGREES 13 MINUTES 35 SECONDS EAST 283.23 FEET TO A POINT A CORNER; THENCE (5) NORTH 68 DEGREES 46 MINUTES 25 SECONDS WEST 40.86 FEET; THENCE FROM THE SAID POINT OF BEGINNING, ALONG THE SAID LOT 24 PASSING THROUGH A PARTY WALL NORTH 68 DEGREES 46 MINUTES 25 SECONDS WEST 82.10 FEET TO A POINT A CORNER; THENCE NORTH 21 DEGREES 13 MINUTES 35 SECONDS EAST 16.02 FEET TO A POINT A CORNER OF LOT 26; THENCE ALONG THE SAID LOT 26 AND PASSING THROUGH ANOTHER PARTY WALL SOUTH 68 DEGREES 46 MINUTES 25 SECONDS EAST 82.10 FEET TO A POINT A CORNER; THENCE SOUTH 21 DEGREES 13 MINUTES 35 SECONDS WEST 16.01 FEET TO THE POINT OR PLACE OF BEGINNING.

PARCEL NUMBER 27-8-5-217.

BEING KNOWN AS 204 BUCKS ROAD.